the Unofficial Guide® to the World's Best Diving Vacations

1st Edition

Also available from Hungry Minds

the Unofficial Guide®to the World's Best Diving Vacations

1st Edition

Jean Pierce

with Brenda Fine

Please note that prices fluctuate in the course of time, and travel information changes under the impact of the many factors that influence the travel industry. We therefore suggest that you write or call ahead for confirmation when making your travel plans. Every effort has been made to ensure the accuracy of information throughout this guidebook, and the contents of this publication are believed correct at the time of printing. Nevertheless, the publishers cannot accept responsibility for errors or omissions, for changes in details given in this guide, or for the consequences of any reliance on the information provided by same. Assessments of attractions and so forth are based upon the author's own experience, and therefore, descriptions given in this guide necessarily contain an element of subjective opinion, which may not reflect the publisher's opinion or dictate a reader's own experience on another occasion. Readers are invited to write to the publisher with ideas, comments, and suggestions for future editions.

Your safety is important to us, however, so we encourage you to stay alert and be aware of your surroundings. Keep a close eye on cameras, purses, and wallets, all favorite targets of thieves and pickpockets.

Hungry Minds, Inc.
909 Third Avenue, 21st Floor
New York, New York 10022

Copyright © 2001 Bob Sehlinger

Produced by Menasha Ridge Press

ISBN 0-7645-6220-7

ISSN 1532-9917

Manufactured in the United States of America

10 9 8 7 6 5 4 3 2 1

First edition

Trademarks: Unofficial Guide is a trademark or registered trademark of Hungry Minds, Inc. All other trademarks are property of their respective owners.

PADI (Professional Association of Diving Instructors) is the world's largest recreational diving membership organization that makes underwater exploration and adventure accessible to the public while maintaining the highest industry standards for dive training, safety, and customer service. Visit padi.com for program information and dive center listings.

In memory of Ed Haxby of Great Exuma, Bahamas—
my instructor and eco-diving inspiration.

—J.P.

Contents

9   Mexico's Cozumel   223

10   Curaçao   245

11   Fiji   267

12   Florida: The Keys   293

List of Maps

Acknowledgments

I can't possibly thank every individual or entity that helped with the research for this book. There are simply too many. But I would like to acknowledge the Society of American Travel Writers, and especially all the Associate members who worked so hard to put together press trips and answer countless questions. These people are invaluable, and without them, this book would never have been written.

I would also like to thank the industry manufacturers whose equipment we rely upon so much: the Oceanic team for their excellent regulators, BCDs, and computers; Atlan Productions for wetsuits; National Divers Manufacturing for all the clips, hoses, and accessories; and Force Fins for our favorite footwear.

Finally, thank you to the editors at Menasha Ridge Press for the honesty and integrity you bring to our profession.

—*Jean Pierce*

About the Authors

Author **Jean Pierce** has been diving since 1985. She now works as a divemaster with her husband Kris Newman. Reeldivers, their California dive business, provides dive support to underwater film productions, such as the Warner Brothers movie *Sphere*. In addition to being a PADI divemaster, Pierce is Nitrox-certified with the International Association of Nitrox and Technical Divers and cave-certified with the National Speleological Society/Cave Diving Section. She has written for scuba magazines like *Dive Training* and *Sport Diver*, and she authored the dive guide *Diving and Snorkeling Cayman Islands*. She is a member of the Society of American Travel Writers and is a recipient of a Lowell Thomas Award, a Maggie Award, and the Bahamas Discovery Award. Pierce and her husband are also avid underwater photographers, supplying much of the photography for their published work.

Contributor **Brenda Fine** wrote the chapter on Fiji Islands diving. Also a member of the Society of American Travel Writers, she has been diving since 1986. Her byline appears regularly in a variety of national travel publications.

Introduction

It's All About Honesty

You should know, right up front, that as the author of this guidebook, I am highly biased. I selected the destinations because I like them and figure you'll probably enjoy them too. I sincerely hope so. Moreover, thanks to our publishers, we writers have been sworn to honesty, to state the truth, whatever that may be.

This not meant to imply that other guidebooks are not honest—they probably are. It's just that most do not give the entire picture. The positive attributes are described in detail, but the less-than-stellar qualities simply are not mentioned. And that's the problem—the information that you don't get.

We will give you both—the good and the not-so-good. So if a resort is getting run down, it's important to let you know that. Or if a reef has experienced some coral bleaching or storm damage, then you should be aware of that before making your traveling plans.

But fairness is important, too. We've all had divemasters who occasionally slip up. Here's an example: I like to assemble my own gear before a dive, but often divemasters will take care of it without asking. On one particular dive trip in the Caribbean, my divemaster got everything together but neglected to hook up my inflator hose (I caught the mistake in time). Then, unbelievably, he turned my air *off* just before I made my giant stride into the water. Now to me, that's unacceptable, and it indicates that the dive shop's standards need to be improved. But what about the new divemaster who is leading a tour and can't find his way back to the boat without surfacing? Should we rate a dive shop poorly because of that one incident? If that was the only problem noticed, then of course not—things happen. So it's also our responsibility to be fair to the places and people we write about.

All of the destinations in this book are highly recommended, but not every aspect of them is perfect. What we try to do is describe them as accurately as we can, so that you can make choices. Except for getting hard data, we are not influenced in any way by publicists, tourism departments, resorts, dive shops, etc. Unfortunately, we cannot try out every restaurant, every dive shop, or every lodging. So we have to rely occasionally on recommendations by others.

MAKING COMPARISONS: THE RATING GAME

Another bonus that we can offer to you readers (part of the honesty thing) is our ability to compare.

Do you remember your first couple of dives? How exciting and wonderful they were? As a divemaster, I've helped instruct new students in the most awful underwater conditions—in bone-numbing cold, or stomach-churning surge, or completely mucked-up vis—conditions so bad that I desperately wanted the students to hurry up with their skills, just so I could get out of the water! But amazingly, they're always enthusiastic after a training dive. When asked how their dives were, invariably they'll say something like, "Wonderful! We saw so much—it was a blast!"

I'm always really happy they feel that way, but also amazed by it. Much of their reaction is undoubtedly due to adrenaline and perceptual narrowing (remember that in your Open Water class?). Perceptual narrowing is a decreased level of awareness. It can be due to stress, but usually it's just inexperience. You aren't noticing things around you, as you normally would. But the inability to make comparisons is another reason for that reaction. How do you know it's a lousy dive if that's the only thing you've seen?

That's where we writers come in handy. Not only can we describe a destination, but we can also compare it to the myriad other sites we've dived around the globe. And we can evaluate the dive shops, dive boats, and divemasters from a dive-professional's perspective—we know how they are *supposed* to do their jobs, because that's how we were trained. And having stayed in umpteen awful dive resorts, we know what to expect from a good one.

Each chapter in this guide ranks the diving in the area, the dive centers and dive boats, and the lodgings. Farther along in this introduction is a complete description of how the rankings work. If you disagree strongly with any of these, certainly let us know. Also, feel free to make recommendations, and we'll check them out for the next go-around.

AUTHORS' CREDENTIALS

Jean Pierce, Author I have been diving since 1985, the year I was certified in a mucky quarry in Wisconsin (yes, it was great!). My initiation into ocean diving was off Heron Island, Australia, where I'm remembered for vomiting immediately after the dive. Fortunately, I was one of the first divers back on the boat, having sucked my tank dry in record time, so few actually witnessed the event.

My skills have improved greatly since those best-forgotten days, and now I work as a divemaster, assisting my instructor/husband, Kris Newman. We own a dive business called Reeldivers®, and we work in the film industry in California, providing dive support to underwater film productions. For instance, we managed the Dive Unit for the Warner Brothers' film *Sphere*. I worked on the five dive decks, organizing safety teams, dive equipment, air tanks, and such, while Kris was having fun training the cast—Sharon Stone, Dustin Hoffman, Samuel L. Jackson, Peter Coyote, and Liev Schreiber—to helmet-dive. Oh, yes, and I can't forget his favorite pupil and duet-partner, Queen Latifah.

Besides being a PADI Divemaster (DM 154879), I am Nitrox-certified with the International Association of Nitrox & Technical Divers (IANTD) and cave-certified with the National Speleological Society/Cave Diving Section (NSS/CDS).

I write for scuba magazines, such as *Dive Training* and *Sport Diver,* and I authored the dive guide *Diving and Snorkeling Cayman Islands,* published in January 2000 by Lonely Planet/Pisces. Kris and I took most of the photographs in the book. We absolutely love underwater photography and spend way too much money on equipment. Before I became a freelance travel journalist, I was stuck behind a desk at Rand McNally & Co. (senior editor) and Prentice Hall (editor-in-chief). I was also editor of *Odyssey* magazine. I've been a member of the Society of American Travel Writers (SATW) since 1985 and am the recipient of an SATW Lowell Thomas Award, a Maggie Award, and the Bahamas Discovery Award.

Brenda Fine, Contributor   (Fiji chapter) Brenda was a stay-at-home mom with three kids in New York City until a good friend enticed her to write a magazine story about her family's experience in Disney World. That good friend was Steve Birnbaum, a familiar name in travel publishing. Suddenly her life became a whole lot more exciting. Now Brenda is a highly respected and recognized travel journalist. She has been a member of the prestigious Society of American Travel Writers since 1987, and her byline appears frequently in national travel magazines. She was scuba certified in Grand Cayman in 1986, but still lives in New York City—much too far, she says, from the "blue-water-warm-water kind of diving" she loves to do. Brenda has dived extensively in the Fiji islands.

LETTERS, COMMENTS, AND QUESTIONS FROM READERS

Many who use the *Unofficial Guides* write to us with questions, comments, or their own strategies for planning and enjoying travel. We appreciate all such input, both positive and critical. Readers' comments are frequently incorporated into revised editions of the *Unofficial Guides* and have contributed immeasurably to their improvement. Please write to:

Jean Pierce
The Unofficial Guide to the World's Best Diving Vacations
P.O. Box 43673
Birmingham, AL 35243

Please put your return address on both your letter and envelope; the two sometimes become separated. Also, include your phone number if you are available for a possible interview. And remember, our work often requires that we be out of the office for long periods, so forgive us if our response is slow.

A Reader Survey is included at the end of this book. We urge you to copy or clip it out, add your impressions, and send it in.

RATIONALE FOR SELECTING DIVE SITES, DIVE SHOPS, AND RESORTS

Dive Sites   That's easy. They were chosen for quality, pure and simple. They are among the most beautiful and most exciting places that I know of. I don't want to waste your time (and mine) describing places that have been destroyed by cruise ship anchoring, soil runoff, massive development, and so on. At these sites, you'll find healthy reefs, abundant marine life, exciting shipwrecks, and intriguing caves and caverns.

A couple of other important factors went into the selection: accessibility and infrastructure. Some dive sites are really terrific, but they are next to impossible to get to. Others simply don't have the infrastructure to support much tourism, and they lack reputable dive operations. In both these situations, safety can be compromised. So I have omitted places that I feel wouldn't be safe, even for experienced divers.

Some of the selections really are for experienced divers, and that is stated clearly in the chapters. A reef could be very deep, or there could be strong currents. At cave sites, divers need to have special cave diving training. However, almost all destinations have some variety, and can offer a lot of fun for new divers, snorkelers, and even technical divers. For instance, a place that features wall diving usually has great diving and snorkeling on top of the reef and right at the drop-off. So you can dive deep along the wall or stay on top in the shallows.

Dive Shops   We're really picky about our dive shops. It's important to keep in mind, though, that we are reporting what we see and experience. Quality can easily change for the better or for the worse. So it is important to try to evaluate a dive shop, and a dive boat, yourself. There are some specific things you can look for—some telltale clues. Refer to the section "Evaluating Dive Shops and Dive Boats" to learn what these are.

What we look for is a dive shop that has been around for a while, with little turnover and a loyal staff. Obviously, we can't try out every shop in an area, but we do try to sample several, for comparison. Usually we select those that are the most complete—the ones that have a particularly good reputation for service, instruction, rentals, and so on.

Because we are underwater photographers, we also look for dive operations that are especially attuned to those needs. As photographers, we like to see divemasters who know how to handle the equipment, and who know how important it is to have a large container of fresh water on board reserved strictly for cameras. Ideally, we like to see a camera table where we can easily change film after a dive and keep everything dry. Also, it's nice to have a dry storage area for the land cameras.

Good pre-dive briefings are extremely important, so we can have adequate preparation for the dive and a good understanding of the site's topography and marine life before we ever get into the water. It also helps to know what type of camera lens to use. If we're going to be looking at sea horses, we certainly don't want to go down with our wide-angle lenses.

We definitely prefer dive shops that are on the premises of the resort where we're staying. The less we lug around our dive gear and camera equipment, the better. It's also a real advantage having the dive boat leave directly from the dock at the dive shop or the resort, rather than having to take a bus or van to some marina. Ideally, the dive shops will have large tanks for rinsing gear and storage lockers for leaving gear overnight. We also like shops that pump their own air, including Enriched Air Nitrox, and have an efficient system in place for ordering and testing the mixture of choice.

Unless we state otherwise, however, do not assume that a dive shop will offer Nitrox or any other mixed gas or technical diving equipment. You can assume that most of the dive operations listed will have a storefront, at least one boat, a retail section, a rental section, and some repair service. Some, however, are charter operations that have no storefront (which will be stated). And many, especially in remote areas, will have a meager retail line and little ability to make equipment repairs. We have tried to give as much information about dive boats as possible, but for specific concerns, be sure to contact the facilities directly.

Resorts   First, don't be overly concerned about the star rankings, since they are based on quantitative (not qualitative) data. Better to base your choice on the type of facility (large or small, personal or impersonal, etc.) and the rate. If a hotel or accommodation has no star rating given, it means that while it might be a fine place to stay otherwise, it doesn't cater to or have facilities for divers.

The dedicated dive resort is definitely our lodging of choice. These resorts understand divers and are well set up to accommodate them. Most of the lodgings recommended in this guide actively market themselves to the diving and snorkeling public. Most provide diving packages that include special rates for the lodging, the diving, and sometimes a certain number of meals. Usually the dive/resort packages have a minimum of two dives per day (a two-tank dive), an occasional night dive, and, if they are on the beach, unlimited shore diving. The dive package is almost always less expensive than paying for the diving separately.

Because there are so many variables with regard to packages, we generally give only the room rate for a single night (or the minimum number of nights), to use as a comparison. From there, you can contact the resort for more details or simply look up the rates on the website. Factors such as the type of room you want, the season in which you're traveling, the length of your stay, or the meal plan will all contribute to the final rate, making comparisons difficult in a guidebook like this one. Therefore, the simplest measurement is to take the rate, or the rate range, for a one-night stay, to use as a comparison. Rates are current at press time, but remember to call ahead and check when planning your trip.

We like to see guest rooms that are spacious, for accommodating all the "stuff" we have. A patio or balcony is practically a necessity, for drying out towels, swimsuits, wetsuits, and gear. Even if the resort has lockers (which they should have), you occasionally want to bring your wetsuit back to the room to wash out, or to get it nice and toasty-warm.

I stayed at a gorgeous resort in Palau that had a dive shop on the premises and actively advertised in all the dive magazines. However, I was told not to put my dive gear out on the balcony—it looked too tacky. The general manager explained that the drying line in the bathroom was for hanging dive gear—yes, that flimsy little piece of string that extends from the wall. Now, we divers know how silly that is! Obviously, he was not a diver. In contrast, I stayed at a very nice resort on Bonaire that provided buckets for getting your wet gear from the bathroom to the balcony—very thoughtful, plus it protected their floors.

A good dive resort needs to state clearly their procedures for diving—including where the dive shop is located, how to get checked out, where to sign up for trips, rent gear, and so on. In other words, the diving logistics should be given high priority. A boat dock on the premises is a definite bonus, as are lockers for dive gear, a retail shop, camera rentals, and a repair facility. If there is E-6 film processing, that's terrific.

Phone Calls from the United States and Canada

Where possible, the toll-free 800 numbers are given for resorts, dive shops, etc. These can be used from the United States and frequently from Canada. Unfortunately, though, not all 800 numbers can be accessed from Canada. When calling the local number at an international destination from the United States or Canada, you usually have to first dial 011, the international number. However, many Caribbean islands—the Bahamas and Cayman Islands, for example—are direct-dial and do not require the 011 prefix.

Dive Trips:
Some Considerations before You Go

Scuba Certification   Never use scuba equipment unless you are scuba-certified with one of the reputable agencies (NAUI, PADI, SSI, YMCA, TDI, etc.) or you are under the care of a diving professional certified by one of these agencies. If you want to "test the waters," so to speak, before getting certified, make sure you take a legitimate course that's sanctioned by one of these agencies. The popular Discover Scuba Diving program by PADI (Professional Association of Diving Instructors) is one example. These types of classes used to be called *resort courses,* and many were not standardized. A few places still use that term. Make sure that your course is a standardized one, with a syllabus, from one of the certifying agencies. *Also, unless you are certified, never dive with a friend or use scuba equipment borrowed from a friend who is not a diving professional.*

Be a Good Diver   Because scuba diving involves life-support equipment, it's important to do some serious planning before taking off. A dive trip involves quite a bit more work than a regular trip—yes, work. Although most of the certifying agencies tend to portray this sport as effortless, it is not. It does require work—getting trained, staying in shape, keeping equipment serviced, and generally being a responsible diver. Certainly, this sport is not for everyone, and that's OK.

Dive professionals are accustomed to dealing with students who are in their classes solely because of pressure from a spouse or friend. Let me tell you, *it never works.* You have to *want* to dive. Someone who is doing it primarily to please someone else is just going to be miserable and could turn out to be a dangerous dive buddy. Divers need to be responsible for themselves, and they need to put some effort into it.

What are the signs of a good diver? I'm always impressed when someone on the dive boat can pull out an extra O-ring if it's needed, can produce a cable tie in a pinch or a diver's tool to tighten a hose fitting. That takes some pre-planning and organization. Simply putting all the dive gear neatly in a mesh bag and keeping it out of the way under the benches is a definite sign of a good diver. Same for not leaving a tank standing by itself, and for not putting lead weights in places where they can fall off and break a toe.

So after making your reservations, start to do some pre-planning for your trip. If you dive only once or twice a year, your planning should start earlier than if you dive frequently. And if you haven't dived in a couple of years, start even earlier. The following guidelines might be helpful.

Service Your Equipment   Manufacturers recommend that divers have a regulator service check *at least* once a year, even if the regulator has not been used. Don't think that this is just a way for them to make money—it's really very important. Have you ever grabbed an item from your closet, put it on, and discovered that the elastic was completely worn out? That's similar to what happens with regs—some of the parts simply deteriorate. And you wouldn't want to discover it while you're underwater. It helps to keep a service record in your logbook, so you know how long it has been since the last service. If you dive a lot, then have your regulator serviced more often.

Make sure you have the work done at a dive center with a highly trained technician, not someone who will simply rinse out the sand, grease the O-ring, then put it back together. How do you know how good the person is? One way is to make sure that old parts are returned. Also, don't be shy about asking for credentials. Manufacturers have repair schools and give students "diplomas," but that does not make them technicians. It takes a lot of training, experience, and know-how. The best dive centers will use a technician who does nothing but service and repair work. They might have someone in-house, or they might use an outside business, which is fine.

If you don't have a good dive center to handle services near you, then you can simply send your reg out to the experts that a lot of the shops use. There are several around the country. The following have excellent reputations and can repair just about anything:

For those in the west, contact Dive Tech West. The website, at www.divetechwest.com, will give mailing instructions, price lists, etc. Phone or fax them at (831) 336-0137 or e-mail: repair@divetechwest.com. In the east, contact Diving Technologies International, which normally has a one week turnaround time. Summer, however, is the busiest time, so it might take as long as three weeks to get your gear back (plan accordingly). Call (954) 748-4772; fax (954) 748-0637; e-mail: divetec@aol.com; website: www.divingtechnologies.com.

Just before taking off for a dive trip, it's a good idea to have a dive center bench-check your regulator, even if it has been serviced within the year. This will assess the manahelic pressure, or "breathability," which frequently can be adjusted on the spot. It will also detect if there's a more serious problem.

Keep Learning Don't settle for being an ordinary diver—try to be a *good* diver. Dive as much as you can and get as much extra training as you can. Definitely venture beyond the basic level of certification. I always recommend to students that after certifying they should get some practical experience in the water to master their buoyancy and feel comfortable with their gear. Then they should take an advanced course, which will introduce them to night diving and deep diving. But to be really good divers, they should take the rescue course. It's a lot of fun, and students usually feel very confident after going through it. These three levels will make you a much better diver and you'll definitely get a lot more enjoyment from your diving excursions.

Even this extra training will not be sufficient, though, with some types of diving. Cave diving and shipwreck penetration, in particular, can be very dangerous if you are not properly trained. If you want to cave dive, it is critical that you get cave-certified. Or if you just want to cavern-dive (always keeping within range of a natural light source), you can take a specialty course to earn cavern certification. For wreck diving, take the wreck diver specialty course. Other types of diving require special training. Drysuit diving is one example. Getting used to diving in a drysuit takes a lot of practice, and it can be dangerous to try it on your own. The important thing here is that formal instruction is the safest way to learn these special skills.

Nitrox Diver is a good certification to get while you're traveling. Many dive centers are now teaching the course, and it takes little time to complete it. Most of the certifying agencies have Nitrox certifications. The more technically oriented agencies, however, tend to have more complex manuals, simply because most of their students go on to take advanced Nitrox and classes in other kinds of mixed gases. For recreational divers who simply want to use basic Nitrox (which is usually between 32 and 36 percent oxygen), the simpler classes given by the recreational agencies is probably the best way to go.

To help keep you up-to-date and informed, an excellent resource is *Dive Training* magazine, which you can order through your local dive center. Another excellent publication is *Sport Diver* magazine, which is now the magazine of the PADI Diving Society.

Certification Agencies—What's in an Acronym?   If you are not yet certified, perhaps you're wondering which agency to go with. Is one agency better than another? Actually, there is not a great deal of difference among them, and there are plenty to choose from—probably many more than you realize. There is a dive industry standard, written by the Recreational Scuba Training Council and accepted by ANSI (American National Standards Institute). Most of the certification agencies (perhaps all) in the United States adhere to those minimum standards. Some exceed the standards. Also, instructors are free to exceed any agency's minimum standards. My recommendation is that you worry less about the agency and more about the individual instructor. Find an excellent instructor and get the best training possible.

The following abbreviations are the primary ones used throughout this guide to describe the various certification agencies with which the dive shops are affiliated: ACUC (American Canadian Underwater Certification, Inc.), BSAC (British Sub-Aqua Club), ANDI (American Nitrox Divers International), IANTD (International Association of Nitrox & Technical Divers), IDEA (International Diving Educators Association), NASE (National Academy of Scuba Educators), NAUI (National Association of Underwater Instructors), PADI (Professional Association of Diving Instructors), PDIC (Professional Diving Instructors Corporation), SDI/TDI (Scuba Diving International/Technical Diving International), SSI (Scuba Schools International), YMCA (Young Men's Christian Association), and WASI (World Association of Scuba Instructors).

Whew! And there are more, but these are the primary ones used by divers in North America and the U.K. In the U.S., PADI issues more C-cards than all the others and has specific levels for its affiliate dive centers and resorts. Altogether there are seven categories, four are of primary concern to traveling recreational divers.

The first, the PADI Dive Center, offers the basic services you would expect from a dive shop—instruction, tours, equipment sales, rentals, and so on. The PADI 5-Star Dive Center (no, there are no 1, 2, 3, or 4-star categories) requires that a business have, among other things, an increased level of community involvement and diver recruitment and at least 30 percent of its certifications above the Open Water level. It also must issue and advertise PADI certifications only (with some exceptions) and use PADI training materials exclusively. A PADI Resort is essentially a resort that specifically caters to divers and snorkelers; a PADI Gold Palm Resort is similar but offers higher-quality lodging and dive service. The other three categories are oriented toward diving professionals. These include the PADI 5-Star IDC (Instructor Development Center), PADI Career Development Center, and PADI Gold Palm IDC Resort (Gold Palm Resorts that offer instructor-level training).

Five certification agencies have formed a Universal Referral Program whereby students are able to take their classroom and pool instruction at home with one agency, then travel to another destination to complete their open water dives with any of the others. The agencies participating under this umbrella are IDEA, NAUI, PDIC, SSI, and YMCA.

With such agency diversity and world-wide representation, divers shouldn't find it difficult to certify at home—or begin their instruction at home, then find a dive center to meet their needs virtually anywhere in the world. For further information, visit the following agency websites: idea.com, scuba-idea.com/us, nasescuba.com, naui.org, padi.com, pdic-intl.com, ssiusa.com, ymcascuba.org, divewasi.com, and sditdi.org.

CHOOSING YOUR DESTINATION

Definitely use this guidebook to determine where to take your vacation, where to stay, and which dive shop to use. If you're a new diver or a "rusty" diver, try to choose a location that has excellent services and is accustomed to seeing a lot of inexperienced divers. You can always graduate to the more challenging sites. It's not a good idea to "get in over your head," so to speak.

Dive shop and dive boat standards vary considerably around the world. Some destinations have extremely high standards, usually influenced, or imposed, by some entity. For instance, in the Cayman Islands, it's the Watersports Operators Association. In the Bahamas, it's the Bahamas Dive Association. In other areas, the standards might be whatever each dive shop decides on (regardless of its affiliation with a certifying agency). So that can be a critical consideration.

Some areas simply require more self-reliance than others. In these, it's best to be an experienced diver and to have your own dive equipment, including some redundant equipment. You should also have a tool kit and first-aid kit, in addition to a handy save-a-dive kit.

New or inexperienced divers should choose a location where they can be fairly certain the rental equipment will be excellent and well maintained and they'll have experienced divemasters that can assist them. Do not be afraid to let the staff know that you would appreciate some extra assistance—to give advice or to dive with you—they will appreciate it, and your personal enjoyment will be enhanced. *Swallow your pride. Don't pretend to be confident if you are not.* It takes only a couple of dives to re-establish your buoyancy skills and become more confident, then you'll be diving like a pro again, and helping others.

One resource for planning your dive trip (or just for poking around among the options) is the PADI Travel Network. This organization represents over 200 resorts in more than 90 destinations worldwide. They can handle everything from simple tours to complete airfare-inclusive resort packages. Check them out at www.padi.com/ptn.

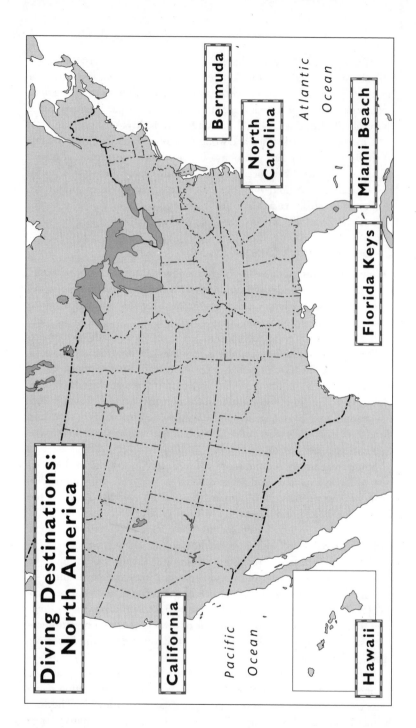

Diving Destinations: North America

Bermuda

North Carolina

Miami Beach

Florida Keys

California

Hawaii

Atlantic Ocean

Pacific Ocean

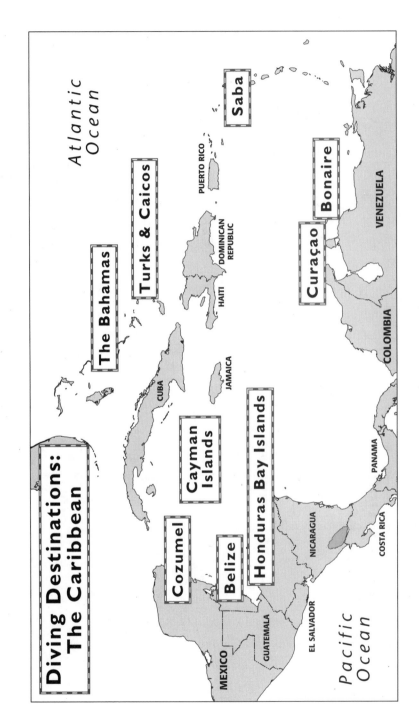

Diving Destinations: The Caribbean

Atlantic Ocean

Pacific Ocean

The Bahamas

Turks & Caicos

Saba

Cayman Islands

Cozumel

Belize

Honduras Bay Islands

Curaçao

Bonaire

CUBA

JAMAICA

PUERTO RICO

DOMINICAN REPUBLIC

HAITI

MEXICO

GUATEMALA

EL SALVADOR

NICARAGUA

COSTA RICA

PANAMA

COLOMBIA

VENEZUELA

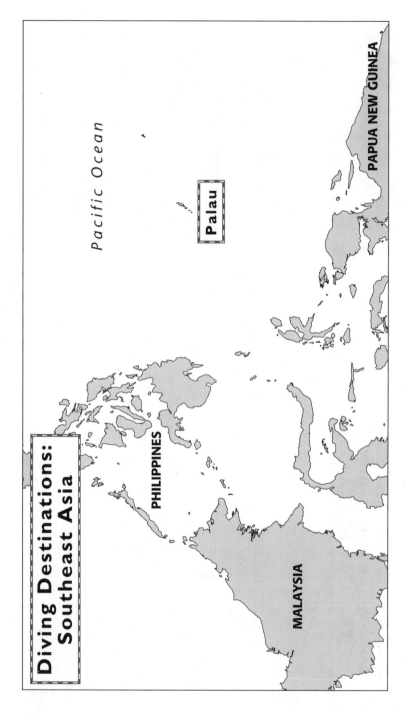

Diving Destinations: Southeast Asia

Pacific Ocean

Palau

PHILIPPINES

MALAYSIA

PAPUA NEW GUINEA

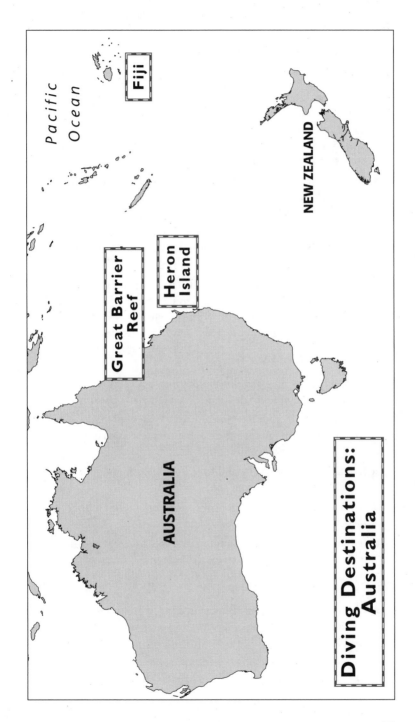

Pacific Ocean

Fiji

NEW ZEALAND

Great Barrier Reef

Heron Island

AUSTRALIA

Diving Destinations: Australia

PRE-TRIP COUNTDOWN

Several Months before Your Trip

- If you are an infrequent diver, or an out-of-shape diver, consider contacting an instructor or divemaster for a scuba review course. This can be done either at a swimming pool or at the ocean (or lake). Or you can contact the resort where you're staying to schedule a scuba review immediately after your arrival.

- Get in shape and exercise frequently. Find a swimming pool, grab your mask, snorkel, and fins, and start doing laps without lifting your head out of the water.

- Find out if you need any special immunizations for the area you're visiting. A quick way to do this is to log on to www.cdc.gov, the website of the Center for Disease Control.

- Check the date on your passport. If it has expired, get a renewal form from the post office. If you're using a birth certificate, make sure it's an original (certified) certificate with a raised seal. A good resource for foreign entry requirements is: www.travel.state.gov.

Two Months before Your Trip

- Find out about the conditions in the area, especially the water temperature, to determine what type of wetsuit you'll need.

- Determine all of your equipment needs. Either purchase your equipment or find out if the dive shop you're using has all the rental equipment you'll need.

- If you are an unusual size and have trouble fitting into a wetsuit, consider ordering a custom suit.

- If you have severe vision problems, consider ordering a prescription mask.

- If you have any medical condition that could prevent you from diving, ask your doctor for a medical release that you can take along.

One Month before Your Trip

- If you use your own dive equipment, check it over carefully to make sure it's in good working order and that you have everything you need for the trip.

- Find out if the dive shop rents or can service the type of gear you own. If not, consider taking spare parts or even spare gear.

- Purchase extra gear that you might need, such as an extra mask, a dive light and tank marker light for night diving, a line reel for wreck diving, and so on.

- If you're shore diving, pack a tarp to make changing easier and cleaner, and some hard-soled booties for walking on rocks and rough ironshore.

- Make sure that you have a mesh bag for your dive gear, and get a rolling dive bag for transporting gear to the destination.

- *Don't forget emergency equipment. At a minimum, you should have a whistle to attach to your BCD and a knife. Consider a small strobe light that you can put into the pocket of your BCD. A safety sausage (sometimes called a come-to-me) is highly recommended, especially if you're going to be doing any drift diving. This can be attached to a D-ring on your BCD.*

- Have your regulator serviced. Regs need to be serviced annually, *whether they have been used or not.* If it has been serviced, just ask the shop to bench-check it; that is, to test it for breathing consistency and reliability. Frequently this is a free service. It's especially important if you feel that you might have gotten some sand or grit in it.

- If you use a dive computer, check the battery. Better yet, change it before the trip (if it's one you can change yourself) or buy a spare one to take along. Otherwise, send the computer to the manufacturer for a battery replacement.

- Consider getting insurance for yourself and your dive gear. Chances are, your normal health insurance will not cover treatment in a recompression chamber. And if you need to be airlifted anywhere, you could get a mondo bill! You can also get coverage for your dive and photo equipment. Refer to the section "Insurance and Medical Emergencies" for information about specific insurance coverages.

One Week before Your Trip

- Make a final gear-check: grease O-rings, check batteries and light bulbs.

- Assemble a save-a-dive kit containing at a minimum: extra mask and fin straps, extra mouthpiece, selection of O-rings, mask defog, O-ring lubricant, cable ties (very important), sea snips, and scuba tool. Optional items: computer batteries, contact lenses, meat tenderizer for jellyfish stings.

- Make sure you have all the clips you need to secure your console and your octopus—don't let them dangle.

- Assemble a first-aid kit if you think you might need it at your destination.

- Get suntan lotion and any medications you'll need, such as antihistimines, seasick pills, and ear drops.

Right before Your Trip

- Double-check to make sure you have your C-card.

- Ditto your passport or birth certificate, airline tickets, and money.

- Cancel the paper, turn off the electric blanket, change the message on your answering machine, grab a water bottle for the flight, and you're on your way!

TRAVEL TIPS

Pack a carry-on with items you'll want in case your checked bags don't make it to the destination right away. Pack a swimsuit, extra underwear, shorts and T-shirt, medications, etc. Consider packing an extra dive mask—even your regulator if you want.

At the airport, always check to make sure the ticket agent attaches the correct baggage sticker. In other words, make sure the luggage tag is for your final destination, not destinations en route. I have had to correct the reservationist a couple of times. On the way to Saba, for instance, my bags were ticketed for St. Barts!

Put secure locks on your bags. I like the combination locks; that way I don't have to futz with trying to locate keys. Make a photocopy of your passport or birth certificate and keep it in a separate place, in case the original is lost or stolen.

After getting to your destination, always watch to make sure your luggage is transported into vans, buses, etc. Don't simply assume that it will be done. Actually see the bags go in, and watch as the door is closed behind them.

Once You Arrive

BUOYANCY CHECKS

After arriving at your destination, take time to do a buoyancy check before making your first dive. Maintaining neutral buoyancy is important, not only for comfortable diving but also to avoid damaging the environment. If you're too heavy, you'll probably be kicking and bumping into living corals and sponges, causing damage that takes years to repair.

Incorrect weighting will cause you to work harder in the water. If you're not relaxed, you'll breathe more heavily and use up air more quickly. When you're neutrally buoyant you can have a longer dive, as well as a more controlled and comfortable dive.

Once, on a dive in Tobago, it was obvious from the start that my dive buddy was much too light, and was fighting hard to stay down and keep up with us. He signaled the divemaster, who took him down to the sandy bottom at 90 feet. While kneeling on the sand, the divemaster took weight off his own dive belt and gave it to my dive buddy—not something that can be done quickly. I kneeled next to them, watching this procedure in complete amazement, while holding onto our float and line reel (the boat was following our bubbles). Occasionally I'd glance at my computer to see the pixels bouncing along at a fairly steady rate through the green zone. Then they went into the yellow caution zone, right to the edge of the red deco zone! This scenario points out a lot of mistakes that were made, all of which could have been avoided if the guy had just been properly weighted from the start.

To check your buoyancy, the standard test is to wear all of your equipment into water that is too deep to stand in. Deflate the BCD completely. Don't move, hold your breath, and hang vertically. If you're neutrally buoyant, you'll float at about eye level, and when you exhale, you'll sink slowly.

There's one problem with this test, however. It doesn't account for the type of tank you're using (steel or aluminum) and the fact that tanks become more buoyant toward the end of the dive, as the air is consumed. Aluminum tanks, especially, are quite buoyant. So keep that in mind when you're doing your buoyancy check. You might want to wear a little more weight to compensate, especially if the dive boat is not anchoring, but running "live." In that case, you'll be making a safety stop in open ocean, without a line to hold onto, so being able to hover at 15 feet is important.

Even if the shop you're diving with doesn't require an initial buoyancy check, you should do one on your own, if possible, before starting to dive in any unfamiliar location. This should be done in the open ocean, not the swimming pool. Even if you're a comfortable diver, performing a buoyancy check is important for several reasons:

- The salinity of the water varies from one location to another. The higher the salt content, the more buoyant you will be, so you might need to add a bit more weight to your belt or in your weight pockets. And, of course, if you're switching between salt water and fresh water diving, there will be a tremendous difference.

- The buoyancy of wetsuits also varies. Some of the warm-water trilaminate and lycra suits have no buoyancy at all. Neoprene, of course, is very buoyant. We all know that the thicker the neoprene wetsuit, the more buoyant it is. A 6-mm suit is a lot more buoyant than a 3-mm warm-water suit. But you might not realize that a brand-new neoprene suit is also a lot more buoyant than an old suit of the same thickness. Neoprene cells break down over time, and the older suits compress more as you dive deeper, becoming less buoyant. This is particularly relevant if you're renting your wetsuits.

- Also, if you rent your dive gear, you should be aware that all BCDs are not alike when it comes to buoyancy. Some do not vent as well as others; some bladders actually trap air. That's not to say that these are inferior BCDs—actually, some excellent brands will do that. That's just one reason why it's best to have your own equipment, so that you're familiar with it.

- Finally, as mentioned before, the type of tank and the tank size will affect buoyancy. Generally, steel tanks are heavier and do not get as buoyant as aluminum tanks as the air is consumed. An 80-cubic-foot aluminum tank is usually the tank-of-choice for most dive shops, and those are quite buoyant toward the end of a dive.

DIVE SHOPS AND DIVE BOATS

Remember that the quality of dive shops and dive boats is only as good as the individuals who manage and work in them. Sometimes turnover is high and standards slip. In most other sports that could be inconvenient, but for scuba diving it can be disastrous. So it's important to observe and to evaluate. Here are some minimum standards that we can expect for dive businesses and some telltale signs to watch for:

Professionalism   Does the shop appear to be efficient and professionally run? Is it clear what their procedures are? Does it display prominently its dive affiliation, such as NAUI, PADI, SSI, etc.? If it does, that's a pretty good indication that the shop has high standards.

Paperwork   Every dive business should check divers' certification cards before selling air or arranging a boat dive. They should also ask you to provide basic information about your age, general state of health, home phone and address, and someone to contact in case of emergency. Usually all of this is accompanied by a liability release form.

Assessing Skill Level   Dive shops will do this in a variety of ways. Sometimes they simply ask when you last dived. Some will actually want to take a look at your log book. Others will give you a quick skills test in the water. I've experienced the latter only twice—once on the island of Andros (Small Hope Bay Resort) in the Bahamas, and again on the island of Roatan in the Bay Islands of Honduras (Anthony's Key Resort). Both times I was impressed with how quickly and efficiently the divemasters performed the test. It didn't interfere at all with the dive, and I wasn't a bit inconvenienced.

Buoyancy Check   Some of the best-run resorts and dive shops will require that you make a preliminary dive from shore to check your buoyancy. This is a good sign that not only are they concerned that you're properly weighted (eliminating potential problems later on when you're diving from their boats), but also concerned that you won't be bouncing along the bottom, destroying corals and other marine life.

Rental Equipment   Be very suspicious of rental equipment that looks like it has not been rinsed. If you see sand or salt crystals on the regulator, watch out. This is an obvious sign that the equipment is not being adequately maintained. A worn and shabby appearance is another danger signal.

Inspect the gear thoroughly while you're still in the dive shop. Check the hoses for wear and make sure the mouthpieces are secure. Make sure you have your primary regulator, an octopus, an inflator hose, and an air pressure gauge and depth gauge. I have seen shops rent regs with no depth gauges or octos! Remember that some shops in remote locations have a hard time getting parts for their equipment, so if something breaks, there's not much they can do about it until parts or replacements arrive. Nevertheless, you should not have to compromise your safety because of their problems.

Next, test the gear before you use it (again, in the shop is best). Assemble your BCD and reg on the tank and connect the inflator hose. Slowly turn the tank valve until you hear the rush of air, then go ahead and turn it all the way until it stops. Listen for air leaks. Then test your power inflator and BCD. Push the inflator button to make sure it functions (and doesn't free-flow) and inflate the BCDs. Make sure it holds air. If the power inflator does not work, get another BCD—do not attempt oral inflation underwater unless there's an emergency. Then purge the regulator a bit and smell the air. It should be odorless. But if you detect an oily or "bad" odor, get another tank to test. When you're finished, turn off the air and purge the regulator.

If there's a persistent problem with air or equipment, it's time to switch to another dive operator.

Dive Boats   Many countries have rigorous standards for vessels that carry passengers for hire. In the United States, boats must be Coast Guard certified if they carry more than six paying passengers. This requires them to have specific safety equipment on board, which is inspected yearly. Keep in mind that the requirements in some countries might not be so rigorous, and there might not be any at all. Before throwing your dive gear into that little skiff, at least be aware of what it probably does not have on board:

Communications with shore. What would happen if the vessel broke down, and it couldn't pick up its divers?

Oxygen supply. Suppose a diver needed oxygen immediately, but the vessel was an hour or more from shore?

First-aid kit. What if someone leaped off the boat during the surface interval and cut themselves seriously on sharp coral?

Recall device. What if a diver has an emergency and needs to be taken to shore, but everyone else is still in the water?

Dive boats carrying more than six passengers should have this kind of equipment and more. They should be able to throw out a drift line (or "tag line") from the stern, for divers to hold onto in strong currents. They should also have special descent lines for challenging situations and at least one extra scuba cylinder that can hang at 15 feet, in case a diver runs low on air. For night dives, they should have powerful lights, including a good strobe light, that can be seen easily from the water. If the boat is going out for more than a single dive, it should be able to provide some shade, and have fresh drinking water.

Dive Boat Procedures   The boat crew should explain the various features of the boat. They should also explain their emergency procedures. Pre-dive briefings should specify how divers should enter the water and how to get back on board, as well as what the divemaster expects once they're in the water. For instance, is there a time limit? a depth limit?

One of the most important tasks for the boat crew is to account for all the divers. With groups, they should have a dive roster with the name of every diver on board. Before leaving the dive site, they need to account for everyone on the roster. Always make sure that *your* name is on the roster.

Wait for Me!

If you want to increase the odds of *not* being left "in deep water" by a dive boat, a nifty little plastic ID card will help. It says, "Dive Boat Captain WAIT FOR ME [your name] Is Not Yet Back on Board." And it has a cute graphic of a diver. Each time you enter the water, simply leave it with the crew member in charge of head counts. Retrieve it when you climb back on board. The card was created by dive journalist Joyce Huber, who got the idea in 1975 while on a dive trip in Honduras. She and her dive buddy were forgotten a couple of times, but were eventually picked up when their C-cards were discovered by the water fountain (it was a big yacht). Since the crew's English was poor, they didn't use a roster. Instead, they instructed the divers to drop their C-cards in the water fountain each time they made a dive and to pick them up when they climbed back on board. Simple!

The cards are only $3 each or four for $10, plus 50 cents for shipping and handling. Obviously, Huber is not making a fortune from this. "If it saves just one life, it's worth it," she says. Order the cards by sending a check or money order to PhotoGraphics Publishing, 629 Edgewater Avenue, Ridgefield, NJ 07657. Phone (201) 945-5477 or fax (201) 945-6105.

Live-Aboard Diving

Live-aboard dive boats ply the waters around the world, from exotic locales around Indonesia to familiar sites like the Cayman Islands. And the live-aboards have really come a long way since the early days of diving. When live-aboard diving was in its infancy, divers had to give up a lot of creature comforts. They slept in bunkrooms and generally shared a single head and shower. Some are still like that; they can be a lot of fun, and are inexpensive. But now there are entire flotillas of far more comfortable, even luxurious boats. They feature individual staterooms with private heads and showers, individual air conditioning, and picture windows. They might feature lavish buffets and hot tubs. Some even have satellite phones and stereo systems.

Some, such as the Aggressor Fleet, cater to underwater photographers and videographers. Their photo labs might feature Nikonos or Sea & Sea cameras, multiple lenses, macro and close-up kits, plus daily E-6 processing. For videographers, there are professional editing bays with special effects generators and sound track mixing equipment.

The prices for live-aboard trips might sound expensive—they certainly can be. But remember that most live-aboard trips are all-inclusive. When you're comparing them to resort/dive packages, be sure to include all the extras at the resorts—the meals, taxi fares, extra costs for night dives, rental gear, etc. Some countries have a very high cost of living, so the shore-based options might be more expensive, especially in the high season.

Still, you might ask, "What, really, is the benefit of a live-aboard, especially now that there are so many excellent resorts that are totally, or at least partially, dedicated to the diving market?" The answer to that question really depends on the area where you're diving, as well as the type of traveler you are.

In order to dive some parts of the world—the Galapagos, or the Coral Sea, for instance—you *have* to dive from a live-aboard. There simply are no land-based lodgings. However, even in areas where there are plenty of lodgings on land, many divers still prefer to dive from a live-aboard. There usually are a number of advantages, although not always, so definitely ask a lot of questions before you commit to one of these trips.

The time spent getting to dive sites can be greatly reduced, since your floating resort could be anchored right on top of one. On the other hand, tenders are frequently used to transport divers from the ship to the dive sites, so the time en route might not be terribly different than leaving from shore. Also the convenience of flexibility—diving virtually any time you want—may not be possible on some boats.

Live-aboards can offer a greater selection of dive sites and take you to special places that boats cannot get to from shore. The advantage can be more pristine underwater conditions and fewer divers in the water. Some live-aboards, however, use pretty much the same sites and moorings as do the boats from shore, so there's not much of an advantage.

Convenience can be a big factor. There's no trudging around with equipment, taking it from your resort to the boat or dive shop. It's always on the ship, right when you need it. However, many dive shops and resorts have convenient storage lockers where you can rinse your gear and hang it up to dry. Some of them will even do those tasks for you.

Regardless of all these pros and cons, the final yea or nay for many will be based on other personal considerations. Do you want to be around the same small group of people for an entire week? Do you mind being on a rocking vessel night and day? Do you want to dive in practically virgin waters, to encounter whale sharks and hammerheads? Do you enjoy exploring new territory, meeting the locals, experiencing a new culture? All of these factors should be considered.

Also, check out www.liveaboard-diving.com. You can search the site for live-aboard availability and book and pay by credit card, all online.

Tipping on Dive Boats

If you feel that the crew on a dive boat has given good service, by all means leave them a tip. They have a tough job—a lot is expected of them—and they definitely deserve our thanks, as well as some extra compensation. If we tip waiters for simply delivering food, surely we should tip divemasters who watch out for our well-being, and who perform tasks that range from hosing down shipboard vomit to rescuing panicked divers.

On dive boats it's customary to tip the crew about 15 percent of the cost of the dive. You could give the tip to the boat captain to split evenly with the crew, or you could tip a specific person and say "This is for you." If you're diving with the same crew each day, it's acceptable to tip at the end of your trip.

FLYING, DIVING, AND HIKING

Before flying, divers must allow time after diving for their bodies to "off-gas." Due to lower atmospheric pressures at altitude, there is an increased risk of decompression sickness (DCS) after diving. Most certifying agencies now recommend that before flying, divers wait at least 12 hours after a single no-decompression dive (24 hours is better). However, if the diving pattern has been repetitive or deep, or includes decompression diving, then divers should wait *at least* 24 hours before flying.

Remember that the rules for flying after diving also apply to hiking, biking, and driving to high altitudes. But also keep in mind that other factors besides altitude enter the equation. Rigorous exercise, in particular, is thought to increase susceptibility to DCS.

So even if, for instance, you do not hike to 8,000 feet, you could still be at risk, especially if you're not in good physical condition or you smoke, drink alcohol, or have been ill. It's important to make a self-evaluation and consider your personal health habits.

ENRICHED AIR NITROX: AN ADDED MEASURE OF SAFETY

One way to help minimize the effects of nitrogen is to dive with Enriched Air Nitrox while using standard dive tables or computers. This is especially attractive to divers who travel and fly to their destinations. You must be certified to use it, however, because if used improperly Nitrox can be extremely dangerous—even more dangerous than decompression sickness. Also, Nitrox air fills will cost more—usually an additional eight to ten dollars per tank.

Nitrox is basically oxygen enriched air. Normal breathing air contains 21 percent oxygen, whereas Nitrox is usually between 32 and 36 percent oxygen. So you're getting more oxygen and less nitrogen into your system.

The benefits can be extended bottom times and more dives per day, as well as shorter surface intervals and decompression stops. There is also a decrease in dive fatigue and a reduced risk of nitrogen narcosis. Nitrox is ideal for divers who are older or not physically fit, if used with standard dive tables or computers, for that extra margin of safety. However, it's getting popular with even young, fit divers, who are using it in the more conservative manner.

On the downside, Nitrox is extremely dangerous if it is used for deep diving (usually past 100 feet). Oxygen toxicity can quickly result in convulsions and death.

Each Nitrox mix has a maximum operating depth. The higher the percentage of oxygen, the shallower the maximum operating depth. That's why Nitrox users must be certified in order to understand the physiological effects of the gas and how to use it properly. They must present their Nitrox certification before getting Nitrox fills, and they are required to test their own gas mixture before using the tank. Never attempt to use Nitrox, or any mixture other than normal air, unless you have the proper training and certification.

INSURANCE AND MEDICAL EMERGENCIES

Emergency Medical Insurance   Special dive insurance is a good idea if you're going to be traveling and diving. Check with your health insurance company, but chances are it will not cover you for hyperbaric treatment of diving-related injuries or air evacuation to a chamber or hospital. And *that* can be very expensive.

DAN, the Divers Alert Network, has an excellent reputation in the diving community and offers a couple of benefit options that are not outrageously expensive. DAN is an international nonprofit diving safety organization that functions primarily to assist in the treatment of underwater diving accidents. It provides 24-hour emergency telephone access to physicians skilled in diving medicine.

DAN does not maintain any treatment facility or directly provide any form of treatment. It functions primarily as a facilitator, coordinating the efforts of everyone involved in order to get the injured diver into the hyperbaric trauma care system. If a diver is injured, call DAN's emergency hotline, and they will take care of the rest. Emergency calls go straight to DAN headquarters at Duke University Medical Center in Durham, North Carolina.

DAN also has a nonemergency phone number that you can use for advice. For instance, if you have a question about some medication you're taking and would like to know if you should be diving, they are available to help you out. DAN also keeps statistics on diving-related accidents, which can be helpful in the prevention and also the treatment of the injuries.

For membership questions call (800) 446-2671 in North America. Elsewhere call (919) 684-2948; fax (919) 490-6630. Contact them online at www.diversalertnetwork.org.

In case of a diving emergency, call DAN at (919) 684-4DAN (4326) or (919) 684-8111. PADI offers a similar plan with its Diver Protection Plan. For information, check out www.padi.com.

Equipment Protection   Equipment insurance also might be a good idea. First check your homeowner's policy to see if you are already covered for loss while traveling. The airlines cover a certain amount, but if you have dive gear and camera equipment, the value could be in the thousands. The Divers Equipment Protection Program (DEPP) is a reputable organization. With them, you can also get flood coverage for cameras, lenses, and strobes. Call (760) 360-9781 or (888) 678-4096.

Protecting the Reefs— What are Reefs, Anyway?

Reefs are made up largely of hard corals, which are animals—tiny polyps, actually related to the sea anemone. The polyps build calcium carbonate structures around themselves, and as they divide and grow, the colonies build up on top of one another, gradually forming a coral reef. Marine biologists will probably cringe at this explanation. Surely it's much more complicated than that! Nevertheless, the important fact is that it takes a long, long time—thousands of years, it is said—to build a coral reef. Certainly they deserve our utmost respect.

Unfortunately, the hard coral is extremely fragile. Soil runoff, chemicals, urine, sand—and even human touch—can kill it. As divers and snorkelers, our responsibility is to protect the reefs and the entire marine environment. Minimizing kicking and establishing good buoyancy are extremely important, as is not touching the reef. New divers and underwater photographers, especially, can do a lot of damage.

To get good pictures, photographers are required to shoot upward, toward the light. In order to do that, they have to be low, which puts them closer to fragile marine life. So photographers need to be especially careful and realize that getting the shot is not worth damaging the subject matter. I confess that I have bumped into coral, by accident, and I feel terrible when I do it. Usually coral encounters are accidental, caused by currents or surge, or simply getting distracted. With the growing number of photographers, however, it's even more important for us to be extremely careful to protect these beautiful living organisms.

Snorkelers also can be guilty of damaging the shallow coral reefs. I love reading about the colorful coral that snorkelers can see in popular Hanauma Bay, Oahu, in the Hawaiian Islands. Well, I am here to report that the only coral that snorkelers can see in Hanauma Bay is dead coral. It has been killed by its admirers walking on it. There are some beautiful corals farther out in the bay, but so deep that snorkelers would not be able to see it (it is a terrific place to dive).

Snorkelers and shore divers should always remember to walk out into the water *only* on sand or rock, then don their fins before getting to the coral. We should remember that this is their turf, not ours. Try to think of diving (and snorkeling) as a privilege, not a "right."

In your dive travels, it's likely that you will come upon a phenomenon commonly called coral bleaching. It's easy to recognize, since huge areas can look ghostly white. The devastation is sickening. It is assumed that high water temperatures cause this bleaching, and it can occur quickly. In fact, some of the dive sites described in this book might be bleached out when you see them—it wouldn't surprise me, since the phenomenon is occurring all around the world. I have personally seen huge areas of complete coral devastation in the Indian Ocean and in the Caribbean.

The good news, though, is that bleached coral is not necessarily dead, and it can recover. I've been told by experts, including marine biologists, that in the early stages of bleaching, the coral is actually stressed. Divemasters have told me that they have seen huge areas recover almost as quickly as they became bleached. In 1998, an organization called Reef Check reported that 15 percent of the world's reefs had died off. In May 2000, they issued a new report revealing that a third of those reefs had since recovered—very good news.

Sedimentation also damages reefs extensively. This can come from coastal development or natural runoff. Sandy beaches can be detrimental, especially when storms arise. The sand particles, and any sedimentation, reduce light and nutrients and can actually smother the corals. So keep that in mind when you're looking for those great dive spots: stay away from areas with a lot of sand, rivers, and shoreline development. We all can help by fanning sand and silt off corals and sponges when we see that they're in danger of being smothered. Dee Scarr, an environmentalist on Bonaire, says that the sponges are the most vulnerable. Corals seem to be better able to cleanse themselves.

CLIPOLOGY

Never heard of it? That's the official term for the science of clipping off dive gear to keep it from dangling. And it's important. To protect the reefs, please have clips for your octopus and gauges. Don't leave anything dangling. Also, remember that when you're diving walls, the drop-offs can be deep. So when you're wall diving, be sure to attach your light, slates, cameras, etc., to a cord or lanyard, because if you drop anything, it's *hasta la bye-bye*.

DON'T EAT THE WILDLIFE!

Would you ever consider eating a cheetah or a jaguar? Or a chimpanzee or a parrot? Think about that before sinking your teeth into swordfish, shark, Atlantic lobster, or haddock. These, as well as red snapper, cod, and many marine fish, are disappearing quickly. Because they are delicious and healthy for us, they're in great demand. But serious overfishing around the globe has brought their numbers to an all-time low.

Fortunately, there are alternatives. We can choose to eat species that are more abundant, such as Alaskan salmon, mahi-mahi, and rainbow trout. Also, farm-raised fish is now plentiful and just as nutritious.

In June 2000, Ocean Wildlife Campaign reported that fishermen kill about 60,000 Pacific sharks every year (mostly the beautiful and shy blue sharks and the gentle whale sharks) by slicing off their fins and throwing the dying bodies back into the sea. Why? To satisfy the voracious human appetite for shark's fin soup. It makes me sick. Please, do not contribute to this type of cruel and wasteful practice.

Fisheries also are contributing to the near-extinction of the leatherback turtle, the world's largest sea turtle and the only ones found off the coast of

California. The scientific journal *Nature* reported that in 1982 there were 115,000 adult female leatherback turtles in the world's oceans, according to a study by Drexel University in Philadelphia and the Center for Marine Conservation. That number declined to 34,500 by 1996, and now these organizations figure there are no more than about 5,000.

So the situation worldwide is pretty serious. While I'm on my soapbox, I'd like to encourage you to support organizations like the Center for Marine Conservation, the Ocean Wildlife Campaign, the Project AWARE Foundation, and REEF. They are highly respected, and their work is making a significant impact toward protecting our oceans and their marine inhabitants.

One way to learn more about this is to log onto the Monterey Bay Aquarium's website (www.montereybayaquarium.org) and take a look at their Seafood Watch chart. It will help you to make wise choices and contribute to the health of our oceans.

PICK UP TRASH AND PROTECT YOUR FRIENDS

Another way you can do your part to protect marine life is to pick up trash that you see in the water. Some items are a lot worse than others, such as plastic bags, fishing line, and plastic carriers that hold sodas and beer. If you see bottles or cans with a lot if growth on them, it's probably best to leave them alone. Sometimes these can be good habitats for marine animals.

Usually diving is a joyous sport, but occasionally it can be heartbreaking. In Monterey, for example, I've seen plastic rings around the necks of sea lions, which have become deformed as a result. They are the victims of our carelessness. If you see these rings in the water, or anything that could trap marine life, always pick them up and take them back to shore with you. Then cut them up before disposing of them. Even nondivers and snorkelers can help out by simply cutting up plastic carriers before putting them in the trash. Tell all of your friends, and perhaps you'll save some helpless marine animal from an agonizing death.

Understanding the Ratings

Use the ratings to help make comparisons and to determine whether the diving environment is appropriate for your skill level and whether the support services are adequate. These are general guidelines, but they should help you get a quick "read" on a place.

Remember that businesses change for the better or worse, so by the time this book is published, some of the services on which the rankings are based might have changed. Similarly, underwater conditions change due to such factors as coral bleaching, shoreline development, and over-fishing.

PHYSICAL CHARACTERISTICS OF THE DIVE AREA

These ratings refer to underwater conditions under normal circumstances at the dive destination. We're actually evaluating (but not scientifically) a typical day. During certain times of the year, these conditions can quickly deteriorate. Some areas, for instance, experience red tides, or plankton bloom, which reduce underwater visibility. Storms also can stir up the sea bottom, contributing to reduced visibility, and stronger surge. Hurricanes in the Caribbean and typhoons in the Pacific are typical occurrences that cause havoc underwater, but some islands are hit by these more than others. That's where these rankings can be helpful.

Some divers like cold water and strong currents, and they don't mind poor visibility. They might claim that they actually see more marine life in those conditions. Nevertheless, we believe that most divers are looking for calm, gin-clear, bathtub-warm waters, and these rankings are based on those criteria.

Water & Weather Conditions

Visibility   Good visibility is a definite plus in any area. Fewer particles in the water enhance our viewing and certainly improve photography. Typical horizontal visibility on a typical day at the site is the determining factor. Because visibility has unlimited possibilities, the rankings we use pertain to the low end of the spectrum.

Visibility of around 100 feet and beyond is *Excellent*. About 85 feet is *Good*. Somewhere around 65 feet is *Adequate*. Consistently less than 50 feet of visibility gets a *Poor* rating.

Current and Surge   Usually we do not like surge, and we might or might not like current. Unusually heavy current can be dangerous, but a moderate current can be great for drift diving. For instance, off of Cozumel, which is known for its drift diving, a moderate current is a definite plus, but a strong current is not. Therefore, in some areas a moderate current might actually be preferable to a minimal current.

We will not attempt to apply specific velocity measurements but will instead make do with: *Minimal, Moderate, Strong,* and *Ripping*.

Temperature   Generally, the warmer the water temperature, the more pleasant the diving. In warm water, we need less protection from an exposure suit, and therefore need to carry less weight. Also, when we dive in warm water our air consumption decreases and we can have longer dives. Some divers are accustomed to wearing thick wetsuits or drysuits with hoods and gloves, and they don't mind at all diving in water below 50 degrees, or even ice diving. However, we think that most divers, particularly women, children, and older people (who tend to chill more easily), enjoy warm water.

Therefore, for our rankings, around 80° Fahrenheit is *Comfortable.* About 70° is *Chilly.* Below 70° it's definitely getting pretty cold for most people. Therefore, about 60° is *Cold.* Approximately 50° and below gets a ranking of *Numbing.*

Storms   Storm rankings refer to the frequency of storms in the area. Some destinations are constantly being hammered, and others rarely see a storm. Obviously, the fewer the storms, the better. So a place that hardly ever sees a storm gets a ranking of *Calm,* whereas one that experiences seasonal storms gets a ranking of *Occasionally Stormy.* A place that consistently experiences stormy or turbulent conditions gets a *Stormy* ranking.

Site Conditions

Mooring Buoys   Mooring buoys are extremely important for reef preservation. The more buoys, the better. When boats can tie up to a buoy rather than dropping anchor, not only is the reef protected, but it is also safer and more convenient for the boat operator. There's nothing more annoying than attempting to pull up the anchor only to find it stuck on some obstacle—a rock, some kelp, or a beautiful stand of coral. That means that someone has to get back in the water and extricate the anchor.

An area with a lot of mooring buoys is also a good sign that reef conservation in general is deemed important. It takes a lot of money to put in these buoys and maintain them. So if they are being funded by some entity, it usually means there are other conservation efforts going on. The bottom line to all this: better diving. Keep in mind, however, that in some areas where drift diving is popular, boats run live and do not anchor at all. In these areas mooring buoys are not needed.

A vast system of mooring buoys that are well maintained gets an *Extensive* ranking. A scattering of mooring buoys gets an *Average* rating. And no buoys at all gets a ranking of *None.* In areas where buoys are not needed because boats are not anchoring, the ranking is *N/A* (not applicable).

Fishing, Collecting, & Hunting Restrictions   In diving areas, the more restrictions regarding fishing, collecting, and hunting, the better. Also, the more extensive the underwater area covered by these restrictions, the better. These activities might be prohibited altogether, there could be seasonal restrictions, or no restrictions at all. Therefore, for our rankings, where there are vast areas of fishing, collecting and hunting restrictions, the ranking is *Widespread Restrictions.* Where there are some protected areas, the ranking is *Some Restrictions.* And no regulations at all for fishing, collecting, or hunting gets a ranking of *No Restrictions.*

Ease of Access   Generally, divers do not want to spend a lot of time being transported to dive sites. They might want to share time with nondiving family and friends during part of the day. Also, divers don't want to have to experience rough, heavy seas for long periods of time. It's an important consideration for someone prone to seasickness. Unfortunately, in some areas, both of these scenarios are unavoidable. For instance, the reef drop-off could be a long way from shore and shipwrecks might be way out in deep ocean. There are gung-ho divers who don't mind long rides and choppy seas in order to get to desirable dive spots, but we feel that most divers prefer easy, quick access.

Therefore, quick access (15 minutes or less) gets a ranking of *Very Easy.* About 30 minutes gets a ranking of *Convenient.* Transportation taking close to an hour, which would probably entail some choppy seas, gets a ranking of *Moderate.* Anything longer would have a ranking of *Inconvenient.*

Boat Traffic/Diver Congestion   Boat traffic and diver congestion at dive sites are definitely unpleasant situations. These are annoying, and they can mean that the dive sites themselves could be getting stressed and possibly damaged. Therefore, where there is virtually no problem with competition from dive boats, the area gets a ranking of *None.* Where there is occasional competition, the area gets a *Light* ranking. And where this is a real problem, the ranking is *Heavy.*

Marine Life

Certainly, the more the better, when divers talk about marine life. We want to see as many of these critters as we possibly can. The exception to this can be the predominance of a single species to the detriment of other marine life. For instance, there are entire areas of ocean floor in Southern California where there is little marine life except for sea urchins, and these are prolific. That's because the urchins themselves have wiped out other species, devouring everything in sight. So when we talk about abundance, we mean a *healthy* abundance of life.

Abundance of Invertebrates   Invertebrates are those animals that do not have spinal columns: the beautiful gorgonians, corals, and sponges; the worms, mollusks, tunicates, sea stars, octopus, shrimp, and so on. We're ranking these: *Prolific, Abundant, Common,* and *Uncommon.*

Abundance of Vertebrates   These are all the animals with spinal columns—namely, the fish. This category would also include pelagic life, but we've broken these out separately. The same rankings apply: *Prolific, Abundant, Common,* and *Uncommon.*

Abundance of Pelagic Life   Pelagic animals are those that are not habitués of the benthic, or bottom, regions, such as ocean reefs. The pelagic animals will visit reefs from the deep ocean where they roam and travel long distances. Examples are whales, sharks, manta rays, turtles, and dolphins. Usually we can see them off in blue water when we're cruising along deep walls, but occasionally they'll come in to a shallow reef to feed or have their young. Again, the same rankings apply: *Prolific, Abundant, Common,* and *Uncommon.*

Health of Reef/Marine Life/Marine Structure   Due to all sorts of circumstances, some marine environments are healthier than others. We've ranked these *Pristine, Healthy,* and *Mixed.* The *Mixed* ranking would apply to areas that have experienced some coral bleaching, storm damage, anchor damage, and so on; however, most of the diving environment would be in a healthy state. Any area that has widespread damage would be omitted from this guidebook.

CHARACTERISTICS OF DIVE OPERATIONS

The dive operations in this guide have been chosen for their overall *reputation* in the region in which they work and among the divers they serve. However, remember that standards vary considerably in different parts of the world. We do not attempt to measure qualities such as professionalism, reliability, safety, and so on, simply because these can change from one day to the next. Also, it's impossible for us to dive with all the businesses included in this guide and to evaluate them. Therefore, the rankings are based on tangibles that we can measure to some degree.

Unfortunately, we simply can't include all the excellent dive centers that exist. In many areas, there are simply too many for us to handle. Consequently, if you don't see a business listed here, do not automatically presume that it is not on par with the others. Your personal evaluation may be the best, so take some time to observe some of those telltale signs that we have described in the previous section, "Evaluating Dive Shops and Dive Boats."

Retail Sales   If a shop has a complete line of up-to-date scuba inventory, the ranking is *Extensive.* A selection that would help customers to just "get by" would receive a ranking of *Adequate. None* is for those that have no retail sales at all, that we are aware of.

Rentals   The same rankings apply to rental equipment. *Extensive* rentals would include everything you could possibly need for diving or snorkeling, and probably some extras, such as scooters, rebreathers, and underwater cameras. *Adequate* rentals would be just the basics: wetsuits, BCDs, and regulators. *None* means no rentals at all, that we are aware of.

Scuba Training   The range here is vast. Some dive centers simply provide introductory scuba courses; others are prestigious centers for training future scuba instructors. Most divers don't care about the latter. Typically they simply want to improve their diving skills by getting an advanced certification, or perhaps they are not yet certified and have a referral from an instructor at home, to do their ocean dives while on vacation. Some centers specialize in the latter and do an excellent job with new divers. But training is only as good as the instructor doing it. Here, we are ranking centers on *how much* training they do, not how well they do it.

The rankings are *Extensive, Moderate, Limited,* and *None. Extensive* training would include centers that offer courses at least through the divemaster level and that also offer specialty courses. *Moderate* training includes centers that offer the basic open-water course (and referrals), an introduction to scuba and snorkeling, and some specialties. *Limited* training would include those centers that offer only introductory courses (intro to scuba and snorkeling). *None* is no training at all, that we are aware of.

Photo Services   Our categories are *Extensive, Moderate, Limited,* and *None.* These also vary quite a bit. Some shops not only rent cameras but also have E-6 processing and terrific photo classes. *Extensive* photo services would include camera, video, strobe and lens rentals, photo instruction, camera repair service, and E-6 processing. *Moderate* services would include those centers that have a good rental line of underwater still and video cameras and strobes, and that usually have some repair services. *Limited* photo services would include those shops that have a few pieces of equipment for rent. And *None* would be those that, to our knowledge, offer nothing.

Dive Boats

Again, we're not attempting to rank safety and professionalism here, since these are so variable. Be sure to try to evaluate those yourself. To help, refer to the earlier section, "Evaluating Dive Shops and Dive Boats." The following rankings are based on the tangibles that we can measure to some degree of accuracy. In the case of dive operations that run several dive boats, our rankings refer only to their top-of-the-line fleet.

Dive Boat Comfort   With regard to comfort, there are no absolutes. A large boat is not necessarily better than a small one, and vise versa. Sometimes people refer to large boats as cattle cars. However, a crowded small boat can be a lot less comfortable than a typical load on a large boat. The most important factor is that the type of boat used be the most appropriate one for the area. If dive sites are a long way from shore, a larger boat is usually more comfortable, as long as it has a lot of power and can really scoot. On the other hand, if sites are just minutes from shore, smaller boats are fine, since they don't need to carry as many tanks. You're not going to be on board long, and you'll probably be brought back to shore for the surface interval.

Our boat categories are *Excellent, Good,* and *Adequate. N/A* is used for dive centers that do not run boats at all. Boats with the *Excellent* ranking should be stable in the water, be able to get you to the site as fast as possible, and have a configuration that suits the diving environment. All boats in this category should have a solid diving platform, handrails for stability, and a good, solid ladder. Tank racks should be easy to slip into and should keep tanks secure, not banging about. There should be adequate space for the divers on board, with plenty of room to don equipment and store gear.

For lengthy rides, a marine head on board is a necessity, as is fresh drinking water and an area for getting out of the sun. A freshwater shower is also expected. Plenty of comfortable seating and a lounging area are important.

Most boats will fall into the *Good* category. This is hard to define, because it is usually the boat's configuration that doesn't measure up to the *Excellent* category. Perhaps there's no area to store dry gear, or it's difficult to move about and get around passengers. The boat also might be lacking in speed and performance.

The *Adequate* category indicates that the boat offers no-frills, just the basics: a bucket for masks, a cooler for soft drinks, a serviceable diving platform and ladder. Usually there's little sitting or lounging space. Boats in the *Adequate* category, regardless of their size, will not have much speed.

On-Board Facilities for Photographers Categories are *Superior, Good,* and *None. Superior* accommodation for photographers will have a large rinse container that can easily accommodate all the cameras, and a large, well-equipped table for changing film. The table should have railings to prevent cameras from sliding off and be out of sea spray range. There should be dry storage for film and other equipment. A *Good* rating usually means the boat is carrying a freshwater container for rinsing and leak-testing cameras. Many boats do not accommodate photographers at all. *N/A* is used for those centers that do not run boats at all.

LODGING

The lodgings selected for this guide are those in the area that are the most suitable for divers. That is not to say that others, which we have not included, do not measure up or are not quality establishments. It's just that our selections are the most *convenient* for divers, who need specific accommodations due to the nature of the sport. We feel that most divers will be happiest at the lodgings that are really working to attract diving travelers. If you have ever lugged dripping wet dive gear through a gorgeous lobby in order to get to your room, with salt crystals and sand still clinging to your body, you know what we mean!

A ranking of five stars (★★★★★) is the highest and signifies that the resort is truly dedicated to providing exceptional accommodations and services for divers and snorkelers. A four-star ranking (★★★★) indicates that the lodging accommodates divers very well. Lodgings receiving three stars (★★★) might be small but still offer very good service to divers, and might even be preferable to a four- or five-star property if very personal service is what you're looking for. Two stars (★★) would offer a moderate amount of service to divers and snorkelers, and one star (★) ranking signifies that the resort offers minimal service. No stars means that the property offers no facilities or amenities for divers.

Coordination of Dive Service   The best dive resorts have a dive shop right on the premises that is easy to locate. Moreover, information about the dive shop and diving procedures should be placed prominently in guest rooms. The best shops have a section for retail sales, another section for gear rentals, a repair service area, a classroom, and a central desk with knowledgeable employees who can help you sign up for dives, fill out paperwork, check your certification, and answer your questions.

The best resorts have air compressors and fill their own scuba tanks with top-graded breathing air. If they also pump Nitrox, it's a real plus. The air fill station should be set apart from the retail shop for safety reasons and to avoid noise from the compressors. The route from the shop to the diving area should be clearly defined. The shop should have a convenient and spacious rinse area for gear, as well as showers, and good storage lockers for leaving gear overnight. The shop should provide locks for guests.

Meal service is also important, vis à vis diving, especially when dining rooms are open only at specific times. There is nothing more irritating than returning from a dive (ravenous, of course), only to find the restaurant closed, and you can't get lunch! If dive boats do not return to shore in time for lunch, box lunches should be an available option, which people can order the night before. Breakfasts should be set up at least 45 minutes before boat departure time. A buffet is the best, to speed up service. Similarly, after night dives the dining room should give divers time to shower, change into dry clothes, and get down to the restaurant and have dinner before closing down. If entertainment is offered, it should coincide with divers returning from the night dive.

Access to Docks, Boats, Diving Area   Whether there is a dive shop on the premises or not, access to the dock, to boats, or to the shore should be effortless. The best scenario is to have a boat dock or dive spot directly at the resort, with easy access by guests. Boats could be docked or anchored at the site or they could be brought in from another location. The dock itself should be wide enough to accommodate at least two divers side by side with all of their gear, and should have sufficient bumpers and cleats for tying-off.

Dive Packages   A resort that caters to divers would typically have pricing options that would include lodging and diving. The package should clearly state everything that is included: the number of dives per day, including shore diving options, the type of room, any meals included, airport transportation, taxes, and so on.

One problem to watch out for is resorts that do not make clear exactly how many dives are included in their packages. For instance, a resort might state that six dives are included in their one-week package. Most divers would assume that would mean six two-tank dives. Unfortunately, some resorts count a single two-tank dive as two dives. So clarity is important. Also, packages should be available for nondivers and for snorkelers.

Australia's Great Barrier Reef & Heron Island

Physical Characteristics of the Dive Area

WATER & WEATHER CONDITIONS

Visibility	*Good to Adequate*
Current and Surge	*Moderate*
Temperature	*Comfortable to Chilly*
Storms	*Occasionally Stormy*

SITE CONDITIONS

Mooring Buoys	*None*
Fishing, Collecting, and Hunting Restrictions	*Widespread Restrictions*
Ease of Access	*Very Easy*
Boat Traffic/Diver Congestion	*None*

MARINE LIFE

Abundance of Invertebrates	*Prolific*
Abundance of Vertebrates	*Prolific*
Abundance of Pelagic Life	*Abundant*
Health of Reef/Marine Life/ Marine Structure	*Pristine*

The Great Barrier Reef

Whether you are a snorkeler or a diver, at some point in your life you really should visit this great Natural Wonder of the World. There are 238,899 miles of reef—just imagine how many tiny coral polyps contributed! The Great Barrier Reef (GBR) is said to be the only living structure on earth visible from the moon.

Actually, 2,900 individual coral reefs make up the Great Barrier Reef, strung out in a long chain that parallels the state of Queensland on Australia's east coast. The chain stretches an incredible 1,250 miles—the distance from New York to Florida! The reef starts at the southern extreme near the city of Bundaberg and continues north along the Queensland coast past Cape York to Papua New Guinea. At some points along the way, it reaches more than 200 nautical miles into the Coral Sea.

Back in 1770, Captain Cook was the first European to explore this area and to learn what disastrous results can befall seamen who get too close to the coral reef. He probably destroyed quite a few polyps when he ran his ship *Endeavor* aground on what is now called Endeavor Reef, up in northern Queensland.

It is a common misconception that you can just fall into the water from various points on the mainland and be able to dive on the Great Barrier Reef. Actually, the main structure of the reef is miles away; only shallow fringing reef grows along the coast. This main Outer Reef lies an average of 41 miles off the coast, and by high-speed catamaran you'll reach it in about an hour or an hour and a half. Cairns is a major jumping-off point for 300-foot catamarans that have enough power to take visitors out to the reef and back in a single day.

The main gateways to the GBR, from north to south, are Port Douglas, Cairns, Mission Beach, Townsville, and Gladstone. Because it is so large, the Marine Park is divided into four sections: Far North Section, Cairns Section, Central Section, and Capricorn Section. This latter section is where the subject of our chapter is located: Heron Island.

The reef consists of three kinds of coral structures: fringing reef, ribbon reef, and platform reef. In most cases, you'll be diving in the platform variety, which consists mostly of patch reef. It grows up from the continental shelf and extends the length of the Queensland coastline. This is the most common type—the primary structure of the Great Barrier Reef. Fringing reef exists close to the mainland and around the islands. Ribbon reefs are "streamers" of long thin reef along the outer edge of the GBR and are only found north of Cairns.

The islands in the GBR are either "continental," meaning they are part of the Australian landmass, or "cays," meaning they are made of coral. Over the years, corals died, were mixed with sand, and the whole lot was under great pressure from water action. As you would expect, the cays are all surrounded by vibrant coral and fish life. Continental islands may be surrounded by coral or they may have no coral at all. Experts say that the Great Barrier Reef has 1,500 species of fish, 4,000 types of mollusks, and 400 species of hard and soft corals.

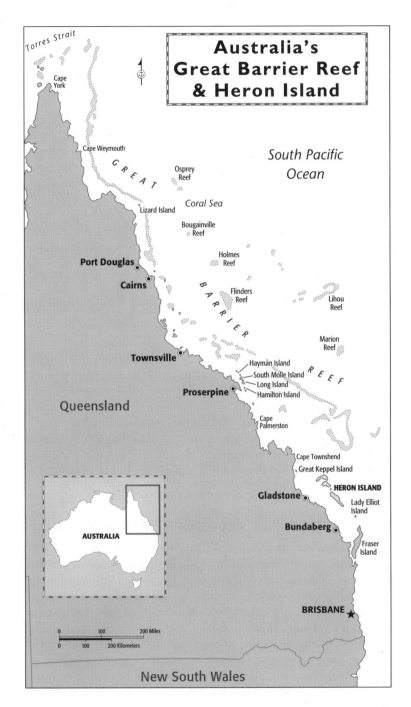

Australia's
Great Barrier Reef
& Heron Island

Torres Strait

Cape York

Cape Weymouth

GREAT

Osprey Reef

South Pacific Ocean

Coral Sea

Lizard Island

Bougainville Reef

Holmes Reef

Port Douglas

Cairns

BARRIER

Flinders Reef

Lihou Reef

Marion Reef

Townsville

Hayman Island
South Molle Island
Long Island
Hamilton Island

REEF

Proserpine

Queensland

Cape Palmerston

Cape Townshend

Great Keppel Island

HERON ISLAND

Gladstone

Lady Elliot Island

AUSTRALIA

Bundaberg

Fraser Island

BRISBANE

0   100   200 Miles
0   100   200 Kilometers

New South Wales

The northern section of the reef has the warmest water. It also has the best visibility, and the sites are closer to shore. That doesn't necessarily mean that the diving is better, however. Heron and Lady Elliott Islands down south are outstanding dive spots and see far fewer polluters in the form of people, boats, and airplanes.

Heron Island was chosen for this chapter because it is one of only three coral islands among the GBR where guests can stay overnight. The others are Lady Elliott Island and Green Island. Heron is made of coral, surrounded by coral, and contains so much variety and abundance of marine life that a research station operates right there. There is only one lodging on the island, filled with excited divers and snorkelers, and there is a dive shop. That's it. If you don't like the water, you'd better enjoy birdlife or taking tidepool treks.

Most of the GBR's visitors access the reef from Cairns, much farther north. Green Island, a 32-acre coral cay, is a popular site just offshore, but it's besieged by crowds of tourists—hardly a wilderness experience. That leaves Heron Island much more isolated, with little boat traffic and no day-trippers, which is another reason why I rate it so highly.

Since the Great Barrier Reef is so huge, there are other islands that could be recommended, but I feel that for divers Heron Island is as good as it gets. If you'd like to sample some others, I would recommend (for diving) Lizard Island in the far North, Hayman and Daydream in the Central Section, and Lady Elliot, another coral island just south of Heron. For another possible excursion, I highly recommend Fraser Island. It's the world's largest sand island and a fascinating place for eco-minded tourists.

Don't forget that Australia's winter is the Northern Hemishpere's summer, and June to August is high season in Queensland. When planning your trip, definitely keep weather conditions in mind (see the Quick Stats below), but also consider the dates of several exciting biological events that occur around Heron Island.

Heron Island: A Wonder Down Under

From the air this tiny bit of land looks like a head of broccoli surrounded by bright white sand. It sits smack dab on top of a massive reef structure that sprawls out for more than ten square miles. The diving is just minutes outside the harbor entrance on a series of shallow bommies (that's Aussie-speak for "coral heads") or along the steep walls of a deep channel that separates Heron Reef and adjacent Wistari Reef. Turtles, manta rays, an astounding number of reef fish species, and gorgeous hard and soft corals will definitely keep you happy underwater. But that's not all that Heron has to offer.

You should know straight off that you're going to be sharing this island with thousands of visitors. No, not the day-trippers that are motored over to the reef for a few hours of snorkeling and diving. (In fact, there is no day-tripper service to Heron Island at all.) I'm talking about the feathered variety, primarily, but there are others, as well. Migratory birds, egg-laying turtles, and migrating whales all visit the island at various times throughout the year. It is a major seabird rookery and a nesting site for giant green and loggerhead turtles.

When I visited Heron Island in late October, for instance, it was filled with the noises (and musty odors) of nesting silver eyes, black noddy terns, white herons, and wedge-tailed shearwaters. Shearwaters, also called muttons, really cause a commotion at night, when they do their amorous courtship thing. It's downright spooky! Anyway, our helicopter from the mainland touched down, practically on the beach, and after the rotors stopped whirring, the chorus of birdcalls flew through the air. It seemed as though every tree contained hundreds of these visitors. I couldn't stop looking skyward, despite the beauty of the surrounding waters. But these were not the only visitors. October also begins the season for sea turtles to make their way up the beach at night to deposit their precious cargo of eggs. Later, in December, the hatchlings begin to emerge from the warm sand. All of this continues through January, February, and most of March.

By May, most of the birds and the last of the turtle hatchlings have left the island, but a new species appears— the humpback whales. When these huge creatures begin their northern migration, they can be seen all around the island through September. And in September most of the migratory birds return to Heron Island to begin building their nests once again, and the cycle continues.

QUICK STATS FOR AUSTRALIA & HERON ISLAND

Size   Australia's landmass is almost 3 million square miles, almost the same size as the continental United States. Tiny Heron Island is less than one-third of a mile long and 330 yards wide, for a total of only 42 acres.

Population   Full of Aussies—about 18 million of them; Heron Island has a few people and around 40,000 seabirds.

Location   It is about 7,500 miles from Los Angeles to Sydney and 10,000 miles from New York to Sydney. Australia is south of the equator (the seasons are opposite of North America's) and west of the International Date Line. Heron Island lies on the Tropic of Capricorn, 45 miles northeast of Gladstone, in the State of Queensland.

Time   There are three time zones in Australia. Queensland does not observe Daylight Savings Time, but several states do. The east coast of the continent (where Heron Island is located) is Greenwich Mean Time plus ten hours. If you were to phone from Los Angeles at 4 p.m. on Monday, it would be 9 a.m. Tuesday in Sydney.

Government   Member of the British Commonwealth

Language   English

Electrical Current   220 to 240 volts, 50 cycles AC current. The outlets accept a two- or three-pin plug that has flat blades in a V-configuration. They will not accept plugs made for American outlets. U.S.-made appliances will require an adapter plug and a voltage converter.

Weather   In this land down under, December through March are the hottest and wettest months; the winter months of June to August are the chilliest and the driest. November or December through March or April is monsoon season, with heavy rains and cyclones, but this is mostly a problem in north Queensland. On Heron Island, you'll find yourself in a perpetual summer, with the air temperature generally in the 80s and a light sea breeze blowing.

Water Temperature   Note that summer water temperatures are chilly; the winter temps are perfect. The temperatures range from 65° in June to a high of 78° in December. In winter, plan to wear a 3-mm neoprene wetsuit, and in summer a 5- to 6.5-mm suit (or the equivalent level of warmth in another material).

Underwater Visibility   August through January are the months of peak underwater visibility. On Heron Island, tidal flow determines the quality of the visibility. It ranges from around 90 feet to as low as 40 feet.

Best Diving Months   September and October are terrific, but any time you can get here is great; just remember that the water is very chilly in summer.

PLANNING THE TRIP

Phoning Australia   From North America, dial the international access code (011), then Australia's country code (61), then the area code (7 for Heron Island), then the local number. Most local numbers have 8 digits. For calls to Heron Island dial: 011+61+7+ the local number.

Getting to Heron Island   Fly into Sydney, then take a local carrier to Gladstone Airport for transport by either sea or air to Heron Island. Brisbane, which is closer to Gladstone than Sydney, is the better airport to fly into; however, from North America there probably will not be any direct flights. Nevertheless, it's worthwhile to check. Driving from Brisbane will take about six hours. Covered and secure parking is available at the marina in Brisbane. Remember that Australians drive on the left side of the road.

To Sydney: From North America, the major carriers are Air New Zealand (800) 262-1234, www.airnz.co.nz; Canadian Airlines (800) 665-1177, www.cdnair.ca; Qantas (800) 227-4500, www.qantas.com.au; and United Airlines (800) 538-2929, www.ual.com.

To Gladstone: Fly either Qantas or Ansett (13-13-00; www.ansett.com.au). The airfares are usually the same. Also, both offer discounts for international travelers and special air passes for visiting several destinations. These must be purchased before arriving in Australia.

To Heron Island: Helicopter service (book through the resort) is about A$395 round-trip. There's a 15-kilogram luggage limit; excess baggage can be stored for free at Gladstone Airport. For ferry service, a courtesy coach meets morning flights at Gladstone Airport at 10:30 to take guests to Gladstone Marina for the two-hour catamaran trip to the island. Launches depart at 11 a.m. daily (except Christmas) and return at 3:45 daily. Check in at the marina 30 minutes prior to departure. Round-trip: A$156.

Getting Around   On two feet! It takes only 30 minutes to walk around the island.

Entry Documents   A current passport and a visa are required of all foreign nationals, with the sole exception of citizens of New Zealand. An electronic visa can be issued by a travel agent or your airline booking agent and takes only seconds, assuming you are approved. The Electronic Travel Authority's website is located at www.immi.gov.au/eta/eta.htm.

Currency   The Australian dollar (A$1) is roughly equal to U.S. 70 cents, but it fluctuates.

Tourist Information   The Australian Tourist Commission has the Aussie Helpline at (805) 775-2000; fax (805) 775-4448. Request a copy of the *Australian Vacation Planner* and *Australia Unplugged*. The website is www.australia.com. Another good website, especially if you're planning to explore more of the Queensland area, is www.queenslandislands.com. The Great Barrier Reef Visitors Bureau is a private company and also has an excellent website: www.great-barrier-reef.com.

THE UNDERWATER SCENE

Around this tiny speck of an island in this largest coral reef system in the world, you'll find 1,200 of the possible 1,500 species of fish that are on the

Great Barrier Reef. Just walk out of your room to the water's edge, and say g'day to a reef teeming with life. This is it—you're on the reef itself.

Heron Island sits on a shallow coral flat and is completely encircled by a coral ledge that drops vertically from only 2 feet to depths of 20 to 90 feet. The waters are nutrient-rich, with winds and currents sweeping in toward the shoreline, and it is this that results in a flourishing marine ecosystem. Plankton and other nutrients multiply as they pass through the reef system. This can result in reduced visibility; GBR waters are not as crystal clear as in the Coral Sea. However, these nutrients are what attract the dense schools of fish and the healthy profusion of invertebrate life.

Because Heron is a protected turtle nesting site, sea turtles are commonly seen on just about every dive here; not just one turtle—many. The most common to the area is the green turtle, which has a large body and small head, and the loggerhead turtle, characterized by a large head with a black ring around the eyes. Another pelagic visitor occasionally seen is the white-tip reef shark. But what really catches your attention is the huge variety of fish. Also, the size of these reef fish, especially the butterflyfish and the angelfish, is amazing.

Health Score Card

Pristine. You know it's great if there's a research center on the island!

Diving Conditions

Just about perfect. Most dives are very shallow, which gives plenty of opportunity to observe and to take pictures. Underwater photographers should bring close-up framers and macro tubes. Usually there's a slight current, so drift dives are fairly common. The water can be chilly, especially in summer, so be sure to bring at least a 3-mm neoprene wetsuit. If you are prone to getting cold easily, consider a 6-mm wetsuit, hood, and gloves. The temperatures range from 65° in June to a high of 78° in December. The underwater clarity is affected by tidal flow and varies with the conditions. It can be 90 feet on an incoming tide or as low as 40 feet on an outgoing tide.

Recommended Level of Experience

Any level at all would have a superb experience here. Almost all the dives are easy enough for beginners but have enough underwater variety to keep everyone happy. It's always exciting to encounter new species, and this certainly is where you'll find them.

Great Dive Sites

Heron Reef and nearby Wistari Reef, separated from each other by a small deep-water channel, have an abundance of fascinating sites. Actually, diving anywhere along these reefs could keep you sublimely happy watching nudibranchs, clams, corals, and loads of fish. There are a few sites, though, that are noteworthy, and these are on the south side of Heron.

Wistari I and *Wistari II* are fast-moving drift dives in Wistari Channel, on the south side. The channel is shaped like a funnel, being about a mile wide at the southeastern end and narrowing considerably at the opposite end. The effect is a ripping flow at the narrow end. As you drift by, then fly by, you'll have plenty to admire on both sides of the reef, and have some fun pelagic fish encounters, too. You'll undoubtedly see schools of trevally here, known as jacks in the Caribbean. *Wistari I* is a steep slope covered in staghorn and boulder corals and anemones, with visiting barramundi rock cod and pelagics. *Wistari II* is a 20- to 60-foot dive along a slope broken by boulder corals and swept with schools of baitfish. If dived during the latter half of an incoming tide, water conditions are more placid.

Big Bommie is just a few minutes from the resort and the first dive site from the harbor. Coral heads rise 50 feet and stairstep along the sloping sandy bottom. Big Bommie itself is one immense coral head decorated with vibrant soft corals. The astounding variety of fish is what really accentuates this spot. There could be everything from manta rays to sweetlips, coral trout, spangled emperors, grouper, moray eels, barracuda, and barramundi. The barramundi are those strange-looking polka-dotted fish with the smashed heads. By the way, a bommie is essentially a patch reef consisting of many coral heads.

At *Pam's Point* and also at *Coral Cascades,* giant manta rays are frequently spotted cruising over the tops of the bommies. These are shallow sites with gorgeous plate coral and blue-tipped staghorn coral covering the reef. Look for the elusive lionfish (but don't touch!) and black-and-white-banded humbugs.

Gorgonia Hole is another shallow site (about 45 feet) and a terrific spot to find colorful nudibranchs and seahares. It's around the tip of Heron Reef on the north side. A small wall runs parallel to the reef edge and features a great variety of both soft and hard corals, including large plate and brain coral. Of course, true to its name, gorgonian soft corals abound, covering the overhangs. Holes and swim-throughs cut into the wall and provide excellent habitat for octopus and spotted sweetlips. You'll also see huge angelfish and red-and-orange-speckled coral trout. Green turtles will probably want to check you out. This is a popular night dive.

Excellent dive sites are all along this north side. *Blue Pools* is a semi-enclosed tidal area the size of a big swimming pool. Horizontal ledges of the reef overlap the sandy bottom, sheltering all sorts of colorful fish, including some large trumpetfish. You could also see fat grouper (called groper here), potato cod, and spotted sweetlips. Actually, potato cod are a type of grouper—among the largest. Squid, octopus, and probably hundreds of different types of fish can be seen, as well as white-tip reef sharks.

Tenements (about three of them) are popular spots with photographers, for the clownfish found here, as well as the batfish. If you want to find a clownfish, just look for anemones. These guys have a fascinating symbiotic relationship, which really simplifies the work of a photographer. The fish has a mucous coating that tricks the anemone into not firing its nematocysts, which normally would be deadly. In turn, the clownfish cleans the wiggly tentacles of its host. There are also several varieties of batfish here (also called spadefish). These look like silver swimming plates and almost all have vertical stripes running across the eyes. You'll probably see schools of blue and turquoise fusiliers, turtles, and perhaps mantas, as well. This is another northern site, and features a wall that drops to 70 feet, cut with a number of swim-throughs. A variety of sharks might be cruising along the wall, including leopard sharks, gray reef, white-tip and wobbegong.

The wobbegong is a rather strange-looking shark that reminds me a little of horn sharks in California. They have a flat body, a broad head with barbels, and flaps of skin around the mouth. Their varied color patterns keep them camouflaged on coral and rocks, so they're primarily bottom dwellers and lie in wait for passing prey. Be careful; they might look harmless, but they have been known to bite.

Marine Park

The Great Barrier Reef Marine Park is the biggest marine park in the world, and possibly the most biologically diverse aquatic habitat on earth. It was established in 1975 to protect the reef system and the water that surrounds it from the outer rim to the Queensland coast. In 1981 it was dedicated as a World Heritage Site because of its status as the largest reef and for its species diversity—1,500 kinds of fish, 4,000 varieties of mollusks, and 400 types of hard and soft corals.

In certain areas the park allows commercial and sport fishing, shell collecting, spearfishing, and fish collecting. Oil drilling and mining, spearfishing with power heads, and littering are outlawed.

Passengers over four years of age must pay a A$4 Environmental Management Charge (EMC), commonly called the "reef tax," every time they visit the Great Barrier Reef. This money, which goes toward the management and conservation of the reef, is collected by the tour operator when you pay for your trip.

Heron Island is not only protected by the GBR Marine Park Authority, it is an Australian Wildlife Sanctuary as well. Park rangers give wonderful tours and slide shows. Queensland University operates a research facility here, where scientists come to study Heron's amazing treasures and keep track of ecological changes along the reef.

DIVE SERVICES & PACKAGES ON HERON ISLAND

Heron Island Dive Center

The dive shop is a full-service facility. The staff of instructors and divemasters can handle up to 100 divers at a time. Four boats run two dive trips daily to a choice of more than 20 dive sites. Boats are wide, flat-bottom types. There are also night dives and special full-day adventure dives to remote reefs, all for advanced divers. The facility (a PADI resort) has a retail dive equipment sales area, a large rental department (including lights), and a training center, where NAUI and PADI certification courses are taught, as well as introductory courses. Be sure to schedule the courses before leaving home; you'll need a medical certificate (the facility will supply the form) and two passport-size photos. For referrals, you'll also need the certificate and referral papers. There are camera rentals and photo instruction. Large rinse tanks and gear storage are conveniently located near the dock. Dive packages for two to ten days of diving are available. Phone (800) 225-9849 or 7-3876-4644; fax 7-3876-4645; e-mail: visitors@ greatbarrierreef.aus.net; website: www.heronisland.com.

Retail Sales: *Adequate*　　　**Dive Boat Comfort:** *Good*

Rentals: *Adequate*　　　**On-Board Facilities**

Scuba Training: *Moderate*　　**for Photographers:** *Good*

Photo Services: *Limited*

WHERE TO STAY ON HERON ISLAND

Heron Island Resort ★★★★   There is only one dedicated dive resort on the island—whoopee! Heron Island Resort (a PADI Resort) is a cluster of some 35 small buildings tucked away in a corner of the island. The rest of the island is literally for the birds. The resort is casual, fun, and family-oriented. Heron Island is a place to completely unwind; leave real shoes and socks behind, and leave behind anything that needs to be ironed. If you like glamour, better go elsewhere. There are 117 rooms, not one with TV or telephone.

Turtle Cabins (30) have shared bathroom facilities and bunks. Reef Suites (44) have a queen and a twin bed, balcony, shower, and toilet; each accommodates three people, and adjoining suites are available. Heron Suites (38) are beachside and are two-room units with a queen and a twin bed, balcony, shower, and toilet; each accommodates three people. A Beach House has a bedroom and sitting room, balcony, queen bed, bath, and toilet; it accommodates two adults. Point Suites (4) are extra-large one-room units, each with balcony (premium views), king bed, shower, and toilet. Most of the rooms have a refrigerator, hairdryer, and clock radio, and all have ceiling fans and tea and coffee makers.

Facilities here include a swimming pool (towels provided), lighted tennis court, game room with snooker table, board games, boutique/shop, guest laundry, complimentary cots, free child care and baby-sitting, conference facilities, and currency exchange. The resort shop and boutique carry clothing, souvenirs, snacks, magazines, newspapers, toiletries, and voltage adapters. The Wistari Room is an air-conditioned room for evening nature presentations and late release movies.

All meals and snacks are included in the package price. Breakfast and lunch are buffets, and dinner is usually a four-course spread. A cocktail bar overlooking the reef is a popular gathering spot, and some kind of entertainment is featured nightly. It could be a bush band, movies, or games. Grab a Fourex, wet your whistle, and get ready for a rousing round of *Bound for Botany Bay.*

Daily rates, which include all meals: Turtle Cabins (per person) $98–$119, Reef Suites $343, Heron Suites $389, Beach House or Point Suite $504. Dive/lodging packages are available. Phone (800) 225-9849 or (408) 685-8902 or 7-3876-4644; fax (408) 685-8903 or 7-3876-4645; e-mail: visitors@greatbarrierreef.aus.net; website: www.heronisland.com.

Live-Aboards

Almost all the live-aboards operate from way up north in Cairns or Port Douglas. If you're interested, here are a few to check out:

Auriga Bay   Cairns (011-6-7-4058-1408)

Down Under Dive   Cairns (011-61-7-4031-1288)
www.ozemail.com.au/~dudive

Mike Ball Dive Expeditions   (PADI Gold Palm Resort) Cairns and Townsville (phone (888) MIKE-BALL or (520) 556-0747) www.mikeball.com

Nimrod III   Cairns (011-61-7-4031-5566)
www.internetnorth.com.au/nimrod

Rum Runner   Cairns and Cape Tribulation (011-61-7-4050-999)
www.rumrunner.com.au

Taka II   (PADI Resort) Cairns (011-61-7-4051-8722) www.taka.com.au

Tusa Dive Connection   (PADI Resort) Cairns (011-61-7-4031-1248)
www.tusadive.com

LIFE ON HERON ISLAND

When you're not diving, snorkeling, or snoozing, the island's natural attractions should keep you busy. Reef walks are a lot of fun, and on Heron Island they're complimentary and you'll get experts who really know what they're talking about. You'll be amazed how much you'll learn. The tides around the island create large exposed tidal flats, so when the tide is out visitors can actually walk (carefully) on the reef. The flats have a virtual smorgasbord of marine animals. You'll find fish, anemones, snails, lobsters, crayfish, jellyfish, prawns, starfish, giant clams, and the unique pearlfish. When the tide is in, it's time to snorkel. The resort offers snorkeling lessons in the swimming pool (complimentary) and snorkeling excursions to the edge of the reef (that's extra).

Other activities are complimentary turtle walks during the nesting season, whale spotting walks in season (bring binoculars), and island ecology and bird-life walks. Otherwise, just walk around on your own (it only takes about 30 minutes to get all around the island), and enjoy. Watch out for gooey stuff that can fall from the sky or from under a tree; in fact, a hat is not a bad idea.

Sea-Safari day cruises include lunch, snorkeling, and fishing, and full-day barbecue cruises stop at nearby Wilson Island. Nondivers can take a semi-submersible to learn more about what excites us under the water. There's excellent commentary by a reef interpreter. Even divers will enjoy this. There are also fishing trips, and if you need more exercise, grab a racket and check out the tennis court, day or night.

In the evening the resort has sunset wine and cheese cruises for ages 18 and over. Sunsets are awesome. Photographers will be in shutter heaven.

Caution: strolling around here at night, where there are few artificial lights, can be downright spooky when the muttons are in an amorous mood. I made the mistake of taking a moonlight stroll by myself and ended up practically running back to the room!

Note: It's interesting to see some of the environmental safeguards on Heron Island, namely: use of recycled or biodegradable products whenever possible, returning all waste to the mainland and storing for recycling, keeping all building below treetop level and designing it to blend unobtrusively into the natural surroundings, removing non-native plant species, and more!

Medical Facilities

The resort has a registered nurse and first-aid center. In case of a diving emergency call DAN (Divers Alert Network) at (919) 684-4DAN (4326) or (919) 684-8111.

The Bahamas

Physical Characteristics of the Dive Area

WATER & WEATHER CONDITIONS

Visibility	*Good*
Current and Surge	*Minimal*
Temperature	*Comfortable*
Storms	*Occasionally Stormy*

SITE CONDITIONS

Mooring Buoys	*Some*
Fishing, Collecting, and Hunting Restrictions	*Some*
Ease of Access	*Very Easy*
Boat Traffic/Diver Congestion	*Light*

MARINE LIFE

Abundance of Invertebrates	*Abundant*
Abundance of Vertebrates	*Abundant*
Abundance of Pelagic Life	*Abundant*
Health of Reef/Marine Life/ Marine Structure	*Pristine*

Islands of Discovery

Christopher Columbus, his entourage, and their three vessels landed in the Bahamas on October 12, 1492. For many years archaeologists have been trying to figure out exactly on which island they landed first. San Salvador is generally assumed to be the landfall, but it's a difficult fact to prove. Could the actual landing have been on Cat Island? Or how about Long Island?

What about tiny Conception Island? How about Rum Cay? The point is, it could have been any one of scores of islands, because there are hundreds of islands that make up this single nation—around 700 actually!

In Columbus's log we can read that he saw so many parrots, the skies were dark with them. He also wrote that he saw lizards, snakes, and fruit-bearing trees such as the plantain, guava, sugar apple, and sapodilla. He appreciated the whales and the beautiful fish. Of these he wrote, "Here there are fish, so unlike ours that it is a marvel; there are some like dories, of the brightest colours in the world, blue, yellow, red and all colours, coloured in a thousand ways, and all the colours so bright that no man would not wonder at them."

For sport, his men enjoyed shooting the parrots from the sky, so we're lucky they couldn't scuba dive. Although the parrots came close to extinction and many of the islands were long ago stripped bare of trees, lush vegetation remains, including the fruit trees, and the marine life is still a wonder. What Columbus could not see, what would really have knocked his leggings off, are the intricately carved coral reefs, the walls that plummet hundreds of feet into the abyss, and subsea canyons more than a mile deep. Fortunately, these are for us to explore.

With so many islands, there are so many choices, giving us so much variety. There are shipwrecks, caves, and blue holes to explore; patch reef, spur and groove reef and underwater canyons; dolphin dives and shark dives. And the great news is that for U.S. divers this is all practically in our back yard. Indeed, the Bahamas are our neighbors—not quite within over-the-fence shouting distance, but Bimini, for instance, is only 50 miles off the Florida coast.

East Coast divers think nothing of hopping over to the islands for a weekend. Although close enough, they're still a world away in terms of atmosphere and the pace of life. Surprisingly, it seems that the rest of the United States is sublimely unaware of this incredible treasure that stretches across 750 miles of ocean. While flying above them on Bahamas Air, the sight is simply magnificent—one little island and cay after another surrounded by white sandy beach, fringing reef, and waters ranging in color from bottle green to midnight blue.

Nassau, located on New Providence, is the capital of the islands and the name most people recognize as being "the Bahamas." This is where you'll find behemoth cruise ships, high-rise resorts, gambling, glittery nightlife, and, well, you get the idea. There are plenty of activities for nondivers, including shopping and touring. The historic downtown area is a beautiful blend of architecture and color, from grand government buildings in the classical style to traditional Caribbean-type pastel cottages. The dive shops and dive sites

are on the opposite end of the island from Nassau and the big resorts, which can be either good or bad, depending on what you're looking for.

If you prefer sunsets to slot machines, head for the Bahamas Out Islands. Five-star service is in short supply, as is much of anything running like clockwork, but you might have a lot more fun and will probably save some dollars. Note: Nassau is not cheap, especially for food. The Out Islands are the great lands of trade winds and quaint resorts, honor bars and conch fritters. Entertainment is a game of dominoes, and serious shopping is buying a lovely handmade basket at a place like Winifred's Dry Goods, which is across the street from the Pass Me Not Pool and Bar.

The Out Islands are considered to be any island except New Providence or Grand Bahama Island, so you have plenty of options there. Most of the islands described in this chapter are in the southern Out Islands, which happen to be the most remote. But they also have the most magnificent diving, in my opinion.

Thanks to the advent of live-aboard diving, almost all of the Bahamas is now accessible to the traveling diver. Seldom-dived destinations such as Great Inagua, where it's still possible to encounter tuna during a dive, are within reach of those who have the ability to plan their trips well ahead.

Although remote, the Out Islands in this chapter have regular air service and excellent lodgings. In fact, I'm thrilled to be able to write about some of my very favorite places to stay, whether you're diving or not. They are loaded with charm, have gorgeous natural settings, and are exceptionally romantic. Oh, yes—they definitely cater to divers. In fact, some, such as Small Hope Bay on Andros, were built by diving pioneers.

Out Island people are casual and welcoming. Even at the nicest resorts, you wouldn't be admonished if you came to dinner sans shoes. However, it would be a definite *faux pas* if you walked in with *sandy* feet. That's what the pail of water is for outside the front door. Most resorts in the Out Islands are very intimate, with only a few rooms. Many have honor bars where you simply take whatever you want to drink and write it down on a sheet of paper. Evening entertainment might be a rake 'n' scrape band or a rousing game of dominoes. Lounging in a hammock or on the beach and gazing up at the starlit sky is an option I personally enjoy.

Dive boats in the Out Islands rarely carry more than six passengers. The obvious benefits are diving freedom and flexibility. On the negative side, dive shops typically will have sparse rental gear and few employees, and their ability to make repairs and supply parts also will be limited.

Although the islands of the Bahamas are not technically in the Caribbean Sea (they're in the Atlantic Ocean), from a psychological and diving perspective, they might as well be; they are certainly Caribbean-like in most respects. Warm Gulf Stream waters flow around the south and west of the islands, whereas rougher Atlantic waters hit the windward northern and eastern sides.

I have not visited all of the inhabited islands in the Bahamas, so don't assume that I'm not including some in this chapter because I don't recommend them. That is not the case at all. I can only write about those with which I am personally familiar.

QUICK STATS

Size   The 700 or so islands and more than 2,000 cays are spread out over roughly 100,000 square miles of ocean. Together, the total land area is about 5,300 square miles. Sizes: New Providence, 80 square miles; Andros, 2,300 square miles; Cat Island, 150 square miles; Exumas, 100 square miles; Long Island, 230 square miles; San Salvador, 63 square miles.

Population   The population of the Bahamas is 302,836. About 80 percent of the population is black, 17 percent white, and 3 percent Asian or Hispanic. Island populations: New Providence, 172,000; Andros, 8,155; Cat Island, 1,678; Exumas, 3,539; Long Island, 3,404; San Salvador, 465.

Location The long archipelago spreads out from the southern part of Florida, extending southeast 750 miles into the Atlantic Ocean. The Turks and Caicos islands are part of the same archipelago and lie at the southern end of the Bahamas chain.

Time The islands in the Bahamas are all in the Eastern Time Zone and observe Daylight Savings Time.

Government After nearly 250 years of British colonial rule, the Commonwealth of the Bahamas declared its independence in 1973. It is now a parliamentary democracy with a governor-general as head of state.

Language English

Electrical Current 120 volts, 60 cycles AC, compatible with American appliances, but surge protectors are recommended for sensitive equipment.

Air Temperature The Gulf Stream and trade winds help to maintain a fairly even temperature throughout the year, ranging from 68° to 86° during the day and 62° to 70° at night. The southern Out Islands are a few degrees warmer than those in the north.

Water Temperature Water temperatures range from 73° in February to 82° in August.

Underwater Visibility Averages around 80 feet.

Best Diving Months Excellent year-round, but June through September is hurricane season.

PLANNING THE TRIP

Phoning the Bahamas The area code for the Bahamas is 242. From the United States it is not necessary to dial the international access number. Just dial 1+242+the local number.

Getting to the Bahamas Most major carriers fly directly into Nassau from many U.S. cities, with Miami and New York being the most-used route. American Airlines, Bahamas Air (phone (800) 222-4262; www.bahamas air.com) and Gulfstream International (phone (800) 992-8532 or (305) 871-1200) also fly directly into a few of the Out Islands from Florida. In addition, many of the resorts in the Out Islands offer their own charter service.

Flights on Bahamas Air to the Out Islands usually have to emanate from Nassau, which serves as a hub. Consequently, if you want to fly from Long Island to Cat Island, for instance, you'll probably have to fly to Nassau, then catch another flight to Cat Island. Bahamas Air also has a

"Great Value Airpass," good for flights from Florida or from Nassau. This allows you to purchase a round-trip ticket and add on one, two, or three islands without having to pay full fare for each leg. This ticket cannot be purchased in the Bahamas and is good for a stay of up to 21 days.

Note: On Bahamas Air flights, it is easy to get confused about where to get off! Twice now, I've seen passengers disembark at the wrong airport. One actually disembarked on Cat Island, when her intended destination was San Salvador. Another got off at Deadman's Cay, Long Island, when his intended destination was Stella Maris, Long Island. Bahamas Air announcements are sketchy at best. Before landing, they usually announce the airport name, which tourists generally don't recognize. Often the island name itself is not mentioned at all.

Of course, for the Out Islands there's always the option of taking the Mail Boat out of Nassau (from Potter's Cay). Why not try it if you have plenty of time? Just remember, this is not cruise-ship travel and the accommodations are spartan. Call (242) 393-1064.

Bahamas Air Baggage Requirements This is difficult. Each time I check with the airline, I get a different answer. Each passenger is allowed two pieces of baggage not exceeding 70 pounds on international flights or 42 pounds on domestic flights. Some reservationists say that poundage is for each bag, some say it's for both. Another problem: frequently the international baggage allowance does not apply if you're connecting in Nassau (depends on how full the flight is). For the excess baggage charge, I've been told that 1) it depends on the size of the bag, in which case, it can be $40 and up, and that 2) it can be by weight, with an added $1.40 for each pound in excess of the allowance. Carry-on baggage is limited to two pieces per passenger and must fit into overhead bins or under the seats, both of which have restricted space. Most rolling-type carry-on bags, for instance, will not fit.

Entry Documents A passport is preferred, but U.S. and Canadian citizens may use a certified, original birth certificate (with a raised seal), and a driver's license (photo ID).

Getting Around This is always a challenge, and worth spending some time to plan in advance. Few resorts offer airport shuttle service, but taxi service at the Nassau airport is very good. Hardly any of the islands have public transportation. All have taxi service, but it is expensive. Rental cars, also, are expensive—$70 per day is not unusual. So it's important to stay in an area where you're close to restaurants and services, or else make sure the dive shop or the resort can provide transportation. Driving here is on the left side of the road.

Currency   The Bahamian dollar is roughly equivalent to the U.S. dollar, which is also accepted throughout the islands.

Bahamas Ministry of Tourism   The Islands of the Bahamas can be reached at (800) 4-BAHAMAS; website: www.bahamas.com.

Bahamas Diving Association   PO Box 21707, Ft. Lauderdale, FL 33335-1707; (800) 866-DIVE or (305) 442-7095; website: www.bahamas diving.com. Call the 800 number to receive a free *Bahamas Dive Guide* or CD-ROM Diving Brochure.

Other Sources   Out Islands Promotion Board: (800) OUT-ISLANDS (688-4752) or in Ft. Lauderdale at (954) 359-8099; fax (954) 359-8098. Another good source of information is the website: www.bahamasvg.com.

Marine Conservation in the Bahamas

In 1986, an extensive set of conservation regulations was established protecting Bahamian crawfish, conch, turtles, scalefish, stone crabs, marine mammals, and sponges. These regulations include prohibitions against taking any marine resource while on scuba, and include the outlawing of spearguns within principal diving areas near New Providence and Grand Bahama and in nearshore areas elsewhere throughout the Bahamas.

There is also a ban on long-line fishing. Long-lines, often used to commercially take sharks for their fins, for a time severely depleted shark populations in several areas around the Caribbean. Also, laws prohibit marine dumping from shore or from ships.

When the Exuma Cays Land and Seas Park was instituted in 1958, it allowed only limited fishing within its boundaries. But since 1986 all fishing has been banned. A number of mooring buoys have been placed within the park.

For several years, various conservation groups in the Bahamas pressed for a network of No Take Marine Reserves, which would be large enough to adequately represent the different habitats and close enough together for there to be linkages for marine animal and plant life as they move through their life cycles. In 1999 the Department of Fisheries, the Bahamas Reef Environmental Education Foundation, the National Trust, and others were successful establishing the first five No Take Marine Reserve sites. These are in the areas of North Bimini, the Berry Islands, South Eleuthera, Northern Abaco Cays, and Exuma Cays (south of the Land and Sea Park in the Lee Stocking Island area).

People to People

One way to experience the true Bahamas lifestyle is to participate in the *People-to-People* program run by the Ministry of Tourism. Visitors are matched with residents of similar age groups, interests, and professions. You might be invited to join them at home, at a sporting event or a social club, among other possibilities. It won't cost a thing and will provide you with lasting friends and memories. More than 1,000 volunteers are available in Nassau alone.

I had a wonderful time when I was invited to a Bahamian family's home for dinner. I learned about the native dishes, their system of education, leisure activities, etc. In the process I gained a much better appreciation for the culture. If you're traveling with children, this would be an especially valuable educational experience.

To participate, you can register with the Social Director at participating hotels or call the People-to-People coordinator, Ministry of Tourism, at (242) 326-5371 or (242) 328-7810 or (242) 326-9442; fax (242)356-0434. The program is also available in Exuma and San Salvador.

New Providence (Nassau)

THE UNDERWATER SCENE

Off New Providence, you can dive the same wrecks and reefs seen in the James Bond films and even experience some of those high-adrenaline shark dives that you see on the Discovery Channel. The island is ringed by good dive sites, many preserved under a harbor protection regulation.

The best diving on New Providence is around the Coral Harbour area on the southern side toward the west end, and also at Lyford Cay on the western tip. These are on the opposite side of the island from Nassau, Paradise Island, and Cable Beach, where most of the big resorts are located. Still, the distances are not great here. For instance, to drive to Coral Harbour from the Cable Beach area takes only about 20 minutes.

The southwest area is where scenes from several movies have been filmed, and you can actually dive some of the waterlogged sets. Also on this side are shipwrecks sitting in shallow water. Some have been put down intentionally to provide artificial reef. By far the greatest attractions here are the sharks, and there are sites where you can see them in their natural habitats, in addition to the rather contrived organized shark dive.

Actually, the most noteworthy feature of this side of the island is the underwater topography. All of the islands of the Bahamas sit atop a series of enormous underwater platforms that rise thousands of feet from the seabed. Together, these platforms are called the Bahama Banks. New Providence belongs to the largest of these, called the Great Bahama Bank. The composition of the banks is primarily limestone, created from marine organisms deposited over thousands of years (that's the explanation in a nutshell).

Between New Providence and its neighboring island, Andros, an enormous and extremely deep trench cuts through the Great Bahama Bank. On a map that shows some of these features, this trench looks like a large extended tongue. Dark blue ocean water cuts into the light-colored shallow bank. Consequently, this marvel is called the Tongue of the Ocean, and along its mountainsides, from both islands, are some thrilling wall dives. From New Providence, the most popular wall sites are off the southwest of the island and off Lyford Cay on the west end.

Diving Conditions

The conditions couldn't be better: bathtub-warm water, little current, and shallow depths. About the deepest you'll get is 70 feet, with normal cruising depths at around 50 feet.

Recommended Level of Experience

Most dive charters in Nassau are equipped and staffed to do a great job with newly certified divers or even those who are coming down to complete their open water training dives. There are plenty of shallow sites with outstanding visibility and a healthy marine environment, for both novice divers and snorkelers. Still, the wall sites along the Tongue of the Ocean are sufficiently adrenaline- and nitrogen-producing to excite the most gung-ho divers. Always make sure you know what you're getting into before just hopping on a dive boat, so that you're happy with the dive experience and not "getting in over your head."

Great Dive Sites

Off the north side in about 40 feet of water is a huge cavity in the ocean floor—the *Lost Ocean Blue Hole,* which descends to about 300 feet. The rim is a perfect place to hang out to see both tropicals and pelagic visitors. The north side is also wreck diving territory, just off Nassau and Paradise Island. Two favorites are the *Mahoney,* a 212-foot freighter, and the *LCT,* in only 20 feet of water. The initials stand for Landing Craft, Tanks.

Shark Alley is undoubtedly the most talked-about dive off New Providence, and for good reason. The marine visitors will certainly get your attention and raise your adrenaline level considerably. You'll drop down to a coral rubble bottom at 50 feet and form a semicircle with the rest of the divers. The unfortunate divemaster chosen for the task will bring down a bucket of frozen fish. He'll take a piece at a time on a long metal rod and extend it to the sharks. On this dive, and any shark dive, it's a good idea to use a little extra weight. You don't want to be having buoyancy problems, and odds are good you'll suck that tank down faster than usual!

However, you don't have to work hard to find sharks around here. Just go to *Shark Wall* and you'll probably be able to see them in their natural habitat, which I enjoy a lot more than the contrived shark feeds. It is more difficult to get those great close-up portraits, though.

Razorback is a typical wall dive for this area, with a ridge of corals rising to 45 feet on the edge of the awesome Tongue of the Ocean. Brain coral, lettuce, and star corals create a miniature mountain range. Along the wall are schooling jacks and Bermuda chub. Nurse sharks hunker down under the coral ledges. *Hole in the Head* and *Wreck on the Wall* are two more great wall dives.

Shark Buoy is a most unusual dive that features an actual buoy set in the middle of the Tongue of the Ocean. Used by the U.S. Navy for submarine exercises, it is huge (about the size of a small boat) and consequently attracts a wide variety of pelagic marine life. You could see dolphinfish, jacks, rainbow runners, and silky sharks—lots of silky sharks, in fact. Compared to other sharks, these guys are fairly small and actually like to school. The divemasters will hand feed them ballyhoo and frozen squid, with divers positioned nearby. It's pretty exciting stuff and in an area that typically has outstanding water clarity.

Shallow Diving and Snorkeling

The choices for shallow diving and for snorkeling here are practically endless. Both the north and the south sides have many possibilities. Here are a few suggestions, just to whet your appetite. *Southwest Reef* offers large coral heads in only 15 to 30 feet of water. The highlights are elkhorn and staghorn corals that attract schooling grunts, squirrelfish, and barracuda. *Nari Nari* is a shallow reef dive, and eagle rays are frequently spotted here.

Off the west end is *Gouldings Cay,* a bird sanctuary topside. Underwater it features stately elkhorn coral and is a great place to snorkel as well as dive. The shallow reef was filmed for the productions of both *Cocoon* and *Splash.* Eagle rays and turtles usually visit the deeper part of the reef here.

Speaking of movies, on the southwest area are several sites of movies you'll recognize. There's the *Vulcan Bomber* from *Thunderball* and the *Tears of Allah* from *Never Say Never Again.* The *Bahama Mama* is a small wreck that's not particularly exciting, but it attracts a beautiful assortment of tropicals. You're likely to see blue tangs, French grunts, rainbow, and midnight parrotfish, as well as a variety of jacks. And naturally this is the domain of the Nassau grouper. The wreck is in less than 50 feet of water, so there's plenty of time for photographers to set up shots.

DIVE SERVICES & PACKAGES ON NEW PROVIDENCE

The following dive services are all located on the south side of the island. All provide free shuttle service back and forth from the major resorts on the north side.

Nassau Scuba Centre (a PADI 5-Star IDC) is located on the south side of the island in Coral Harbour. It operates a 42-foot Burpee, which accommodates 20 divers, and a 42-foot Newton. Both have freshwater rinse buckets for camera gear and are U.S. Coast Guard approved, with DAN oxygen units. The shop supplies Enriched Air Nitrox and has a complete line of rental gear, including underwater cameras. Certifying agencies are BSAC, NAUI, PADI, and SSI. PADI Enriched Air Nitrox certification is offered, as well as some interesting shark diving specialties, including a Shark Suit Adventure. During this unusual experience divers can actually feed the sharks while wearing a stainless steel shark suit. The shop has packages with Orange Hill Beach Inn and provides transportation to and from. Gear lockers are available at the dive shop. Phone (888) 962-7728 or (954) 462-3400; fax (954) 462-4100; e-mail: nealwatson@aol.com; website: www.nealwatson.com/nassau.htm.

Retail Sales: *Adequate*	**Dive Boat Comfort:** *Good*
Rentals: *Adequate*	**On-Board Facilities**
Scuba Training: *Extensive*	**for Photographers:** *Good*
Photo Services: *Moderate*	

Stuart Cove's Dive Bahamas (a PADI Gold Palm Resort) is the local outfit trusted by Hollywood producers in search of reliably calm, clear water for underwater filming. South Ocean is on the south side of the island, near the western tip, and within extremely easy proximity to the dive sites. Stuart runs two 30-, four 40-, one 44- and one 54-foot boat. Enriched Air Nitrox is supplied. Certifying agencies are NASDS, NAUI, PADI, PDIC, SSI, and YMCA. Courses are taught through the advanced level, and specialties are offered, including the use of DPVs (called Wall Flying), Nitrox, and rebreathers. The shop also organizes several shark specialty dives, including one in which you can feed the sharks yourself (with a stainless steel suit). Stuart himself has served as a shark wrangler for Hollywood productions, so these guys are the experts. The shop also has an extensive photo facility called Fin Photo, with still and video rentals, photo and video classes, E-6 slide processing, print processing up to poster size, and more. Dive packages are with the Clarion Resort (right next door), Nassau Marriott Resort and Crystal Palace Casino, Radisson Cable Beach Resort, and the brand new Holiday Inn Junkanoo Beach. Phone (800) 879-9832 or (954) 524-5755; fax (954) 524-5925; e-mail: info@stuartcove.com; website: www.stuartcove.com.

Retail Sales: *Adequate*	**Dive Boat Comfort:** *Good*
Rentals: *Extensive*	**On-Board Facilities**
Scuba Training: *Moderate*	**for Photographers:** *Superior*
Photo Services: *Extensive*	

WHERE TO STAY ON NEW PROVIDENCE

The beachfront **Clarion South Ocean ★★★★** couldn't have a better location for divers. It's right next door to Stuart Cove's Dive Bahamas, with which it offers dive/lodging packages. The Clarion (a PADI Gold Palm Resort) is in a 195-acre compound and has 249 air-conditioned rooms. Recently it went through a major renovation. There are three restaurants on the premises, two swimming pools, four tennis courts, and a golf course. Rooms are either gardenview or oceanfront. A three-night stay with two days of diving ranges from $337 to $446, depending on the type of room and the season. This includes all taxes and service charges, and is based on double occupancy. Phone (800) 646-3333 or (954) 524-5744; fax (954) 524-5925; e-mail: info@stuartcove.com; website: www.stuartcove.com/dso/rp-02-a.htm.

Orange Hill Beach Inn ★★★, with 32 air-conditioned rooms, is especially popular with divers. It is close to the airport on the north side, just west of Cable Beach. Nassau Scuba Center provides transportation down to its dock on the south side, which takes about 15 minutes. Orange Hill was a former orange orchard plantation built in the early 1920s; consequently, the grounds are lovely, with tropical fruit trees, flowering bushes, and expansive lawns. Rooms overlook either the ocean (the beach is about 250 feet away) or the pool garden area. A restaurant on the premises serves breakfast, lunch, and dinner. A two-night stay here with one day of diving is $211, which includes breakfast, transportation, taxes, etc. Phone (800) 805-5485 or (242) 327-5184/5; fax (242) 327-5186; e-mail: info@orange hill.com; website: www.orangehill.com.

ISLAND LIFE ON NEW PROVIDENCE

Many people visit this central Bahamian island without ever learning its real identity. They just call the entire island by the name of the Bahamian capital located here—Nassau. No matter, one can only wonder how many diver/nondiver marriages have been saved by vacation trips to Nassau. Just about anyone can have an absolutely wonderful time here without ever setting foot in the water. There are world-class golf courses, tennis clubs, and enough shopping to melt down your Visa card.

For many, New Providence could merely be a stopover on the way to the Out Islands. But if you have some time, definitely try to see **Nassau,** a wonderful, vibrant city. It is perfect for exploring on foot. Start at Rawson Square near the stalls of the Straw Market, then go over to the native market on the waterfront before noon, to see the local fishermen unloading their saltwater catch and crates of tropical fruit.

At Government House, watch the bands perform at the changing of the guards every other Saturday at 10 a.m. See Parliament Square with its statue of Queen Victoria; and the Nassau Public Library, built in 1797, which was once the city's jail. The Queen's Staircase, 66 steps leading to Fort Fincastle was cut into the limestone hill and bricked up by slaves. Balcony House is an authentically furnished eighteenth-century home and the oldest residential structure in Nassau. These are just a few of the interesting sites. Latch onto a tourist map or better yet, take an organized tour of the island.

Try to visit **Crystal Cay** if you possibly can. This is a marine park with a network of 24 saltwater aquariums, landscaped park areas, nature trails, and more. There's an outstanding Underwater Observation Tower, where nondivers can see what enthralls us about our sport. This is also the home of the world's largest man-made living reef. A shark tank can be viewed from an overhead deck or from an underwater observation area. Stingrays and sea turtles swim about in pools. Crystal Cay is located off the northern side of the island, connected by a bridge. For information call (242) 328-1036.

Dining and Entertainment

Restaurants cater to virtually every taste, but be forewarned: they are expensive, especially in the city and the resort areas. Also, here and throughout the Bahamas, it is customary for restaurants to add the service charge to the bill, so a tip is not necessary.

If this is your first time in the Bahamas, then you should be initiated to conch (pronounced konk), which could be considered the national dish. It is served in a multitude of ways, from conch salad to fritters to soup. Other popular seafood dishes are stewed fish and crawfish. A typical Bahamian dish is served with peas and rice (small pigeon peas or beans are used in this dish), cole slaw, or macaroni salad. Nassau, however, is a cosmopolitan city, so you'll find everything from these down-home native dishes to haute cuisine.

Since the growing season is year-round, tropical fruit is always available, grown on many of the Out Islands. Choose from avocados, mangoes, pineapple, bananas, coconuts, and plantains, for starters.

Resorts on Paradise Island and Cable Beach offer Las Vegas-style casinos and floor shows. Besides the slots, there are crap and blackjack tables, roulette, and baccarat. Dance the night away at all-night discos or catch some local talent at one of the pubs.

Medical Facilities

The Doctors Hospital in Nassau can be reached at (242) 322-8411. In case of a diving emergency call DAN (Divers Alert Network) at (919) 684-4DAN (4326) or (919) 684-8111.

Andros

THE UNDERWATER SCENE

Andros is only 175 miles from Ft. Lauderdale, and amazingly, there is absolutely no diving traffic pressure here. Amazing, because just offshore is the third largest barrier reef in the world, stretching over 100 miles. For years a single dive business catered to the lucky divers who found it, but just in the last couple of years new businesses have sprouted. Divers have a lot of individual attention and dive sites remain pristine and uncrowded.

Andros is huge (104 miles long, 40 miles wide) compared to the other islands, but my guess is you probably have not heard much about it. It has fewer people per square mile than any other populated island in the country. The island itself consists of coral limestone covered with impenetrable bush. It is sliced through in some sections by inland waterways, with all of the land bits edged by mangrove swamp. But the really noteworthy feature of Andros is what lies off its eastern coast, namely, the third largest barrier reef (140 miles long) in the world, and the second largest in the western hemisphere. And that's not all. On the outer edge of this reef is a plummeting wall that drops off into the mile-deep trench that's called the Tongue of the Ocean.

As described in the New Providence section, this tongue-shaped trench cuts into the Great Bahama Bank between New Providence and Andros. It is so deep that the U.S. Navy has been using it for years to test its submarines.

Andros has gained a reputation among advanced divers for its spectacular blue hole dives, which are vast underwater cave systems. But even the less experienced, without special certification, can still see wonderful geologic formations in the underwater caverns.

Diving Conditions

Most dive sites are only a 15-minute boat ride from Small Hope Bay. The waters are nice and calm on the east side, with little current and excellent visibility most of the time.

Recommended Level of Experience

It sounds like the diving here is all hard-core, but don't worry, it is not. Actually, it's an excellent place to learn to dive. Prospective divers can even take a free resort course at Small Hope Bay. Andros' inland blue holes provide excellent cavern experiences, and specialty guides can introduce you to the world of overhead environments.

However, for the high-voltage, deep-wall dives, you should be a confident, experienced diver. For any of the specialized blue hole sites you'll definitely need a guide.

Great Dive Sites

On Small Hope Bay's *Over the Wall* dive (a.k.a. *Nitro Express*) you can soar over the Tongue of the Ocean and peer down into the great black abyss. To do it, though, your depth gauge will reach previously untouched numbers, and you'd have to be superhuman not to get really, really narked. Dick Birch described it to me once as "like having a martini on an empty stomach." Divers head down to about 120 feet, and meet up. Then they descend to a sandy shelf at 185 feet. From there you can leap off the ledge and soar out over the vast darkness. It's an amazing feeling at that depth. Believe it or not, this is a no-decompression dive. You'll stay at depth just a couple of minutes before heading back up to the 120-foot level. Although this is a supervised and very controlled dive, I'm not encouraging you to do this. It is way beyond normal sport-diving limits. I actually got dangerously narked on this dive and would never go down that deep again, at least on regular air. But Small Hope Bay has been leading divers over the wall for decades, and they claim they've never had a single incident or injury.

Turnbull's Gut doesn't sound appealing, but it's another thrilling wall dive. This one is a crevice at 90 feet that spits you out at 120 feet over the seemingly bottomless void. At 120 feet, *Giant's Staircase* drops down by giant steps into the 6,000-foot abyss.

Shepherd's Pie is a particularly beautiful wall dive on the north end, where at 120 feet you can peer out over the mysterious velvet void beyond. The wall is gorgeous, with soft and hard corals everywhere.

Diana's Dungeons, in the 90-foot range, is noteworthy for its interesting structure rather than an abundance of marine life. Divers weave through arches and tunnels, like being in a playground. It can be a lot of fun, if you enjoy that kind of thing.

Andros has developed a reputation for its specialty dives, with only one or two divers to a guide. These take advanced and technical divers to both ocean and inland blue holes. Some, such as *Guardian Blue Hole* (named after a resident brackish-water-adapted barracuda), provide entrances to wonderland caves and caverns.

Shallow Diving and Snorkeling

Between Andros and the cobalt waters of the Tongue of the Ocean lie more than 100 miles of mostly shallow reef. This area provides a multitude of great shallow diving and snorkeling sites in depths from 15 to 70 feet. You'll see a full range of tropicals, including schooling grunts and jacks, gorgeous stands of sun-kissed elkhorn coral, and more little critters than your close-up lens could possibly document in a single visit. *Kleins Place* is a 50-foot coral garden with almost every variety of sponge found in the Bahamas.

Marine Protection

The Andros Barrier Reef is protected from spearfishing and collecting.

DIVE SERVICES & PACKAGES ON ANDROS

The **Small Hope Bay Diving Facility** is an experienced shop; they've been here an astounding 36 years! They offer wall dives, blue hole and cavern dives, shark dives, wreck dives, and coral garden dives. They also provide special snorkeling excursions, including snorkeling with wild dolphins. Custom-tailored specialty dives can be arranged. Three dive boats are used and more than 60 sites visited. The PADI open water and advanced courses are offered. Rental equipment is available, including DPV rental. Phone (800) 223-6961 or (242) 368-2014; fax (242) 368-2015; e-mail: shbinfo@smallhope.com; website: www.smallhope.com.

Retail Sales: *None*	**Dive Boat Comfort:** *Good*
Rentals: *Adequate*	**On-Board Facilities**
Scuba Training: *Moderate*	**for Photographers:** *Good*
Photo Services: *Limited*	

WHERE TO STAY ON ANDROS

Small Hope Bay ★★★★ (a PADI Resort) is an island gem. Accommodating no more than 40 guests at any one time, this idyllic resort has ceiling fans instead of air conditioning, hammocks instead of tennis courts, and an all-too-rare form of evening entertainment called conversation. Nestled among the pines and seagrapes, the lodge looks out across the bay to four tiny islands. But the resort's focus is underwater; all meals and activities are synchronized with the arrivals and departures of the dive boats. This is truly a dedicated dive resort.

The late Dick Birch came to Andros from Canada and built the lodge in 1960, when the sport of scuba diving was in its infancy. Actually, most of the guests were free divers at that time. Dick was a pioneer of wall diving and is credited with discovering the Tongue of the Ocean and many of the blue holes. For years he held the world's record for deep diving on compressed air—463 feet—accomplished in 1962. Dick told me that on that dive he stayed down for nine minutes and his decompression time was 51 minutes. At that depth, the visibility was about 70 feet. Dick also mentioned that "it was a really foolhardy thing to do. We were young and stupid." His diving partner was Roger Hutchins of Toronto, who documented the dive.

Mona Birch (Dick's wife) and their son Jeff continue to run the place. The central lodge houses a large living room, a dining room, and an old fishing boat that serves as a bar and gathering spot for munching conch fritters and trading dive tales. The 20 guest cottages, constructed of coral rock and Andros pine, have louvered windows and ceiling fans and are decorated in colorful Androsia batik fabrics. No one bothers much with shoes here, even for dinner.

In addition to diving services, the Birches operate a flats boat and have a complete program for bonefishing, as well as reef and deep-sea fishing. Families can even schedule a unique Overnight Camping Excursion to the west side of the island and explore mangrove wilderness teeming with bird and fish life. The lodge provides transportation, camping equipment, food and beverages, a guide, and a cook.

Small Hope is on the east coast near the town of Fresh Creek. The adult per person, per night rate for a nondiver is $175 during the winter season. The daily dive package rate is $235. Rates include airport transfers, all meals, bar drinks and beverages, nightly conch fritter hors d'oeuvres, all taxes, and service charges. Complimentary activities include introductory scuba and snorkeling lessons, self-guided nature walks, and the use of snorkel equipment, windsurfers, sailboat, kayaks, bicycles, and hot tub. Phone (800) 223-6961 or (242) 368-2014; fax (242) 368-2015; e-mail: shbinfo@smallhope.com; website: www.smallhope.com.

ISLAND LIFE ON ANDROS

From the air, Andros looks like a wide swath of forest, sliced by numerous waterways, which is largely true. Not many terrestrials live here. The island consists primarily of hardwood and pine forests and mangroves, lots of meandering waterways, and few settlements. Most of the population of about 10,000 lives on the eastern coast and are fishers or farmers. Fresh water is a primary resource, and most of Nassau's drinking water comes from here.

In the eighteenth century, pirates who were headquartered on Andros, including Sir Henry Morgan, preyed on ships passing between Cuba and Florida. By the nineteenth century, freed slaves had found their way here, as well as Seminole Indians from Florida. The two groups intermarried and subsisted on farming, lumbering, sponging, and pirating.

The colorful Andros batik fabric is made right on the island, so be sure to leave some room in that dive bag. Dick Birch started the Androsia Batik Factory, and now the cloth is decorating homes, hotels, and bodies throughout the Bahamas. Definitely visit the factory if you have time. From Small Hope Bay, you can hop on a bike and enjoy a pleasant ride to the factory. On the way you'll encounter very friendly folks, including schoolchildren in their cute uniforms, and nice views of the harbor.

If you don't have time to get to the factory, most of the shops on the island will have the cloth. Another item that you might want to tuck in your dive bag is a straw basket. Supposedly the only straw baskets that are waterproof are made here. However, I have not checked it out myself.

Dining and Entertainment

Watching interpretive slide shows and trading dive stories seem to be the most popular forms of entertainment, but there must be others. You'll have to ask around and let me know.

Medical Facilities

The North Andros Community Clinic can be reached at (242) 329-2239. In case of a diving emergency call DAN (Divers Alert Network) at (919) 684-4DAN (4326) or (919) 684-8111.

Cat Island

THE UNDERWATER SCENE

Few travelers find their way to this fascinating island, and it's a shame. Lying in the central-southern chain between Long Island and Eleuthera, Cat Island remains isolated and undeveloped. It draws a modest number of divers—savvy divers, who fly into New Bight Airport, close to the dive resorts and sole dive shop on the south end.

Miles of deserted powder-soft beaches ring the island. The underwater terrain is not only pristine, it's absolutely thrilling. This is some of the most exciting diving I've experienced in the Bahamas, in fact, in the Caribbean, and I can't wait to get back.

Who Is That Chick Charnie?

Chick Charnies seem to get a lot of attention on Andros, and frankly I'm not sure why. But because they do, I thought I'd better mention it. The Chick Charnies (I have no idea as to the origin of the name) are legendary creatures that are half bird and half man (I guess there are no females). Anyway, they drive away evil spirits, so that's a good thing. Legend says that visitors here should explore the island carrying flowers and bright bits of fabric to leave for the Chick Charnies, and they'll reap rewards. Don't worry, you will anyway—just go diving.

This is wall diving at its finest. On the south end, steep cliffs drop down into huge, wild canyons, just begging to be explored. Unfortunately, the walls start deep off Cat Island—in about 50 or 60 feet of water—so by the time you actually get down and start exploring the canyon walls and huge cuts, you're easily at 100 feet and beyond. The marine life is just as wild as the terrain, with sharks ever-present, along with other pelagic visitors.

So why, you might ask, don't divers flock to the island? The reasons are twofold: lack of services and lack of information. Stable dive operations have been a problem. On my first visit in 1994, there was a dive shop and a compressor on the island, but no divemaster or boat operator. My dive buddy and I filled our own tanks and cajoled a native fisherman to show us some possible dive sites. We also struck out on our own to try a variety of areas for shore diving.

Today it's a different story. The Greenwood Inn's Cat Island Dive Center has charted much of the 12-mile wall along the southern coast and takes divers to spectacular sites in the practically virgin territory. However, my guess is that much of the area still has not been explored. Also, I am one of the few dive journalists to have visited Cat Island twice and written about it. For years, dive guides to the Bahamas barely even mentioned Cat Island. And it was pretty obvious the authors had not even set fins in its waters.

Diving Conditions

The coral reef, the walls, and the solitary tropicals are healthy and abundant. Sharks are common sightings on the deep dives. However, there are few schooling fish, for some reason.

Water conditions are excellent, with mild currents and visibility generally around 70 feet. Frequently visibility approaches, and even exceeds, 100 feet. Of course, the occasional storm can impair the vis, especially in sandy areas.

Cat Island also has many inland waterways and miles of healthy mangroves, all of which provide wonderful environments for nurturing marine life. Inland, the island is chock-a-block with blue holes, which have some access to the sea. Generally on top of the "hole" there is a layer of brackish water mixed with decomposed matter. Visibility is not very good on this top layer, which is usually 20 to 30 feet in depth. Frequently you can barely see your hand in front of your mask.

Recommended Level of Experience

This is a place for experienced divers, technical divers, and snorkelers. Divers coming here should bring their own equipment and make sure it's in good working condition. Repairs here are difficult, and the rental equipment is pretty sketchy. I saw several divers using rental equipment that did not include depth gauges, for instance.

Also, the best wall dives here are deep—about 65 feet at the shallowest. In some areas the wall begins at 70 or even up to 100 feet. So when you begin the dive, you're already deep. This requires long safety stops, which usually are made in blue water without an anchor line to hold onto. Therefore, good buoyancy control is essential.

Technical divers who dive deep would love Cat Island, but there is no place to get special air mixes. However, there are a number of inland blue holes that have never been explored. I went down to the entrance of one and immediately saw stalagtites. Unfortunately, we didn't have the proper equipment to continue our exploration. While we peered into the cave, straining to see it with our small lights, our air bubbles hit the ceiling and silting almost obscured the entrance. We left immediately while we could still see ambient light. These caves can be extremely dangerous without the proper cave diving training and the proper equipment. Line reels should be tied up well outside a cave's entrance.

Great Dive Sites

Devil's Point 1 and 2 and *Black Coral Spot* are really heart-pounding wall dives. The top of the wall ranges from about 50 to 60 feet and has a take-your-breath-away sheer vertical drop into the deep blue. Sea fans and black coral trees grow in profusion, and layers of plate coral stairstep down the plummeting face. Huge channels slash into the walls, tempting divers to explore every nook, cranny, and crevice. Vague images of reef sharks weave in and out among the channels and enormous coral escarpments. At the shallower depths, angelfish and parrotfish munch away at the coral and grouper lie in wait for a passing meal. Bermuda chubs gather inside a huge crevice, swaying in the moderate current.

First Basin Wall, just offshore from the Greenwood Inn, starts at 65 feet and plunges to about 200 feet. A prolific amount of hard coral covers the shallower areas. Down the wall are giant sponges, deep water sea fans, and bushes of black coral. Huge grouper and jewfish keep a wary eye on divers, and every now and then a nurse shark will be seen slumbering in a crevice.

Shallow Diving and Snorkeling

Some of the best snorkeling on the island is near Fernandez Bay at a place called *Dry Head.* It is known for having very large coral heads that attract a nice assortment of marine life.

Shore diving and snorkeling off the *Hotel Greenwood Inn* is excellent. Although there's only a small reef, you'll see grouper, conch, and even flounder. The night dives are superb. Fin out over sea grass and a rocky/sandy bottom. Keep perpendicular to the ripply patterns in the sand, which run horizontal to shore. You'll come to some rocks and probably see the occasional lobster. Kick out about 15 minutes farther and you'll bump into a large coral head that has some wonderful swim-throughs. Weave into and out of the archways and little tunnels, along a sandy bottom. Watch out for jellyfish, though. On my night dive here they and the sea wasps were out in force and attacked any exposed skin. Our entire group was a mess of welts the next day.

Miller Reef, on the southeast side at Big Windy Bay, is a superb shallow site. This is what I wrote in my logbook about it: "This dive rivaled Bonaire for variety of coral and structure. There was a prolific amount of plate and staghorn corals as well as soft corals. It seems that every type of Caribbean reef fish was here, including some beautiful angelfish and rock beauties." Obviously, this is an ideal spot for underwater photography, and the depth is only about 40 feet, which gives you lots of time to set up shots.

Fine Bay (especially the site called *Cat Tail*) on the east side also has some good shore diving from a pretty sandy beach. The trick is in finding it! You'll have to ask for directions.

DIVE SERVICES & PACKAGES ON CAT ISLAND

Hotel Greenwood Dive Centre has an excellent location right on the beach at the Greenwood Beach Resort. Chris Illing has explored these waters on the south end thoroughly and has discovered many of the dive sites. He uses two small dive boats—a 30-footer and a 25-footer—and provides special snorkeling trips. PADI instruction is through the advanced level. Rental equipment is available. Call or fax (877) CAT-7475 or (242) 342-3053; e-mail:gbr@grouper.batelnet.bs; website: www.greenwood beachresort.com.

Retail Sales: *None*	**Dive Boat Comfort:** *Adequate*
Rentals: *Adequate*	**On-Board Facilities**
Scuba Training: *Limited*	**for Photographers:** *Good*
Photo Services: *None*	

WHERE TO STAY ON CAT ISLAND

Fernandez Bay Village ★★ is loaded with charm. Built by Hollywood actress Frances Armbrister, this main house and nine native stone villas face a mile-long, tradewind-swept beach overlooking the calm western shores. From the air, the village is barely discernible, tucked away among casuarina pines. Meals are served in the main house (the home of Tony and Pam Armbrister) or on the beach. Step out of your cottage in your swimsuit and walk just a few steps, past the empty hammocks that you'll fall into in the afternoon, and take a dip in the warm waters of Fernandez Bay. I particularly love the cottage that has the grotto-like outdoor shower! Some of the villas have full kitchens. The resort can customize an island tour, take you fishing, arrange for your diving at the Cat Island Dive Centre, and provide you with a sailboat. Air charters available. Rates range from $165 to $225, depending on the season, and include two meals daily. Call (800) 940-1905 or (954) 474-482; fax (954) 474-4864.

Greenwood Beach Resort ★★★★, although without the structural charm of Fernandez Bay, is lovely, maintains a friendly, casual atmosphere, and seems to draw a younger, more sports-oriented clientele. Located at the southern tip of the island in Port Howe, the dominating feature is the extensive length of chalk-white, powder-fine sandy beach. The resort has the only operating dive shop on the island, and the diving is very good directly from the resort. The 20 rooms are motel-style and comfortable, organized around a swimming pool and gardens. A terrace facing out to sea is the main focus, though, as well as the lounge and dining room. Most dining, however, is outside. Hammocks are strategically placed for excellent napping. Hobie cats, kayaks, and bicycles are available. Fishing can be arranged. The resort also offers air charters. Room rates range from $79 for a single to $119 for a triple. A meal plan can be purchased for $40 or $45. Call or fax (877) CAT-7475 or (242) 342-3053; e-mail: gbr@grouper.batel net.bs; website: www.greenwoodbeachresort.com.

LIFE ON CAT ISLAND

Cat Island is a long 50-mile sliver of rolling limestone hills covered with lush green forests. Every now and then a small settlement will dot the landscape. In 1997 a friendly local named Daisy told me, "Yes, Old Bight is a big town—about 200 people—very big." The beaches stretch for miles, with no interruption and hardly any development. At this time, there are no large-scale resorts, but I have heard that the island is targeted for more tourism services. My hope is that they will be on a small scale.

How the island got its name is not entirely clear. It is shaped like a cat's tail. More likely, though, it was named after one Arthur Catt, a British sea captain-cum-pirate, who used the island as his base of "operations." However, I think the name is appropriate not for either of those reasons, but because it is slightly mysterious, like a cat. Stay here long enough, and you'll surely hear intriguing tales of *obeah,* a type of witchcraft, or voodoo, that is still practiced. And that seems odd, considering the many churches. Driving down the Queen's Highway (the single paved road), you'll pass a church about as often as you spot an islander.

To give you an idea of what you might encounter here, listen to this little tale about island life: On my first visit to Cat Island in 1994, my dive buddy and I rented a car to explore the island and check out the shore diving. For navigation, we used a plastic place mat on which was printed a graphic map showing the bays, the settlements, and a few streets. We filled our own scuba tanks, then set off with our place mat to search for the two-track road that cut across to Fine Bay on the east side. While en route, it started to rain. The windshield wipers didn't work, so the place mat came in handy for clearing away the muck.

Of course, the roads here are not signed, so it's difficult to know whether you're on the right one. We found our way, though, and discovered a long, beautiful stretch of beach. And we had this little piece of paradise all to ourselves. Afterward, we didn't think about filling the gas tank, and the next day were informed that the entire island was out of gasoline. We were paying $80 a day for a car that had no fuel! Fortunately, the local Shell station agreed to siphon gas from another car so we could at least get to the south end for more diving.

Despite these little hiccups, we had a terrific time. One of the joys of being in the Out Islands is encountering the unexpected. If you learn to expect the unexpected you'll have a lot more fun.

A little history: Cat Island was settled in 1783 by British Loyalists who were fleeing the newly formed United States (they picked the wrong side). Actually, many Loyalists fled to the islands of the Bahamas, and many were awarded large tracts of land (for their loyalty) by the Crown. They established cotton plantations, worked by slaves. In 1807 the British Parliament abolished the slave trade and in 1834 ended slavery altogether. That also ended the cotton industry. Many of the plantation owners left the islands

Father Jerome's Legacy

One site that distinguishes itself from the rest is the medieval-style **Hermitage** on Mt. Alvernia. At 206 feet, Mt. Alvernia is the highest point in the Bahamas, and this church/fortress-type structure is truly impressive, albeit incongruous with the surroundings. I would rate it among the Top 10 attractions in all the Bahamas.

Father Jerome, a Franciscan hermit who was trained as an architect, built the Hermitage entirely by hand from local stone. He also built several other churches on the island and on nearby Long Island, some now in rubble, but many still standing. As you walk up the rock staircase hewn into the hill, you pass by the Stations of the Cross carved in stone. Looking at the Hermitage from below, it appears to be massive, but as you approach, you see that it is actually very small. The tower is a tall structure and the most dominant feature. You can explore the little chapel and see the tiny space on a stone floor where Father Jerome's six-foot-plus frame slept. Father Jerome died in 1956 and is buried in a cave on the site, which is where he lived while constructing his masterpiece.

On the top of Mt. Alvernia, glorious 360-degree views surround. This is truly a spiritual place in many respects. Visit the Hermitage at sunset, and you'll be treated to one of the most beautiful sights in all the Out Islands.

and bequeathed their lands to their former slaves. On Cat Island, they turned to farming peas, corn, potatoes, and later, to growing pineapples.

Dining and Entertainment

Visitors have most of their meals at the resorts. One place to check out, though, is **Sailing Club No. 1** for typical local food: fish, chicken, peas and rice, and macaroni and cheese. Of course, a cold Kalik (the local suds) is always a good idea. The place fronts on the ocean, has absolutely no décor to speak of, and the food is mediocre. Nevertheless, it's a cultural experience. While talking to the cook/waitress here, our conversation drifted toward the weather conditions, and I inquired about the forecast. She said, in all sincerity, "Well, it's hard to tell, but it should change Sunday (it was Friday). It usually changes Fridays and Sundays . . . and sometimes Wednesdays."

I have heard that the **Bridge Inn** in The Bight (near Fernandez Bay) and **Cookie House** in Arthurs Town (way up north) are both excellent restaurants featuring local fare. Cookie House is also known for its freshly baked bread.

Fernandez Bay and **Greenwood Beach Resort** are both excellent places to enjoy good meals in friendly surroundings. **Hawk's Nest Resort and Marina,** down at the very southern tip of the island, also has a clubhouse and restaurant, popular with the sailing crowd.

Medical Facilities

The government clinic in Old Bight can be reached at (242) 342-4049. In case of a diving emergency call DAN (Divers Alert Network) at (919) 684-4DAN (4326) or (919) 684-8111.

The Exumas

THE UNDERWATER SCENE

Seasoned sailors were exploring this vast 130-mile archipelago long before the first scuba tank arrived. Great Exuma, Little Exuma, and more than 350 mostly uninhabited cays provide a sailing, boating, and diving tropical paradise. Live-aboards, charters, and those lucky few with their own boats have endless opportunities for exploring virgin dive sites on mile after mile of tropical cays and in shallow coral gardens. Tranquil harbors provide shelter and scenic refuge.

George Town, where yachts pull into Elizabeth Harbor, is also the center for diving activities here, and divers will fly into George Town Airport. Unfortunately, the individual who first introduced divers to Exuma's waters, Ed Haxby, passed away a few years ago. Ed was a well-liked and respected marine biologist (he had worked for years for Morton Salt Company on Great Inagua) known for his fascinating eco-dives. He wanted his divers to experience more than "looking at pretty fish," and his goal was to impart an understanding of marine life behavior. As a result, Ed transformed many a casual diver into an underwater maniac, myself included. Fortunately, Ed's operation has been aptly taken over by the folks who own Small Hope Bay on Andros, diving pioneers themselves.

You don't have to venture far from George Town to find good diving. Even within and near the waters of Elizabeth Harbour, there are shallow patch reef sites, such as *Marker Reef,* good for strobe-free underwater photography. And outside the reef line (easily visible from waterfront hotels), ocean dives offer the chance to see mantas, eagle rays, and all types of pelagic fish. Spur-and-groove reefs and deep blue holes predominate in the Exumas. If there is wall diving here, I have never experienced it.

Diving Conditions

Normally the water conditions are excellent, with great visibility and only light currents. Winter cold fronts, however, can reduce visibility to 30 feet or less. When that happens, the deeper spur and groove sites near the reef line usually improve the odds of better visibility.

Consistent places for clear water are the area blue holes, but you'll need to get local advice as to the best hours to dive them. Better yet, go with a guide. The holes are tidal, and therefore are turbid when they inhale, and clearest after they've been exhaling for a quarter-hour or more.

The clarity of blue holes can be astounding. When one is at peak flow (indicated by a flat spot in the waves on the surface above it), it forms a column of exceptionally clear water. Nearby, the visibility might be 30 feet or so; inside the flow from the hole, 90 or 100 feet can be expected.

Recommended Level of Experience

There is enough variety of dive sites in the Exumas to accommodate every level of diver. The blue holes and caves should be reserved for confident divers, however. Many have a nice flow and therefore do not silt up to any great extent. Nevertheless, unless you are cave-certified, always go with a guide on these dives.

Great Dive Sites

Angelfish Blue Hole near Stocking Island is the signature dive on Exuma. It can be dived in virtually any weather, since it is located in Stocking Island Hurricane Hole No.3, one of a series of small natural harbors. The site is popular with photographers, since there's good growth on the bottom around the hole, and it's easy to avoid stirring up picture-spoiling sediment.

Its cavern starts at about 30 feet and drops to 90 feet. Photographers should position a diver on top, then drop down to shoot what will be a stunning silhouette. Sometimes this is difficult, because of the currents that frequently run through. The cavern is nice and wide, with plenty of light and room to move around. Schools of fish hover near the walls. Look for some swimming upside down on the undersides of ledges.

At just under 100 feet, the blue hole becomes a narrow cave, running horizontally. Although a safety line has been laid, do not attempt to explore the cave unless you have a guide or you are cave-certified. It is very narrow and has no illumination from natural sources. The tightest restriction in the front part of the cave is about two feet high. Inside is a luminous wonderland with white calcite lining the walls and even growth of plate coral, normally found on reefs. Inside you'll probably see lobster, small stingrays, and angelfish. Your maximum depth will be about 96 feet.

Stocking Island Mystery Cave is also a blue hole, and it is a mystery because no one knows how deep it is. It has attracted notable explorers, including the great Jacques Cousteau. Local tidal information is important to have. The cave inhales and exhales, meaning that a strong current typically runs through it, in either direction. During periods of peak inflow, the cave can be difficult to exit. So don't attempt to dive the cave without a guide.

Crab Cay Crevasse is yet another blue hole with large boulders and interesting structure. It can be dived as a cavern to just under 100 feet. It helps to have very good buoyancy control here, because the crevasse is in the middle of a bonefish flat, and a fin brushed against the bottom will instantly cloud out your dive. Caves branch out from the main blue hole, but only the cave-certified should explore them.

Ocean Rock features an underwater valley with huge caves filled with black coral. It's known locally as the Iron Curtain.

Shallow Diving and Snorkeling

Stingray Reef, on the west side of Stocking Island, has a wonderful variety of coral—perfect for cleaning stations. Cleaner shrimp are all over the place. Hold your hand still for a while over a cleaning station and see just how dirty you are.

Marker Reef is another shallow dive on spur and groove coral reef. These shallow areas are super for photography. You might see damselfish darting around protecting their nests, find large purple patches that are the nests of sergeant majors, and view gobies busy cleaning the fish that line up at their fish-washes. The low-relief coral formations are punctuated with beautiful, wave-patterned white sand.

Jeanie's Reef is only ten minutes from the harbor. Rather than fleeing or begging for handouts, fish on this site peek over the tops of corals wondering just what those bubble-blowing visitors are. Huge grouper let divers get within touching distance of their star-coral lairs before turbo-charging away across the sand flats.

A fun place is *Thunderball Grotto* at Staniel Cay, where portions of the James Bond movie *Thunderball* and Disney's *Splash* were filmed.

Marine Park

The Exuma National Land and Sea Park, near Staniel Cay, is a vast underwater preserve stretching for 175 miles. Created in 1958, it was the first marine replenishment nursery in the world, established to forever keep these sites pristine. The Bahamas National Trust protects the whole area and oversees conservation of all underwater wildlife. All commercial fishing and collecting is banned from Wax Cay Cut to Conch Cut and Fowl Cay.

Many of Exuma's distant cays also fall under national park protection. The park is accessible only by boat and is home to many animals that are exclusive to these islands, including "Bahamian Dragons," which are rock iguanas that can grow to two feet in length. Some other exotic species are the long-tailed tropicbird, the nighthawk, and the red-legged thrush.

Stromatolite Reef on the northern (Atlantic) shore of Stocking Island is a virtual living fossil. Stromatolites are a growing reef of layered limestone and are the oldest evidence of life on earth.

Dive Services & Packages on Great Exuma

ExumaScuba Adventures is a new facility located at the Club Peace & Plenty in George Town. Managers of the shop came from Small Hope Bay Resort in Andros. The facility runs daily dive and snorkel excursions and offers PADI introduction and open water certifications. Scuba packages are available with Club Peace & Plenty. Phone (800) 525-2210 or (954) 359-9899 or (242) 336-2893; cell (242) 357-2259; fax (242) 336-2093; website: www.emascuba.com.

Where to Stay on Great Exuma

The tropically pink **Club Peace & Plenty** ★★★★ is the island's most venerable hotel, and one that is kept much the way it was when British Royalty vacationed here in the sixties. At one time this was a private residence and the bar was a slave kitchen. Peace & Plenty was actually the name of the first boat. The kidney-shaped swimming pool overlooking the ocean is a convenient classroom for divers, and the bar seems to always have a lively crowd. A restaurant is also on the premises. Peace & Plenty has 35 air-conditioned rooms, many of which have been refurbished recently. To snorkel here, just carry your stuff down to the dock out back and simply slip into the water—couldn't be easier. There are bicycles, cars, sailboats, and Boston Whalers for rent, and fishing can be arranged. In fact, it's the raison d'etre for most people coming to stay here. A popular bonefishing school is led by P & P's director of sportfishing. ExumaScuba Adventures is now on-site, and dive packages are available. Nightly room rates for double occupancy range from $120 to $140, and meal plans can be arranged. Phone (800) 525-2210 or (242) 336-2551; fax (242) 336-2093; e-mail: ssbpeace@aol.com; website: www.peaceandplenty.com.

Regatta Point has nice waterfront apartments overlooking Kidd Cove and Elizabeth Harbour *and* a private beach. This plantation-style building has only five one- and two-bedroom apartments, all with fully equipped kitchens and daily maid service. Rates are $130 to $160 per night. There is no charge for the use of bicycles, Sunfish, or windsurfers. Call (800) 310-8125 or (242) 336-2206; fax (242) 336-2046.

Coconut Cove Hotel ★★ is just a few miles north of town, overlooking Elizabeth Harbour. The mood here is quiet and romantic. Coconut Cove has only 11 rooms, all air-conditioned, with ceiling fans, mosquito netting over the beds, minibars, and even bathrobes. All have ocean views. Facilities include a swimming pool and poolside bar. Room rates range from $140 to $170. Dive packages are available. Meal plans can be purchased and gourmet picnic baskets arranged. Dining can be in the main dining salon, al fresco, or in your room. Phone (242) 336-2659; fax (242) 336-2658.

ISLAND LIFE ON GREAT EXUMA

Many of the islands and cays in this archipelago are uninhabited, and most of the population live in Great Exuma and Little Exuma, both located in the southern portion of the chain and connected by a short bridge. Exumians for the most part make their living fishing or farming. Moss Town is the airport, located just north of George Town.

This 90-mile string of islets and cays was once a great haunt of buccaneers, with pirates and privateers causing all sorts of mischief. It was also a refitting base for British Men o' War.

The Exuma Cays are quite literally tropical; the Tropic of Cancer bisects the island of Great Exuma at just about the point where **George Town,** the island's principal community, is located. A couple of particularly beautiful structures are in George Town—the pink and white Government Administration Building, modeled after Government House in Nassau, and the 150-year-old St. Andrew's Anglican Church, a busy place on Sundays.

On Little Exuma, **Williams Town** is the largest settlement. Its Salt Marsh is one of the few remaining traces of the once-thriving salt industry housed here. Also here is the Cotton House, the only plantation owner's house still standing in the Exumas.

As wonderful as the diving is here, it is completely eclipsed by two sports that get most of the attention: sailing and bonefishing. The **Out Islands Regatta** is one of the Bahamas most prestigious sailing races (along with Long Island's), and it all begins here in Elizabeth Harbour in April. This is preceded by the George Town Cruising Regatta in March. Both of these are talked about and anticipated throughout the year.

Bonefishing rivals sailing in popularity. Fishing limits are closely monitored in the Land and Sea Park, but the vast shallow flats that run the length of the archipelago provide superb bonefishing habitat. The Club Peace & Plenty's Director of Sportfishing teaches a Bonefishing School, and Bonefish Bonanza Fishing Tournaments are held in October and November.

It's impossible to be on Great Exuma and not bump into a **Rolle.** What's a Rolle? Well, almost half the residents have that name. In the late eighteenth century, Lord John Rolle owned a vast cotton plantation—given to him by the British Government as a reward for being loyal to the Crown during the American colonies' little squabble with them. Working the plantation were more than 300 slaves who adopted their master's surname, which evidently was customary at that time. When emancipation was imminent, he deeded 2,300 acres of the land to his foremen slaves. The land has been passed on to each new generation and can never be sold to outsiders.

For shopping here, visit the **Peace & Plenty Boutique** for Bahamian prints, Androsia batiks, handmade purses, and other native artwork. Definitely walk over to the **straw market,** waterside in George Town. Just look for a group of women gathered in the shade of a large fig tree. I've heard that the **"Shark Lady of Exuma"** (a.k.a. Gloria Patience) sells jewelry and such in her cottage—but you'll have to ask around.

Dining and Entertainment

Club Peace & Plenty is a popular gathering place for both townspeople and visitors. On weekends the place really rocks with calypso music and dancing poolside. Lotsa fun! **Coconut Cove** features fine dining in a quiet, casual atmosphere.

You'll always find some friendly folks at **Eddie's Edge Water** in George Town. Locals mix with visiting divers and yachties to trade tall tales over cold bottles of Kalik. Have a conch salad, grouper fingers with peas and rice, or turtle steak and coleslaw, among other savory options. Eat in or take out. Monday's a special night at Eddie's, when the Rake 'n' Scrape band gets out their washtubs, saws, and screwdrivers to dazzle the patrons. Join in, if you like.

Kermit's Hilltop Tavern in Rolleville also has excellent food and wonderful rooftop views, and it's a popular night spot, as well. A Rolle owns it, of course. Kermit has a terrific establishment, and also gives excellent island tours.

Medical Facilities

The George Town clinic phone is (242) 336-2088. In case of a diving emergency call DAN (Diving Alert Network) at (919) 684-4DAN (4326) or (919) 684-8111.

Long Island

THE UNDERWATER SCENE

Long Island is certainly the most scenic of all the Out Islands. And that includes underwater vistas as well as topside terrain. Amazingly, it has gone virtually unnoticed by North American travelers, including most divers, even though airline access is excellent and the dive and resort facilities are superb.

This 80-mile-long gem is one of the most southerly of the islands, neatly bisected by the Tropic of Cancer. Some claim that Columbus first set foot on the New World *right here*. They've even put up a marker to commemorate the event (one of four such markers you'll find in the Bahamas). Whether it was the first or the third (as most experts now believe), Christopher must have been truly dazzled. Long powdery-white beaches line the calm west coast, contrasted by rocky, rugged headlands on the east that plummet down to small coves and hidden beaches.

Organized shark dives are prevalent now throughout the Bahamas, but the guys who started this slightly insane attraction are located right here, at the Stella Maris Resort. But you don't need a shark dive to get your thrills in these waters. Long Island features what is believed to be the world's deepest blue hole—more than 600 feet straight down. There's more deep diving at nearby Conception Island, where the walls are steep, protected, and pristine. The entire island and the waters surrounding it have been designated a national park.

Relatively few divers find their way to Long Island, but those who do find an unsullied environment and great diversity, coupled with professional dive operations. Divers staying at one of the resorts on the northern end (Cape Santa Maria or Stella Maris) will fly into the Stella Maris Airport. Those coming to central or southern Long Island should fly into Deadman's Cay Airport. Occasionally Bahamas Air has direct service from Ft. Lauderdale to Stella Maris (but not to Deadman's Cay), which might be the most convenient, no matter where you're staying on the island.

Diving Conditions

This is no-stress diving at its finest. Conditions could not be more ideal for sheer comfort. In fact, Long Island is considered to have the most inviting water conditions, coupled with the best climate, in all the Out Islands.

The water is generally calm, toasty-warm, and exceptionally clear. Also, I have never encountered strong currents here. These optimal diving conditions, combined with the exceptional variety of dive experiences—shallow reefs, vertical walls, shark dives, and blue holes—practically guarantees superb diving year-round.

Recommended Level of Experience

Any type of diver would love Long Island, and this would also be an exceptional place to get certified. Dive operations are well equipped and well managed. Also, cave-certified divers and deep-freaks would have a field day diving the deep walls and the 600-foot blue hole at Turtle Cove.

Great Dive Sites

Shark Reef has been both scaring and enchanting divers for many years now. If you've never seen a shark, it'll be a thrill, and if you have, it'll still be a thrill. For photographers it's a wonderful way to get sharks shots and impress your friends back home.

When I first dived *Shark Reef* in 1991, I had never seen a shark in the water, and it scared the wits out of me. About ten sharks milled around as we descended. As soon as they hear the motors, they know it's lunchtime—these guys are not stupid. We divers cowered under the protection of a coral overhang, trying not to hyperventilate, as chum was lowered and there was a feeding frenzy like you wouldn't believe. Through it all, an enormous grouper stayed on the perimeter, but occasionally darted into the melee to snatch some of the scraps. Obviously, he had been scavenging successfully for a long time. One shark darted into the ring, grabbed a bite, and kept on going, bouncing on the sandy bottom before disappearing in the gray mist. After dining, these guys do not go home. They come over and sort of check you out (fortunately they know you're not prey), and as you ascend through the water column to get back to the boat, they're all around you. I have never gotten back on a dive boat as fast as I did then.

Not long ago I went back to *Shark Reef,* and it still scared the wits out of me, even though by that time I had encountered many sharks while diving around the world and loved it when I did see them. This time we were all positioned in a circle on the sandy bottom—with no coral head for security—and the 12 gray-tip reef sharks were all around, in every possible place but under us. One brushed my side as it went past me, and as another approached at eye level, I decided it would be an excellent time to hold my large camera housing right out in front. Feeling a little thud and getting a great shot made me happy to have it. While I was photographing the divemaster (a gorgeous, muscular guy in swimming trunks holding a long prod), one of the sharks came right at him, like it had taken aim. This very buffed fellow, however, was looking away, watching another shark that was close to a diver. When he turned back around and looked straight ahead again, he saw a long snout and some very sharp dentures smack in front of his face. I can report that even divemasters, who have probably done this hundreds of times, can get just as frightened as any recreational diver.

Fortunately *Conception Island* is a government-owned and protected national park, because it features some of the very best diving—along its walls and even in the sandy shallows—that the Bahamas has to offer. The Conception Island Wall runs for 15 to 20 miles in a north-south direction and is both vertical and extremely deep. The top of the wall is from 50 to 60 feet, so it also starts deep. Fortunately, large coral heads are in shallow water close to the edge, so after coming up from the wall section, you can get into shallow water easily—a perfect profile for long dive times, nitrogen unloading, and underwater photography.

At the beginning of my first *Conception Island Wall* dive, I spotted a lone reef shark lying on the white sandy bottom. Unlike those at *Shark Reef,* this one scooted off as we descended. At about 70 feet, just off the edge of the wall, a barracuda and turtle were hanging out in blue water. From there all the way down past 93 feet, large orange and red barrel and tube sponges and many species of coral cascaded like a brilliant oriental carpet. Schools of baitfish shimmered in the sunlight. Back in the sandy shallows, pencil-like garden eels waved about in the light current. While we hung at 15 feet for a couple of minutes, the treats just kept coming. In the water column were a helmet comb jelly and a Venus' girdle. Both are transparent and have hairlike cilia running through them called combs. It's the motion of the cilia that propels them. They're not jellyfish and won't sting. The Venus' girdle is particularly fascinating, with a ribbon-shaped body and bluish hue. It can reach up to two feet in length.

As a protected area, *Conception Island* is totally uninhabited. Along its ironshore banks are seagrape trees, scrub, and small palms. Because it takes a good hour to get here from Long Island, divers are deposited on the shore for a picnic lunch. This gives them an opportunity to appreciate the near-shore waters, with gorgeous colors ranging from pale green to turquoise.

The *Long Island Blue Hole,* at about 600 feet deep, is located at Turtle Cove, which is just south of the settlement of Salt Pond and roughly mid-island. The location itself is absolutely gorgeous, with rocky cliffs over-looking the perfectly round dark blue shape that is just a few feet from the sandy shoreline—perfect for easy access and relaxing surface intervals. The hole is shaped somewhat like a funnel, opening up as you descend. Don't attempt to dive this without a guide.

The *West Long Island Wall,* up at the north end, plummets to a ledge at 150 to 180 feet, where black coral trees billow into blue water. All around the northern tip on both the west and east sides are miles of 30-foot coral heads in about 60 feet of water. You'll see grouper, barracuda, schools of jacks, eagle rays, turtles, and the occasional shark.

Along the eastern side of the island, drop anchor (carefully) almost anywhere and you'll discover coral heads, reefs, and walls. Very little of this area has been explored, but the area known as *Kris' Mesa* is exceptional. Deepwater gorgonians flow all around a huge promontory that also has tall stands of pillar coral and, usually, throngs of schoolmaster and blue tang.

Shallow Diving and Snorkeling

Angelfish Reef is a particularly beautiful site on the northwest side of the island, with a one-acre mountain of dense coral sitting in 100-foot-plus visibility. It is surrounded by white sand avenues and teeming with blue tang, lobster, and all varieties of angelfish. Bring plenty of film. *Angelfish Reef* deserves star billing but doesn't get it because it's typically done as the warm-up for *Shark Reef*, which receives all the attention. Swarms of juvenile tropicals and cleaner fish dart in and around the coral structure.

Conception Island, with its strikingly white sandy bottom, has numerous shallow diving and snorkeling sites. Rays of sunlight strike the coral mounds, illuminating brilliant colors.

Gorgeous shallow reefs are found on the west side at both the northern and southern ends. Also, the waters around the tiny cays just offshore from Salt Pond (around mid-island) are excellent for snorkeling and free diving. Just take a kayak, paddle out, and have a great time. You can even take a pole spear and bring home dinner, just like the islanders. Lobsters take refuge in the rocky structure of the cays, just a few feet below the water line. Or, if you can dive down about 25 feet, you'll find reef fish hugging the sandy bottom or taking shelter among the rocks.

There are excellent shore dives and nice snorkeling sites even from the usually more turbulent east side, but it's best to go with a guide. The typical structure is a multilevel shelf configuration. The first shelf is in about five feet of water, then drops about 40 feet to another shelf. Tropical reef fish are numerous, and you'll probably be able to see some pelagic visitors, as well.

DIVE SERVICES & PACKAGES ON LONG ISLAND

For its small size and low population, Long Island has some surprisingly professional dive services and gorgeous resorts.

Cape Santa Maria Beach Resort, up at the north end, has recently established its own dive operation. The shop uses a 38-foot Bertram, accommodating 12 to 14 people. It also has a smaller boat that can be used on the shallow reefs, perfect for special snorkeling trips and introductory dives. Excursions are made to Shark Reef and all the popular sites around the north end, as well as over to Conception Island. The only instruction available is their own resort course, which introduces uncertified divers to the sport. Rental equipment is available, and tanks are filled on the premises with an on-site compressor. Diving is priced separately from the daily room rate. Phone (800) 663-7090 or (242) 338-5273; fax (242) 338-6013; e-mail: capesm@batelnet.bs; website: www.capesantamaria.com.

Retail Sales: *None*
Rentals: *Adequate*
Scuba Training: *Limited*
Photo Services: *Limited*

Dive Boat Comfort: *Good*
On-Board Facilities
for Photographers: *Good*

Stella Maris Resort Club has been serving the Long Island clientele very well for many years. This is one of the oldest dive centers in the Bahamas. Also, although special shark dives are offered on many islands now, Stella Maris gets the credit for being the first to organize such activities and to offer them on a regular basis. The Stella Maris boats: a 65-foot Solmar III that accommodates up to 30 divers on a day trip or up to 18 overnight, and a 32-foot Solmar II that accommodates up to 12 divers. Another small boat is used for just a few divers. This PADI Reort facility offers courses through the advanced level and provides rental gear. Snorkeling is offered from shore or boat. Call (800) 426-0466, or (954) 359-8236 or (242) 338-2051; fax (954) 359-8238 or (242) 338-2052; website: www.stellamarisresort.com.

Retail Sales: *None*
Rentals: *Adequate*
Scuba Training: *Moderate*
Photo Services: *Limited*

Dive Boat Comfort: *Good*
On-Board Facilities
for Photographers: *Good*

At press time, **Reeldivers** was completing construction in Salt Pond. It will be the sole dive center serving the southern end of the island. Californian Kris Newman (the husband of the author) runs this new dive center, which lies on a pristine stretch of coastline with its own dock and launch ramp. Kris managed the Dive Unit for the Warner Brother's movie, *Sphere,* and trained the actors (including Sharon Stone and Dustin Hoffman). He still keeps active in the movie business. This rakish, bearded fellow offers a variety of diving experiences, including kayak diving, blue-hole diving, and reef and wall diving. A couple of offshore cays are within easy kayaking distance, and scuba kayaks can be rented. Kris is a founding member of the International Association of Scuba Technicians, and can repair just about anything. He has a complete line of rental equipment, including dive computers, underwater cameras, and underwater scooters (DPVs). Kris is a PADI Instructor and trains through the divemaster level. He also teaches a variety of specialties. El Grotto is Reeldivers' planned guesthouse, which takes its name from the grotto and enormous cave on the property, complete with stalactites and stalagmites. Divers staying on this end would normally fly into the Deadman's Cay Airport. Phone (707) 254-0307; fax (707) 253-8442; e-mail: reeldivers@aol.com; website: www.reeldivers.com or www.elgrotto.com.

WHERE TO STAY ON LONG ISLAND

When I first saw the beach at **Cape Santa Maria Beach Resort ★★★**, I knew it eclipsed any other that I had seen to that point. The four miles of blinding white sand, soft as talcum powder and set against the sparkling emerald waters, is absolutely stunning—certainly one of the best-kept secrets in the Bahamas. I would describe this place as casually elegant, with its British colonial-style bungalows and attentive service. There are ten beautifully decorated white duplexes. Guest rooms are decked out in rattan furniture, colorful island fabrics, and marble floors. Ten of these have additional side rooms, perfect for families. Each room has a screened-in porch with a ceiling fan—just right for relaxing in the evening and toasting the sunset. Rooms are air-conditioned but have no phones or TVs, since the place is designed for stress-free vacationing. A large Beach House is the center of attention, with a restaurant and cocktail bar (with a 180-degree view) on the second floor. Downstairs is the activity center, gift shop, TV lounge (if you *have* to have it), laundry, and fitness center. Available to guests are kayaks, Hobie cats, windsurfers, snorkeling gear, and bicycles. The resort also has a complete dive shop. Fishing, however, is what draws most of the guests—reef, deep-sea, and bone. A Canadian company that runs several fishing lodges also owns Cape Santa Maria. The resort arranges for taxi pickups at the Stella Maris Airport and can also arrange for car rentals. The per-night rate for double occupancy is from $195 to $260. A meal plan can be purchased for $75 per day. Phone (800) 663-7090 or (242) 338-5273; fax (242) 338-6013; e-mail: capesm@batelnet.bs; website: www.capesantamaria.com.

Stella Maris Resort Club ★★★★, a PADI Resort, really put Long Island on the tourist map, so to speak. Some true adventurers from Germany started building the place in the mid-1960s, and for many years it has attracted a mostly European clientele, with the primary focus always on diving. Americans and Canadians now make up a good percentage of the guest list. The resort is well managed and has a well-established dive operation. The facility is spread out among a nicely landscaped tropical setting and has a wide variety of accommodations, ranging from motel-style rooms to splendid villas with swimming pools overlooking the ocean. Some of the older rooms are starting to look a little tired now, but they are constantly upgrading the place. A clubhouse has an inviting bar/lounge and a new dining room; also a game room and boutique. There are three swimming pools, many nearby coves and beaches, and some brand-new tennis courts, equipped for night-time playing. There's no way to be bored here, so nondivers will have plenty to keep them occupied. The resort arranges complimentary cave parties, beach cookouts, moonlight cruises, nature slide shows, island excursions, and great evening entertainment. Snorkeling and fishing excursions are very popular. Stella Maris has its own marina and landing strip, store, and even a bank. Guests will be picked up at the Stella Maris Airport, and car rentals can be arranged. The basic room rate for double occupancy is about $145 per night and $630 per week. A one-bedroom apartment cottage is $165 per night, double occupancy. Other options are: 2-, 3- and 4-bedroom bunga-lows, and a 2-bedroom villa with car. Because there are so many different lodging options, it is probably best to simply call to discuss your needs. A meal plan that includes breakfast and dinner is $44. Diving and fishing pack-ages are available. Call (800) 426-0466, or (954) 359-8236 or (242) 338-2051; fax (954) 359-8238 or (242) 338-2052; e-mail: smrc@stellamaris resort.com or smresort@batelnet.bs; website: www.stellamarisresort.com.

Sea View Lodge is in Salt Pond, located about mid-island. Six one- and two-bedroom apartments are just off the main road, but not far from the waterfront on the west side. All are air conditioned and have full kitchens; five have ocean views. Scuba diving and snorkeling can be arranged with Reeldivers, found a short distance to the north. The nightly rate is $80. Phone Lucy Wells at (242) 337-0100 during the day or (242) 337-7517 in the evening.

Paul Constantakis (a.k.a. Paul the Greek) runs the **Sea Winds Motel** in the Deadman's Cay area. Although in a motel-like setting, these are complete one- and two-bedroom apartments, and very spacious, at that. Each is air-conditioned and has a fully equipped kitchen. You'll find Paul to be excep-tionally friendly and attentive. His well-stocked grocery store is right next door—perfect! The establishment is just off the main road and does not have a beachfront location. Paul, however, can arrange for scuba diving and snorkeling. Call (242) 337-0644.

Turnbull House ★★ has a spectacular location, on a quarter-mile stretch of secluded beach on the lee of the island. Guests would fly into Deadman's Cay Airport, as the guesthouse is very near the Turtle Cove area, home of Long Island's famous Blue Hole. Turnbull House consists of a great room with kitchen and three bedrooms, each with one double bed, two twin beds, and bath. A sweeping, covered verandah surrounds the building, offering superb views. Bonefish flats are only three miles away (guides can be arranged), and fishing for snapper, bonefish, and other species is as easy as throwing a line right off the beach in front of the house. The water is calm here, perfect for swimming and snorkeling. Scuba diving can be arranged with Reeldivers, in nearby Salt Pond, or with one of the resorts at the north end. The entire house can be rented by the week for $2,500. Call (541) 344-9024; e-mail: bobh@pond.net; website: www.pond.net/~bobh.

A new establishment called **Ritchie's Villas and Bonefish Lodge** is located along the southern shores of Deadman's Cay. This expansive place has individual cottages and wide-open ocean vistas. It's owned by the same family that owns Max's Conch Bar. The bonefishing and snorkeling here are superb. Scuba diving can be arranged with Reeldivers. Rates are $80 for double occupancy, and meal plans are offered. Phone/fax is (242) 337-0056; e-mail: maxconchbar@hotmail.com; website: www.maxconchbar.net.

Lochabar Beach Lodge ★★ is another ideal escape on the south end of the island. If you're looking for seclusion in a perfectly gorgeous romantic setting, this is the place. The lodge, with only three suites, is on an incredible stretch of powder-soft beach that curves around for miles in a sheltered inlet, with hardly any other development—just sea oats waving in the breeze. You'll walk out onto your deck, take a few steps to get to your private beach, then look down into shallow aqua water that slopes into an expansive blue hole (not *the* blue hole). The lodge itself is rustic and comfortable, with fully equipped kitchens. Each downstairs studio apartment is air conditioned (two of them) and combines bedroom area, living area, and kitchen; each can accommodate up to four people. The large luxury suite upstairs, with soaring open-beam ceiling, has a separate bedroom and accommodates up to five people. Since Lochabar is isolated, a rental car is essential and can be ordered. Fishing and snorkeling can be arranged, as well as scuba diving with Reeldivers, in nearby Salt Pond, or with one of the resorts at the north end. Visitors should fly into Deadman's Cay Airport unless you can get a direct flight from Ft. Lauderdale to Stella Maris, and thereby bypass Nassau. The nightly rate for double occupancy ranges from $115 to $150. Phone (242) 327-8323 or 337-3123; fax (242) 327-2567; e-mail: lochabar@hot mail.com; website: www.bahamasvg.com/lochabarbeach.html.

LIFE ON LONG ISLAND

Honeymooners love Long Island. The shoreline is strewn pearl-like with perfect little beaches that seem to have been built for two. In fact, locals call them "love beaches." On the calm leeward side, undeveloped and uninhabited offshore cays ringed with soft white sand are within easy kayaking distance from Salt Pond. More love beaches!

For islanders, the **Long Island Regatta** in June is an event they prepare for yearlong. This and the Exuma Regatta in April attract people from around the world. Serious racing takes place, but it's also a great excuse to party for a couple of weeks. Usually the regatta is about the second week in June, and takes place mid-island from the town of Salt Pond, which on its own is an attraction. For this area, you would fly into Deadman's Cay, and a car rental agency is just across the runway!

Definitely try to be here for the regatta, if you possibly can. Long Island is so unpopulated and so laid back that the event does not get frenetic or overly crowded. It's a wonderful time to see these friendly, fun-loving islanders in their element, enjoying friends and family with a focus on the sea. Just be sure to make your reservations early.

For touring Long Island, you'll need to rent a car, which your resort can arrange. Remember to keep to the left. For some of the not-to-miss sites, I'll start at the north end. Few of these little settlements are signed, so you might have to stop and ask for directions.

It'll take a bit of effort to reach it, but the **Columbus Memorial** is well worth a visit. Long Island was Columbus's third landfall in 1492, and he named it Fernandina, although the native Lucayans called it Yuma. The 15-foot memorial is an imposing site, standing at the northern tip on a tall bluff with wonderful seaward vistas. From the town of Seymours, you can find a sign for the rough 1.7-mile road leading to the monument. A Jeep is recommended for clearing the bumps.

About two miles south of Stella Maris is **Knowles Straw Works,** with artistically crafted baskets, purses, tissue boxes, etc., all made of palmetto palm in a variety of weaves. This is some of the finest straw work that I've seen anywhere in the Bahamas. These make great gifts to take back home.

Continuing along, you'll enjoy the little settlement of **Simms,** which also has straw work. The quaint collection of government buildings is wonderful, so bring the camera. HER MAJESTY'S PRISON (which looks like it never has any "guests") is about the size of a two-car garage; the cute little post office might barely fit a compact car.

The island sort of pinches together at **Salt Pond,** and a road (just north of Harding's Hardware Store) leads east to the shore. You'll reach a headland and be treated to an incredible shoreline vista of pinkish-hued sand and rock that stretches as far as you can see. The salt-pond industry is long gone, but local residents still collect salt for their own consumption at one of the ponds.

The leeward (west) side of Salt Pond has equally stunning vistas, particularly in the evening, toward sunset. Several uninhabited **small cays** just offshore are within easy kayaking distance and just begging for visitors. The water on this side is extremely shallow for miles on end, and with the sugary-white sandy bottom, the water is a breathtaking pale bottle-green. Take a picnic lunch or dinner, and a few bottles of Kalik (or better yet, a Long Island iced tea!) and the odds are very good that you'll have the entire island to yourselves. Make a toast to the setting sun, then keep watch for the green flash on the horizon.

Also in Salt Pond, at the site of a small dive resort under construction at press time, is one of several dry **cave systems.** This one features a beautiful grotto with banana palms growing up through it and a natural stone archway overhead. From the grotto, you enter a tall, open chamber with bats huddled in bunches on the ceiling. A small opening at the end leads into a cavernous chamber with stalactites and stalagmites. Toward the back, another huge tunnel cuts through, then dead ends. There is evidence that the Lucayan Indians used these caves.

Just a couple of miles south of Salt Pond a rough road at the settlement of Pinders leads to **Guana Key,** where an island just offshore is home to curly-tailed lizards. It's an easy swim out and a fun picnicking spot. Don't be surprised if you're suddenly very popular with some curly-tailed beggars.

The landscape all the way down to Clarence Town is prime agricultural area. Long Island is blessed with both climate and soil that are perfect for growing almost anything, and the growing season is year-round. Much of the farming is in potholes (natural holes in the limestone), which the locals fertilize with bat guano from the caves.

Just south of Pinders are the ruins of **Gray's Plantation,** one of several of the old cotton estates. Farther south in Cartwrights (Deadman's Cay area) are **Cartwright's Caves,** once used by Lucayan Indians, and in Hamilton's are **Hamilton's Caves,** which are quite a bit larger. For tours, call (in the evening) Leonard Cartwright at (242) 337-0235; Leonard has discovered some significant native artifacts in the caves. Driving a bit farther south, you'll see the sign to **Wild Tamarind Pottery and Gallery;** stop by to see Denis Knight and Marina Darville, both talented artists. Denis, who was head of the art department at the College of the Bahamas in Nassau, now makes beautiful wheel-thrown pottery, and Marina creates whimsical miniatures of Bahamian cottages.

The vast shallow shelf that stretches west of Deadman's Cay is prime **bonefishing** territory. Definitely try this exciting sport if you enjoy a lot of action in shallow water. Contact Cecil Knowles at Silver Strike Fishing (242) 337-0329 or 336-1555; fax (242) 337-6556; e-mail: judith knowles@hotmail.com or barealty@mail.batelnet.bs. And simply motoring through the pale emerald waters of the Sound here, past dozens of tiny cays, is an absolutely breathtaking experience.

When you're exploring in Clarence Town (as you should), stop by the **Harbour Grocery** and see Ena. She sells some wonderful straw items—baskets, place mats, bags—and has natural sponges from these waters and wonderful homemade jams (I highly recommend the mango). This scenic harbor town also marks the spot of two beautiful mission-style churches: **St. Paul's Anglican Church,** on a hill north of town, and the white and blue **St. Peter's Catholic Church,** south of town. Both were built by Father Jerome, the ascetic architect who constructed the intriguing Hermitage on Cat Island.

Dining and Entertainment

For tasty burgers cooked on an outdoor grill, head for **Burgers and Beer** in Salt Pond. And don't leave Long Island before experiencing **Max's Conch Bar** (between Gray's and Deadman's Cay). Guests venture all the way down from Stella Maris and Cape Santa Maria resorts for a chance to sit outdoors underneath a cover of palm fronds and enjoy Max's legendary conch salad. This is a favorite of the locals, too, and it's a wonderful opportunity to meet them and have some fun. Everyone sits on tall barstools around an octagon-shaped bar. While gentle offshore trade winds brush your skin, mouth-watering aromas waft from a barbecue located in the center. Everyone gets to watch the preparation. But don't call anyone Max here; Gary and Liz are your friendly hosts. While Gary worked as a fisherman he gained quite a reputation for his hunting prowess, so they called him "Mad Max"—hence the restaurant's name. I've seen Gary in action underwater, and he definitely deserves the moniker.

Earli's Hillside Tavern in Hamilton's (between Deadman's Cay and Clarence Town) is a popular local hangout with friendly folks and has good local food, as well as a mean rake 'n' scrape band on Saturday nights. In Clarence Town, the **Harbour Restaurant** is in the center of a hub of activity, near the dockside. It serves excellent native dishes and has a reputation for "the best guava duff in the Bahamas," which is indeed superb. **The Forest Satellite Restaurant & Lounge,** down in Miley (just past Lochabar) also serves excellent local food in a large air-conditioned building that is also a nightclub and disco. The place really rocks on the weekend.

Finally, if you're having difficulty tearing yourself away from this wonderful place and get the hankering for building a little vacation home, you're in luck. The folks who literally "wrote the book" on doing just that live right here. To find out more about ***Building a House on a Tropical***

Island, a Design Guide (by Robert and Dalia Fleming), log on to www. tropichouse.com or e-mail: flemingrobert@hotmail.com.

Medical Facilities

Deadman's Cay Health Centre can be reached at (242) 337-1222. In case of a diving emergency call DAN (Divers Alert Network) at (919) 684-4DAN (4326) or (919) 684-8111.

San Salvador

THE UNDERWATER SCENE

Brilliant white sands encircle this tiny 12-by-5-mile island that is said to contain at least 28 landlocked lakes. Divers will fly into Cockburn (pronounced koh-burn) Town Airport, which is close to the two resorts, Club Med Columbus Isle and the Riding Rock Inn.

The island is actually the exposed peak of a submerged mountain that plunges 15,000 feet to the ocean floor. Loyal American and Canadian divers have been coming back to its shores for years to plummet along its vertical walls, clearly visible for hundreds of feet. In fact, San Sal was one of the first Caribbean islands to develop wall diving and to attract divers specifically for that purpose.

San Salvador's wall stretches from Cockburn Town down the length of the west side (the lee of the island) and around the southern tip to French Bay. A classic wall dive here begins at 40 feet then slopes away, sometimes emerging into caverns and tunnels, plunging down the face of a straight drop-off from about 70 feet on. Frequently, the walls have enormous crevices that slice into the main wall. Huge barrel sponges and layers of spiraling plate coral proliferate at depth. The shallow reefs stand between 15 and 40 feet and they, too, teem with life.

Friendly grouper are the norm on many dives. Manta rays and hammerheads are often seen out in blue water at *Devil's Claw* and similar sites, as are up to 200-pound hawksbill and green sea turtles. Southern stingrays are frequently found rooting around in the sandy bottom, and nurse sharks slumber in the caves. Black-tip sharks, duskies, and bull sharks make occasional appearances.

Both of San Salvador's resorts are on the northwest side of the island, facing the magnificent wall. So boat rides to many of the dive sites are short. For those sites on the south end, the rides can be as long as an hour, but on average, they're about 15 minutes. Altogether, there are more than 70 dive sites to enjoy—enough to intrigue you for several visits—and most of these have mooring buoys.

There is snorkeling from both resorts, and with the exceptional water clarity, snorkelers will really enjoy these waters. The only obstacle, however, is that divers here get all the attention (due to the emphasis on wall diving), and snorkelers are something of an afterthought. Hopefully that will change in time.

Diving Conditions

Conditions here are superb. In fact, they can't get much better. The visibility typically exceeds 100 feet, and waters are generally calm, with little current. The southern and western sides of the island, where most of the sites are located, are on the lee.

Recommended Level of Experience

Although this is wall diving territory, it is not necessary to dive deep here. Most of the sites have a gradual, sloping profile, and the top of the wall is generally shallow, with plenty to keep you occupied. Also, there are plenty of shallow "second-dive" sites that are exceptional. For these reasons, San Salvador is perfect for all levels of divers.

Great Dive Sites

The following dive sites are organized from north to south.

At *Telephone Pole* I actually found myself laughing into my reg when I spotted a parade of grouper-cum-puppies tagging along behind a dive group. These guys are very friendly here and practically beg for attention. From the sandy bottom at about 30 feet, the reef slopes down to coral heads. A crevice cuts through the wall down to about 100 feet. Along with the grouper you might see southern stingrays, snappers, turtles, ocean triggerfish, and black durgon.

Devil's Claw is another wonderful wall dive (one of my favorites). Three great crevasses (the claws) are side by side and lead down the face of the wall from about 45 feet at the top to about 85 feet. At the bottom of the crevices is a plateau from which there is a mighty drop-off, otherwise known as *la la land*. The claws themselves hold all sorts of treasures, such as deepwater crinoids and large red brittle stars. Large pelagics frequently cruise by from the blue beyond.

At *Hole in the Wall,* large deep crevices cut through the wall from 50 feet to 120 feet. In the fissures lurk huge lobsters and Caribbean king crabs. Schools of jacks and schoolmaster snappers flow up and around the structure. Hammerheads and manta rays can often be sighted off in blue water. Stands of beautiful pillar coral billow in the currents on top of the wall—the crowning glory.

For cavern diving, the *Double Caves* site receives the most raves, because of the structure and abundance of both invertebrates and vertebrates. Practically every inch of the wall here is covered with coral and sponge growth. Huge plate corals stairstep down the face and deepwater gorgonians sway in the nutrient-rich currents. The highlights of this dive are two well-lit caverns that start in the shallow sand flats. Both are large enough to penetrate easily, and both are filled with white anemones. You'll enter at about 60 feet, then exit down the wall and into the blue at 110 feet. The caves are close enough together to allow divers to explore the deep sections of the wall, then come up through the second cave. While at depth, you'll see black coral trees, perhaps hammerheads, eagle rays, and manta rays.

Dr. Johns is a wonderful sheer drop starting at about 35 feet. You can shoot right through the big coral heads, down tunnels and chimneys and onto the wall. It's actually adjacent to *Double Caves* and has much of the same marine life. Watch for sharks off the wall. In the sandy shallows you're likely to find stingrays. Grouper here seem to be very curious.

Witches' Cauldron features a sponge that measures an incredible eight feet high and six feet wide. It's on a sandy slope in 70 feet of water. All along the base of the wall are large tube sponges and a variety of long, thin finger sponges. Soft corals, star corals, and brain corals coat the slope, and there are a few small stands of pillar coral.

Shallow Diving and Snorkeling

The *Wreck of the Frascate* is up on the northwest side, convenient to the resorts. This 261-foot freighter ran aground on a shallow reef in 1902, just to the north of the Riding Rock Inn. The highlight is the enormous variety of underwater life that the wreckage has attracted over the years. Two large boilers are covered with sea fans and other soft corals, as well as brain, star, and even pillar corals. The hull is broken open, revealing the round ballast stones inside. Bits and pieces of the vessel are scattered about. Because the depths here range from about 8 to 15 feet, this is a very good site for snorkelers.

Snapshot Reef, not surprisingly, is a site used for photo courses. Close to the surface, large coral heads, yellow tube sponges, and elkhorn coral reach toward the light. The fish are very cooperative, also, so this is a good spot for snorkelers as well as photographers. This is one of the most popular sites, but there are many others, all close to the resorts.

Dive Services & Packages on San Salvador

Club Med Columbus Isle (a PADI Resort) runs three beautiful 48-foot twin hull catamarans, built to accommodate a lot of divers. You could call this cattleboat diving, but that would be a bit unfair. Although the idea is to accommodate large groups, this outfit does it extremely well. Diving management here is excellent (it has to be, given the numbers!), and the crew is professional. I participated in a night dive with them, which drew the largest number of divers over a weeklong trip. The boat was packed, and underwater was a city of lights. Nevertheless, they handled the group expertly and even handed out a very nice dive light to each diver to use for the evening. Impressive! A boat goes out daily, just for snorkelers. The dive center instructs in CMAS, NAUI, and PADI. A lot of introductory courses and basic certifications are taught here, and in several languages. The Sea Center is well equipped, with classrooms, gear rental area, and lockers. The boat dock is right in front. When I was here, a one-person recompression chamber was also on the premises, staffed by a specialist in dive medicine. Phone (800) CLUB-MED or (242) 331-2000; fax (242) 331-2458; website: www.clubmed.com.

Retail Sales: *Adequate*	**Dive Boat Comfort:** *Good*
Rentals: *Extensive*	**On-Board Facilities**
Scuba Training: *Moderate*	**for Photographers:** *Good*
Photo Services: *Limited*	

Riding Rock Divers has been accommodating wall aficionados for many years and gets a lot of repeat, loyal business. Along with Small Hope Bay on Andros, these guys can be credited with being the real pioneers of wall diving. The shop runs a 40-, a 41- and a 42-foot boat, each V-hulls with camera work areas and freshwater rinse. The vessels carry first-aid kits, oxygen, and VHF radio, and have sun protection. A marina complex houses the dive shop, equipment rental facilities, gear storage, and an underwater photo center. Underwater photography has always been a prime emphasis here. They have E-6 processing, camera and video rentals, and a resident photo pro. Certifying agencies are NAUI, PADI, SSI, and YMCA. Instruction includes the advanced level, and specialty courses are offered, including a one-day photo course. Phone (800) 272-1492 or (954) 359-8353; fax (954) 359-8254; e-mail: info@ridingrock.com; website: www.ridingrock.com.

Retail Sales: *Adequate*	**Dive Boat Comfort:** *Good*
Rentals: *Extensive*	**On-Board Facilities**
Scuba Training: *Moderate*	**for Photographers:** *Superior*
Photo Services: *Extensive*	

Where to Stay on San Salvador

Club Med Columbus Isle ★★★★, a PADI Resort, is the most upscale of the Club Med resorts and is particularly popular with Europeans. You can practice your French, German, and Italian here! I have to admit that the Club Meds are "not my style" generally, but I loved Columbus Isle. They have really come a long way since their spartan beginnings in places like Tahiti. This one has beautiful artwork in the public areas and even locks on the guestroom doors—imagine! You still have to use those silly beads, though, to buy drinks. It's on the beach, of course, with lovely tropically landscaped grounds, and the entire village stretches along two and a half miles of beach. Be sure to ask for a room as close to the Sea Center as possible, to avoid long treks back and forth. White, gingerbread-trimmed multicolored villas flank a center building with the main dining room and other public rooms. Rooms are spacious and beautifully decorated. There are at least two additional restaurants, several bars, and a disco. Nightly entertainment outdoors is perfect for all ages. The huge Sea Center at the southern end has all the scuba-related facilities. You could spend a week here and not exhaust all the recreational possibilities (tennis, waterskiing, sailing, windsurfing, etc.), and the equipment is first-rate. The nightly per-person rate is about $170 and includes all meals and most of the recreational activities. When I was here in 1994 the diving was included; now it is extra. Phone (800) CLUB-MED or (242) 331-2000; fax (242) 331-2458; website: www.clubmed.com.

Riding Rock Inn Resort and Marina ★★★★ is a true pioneer in the Out Islands, established back in the 1970s and drawing a primarily American and Canadian clientele. It has grown to 42 air-conditioned rooms (some oceanfront) with mini-refrigerators, and there are five stone cottages with efficiency kitchens. A restaurant on the premises specializes in both American and Bahamian cuisine. The Driftwood Lounge is a fun place to hang out, have a cold one, and swap dive stories. Facilities include a swimming pool, tennis court, marina, and the dive center. The marina has electric hook-ups, fresh water, diesel and gas, showers and restrooms, ice, a laundry room, and even satellite TV connections. The nightly rate range for a double room is $114 to $141 (no meals). Excellent diving packages are available. Phone (800) 272-1492 or (954) 359-8353; fax (954) 359-8254; e-mail: info@ridingrock.com; website: www.ridingrock.com.

Island Life on San Salvador

While touring, don't worry about running into any traffic jams. Telephone listings in the phone directory for year 2000 take up only two pages! Cockburn Town is the island's capital (and only real town), with a cluster of houses, government buildings, and a few shops, restaurants, and bars. A single paved road encircles the island and literally bumps into the airport runway.

Although loyal divers and anglers have been returning to San Salvador year after year for decades, most of the rest of the world heard about it for the first time during preparations for the Quincentennial in 1992, when the island would finally make its mark.

Definitely stop by to see the **White Cross Monument** on the beach just south of Cockburn. This is the spot where it is believed that Columbus made his first landing in the New World in 1492. The native Lucayans called the island Guanahani, but Columbus preferred San Salvador, which means Holy Savior. Unfortunately, the name didn't apply to the Indians, because within 25 years they were decimated by the Spanish colonialists. Most were enslaved and taken off the island to work in gold mines on far-off islands, but all quickly perished. Nevertheless, this is a gorgeous setting, with a backdrop of greenish-blue waters. Some artifacts found here are strong evidence that this was, indeed, the first landing site.

The island's small jail was so little used that it has long since been converted into a museum. An entire room is dedicated to Columbus's discovery; another displays Lucayan Indian artifacts.

Besides the monument and the jail, old plantation ruins that dot the island and the **Dixon Hill Lighthouse** are the primary attractions for visitors. The lighthouse (north end/east side) is kerosene-operated and has been tended by the same family for generations. This is one of nine lighthouses built in the Bahamas by the Imperial Lighthouse Service in the 1800s. Dixon Hill and only two others still operate using the old-fashioned method of hand winding.

Dining and Entertainment

Popular local hangouts for beer and general conviviality are **Ed's First and Last Stop Bar,** up at the northern tip, and the bar at the **Riding Rock Inn.** The **Three Ships Restaurant and Bar** in Cockburn Town is a good choice for trying out some of the local specialties. Also in Cockburn Town is the **Harlem Square Club,** the place to go for a game of pool or island music. Club Med has the best restaurants on the island, but you have to be a guest to even enter the place.

Medical Facilities

Cockburn Town has a clinic. Call (242) 331-2105. In case of a diving emergency call DAN (Divers Alert Network) at (919) 684-4DAN (4326) or (919) 684-8111.

BAHAMAS LIVE-ABOARDS

Blackbeard's Cruises features one-week, all-inclusive cruises around Bimini, the Berry Islands, the Exumas, and Grand Bahama. It has been described as "like camping on a dive boat." Phone (800) 327-9600 or (305) 888-1226; fax (305) 884-4214; e-mail: ro@blackbeard-cruises.com; website: www.blackbeardcruises.com.

M/V Ocean Explorer organizes diving and film explorations to see wild dolphins, whales, shark encounters, and blue hole cave diving. Both Enriched Air Nitrox and Trimix are available on-board and several technical training courses are offered. Phone (800) 338-9383 or (561) 288-4262; fax (561) 288-0183. E-mail: info@oceanexplorerinc.com; website: www.oceanexplorerinc.com.

Nekton Pilot (a PADI Resort) features private cabins with baths for 32 divers. A seven-night package includes all meals, snacks, nonalcoholic beverages, and four to five dives per day. The cruise area is Cay Sal Bank, Freeport area, Rum Cay, Cat Island, San Salvador, Conception Island. Phone (800) 899-6753 or (954) 463-9324; fax (954) 463-8938; e-mail: nekton@nektoncruises.com; website: www.nektoncruises.com.

Belize

Physical Characteristics of the Dive Area

WATER & WEATHER CONDITIONS

Visibility	*Excellent*
Current and Surge	*Minimal*
Temperature	*Comfortable*
Storms	*Occasionally Stormy*

SITE CONDITIONS

Mooring Buoys	*Some*
Fishing, Collecting, and Hunting Restrictions	*Widespread Restrictions*
Ease of Access	*Very Easy*
Boat Traffic/Diver Congestion	*Light*

MARINE LIFE

Abundance of Invertebrates	*Abundant*
Abundance of Vertebrates	*Abundant*
Abundance of Pelagic Life	*Prolific*
Health of Reef/Marine Life/ Marine Structure	*Pristine*

Islands, Atolls, and Wild Beauty

This tiny tropical nation, once part of the British Empire, hugs Guatemala on its long western side, with Mexico's Yucatán Peninsula at the northern end and Honduras to the south. Due east in crystal-clear Caribbean waters lie a mosaic of 200 cayes (pronounced keys) and three atolls punctuating the northern tip of the Great Atlantic Barrier Reef. This reef—second longest in the world—runs parallel to the coast for 180 miles, extending all the way down to Honduras.

Belize is wild and natural—a tempting draw for eco-minded tourists. The thick interior jungle is just as intriguing as the great offshore reef. With more than 20 reserves and preserves, Belize is a virtual safe-haven for marine and terrestrial dwellers. From as far north as Ambergris Caye to the southern tip at the Guatemala border, marine parks and reserves dot the coastline. To date, about 40 percent of the country is under some type of protected-area status. Most travelers who make the trek to Belize come for one of three reasons: to fish, to dive, or to visit the wildlife sanctuaries, home to howler monkeys, iguanas, crocodiles, and even jaguars. But a few also come to explore the mysterious Mayan ruins.

From about the fourth to the ninth century, Mayan Indians dwelled in the Belizean jungle; then, inexplicably, their civilization vanished. Today, we can visit the ruins of Altun Ha and Xunantunich, nestled among huge palm and mahogany trees, and try to imagine this great civilization that spread all the way into central Mexico.

In 1502, Christopher Columbus passed by on his fourth voyage through Caribbean waters and named the bay that borders the southern part of the barrier reef "Bay of Honduras."

Once known as British Honduras (it was formally declared a British colony in 1862), in 1981 Belize became independent from the British Commonwealth. Early on, English Puritans were the first real settlers and set up trading posts all along the coastline. In the sixteenth and seventeenth centuries the coastline's numerous bays and protected coves offered a haven for British privateers. Its bounty of hardwood trees provided the wood they needed to repair their ships, and to allow them to harass Spanish treasure ships at will. By 1638 the British had established a permanent community, and in 1780 a British administrator was appointed. Logging was the dominant occupation.

Both tourists and divers flock to the barrier reef, which is anywhere from 10 to 40 miles offshore. Most are bound for popular Ambergris Caye, a large island at the northern end of the reef. This is where you'll find gentle rolling reefs and excellent spur and groove topography. Wall junkies should head south for the humongous coral atolls—the Turneffe Islands, Lighthouse Reef, and Glover's Reef—accessible from live-aboards or the islands' small dedicated dive lodges. Lighthouse provides the most excitement, with walls that drop down into the great abyss. Half Moon Caye, a conservation area since 1982, provides exceptional wall dives as well as a postcard-perfect landscape of beaches and palm trees.

In this vast expanse divers find enormous basket and tube sponges, black corals, gorgonians and hard corals, groupers, eagle rays, nurse sharks, and barracuda. Whale sharks occasionally present themselves in the spring,

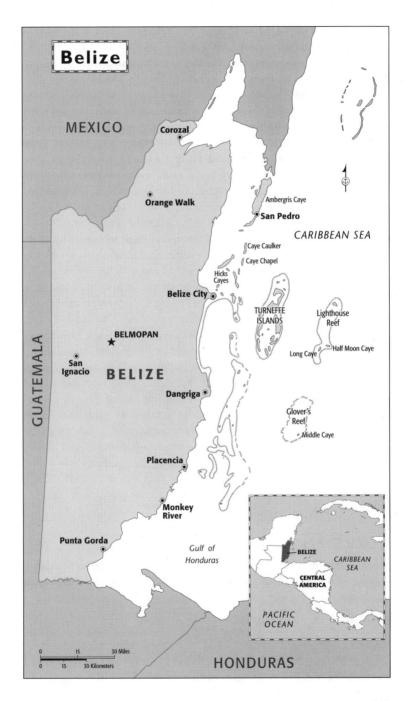

103

and manta rays in August and September. Oh, yes—there is the famous Blue Hole, which plunges nearly 500 feet.

Belmopan, in the center of the country, is the administrative capital, but visitors will fly into the coastal town of Belize City. Not known as the safest place for tourists to walk around, it does have a large selection of nice hotels and restaurants. Actually, its reputation has improved somewhat since my visit, when the owner of the hotel where I was staying absolutely refused to let me walk around on my own. I just wanted to explore for a few hours and take some pictures, and it was broad daylight. He told me not to go, then as I approached the exit, he offered to call a cab, and when I was almost out the door, he said (completely exasperated) that he would drive me around himself. Turned out, he was president of the Chamber of Commerce! Drugs have been the problem, but as I said, the situation has improved.

South of Belize City is the coastal town, Dangriga, whose residents are primarily Garifunas. These people were originally African slaves whose ship ran aground on the reefs of St. Vincent. They came to Belize and also to the Bay Islands of Honduras in the 1800s, to be free of British colonization. Farther south is the seaside resort area of Placencia, the favorite holiday spot for Belizeans, which has only recently been noticed much by outsiders. The area forms a peninsula, with a nice sheltered lagoon. Some new luxury resorts have opened here recently that would be worthwhile to look into.

The many offshore cayes are essentially mangrove islands located between the mainland and the barrier reef. Although mostly uninhabited by humans, they provide wonderful nurseries for marine life and nesting sites for birds. The habitable cayes—six of them—have palm trees, sandy beaches, nice resorts, and a wealth of recreational activities. Besides watersports, birding, fishing, and hiking are extremely popular. Caye Caulker, practically a giant stride away from Ambergris, has a popular dive operation and several lodgings for divers. The dive shop is included in this chapter, and for more information about services on the caye, check out their website: www.gocayecaulker.com.

QUICK STATS

Size   Barely the size of Rhode Island, its landmass is 8,866 square miles, and the islands comprise 266 square miles. It stretches 174 miles on its Caribbean side.

Population   Around 230,000

Location   On the Caribbean coast of Central America, bordered by Mexico's Yucatán Peninsula to the north and by Guatemala to the west and south. It is about 250 miles south of Cancun, Mexico.

Time Belize operates on Central Standard Time all year. Daylight Savings Time is not observed.

Government An independent democratic nation; the capital city is Belmopan.

Language Primarily English, but Spanish and Caribe are also widely spoken.

Electrical Current 110/220 volts AC; 60 cycles. The plugs are U.S.-style.

Air Temperature The mean temperature is 79°, varying from 60° in winter to 96° in summer.

Rainfall January through March is the dry season, but also the season for northers (Belizean term for cold fronts), which bring winds and rough sea conditions. April through June has little rain and low humidity. July through September is rainy season and also the hurricane season. October through December has mild air and water temperatures, and little rainfall.

Water Temperature Ranges from 74° to 84°

Underwater Visibility Frequently exceeds 100 feet

Best Diving Months Spring and fall. In winter, the northers come in, and summer is hurricane season.

PLANNING THE TRIP

Phoning Belize Dial the international access number (011 in North America), then the country code (501), the city code (usually 2), and the local five-digit number.

Getting to Belize The major airlines flying to Philip S.W. Goldson International Airport are American, Continental, and TACA; the primary U.S. hubs are Miami, New Orleans, Houston, and Los Angeles. Flights out of Los Angeles connect through Guatemala and El Salvador. Flying time from Miami is about two hours; two and a half from Houston. There is a departure tax of BZ$22.50. Goldson International Airport in Ladyville is ten miles from Belize City and a 20-minute taxi ride (about $30).

Getting to the Cayes Local airlines, Tropic Air and MayaIsland Air, leave from the municipal airport in Belize City and also the international airport. For Tropic Air, phone (800) 422-3435 or 501-2-62012 or 501-2-62338; website: www.tropicair.com. For Maya Island Air, phone (800) 521-1247 or 501-2-62435 or 501-2-62192; website: www.mayaairways.com. Water taxis can provide transportation to Ambergris Caye and to Caye Caulker. These are open speedboats with outboard engines, and the ride can be anywhere from 45 minutes to 2 hours. Tickets can be purchased at the Maritime Museum (north side of the river) in Belize City. The museum is located at the foot of the Belize Swing Bridge.

Entry Documents   U.S. citizens, as well as British subjects and citizens of Commonwealth countries, will need a valid passport and an onward or return ticket from Belize, but they do not need to obtain a visa.

Getting Around   The least expensive way to get around is by bus. Buses run regular schedules and have extensive routes. Car-rental service is available in the major cities. On Ambergris Caye, taxis are available and golf carts can be rented.

Currency   The local currency is the Belize dollar, which is tied to the American dollar. The exchange rate is two Belize dollars (BZ$2) for each U.S. dollar.

Tourist Information   The Belize Tourism Board can be reached at (800) 624-0686 or 501-2-31913; fax 501-2-31943; e-mail: info@travel belize.org; website: www.travelbelize.org, or www.belizetourism.org. In New York, the Belize Tourist Board can be reached at (800) 624-0686; fax (212) 268-8798.

For a good database of information about Belize, go to www.belizenet. com. For information about Caye Caulker, refer to www.gocayecaulker.com.

Marine Parks

In 1981, the Belize National Parks Systems Act created the Hol Chan Marine Reserve on Ambergris Caye, as well as other parks, with an emphasis on "recreation, tourism and the environment."

In 1996, Ambergris Caye added another park to its list: the Bacalar Chico National Park and Marine Reserve, encompassing 60 square miles on the island's north end. This new section along the barrier reef includes 15,529 acres of marine habitat, where Nassau and yellowfin grouper can spawn in peace, and nesting sites for the green sea turtle and the loggerhead turtle stay undisturbed. An area is also set aside for us warm-blooded snorkel-breathers and bubble-blowers. The ranger station is located among the ruins of Chac-balam, which was an important Maya trading center.

The Caye Caulker Marine Reserve includes the turtle grass lagoon adjacent to the Caye Caulker Forest Reserve and the Belize Barrier Reef that runs parallel to the entire Caye, extending approximately a mile beyond the reef. The area is reserved for snorkeling, scuba diving, and sport fishing.

Half Moon Caye Natural Monument, at Lighthouse Atoll, is a marine reserve and also protects the nesting site of the rare and endangered red-footed boobie bird. Belize's famous Blue Hole, also near Lighthouse Atoll, is another national park. The Belize Audubon Society (www.belize audubon.org) manages these and other sanctuaries, reserves and national parks, encompassing around 150,000 acres. The entrance fee for Half Moon Caye for non-Belizean nationals is $10 and for Blue Hole is $8.

The southern portion of Glover's Reef Atoll has been designated a U.N. World Heritage Site and a National Conservation Zone to preserve its pristine conditions.

The country's departure tax of BZ$22.50 includes $7.50 which goes directly to the Protected Areas Conservation Trust (PACT) used for sustaining the natural and cultural resources of Belize.

Ambergris Caye

Ambergris Caye is the hot spot along this Great Atlantic Barrier Reef, with superb diving and snorkeling and a variety of terrific resorts that are casual and accommodating. All are located beachfront. Ambergris is easy to reach by either boat or plane from Belize City, with the flight time about 20 minutes, and a boat ride about an hour and a half.

At 25 miles in length, it is the largest of about 1,000 cayes. It is so far north that it nearly touches Mexico's Yucatán Peninsula. In fact, experts surmise that the Mayas occupied Ambergris and dug a narrow channel to separate it from the mainland. The island is flat and characterized by mangroves, a large inland lagoon, and white sandy beaches. Its population is about 7,000, with most residents now working in the tourism industry. Previously, the fishing industry was the primary means of income.

At various times in its history, Ambergris was used by British pirates, by Mexican fishermen, the Mayas, and even the Spanish. In 1869 it was purchased for $625! All of these influences have resulted in a very interesting amalgam of cultures. Although English is the official language of Belize, most islanders speak Spanish, or perhaps what could be called pidgin-Spanish.

San Pedro is the only real town on the island; it's where most of the residents live and where the majority of the hotels, restaurants, bars, and clubs are. It is long and narrow, and just about everything is within easy walking distance.

Most resorts and hotels provide transportation from the airport. There is also taxi service on the island as well as ferry service on a regular schedule from San Pedro to both the north and south ends.

THE UNDERWATER SCENE

This entire barrier reef is formed along an ancient underwater fault zone and rises up from the seabed like a great wall. This barrier reef parallels the coastline for roughly 185 miles. Inside the reef (between the reef and the mainland) is a sandy bottom. For dive boats to get to the outer seaward side of the reef, they use a number of convenient cuts. It is this outer fore reef, facing east, that provides the most exciting dive sites.

On Ambergris, the various piers and boat docks all face the east coast, providing quick access to the reef. Usually, rides are around 15 minutes.

Outer reef sites are typically massive spur-and-groove formations in a canyonlike profile, with the spurs being huge crests of coral. The grooves meet a wide sandy shelf usually at around 90 feet. Finning through the valleys, you'll have great walls of coral soaring on either side of you. Tunnels and a variety of swim-throughs cut into these massive coral mounds.

Health Score Card

The coral communities are in excellent shape and the fish population abundant. Also the number of species is impressive. Years ago, the fishing industry did a number on the fish population, but over the years, the marine reserves have allowed the populations to increase.

Diving Conditions

Visibility here is excellent, although generally not as good as farther out in the atolls. Nevertheless, 100-plus is not too shabby. On most of the outer-reef dives, a mild current flows, and boats run live, allowing divers to drift along. This also eliminates the problem of anchor damage. Just make sure your name is on the boat's roster—you wouldn't want to be left drifting. There are sites with mooring buoys, as well.

Recommended Level of Experience

Any level of diver would enjoy the diving from Ambergris. Snorkelers, also, will have a great time, since some excellent sites are in very shallow water.

Great Dive Sites

On the north side, *M & M Caverns* provides one of the most exciting dive experiences from Ambergris. Located about half a mile from Journey's End Dive Center, the prominent features are extensive tunnels and caverns, which begin at around 90 feet. Divers enter one tunnel at 90 feet and follow it for 30 feet up to its exit at 60 feet. Schools of silvery horse-eye jacks (yellow tail fins) like to congregate here, and it's also a good spot to see deep-water pelagics cruising the reef.

At *Renegades,* also on the north, grouper congregate and spawn during the full moons of December and January. And at *Happy Hour Reef,* divers can witness coral spawning once a year. The rest of the year they can drift by large barrel sponges and sea fans. At *Eailman's Reef,* the coral is shaped like a huge mushroom, providing protection for a wide variety of reef fish. Depths at these sites range from 70 to 80 feet.

The walls of *Devil's Canyon* drop off steeply to about 150 feet, and at *Palermo's Point* you'll dive through arches formed by currents that come down from Mexico. Barracuda and large eagle rays enjoy the dining here. Look for stingrays and nurse sharks in the sand-filled canyons of *Angel's Flats,* with depths ranging from 60 to 80 feet. An occasional coral head sticks up out of the great sandy flat, which attracts angelfish and butterflyfish.

At a site called *Mahogany* (from a huge mahogany tree that was once caught on the reef), the coral formation rises about 20 feet higher than the surrounding reef. This is sufficient to attract a variety of reef fish, including tiger and Nassau grouper, triggerfish, and schools of blue tang. At *Mexico Pinnacle,* you'll dive through a cavern, then be deposited in front of this coral pinnacle that attracts grouper and nurse sharks. A drop-off is nicely decorated with tube sponges and beautiful soft corals. The depth here can reach 90 feet.

At *Mata Caverns* and *Tuffy Canyons,* the reef top is about 55 feet, and the canyon cuts descend to the outer reef at 95 feet. All sorts of cuts, swim-throughs, and mini-caverns provide convenient structure for grouper, snapper, and barracuda. Watch out in the blue for cruising spotted eagle rays and black-tip sharks.

Shallow Diving and Snorkeling

The *Hol Chan Marine Reserve,* at the very southern tip of Ambergris and only a few miles north of Caye Caulker, is an excellent spot for snorkeling and shallow diving. This is actually a steep channel through the reef, and since it has been a protected area for years, the fish population has been left alone to increase in numbers. At one time, it was practically fished out, and there was considerable reef damage; hence, the reason for creating the reserve in the first place. The reserve encompasses five square miles of reef, with a maximum depth of 30 feet. Besides fishy stuff, you could see green turtles, and even spotted dolphins. Rays and peacock flounder cruise the sandy bottom. The grouper are fat and happy. One impressive site is called *Pillar Coral* (in a deeper portion of the reserve), where large stands of the coral and friendly grouper are the attractions. You'll also see schools of both schoolmaster and barracuda. The Hol Chan Reserve is an excellent spot for night dives, where giant parrotfish sleep under the reef's ledges wrapped in their cocoons, and squid will flutter up near the surface.

Shark-Ray Alley, in close proximity to *Hol Chan,* is perfect for both snorkeling and diving, and can be very exciting. This is a shallow cut in the reef, where you'll see both nurse sharks and stingrays at depths from eight to ten feet. The divemasters provide lunch to the hungry assemblage. They are not usually aggressive; nevertheless, exercise caution. I had a chunk taken out of my hand by a very large stingray that was supposedly "tame." This is a fun experience, and a great opportunity for underwater photographers.

Amigo's Wreck is an artificial reef site where a 30-foot wreck was sunk in 70 feet of water to attract marine life. Bring your camera with either wide-angle or close-up lens, and be prepared to focus on big Nassau and black grouper, nurse sharks, snappers, hogfish, and morays. *Mexico Rocks* is another popular shallow site at the inside reefs, with coral heads in only 20 feet of water.

Just outside of Hol Chan is *Eagle Ray Canyon,* where more grouper hang out as well as frequent schools of spotted eagle rays. You'll also see enormous barrel sponges. Farther south toward Caye Caulker is the *North Caye Caulker Cut,* where the gentle manatees often swim, in search of food. In summer, bigger visitors sometimes cruise through, as well—the whale sharks!

DIVE SERVICES & PACKAGES ON AMBERGRIS CAYE

Journey's End Dive Center offers NAUI and PADI certifications. Every certification is available, including several specialties. Introduction scuba classes are complimentary. There is a full line of rental gear, including dive lights and underwater Sea & Sea cameras, and Enriched Air Nitrox and Trimix are available. Daily dive-and-snorkel trips are offered as well as sail-and-snorkel trips. Dive trips visit pristine sites around Ambergris, and day trips go out to Caye Caulker, to the Blue Hole, and to the Elbow. Some interesting caves have been discovered in the lagoon just behind the resort. Call (800) 460-5665 or (713) 780-1566; fax (713) 780-1726; e-mail: diving@journeysendresort.com; website: www. journeysendresort.com.

Retail Sales: *Adequate*	**Dive Boat Comfort:** *Good*
Rentals: *Extensive*	**On-Board Facilities**
Scuba Training: *Extensive*	**for Photographers:** *Good*
Photo Services: *Moderate*	

Aqua Dives Belize is located on the beach front in San Pedro at the Sun

Breeze Hotel (a PADI Resort). The shop runs a fleet of six dive boats: two 26-footers, two 43-footers, and two 36-footers. All carry first-aid kits and oxygen. The 36-footers have a marine head and freshwater shower. Packages are available with Mayan Princess Hotel and Sun Breeze. All PADI certifications are taught through the divemaster level, including the Nitrox course. The shop has rental equipment, including dive lights, and Enriched Air Nitrox is available. All sorts of dive trips are offered, from the Hol Chan sites to Turneffe and Lighthouse Reef Atolls (including the Blue Hole). Special snorkeling trips are run, as are day trips to see the manatees and to Goff's Caye for picnicking. Phone (800) 641-2994 or 011-501-2-63415; fax 011-501-62-3414; e-mail: aquadives@btl.net; website: www.aquadives.com.

Retail Sales: *Adequate*   **Dive Boat Comfort:** *Good*
Rentals: *Extensive*   **On-Board Facilities**
Scuba Training: *Extensive*   **for Photographers:** *Good*
Photo Services: *Limited*

Ramon's Village Dive Shop is on the premises of Ramon's Village (a PADI Gold Palm Resort), and is complete with great beach and a pier, where the boat awaits divers. There are six boats, 24- and 30-footers, and a nice Pro-42 for the long excursions. Scuba instruction is through the rescue level with NAUI, PADI, and SSI, and several specialties are offered. The shop offers a full line of rental equipment, including dive lights and underwater still and video cameras. There's also gear for sale. Dive excursions go out to the Blue Hole and to Turneffe Atoll. New divers and snorkelers are taken to Hol Chan Marine Reserve. Phone (601) 649-1990 or 011-501-2-62071; fax (601) 649-1996 or 011-501-2-62214; e-mail: ramons.btl.net; website: www.ramons.com.

Retail Sales: *Adequate*   **Dive Boat Comfort:** *Good*
Rentals: *Extensive*   **On-Board Facilities**
Scuba Training: *Extensive*   **for Photographers:** *Superior*
Photo Services: *Moderate*

On Caye Caulker, **Belize Diving Services** has been in operation since 1978, and is one of the longest-operating dive shops in Belize. A 38-foot speedboat takes divers out to the outer atoll destinations, including the Blue Hole and Turneffe, as well as to sites around Ambergris and the Caye Caulker Marine Reserve. Rental equipment is available. PADI certifications are offered through the divemaster level, as well as 15 specialties. Phone 501-2-22143; fax 501-2-22217; e-mail: bzdiveserv@btl.net; website: www.gocayecaulker.com.

Retail Sales: *Adequate*

Rentals: *Adequate*

Scuba Training: *Extensive*

Photo Services: *Limited*

Dive Boat Comfort: *Good*

On-Board Facilities
   for Photographers: *Good*

WHERE TO STAY ON AMBERGRIS CAYE

A 7 percent hotel tax and a 10 percent service charge will be added to your hotel bill. Also, an 8 percent food tax and a 10 percent service charge will be added to restaurant bills or meal plans.

Journey's End ★★★★ (a PADI Gold Palm Resort) is my favorite place to stay here, but it wouldn't meet everyone's taste, given its distance from most of the activity. On the other hand, if you enjoy a little isolation, this resort is just perfect, and certainly has the best beach. The resort property is 50 acres, sandwiched between the Caribbean and a pristine mangrove community. Note that the property is north of San Pedro and requires a water taxi to get back and forth, since no road connects it. The resort consists of 30 individual cabanas, 40 deluxe guest rooms, and a three-bedroom oceanfront villa. All are air-conditioned and have mini-refrigerators and coffee makers. The dive shop is on the premises. Other than diving and snorkeling trips, activities include bonefishing, guided kayak trips, manatee safaris, cave and river exploration, hikes along the Panti medicine trail, and trips to the atolls. A tour and activity office is on-site for arranging adventure trips into the jungle or wildlife boat excursions. The daily room rate is $137 for a pool or garden cabana, $169 for an oceanfront cabana, and $425 for the villa. Diving, fishing, and adventure packages are available. Full and modified meal plans can also be purchased. Call (800) 460-5665 or (713) 780-1566; fax (713) 780-1726; e-mail: info@journeysend resort.com; website: www.jouneysendresort.com.

The **Mayan Princess Hotel ★★★** is on a white sandy beach in the middle of San Pedro. Studio suites have queen bed, bath, kitchen, living room, and balcony. All are air-conditioned. Services include daily maid service, airport shuttle, hammocks, and beach towels. There is a gift shop on the premises and bicycle and golf cart rentals. Diving is arranged with Aqua Dives Belize, and packages are available. There ia a private dock. Room rates: single, $80–$115; double, $90–$125; triple, $100–$135; quad, $110–$145. These rates do not include the hotel tax or a 10 percent service charge. Call (800) 850-4101 or 011-501-2-62778; fax 011-501-2-62784; e-mail: mayaprin @btl.net; website: www.ambergriscaye.com/mayanprin.

Ramon's Village ★★★★ (a PADI Gold Palm Resort) has the best beach in San Pedro and looks like a South Seas village, with 60 palm-thatched cabanas and a full-service dive shop and pier on the premises. The cabanas have either garden or sea views. The central facility includes a restaurant, the Purple Parrot bar, a boutique, and a swimming pool. In addition to diving, the resort offers fishing—bottom, flats, and deep-sea—and island excursions for snorkeling, picnicking, and bird watching. Rental boats are available for windsurfing, sailing, and kayaking. Bicycles and golf carts can also be rented. A tour desk arranges trips to the mainland. Nightly room rates are $140 to $175 and include airport pickup and drop-off. Hotel tax is additional. Suites are also available and meal plans can be purchased. Dive packages are available. Phone (601) 649-1990 or 011-501-2-62071; fax (601) 649-1996 or 011-501-2-62214; e-mail: ramons.btl.net; website: www.ramons.com.

SunBreeze Beach Hotel ★★★★ (a PADI Resort) has a pretty Spanish colonial look with palm trees and tropical gardens. Although there is no beach here, the hotel is right on the waterfront and the dive shop (Aqua Dives) and boat dock are on the property. There are 39 air-conditioned rooms with two double beds, refrigerator, ceiling fans, and ocean view. Facilities include a swimming pool, restaurant and bar, gift shop, and bicycle rental. Nightly room rates (for double occupancy) range from $100 to $120 for a standard room; $125 to $150 for a deluxe. Rates do not include tax or a 5 percent service charge. Dive packages are available. Phone (800) 688-0191 or 011-501-2-62191; fax 011-501-2-62346; e-mail: sunbreeze@ btl.net; website: www.belizenet.com/sunbreeze.

ISLAND LIFE ON AMBERGRIS CAYE

Walking the sandy streets of San Pedro, the island's only town, won't take long. After you buy a T-shirt and snap off some pictures, there's not much to do except sip a cold beer from a waterfront bar. When I was here, I had to wade through the dope addicts trying (incoherently) to sell me drugs before I could even get into a bar.

To see some of the island, rent a golf cart to zip around in—it's fun! Also, driving is on the right, which is nice for U.S. visitors. You'll need to show a valid driver's license, even for a golf cart.

Other activities are sailing, fishing, and kayaking. The calm San Pedro Lagoon is a perfect place to kayak and observe the wildlife, including crocodiles, raccoons, and of course birds. Tours to Bacalar Chico National Park (see Marine Parks for a description) and other nature-filled areas can be arranged through local tour guides. Also, Ambergris is where you can arrange for an inland tour, and there are some good travel agencies that can help out.

It's a Jungle Out There

The only way to see the famed orchids, hardwood forests, birds, butterflies, and other wildlife in this gorgeous country is to get off the reef and make a trek into the interior. If you're the type that enjoys hidden escapes and a little adventure along with great wildlife viewing, you'll love it. Tropical forest encompasses some 66 percent of the country—at least that's what the tourism folks say, and I don't doubt it. On a bus ride through the country, that's just about all I saw.

As the elevation increases (and the temperature drops) the jungles become forests similar to what one might see in the Appalachian range of the Carolinas. In central Belize, an area called Mountain Pine Ridge, at more than 3,000 feet above sea level, has pine trees and fresh rivers, excellent for rafting. One outstanding tubing experience along the Caves Branch river leads floaters into the dark passages of a Belizean cave system culminating at a Mayan ceremonial site, where footprints from inhabitants of the ancient culture are still embedded in the mud.

During the winter, rainfall is heavy in Belize, feeding several river systems and smaller streams. Both kayaking and canoeing are popular ways to observe the birds and wildlife along the banks. The birds alone will keep you busy; it is said that there are more than 500 species here. Some of the best spots to observe are in the Cockscomb Basin and Crooked Tree Wildlife Sanctuaries.

Belize also has an interesting assortment of creepy crawlies—big ones. During my jungle stay in a gorgeous spot surrounded by hardwoods and tropical growth, I saw insects I never knew existed. My little cottage had no electricity, but I used a kerosene lamp to get around at night. Noticing a dark shadow in the corner of my bedroom one night, I began to reflect that I hadn't put anything there. Deciding I'd better check it out before I turned in, I brought my lamp over and there was an enormous furry spider! Being a prudent individual, I dashed down the hill to alert the owners. They casually told their ten-year-old son to scoot it out with a broom! Guess these visitors are pretty common. At around 4 a. m. the howler monkeys began to make their presence known, and after the entire tribe joined in the dialogue, the jungle was practically shaking.

I had journeyed from Ambergris Caye to Belize City, where I spent a night, then left my dive bag at the hotel while I went into the interior to explore. It was wonderful. First I took a bus, which cost

---

It's a Jungle Out There (continued)

$3, all the way across the country, nearly to the Guatemala border. There a local guide picked me up, took me to the lodging, and then out touring. The most difficult task on this journey was trying to figure out how to use the pay phone to call the guide! Near the Guatemala border, you can stop in San Ignacio for some prime bargain shopping. It's probably best not to cross into Guatemala for safety reasons.

If you make this trek, you'll have the added bonus of seeing the great Mayan ruins of Altun Ha, 30 miles northwest of Belize City, and Xunantunich, some 80 miles southwest. These are some of the remains of the fantastic trade route that extended from Mexico through Central America, all the way to Roatan Island in Honduras. Incredibly, this civilization flourished from about 2000 B.C. to A.D. 1000. The jungle is so thick that Mayan ruins are still being uncovered; it's fascinating to witness the architecture and get a little glimpse of this great culture, when more than a million Mayas populated Belize, and to wonder about the mystery of what caused their demise.

The best way to arrange this is to simply visit a travel agency either in Belize City or on Ambergris Caye. You'll be able to sift through some of the choices for where to stay and get some good advice from the agent.

Dining and Entertainment

This is the Caribbean, so you'll find the ubiquitous peas (beans) and rice, either stewed or barbecued chicken, cole slaw, potato salad, and macaroni and cheese. But it's almost in the lap of Mexico, as well, so just about everything Mexican can be found also. Seafood (including conch and lobster) and a variety of tropical fruit are also on many restaurant menus. Don't just eat at your resort; it's a lot of fun to walk around and discover something new.

Elvi's Kitchen is a favorite spot in San Pedro. When I was here the floor was sand, which I thought was convenient, and the waiters dressed in black-tie! Very good seafood dishes are served here. Other popular spots are **Celi's, The Barrier Reef, Playador Grill,** and the **Green Parrot.**

Ambergris is party central, where the resorts are packed to the gills with excited vacationers. So after the sun sets, the party venues are not difficult to locate. Most of the resorts have nightly live entertainment, and a couple of disco clubs are in town.

The Atolls of Belize

Three very large atolls lie beyond the barrier reef, and all offer superb diving. These tropical beauties feature oblong rings of coral surrounded by shallow turquoise lagoons and punctuated by sandy mounds topped with palm trees. They developed from chunks of earth that at one time were attached to the mainland. As they slide into the sea, corals keep growing and building their structure around them. The outer edges of the atolls have coral walls that plunge thousands of feet.

The closest atoll to the mainland is Turneffe Islands, which is also the largest atoll in the Western Hemisphere. It can be reached by boat from Belize City in about two hours.

Lighthouse Reef lies 50 miles southeast of Belize City. It's the most famous, due primarily to its protected sites—the Blue Hole and Half Moon Caye. However, all the sites in the vicinity of Lighthouse Reef provide tremendous excitement, with walls that drop off into the cobalt abyss.

Glover's Reef is the most remote of the three atolls and can be reached in about five hours by boat from Belize City. It offers pristine conditions and excellent visibility. Nearly uninhabited, Glover's features drift diving along plunging walls, with not another dive boat in sight. The reef is named after John Glover, an English buccaneer who set up camp here in the 1700s.

THE UNDERWATER SCENE

Turneffe Islands

Although this atoll often appears to be a continuous flat island, it is actually an archipelago containing a whopping 32 islands and cayes. All are clustered in the form of an elongated oval measuring 30 miles in length and 10 miles across. The total area is 205 square miles. Inlets lead to large shallow lagoons with gnarled mangrove roots that provide habitat for crocodiles, turtles, and a variety of juvenile fish. The eastern side of the 30-mile-long atoll is lined with flats, sufficiently shallow for wading as well as fishing for bonefish and permit.

Most of the popular dive sites—there are about 70—are clustered around the southern and the northern ends of the archipelago. The long west side has a gradually sloping reef with large coral heads, and the east features a 35-mile wall of coral with some sheer drop-offs. On top of the wall are small tropicals and waving gorgonians. And on the face you'll see healthy tube and barrel sponges, lettuce coral, black coral, and large deepwater gorgonians. There will probably be hawksbill turtles, spotted eagle rays and black-tip sharks cruising by, as well as schools of pelagic fish, such as varieties of jack and snapper.

Around *Rendezvous Point* on the northern end, excellent wall dives start in only 45 feet of water. Pocked with grottoes, they gradually slope into the abyss and are frequently visited by black-tip reef sharks, dolphins, eagle rays, and turtles. Grouper like to hang out here also.

At *Black Beauty,* on the east side of the atoll and at other sites nearby, a spur-and-groove topography drops off at about 70 feet into canyonlike territory with a fun series of swim-throughs and a sheer coral wall plummeting to 150 feet. This site also has huge sponges and black corals. Such shallow areas as *Majestic Alley* and *Coral Gardens* feature giant coral heads that rise from a sandy bottom and attract schooling fish and more solitary tropicals.

At the extreme southern tip of the atoll is the not-to-miss dive here called the *Elbow.* It's a fitting name for an area where two ocean currents merge. Rich nutrients attract abundant life, including the big stuff: eagle rays, sharks, dolphins, and sea turtles. Enormous schools of jack, snapper, grouper, and permit are often sighted out in blue water. The sea fans, sponges, including giant barrel sponges, and anemones are big and healthy. This is an advanced dive due to the strong current and depths up to 120 feet.

The *Sayonara* is a broken-up freighter lying in the southern section of the reef, not far from the *Elbow,* but on the back side. The ship itself is not too exciting, but its marine-life visitors will definitely draw your attention, both in terms of abundance and variety. This is one of the few spots to see the rare whitelined toadfish, which is found only in Belize. They're bottom dwellers, so look for this unusual critter hiding under a ledge or in a crevice. They're dark gray in color, with white stripes running across the head, and barbells under the chin. Approach very slowly and cautiously to get a close look. Usually you can hear their clicking noise before you see them.

Lighthouse Reef Area

Lighthouse Reef is about 28 miles long and has a jagged, irregular shape. The main features are six cayes and a barrier reef that almost encircles a shallow lagoon. The eastern side is nearly unbroken. Up at the northern end are miles of walls that start in only 40 feet of water. South, around Long Caye, are spur-and-groove formations with healthy gorgonians, sponges, and a variety of hard corals. The *North Long Caye Wall* starts at 25 feet, then drops precipitously.

Half Moon Caye Natural Monument is also in the southern portion of the reef, directly across the atoll from Long Caye. It has the distinction of being home to more than 100 bird species as well as a couple of hundred species of fish. Measuring only half a mile wide and one and a half miles long, the caye is ringed with white sand beaches and is lush with vegetation, fertilized liberally by guano from seabirds. Loggerhead and hawksbill turtles come ashore to lay their eggs; otherwise, large land crabs are about the only visitors to these beaches. Thousands of red-footed boobies nest on the caye, which also protects the magnificent frigatebird, ospreys, and many other species. On the east end of the island is an historic lighthouse built in 1848, for which this atoll was named.

At the northern end of Lighthouse Reef Atoll are 42 miles of reef-wall, where divers can roll off and see deepwater gorgonians, corals, and sponges in profusion as well as exciting pelagics cruising by. This area is pristine.

In the center of the atoll is the most famous site in this area, the *Blue Hole*. Almost perfectly cylindrical, it measures 1,000 feet across and 480 feet deep. Two narrow channels lead inside. The hole itself is the opening to a system of caves and passageways that penetrate this submerged mountain. Inside is a beautiful cathedral of huge stalactites formed thousands of years ago before the end of the last Ice Age when this was a subterranean cave. When the ice melted, the sea level rose, flooding the caves. The stalactites range from 20 to 60 feet in length and drop from the "roof" of the cavern. Divers descend past sheer walls to 110 feet, where the stalactites begin. Most dives are to 130 feet, and due to the extreme depth, this one is for comfortable, experienced divers. Around the edge of the blue hole are the meandering angelfish and parrotfish and schools of juvenile tropicals. Some fish feeding (actually, chumming) has been going on here, which has attracted black-tip reef sharks and the occasional hammerhead. Certainly not everyone likes the fish feeding, and it's a controversial issue among dive operators.

At Long Caye's northwest corner, *Aquarium* (isn't there one of these on just about every island?) is known for its wide variety of fish, including large black grouper and midnight parrotfish. Look around and you'll probably see moray eels, Caribbean octopus, and perhaps nurse sharks, all of which are fairly numerous. Eagle rays frequently fly by *Eagle Ray Wall* and other sections on this western side of the reef.

Quebrada Wall, also on the western side, is sheer and projects into the current. As a result, the nutrients flowing by attract a healthy amount of marine life, including lobster, crabs, morays, and a wide variety of fish, including spotted drum. The latter are tough to find and skittish—just look around and under ledges and other structure. They have black bodies, white spots and stripes, and a long flowing front dorsal fin. The younger they are, the longer the front fin.

The outside edge, on the east side, has some exciting vertical drop-offs, with eagle rays and the occasional shark cruising by. *Angelfish Wall*, on the east side, is the domain of the gray angelfish. Nearby *Tarpon Caves* features caves and cuts within a tall reef buttress that rises straight up from a sandy bottom to within 30 feet of the surface. Huge barrel sponges, yellow tube sponges, and even black coral trees are abundant on the vertical wall. Search the sandy floor for garden eels, skittish little razorfish, and southern stingrays. In the shallows are dark-blue midnight parrotfish scraping away at the corals and depositing more contributions on the sandy bottom. You'll find tarpon, as well as grouper, hanging out in the chimneys and tunnels and schooling on the inside edge of the reef.

Half Moon Caye Wall is a huge highlight on the east side. Since the caye is a protected turtle rookery, both hawksbill and loggerhead turtles are common sightings in these waters. Eagle rays are also typically seen. The wall itself is adorned with a gorgeous assortment of sponges in all shapes and colors, and the coral encrusted caverns, canyons, and swim-throughs will have you asking your divemaster to bring you back for another dive. The tremendously healthy reef (along with the area's exceptional visibility) is one of the world's premier dive sites.

Glover's Reef Area

This is considered the wild outpost of the atolls, where you'll drop down stunning vertical walls and enjoy spectacular visibility. Glover's is the most southerly atoll and nearly uninhabited. Drop-offs plummet to 2,000 feet on the east side and patch reefs dot the shallow lagoon. Spotted eagle rays are practically ho-hum, since they are seen year-round. Mantas gather at Manta Reef from December to May. Other common marine types are colorful queen triggerfish and parrotfish, sea turtles, and even dolphins.

At the northeast tip, *Shark Point* is a good place to spot a nice variety of the toothy creatures—black-tips, tigers, and hammerheads. It's a spawning ground for grouper and other tropicals, hence the attraction. The seas can be pretty rough in this area, however. The depth reaches about 90 feet. The *Northeast Caye Wall* has beautiful, sheer drop-offs.

Gorgonia's Gallery is a wall dive that starts nice and shallow in about 40 feet of water before dropping *waaay* down into the abyss. When you get off the wall, look up to the edge to see the profusion of deepwater sea fans and other gorgonians reaching out to catch the nutrients. It's a beautiful sight. Plate corals cascade down the wall, which attracts good-sized trunkfish, schools of creole wrasse, and torpedo-shaped rainbow runners.

Nurse sharks can usually be found at *Elkhorn Forest* and *Grouper Gulch,* along with turtles and Nassau grouper. Schools of silverside pack into a tunnel at *Hole In the Wall.*

Snorkeling is superb in the clear lagoon around Manta Resort. It's home to nurse sharks, southern stingrays, eagle rays, bonefish, snapper, and tarpon, for starters. Fish scraps thrown into the lagoon from the resort keep these guys around.

Diving Conditions

Because the atolls are so remote, both visibility and healthy abundance of marine life around them are normally superb. Barring stormy conditions or rainfall, the visibility can reach up to 200 feet; not bad! Currents running at some of the sites can be strong, but these supply nutrients that feed the corals and sponges.

Recommended Level of Experience

Experienced divers would be more comfortable on these atolls, where the diving is deep and currents can often be strong. More self-sufficiency is generally required out here in the hinterlands. Also, it would be best if you bring your own dive equipment and make sure you have some spare batteries for your computer and other redundant parts that you think might be helpful.

DIVE SERVICES & PACKAGES AROUND THE ATOLLS

Turneffe Island Lodge Dive Shop runs single-tank dives on small skiffs to the nearby sites. It is easy to get back to shore for another surface interval and another load of tanks. The shop's 42-foot dive boat can be used for longer trips. Rental equipment is available, including dive lights. Certifications are through the advanced level, and specialty courses are also offered. Phone (800) 874-0118; fax (770) 534-8290; e-mail: info@turneffelodge.com; website: www.turneffelodge.com.

Retail Sales: *None*	**Dive Boat Comfort:** *Good*
Rentals: *Adequate*	**On-Board Facilities**
Scuba Training: *Moderate*	**for Photographers:** *None*
Photo Services: *Limited*	

Blackbird Caye Dive Shop is on the property of Blackbird Caye Resort (a PADI Resort) on Turneffe Island Atoll. The primary dive boat is a 41-foot Bradley. There is also a 48-foot vessel for transfers and long runs. Call (888) 271-3483 or (305) 969-7945; fax (305) 969-7946; e-mail: dive@blackbird_resort.com; website: www.blackbird_resort.com.

Retail Sales: *None*	**Dive Boat Comfort:** *Good*
Rentals: *Adequate*	**On-Board Facilities**
Scuba Training: *Limited*	**for Photographers:** *None*
Photo Services: *Limited*	

Lighthouse Reef Dive Shop is located on the private island where Lighthouse Reef Resort (a PADI Resort) is found. The shop offers PADI certifications through the advanced level. Rental equipment, including lights, is available, but not extensive. The first dive of the week (for a week-long package) is a morning check-out dive—great idea. Besides wall dives on the north end trip, go out to Long Caye, Blue Hole, and Half Moon Caye. Phone (800) 423-3114 or (941) 439-6600; fax (941) 439-2118; e-mail: reservations@scuba-dive-belize.com; website: www.scubabelize.com.

Retail Sales: *None*	**Dive Boat Comfort:** *Good*
Rentals: *Adequate*	**On-Board Facilities**
Scuba Training: *Moderate*	**for Photographers:** *None*
Photo Services: *Limited*	

Manta Resort Dive Shop is on the 12-acre property that's home to the Manta Resort (a PADI Resort) on Glover's Reef. It runs two dive boats—a 36-foot and a 26-foot Bradley—each carrying about 16 divers. Diving is "live," so you don't have to navigate your way back to the boat. Most of the shop's dives are at depths of 50 to 90 feet. Divemasters "encourage computer diving and independent exploration for more advanced buddy dive teams." There are three daily boat dives, except on Friday when there are just two. A 2,000-foot wall is right in front of the resort. Night dives are twice weekly. Guided snorkel trips are offered daily. Rental gear is limited. Some dive instruction is offered. Phone (800) 326-1724; fax (206) 463-4081; e-mail: info@mantaresort.com; website: www.mantaresort.com.

Retail Sales: *None*	**Dive Boat Comfort:** *Good*
Rentals: *Adequate*	**On-Board Facilities**
Scuba Training: *Limited*	**for Photographers:** *None*
Photo Services: *Limited*	

WHERE TO STAY AROUND THE ATOLLS

The cozy **Turneffe Island Lodge** ★★★★ sits all alone on a 12-acre island. There are 12 beachfront rooms, each with a screened porch, just steps from the water. Kayaks and sailboats are available when you're not diving or snorkeling. This is a lodge, so the decor is island-rustic with attentive service. In 1994 new owners purchased the island and completely renovated the lodge, which was getting pretty tired. For many years, while the public was just learning about the aqualung, Turneffe operated strictly as a fishing lodge. Seven-night packages include three-tank boat dives daily and other recreational activities, all meals, snacks, taxes, and round-trip transfers from

Belize City. The per-person dive package for a week is $1,518.27. Other packages are available. Phone (800) 874-0118; fax (770) 534-8290; e-mail: info@turneffelodge.com; website: www.turneffelodge.com.

Blackbird Caye Resort ★★ (a PADI Resort) is on the east side of Turneffe Island Atoll and consists of 15 thatched-roof bungalows, a main house with restaurant and social area, beachside bar, and docks. All are strewn along a sandy beach and surrounded by palm trees. Rooms have two beds, ceiling fans, and air-conditioning. The sister property is the Royal Mayan, an inland resort in western Belize. Packages are offered that combine stays at both resorts. Call (888) 271-3483 or (305) 969-7945; fax (305) 969-7946; e-mail: dive@blackbird_resort.com; website: www.blackbird_resort.com.

Lighthouse Reef Resort ★★★★ (a PADI Resort) is the only dive resort on Lighthouse Reef Atoll. It is located on a private island at the northern end, with accompanying dive shop and airstrip. The flight over from Belize City is about 20 minutes. The 11 villas, suites, mini-suites, and cabanas are all on the beach and have air-conditioning, ceiling fans, mini-bars, and porches. The cabanas have two queen-size beds; the mini-suites also have a living area with two sofas. Suites have a living room, full-size refrigerator, and breakfast bar. Villas are perfect for two couples, with two bedroom/bath suites, three porches, and a large living room with ten-foot ceilings. Guests have the use of kayaks, perfect for checking out the saltwater crocs in the lagoon. For nature watchers, there are iguanas and plenty of birds. Bring bug spray for the mosquitoes and sand fleas. There is a clothing-optional beach, a volleyball court, and miles of flats for bonefishing. There is no service charge tacked onto the bill. The cost of an upgrade from a cabana to a mini-suite is $150 per person per week and another $25 for an upgrade to a suite or villa. A seven-night diving package (double occupancy in a cabana) is $1,460 and includes 20 meals, 17 dives, taxes, and two air transfers from Belize City. Phone (800) 423-3114 or (941) 439-6600; fax (941) 439-2118; e-mail: reservations@scuba-dive-belize.com; website: www.scubabelize.com.

Manta Resort ★★★★ (a PADI Resort) and its dive shop completely occupy Southwest Caye, a 12-acre private island on the southernmost tip of Glover's Reef. Twelve individual mahogany cabanas are nestled among hundreds of coconut palms (it was a former coconut plantation), right at the water's edge. Each is air-conditioned and has a private porch with inviting hammock. The Manta House is a cabana with two bedrooms, two bathrooms, a living room with pullout sofa, and a TV and VCR. Besides snorkeling and diving, fishing is extremely popular—trolling, fly, and deep-sea. All meals and lots of snacks are included in the rate and served in the thatch-roofed cantina, built at the end of the pier overlooking the lagoon. The cantina also has a bar and lounge area, and, of course, panoramic views. Guests are met at the airport in Belize City and transported by a 50-foot twin-engine motor yacht to the resort. The ride is about three and a half hours. Eight-night, seven-day packages are available for divers, anglers, snorkelers, and beachcombers. Baby-sitting can be arranged. The diving package for a week is $1,150 to $1,350, depending on the season. A four-night stay is $875. This does not include charges for beverages, taxes, and a $10 Marine Reserve Fee. The rate for the Manta House is an additional $200 per person, per week charge ($800 maximum). Phone (800) 326-1724; fax (206) 463-4081; e-mail: info@mantaresort.com; website: www.mantaresort.com.

Medical Facilities

A recompression chamber is located on Ambergris Caye. In case of a diving emergency call DAN (Divers Alert Network) at (919) 684-4DAN (4326) or (919) 684-8111.

BELIZE LIVE-ABOARDS

The **Aggressor Fleet** operates an 18-passenger, 120-foot vessel (a PADI Resort) around the Turneffe Islands, Lighthouse Reef, and the Blue Hole. It features nine staterooms (each with private head and shower, an onboard photo lab, hot tub, Nitrox, and e-mail. There is a full line of rental camera equipment and dive gear, as well as certification and specialty courses. The charters are all-inclusive—meals, tanks, weights, airport transfers—and you get unlimited diving. Call (800) 348-2628 or (504) 385-2628; fax (504) 384-0817; e-mail: info@aggressor.com; website: www.aggressor.com.

Peter Hughes *Wave Dancer* (a PADI Gold Palm Resort) was recently redecorated with a tropical motif and new engines installed. It is also120 feet long and accommodates 20 passengers. It operates at several sites around the atolls. The vessel features ten staterooms, each with private head and shower, TV, and VCR; camera rental, photo instruction, and E-6 film processing; Nitrox and dive gear rental. Certifications are offered through the advanced level, and specialty courses are available. Guests can make up to five dives per day. Charters are all-inclusive—meals, snacks, beverages (including alcohol), airport transfers, nightly slide show and entertainment, and even morning coffee service delivered right to the staterooms. Phone (800) 932-6237; website: www.peterhughes.com.

Bermuda

Physical Characteristics of the Dive Area

WATER & WEATHER CONDITIONS

Visibility	*Excellent*
Current and Surge	*Minimal*
Temperature	*Chilly*
Storms	*Occasionally Stormy*

SITE CONDITIONS

Mooring Buoys	*Some*
Fishing, Collecting, and Hunting Restrictions	*Widespread Restrictions*
Ease of Access	*Very Easy*
Boat Traffic/Diver Congestion	*None*

MARINE LIFE

Abundance of Invertebrates	*Common*
Abundance of Vertebrates	*Common*
Abundance of Pelagic Life	*Common*
Health of Reef/Marine Life/ Marine Structure	*Healthy*

History Down Below

Bermuda is so perfectly prim and proper in that upper-crust English sort of way that if tea and crumpets were served on dive boats, it probably wouldn't raise a salt-encrusted eyebrow. This luscious green island with its gently rolling hills echoes old England. Visitors find red "pillow-box" phone booths, corner pubs, and a strong sense of order and fair play—truly the picture of civility. Some might find Bermuda a bit too neat and perfect, but it can be a refreshing change from the heavy drinking and drug use that mar some islands in this part of the world.

Be aware that perfection comes at a steep price; room rates here are high, so plan accordingly. Families might want to opt for a self-catering cottage rather than one of the resorts. Just make sure you'll be conveniently near the dive shops.

Contrary to what you might have heard, Bermuda is not really a single island. Nor is it in the Caribbean, another common misconception. Bermuda is actually a collection of more than 100 small islands and islets, with the seven major ones connected by bridges and causeways—and it's in the Atlantic Ocean, directly east of North Carolina.

If you don't know much about the diving on Bermuda, it wouldn't be at all surprising. Don't worry, the lack of information has nothing to do with the quality of what you'll see underwater; it is only dive promotion that has been lacking. For years Bermuda has drawn tourists to its spectacular golf courses, pink sand beaches, and relaxing resorts. Tourism and other healthy industries have endowed the island with a high standard of living; consequently, it has not had a great need for diving dollars. Bermuda began actively promoting its diving resources only about five years ago.

Climatically, Bermuda benefits from the Gulf Stream, which swoops around from the north and the west. This effect insulates these little peaks from extremes in weather and creates the northernmost region in the Western Hemisphere where coral reefs grow. That means that divers will find plenty of tropical fish and some nice reefs here, but the reefs are not nearly as lush as those in true Caribbean waters. Nevertheless, those are just the appetizers, anyway.

The entrees—the real reason you will want to feast on Bermuda—are its shipwrecks. These "turtles in the net," as the early wrecks were called, have been running into Bermuda's hazardous barrier reefs for centuries. It is said that there are more than 300 resting on Bermuda's sugar-white sands. Shipwreck survivors were, in fact, Bermuda's first settlers. Not only are these wrecks plentiful, they are also very accessible, lying in clear shallow waters. So if you love to dive wrecks, or if you have diving or snorkeling children, this place is paradise. With ships dating from the Civil War to modern freighters, Bermuda's waters serve up a fascinating underwater history lesson.

Fortunately, this gripping and colorful heritage has been preserved and is on view all around the island as well as beneath its waters. Divers and landlubbers alike will have a great time exploring scenic old stone-walled forts with moats and iron gates; and town squares with stocks, dunking stools, and whipping posts. Definitely leave time to do some sightseeing

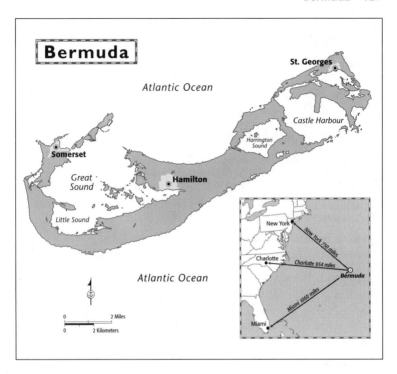

here—at least a couple of afternoons and a full day before you leave. And don't forget the camera!

QUICK STATS

Size   Shaped like a fish-hook, Bermuda covers 22 square miles; length is 21 miles, maximum width is two miles.

Population   Approximately 58,460, of which nearly 61 percent are black and 39 percent are white.

Location   In the Atlantic, some 650 miles east of Cape Hatteras, North Carolina, and 774 miles from New York City.

Time Zone   Atlantic

Government   Bermuda is the oldest British Colony and has the second oldest parliamentary democracy (after England) in the world.

Language   English

Electrical Current   110 volts, 60 cycles AC (same as the United States); adapters are necessary for United Kingdom and European appliances.

Climate   With its Atlantic location, Bermuda does not get as hot as the islands in the Caribbean. It has a mild semitropical climate with temperatures ranging from 68° to 84°. Relative humidity is 71 to 84 percent and annual rainfall is 57.6 inches.

Water Temperature   Mid-70s to low 80s in summer; high 60s in winter.

Underwater Visibility   From about 70 to 100 feet

Best Diving Months   Mid-March through November

PLANNING THE TRIP

Phoning Bermuda   From North America, simply dial 1 + area code + phone number. It is not necessary to dial the international access number.

Getting to Bermuda   By air, Bermuda is served by American, Continental, Delta, USAir, Air Canada, and British Airways. Direct service is available from Baltimore, Boston, Chicago, and Philadelphia. Nonstop service is available from Atlanta, Newark, and New York. A $20 tax is collected upon departure.

Getting Around on Bermuda   There are no rental cars on the island. You'll have to rely on taxis, ferries, buses, bicycles, and horse-drawn carriages. You can rent mopeds.

Entry Documents   Proof of citizenship is required. A passport is the preferred document, but an original certified birth certificate with photograph ID is acceptable. The birth certificate cannot be a copy and must have a raised seal.

Currency   The Bermuda dollar (BD$). It is divided into 100 cents and is pegged, through gold, to the U.S. dollar, which is accepted throughout the island. Note that some hotels do not accept credit cards.

Bermuda Tourist Office   From North America, call (800) 223-6106. The website is www.bermudatourism.com. The Bermuda Vacation Planner at www.keyguide.com/doc/planner.htm is also an excellent resource.

THE UNDERWATER SCENE

The Bermuda islands are volcanic mountains that rise from the ocean floor, about two and a half miles down. But rather than diving the sides of submerged mountain walls, as you would in the Cayman Islands, for instance, you'll most likely explore the fringing reef and sandy-bottom area that immediately surrounds the islands.

And when you dive here, you'll find the same species of marine life that inhabit Caribbean waters. The only difference is in the abundance, since Bermuda is the northernmost place in the Western Hemisphere where coral reefs grow. You won't find the large branching corals or basket sponges, but soft corals are especially prolific, particularly the gorgonian sea fans and plumes. Also, except for Bermuda chub, grunts, and jacks, you won't see as many schooling fish. Most of the tropicals here are the paired variety—the butterflyfish, parrotfish, trumpetfish, and so on. As for open-water pelagic life, four species of marine turtles ply these waters, and humpback whales migrate past the islands in March and April.

Also intriguing are the caverns, caves, arches, and tunnels found throughout the area. Most of the caves are technically caverns, which do not require any special training to explore. Having a light is nice, but it's usually not necessary. Wherever there's structure like crags and overhangs, look for schools of jacks and fry as well as grouper, tarpon, and spiny lobsters.

For photographers who enjoy macro life, there are plenty of little critters. The most common are flamingo tongues, usually found clinging to the back sides of sea fans, and you'll find arrow crabs and banded coral shrimp.

But truthfully, the coral reef and the tropical marine life are only the perks. The real prizes are Bermuda's shipwrecks, and they are found in abundance and usually in shallow waters on nice white sandy resting-places—perfect backdrops for photography. The vast reef system—about 230 square miles of it—surrounding Bermuda was a navigator's nightmare, bringing down untold numbers of ships. Of course, that same shallow reef is now a glorious playground for us, with dive trips averaging only a half-hour or so from shore.

Health Score Card

Except for storm damage, the natural reefs and the artificial ones—the shipwrecks—are in good condition. You won't find trash underwater, unless it was originally on a ship that went down.

Diving Conditions

The Gulf Stream insulates to the north and west, minimizing weather extremes, thus creating its subtropical climate. Still, the water is cold in winter, and it is amazing how healthy the corals are given the extremes in temperatures—in the 80s in summer to mid-60s in winter.

A wetsuit is an absolute necessity most of the time. From April through November, only a 3mm suit would be needed, but from December through March, a 6mm suit (quarter-inch) is necessary, along with hood and gloves. Bermuda's waters are very salty, so you might have to wear a little more lead than you are accustomed to.

Because most of Bermuda's shipwrecks went down on shallow reefs, divers generally enjoy a longer bottom time, unlike places like Chuuk or North Carolina, where most wrecks are 100 feet plus.

Underwater visibility here is excellent. The average summer vis on the north and west shores is 100 feet, increasing to 150 feet from November to March. The south and east shores average 80 feet year-round.

Recommended Level of Experience

With nice shallow dive sites, relatively warm clear water, and lack of strong currents, Bermuda is truly a perfect spot for all levels of divers. Dives are not challenging, so new divers and those who are rusty on their skills will still feel comfortable. In fact, you could easily log your very first ocean dive on one of Bermuda's shipwrecks.

Bermuda dive shops offer what they call a Shipwreck Certificate Program, but I'm not really sure what benefit that has other than to give divers something to take home. Many of the wrecks do not require any special skills at all since they are so broken up that penetration is not an issue.

This would be an excellent place, however, to complete a scuba certification. Students will find open-water dives here a real dream, with the welcoming underwater conditions and seasoned instructors.

Several shipwrecks also lie in deep water, offering some nice opportunities for experienced divers with bona fide wreck-diving certifications.

Bermuda's Legendary Shipwrecks

The following shipwrecks are listed starting in the northwest and progressing counterclockwise around the island to the west, the south, and the east. Remember, this is only a selection—there are believed to be more than 300 wrecks in Bermuda's waters, ranging from Spanish galleons to modern-day vessels.

On the island's northwest side are two wonderful shipwrecks: the *Constellation* and the *Lartington.* The *Constellation* was a 192-foot American four-masted schooner that sank in 1943 when it was bound for Venezuela with a general cargo. Actually, you don't see much of the *Constellation,* since wave action has broken it apart and the wreckage is strewn about over a large area. You can easily miss the ship itself, but not its cargo of huge bags of cement (now concrete), medical supplies, bottles, and china.

The ship played a large role in the film *The Deep,* which wouldn't have caused much notice were it not for Jacqueline Bisset's clinging T-shirt.

Actually, we should give credit to Peter Benchley, who wrote the novel on which the film was based. The characters in *The Deep* were searching for drug ampoules. Now, divers can easily find bottles of all sorts, including Elizabeth Arden cosmetic products, as well as broken crystal, gramophones, broken china, and much more strewn about the bottom and in full view. The area is protected, so divers cannot take "souvenirs."

After my dive here, when we were all back on board, one of the divers exclaimed that it was a terrific dive, but she didn't see any of the bags of cement. We all laughed, because she literally swam over hundreds of them, stacked one on top of another—an entire mountain of cement!

The 236-foot *Montana,* the sister ship to the *Marie Celestia,* lies just a short swim from the *Constellation.* In fact, exploring both of these ships in a single dive is easy, since the depths here range from 25 to 30 feet. A paddlewheel steamer built to penetrate the Union blockade during the Civil War, the *Montana* is greatly broken up, so there's not much to see. It ran aground in 1863, having missed the channel leading to the dock. Some of the bow is intact, or was when I dived it. There were also large snappers and grouper here, typical of protected areas. By staying in these waters, they'll never end up on someone's dinner plate.

The 245-foot *Lartington,* which sank in 1879, is also seriously broken up, but there is enough structure for some fun exploring and good photo compositions. Lying in waters of only 15 to 35 feet, boilers, a stern section, and a propeller can still be seen. The marine life is prolific, with schools of yellow grunts, parrotfish, large anemones, and some good-sized barracuda. There's more brain coral here than at most sites, and the sea fans and rope sponges are also abundant. I missed it, but look for the wreckage that has the ship's name on it.

On the west side is the *North Carolina,* a 205-foot English iron-hulled sailing bark that ran aground in 1880. It was laden with cotton from the United States and bound for England. This is a most photogenic wreck in only 40 feet of water, with a nice bowsprit, sail rigging, and several deadeyes still in place. A deadeye (this one was new to me) is a flat block of wood (used in pairs) with three holes for a lanyard. They were used on sailing ships to hold the shrouds and stays taut, similar to the function of a cleat on boats today. The bow and stern are still intact, but the mid-section has collapsed.

On the southwest side of the island is a beautiful little paddle wheeler, the *Marie Celestia.* During the Civil War it worked as a blockade-runner, exchanging guns and ammunition for cotton, until it was brought down in 1864. Unfortunately, one of the crew went down with the ship, which was unusual for shipwrecks here on the shallow reef. Evidently, after it struck the reef, the cook went back to retrieve his cat and became trapped inside. The *Marie Celestia* is one of three or four other paddle wheelers that sank in the area.

The *Marie Celestia* sits on bright white sand in 55 feet of water. A section of it, however, is in water as shallow as 10 feet, so this is a nice wreck for snorkelers, also. The ship is 225 feet long, with a narrow beam and two big paddle wheels on either side. One wheel sits upright in the sand, offering a dramatic photo opportunity, with soft corals waving in the surge. You can also still see an anchor. Trumpetfish and Bermuda chub wander among purple sea fans and golden whips. Divers should be extra careful not to kick up sand, because the visibility can easily get murky in these shallow waters. You might encounter some surge or current.

Farther along the south side lies the *Minnie Breslauer,* a 300-foot steel-hulled English freighter. Bound for New York, it wrecked on its maiden voyage in 1873. Still visible are the ship's propeller, steam boilers, and wheelhouse.

One of the deeper wreck dives is the *Hermes,* a 165-foot U.S. freighter that was abandoned in Bermuda and scuttled in 1985. Thus, it is the most intact wreck in Bermuda. It sits upright, on the south side about mid-island, offering some nice photo ops, in about 75 feet of water. The *Hermes* can be penetrated, but don't try this without a guide unless you are certified for wreck diving. The mast, wheelhouse, and deck winch are particularly visible features.

The *Cristobal Colon* is a 499-foot Spanish transatlantic luxury liner that ran aground in 1936. It is now assumed that it was used for smuggling Loyalists out of Spain during the Spanish Civil War and was bound for Cuba. It's the largest shipwreck in Bermuda, and lies in about 55 feet of water. During World War II it was convenient for bombing practice; consequently, sections of it are scattered across the reef. But its six boilers are still visible.

A 228-foot Norwegian freighter called the *Taunton* was wrecked on the North East Breakers in 1920, with a load of coal from Virginia. It rests at a depth of 40 feet, but comes up to within 10 feet of the surface and has a photogenic bow section.

Two cargo steamers bound for Baltimore with holds full of manganese ore sank just offshore at different times. The Greek 385-foot *Pelinaion,* located on the East End, offers some nice swim-through arches on either side of the wreck. It went down in 1940 and now lies at 55 feet. Its giant boiler and engine are visible. The *Rita Zovetta,* currently residing at a depth of 70 feet, was a 50-foot Italian ship that sank during near-hurricane conditions off the East End in 1924. It is semipenetrable and also has nice swim-throughs.

The *L'Herminie* is one of Bermuda's most impressive warship wrecks. This French 60-gun man-of-war sank in 1838 and rests in 25 to 30 feet of water. Photographers get ready: its nine-foot-long cannons are still on board and visible, and many other cannons lie scattered around the reef and sand.

Bermuda's newest dive is the *Xing Da,* a Chinese smuggling ship 200 feet long. It was scuttled in 1997 and sits upright in 100 feet of water.

Shallow Diving and Snorkeling

The site called *Southwest Breaker* is an interesting as well as pretty second dive with a depth of only about 28 feet. Caverns are the featured attractions here, and they're safe to explore, with natural light nicely illuminating them. One is a very small cavern that dead-ends, and the other is a fun swim-through. The sand here is white and gorgeous. If the sky is clear, a brilliant light shines on top of the reef, where some hard corals thrive, as well as sea fans and plumes. Trumpetfish and parrotfish are common visitors.

Near *Southwest Breaker* is *Three Little Reefs,* with a depth of about 45 feet. Like *Southwest Breaker,* the sand is sugar-white. A transatlantic phone cable runs out to the reef. On a dive here, a congregation of sergeant majors swarmed around me and my dive buddy, then tagged along as we followed the cable. Either they didn't have anything better to do or they were escorting us away from their egg nests. In any case, it was a lot of fun. We also spotted a beautiful queen angelfish, an enormous trumpetfish, and a large and very bold lobster, strutting its stuff on the sandy bottom.

For shore diving and snorkeling, *Church Bay* in Southampton is a particularly beautiful site, with pink sand and good swimming. *Horseshoe Bay,* located a little farther east, is one of the most beautiful local beaches; it also has good swimming conditions, as well as opportunities for exploring a cavelike formation. Also on the south shore is a good shore diving and snorkeling jumping-off spot called *Elbow Beach.* From here, you can swim out to the wreck *Pollockshields,* a German naval supply vessel captured by the British in World War I. In 1915 it was hit by a squall and then captured by Bermuda's treacherous reef. There's also good shore diving at *Watch Hill,* on the southeast part of the island.

Marine Park

In 1966 the Coral Reef Preserve Act was instituted to protect the reefs and marine life species within the two preserve areas—the South Shore Coral Reef Preserve and the North Shore Coral Reef Preserve. These two areas encompass most of Bermuda's fringing reef.

The act prohibits the removal or damage of any marine life in the preserves. Also, don't try to bring home any souvenirs from your wreck dives, as law forbids the removal of shipwreck artifacts in Bermuda. A comprehensive mooring system is being implemented to mark and protect the dive sites.

Fishing restrictions apply to several protected areas, including the shipwrecks *Vixen, Constellation, Pelinaion, Rita Zovetta, Kate, Hermes,* and *Minnie Bresslauer.* They also apply to Eastern Blue Cut, North Rock, and South West Breaker. A 200-mile exclusive fishing zone also prohibits the taking of all species of marine turtles, marine mammals, and corals. A number of species of mollusks are also protected.

Spearfishing on scuba is illegal, and only pole spears (no spearguns) are allowed. Also, spearfishing is not permitted within one nautical mile of the shore. Lobster diving is permitted with a license, but only under specific conditions, one of which is the two-lobsters-per-person-per-day bag limit.

DIVE SERVICES & PACKAGES

Blue Water Divers, & Watersports (a PADI Gold Palm IDC Resort) covers a lot of territory, with three locations—the western edge at Robinson's Marina, Somerset Bridge; the south, at Elbow Beach; and the east end at Castle Harbour. Their boats, which include a Newton 36 Dive Special, carry oxygen, first-aid kits, communications radios, and GPS. The Newton has an upper deck with seating, freshwater shower, electric marine head, coolers, and dry storage. All crews are certified as engine drivers by the Bermuda Government Marine and Ports Department. Captains are also certified as pilots with the MPD. Dive staff are all rated at instructor level or above. They offer an extensive range of rental equipment, including underwater still and video cameras. There is a retail section and a repair facility. Instruction is with PADI, NASDS, and SSI. They offer classes from introduction to scuba to divemaster, as well as specialty courses, including CPR and first aid. Exclusive snorkel trips are offered as well as such watersports activities as personal watercraft, sailing, and guided kayak and snorkel tours. On its south side location at Elbow Beach resort, divers can rent underwater scooters. There are dive packages with 13 lodgings, in addition to the business's on-property locations at Elbow Beach and Castle Harbour. Phone (441) 234-1034; fax (441) 232-3670; e-mail: bwdivers@ibl.bm; website: www.dive bermuda.com.

Retail Sales: *Extensive*

Rentals: *Extensive*

Scuba Training: *Extensive*

Photo Services: *Moderate*

Dive Boat Comfort: *Excellent*

On-Board Facilities for Photographers: *Good*

The other major dive business is **Fantasea** (a PADI 5-Star Dive Center and Resort), with two island locations, one in Hamilton, at Albuoy's Point, and another at the Sonesta Beach Resort, in Southampton. The shop operates a 42-foot custom dive boat for up to 30 divers, and several other boats for snorkeling, kayaking, sailing, and whale-watching. A PADI and NAUI dive center, the shop offers courses through assistant instructor level, as well as the DAN oxygen provider specialty course and the Enriched Air Nitrox course. Equipment sales, service, and rentals (including cameras) are available, as is Nitrox diving. Whale watching cruises go out in March and April with the custom glass-bottom boat *Looking Glass*. That's when the humpback whales are making their northward migration. The shop has dive packages with the Sonesta Beach Resort. Call (800) DO-A-DIVE or (441) 238-1833; fax (441) 236-0394; e-mail: info@fantasea.bm; website: www.fantasea.bm.

Retail Sales: *Extensive*

Rentals: *Extensive*

Scuba Training: *Extensive*

Photo Services: *Moderate*

Dive Boat Comfort: *Excellent*

On-Board Facilities for Photographers: *Good*

WHERE TO STAY

Most accommodations are located along the south shore, in Paget, Warwick, and Southampton, where the best beaches are located. The West End is more remote, but is a very nice location that caters to the boating and fishing set. Bermuda has a wealth of small guest houses, cottage colonies, and house-keeping cottages, in addition to its grander resorts. For these, check out www.bermudatourism.com or contact the Bermuda Tourist Office at (800) 223-6106. Locate both at the end of this chapter. All room rates are subject to a 7.25 percent Bermuda Government Occupancy Tax.

An intriguing new resort recently opened on the northwest peninsula. The environmentally oriented **Daniel's Head Village ★★** offers over-the-water and along-the-coast tent-cottages, all with verandahs and expansive ocean views. The resort sits on a 20-acre peninsula scattered with casuarina trees, cedars, and flowering bushes and plants. The surrounding coastline is all protected. Some of the cottages are on stilts and have glass floors, just in case you can't get enough marine life viewing. The one- and two-bedroom suites sit on a hillside and also have ocean views. The cottages have indoor-outdoor living areas, wide porches, and private baths. Literature states that the resort practices ecologically-sensitive care of the surrounding environment, including the nearby seagrass beds. The water sports are strictly nature- and people-powered. In addition to shore diving and snorkeling (gear is available), the resort offers swimming, sea-kayaking, windsurfing, and small sailboating. Fishing trips, catamaran cruises, parasailing, and eco-tours can also be arranged. Bicycles and scooters can be rented at the resort. Dining is in the Village restaurant, with grilled specialties and vegetarian options, and there is a lounge. Prices look good for Bermuda standards—starting from $135 to $250 daily for a tent cottage for two during the high season. All watersports are extra, and a watersports package is available. Call (877) 418-1723 or (203) 602-0300; fax (203) 602-2265; e-mail: info@danielsheadvillage.com; website: www.danielsheadvillage.com.

The Reefs is a small hotel, located on a private beach on the south shore. Facilities include a swimming pool and sun deck, two tennis courts, fitness center, shuffleboard courts, dining room, cocktail lounge, beach bar, and restaurant. There's entertainment nightly. Nightly rates range from $181 to $286 per person, double occupancy, and this is typical of most of the resorts along the south shore. Phone (800) 742-2008 or (441) 238-0222; fax (441) 238-8372.

The sprawling 25-acre **Sonesta Beach Resort** ★★★★ is perched on the island's south shore. It encompasses several secluded coves that invite exploring as well as a couple of nice crescent-shaped beaches. Most of the 400 rooms and suites have private balconies and ocean views. There are restaurants, bars, and nightlife aplenty, as well as activities ranging from kayaking to croquet. Also on the property is a European Health and Beauty Spa, outdoor and indoor swimming pools, tennis courts, and shops. The on-site dive operation is Fantasea Bermuda Ltd. The resort offers a five-night South Side Scuba Dive Package that includes either Discover Diving or Divers Wreck programs. The more advanced package is $496 to $566 for two people per night. In summer, room rates start at $290 for an island view room; the winter rate starts at $135. From North America, call (800) SONESTA, or the local number (441) 238-8122; fax (441) 238-8463; website: www.sonesta.com.

The Fairmont Southampton Princess ★★★ sits high atop a 100-acre estate, surrounded by ocean and bay. With 600 rooms and nine stories, it's one of the biggest resorts on the island. All rooms have a private balcony with ocean or bay views. There are numerous dining and shopping options, and, of course, sports, including tennis, golf, and diving. A five-night wreck-diving package consists of daily buffet breakfast, three two-tank dives, a Wreck Diving Certificate, and more. In high season (summer) prices start at $1,276 per person. Call (441) 238-8000; fax (441) 238-8968; e-mail: southampton@fairmont.com; website: www.fairmont.com.

Elbow Beach Resort ★★★★ is located near the center of the island on the south shore. With 250 rooms, it is one of the largest resorts on Bermuda. It sits among 50 acres of lush gardens and has its own pink sand beach, as well as a swimming pool. Also on the property are a shopping arcade, beauty salon, health club with Jacuzzi, and five tennis courts. For dining, there are five restaurants and a beachside bistro with entertainment and dancing. The resort's on-property dive operation is Blue Water Divers and Watersports. Convenient shore diving is right off the beach. High season rates (summer) range from $217.50 to $307.50 per person, double occupancy. Phone (800) 344-3526 or (441) 236-3535; fax (441) 236-8043; e-mail: elbowbch@ibl.bm; website: www.elbowbeach.com.

The **Whale Bay Inn** ★★ is a good choice for divers looking for an affordable place to stay, even though there is no on-site dive shop. The Blue Water Divers' Somerset Bridge facility is located about ten minutes away. The five one-bedroom apartments each have three rooms: a bathroom with full bath and shower, bedroom with both double and single beds, and kitchen/sitting/eating room. The kitchen portion has a two-burner stove, fridge, toaster, microwave oven, coffee maker, and all cooking and eating utensils. Units are air-conditioned, have cable TV, radio, telephone, and ceiling fans. Each apartment has its own patio with views facing Port Royal Golf Course and Whale Bay Beach (just a few minutes' walk away). Little barbecues are available for outdoor cooking.

The property is close to the main bus route, ferry, restaurants, supermarket, and moped rental. No credit cards are accepted, and a two-night deposit is required. The nightly single rate is $100; a double is $70 per person. Children under 12 are $20 per night. A 10 percent maid service charge is tacked onto the bill. The diving package for three nights (more nights are available) during the summer season is $418. That is a per-person rate based on two people sharing a room. It includes two-way airport transfer, room tax and hotel gratuities, two two-tank dive trips, tanks and weights. Additional dives can be purchased for $60 per two-tank trip. Other equipment rentals and dive store gratuities are extra. All dive packages that include six dives or more also include free unlimited shore diving at the Elbow Beach Dive Center. Phone (441) 238-0469; fax (441) 238-1224; e-mail: whalebayinn@northrock.bm.

Other packages with Blue Water Divers, similar to Whale Bay Inn's, can be arranged with the following lodgings: Angels Grotto, Astwood Cove, Brightside Apartments, Cambridge Beaches, The Clearview Suites, Dawkins Manor, Edgehill Manor, Munro Beach Cottages, Pompano Beach Club, Sandpiper Apartments, Sky Top Cottages, Syl-Den Guest Apartments, Tarrafal Apartments, and Top Hat Guest House.

ISLAND LIFE

On my first visit to Bermuda, I arrived from California completely jet-lagged but still wanting to walk outside my lodging and survey the grounds. As I was admiring the lush tropical foliage and meticulous land-scaping, the manager of the small hotel came out to welcome me, and he apologized for the sorry state of the landscaping. "The last hurricane that came through spared structures but stripped foliage of leaves and flowers—it's all a mess," he bemoaned. Well, you could have fooled me; my yard should look so good. In fact, I had just been thinking that if ever there were an Eden, it would be just this way—with a healthy, manicured lawn, herb garden, an enormous spreading poinciana tree, and a white wooden trellis draped with flaming bougainvillea.

Bermudians obviously take great pride in their island and institute strict measures to protect its natural beauty. Pollution here is not an issue. Indeed, that's one of the reasons you'll see so many people driving mopeds; the government allows only one car per household. It might seem harsh, but the restriction is one way to make sure that the island doesn't have huge traffic or air pollution problems (Grand Cayman, take note!). So when touring the island, you'll see the incongruous sight of businessmen dressed in coat and tie coupled with—what else?—Bermuda shorts (always with knee-high socks), their ties flowing like wind socks behind the scooters. And the women? As my guide explained, "The wife gets the car."

Motoring around, you'll pass pastel-colored cottages and stone forts with cannons pointing out to sea; manicured golf courses and spotless public gardens (in fact, everything is spotless here); and lots of color—from golden hibiscus to lavender oleanders. There are no rivers or freshwater lakes, so residents catch rainwater on their roofs, all coated with stark white limestone.

Bermuda is all spit and polish, prim and proper, with everything seemingly in its place, at least to a visitor's eye. The economy of the island is extremely prosperous. Visiting definitely will put a significant dent in your vacation budget. Tourism is one of the biggest industries, but international business, including insurance, oil, computer software, investment holding and finance, shipping, and communications are also significant. In fact, there are more than 8,000 offshore companies based on the island.

Also, remember that Bermuda is tiny, and with a population of about 58,000, there are an estimated 3,000 people to the square mile. That gives it one of the highest population densities in the world—another good reason for mopeds. The racial mix is approximately 61 percent of African heritage, and 39 percent white. Bermudians—about 64 percent of the population—have a heritage of several generations in Bermuda. Other ancestral groups include British (16 percent), West Indian (11 percent), and Portuguese (9 percent).

For such a small island, Bermuda has an impressive amount of land that is protected. In 1986 the National Parks Act established a national parks system. Now Bermuda has 79 national parks and nature reserves that cover more than 800 acres. This "ribbon of green" stretches from the eastern to the western ends of the island. One of the 150 smaller islands around Bermuda, called Nonsuch Island, has been restored as a living museum. This 30-year enterprise has restored the land to a lush, subtropical island similar to its precolonial times.

Hotel development is strictly monitored. Cruise ships are also restricted to an extent. The number of ships is limited; those that come in are required to hook up to the local sewage systems, and they are prohibited from emitting soot while in port.

For touring, remember that there are no rental cars, but public transportation and taxi service are readily available. If you want to explore the island on your own, you can rent mopeds at all the major hotels, but don't forget that driving is on the left. Also, most roads are two-lane, winding, and narrow. With a speed limit of only 20 m.p.h. (or 35 k.p.h), you can't get into too much trouble; nevertheless, if you're not used to left-lane driving, better stick to buses, taxis, and ferries.

Buses (they're all pink) are inexpensive and a great way to get around. Bus stops are marked by striped poles at the side of the road. The pink-topped poles indicate buses heading into Hamilton, the capital, and those with blue tops are heading out of Hamilton. If you'd like a tour guide, look for taxis displaying a blue flag on the front of the vehicles. That means that the driver is qualified as a guide.

The ferry is convenient, quick, and scenic. From Newstead, for instance, it's only 15 minutes to Hamilton, and the fare is just a couple of dollars. You don't even have to get off. Just stay on and you'll have a fun sightseeing tour of Great Sound.

Walking here is also wonderful, since the island is so pristine. If the weather is nice, definitely lace up the tennis shoes, grab a map, and explore.

Topside Attractions

It doesn't take long to learn the lay of the land, or the primary thoroughfares. Just a few major roads run the length of the main island and its nine bridged adjacent islands, and they're all sensibly named. For instance, you'll find South Road, Middle Road, and North Shore Road. The names are not imaginative, but for visitors, they are perfect. Starting at the western tip, definitely visit the **Royal Naval Dockyard.** The quickest and easiest way to get there is by ferry. It was once the largest naval base in the Western Atlantic, with much of it constructed just before the War of 1812.

You'll enter the Keep (with walls 20 feet wide) by crossing a concrete draw-bridge over the surrounding moat—fun! The Dockyard is now loaded with activities, many for kids, with a wet and dry playground, snorkeling park, train ride, restaurants and pubs, shops, and the wonderful **Maritime Museum.** There you'll learn that Bermuda's early settlers literally washed ashore (visit the sidebar that follows to learn more). And then at the **Old Cooperage,** shop for Bermuda-made crafts, such as candles, sculptures, stained glass, watercolors, jewelry, weaving, and so on.

For further touring around the West End, take the Route 7 bus, which will pass Somerset Draw Bridge, with stops at Elbow Beach Hotel, Gibbs Hill Lighthouse, Horseshoe Bay Beach (beautiful pink sand), Sonesta Beach Hotel, and the Southampton Princess. For a small fee you can climb up into **Gibbs Hill Lighthouse,** enjoy some sweeping views, and take pictures. Put in service in 1846, it stands 117 feet high, and is said to be the oldest cast-iron lighthouse in the world. Its beam can be seen up to 25 miles away. Route 7's terminus is the city of Hamilton. If you want to continue on to see more of the island, you have to transfer to another bus at the terminal.

A central tour of Bermuda would encompass the **Botanical Gardens,** where you can walk among subtropical fruit groves, cedar and banyan trees, and 36 acres of lush exotic plants. There's also an aviary and the Premier's official residence, called Camden. From here you can trek over to the **Bermuda Underwater Exploration Institute,** located waterside in Hamilton. Experience the thrill of a simulated dive 12,000 feet to the bottom of the Atlantic and participate in a variety of simulations of underwater explorations. Even nondivers can experience deepwater exploration without ever getting wet! Visitors can take a multimedia visit to key dive sites around Bermuda and see a display of dive technology that includes explanations of SCUBA, the science of air, depth control, physical diving, and dive equipment. A variety of submersibles are on display, as well as artifacts recovered from many of the 300 wrecks that lie in Bermuda's waters. And in **Hamilton,** you can visit the Bermuda Cathedral (good views from the tower), City Hall, and Bermuda National Galleries. This would be an excellent place to shop. Typical store hours are 9 a.m. to 5 p.m. Monday through Saturday, but this varies somewhat with the type of store.

I would start an East End tour in the fun harborside town of **St. George,** where the center of attention is the town square. Have your picture taken in the wooden stocks, check out the ducking stool, and if you have time, take a walking tour through the narrow streets and alleyways of the old town. Typically on Wednesday at noon the town crier holds a mock

Turtles In the Net

It's ironic that this island which is the quintessential picture of British order and civility was born from a horribly violent, decidedly disorderly event—the wreck of the *Sea Venture* in 1609. Definitely visit the Maritime Museum to learn more about it, but in a very abridged version it happened thus:

Sir George Somer's flagship the *Sea Venture,* along with a fleet of seven ships, was bound for Jamestown, Virginia. Laden with supplies and colonists, it had been on the seas for about two months when a hurricane struck. The ship became separated from the fleet and ran aground on Bermuda's hazardous barrier reef. Fortunately, the survivors found plenty of things to eat. There were berries, wild hogs, flocks of birds, turtles, and, of course, fish.

Using Bermuda cedar and timber, the castaways built two smaller vessels, the *Deliverance* and *Patina,* and sailed for Virginia, arriving in Jamestown in 1610. But several of the *Sea Venture's* crew decided to remain on the island, and in 1612 they were joined by 60 additional settlers.

Interestingly, Shakespeare's last play, *The Tempest,* was written in 1610, shortly after the news of the *Sea Venture* reached England. It is therefore assumed that the play was based on those reports.

Another early turtle caught in Bermuda's net was the *San Pedro,* a 350-ton merchant ship of the 1596 Spanish fleet. Yet another Spanish ship, the *San Antonio,* foundered off the southwestern reefs in 1621. Both of these were discovered in the 1950s by a local salver named Teddy Tucker. Visit the Treasure Room of the Maritime Museum to see some of their precious cargo.

Over the years, residents benefited from a number of maritime misfortunes. In the 1930s, it is said, they literally made their living off the *Cristobel,* which was wrecked on the shallow shoals. As the incredible story goes, they would board her and actually picnic on her decks. When ships saw them, the skippers assumed that that the waters were safe and thus were lured in to shore. Disaster was the result for them, and huge profits for the malicious picnickers.

tribunal in the square and metes out justice to petty offenders. Some are sent to the stocks and pillory or ducked in the ducking stool—all the tools of eighteenth-century justice.

This is where you'll find the **Old State House,** constructed in 1620, as well as a full-scale replica of *Deliverance I* (on Ordnance Island, across the bridge). Visit **Bridge House** to see antiques and collectibles. The forts on this end are stunning. High up, towering over the beach where the ship-wrecked crew of the *Sea Venture* came ashore in 1609, is **Fort St. Catherine.** Not far away is **Tobacco Bay,** with a beach set in a coral cove. It's an excellent place to spend an afternoon, especially with kids, since there is food here and restrooms nearby.

Leaving St. George, on the other side of Castle Harbour is **Tucker's Town,** where the multimillionaires live—mostly Americans, including Ross Perot. Several large resorts are here, as well as small coves with nice beaches. Naturally, they're all immaculate.

If you still have the stamina, go around Harrington Sound to visit **Crystal Caves,** the Bermuda **Perfumery,** the **Aquarium, the Natural History Museum,** and the **Zoo.** One of the highlights at the aquarium is a 140,000-gallon tank with a living coral reef and sharks. Kids will like the touch tank.

The island's **golf** courses are a big, big draw for visitors from around the world. There are about eight private courses on these tiny islands! Frankly, I don't know much about them (except they're gorgeous!), but I have a feeling that a day of golf far exceeds the cost of diving.

For spectator sports, there's the World Rugby Classic in mid-November, and power boat racing and yacht racing throughout the summer months.

If your visit coincides with the **Bermuda Tattoo,** which usually takes place in early November, don't miss it! I saw it at the National Stadium in Devonshire (about mid-island) during a drenching, relentless rainfall, and had an absolute blast. This Tattoo has nothing to do with the craze of body-adorning. Rather, it is a military display at night—the beating of retreat, which dates back to sixteenth-century British military history. In those days, towns and encampments were protected by battlement and for-tifications, and at sunset each day a warning call was made on a horn to collect the guards for the night. It also warned all those outside the walls to return to the security within. In this ceremony, bands play, soldiers march, and sabers rattle. It's a grand display and a lot of fun for all ages.

Dining and Entertainment

Frequently the gratuity is included in the bill.

You won't go hungry on Bermuda; there are many options, from pubs to fine restaurants. Pop into anything that looks appealing, since the selections are practically endless.

Definitely try a Dark and Stormy, the island drink. It consists of black rum and ginger beer with some fresh ginger grated on top. Occasionally it's mixed with fruit. Yum!

For music under the stars, a steel band just can't be beat. Just ask around to find one—shouldn't be difficult. The **Swizzle Inn** is usually a good bet; also **Ariel Sands,** owned by the Douglas family (Kirk, Michael, etc.) Nighttime cruises usually offer calypso and steel pan music; sometimes even limbo dancing. Of course, all the major resorts will have plenty of options for evening entertainment.

Medical Facilities

The island's main hospital is King Edward Memorial Hospital on Point Finger Road in Paget. Phone (441) 236-2345. The hospital is equipped with a recompression chamber (at press time). For scuba related emergencies, you can call DAN (Divers Alert Network) at (919) 684-4DAN (4326) or (919) 684-8111.

Bonaire

Physical Characteristics of the Dive Area

WATER & WEATHER CONDITIONS

Visibility	*Excellent*
Current and Surge	*Minimal*
Temperature	*Comfortable*
Storms	*Calm*

SITE CONDITIONS

Mooring Buoys	*Extensive*
Fishing, Collecting, and Hunting Restrictions	*Widespread Restrictions*
Ease of Access	*Very Easy*
Boat Traffic/Diver Congestion	*Light*

MARINE LIFE

Abundance of Invertebrates	*Abundant*
Abundance of Vertebrates	*Abundant*
Abundance of Pelagic Life	*Common*
Health of Reef/Marine Life/ Marine Structure	*Pristine*

Diver's Paradise

Bonaire—the memories are vivid: There was the night dive at Captain Don's, when I jumped off the pier before turning on my air. And the time when we were halfway to Karpata to do some shore diving before we realized we had forgotten our scuba tanks! Fortunately, there were many more positive memories, as well, like seeing the green flash at sunset for the first time and diving among the most abundant coral-covered hillsides I could ever imagine.

That's the effect that Bonaire has on you. It evokes memories. And that's why divers make the trek to this Caribbean speck of an island, then return, and return again. This, truly, is a diver's island—and a snorkeler's, as well. Here, and also on neighboring Curaçao, the fringing reef is just a few quick kicks from shore, and in a matter of minutes you can swim off from the beach and say hello to the abyss.

Also, this easternmost of the ABC islands (Aruba, Bonaire, and Curaçao) located close to the coast of Venezuela, is a giant when it comes to reef protection. Buoyancy control workshops are offered free of charge by every dive operator on Bonaire, and an ambitious Marine Park, supported by a modest $10 per annum dive-permit system, protects and oversees the marine ecosystem all around Bonaire and its smaller neighbor, Klein Bonaire.

Underwater, visibility often approaches 200 feet, fish act like fish (rather than reef-bound panhandlers), and the beautiful coral reefs and walls go on for miles. It is no wonder that the island's license plates proclaim "Diver's Paradise."

On many Caribbean islands, scuba diving is an important industry; on Bonaire, dive tourism is *the* industry. Just about every hotel of any size has a dive shop on premises (and at least one hotel has two), and air stations are standard equipment

You won't find elegant resorts or glitzy casinos here, although the resorts in recent years have become quite fashionable. Also, you won't find much in the way of shopping or even sightseeing. What you will see are lots and lots of dive shops, divemasters, roadside dive markers, and excited divers. In years past, there was not much reason to visit Bonaire if you were not planning to don scuba gear or at least a mask and snorkel. Now there are many more diversions, and resorts make sure that even if you're not a water hound, you'll still have a great time. Windsurfers, especially, will love it. Bonaire is considered one of the top spots in the world to enjoy this sport. And just recently, mountain biking has really caught on.

If you do visit Bonaire with nondiving companions, encourage them to at least try snorkeling. The learn-to-snorkel programs here are excellent, and snorkelers are given top priority, with dedicated snorkeling boats, in-water training, and marine life education programs.

QUICK STATS

Size   Shaped like a boomerang, Bonaire is only 112 square miles in area—3 to 7 miles wide and 24 miles long.

Population   About 15,000

Location   50 miles north of Venezuela, 86 miles east of Aruba, and 30 miles east of Curaçao.

Time   Atlantic Standard Time. During Daylight Savings Time in the United States (mid-spring to late fall), it is the same time as the U.S. East Coast.

Government   Bonaire is one of five islands—Bonaire, Curaçao, St. Maarten, Saba, and St. Eustatius—that comprise the Netherlands Antilles, an autonomous part of the Kingdom of the Netherlands.

Language   The official language is Dutch, and the native language is Papiamentu, with English and Spanish widely spoken.

Electrical   Current 50 cycles, 127 volts; camera and computer batteries should be recharged only at designated charging stations at dive shops and resorts.

Climate   The average air temp is 82° and the average humidity is 75 percent. Rainfall averages 22 inches per year. There is a constant trade wind, making the evenings cool and comfortable. Average wind speed is 15 m.p.h.

Water Temperature   The average is 80°.

Underwater Visibility   Usually around 100 feet, but frequently even greater

Best Diving Months   Bonaire is outside the hurricane belt, so just about any time is perfect.

PLANNING THE TRIP

Phoning Bonaire   In 2000, the phone system on Bonaire was upgraded. All local numbers now have the prefix 717. To call from the United States or Canada, you need to dial 011 (international access code), 599 (Netherlands Antilles country code), 717 (Bonaire prefix), and then the four-digit local number.

Getting to Bonaire   Airlines from the United States, Europe, Aruba, and Curaçao serving Bonaire's Flamingo Airport are Air ALM, (800) 327-7230; Air Aruba, (800) 882-7822; and Air Jamaica (800) 622-3009. Air ALM and Air Jamaica fly from all major gateway cities in the United States. The airtime from Miami is approximately two hours and 45 minutes. The airport's designation is BON.

Getting Around the Island   Taxis, rental cars, and vans are widely available. Taxis are available at the airport.

Entry Documents   U.S. and Canadian citizens must have a valid passport, or a birth certificate and photo ID, and a return or ongoing plane ticket.

Currency   Netherlands Antilles guilder is approximately 1.77 to the U.S. dollar. U.S. dollars are accepted everywhere, but you'll get change in guilders.

Tourism   Corporation Bonaire. From North America, call (800) BONAIRE or (212) 956-5912; fax (212) 956-5913. To call the island, dial (599) 717-8322 or 8649; fax (599) 717-8408. E-mail: info@tourism bonaire.com; website: www.infobonaire.com. From Europe, e-mail: inter rep@interrep.demon.nl.

THE UNDERWATER SCENE

Bonaire was created through volcanic eruptions, so the entire island is actually an underwater mountain. It is completely encircled by fringing reefs, therefore assuring that there is plenty to see by divers and snorkelers from virtually any shoreline spot. Most boat trips to dive sites take only about 15 minutes.

Less than a mile off the south coast is the uninhabited Klein Bonaire (Little Bonaire), which acts like a barrier reef, creating calm, leeward waters. On most sites south of town, the top of the reef slopes gently down to about 100 feet and features a wide belt of pretty soft corals. The north coast, on the other hand, is battered by strong waves that pound the rocky coast. These northern sites have a narrow-topped reef to about 35 feet, and then they drop abruptly. This is not exactly a wall, but it is steep nonetheless.

The best reefs are found within the protected lee of the island. Because the sites are so close to shore and the water is so calm, it's possible to dive almost every day and night. Night dives are particularly spectacular, since the water is clear and the corals vibrant.

Noticeably absent at most sites here are big fish. You'll see primarily small- to medium-size fish, as well as numerous eels. At some sites there are tarpon, and you will see the occasional grouper. Pelagic life is only occasionally spotted at the Klein Bonaire sites. That's the one slightly disappointing feature about diving here, and it does seem strange, after two decades of marine park protection.

Most divers here will dive "out of the boot" rather than from a boat. However, you do need a boat to get to the sites around Klein Bonaire and a few other sites, such as *La Donia's Leap* and *Rappel,* where, as the names imply, the terrain makes shore access difficult. But for the most part, you can dive right out of the trunk of your car all up and down the island, and be on the reef in a matter of minutes.

To get to dive sites (there are more than 80 from which to choose), all you have to do is get a map (a copy of the *New Guide to the Bonaire Marine Park* is a good idea), grab your gear (don't forget the tanks!) and go. Sites are marked along the roadsides by distinctive yellow-painted, duffelbag-size rocks with the names of the sites hand-lettered on them. Also, most dive operators allow unlimited beach diving any time day or night, with tanks available around the clock.

Health Score Card

Bonaire's reefs are extremely healthy, due in part to the strong environmental ethic, but also due to the effects of nature, or lack thereof. Because Bonaire lies outside the hurricane belt, the reefs are protected from storm damage. So even its shallowest reefs, which tend to get pounded on most other Caribbean islands, remain in excellent condition.

Restrictions on commercial fishing and spearfishing have obviously made a significant impact. In 1995 the Reef Environmental Foundation

(REEF) revealed that Bonaire is inhabited by more species of fish than any other Caribbean island. Trained "fish spotters" studied 30 sites and identified 197 species of fish. Moreover, an abundance of fish was found both at sites less frequently visited and at sites heavily visited by divers, suggesting that that high diving traffic has little impact on the reef and fish population.

Diving Conditions

Most of the 90 or so identified dive sites are scattered along the leeward, southwest side of the island. This is where the conditions are calmest and visibility is excellent. With only 12 inches of annual rainfall, there is no appreciable freshwater runoff, so water visibility is typically 100 feet or much more.

Divers will find a dense, healthy fringing reef that starts in about 20 feet of water. At that depth, coral heads are dotted along a mostly flat, sandy bottom. About 35 yards offshore, the topography changes and the reef suddenly drops off into the blue depths. In some areas the lush reef slope is occasionally broken by mini-walls.

Come to Bonaire prepared for shore diving. That means you'll need hard-soled dive booties for walking on rocky beaches, although many sites have nice sandy shore entries. Also bring a tarp or mat for spreading out your dive gear. Later on in this chapter you'll find more recommendations for making shore dives.

Recommended Level of Experience

Bonaire is a terrific place for all levels of divers. Everyone will be happy. New divers, rusty divers, and snorkelers will love the lush, shallow fringing reef with its calm conditions. More confident divers will thrill at the prolific amount of life on the deeper slopes. And photographers will be delighted with great visibility and plenty of opportunities for both macro and wide angle shots.

This would also be the perfect place to get certified. Take your entire class here, or bring a referral from your instructor back home and enjoy your open water dives in a bathtub-warm paradise!

Bonaire's Great Boat Dives

Some of the most exciting dives are around Klein Bonaire, the little uninhabited island that's now a wilderness park, some 500 yards offshore. It has about 24 sites, and all are excellent. *Carl's Hill,* off the northwest tip of Klein Bonaire, is carpeted with colorful encrusting sponges, multicolored tube sponges and wire coral, and teeming with bar jacks. The reef here is so steep that it can be considered a wall. Not surprisingly, this site is popular with photographers.

For some reason, frogfish are plentiful here around both Bonaire and Klein Bonaire, and with a little practice you'll be able to spot them fairly easily. They sit motionless and camouflaged on sponges, and they're spongy-looking tehmselves, thus tough to discern. Ask your divemaster to show you one, then you'll be spotting them for yourself.

Near *Carl's Hill* is *Sharon's Serenity,* another popular Klein Bonaire site, with mounds of star coral, branching gorgonians, and terraced sheet coral. At shallower depths here, the staghorn coral and sea fans are particularly striking, and watch for the ubiquitous fire coral, especially if you're snorkeling. Another good snorkel site is called *Knife,* where the staghorn and elkhorn corals are prolific. These types of corals thrive in shallow waters where they get plenty of sunlight, and they always attract a healthy assortment of fish. Typically you'll see throngs of blue tangs, perhaps some chromis, and horse-eye jacks.

Farther south the site called *Forest* features a wall that is unusually vertical for Bonaire standards. Thick colonies of hard corals cover the edge. Off the wall are the convoluted orange elephant ear sponges and a plethora of gorgonians reaching out into the open ocean to snatch up nutrients passing by. You'll see billowy black coral at the deeper levels, as well as swirling plates of sheet coral—beautiful!

Back on Bonaire, the *Invisibles* is a deep dive that features a prolific amount of mountainous star coral and numerous eels and flounder. The double reef here, separated by a sandy field, runs parallel to shore. Look for the swaying pencil-like garden eels sticking up from the sand. In the shallows, enjoy the gorgeous stands of staghorn and elkhorn coral glowing in the bright sunlight. Although this site can be accessed from shore, the entry is tricky, so it's best reserved for a boat dive. After one dive here, our boat was surrounded by a pod of dolphin!

Bonaire's Legendary Shore Dives

At the northern end of Bonaire, within Washington-Slagbaai Park, are two excellent sites—*Playa Funchi* and *Boca Slagbaai*—with easy entry and a lot to capture your attention. These are also good snorkeling areas. At Playa Funchi it doesn't take long to drop down the gradually sloping wall and encounter all the reef inhabitants schooling among the condo-like formations of star coral. Just a little south is Boca Slagbaai, one of the few shore dive areas that sells food and drinks. You can easily dive both these sites in half a day, but you'll need to enter the park and pay the $5 entrance fee.

The site called *Karpata,* named after the marine study station of the same name that sits above it, can be tricky to enter when the surf is running rough, but normally it's easy and the rewards are great. After I dived Karpata for the first time, I wrote in my logbook, "Everywhere we looked was exciting." To access the site, walk down a short cement stairway to a small dock. Drop into the water and you'll see a small channel about five feet wide by about 20 feet long etched out of the coral. Follow it and swim out to the reef. About 50 feet from shore the reef slopes down abruptly and the bottom takes a steep, almost vertical drop to more than 130 feet. Because the water is so clear here it's easy to get deeper than you might have planned, so be cautious. The drop-off is completely carpeted with an enormous variety of corals and sponges—truly a stunning kaleidoscope of color. The tropical fish are abundant here, as well.

Windsock, near the airport, has an easy, sandy shore entry. Because of the sand, though, the shallows are silty, so you'll need to get down to at least 50 feet before the visibility really improves. Angelfish and parrotfish are frequent visitors. This place holds wonderful memories. After a dive here on a late afternoon, my dive buddy and I decided to sit on the sand to watch the sunset. And there it was in all its glory: the Green Flash! We were speechless for a few moments, amazed to discover that what we had always heard about really did happen. As the last of the sun slipped below the watery horizon, a flash of green light shot up into the sky. Great dive and a green flash—what a day!

One of the most popular dives on the island, and for good reason, is the *Hilma Hooker,* a marijuana smuggler's boat that made the transformation from reefer to reef after she limped into harbor with engine problems and very nearly sank at the dock. Local dive operators convinced the government to scuttle the boat near shore, and she can now be dived from the beach or from a boat. Submerged since about 1984, she displays a lot of growth, including orange cup corals and tube sponges. Fortunately, it is shallow enough for divers to have plenty of time to really look around all 236 feet of her. The railings are at about 60 feet. The sandy bottom is at 100 feet. At the helm you can see the steering wheel and the huge prop. More than one dive boat can moor here, so make sure you go up the same mooring line you came down and get back on the right boat!

The ship lies within the dive site called *Angel City,* which is actually a section of the larger area known as *Alice in Wonderland. Alice* is a double reef complex, separated by a sand channel, that extends from Point Vierkannt south toward *Salt Pier.* The Salt Pier, with its vast network of limbs, is a tremendous attraction for invertebrates. Multicolored corals and sponges completely cover the structure, and tropicals play all about.

It's almost criminal to come to Bonaire and not do at least one night dive. They really are a lot of fun, so do yourselves a big favor! Some of the most popular sites are those that display the orange cup corals in all their glory. That usually means anywhere you'll find structure. *Town Pier* is a very good spot. So is the *Hilma Hooker,* but that's pretty deep for a night dive. Of course, it's nice to be able to dive right from your resort, where it's convenient to get back to your room easily. Captain Don's Habitat features excellent night diving at its site called *La Machaca.* Just giant-stride right off the dock. Don't do what I did, though, and forget to turn on your air before making that leap! *Bari Reef,* at Sand Dollar, and *Buddy's Reef,* at Buddy Dive, are two more good ones. On these night dives, watch for octopus, which will change color as they move along, and decorator crabs, all dressed up with marine flotsam. The goldentail moray is also a frequent nighttime forager.

Snorkeling

For snorkeling, just wade from the shore out to the reefs at any of the designated dive spots, or right off your resort. *Bari Reef,* at Sand Dollar Condominium Resort, is one of the best. Corals off the island are within easy finning distance, especially elkhorn coral, which thrives in the sun-bathed shallow water. Fish also are bountiful, particularly the beautiful pastel-colored parrotfish, yellow snappers, cute little black-and-white trunkfish, and the feisty little blennies. Eels, too, are plentiful, so don't go sticking your hand into any crevices!

Excellent walk-in dive sites are *Playa Funchi* and *Nukove* at the northern end; *Thousand Steps, Cliff,* and *Windsock* at the center of the island; *Invisibles* at the southern end; and *Mangroves* at Lac Bay. Klein Bonaire and Washington/Slagbaai National Park also offer splendid snorkeling.

Guided snorkel programs on Bonaire are light-years ahead of most Caribbean islands, where lowly snorkelers are typically left to fend for themselves. Here, not only do visitors learn the skills of snorkeling, they also can learn about the marine environment, particularly the virtues of protecting it, from experienced guides. Most local dive shops run dedicated snorkel boats that are fully equipped with excellent snorkel gear, and they can offer slide presentations on fish and coral identification.

The Tourism Corporation has produced a free eight-page snorkel guide that can be ordered by calling (800) U-BONAIR. You can also visit the website at www.interknowledge.com.

Shore Diving Tips

Because shore diving here is some of the best in the world—that is, both easy and scenic—you really should take advantage of it. It does require more planning, though, than boat diving, so here are a few tips to help ensure that your experience is safe and that you get the maximum enjoyment from it.

Car Rental   Before renting that cute little open jeep, remember that it will not be secure if you want to leave things in it while you're in the water. The tourism department doesn't like to advertise this on the island, but there is a problem with theft, and the shore-diving locations are prime spots for break-ins. While you're having a great time in the water, your vehicle is a sitting duck. So if you want to bring things along, it's best to rent a car with a trunk that can be locked. Definitely put all your personal belongings (especially valuables) in the trunk.

Valuables   Even if you do have a secure vehicle, take only what you'll really need and leave valuables behind. That means passports, airline tickets, identification, cash, cameras, and other expensive equipment.

What to Take   Be sure to take drinking water, sunscreen, a save-a-dive kit, and scuba tools Oh, yeah—the tanks! Sunglasses and a hat are also a good idea. If you're using an underwater camera, take along some fresh water for rinsing. Also take a tarp to put on the ground to keep your gear clean, and some towels. Finally, take an island map that shows all the dive spots.

Booties   It's usually a good idea to wear booties—preferably the hard-sole type—when you are shore diving. Sometimes you'll enter the water from a rocky or ironshore coastline rather than from a sandy beach.

Evaluate the Water Conditions   Most of the dive sites are on the lee of the island where the water is usually calm. You won't find strong currents or rough surf. Nevertheless, on some sections, and at certain times, you might find both—the current and surf can get pretty rough. So check it out carefully before getting in.

The Heat   Remember that this island is hot, hot, hot and very dry. Besides having plenty of drinking water, don't get overheated before you even begin the dive.

Plan Your Dive   Agree with your buddy how you intend to plan the dive. Usually you'll want to kick out to the buoy on the surface, then

Shore Diving Tips (continued)

drop down. As you follow the slope down, check the direction of the current, then head into it. Usually it's best to turn around when you get to about 1,500 psi. Then, start to ascend gradually as you return. Since there's plenty to see in the shallows, you can play around and gas off at the same time.

Navigate Remember, you have to get back to your point of departure on shore, so navigation is important. Take a compass heading and note natural landmarks before heading into the current. Also note the position of the sun.

Marine Park

Bonaire was the first Caribbean island to establish a national park, so it's not surprising that an underwater park would soon follow. The Bonaire Marine Park is an ambitious system begun by virtual legends in the dive world and run by equally capable and dedicated managers. Tom Van'T Hof, who now resides on the island of Saba, was the guy who spearheaded the entire marine protection effort in the Netherlands Antilles. He began his work here on Bonaire in the 1970s, then moved on to Curaçao and up to the Windward Islands of Saba, Statia, and St. Maarten, which comprise the rest of the Antilles. Funding for the Bonaire Marine Park came in 1979 from the World Wildlife Fund (WWF) and the Bonaire government.

In 1971 spearfishing was banned in Marine Park waters; in 1982 moorings began to be installed; and in 1975 it became illegal to break coral, take it from the water, or sell it. The Marine Park now has National Park status. Rangers actively survey the park, verifying valid Marine Park tags and making sure that the rules are observed.

In December 1999, a monumental purchase was made by WWF, the Dutch government, and the Foundation Preservation Klein Bonaire. After years of negotiations, these three groups purchased the entire island of Klein Bonaire from private developers. This was a big victory for conservationists, ensuring that the uninhabited island will be saved from development. So it, too, is now a national park.

The reef conservation ethic is evident everywhere around Bonaire. Every dive operator on the island offers buoyancy control workshops free of charge. Divers are asked to check their weighting before making their first dive on the reef here. Divers also purchase a $10 per annum dive permit that helps support the Marine Park. The little disk that they wear on their BCDs then becomes a proud souvenir of their visit to the island, and many continue to wear them long after they leave—a badge of honor, so to speak. Marine Park protection extends all around Bonaire and its smaller neighbor, Klein Bonaire, from the high-water mark down to the 200-foot depth contour.

Another diving pioneer, educator, and conservationist on Bonaire is Dee Scarr. Her *Touch the Sea* program has introduced thousands of divers to the beautiful and fragile intricacies of the marine ecosystem. Many years ago Dee helped restore Town Pier to its former glory by transplanting sponges onto pilings that had been repaired.

An important task of the Marine Park is to monitor shore construction projects to make sure they are not endangering the reef. Bonaire requires the use of mooring buoys (except on wreck dives), and the waters are patrolled, assuring compliance. The least of their problems, according to Kalli DeMeyer, Marine Park Manager, is divers. She claims that much of their patrol time is spent making sure that the owners of private yachts understand how the mooring system works. As Scarr pointed out to me in this poignant and pithy statement a few years ago: "There are yachties who are ignorant, and yachties who are stupid—some are both ignorant *and* stupid."

Don't be surprised when diving here if you are advised to pick up dangerous debris on the ocean floor. Where divers elsewhere might put shells or sand dollars into their BCD pockets, here they routinely pick up bottle caps and batteries, and they have even been known to fan the sand off sponges to make it easier for them to filter-feed. This is the ethic that Bonaire has engendered, and it's a good one for other diving destinations to emulate.

Dive Services & Packages

Bon Bini Divers is a PADI and SSI dive center at the Lion's Dive Resort (a PADI Gold Palm Resort). There are daily boat dives, as well as instruction from basic to instructor. Underwater photo and video instruction is also available. The boats are all small, like the 28-foot V-hulled vessel *Bon Danki,* which holds 12 divers. Special trips are made to Washington-Slagbaai Park and to the southern tip of the island. Equipment rental and sales are available, as well as Nitrox and dedicated snorkel programs. Call (599) 717-5425; fax (599) 717-4425; e-mail: info@bonbinidivers.com; website: www.bonbinidivers.com.

Retail Sales: *Adequate*	**Dive Boat Comfort:** *Good*
Rentals: *Adequate*	**On-Board Facilities**
Scuba Training: *Extensive*	**for Photographers:** *Good*
Photo Services: *Moderate*	

Buddy Dive Resort's PADI Gold Palm Resort facility is known for what it claims is "the world's only drive-thru air fill station," which also provides Nitrox. The resort runs two 18-passenger dive boats and has snorkeling and diving equipment rentals and a repair facility. Instruction is extensive, ranging from a "Bubble Program" for children ages 8 to 11, all the way through divemaster. There are also guided snorkeling programs. Call (599) 717-5080; fax (599) 717-8647; e-mail: info@buddydive.com; website: www.buddydive.com.

Retail Sales: *Adequate*	**Dive Boat Comfort:** *Good*
Rentals: *Adequate*	**On-Board Facilities**
Scuba Training: *Extensive*	**for Photographers:** *Good*
Photo Services: *Limited*	

Captain Don's Habitat, on the property at good old Captain Don's, is a venerable PADI 5-Star IDC, so if you're thinking of going pro, this could be the place to do it. It now offers semiclosed-circuit rebreather training and rentals, Nitrox instruction, and underwater camera/photo lab facilities. Call (800) 327-6709 or (599) 717-8290; fax (599) 717-8240; e-mail: bonaire@habitatdiveresorts.com; website: www.habitatdiveresorts.com.

Retail Sales: *Adequate*	**Dive Boat Comfort:** *Good*
Rentals: *Adequate*	**On-Board Facilities**
Scuba Training: *Extensive*	**for Photographers:** *Good*
Photo Services: *Extensive*	

Dive-Inn Bonaire (a PADI 5-Star Dive Center) operates several dive shops, one at Kralendijk and others at the dive locations of the Bonaire Caribbean Club. It has exclusive arrangements with various blocks of apartments, and offers packages with rooms, apartments, or villas. At each of those is a satellite tank station, where you can get full tanks every day. They also have equipment rentals, snorkel instruction, PADI dive instruction, and boat diving. Contact them at (599) 717-8761; fax (599) 717-8513; e-mail: diveinn@bonairenet.com; website: www.diveinn-bonaire.com.

Retail Sales: *Adequate*	**Dive Boat Comfort:** *Good*
Rentals: *Adequate*	**On-Board Facilities**
Scuba Training: *Moderate*	**for Photographers:** *Good*
Photo Services: *Limited*	

Touch the Sea with Dee Scarr

PADI dive instructor Dee Scarr has the unique distinction of having started her own PADI specialty course called Touch the Sea. But more than an instructor, Dee is an ardent environmentalist and experienced naturalist, as well as being something of a Bonaire ambassador.

During her underwater outings, participants learn to interact with marine life in a gentle way, and in the process learn about the natural behaviors of marine creatures. Her favorite participants are kids, who are inevitably enchanted with Dee's unique "syllabus." They will have their hands manicured by cleaner shrimp, they'll feed anemones, play with octopus and meet Mr. Magoo, the sharptail eel, as well as the scorpionfishes named Ruby and Rodney Dangerfield. In the process Dee gets across her message of conservation and protection of these species, and how we must all do our part.

What Dee started years ago (1982) has now spread across the island and throughout the Caribbean: Don't let gauges dangle, watch your buoyancy, don't kick corals. She explains that kicking up silt is damaging to sponges, which are filter feeders. "When silt lands on a sponge," she explains, "it inhibits the animal's ability to suck in water and to feed and breathe." Coral has the same problem. She'll show you how to fan sponges and corals to remove the sand.

"It's important to be a role model," says Dee. "Start picking up garbage that you see underwater and stuff it into your BCD pockets. Remove fishing line by coiling it around your hand, then putting it in your pocket. You'll be surprised how people will start to copy you.

"A lot of people think the ocean is an enormous garbage can," she says. She warns, however, to be careful about the "old" garbage, like cans and bottles, in which creatures might already have made their homes. These, she says, should not be disturbed.

She encourages people to be activists—to tell others not to stress pufferfish, for instance, just to get that one good photo. She'll explain what happens when you touch coral: that the delicate, thin membrane covering it is smashed against the coral skeleton. Ouch!

You don't even have to go to Bonaire to talk to Dee. She and her husband will come to you if you'd like to bring a Touch the Sea experience to your child's school, or if you would like to sponsor one for a symposium, school, or dive club. You can also learn more by reading her monthly column in *Dive Training* magazine, or looking it up at www.divetrainingmag.com.

> ### Touch the Sea with Dee Scarr (continued)
>
> She requires a minimum of two divers for her educational dives. You can have a single dive for $90 each, or take the three-dive specialty course, which includes presentations and postdive discussions for $180 per diver. She also teaches another specialty course, called Future Perfect Diver, to learn about reef caretaking. This involves two dives with presentations and postdive discussions, and is also $180 per diver.
>
> Dee is usually on Bonaire from November through June, and in Colorado the rest of the time. Her Bonaire address is PO Box 369, Bonaire, Netherlands Antilles; her U.S. address is PO Box 369, Conifer, CO 80433. On Bonaire, call (599) 717-8529; in Colorado, (303) 816-1727. Year-round, her e-mail address is dee@touchthe sea.com. Check out her fun website at www.touchthesea.com.

Great Adventures is the on-property PADI and NAUI dive operation at Harbour Village. The shop runs four dive boats, and now has a 42-foot Newton equipped with a camera table, rinse tank, showers, etc. Great Adventures is another PADI Gold Palm IDC Resort—something for the pros to think about. They now have the Great Photo Adventures professional photo service with rentals featuring Nikonos and Sea & Sea camera gear, as well as Sony Hi-8 digital video in Gates underwater housings and Underwater Kinetics lights. Personalized photo and video classes are taught with or without certification, with only one or two students per class. Call (800) 868-7477 or (305) 567-9509; fax (305) 567-9659; e-mail: reservations @harbourvillage.com; website: www.harbourvillage.com.

Retail Sales: *Adequate*

Rentals: *Extensive*

Scuba Training: *Extensive*

Photo Services: *Extensive*

Dive Boat Comfort: *Excellent*

On-Board Facilities for Photographers: *Superior*

Sand Dollar Dive & Photo is a PADI 5-Star IDC with several small boats serving guests at the Sand Dollar Condominium Resort. It offers an Unlimited Dive Package that includes six days of boat diving and unlimited tanks for on-your-own shore diving with a buddy. Instruction is PADI, NAUI, and SSI, from beginner through advanced levels. It also has an underwater photography course, camera rentals and sales, film processing, a slide-viewing room, and custom dive videos. A naturalist teaches a course called Introduction to Fish Watching, which includes 15 hours of classroom slide presentations, 2 snorkel field trips, and 6 shore dives. Ocean's Classroom is a special snorkel class for kids, which teaches them about the ocean and its inhabitants. A full line of equipment sales and rentals is offered. Contact the resort at (800) 288-4773 or (599) 717-8738; fax (599) 717-8760; e-mail: sanddollar@bonairenet.com; website: www.interknowledge. com/bonaire/sand-dollar.

Retail Sales: *Extensive*   **Dive Boat Comfort:** *Good*
Rentals: *Extensive*   **On-Board Facilities**
Scuba Training: *Extensive*   **for Photographers:** *Superior*
Photo Services: *Extensive*

Toucan Diving is on the property of Plaza Resort Bonaire (a PADI Gold Palm IDC Resort). If offers IDD, PADI, and NAUI instruction, several dive boats, rental equipment, and has a classroom/meeting facility for ten people. The facilities are great, including a full-service retail area. Nitrox is available, as well as photo instruction. Special trips are offered to the eastern side of the island, which is rarely dived, and also to Washington-Slagbaai Park. Call (800) 766-6016 or (599) 717-2500; fax (599) 717-7133; e-mail: info@plaza resortbonaire.com; website: www.plazaresortbonaire.com.

Retail Sales: *Extensive*   **Dive Boat Comfort:** *Good*
Rentals: *Extensive*   **On-Board Facilities**
Scuba Training: *Extensive*   **for Photographers:** *Good*
Photo Services: *Moderate*

WHERE TO STAY

Note that there is a room tax of $5.50 to $6.50 per person per day, and many lodgings tack on a service charge as well. When comparing prices, be sure to inquire if the extra charges are included in the rates quoted.

Buddy Dive Resort ★★★★ (a PADI Gold Palm Resort) is an oceanfront, casual place with an on-property dive center. Accommodations range from six hotel rooms to 40 one-, two-, and three-bedroom apartments with either ocean view or garden view. All apartments have a fully equipped kitchen, spacious living area, air-conditioning, and balcony or patio. Facilities include two swimming pools, a waterside bar and restaurant, retail shop, car rentals, equipment rental and storage, and a coin-operated laundry. Kayaking, hiking, biking, sailing, fishing, cruising, and parasailing are offered. A special

Drive and Dive Package features seven nights accommodation, seven days rental vehicle, six days of unlimited air fills, daily breakfast buffet, airport transfers, and all taxes. Nightly room rates start at $110 in summer and fall, and at $113 in winter and spring. Call (599) 717-5080; fax (599) 717-8647; e-mail: info@buddydive.com; website: www.buddydive.com.

Captain Don's Habitat ★★★★★ (a PADI Resort) led the pack years ago when it began offering 24-hours-a-day, 365-days-a-year diving freedom. Reefs and wrecks are only 90 feet offshore, and night diving here is superb. There is a choice of deluxe oceanfront junior suites (sleeping two), two-bedroom garden-view cottages (sleeping four), and a variety of ocean-view villas (sleeping two to four). All are air-conditioned and have patios. Most have full kitchens. Facilities include an oceanfront restaurant, bar, swimming pool, and, of course, beach. Daily rates start at $92 per person for a two-person unit. Dive packages include accommodations in any of the units, buffet breakfast, boat dives, unlimited shore diving, unlimited air fills, airport transfers, government taxes, service charges, gratuities, and more. Call (800) 327-6709 or (599) 717-8290; fax (599) 717-8240; e-mail: bonaire@habitatdiveresorts.com; website: www.habitatdiveresorts.com.

The new **Eden Beach Resort** has 38 condominium units, including 18 studios and 20 two-bedroom town houses. All have full kitchens and air-conditioning. This would be ideal for families. Call (599) 717-6720.

Harbour Village ★★★★, a PADI Gold Palm IDC Resort, is one of the more upscale resorts on the island, with a veteran dive operation. It's on a pretty quarter-mile stretch of beach and features a spa/fitness center, four restaurants, swimming pools, a tennis center with night lighting, shops, and a marina. All rooms have private balconies that overlook the beach. Dive packages include beachfront junior suite accommodations, buffet breakfast, six days of diving and unlimited shore diving, one-day car rental, and more. Nightly room rates start at $275 in summer, $310 in winter. Call (800) 868-7477 or (305) 567-9509; fax (305) 567-9659; e-mail: reservations@harbourvillage.com; website: www.harbourvillage.com.

Lion's Dive Resort ★★★★, a PADI Gold Palm Resort, with its Bon Bini Divers, is located north of Kralendijk, between Captain Don's and Buddy Dive. It's a short walk to the sandy beach and restaurants. There is a swimming pool, and the 31 air-conditioned condos all have fully stocked kitchens, room safes, and balconies with ocean views. They sleep up to six people. Per room rates begin at a very reasonable $120 per night. Call (599) 717-5580; fax (599) 717-5680; e-mail: info@lionsdivebonaire.com; website: www.lionsdivebonaire.com.

Palm Studios is a nice place for those on a budget. It's located near the capital, Kralendijk, and Blue Divers is right next door. Each of the ten air-conditioned apartments has a kitchenette, and although it's not on the beach, the property does have a swimming pool, and the beach is within walking distance. The price is about $65 for a double, including tax and service. The on-island phone number is (599) 717-6860.

Located on a pretty stretch of white sand beach is **Plaza Resort Bonaire** ★★★★, a PADI Gold Palm IDC Resort featuring 24-hour tank access and complete packages. This 224-unit luxury hotel has a casino, restaurant, fitness center, racquetball and squash court, basketball court, beauty shop, mini-market, jogging track, and kid's club with playground. The Sports and Entertainment Department offers snorkeling, waterskiing, windsurfing, kayaking, tennis, beach volleyball, aqua jogging, water-polo, and body-fitness training. Boston Whalers and catamarans are available to rent. The dive package includes stay in a junior suite, six days of single-tank diving, unlimited shore diving, airport transfers, hotel taxes, and service charge. Call (800) 766-6016 or (781) 821-6016 or (599) 717-2500; fax (781) 821-1568 or (599) 717-7133; e-mail: info@plazaresortbonaire.com; website: www.plazaresortbonaire.com.

Sand Dollar Condominium ★★★★ is especially popular with families. Choose from deluxe air-conditioned studios or one-, two-, or three-bedroom condos, all facing the ocean. Rates start at $180 per day. The resort recently upgraded, adding an ice cream parlor, bank, and grocery store. Other features are a swimming pool, lighted tennis courts, and restaurant. On the property is Sand Dollar Dive and Photo. Besides diving (shore diving is only 50 yards "out back") they offer kayaking (including kayak trips to the mangroves), guided snorkel trips, weekly birdwatching excursions, and mountain biking adventures—plenty of fun for everyone. Contact the resort at (800) 288-4773 or (599) 717-8738; fax (599) 717-8760; e-mail: sanddollar@bonairenet.com; website: www.interknowledge.com/bonaire/sand-dollar.

SunRentals rents out homes for both short and long stays in a number of price ranges, and this might be another option for your family or a group. Prices start at $75 per night. Contact them at (599) 717-6130; fax (599) 717-6136; e-mail: info@sunrentals.an; website: www.sunrentals.an.

ISLAND LIFE

At first glance, this mostly flat, arid island seems to offer little to the tropical tourist. Nevertheless, when it's time to gas-off before heading home, there are a few terrestrial options besides reading a good book. What you will not find here, as you're exploring, is litter, billboards, or neon signs. What you *will* find are unpaved side roads, a lot of goats and cactus, and friendly people honking and waving as they pass one another.

Since Bonaire is one of the five islands that comprise the Netherlands Antilles, the Dutch influence is very evident, reflected mostly in its architecture. But Bonaireans exhibit an interesting combination of cultures, including Spanish and Portuguese, having been ruled by both countries, and also African, as a result of the slave trade.

When the Spanish seafarer Amerigo Vespucci discovered Bonaire in 1499, it was inhabited by the Arawak Indians. The Spanish colonized it in about 1527, and the Dutch snatched it away in 1634. They used it mainly for salt mining and brought in many slaves from Africa—as well as from neighboring islands—to work in the salt flats. In the 1800s, the British briefly occupied the island. This also was a time when British and French pirates were playing havoc with the shipping trade. In 1816 the Dutch regained control, and in 1863 slavery was outlawed. In 1951 the Netherlands Antilles were granted self-rule.

The local patois, called Papiamentu, is an intriguing blend of at least six languages! But English is spoken everywhere, so you won't have any problems communicating. Nevertheless, try learning a few words like *Bon Bini* (welcome) and *Bon Dia* (good day), then watch the reaction!

Topside Attractions

Drive to the dive site called *White Slave* and see for yourself the stark white **slave huts,** still alone on the sand and facing the sea, as if searching for another place. These are actually reconstructed huts from the early salt mining days when the slaves worked as rakers, and are sad reminders of those unhappy times. The obelisks that you'll see along the shore were navigational markers for the ships that carried the salt and the slaves.

Just north of this site is **Pink Beach,** which is one of the few nice stretches of beach on the island, so it's popular with families and snorkelers. Just around the southern tip is the lonely **Willemstoren Lighthouse.** Beyond this point begins the windward, therefore rougher, side of the island. As you drive around, you'll come to **Lac Bay,** a shallow lagoon. This is where windsurfers will want to try their skills, since it's one of the best such sites in the world. In the mangroves fringing Lac Bay, sea kayaking and bird watching are popular.

Where there's windsurfing, there's also sailing, and this is equally popular on Bonaire. Just make sure you never throw anchor onto the coral bottom and incur the wrath of Dee Scarr and Kalli DeMeyer! Mooring buoys are conveniently located in 20 feet of water. You simply take your own length of line and slip it through some PVC pipe to tie off.

Up at the northern end of the island is **Washington-Slagbaai Park,** where the attraction is beautiful pink flamingos. The park was the first one established in the Caribbean (1969) and it is huge, covering 13,500 acres. It once consisted of two plantations—Washington and Slagbaai—hence the hyphenated name. Miles of nature trails wind through the park, and pretty secluded beaches have terrific snorkeling and diving. You'll find the pink flamingos wading in the lakes of the saltpans. This is the home and breeding ground for between 5–6,000 of the beautiful birds. Frequently they're far from view, so take binoculars if you have them. Of course, you'll find other feathered friends, as well—look for parrots and parakeets. It is said that Bonaire has as many as 170 species of birds! Entrance to the park is $5, and it's open daily from 8 a.m. to 5 p.m. Be sure to take drinking water and food if you plan to stay a while. Much of the park can only be explored with a four-wheel-drive vehicle.

Look for restored plantation houses in the beautiful Dutch design. If you drive up to Karpata, you'll be able to see one. This is a scenic drive, where you'll also see one secluded cove after another. Many will have divers on the beach, gearing up.

Definitely stroll around the capital, **Kralendijk,** to see Fort Oranje, Museo Boneriano, and the Fish Market. Browse some of the galleries and boutiques on Main Street. Normal store hours are from 8 or 9 a.m. until noon, when they close for one to two hours, then remain open until 6 p.m.

Dining and Entertainment

When dining out, check out the bill before tipping. Many restaurants add a 10 to 15 percent service charge.

Most of the resorts have good restaurants and many have entertainment as well, usually al fresco. **Captain Don's** always has something fun happening in the evenings. Also, the **Green Parrot** at the Sand Dollar Condominium is typically bustling with hungry divers downing burgers, Mexican food, and grilled fish.

Harbour Village has a couple of good restaurants. **The Admiral's Tavern** at the Harbour Village Lighthouse, features seafood specialties. **Compadres Mexican Grill** and **Capt. Wook's** serve good Tex-Mex dishes.

In Kralendijk, for some local flavor that's easy on the pocketbook try **Mi Poron Bar and Restaurant** in a pleasant courtyard on Kaya Caracas 1. Menus featuring local cuisine usually include goat stew, soups, and gumbos. On Kaya Craane, **Shamballas** has an eclectic selection of Caribbean dishes, sushi, and tapas.

At Lac Bay, you'll find the **Kontiki Beach Club** at Lac Bay Resort. And on the waterfront in Kralendijk is **Karel's Beach Bar,** which attracts an always-interesting assortment of divers, locals, and yachties. There's live entertainment and dancing on weekends. Have dinner across the street at Zeezicht (same owners), where they serve seafood and local specialties.

Medical Facilities

Hospitaal San Francisco, with 72 beds, is located in Kralendijk. The island's emergency phone number is 191. There is an ambulance plane for emergencies, as well as a recompression chamber adjacent to the hospital. To contact either the hospital or the chamber, call (599) 717-8900. In case of a diving emergency call DAN (Divers Alert Network) at (919) 684-4DAN (4326) or (919) 684-8111.

California

Physical Characteristics of the Dive Area

WATER & WEATHER CONDITIONS

Visibility	
Catalina	*Adequate to Good*
Monterey	*Poor to Adequate*
Current and Surge	*Moderate*
Temperature	
Catalina	*Cold*
Monterey	*Numbing*
Storms	*Occasionally Stormy*

SITE CONDITIONS

Mooring Buoys	*Some*
Fishing, Collecting, and Hunting Restrictions	*Widespread Restrictions*
Ease of Access	*Convenient*
Boat Traffic/Diver Congestion	*Light*

MARINE LIFE

Abundance of Invertebrates	*Prolific*
Abundance of Vertebrates	*Abundant*
Abundance of Pelagic Life	*Abundant*
Health of Reef/Marine Life/ Marine Structure	*Healthy*

Kelp Cathedrals along the Coast

Diving is possible along practically the entire length of California, from San Diego all the way to Eureka. But there are two areas that stand out as exceptional places for recreational diving and for dive training. These are Catalina Island in the south and Monterey in the north. Underwater, magnificent forests of spreading kelp provide nourishment and refuge for a wide array of native marine life. Divers here will discover creatures ranging from the cute big-eyed harbor seals to tiny shimmering sardines.

The two jumping-off spots for Catalina are Long Beach and San Pedro, both just south of Los Angeles. Monterey is south of San Francisco and San Jose. Of course, there are many other excellent places to dive in California. I highly recommend Santa Barbara and the northern Channel Islands, Laguna Beach, and San Diego. Actually, Catalina is one of the eight Channel Islands in the southern group of four around Los Angeles.

Both Catalina Island and the Monterey/Carmel area provide calm conditions most of the year, and they are wonderful vacation spots even for those who feel that a morning shower is about as damp as they'd like to get. Both are exceptionally scenic and show, I think, some of the best of California's attributes—its mild climate, natural beauty, and interesting historical and cultural heritage.

As a diver, you'll have to work a little harder to see what California's waters have to offer. The water is cold—very cold. Divers here wear two-piece wetsuits, (a farmer-john and a jacket) each of 6.5-mm thickness, with a hood, gloves, and heavy booties. And many wear dry suits, which are even warmer. To make things more difficult, the visibility is frequently poor, and Pacific swells can create challenging surface conditions. Shore diving, especially, can be difficult, and even dangerous. But it's interesting—I overheard a dive instructor comment that she had moved from California to teach in Florida; now she was glad to be back in California. Why? She said that Californians are much better divers. It makes sense, since the diving environment is so much tougher.

Don't let the harsh conditions deter you. With the appropriate equipment, you'll stay warm and have an entrée into a truly enchanted world dominated by soaring forests of flowing kelp and the prolific marine life that it attracts and shelters. Of the two destinations, Catalina Island has the most comfortable diving. The visibility is a lot better than in the Monterey area, and the water is warmer. I've actually dived in Catalina without a hood and gloves, but would never dream of doing such a thing in Monterey.

Quick Stats for Catalina

Size Catalina is 21 miles long and 8 miles at its widest point. It covers about 76 square miles. Its highest elevation is 2,069 feet.

Location About 20 miles east of the Los Angeles area

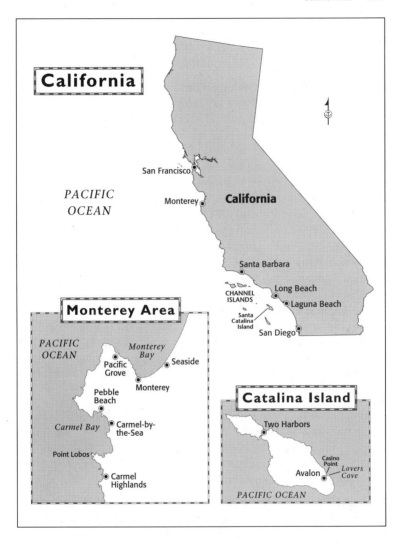

Air Temperature   Usually around 70°

Water Temperature   From 56° to 63° in winter; from 63° to 73° in summer

Underwater Visibility   Usually around 50 feet; occasionally up to 100 feet

Best Diving Months   Late summer and fall for best visibility and warmer temperatures

Planning the Trip

Getting to Catalina   Ferries leave from Long Beach, San Pedro, Newport Beach, and Dana Point. From LA International Airport, take the Best Shuttle, (800) 606-RIDE, to get to the harbor at either Long Beach or San Pedro.

The least expensive ferry transportation is with Catalina Cruises, which leaves from Long Beach and has service only to Avalon. This one is best if you're carrying a lot of gear. The trip takes only two hours, and the round-trip fare is $25. The company can also get you there in half the time (on a faster boat) for $35. Call (800) CATALINA; website: www.catalina cruises.com.

Catalina Express has high-speed catamarans that leave from Long Beach, San Pedro, and Dana Point, with service to Avalon and Two Harbors. The round-trip fare is $38. Call (800) 618-5533 or (310) 519-1212; website: www.catalinaexpress.com.

The Catalina Flyer leaves from Newport and has 75-minute service to Avalon. The round-trip fare is $38. Call (800) 830-7744 or (949) 673-5245; website: www.catalinainfo.com.

If you're in a big hurry, take a helicopter and get there in 15 minutes from Long Beach. Call Island Express Helicopter Service at (310) 510-2525; website: www.islandexpress.com.

Getting Around   There are no rental cars on the island; in fact, there are hardly any cars at all. However, there are taxis, and you can rent a golf cart in Avalon or simply walk. Some excellent tours are available through the Santa Catalina Island Company. Call (800) 626-5440; fax (310) 510-7254; website: www.catalina.com/scico.

Tourist Office   The Visitor's Bureau has an office on the Green Pier in Avalon. For a packet of information, write Catalina Visitor's Bureau, PO Box 217, Avalon, CA 90704. Call (310) 510-1520 (five-ten-fifteen-twenty) or fax (310) 510-7607; e-mail: info@visitcatalina.org. The excellent website is www.catalina.com.

Catalina Island

Only 20 miles from the frenetic world of Southern California is Santa Catalina Island, a pristine place of refuge where buffalo still graze on high bluffs overlooking blue Pacific waters. Beyond the little harbor town of

Kelp! I Need Somebody

Almost all California dive spots contain kelp beds to some extent, and unless you understand how to dive in kelp, it could cause anxiety. First, streamline your gear, and don't let anything dangle (you should be doing this all the time, anyway). Tape or tie down the loose ends of mask and fin straps if they are long and dangling.

Try to move slowly through the water and between the large trees of kelp, spreading them apart with your arms as you move along. If you don't kick much and move slowly with the rhythms of the water, you'll find that the strands will simply slide right off. It is very natural, however, for the stipes (stems) and blades (like leaves) to wrap around your tank, hoses, or fins; it just happens. When it does, just relax, keep still, and don't tug; frequently, the strand(s) will simply drift off with the movement of the water.

Also, masses of kelp always collect near the surface, so that's where it will be the thickest. Therefore, it helps to stay well below the surface and toward the rocky bottom, close to the holdfasts. These masses of stringy things look like roots, but holdfasts are actually what anchors the kelp to rocks. They don't gather water and nutrients at all.

Also, the most difficult situation to extricate yourself from is being entangled in kelp while you're coming to the surface in a vertical position. Always look up and around to make sure you're not coming up right in the middle of a thick bed of kelp. But if you do, remember that struggling usually makes it worse. Just relax and try to figure out the problem. If you have enough air, it might be best to go back down and find another spot to come up.

Low tide is absolutely the worst time to try to make your way through kelp on top of the water. Sometimes vast beds of the stuff spread far out on the surface. If you happen to find yourself in a situation where you have to make your way through such a bed, don't worry—it can be done. Known among divers here as the "Kelp Crawl," the technique goes like this: lie horizontally on top of the water and tuck anything in that might be dangling; then move your arms as if you're swimming the Australian crawl, pushing down the kelp while you're being propelled forward. This technique works surprisingly well—just make sure you don't hang vertically in the water.

(continued)

> ### Kelp! I Need Somebody (continued)
>
> Always try to reserve enough air to get back to shore from under water, and you'll avoid having to swim through kelp on the surface. If you do become entangled in kelp, the situation usually gets worse if you tug on it and try to fight it. Calmly try to find out where the tangle is and move as little as possible. Stay neutrally buoyant, without kicking. Locate the culprit and either pull gently out of the way or try to snap the stipe in half—grab it with both hands, fold it over, and break it. Or use your knife. Dive buddies should stay in view of one another and be ready to help the other out. A signaling device (like a tank banger) is a good idea. If you can't locate your buddy, be prepared to take off your scuba unit, leaving your regulator in your mouth, so you can clear the kelp yourself.

Avalon and another small resort and marina at Two Harbors, most development on these 48,000 or so acres consists of hiking trails and campgrounds.

At one time the Wrigley family—the guys who started America's love affair with chewing gum—owned the entire island. Fortunately, these were people of vision, with a strong interest in conservation coupled with philanthropic tendencies. Rather than selling the land and watching the inexorable progression of condos and high rises, they turned most of it over to the Catalina Island Conservancy in 1974. The Conservancy was charged with preserving the native plants and animals, and managing the open-space lands for the pure enjoyment of the island's scenic beauty and for its controlled recreational purposes.

I can report that the Conservancy has done a superb job. It maintains the interior roads and the airport, and provides a ranger service on land and along the shore. The service not only protects the endemic plants and animals, it provides excellent tours of the island. On one tour I saw bald eagles flying overhead and a native fox trotting through the brush. All this, just a few miles from one of the world's largest metropolitan centers.

THE UNDERWATER SCENE
Health Score Card

Over the years, commercial fishing around Southern California and Catalina Island has taken a toll on certain species. Several years ago, native Randy Bombard told me that the whales' feeding grounds, for instance, have been wiped out. "As a kid, I used to watch the whales scoop up mouthfulls of squid by the ton after they spawned; now the squid fishers have bright lights all around their boats, which attract the squid. So they catch the squid before they've spawned, which reduces the population even more. They don't replenish themselves. The further ignominy is that the squid usually aren't even used for food—they're ground up for fertilizer!" Randy says that as a result, he rarely sees whales anymore.

The beautiful and nonaggressive blue shark, also, is in serious decline, and all species of abalone have been wiped out in Southern California. Fortunately, there are pockets of preservation, such as the one at Casino Point, where divers can still see enormous sheephead, triggerfish, garibaldi, calico bass, convict perch, and rock wrasse. Octopus, lobster, bat rays, and horn sharks all seem to know they are protected here.

The area has few mooring buoys, so anchor damage occurs to the marine floor and the kelp forest. Permanent moorings would eliminate such anchoring problems. A mooring program was begun in February 1998; about 60 sites are targeted, but the schedule depends largely on fund-raising efforts.

Diving Conditions

Conditions here are generally excellent for California waters. Indeed, this is about as good as it gets. Most of the diving takes place on the east side, which is more protected. The shoreline is scalloped by numerous small coves, which provide even more protection. Avalon's cove is typically very calm, and the visibility is normally around 50 feet, frequently better. Within the Casino Point Underwater Park, the vis is noticeably better mid-week when there are not so many divers.

Recommended Level of Experience

Most of Catalina's sites are perfect for any level of diver. In fact, it is one of the most popular training sites in California. The Casino Underwater Park is ideal for showing new divers a variety of environments. It has shallow rocky reefs, both shallow and deep kelp forests, a deep drop-off, some wrecks, and even a nice flat sandy bottom. This variety is also ideal for teaching underwater navigation, search and salvage, and deep diving—all part of the advanced certification.

Catalina also has some challenging sites, such as *Farnsworth Banks,* on the west side, and *Little Farnsworth,* on the east. These are deep dives and therefore best for advanced divers. Strong currents are also typical in some areas. Diving with one of the local operators is the best way to make sure you'll dive the sites that are best for your level of ability.

Great Dive Sites

Avalon Area   On most days, bright rays of sunshine shoot through the kelp forest in Catalina's *Casino Underwater Park.* To be close to the rocky bottom and look up through the vast illuminated forest is practically a religious experience. Rarely have I seen anything more gorgeous. The effect is absolutely calming and otherworldly. Moreover, the life forms that make their homes among the kelp are prolific. There's no chance of getting bored in these forests! From the holdfasts, along the stipes and on the blades, there are little critters everywhere. Seeking shelter and nutrients below the kelp canopy are top snails, sea stars, sponges, sea urchins, hermit crabs, and nudibranchs, for starters. Giant kelpfish hide among the kelp structure, blending in and swaying along with it. Rockfish prowl stealthily, and cigar-shaped señoritas dart quickly through the forest, picking off small invertebrates.

One of the more beautiful fish here is the brilliant orange garibaldi, which is California's state fish, and therefore protected. These are feisty and fiercely territorial damselfish. If you get too close to their nests, they'll certainly let you know. As a result, they're fairly easy to photograph. The males of the species protect the nests, and they are extremely fastidious housekeepers. It's fun to watch them cleaning up and removing unwanted bits of rock and algae. Juveniles have blue spots all over their bodies. The pink and grey male sheephead is another gorgeous fish, and it grows to huge proportions here in the park. The greenish colored opaleye is another distinctive fish, this one with blue-green eyes. These three species—garibaldi, sheephead, and opaleye—are rarely found up in colder northern California waters.

Kelp bass, blacksmiths, and a variety of rockfish all thrive here. Schools of mackerel usually get the attention of hungry barracuda. Among the bottom dwellers are moray eels, speckled horn sharks, lobsters, decorator crabs, and octopus.

The *Underwater Park* is where I first saw what looked like fish either kissing or giving mouth-to-mouth resuscitation. Their mouths were gaping wide and pressed against each another. They were anything but kissing, however. Ned DeLoach, the author of the excellent resource *Reef Fish Behavior*, explained to me that this is an aggressive stance, where male fish are striving to establish rank, usually within a harem.

If possible, try to dive here midweek when there are fewer people. Because the site is so popular for training, it does get crowded. Midweek, the visibility is greatly improved and you'll see a lot more marine life. On one particularly beautiful midweek dive here, I saw a group of eight bat rays flying over the sandy bottom.

For years, divers had to enter and exit the water here over huge slippery boulders. It was messy. Getting bashed against the rocks when the water was rough was just part of diving the Casino; in fact, I almost destroyed a camera housing that way. Fortunately, those days are gone. Now a walkway and stairs make access much safer.

The Casino, of course, is the beautiful round building that was never a real casino. You can rent tanks and equipment on the pier, or from one of the dive shops fronting the beach, and use a little pushcart to take your stuff to the point. It's about a 15- to 20-minute walk. Behind the Casino is a huge parking area with plenty of room to spread out gear and change, and there are large lockers for storing gear. An air station also operates in back, where you can get your tank fills. There are restrooms in the Casino, with outside access, and a waterside restaurant. If you dive at night here (which is an excellent idea), you can have dinner outdoors at the Descanso Beach Club, right next to the Casino. It's just a short walk and very convenient. For night dives, be sure to leave a lantern on shore that is clearly visible from the water. Also, it's best to have someone stay shore-side during your dive, in case you need assistance.

The entire park is roped off, to keep out boaters and fishers, so you don't have to worry about bumping into a dangerous prop when surfacing. The underwater terrain slopes down from a rocky bank to about 90 feet at the outer edge, and most of the area is covered in beautiful kelp forest. Along the right edge of the park in 60 to 90 feet of water is the wreck *Sue-Jac,* a 70-foot-long freighter that's on a steep bank and covered with kelp and gorgonians. Don't let your expectations get too high; there's not much here, since storms have really torn it up. You can find it easily by locating the far right buoy and following the anchor chain down. Smaller wrecks are scattered about the park. On the left side of the park is a flat sandy area with a depth of about 60 feet. Navigation is fairly simple here because of these features.

Two terrific dive spots near one another on this side of the island are *Little Farnsworth* and *Jewfish Point,* both with exciting narcosis-producing depths. You'll need a boat to get to these. I went out with Jon Hardy's Argo Diving Service. Jon writes the gear reviews for Rodale's *Scuba Diving* magazine. His divemaster, Jason, led us down the anchor line at *Little Farnsworth* to about 40 feet. After a short swim we saw the enormous outline of a rocky pinnacle, with smaller flanking pinnacles. After getting closer, we could see that every inch was covered with invertebrates. Jason signaled to us to follow him through a cut in the rock, just wide enough for a single diver to go through. Within the cut were flowing sea fans and other gorgonians. We made our way around the pinnacle at about 90 feet, then descended closer to the base at about 127 feet. At that point, a large California electric ray soared right over my head. "Don't touch!" signaled my dive-instructor husband—"dangerous!" I settled for a shot of its nice white belly. At that depth in mid-November the water temperature was a chilly 59°. And, yes, narcosis definitely set in. Our shallower second dive was at *Jewfish Point,* which can also be a deep dive. Here we found plenty of bladder kelp, a moray eel, some lobster, and another fish couple in mouth-to-mouth aggression.

On the rough windward side of Catalina, a dive site called *Farnsworth Bank* gets raves. I have never experienced it, but can tell you that it is an ecological reserve where no coral or geologic specimens can be taken. An undersea mountain here reaches within 55 feet of the surface and is covered with rare cold-water purple coral. Unfortunately, it is so rough on this side that boats rarely venture out here. This is for advanced divers only.

Two Harbors Area The skinnier eastern side of the island, around *Isthmus Cove,* has a nice array of dive sites, with depths up to 130 feet. The guano-covered *Ship Rock* stands 70 feet above the surface. Below, a sheer rock wall descends very deep. You'll see greater numbers of schooling fish in this area, as well as sea lions gliding along the wall. Also look for bat rays and angel sharks. On the rocks are beautiful soft corals and anemones in various shades of red, pink, and orange. The remains of the 100-foot, 95-year-old schooner *Diosa del Mar,* are nearby. These "rock" dives provide nice oases from currents that can get pretty strong. *Bird Rock* is another popular spot, which has a reeflike area and a wall drop-off.

Blue Cavern Point is a rocky promontory with a small wall that plummets beyond 100 feet. Currents sweep the area, keeping the water clear. A profusion of bright gorgonian fans grow throughout the area, and in vivid colors of yellow, purple, red, and orange—a real kaleidoscope. A couple of caves here extend way back into the island, and boats can actually go inside if conditions permit. Underwater are smaller caves. The wall is absolutely buzzing with marine life; you'll find greenling, rock fish, kelp fish, sculpin, and bright blue gobies. Morays and lobster hunker inside crevices. Cup corals, nudibranchs, and starfish add even more color.

Snorkeling

Lover's Cove Marine Reserve is a special cove—the next one over (east) from Avalon Bay—that's just for snorkelers and swimmers. Diving is not allowed, nor is fishing, anchoring, or taking any marine life. Catalina Snorkeling Adventures is on the shore and can rent snorkeling equipment and lead tours. Their phone number is (877) SNORKEL. There is also snorkeling from the Descanso Beach Club, on the other side (west) of Avalon Bay, where you can also rent snorkeling equipment. Phone (310) 510-1226.

Marine Park

The Catalina Island Conservancy maintains the Casino Point Underwater Park, a marine reserve off-limits to boating, fishing, and collecting. The corals and geologic specimens at Farnsworth Bank Ecological Reserve are protected.

DIVE SERVICES & PACKAGES ON CATALINA ISLAND

Argo Diving Service operates a Sea Way 25-foot, six-passenger vessel that can be chartered for $500 per day. The price includes a two-person crew, guided underwater tours (if desired), tanks and air fills, weights, lunch, beverages, and ground transportation. An open-ocean marine life encounter is also offered for $600 per day. On these open-ocean dives, the crew chums for sharks, but if sharks do not appear (they're being wiped out by commercial fishing), the chum is dropped in other areas, where divers can observe bat rays, sea lions, and morays. Argo Diving Service also offers private instruction with NAUI, PADI, and SSI certifications, and numerous specialty courses. Phone (888) SCUBA 99 or (310) 510-2208; fax (310) 510-2337; e-mail: scubalab1@aol.com.

Retail Sales: *None*	**Dive Boat Comfort:** *Good*
Rentals: *None*	**On-Board Facilities**
Scuba Training: *Moderate*	**for Photographers:** *Good*
Photo Services: *None*	

Catalina Scuba Luv (a PADI Resort) owns and operates the *King Neptune* and *Prince Neptune* dive boats. On the 32-foot *Prince Neptune,* divers will receive a guided tour through kelp forest, have a complimentary lunch during the surface interval, and get fresh towels. A videographer usually comes along, and tapes can be purchased after the dives. The second dive is often a special eel-feeding experience. Trips are designed for photographers, single divers, divers with special needs, newer divers, and "rusty" divers. Shark dives are also among their trip offerings. Hot indoor showers are available onboard, as well as camera rinse tanks, camera racks, and a soda bar. The shop repairs, sells, and rents dive gear, including underwater cameras. They also offer all levels of PADI instruction, and this is a 5-Star IDC where you can turn pro. You can get your Enriched Air Nitrox here, rent rebreathers and dry suits, and have instruction for all. Scuba Luv also offers photo and video classes. Their *King Neptune* is a live-aboard that takes up to 12 passengers. See the section on Live-Aboards for more information. Call (800) 262-DIVE or (310) 510-2350; fax (310) 510-0821; e-mail: prneptune@ aol.com; website: www.scubaluv.com.

Retail Sales: *Extensive*

Rentals: *Extensive*

Scuba Training: *Extensive*

Photo Services: *Extensive*

Dive Boat Comfort: *Excellent*

On-Board Facilities for
Photographers: *Superior*

Catalina Divers Supply (a PADI Resort) has a new 46-foot Newton with flybridge, which can accommodate 49 divers but is limited to 25. The boat features three showers, a marine head, camera table, and rinse tanks. Another 42-foot vessel has a shower, marine head, galley, and freshwater rinse. Two-tank morning dives and all-day three-tank dives are scheduled, and the latter includes lunch. Introductory and guided dives and snorkel tours are also offered. The shop has a full line of rental gear, and also rents tanks and weight belts for shore diving. Catalina Divers Supply has two locations: one on the Green Pier and the other down at the Casino, where they rent and fill tanks, rent an assortment of other gear, and sell snacks. They also rent handy dive carts at the pier. Certification classes are available through NAUI, PADI, and SSI. Call (800) 353-0330 or (310) 510-0330; fax (310) 510-0695; website: www.catalina.com/cds.

Retail Sales: *Adequate*

Rentals: *Adequate*

Scuba Training: *Moderate*

Photo Services: *Limited*

Dive Boat Comfort: *Good*

On-Board Facilities for
Photographers: *Superior*

Catalina West End Dive Center is located at Two Harbors, down the hill from the Banning House Lodge. This is a PADI Resort with equipment rentals, dive and snorkel boat trips (on a 46-foot dive boat), and instruction. Dive sites are just a few minutes from the harbor. You can also dive right off the beach here and stay at either the campground or the Banning House Lodge. Resort packages are available. Ocean kayaks are also available for rent. Phone (800) 785-8425 or (310) 510-2800; website: www.catalina.com/twoharbors.

Retail Sales: *None*

Rentals: *Adequate*

Scuba Training: *Limited*

Photo Services: *Limited*

Dive Boat Comfort: *Adequate*

On-Board Facilities for
Photographers: *Good*

WHERE TO STAY ON CATALINA ISLAND

Hotel Atwater ★ is just half a block to the little beach in Avalon, and more importantly for divers, it has easy access to the underwater park behind the Casino. Most rooms (26) have been renovated, but it has older, tired rooms at budget prices. The new rooms are air-conditioned, the old ones are not, and can be stifling in summer. There is a storage area for dive gear, and the hotel provides baggage service to and from the boat. Dive packages are offered with the Santa Catalina Island Company and include round-trip ferry transportation, and such options as the Undersea "semi-sub" Tour and the Inland Motor Tour. Another weekend package includes a full-day boat dive, shore diving at Casino Point, round-trip transportation on Catalina Express, and two nights lodging in a budget room—from $218 to $234 per person. Phone (800) 414-2742 or (310) 510-2500; fax (310) 510-7254; website: catalina.com/scico.

At the more remote area of Two Harbors—a wonderful, peaceful place—the **Banning House Lodge** ★ ★ ★ provides large attractive rooms and terrific views. There are only 11 rooms and most have patios. From my room here I could see both harbors down below, and palm trees nicely framed the view. A large, rustic living room features a huge stone fireplace. The lodge provides free transportation from the boat dock and offers diving packages. There is a restaurant (Harbor Reef) just down the hill, and a general store near the dive shop. The weekend package rate for two nights in the lodge with a day of diving, a day of kayaking, and round-trip transportation on the Catalina Express from San Pedro is $174 to $235 per person, depending upon the season. Call (800) 685-8425 or (310) 510-2800; website: www.catalina.com/twoharbors.

Pavilion Lodge ★ is another popular place for divers, but it's a bit farther than the others from the Underwater Park. Rooms are all situated around a central garden area and swimming pool, and have sliding glass doors that lead outside. A diver package includes a full-day boat dive, shore diving at Casino Point, round-trip transportation on Catalina Express, and two nights lodging—from $229 to $353 on the weekend, per person. Phone (800) 414-2742 or (310) 510-2500; fax (310) 510-7254; website: catalina.com/scico.

Seaport Village Inn ★ has a convenient facility for divers, in close proximity to the Casino Underwater Park. You'll have to walk one block up a hill, but it's still closer than many of the other lodgings. Most of the rooms are spacious, and there is a nice variety. There are one- and two-bedroom units and also units with full kitchens. Since many of these connect, you can combine several rooms with a full kitchen and living room, which is nice for groups. There's a gear rinse area and storage lockers and an outdoor spa. A courtesy shuttle provides dockside transportation. Phone (800) 222-8254 or (310) 510-0344; fax (310) 510-1156; e-mail: seaport@cata linacatalina.com; website: www.catalinacatalina.com.

Live-Aboard

Catalina Scuba Luv runs the *King Neptune,* which takes up to 12 passengers. It has a subsurface swim platform, sun deck, on-deck shower, gear storage, live game well, deck freezer, camera rinse system, full galley, interior seating, TV and VCR, and unlimited beverage bar. There are three air compressors on board, and soft weights are provided. Below deck are several berth/dinettes, showers, sinks, and heads. Call (800) 262-DIVE or (310) 510-2350.

LIFE ON CATALINA ISLAND

Of the Channel Islands, Catalina is the only one with any towns or visitor services other than basic camping. Still, simply journeying to this island seems like a grand adventure. Getting down to the pier, anticipating the ride across, then settling in. If you're like me, you want to be outside, enjoying the sunshine and fresh air. Although some boats scoot over really fast, as far as I'm concerned, a relaxed two-hour trip is just fine. One of the thrills that hopefully you'll have is being escorted by dolphins along the way. They'll race and jump alongside as if they're trained. It's great fun and sets the tone for the rest of the trip. When we return, it's usually dark, so we'll bring a deck of cards or some dominoes to entertain ourselves. Sometimes the crossing can be rough, so if you're prone to seasickness, better take the meds.

Some ferries (not all) will dock at **Two Harbors,** up on the west end, otherwise known as "the isthmus." This is a gorgeous spot, where the two perfect harbors are separated by a narrow strip of land. Watch the sun come up over one harbor, then set on the other! Overlooking it all are hiking trails and grazing buffalo. The Banning House Lodge is the perfect escape from the frenetic pace, just 20 miles away. In fact, you can see the lights of Long Beach and LA from here at night.

The facilities at Two Harbors include a campground—call (888) 510-7979—the lodge, a store, West End Dive Center, and restaurant. **Kayaks** can be rented from the dive shop. The campground has tent cabins and equipment rentals, so you won't have to bring everything in. You can also kayak from Avalon by renting at the Descanso Beach Club, where guided kayak trips are provided. Snorkel gear and wetsuits can be rented too. Call (310) 510-1226.

Of course, **Avalon** is the center of attention on the island. Cruise ships on their way to Mexico stop by and let passengers off for a few hours before pulling out again. There are shops, restaurants, motels, hotels, lodges, and B&Bs. But it's all very quaint. Actually, Avalon is a pleasant reminder of the small beach communities that existed on the mainland during pre-World War II days. All along the beachfront you'll see colorful ceramic tiles, with images of birds and fish, that were made here on the island around the turn of the century. You won't see cars, though, since these are restricted. Only certain businesses are allowed to run anything except golf carts. It's a lot of fun to see some of these carts dressed up like corvettes or surreys with-the-fringe-on-top.

The beautiful white art deco **Casino** for many years was a ballroom, which hosted some of the famous big bands. It has never seen any gambling at all. When my parents were in high school in Long Beach, they loved taking the ferry over here for dances. Now the former ballroom hosts a variety of community events, and the Catalina Island Museum is inside.

Oceanside, Avalon is a relaxing place where you can sit on a bench and look out to sea, with seagulls squawking overhead. Watch boats pull in and out of the harbor and breathe some of that clean fresh air. Nondivers would enjoy the semisubmersible **Nautilus.** The environment tour and the fun narration about the marine life are really fascinating. Even divers would enjoy it, and definitely your kids. It's a good way to get them interested in our sport. The company is Catalina Adventure Tours at (310) 510-2888; website: www.catalinaadventuretours.com.

When you're pushing scuba tanks over to the Casino, you might notice a sign for the **Avalon Tuna Club.** Founded in 1889, it was the very first fishing club in the United States and attracted the likes of Zane Grey, Cecil B. De Mille, John Wayne, and even Winston Churchill. In 1924 **buffalo** were brought over for the making of a film. There was an attempt to round them all up and ship them off, but thank goodness it was not entirely successful.

Definitely take an **island jeep tour** if you possibly can, and you'll see some of these beautiful big guys, as well as a number of indigenous animals like the Catalina Island fox. The Island Conservancy runs these tours with a trained naturalist guide, and they are terrific. I toured with Jan, who grew up in the Casino—her dad was the caretaker! All proceeds benefit the Conservancy's efforts to preserve and protect the island. Call (310) 510-1421.

Dining and Entertainment

The **Green Pier** is a fun place for sitting on barstools outdoors and eating fish 'n' chips. Somehow, they just taste a lot better outdoors. For dining with waiter service, try the **Ristorante Villa Portofino** (next door to the hotel at 111 Crescent), which has wonderful Italian food.

Around the Casino area are several fun places to eat or to sit outside and have a cold one. There's the **Casino Dock Café** for either breakfast or lunch. **Luau Larry's** (509 Crescent Avenue) is another place on the water with patio seating. At night they have live music and dancing. The **Descanso Beach Club,** at the little cove adjacent to the Casino, has a bar right on the beach and serves lunch daily. On weekends they have a night-time barbecue.

For a great view of the bay and some equally great seafood, go to **Armstrong's Fish Market and Seafood Restaurant.** It features mesquite broiled selections, fresh sashimi, clams, oysters, and mussels. You'll find it at 306 Crescent Avenue.

There is undoubtedly some fun nightlife here, but frankly, I'm usually so beat after a day of diving that I'm not exactly Ms. Party-Animal, so I'm not the expert. It should be easy enough to find out, though. My evening excitement is having an ice-cream cone, strolling around for a little while, then collapsing into bed.

Medical Facilities

The local hospital phone is (310) 510-0700. In an emergency, call 911. The University of Southern California (USC) operates a hyperbaric chamber near Two Harbors. In case of a diving emergency call DAN (Divers Alert Network) at (919) 684-4DAN (4326) or (919) 684-8111.

Monterey

Monterey, and specifically the Breakwater area in Monterey, is northern California's primary dive training ground. It's an exciting place to be, with divers from all over northern California donning wetsuits and heavy weight belts, launching boats, practicing navigation skills, getting predive briefings and intently taking quizzes. While all this is going on, the sea lions are honking on the long rocky breakwater or frolicking among delighted kayakers; the otters are plopped in the middle of kelp beds, floating along on their backs; and seagulls are on the watch for someone's leftover sandwich.

Beautiful wind-swept Monterey pines bend over and point like windsocks away from the prevailing winds. Mornings are usually fogged in, but the sun gradually starts to show itself around noon and is a welcoming sight when it is full-force. Because these waters are cold, keeping warm is an important task at the Breakwater, so it's fortunate that the facilities are excellent.

Above water, Monterey is a scenic resort area with rocky cliffs, sandy beaches, and shoreline parks. Accommodations range from budget motels to upscale Cannery Row hotels and quaint B&Bs. Your nondiving companions will love it. They can kayak in the cove, explore Fisherman's Wharf, the historical center, and Cannery Row. And they'll certainly want to visit the Monterey Bay Aquarium.

QUICK STATS FOR MONTEREY

Location   About 125 miles south of San Francisco

Air Temperature   The climate is temperate (around 70°), never getting very hot or very cold. Expect mornings to be foggy; around 11 a.m., the fog usually lifts and the sun appears.

Water Temperature   High 50s in summer; average is 53°.

Underwater Visibility   Averages around 30 feet

Best Diving Months   Late summer and early fall

PLANNING THE TRIP

Getting to Monterey and Getting Around   The Monterey Peninsula Airport is six miles from downtown Monterey and is served by airlines from San Francisco, San Jose, and Los Angeles. Most visitors fly into one of these larger airports, rent a car, and drive to Monterey. From Monterey, San Jose International Airport is 60 miles north (phone (408) 277-4759); Oakland International Airport is 115 miles north (phone (650) 876-2377); and San Francisco International Airport is 120 miles north (phone (510) 577-4000). When driving, from US 101 take Highway 68 west to Highway 1, if you're coming from the south. If coming from the north, from US 101 take Highway156 to Highway 1.

Weather   Marine Forecast (831) 656-1725

Tourist Office   Monterey County Convention & Visitors Bureau, (877) 666-8373; fax (831) 648-5373; website: www.877monterey.com.

THE UNDERWATER SCENE

Make a mental image of the Grand Canyon, then visualize it underwater. That's what you get when you dive Monterey; this canyon is more than 10,000 feet deep. Of course, you don't really see it that way, since the sites are on the edge of the canyon in shallow depths; also, the visibility is insufficient to get long, Caribbean-like vistas. But this type of structure is important for harboring life as large as giant squid and endangered blue whales, and as small as plankton, the basis for this healthy ecosystem.

Different habitats exist here, but the kelp forest is the one you'll encounter most often. Giant kelp supports a huge variety of life, from the tiny kelp crab to hefty blue rockfish. The giant kelp grows in water about 100 feet deep or less, and also grows extremely fast—up to two feet per day!

It's anchored to the rocky bottom with holdfasts and soars toward the sunlight with the help of buoyant bulbs called pneumatocysts. The flat leaflike blades grow from them. On the surface of the water, the kelp collects in a dense canopy, which gets even denser at low tide. It's that canopy that you would want to avoid because it's a big nuisance to struggle through it. Be sure to leave yourself plenty of air to be able to get back to shore or to the boat without having to swim on the surface through kelp beds.

Underwater, though, the kelp is gorgeous, especially on a sunny day when sunlight filters through the forests of gracefully waving blades. Along the entire length of the kelp plant, from its rocky base to the surface, are fish and invertebrates, all part of the community. This habitat also teems with marine life. You'll see billowy white metridium anemones and little strawberry anemones, sea stars and enormous sun stars, sea hares and gum boot chitons. Abalone also cling to the rocks, but don't touch! You cannot collect these delicacies on scuba.

Just underneath the spreading kelp canopy and close to the surface are all sorts of creatures that you won't see deeper. Kelp crabs and juvenile fish live among the giant kelp blades, sheltered from predators. Schools of slightly larger fish also swim under the canopy. Try to find the giant kelpfish, which are easily missed because they look so much like the blades. Farther down in midwater are kelp and olive rockfish, schools of blacksmith, senoritas, mackerels, and smelt. You'll even see sardines, which were nearly wiped out from these waters after Steinbeck wrote *Cannery Row*. At certain times of the year, jellyfish collect around the stalks.

If you happen to feel as though someone or something is watching you, that could very well be true. Cute, wide-eyed harbor seals frequently observe divers from a distance, hiding among the kelp. Then they might swoop down and playfully hang out with you. I've had the young ones grab my fins in their mouths and play tug of war. Kris, my dive instructor-husband, for some reason seems to have an enviable rapport with these guys. He'll actually scratch them under their chins; then they'll roll over for more scratches on their bellies! It's only the grey speckled harbor seals that will do this. The sea lions are not as friendly.

Down on the rocky bottom of the kelp forest, there are often cabezon and lingcod. Cabezon are brownish or reddish and are noted for their large head and "stalks" rising just behind their eyes. They eat crab, shrimp, and molluscs. The sleeker lingcod are spotted, gray to green in color, have a longer head and jaw, and eat other fish.

Health Score Card

Most of this area is extremely healthy, although boating, fishing, and near-shore dive training have certainly taken a toll. Nevertheless, sanctuary protection helps ensure that the area remains healthy. There was good news in September 2000, when Monterey Bay became off-limits to commercial gill-net fishing for halibut. These nets entangle and kill many species besides halibut, such as common murres, sea otters, and harbor porpoises.

Diving Conditions

In late summer and early fall the conditions are the best. Kelp growth will be at its thickest, and since the kelp forest serves as a nursery for marine life, you'll see the greatest number of species in abundance. Calm weather at this time brings the best visibility, and the water is warmest, reaching its peak in late summer and continuing for a while into the fall. At other times of the year, plankton bloom reduces visibility and storms stir up the sea bottom and make surface conditions miserable. Count on the visibility to be anywhere from 10 feet to 45 feet.

To dive here you'll need a well-fitting heavy wet suit. The usual ensemble is a farmer john worn under a long-sleeve step-in jacket that comes down almost to the knees. Each piece should be 6.5 mm in thickness. You'll also need a close-fitting hood with no big gaps, warm booties, and gloves. The alternative is to wear a dry suit, but they require some instruction and quite a few dives before you begin to feel comfortable in them. Wearing a dry suit is like having on a giant BCD, since the entire suit fills with air from a separate inflator hose attached to your regulator's first stage. You can wear warm underwear, since everything stays dry, and the air that's pumped in adds even more warmth. On the downside, dry suits require a lot more weight to counteract the extra buoyancy, and you won't have as much mobility.

Recommended Level of Experience

Any level of diver would enjoy this area, and it is perfect for training. The more challenging conditions actually tend to produce better divers. Shore diving, however, can range from tricky to dangerous, depending on the area, and it's a good idea to have a site orientation with a divemaster before making your first one. To avoid shore diving, try to hook up with one of the dive operations listed here, which have comfortable, fast boats. It's safer and you'll be able to get to deeper, healthier areas with a lot better visibility.

Great Dive Sites

An easy site to reach from the Breakwater (more description follows) is the *Metridium Field,* in 40 to 60 feet of water. I love these gorgeous anemones with their billowy white plumes and long-necked tubes. Usually they grow in large colonies and appear very regal, perched high atop the rocky pinnacles. This particular colony is quite large, but since visibility is usually limited to 20 or 30 feet, you don't exactly get panoramic views. Nevertheless, the site is beautiful. You'll find it a few hundred yards northwest of the Breakwater. This is a long way out, so access by boat is best.

Deep Hopkins, Inner Chase Reef, Outer Chase Reef, and *The Pinnacles* are all very popular boat dives in deep water where the visibility is improved over the inshore sites, and pelagic visitors more numerous. *Deep Hopkins* is the site closest to the Breakwater launching area and is considered an advanced site, due to strong currents. The large boulders here are decorated with beautiful metridium anemones, harbor wolf eels, and a wealth of invertebrates.

Chase Reef is farther from the Breakwater; it's west of Lover's Point and north of Pt. Pinos. *Inner Chase* has a rocky topography at depths of 40 to 60 feet; *Outer Chase* has a deep rock drop-off to beyond 100 feet. Conditions here can be dicey, with frequent swells and strong current, especially at *Outer Chase.* Surge is generally the problem at *Inner Chase.* Nevertheless, the charter boats frequently come here when conditions are good, and neither is considered an advanced site. However, I would rate *Outer Chase* as an intermediate site. The tapestry of invertebrates here is amazing and includes the imposing metridium anemones. Large fish and pelagic visitors are common. This is where I saw a beautiful leopard shark cruise right by me, at about waist level in 40 feet of water. These sharks are not at all threatening.

The Pinnacles (again, Inner and Outer) is way around the peninsula in Carmel Bay, and about three-quarters of a mile from Pescadero Point. It's part of the Carmel Bay Ecological Reserve. The actual pinnacles of the outer area are quite a bit deeper. I personally like this area a lot because it combines extremely scenic shoreline vistas with terrific diving. You can see golfers taking swings on the Pebble Beach golf course while you're suiting up. The invertebrate life is truly amazing. You'll see the rocks completely covered with sea slugs and nudibranchs, strawberry anemones, and other anemones in a kaleidoscope of colors. There are also cup corals here. Every now and then you can spot a wolf eel curiously checking you out, and the waters are teeming with schools of blue and olive rockfish underneath the kelp canopy, and other rockfish closer to the rocky bottom. Large lingcod and cabezon will be waiting for you at depth. If you're heading back to the Breakwater, it will be a long excursion but well worth it.

Monterey Beach Dives

Monterey's most popular beach dive is at the *Breakwater Cove Marina,* on the northeast side of Monterey Harbor, where the services are excellent and the conditions generally nice and calm. For these reasons, the *Breakwater* is the primary site in northern California used by instructors for classes.

The name for this area is San Carlos Beach Park, but call it that and no one will have a clue what you're talking about.

The entry here is very easy, with a short set of stairs leading down to a nice wide sandy beach. Visibility isn't always the greatest, but this is a protected location, and the surf is generally manageable.

Look for the kelp beds and that's where you'll find most of the interesting marine life. You'll usually want to kick out about to where the jetty starts to bend, then drop down to the rocks. Sea lions and diving cormorants might come around to check you out. It can also be interesting to explore the rocks around the jetty itself, since these provide nice habitat for octopus, monkeyface eels, nudibranchs, brittlestars, crabs, and such.

For directions from Highway 1 driving south, take the Del Monte exit; follow Del Monte through the tunnel and take the first right fork; then take the next right to the lower Breakwater parking lot. Everything a diver needs is close at hand: two launch ramps, a place to buy food (Casey's Deli and Market), including hefty sandwiches and hot soup; showers, toilets, and changing areas; a dive shop and fill station (Aquarius); a superb underwater photo shop (Backscatter); and parking for boat trailers and cars. Kayak Tours and Rental is also down here. A large parking area is just above all this, and is close to picnic tables and nice grassy areas. *It helps to have a lot of quarters for parking and for the showers. Also, bring a tarp to keep all your gear clean.*

Because this is such a popular training site, it can get pretty crowded, especially on weekends. Nevertheless, it's always a lot of fun, with divers constantly running into old friends.

Just a short distance up the beach from the Breakwater is another very popular dive, also used for training, called *McAbee Beach*. Again, the entrance is easy, from a nice sandy beach that generally has light surf. *McAbee Beach* fronts the famous Cannery Row, between Prescott and Hoffman Streets next to El Torito restaurant. Pay parking is across the street, so to save a lot of lugging, it's best to unload your equipment before parking (and keep someone with it). This area is close to the Monterey Bay Aquarium, so the lot fills up quickly. Also, there are restrictions regarding hours of operation and the unloading and loading of gear. Again, kick out for a while, then drop down before reaching the kelp beds. You might notice some old pipes that harken back to the days of Steinbeck. This area was really bustling with sardine canning until the sardine population crashed in the 1950s. Back then, the catch was literally pumped into the cannery through these submerged pipes. Now they make handy habitats for all sorts of marine creatures. Keep watch for colorful nudibranchs. It's likely that you'll encounter some playful harbor seals and perhaps some lounging sea otters in their best tummy-up position.

Over in Pacific Grove, *Lover's Point* is another popular shore-entry area that is acceptable for all skill levels. The depths range from 20 to 60 feet; visibility is usually 20 to 40 feet. The site is located at the end of Ocean View Boulevard and is within the limits of the Pacific Grove Marine Gardens Fish Refuge. No invertebrate may be taken in waters above 60 feet. There is a large parking area close to the water. Two small sandy beaches are on the east side of the point and have a few stairs leading down to the sand. Offshore are rocky pinnacles that reach from 10 to 20 feet, and here is where you'll find a tapestry of invertebrates, small fish, and octopus. Harbor seals enjoy cavorting here, also.

Marine Park

In 1992 the Monterey Bay and surrounding Central California coastal water became the largest National Marine Sanctuary. It spans over 5,300 square miles from San Francisco to San Simeon and its boundaries extend from the high tide line to 50 miles offshore. Due to the reduction in the sea otter population, sanctuary regulations require that kayakers and divers remain at least 100 yards away. Also, remember that sea lion pups alone on the beach generally are not abandoned animals and should be left alone.

Some areas of the sanctuary allow spearfishing, which is regulated by the California Department of Fish and Game. Hunters will need a fishing license and should take only what they can use, within the limits of the law. In the winter months, male lingcod and cabezon guard nests of the female's eggs. At these times, males are very territorial and will not leave the nest. This makes them easy targets. Hunters should be mindful of good conservation practices and refrain from taking lingcod and cabezon during the winter. Let's allow these species to increase in number.

In 1995 I read in the *San Francisco Chronicle* some very good news—the return of the sardines to northern California waters. In 1936 the sardine catch was at its peak, but due to overfishing, these tiny schooling fish almost disappeared. Fortunately, the numbers are increasing, and commercial fishing crews are bringing up perch and also catching sardines in their nets.

Speaking of commercial fishers, in September 2000 state regulators closed much of the California coast to commercial gill-net fishing to protect endangered seabirds and marine mammals, particularly common murres and the southern sea otter. The area includes Monterey Bay, parts of Marin County, the entire San Francisco Peninsula, and portions of Santa Barbara County. It was a sweeping piece of legislation. Gill nets are suspended like curtains in the water, and fish become entangled in the mesh. Unfortunately, murres, sea otters and harbor porpoises also become entangled and drown when they hunt for food. In recent years, the numbers of murres and otters, especially, have drastically dropped.

Dive Services & Packages in Monterey

The *Monterey Express* (a PADI Resort) is a unique service in that it is not a dive shop at all; it is strictly a boat operation. So what you get is a business that is highly organized and gives excellent service. The *Monterey Express* is a custom Newton 42—42 feet long and 16 feet wide. The nice wide beam means that it is stable in the water, minimizing rocking in rough seas. Nevertheless, seasickness can be a problem in these waters in any boat (or even on the surface of the water), so consider taking seasick medication before going out. With its twin diesels, the *Monterey Express* can really scoot, getting to the dive sites quickly. The boat can hold 30 divers, but Capt. Tim takes a maximum of 20. It is Coast Guard certified, which means it comes well equipped with safety and survival equipment, including plenty of oxygen tanks. The *Express* leaves from the "K" dock down at the Breakwater, just in front of the London Bridge Pub. Normal "open" weekday departures are on Wednesday and Friday mornings (frequently other days, as well) year-round, with a minimum of eight divers. All weekday dives (including national holidays) have 9 a.m. departures. Two two-tank trips are scheduled every Saturday and Sunday, leaving at 8 a.m. and at 1:30 p.m. Boarding times are 15 minutes prior to departure. Night diving is also offered.

Both aluminum and steel tanks are provided. Hot and cold beverages and snacks are included in the price. There are three hot freshwater showers (note: *hot*), a camera table, and a camera wash. Divers should partially gear-up before getting on the boat, and should have all dive equipment, except tanks. This business does not rent or sell scuba gear. The dive sites chosen are appropriate for divers up to the intermediate level; advanced sites are not dived. The crew consists of a USCG-licensed captain, a senior deck hand, and a certified divemaster (usually also paramedic or EMT certified) or an instructor. The divemaster enters the water to assist divers, or to aid in emergencies, but normally stays on the boat. A tour guide can be arranged for an additional charge.

Most trips are a very reasonable $70. Night dives are less. Of course, tips for the crew are appreciated. Book through one of the dive shops or with *Monterey Express* directly. An excellent website has their complete schedule and lots of details about the diving, as well as loads of information about Monterey lodgings, dive shops, restaurants, and current weather conditions. Phone (888) 422-2999 or (831) 659-3009; fax (831) 659-3110; e-mail: capttim@montereyexpress.com; website: www.montereyexpress.com.

Retail Sales: *None*
Rentals: *None*
Scuba Training: *None*
Photo Services: *None*

Dive Boat Comfort: *Good*
On-Board Facilities for Photographers: *Superior*

Aquarius Dive Shop is a PADI 5-Star Dive Center and NAUI Pro facility conveniently located within the Breakwater area. You can get all your rental gear here, have your tanks filled, get equipment serviced and repaired, and purchase gear. They also have a location at 2040 Del Monte Avenue where they can supply Enriched Air Nitrox fills (with a certification). The shop provides guide service for dives in the Sanctuary, keeping the groups to a maximum of four divers—but the shop does not operate its own dive boat. Phone (831) 375-1933 (Del Monte) or (831) 375-6605 (Breakwater); fax (831) 375-3051; e-mail: aquarius@montereybay.com; website: www.montereybay.com/dive.

Retail Sales: *Extensive*
Rentals: *Extensive*
Scuba Training: *Extensive*
Photo Services: *Moderate*

Dive Boat Comfort: *N/A*
On-Board Facilities for Photographers: *N/A*

Monterey Bay Dive Center is also conveniently located near the Breakwater, at 225 Cannery Row. The shop has an extensive rental service, which includes dry suits and undergarments, computers, dive lights, and Enriched Air Nitrox fills. Its repair and retail centers are also extensive. Scuba instruction is through the divemaster level, and this is a PADI 5-Star Dive Center. Specialty courses include Nitrox, drysuit diving, medic first aid, and the DAN oxygen course. The shop also gives guided tours from the 40-foot by 12-foot *Silver Prince,* which is Coast Guard certified for 20 passengers. Hot coffee and soup are provided. A two-tank dive is $80. Snorkelers are welcomed. Phone (831) 656-0454; fax (831) 656-9535; e-mail: mbdc@mbay.net; website: www.mbay.net/~mbdc.

Retail Sales: *Extensive*
Rentals: *Extensive*
Scuba Training: *Extensive*
Photo Services: *Moderate*

Dive Boat Comfort: *Good*
On-Board Facilities for Photographers: *Superior*

WHERE TO STAY IN MONTEREY

Room rates in Monterey vary considerably, depending on the season and events, such as the Jazz Festival, Laguna Seca race, etc. Generally, summertime is the most expensive; also, weekends are more expensive than midweek.

Best Western Monterey Inn is a lovely place at 825 Abrego Street. The 80 rooms are spacious and comfortable; some have fireplaces and ocean views. Each has a coffeemaker and refrigerator, and all are nonsmoking. There's a heated pool and Jacuzzi and a covered garage with elevators. Room rates (double occupancy) during the summer are $119 to $139 midweek and around $200 on the weekend. Phone (800) 528-1234 or (831) 373-5345; website: www.bestwestern.com.

Cypress Tree Inn ★ at 2227 North Fremont Street is welcoming to divers and just ten minutes away from the Breakwater. Some rooms have kitchenettes, sofa sleepers, hot tubs, fireplaces, and decks. A deluxe two-room suite has all of these. For divers, there are dip tanks and a hanging area, and to get warmed up again, a hot tub and sauna. There is also parking for boats and trailers, as well as an RV overnighting area with hookups, dump station, showers, and bathrooms. Also on the premises are guest laundry room, barbecue and picnic area, and bake shop with complimentary coffee service. Mid-week room rates range from $46 to $170; weekends, from $54 to $239. Cypress Tree offers discounts to divers. Call (800) 446-8303 (in CA only) or (831) 372-7586; fax (831) 372-2940; e-mail: info@ cypresstreeinn.com; website: www.cypresstreeinn.com.

Monterey Bay Inn is a terrific place to stay if you feel like splurging. It has an ideal location at 242 Cannery Row. If you're fortunate enough to have an ocean-view room, you can go out on your balcony and use the binoculars provided to watch the sea otters and search for whales. There are 47 attractive rooms (contemporary style), all with king beds and a foldout sofa bed, plus lots of nice amenities. Rooms have Cannery Row (street) view, park view, coastline view, or full bay view. Complimentary continental breakfast is delivered to the room, and there are apples and cookies in the afternoon. Room rates include garage parking. Rates range from $199 to $389. Phone (800) 424-6242 or (831)373-6242; fax (831) 373-7603; e-mail: reservations@innsofmonterey.com; website: www.coastalhotel.com.

Monterey Fairgrounds Travelodge, at 2030 North Fremont Street, is a comfortable 104-room motel with modest prices that is popular with divers. Some of the rooms are large, and you can request a microwave and refrigerator. There's a heated pool, restaurant, and lounge. Rates range from about $59 to $169 for standard rooms, depending on the season. Phone (800) 578-7878 or (831) 373-3381; fax (831) 649-8741; website: www.travelodge.com.

Campgrounds

The 500-acre, 175-site **Laguna Seca Recreation Area** has tent sites as well as RV sites with electrical and water hookups. The facility also includes restrooms and hot showers, group barbecue areas, a dump station, and beautiful views. The recreation area is located between Monterey and the

Salinas Valley, just off Highway 68. Call (888) 588-2267 or (831) 755-4899; e-mail: parks@co.monterey.ca.us; website: www.co.monterey.ca.us/parks.

LIFE IN MONTEREY

Definitely visit the great **Monterey Bay Aquarium** at 886 Cannery Row. Its three-story-high, 330,000-gallon kelp forest tank is absolutely mesmerizing—I guarantee you'll have a hard time tearing yourself away. It's almost as good as diving the real thing. A special temporary exhibit is always being featured, but the aquarium really outdid itself with the wonderful jellyfish exhibit several years ago. Fortunately, it has been able to permanently display many of these species. The huge million-gallon Outer Bay display has an enormous single piece of glass enclosing this tank that is home to creatures of Monterey Canyon's deep-ocean environment. There's also a fun sea otter tank, where you can see these whiskered guys cavort underwater. A giant outdoor artificial tidepool is filled with starfish, anemones, and other invertebrates. A new attraction is called Splash Zone, and is designed for families with children from infants up to nine years old. It blends live-animal experiences with hands-on learning, and features nearly 60 species, from South African blackfooted penguins to leafy sea dragons, corals, moray eels, and tropical sharks. We can thank conservationist Julie Packard (one of the Hewlett-Packards) for founding her aquatic dream. The aquarium has a couple of excellent gift shops with a terrific variety of both fun and educational items, so be sure to leave time to browse.

Fortunately, Monterey has preserved its early structures, and it is fascinating to tour some of these. You might be surprised to know that when California was under Spanish rule in the late eighteenth century, Monterey was the capital and an important center of Alta California. The U.S. flag was officially raised on July 7, 1846, bringing 600,000 square miles into the Union. I particularly enjoy the old **Customs House,** which will take you right back to the nineteenth century, when this was the busiest port in California. It was built by the Mexican government in 1814 and is considered to be the oldest government building west of the Rockies. If you really enjoy this kind of thing, find a copy of the brochure *The Path of History,* from the Old Monterey Business Association at 20 Custom House Plaza near Fisherman's Wharf, which describes a two-mile self-guided walking tour. It features a wonderful collection of ten preserved adobe buildings built in the 1830s that are all part of **Monterey State Historic Park.** Special walking tours leave several times a day from the Stanton Visitor Center near Fisherman's Wharf. The **Maritime Museum,** at 5 Custom House Plaza, is another fascinating place to explore.

To locate the waterfront, just listen for the barking sea lions. They're all along the coastline, including **Fisherman's Wharf,** an aging pier with souvenir shops, fish markets, and seafood restaurants. From the wharf, a scenic recreational trail along the shore leads past the breakwater area and over to **Cannery Row.** John Steinbeck, of course, chronicled this area beautifully during its heyday, when tin-roofed sardine canneries lined the street. Many of the canneries have been converted into restaurants, art galleries, shops, and a new Culinary Center. Fortunately, the area still has that rustic "earthy" feeling.

For great shopping in either Monterey or Carmel, look for sculptures by Dale Evers, who sculpts gorgeous wood and bronze marine figures.

A little farther afield, in Salinas, is the National Steinbeck Center at 1 Main Street. It's an interactive museum with seven theaters. Steinbeck, born in 1902, is the great American writer who chronicled in fiction the lives of Salinas Valley farm workers and Monterey Bay cannery workers in *The Grapes of Wrath, East of Eden,* and many more wonderful works. For details call (831) 775-4720. The website is www.steinbeck.org.

Dining and Entertainment

The dining is superb—you'll find everything from sushi to fajitas. Take a stroll along Fisherman's Wharf and have a chowder bowl with a glass of buttery chardonnay. Yum! **Old Fisherman's Grotto** or **Bubba Gumps** would be good choices. My favorite spot for both food and atmosphere here is **Wharfside Restaurant & Lounge** on the second floor, which has a warm old Monterey feel about it.

For fine dining, the following are highly recommended: **Fresh Cream** (99 Pacific Street) for French/California cuisine; **Stokes Adobe** (500 Hartnell Street, at Madison) for California/Mediterranean cuisine in a historic adobe; **Montrio** (Calle Principal, at Franklin) for California/Continental cuisine in a circa-1910 firehouse; and **Tarpy's** for country-style favorites in a vine-covered stone house. Two recommended restaurants in the Cannery Row area are **Paradiso Trattoria** and **Whaling Station Inn.**

If you're a sushi lover like I am, definitely go to **Jugem Japanese Restaurant** (409 Alvarado Street), which has an inviting contemporary decor. There are both tables and a sushi bar. If you still have salt clinging to your body and don't feel like getting cleaned up before dinner, head for **Gianni's Pizza** at 725 Lighthouse Avenue This is a fun family-owned place (since 1974), and besides a wonderful variety of pizza offerings they have good salads, calzones, and pasta dishes. My personal favorite is the fettucine and clams Sicilian. There's beer on tap, and if you're with a group, you can get pitchers. Seating is at long picniclike tables.

For good Mexican food overlooking the ocean, walk over to **El Torito** at 600 Cannery Row, adjacent to a popular dive area called McAbee Beach.

Medical Facilities

Doctors on Duty is located at 389 Lighthouse Avenue, close to the Breakwater and open from 8 a.m. to 9 p.m. daily. Phone (831) 649-0770. The Community Hospital of the Monterey Peninsula is at 23625 Holman Way (off Hwy 1) in Monterey. Call (831) 625-4900 (direct line) or (831) 624-5311 (general line). A recompression chamber is located in Pacific Grove. In case of a diving emergency call DAN (Divers Alert Network) at (919) 684-4DAN (4326) or (919) 684-8111.

Cayman Islands

Physical Characteristics of the Dive Area

WATER & WEATHER CONDITIONS

Visibility	*Excellent*
Current and Surge	*Minimal*
Temperature	*Comfortable*
Storms	*Occasionally Stormy*

SITE CONDITIONS

Mooring Buoys	*Extensive*
Fishing, Collecting, and Hunting Restrictions	*Widespread Restrictions*
Ease of Access	*Very Easy*
Boat Traffic/Diver Congestion	*Light*

MARINE LIFE

Abundance of Invertebrates	*Prolific*
Abundance of Vertebrates	*Abundant*
Abundance of Pelagic Life	*Abundant*
Health of Reef/Marine Life/ Marine Structure	*Healthy*

Mountain Peaks in Paradise

Grand Cayman, like its farflung sister islands, Little Cayman and Cayman Brac, is the top of a steep underwater mountain, sitting alongside the Cayman Trench, the deepest water in the Caribbean. This magnificent mountain range, which starts just southeast of Cuba and stretches nearly to Belize on the Central American coast, is easily equal to the great Rockies in size.

Though diminutive, the Caymans are springboards to a vast magical domain of canyonlike terrain and vertical walls that drop thousands of feet into the dark nether regions. Stunning black coral and gorgonians jut out from sheer walls over ledges bulging with giant barrel sponges and bright-orange elephant ear sponges. Divers romp through canyons, chimneys, and swim-throughs like kids in a playground. New divers cut their teeth in shallow waters teeming with tropicals. Underwater photographers eagerly seek out eagle rays and sting rays, sea turtles, barracuda, and the occasional black-tip shark prowling the deep. Underwater, the Cayman Islands really do have it all.

All this, in combination with almost perfect water conditions—warm, crystal-clear, and free of strong currents—should be sufficient reason to place the Cayman Islands high on any diver's wish list. But the final winning element here is accessibility. The concept of the dive package was literally invented by Cayman pioneer Bob Soto. So arranging a trip is about as easy as making a phone call to your local dive shop or travel agency.

But before you do, be forewarned: the Caymans are not cheap—a free fall this is not! This British Crown Colony enjoys a high standard of living, and the fixed exchange rate is US$1.25 to the Cayman dollar (CI$). But in return you'll get dive operators that are about as professional as any you'll find in the Caribbean. Whether you're a newbie, a techie, or somewhere in between, you'll be accommodated and receive good value for that hard-earned dollar. Also, the Caymans run safe operations, thanks in large part to the high standards imposed by the Watersports Operators Association.

High standards, however, have not always been the islands' legacy. Cayman's official logo—"Sir Turtle"—depicts a sea turtle in pirate garb, and for years both elements helped shape the islands' economy and culture. After Columbus accidentally discovered the islands in 1503, he named them Las Tortugas for the large number of sea turtles he found. From the late sixteenth into the eighteenth century, the huge turtles provided sustenance for European sailors, and the islands became a replenishing center for merchant ships, explorers, and buccaneers.

Meanwhile, in the untamed lawless days of the eighteenth century, Blackbeard the pirate, Sir Henry Morgan, and other unsavory characters preyed on Central American shipping that had to pass by the Caymans on the way to and from Jamaica. Eventually, the British became fed up with the situation, and the result was a bloody battle off the north coast of Little Cayman—hence the name of that adrenaline-producing dive spot, Bloody Bay.

With a stable government and tax-free status, the islands began to prosper, eventually establishing themselves as one of the most successful off-

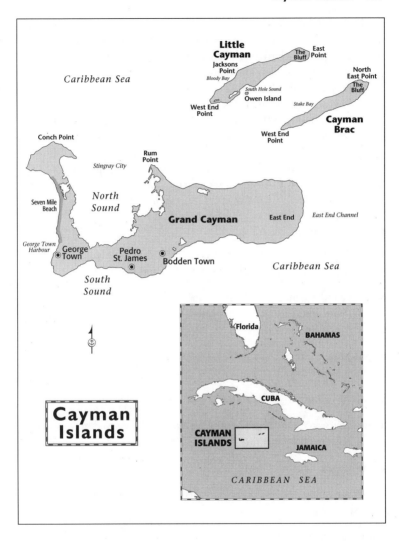

shore financial centers in the world. In the 1950s, with the development of scuba, the construction of the airport, and Bob Soto's first dive operation, tourists started arriving to dive and to fish. In the 1970s tourism really took off, and now, next to banking, it is Cayman's top industry.

Unlike many Caribbean destinations, it is possible to enjoy a first-class meal every night of the week on Grand Cayman. Lodgings range from low-budget, no-frills rooms off the highway to sumptuous resorts along the beach. And there's plenty in between. Nondivers can golf, take submarine rides to 1,000 feet, shop for fine jewelry or local crafts, and visit museums, parks, and galleries. Driving is a dream on all the islands, although Grand Cayman is getting so developed now that it's experiencing traffic jams. In fact, the quaint island image is long gone. Fast-food chains, enormous cruise ships, land developers, and shopping malls have taken care of that. You'll need to travel to the Sister Islands (you should anyway) to find true island life. But if it's nightlife you are after, plus shopping and lots of activity, then Grand Cayman is the place to be.

And there's the dilemma: three islands, three choices, and only one trip. Which to choose? My advice is to see them all if you possibly can. They're as different as New York, New Jersey, and Vermont.

QUICK STATS

Pronunciation Locals frequently accent the second syllable (kay MAN) when they're referring to Little Cayman or Grand Cayman.

Size Grand Cayman is 22 miles long and seven miles wide; the sister islands, both somewhat torpedo-shaped, are each about 12 miles long and one and a half miles wide.

Population Grand Cayman, 34,000; Cayman Brac, 1,500; Little Cayman, fewer than 100

Location South of Cuba and 460 miles south of Miami

Time Eastern Standard; Daylight Savings is not observed, so in summer the islands are an hour earlier.

Government British Crown Colony

Language English; many residents have a Gaelic brogue due to their Scottish heritage.

Electrical Current 110 volts/60 cycles; plugs are U.S. standard

Air Temperature 70° to 86° in winter and from 85° to 90° in summer

Water Temperature Typically a toasty 80° to 85°, but a light wet suit is a good idea, especially for those deeper dives.

Underwater Visibility Usually ranges from 75 to 100 feet.

Best Diving Months The dry season runs from February to mid-April.

PLANNING THE TRIP

Phoning the Cayman Islands   The area code for all three islands is 345. To call from the United States and Canada, dial 1 + 345 + the local number. From elsewhere, use the country's international access code, then repeat these numbers.

Getting to the Caymans   The major U.S. carriers fly from gateway cities in the United States directly into Grand Cayman's Owen Robert's International Airport, a modern, efficient facility. Carriers also fly directly into Cayman Brac, bypassing Grand Cayman. Cayman Airways—(800) G-CAYMAN—flies from Houston, Orlando, Tampa, and Miami. Recently, Lynx Air International began service from Fort Lauderdale to Cayman Brac on Wednesdays and Saturdays. Phone (888) 596-9247; website: www.lynxair.com.

The only air service to Little Cayman is on Island Air, from Grand Cayman or Cayman Brac. But be forewarned: Island Air uses small turbo-props that can touch down on the grass-and-gravel landing strip. Their baggage allowance is a strict 55 pounds per person. Excess weight will cost you 55 cents per pound ($CI), and your baggage might be put onto a different flight. Even journalists are not spared!

Unfortunately, and inexplicably, there is no ferry service between the islands.

Getting Around   Grand Cayman has no airport shuttles, but taxis are plentiful. On Cayman Brac, most lodgings pick up their guests, but taxis are also available at the airport, in case there's a mix-up. And on Little Cayman, your resort will pick you up. All three islands have car rental agencies. Driving is on the left, and you'll probably have to shift with your left hand if you rent a car (since the steering wheel is on the right). Bikes are fun for getting around Cayman Brac and Little Cayman.

Entry Documents   U.S. citizens must have a return ticket and proof of citizenship, which can be a passport or original birth certificate (with a raised seal) and photo ID. A departure tax of CI$10 is included in the ticket price.

Currency   The fixed exchange rate is US$1.25 to the Cayman dollar (CI$). You can use U.S. dollars everywhere, but change will be in the local currency. Traveler's checks and credit cards are accepted.

Cayman Islands Tourist Office   For more information call (800) 346-3313. On Grand Cayman, phone (345) 949-0623; fax (345) 949-4053. The website is www.caymanislands.ky. For the Sister Islands Tourism Association, call (345) 948-1649.

Cayman Islands Diving Website   Check out www.divecayman.ky to search more than 250 dive sites.

Cayman Islands Watersports Operators Association   Phone: (345) 949-8522; e-mail: ciwoa@candw.ky.

Marine Conservation in the Cayman Islands

Most sites dived off of Grand Cayman, as well as those in the Sister Islands, are in protected waters. Fortunately, the Cayman Islands recognized that it possessed a submerged treasure and established the Marine Management System in 1986 to protect its resource. That means prohibitions and restrictions on fishing, spearing, collecting, etc., and a vast system of about 265 mooring buoys. The mooring system is so extensive that some parts of the sea look like a giant has spilled a box of Ping-Pong balls. The Cayman Islands Watersports Operators Association specifies no glove use when diving, a policy that encourages a look-but-don't-touch approach.

Diving in the Bloody Bay Marine Park on Little Cayman is restricted, to avoid stressing the popular dive sites. Only two 20-diver boats per day are allowed.

Grand Cayman

THE UNDERWATER SCENE

The Caymans offer just about the most perfect conditions you can imagine, and the most exciting. With their fringing reefs, shallow shelves, and quick shoreline drop-offs, snorkelers and divers alike have almost instant access to practically every type of reef environment. Boat rides are seldom more than 20 minutes out, and (this is a hot tip) shore diving is superb, particularly on the Brac and Grand Cayman.

Ringing each island is a narrow, shallow shelf with both spur-and-groove and patch reef coral formations. The spurs, or fingers, are separated by sandy grooves and extend perpendicular to the shoreline, reaching out to the shelf edge. Just beyond the shelf is where the precipitous walls drop off some thousands of feet into the Cayman Trench, the deepest water in the Caribbean (also known scientifically as *la la land*).

Corals and sponges carpet the walls. Everywhere, you'll find formations of mountainous star coral, brain coral, and shinglelike sheet coral. Gorgonians—the sea whips, plumes, and fans—stretch out for sunlight over ledges bulging with giant barrel sponges and tube sponges. Waters teem with tropicals, rays, schools of tarpon, sea turtles, and the occasional black-tip.

The divemasters (frequently instructors) here work hard and generally do a superb job with the enormous variety of diving skills they encounter.

These guys and gals are adept at pleasing everyone, from the newly certified who scarcely know which island they're on, to the very experienced, equipped with expensive camera setups and Nitrox certs. They answer an infinite number of questions, deal with every conceivable problem, and perform multiple tasks with extraordinary patience. They definitely deserve at least hefty tips, if not medals.

Health Score Card

The diving industry draws more than 80,000 visitors here annually. What's surprising is that, underwater, signs of this pressure are difficult to find. Healthy corals, giant grouper, and free-swimming hawksbills and green sea turtles are the norm on most Grand Cayman wall dives. It is precisely because many of the dives here are along walls that the reefs stay in such good condition. Alongside a wall, rather than on top of it, divers are less likely to brush against corals and sponges. Where damage is seen is usually in the shallow areas. However, that's also where storms are most destructive.

Much of the credit for the excellent conditions here should go to the forward-thinking action of some key players who were instrumental in establishing the Cayman Islands Watersports Operators Association. Recognizing early on that they literally sat upon a national treasure, they took the steps needed to preserve it. The preservation mentality is strong. On a dive here in 1994, a divemaster told me, "Much of the water surrounding the island is marine park, but as far as the divemasters are concerned, it's all marine park."

Diving Conditions

Of the three islands, Grand Cayman provides the greatest certainty for good dive conditions. Its shape practically guarantees that a sheltered area can be found somewhere, so barring hurricane conditions, a no-diving day is practically unheard of. Most of Grand Cayman's diving takes place in one of three areas: the Northwest, the West End, and the East End. Each has its unique diving conditions, and that's important to know before setting off.

On the Northwest Side is the huge shallow lagoon that is home to *Stingray City*—but don't be fooled. Although this area is shallow and calm, going outside the lagoon is quite different. The North Wall lies just outside the fringing reef. It crests at about 40 to 60 feet and runs parallel to the coast, practically in a straight line. And it can be rough-and-tumble getting out to it. The seas are frequently very choppy, which can be tough on divers. Often boats don't even make the attempt.

West End dive sites are another matter entirely. Conditions usually are excellent—nice calm water, little current, excellent visibility, and sites just minutes from shore. The shallow reef is typically a spur-and-groove configuration, with the spurs running perpendicular to shore and running parallel to one another out to the West Wall. The wall crests at about 50 feet and descends gradually in a soft slope, perfect for intermediate divers. The Southwest is dived infrequently, but on those rare occasions when the West End is blown out, that's where dive boats head. Like the West Wall, the South Wall slopes gradually, but it starts deeper—about 75 to 85 feet, plunging to 6,000 feet! Consequently, most diving in the south is on the shallow reef, which is really spectacular. The surge, though, can be a problem.

Along most of the East End, the reef is deeper, with the wall cresting at 60 to 80 feet—definitely an area for divers who are easy on air consumption. Somewhat choppy seas are the norm, but underwater conditions are fine—a lot like California diving. And the structure? Think of kicking effortlessly through the Grand Canyon, around huge pinnacles and through narrow cuts, with canyon walls soaring high, high above you. It's great drama and wildly exciting.

Recommended Level of Experience

Grand Cayman is a perfect host—making everyone comfortable, accommodating every style. Because so many of the sites are shallow, they're perfect for new divers and those who need to brush up on their skills. But these dives can be just as much fun for more advanced divers, too. Observing fish behavior, doing underwater photography, and just having ample time to appreciate the beauty are all great reasons for diving Cayman's shallow walls and "second sites."

And of course, there is plenty of excitement for more experienced divers on the North Wall, and even more on the East End. Rough waters and deep dives are characteristic at some of these sites, so new divers should avoid them.

Grand Cayman is a perfect place to get certified or to get further training. Most of the dive operations are superb, with highly skilled divemasters and instructors and safe equipment. The West End, especially, is calm, shallow, and perfect for students.

Techies will love it, too. You'll have access to Nitrox fills, and at least one shop—Dive Tech—offers special mixes and training for very deep diving, as well as rebreather training. They even offer a certification course in free diving. The shops that cater to more advanced divers are located north of 7-Mile Beach.

Dive Sites for the Adventurous

Outside the lagoon the seas get churned up, but diving the wilder North Wall is highly recommended for comfortable divers. *White Stroke Canyon,*

Robert's Wall, Leslie's Curl, Eagle Ray Pass, and *Princess Penny's Pinnacle* are all wonderful sites with structure and adornments that will take your breath away. Huge barrel sponges and bushes of black coral protrude into the blue water. The wall starts at about 60 feet, so these dives are deep, but there's also more pelagic life coming in from the deep ocean. Hammerheads and black-tips, spotted eagle rays, and hawksbill turtles all cruise by.

Because the North Wall is typically rough, be prepared for a bouncy ride on the dive boat. Take some seasick medication in the morning if you are prone to seasickness or even have a suspicion that there could be a problem. Something to snack on and a cover-up are also wise to have.

The East End, definitely the more serene section of the island topside, gets a small fraction of Grand Cayman's divers. Dive sites are absolutely pristine and definitely exciting! Visualize yourself soaring through a huge canyon, with winding craggy walls looming high above. The top of the wall is deep here, cresting from 60 to 80 feet, so dives unfortunately are over much too soon. Definitely keep a watch out in blue water for passing pelagic life, which is abundant on this end of the island.

The Maze, McKennedy's Canyon, Pat's Wall, and *Babylon* all provide endless joy along this deep stretch of wall. Even the shallow sites—*Playing Field, Scuba Bowl, Grouper Grotto,* and *Snapper Hole*— are mazes of tunnels, caverns, cuts, and coral buttresses. You could never be disappointed or bored.

You'll probably hear that the East End is usually rough, with high surf and currents, but that's true primarily at the very eastern tip. So don't let that dissuade you from diving here. Most of the dive sites are clustered on the northeast and southeast, which are more sheltered. You'll find comfortable lodgings here, although the choices are limited. From West End resorts, it'll take you about 30 to 45 minutes to drive to the East End—not a problem.

Ordinary Great Sites

Most divers will cut their teeth, so to speak, on the West End. This is where conditions are most stable and also where the resorts are conveniently located—off 7-Mile Beach and the George Town area. Coral mounds are shallow, typically in about 35 feet of water, and the wall crests at about 50 feet, descending in a gradual slope. This profile means nice long bottom times, easy off-gassing, and great photo conditions. Many of the sites do double duty, with wall or canyon dives below 60 feet, and patch reef or spur-and-groove formations on the flats above the wall.

Big Tunnel and *Little Tunnels* on the Northwest Wall is exciting canyonlike territory, riddled with swim-throughs. Several arches provide ample coral-framed photography. At the rim (about 55 feet) stingrays search in the sand for crustaceans, occasionally sporting a bar jack hunting alongside.

Dropping down the wall are canopies of plate coral, yellow and purple-tipped anemones, sea fans, and massive elephant ear and barrel sponges. Bushes of black coral billow at 90 feet. Out in blue water, the vague outlines of sharks and eagle rays are frequently seen.

At West Bay, *Round Rock* and *Trinity Caves* provide even more great wall excitement—deep canyons, formations of overlapping plate coral, and narrow passageways lead down the wall. Schools of blue chromis soar over and around the pinnacles. Elephant ear sponges jut from the wall. And on top, swaying gorgonians harbor camouflaged trumpetfish.

Farther south at *Eagle Ray Rock,* divers negotiate through a canyon with soaring walls of coral on either side. In the distance eagle rays frequently are spied. Wide-eyed balloonfish and gray and queen angelfish appear to check you out, but always keep a respectable distance. The sponge life is prolific and enormous.

As stunning as the scenery is, the laid-back attitude of the fish is what really makes the West End popular. Underwater photographers will enjoy the fact that most of these dive sites harbor Nassau grouper and hinds that tolerate close-ups at cleaning stations. Also, the angelfish, always curious, are particularly bold here.

The Southwest is where dive boats point their bows when winter storms blow. The South Wall, like the West, has a gradual slope, but its crest is much deeper—about 70 to 80 feet—plunging to 6,000 feet! A nice shallow dive here is *Japanese Gardens.* In this labyrinthine structure, you can have a lot of fun venturing down sand chutes, through cuts, and into caverns.

Shallow Diving and Snorkeling

Shallow sites, or "second dives," on the West End are terrific for photographers. At *Aquarium, Governor's Reef, Rhapsody,* and *Royal Palms Ledge,* angelfish are literally in your face; grouper line up at cleaning stations; and the grunts, snapper, jacks, and Bermuda chub school among the coral heads. Eels, lobster, and spotted drum hunker under coral overhangs, along with the occasional slumbering nurse shark.

For excellent shore diving, head over to the Eden Rock Diving Center, Parrots Landing Watersports Park, or Sunset House where you can pick up a tank, then simply drop down and begin to explore, day or night. *Eden Rock* and *Devil's Grotto* are playgrounds of mazes and grottoes. Schools of silversides attract their large predators, the tarpon.

Don't leave Grand Cayman without taking an excursion to the enormous shallow lagoon called the North Sound. This is where you'll find one of the world's most popular dive and snorkel sites—*Stingray City.* You should wear a little extra weight here, so you can plop down comfortably on the sand without being too buoyant. Hold your little package of squid close to your body, and rays will literally suck up to you. Stroke their soft bellies and rub the area between their eyes, and they'll be your best friends. Don't worry about those menacing-looking barbs on their tails. They are purely for defense, and as long as these guys know you're providing lunch, you'll have no problems. Do watch out for the pesky yellowtails, though. They can nip, and even draw blood. This is really a terrific site for snorkelers, too, since the rays will come right up to the surface!

DIVE SERVICES & PACKAGES ON GRAND CAYMAN

Pre-booked packages are always cheaper. Walk-in rates range from $65 to $75 for a two-tank dive. Grand Cayman has first-rate photo services, many located in the resorts or dive shops. Many rent both still and video cameras and provide E-6 processing.

Aqua'nauts, a PADI 5-Star Dive Center just north of 7-Mile Beach, specializes in small groups and more experienced divers. Its 42-foot and 50-foot boats take divers to North Wall and West Wall. Dive instruction is through the advanced level and also includes Enriched Air Nitrox, rebreather, and photo/video instruction. Certifying agencies are IDEA, NASDS, NAUI, PADI, and SSI. Nitrox is pumped on the premises. Phone toll free (888) SUN-NUTS or (345) 945-1990; fax (345) 945-1991; e-mail: aquanaut@candw.ky; website: www.aquanauts.com.

Retail Sales: *Adequate*	**Dive Boat Comfort:** *Good*
Rentals: *Extensive*	**On-Board Facilities**
Scuba Training: *Extensive*	**for Photographers:** *Good*
Photo Services: *Moderate*	

Bob Soto's Diving is an impressive business that has really perfected the art of pleasing its customers. The shop takes time to determine your skill level and the types of dives you want to do. By running several boats (about seven, ranging from 17 footers to 59 footers), Soto's makes sure that you don't return to the same dive sites unless you want to. The entire island is covered, including the East End. Boats are not crowded, and a healthy ratio of divemasters to divers is maintained. If you're inexperienced and would like a little more attention, Soto's makes sure you get it. On the other hand, if you're thinking of going pro, this would be a good place to do it, since Soto's is a PADI 5-Star IDC. The full line of rental gear includes camera rentals at the Treasure Island location. Other locations are the Strand Shopping Center, Coconuts Shopping Center, and the Lobster Pot. Phone

(888) 698-7400; fax (345) 949-8731; e-mail: bobsotos@candw.ky; website: www.bobsotosdiving.com.ky.

Retail Sales: *Extensive*	**Dive Boat Comfort:** *Good*
Rentals: *Extensive*	**On-Board Facilities**
Scuba Training: *Extensive*	**for Photographers:** *Good*
Photo Services: *Extensive*	

Divetech, a PADI Resort north of 7-Mile Beach, definitely caters to advanced and technical divers. You can rent rebreathers, twin and deco tanks, scooters (DPVs), communications equipment, metal detectors, and cameras. The shop provides Nitrox mixtures and special mixes for deep diving. The extensive course selection includes certifications through the instructor level, Nitrox, advanced Nitrox, technical Nitrox, Trimix, rebreather, and even free-diving. They've developed the first free-diving certification course, and the shop organizes and provides safety divers for free-diving competitions. Their diving vessel is a 34-foot Delta for diving the North Wall and Northwest Point. They also have a few apartments for rent. Call (345) 949-1700; fax (345) 949-1701; e-mail: divetech@candw.ky; website: www.divetech.com.

Retail Sales: *Adequate*	**Dive Boat Comfort:** *Good*
Rentals: *Extensive*	**On-Board Facilities**
Scuba Training: *Extensive*	**for Photographers:** *Good*
Photo Services: *Limited*	

Don Foster's Dive Cayman, the in-house watersports operator for the new Comfort Suites (a PADI Resort), is a veteran on-island, established in 1982. Daily two-tank dives go to the North, West, and South walls, reefs, and Stingray City. Instruction is offered to the advanced open water level, and includes several specialty courses. Call (345) 945-5132; fax (345) 945-5133; e-mail: donfosters@cayman.org; website: www.cayman.org/donfosters.

Retail Sales: *Adequate*	**Dive Boat Comfort:** *Good*
Rentals: *Extensive*	**On-Board Facilities**
Scuba Training: *Moderate*	**for Photographers:** *Good*
Photo Services: *Limited*	

Ocean Frontiers (a PADI Gold Palm IDC Resort) serves the East End, and does it very well. The shop itself needs some work, but a new one is being built, and there is a new training pool. A 38-foot custom catamaran (which gives greater stability in choppy waters) takes divers to sites on the East End, as well as Stingray City. A full rental line, including cameras and videos, is offered, and Nitrox fills are provided. This would be an excellent place to go pro, since a course director heads their new scuba college. Nitrox and rebreather classes are also given. Phone (345) 947-7500; fax (345) 947-7600; e-mail: oceanf@candw.ky; website: www.oceanfrontiers.com.

Retail Sales: *Adequate*

Rentals: *Extensive*

Scuba Training: *Extensive*

Photo Services: *Moderate*

Dive Boat Comfort: *Good*

On-Board Facilities for Photographers: *Good*

Sunset Divers operates out of Sunset House (a PADI Gold Palm Resort) and has a fleet of six boats, ranging from 36 to 45 feet in length. Trips go out to the West End, North Wall, and South Sound. The boats dock right in back of the property, where there's also excellent shore diving and snorkeling. Enriched Air Nitrox is offered as well as a full line of rental gear, including rebreathers. Cathy Church's Underwater Photo Center has camera, lenses, and strobe rentals, E-6 processing, and extensive photo instruction. Courses given are through the advanced level, and they include some specialty courses with NASDS, NAUI, PADI, and SSI. Phone (345) 949-7111; fax (345) 949-7101; e-mail: sunseths@candw.ky; website: www.sunsethouse.com.

Retail Sales: *Adequate*

Rentals: *Extensive*

Scuba Training: *Moderate*

Photo Services: *Extensive*

Dive Boat Comfort: *Good*

On-Board Facilities for Photographers: *Superior*

WHERE TO STAY ON GRAND CAYMAN

Watch out for the 10 percent tax, and frequently a 10 percent service charge, tacked on to the price of these rates. Packages are really the way to go in the Caymans. Also, meals are expensive on the island, so having a kitchenette in your room is a good way to save some money.

Cayman Diving Lodge ★★★★, a PADI Gold Palm IDC Resort located right on the beach, is one of the few resorts serving the East End. It is small, all-inclusive (meals, diving, transfers, etc.) and very friendly—a perfect dedicated diving lodge. The lodge operates two dive boats (one is a Pro-48) crewed by PADI divemasters and instructors. Some instruction is offered, and scuba rentals, underwater camera rentals, and full repair facilities are available in-house. The private dock and shallow lagoon facilitate both diving and snorkeling. A large walk-in gear room is very conveniently located right at the end of the dock. The lodge's 14 rooms are air conditioned and have private baths. All-inclusive packages, double occupancy, for 7 nights are $1,361 for daily two-tank dives or $1,546 for daily three-tank dives. Phone (800) TLC-DIVE; fax (806) 798-7548; e-mail: divelodge@aol.com; website: www.divelodge.com.

Comfort Suites and Resort ★★★★, a PADI Resort which uses Don Foster's Dive Cayman for its dive service, is one of the newest dive-lodgings on Grand Cayman. It's an all-suite hotel on 7-Mile Beach (next door to the Marriott), with 110 units: junior studio and deluxe studio suites, one- and two-bedroom suites, and a master suite. Many have ocean views. Each has either a kitchenette or a full kitchen. The rooms are air-conditioned, have two phone lines for data ports, and irons and ironing boards (do divers iron?). Facilities here include a swimming pool, bar/restaurant, dive/gift shop, child-care center, fitness center, and a coin-operated laundry. A continental breakfast is included in the rate. Rooms range from about $145 to $350, depending on the season. Most suites accommodate from four to six people. Phone (345) 945-7300; fax (345) 945-7400; e-mail: comfort@candw.ky; website: comfortinn.com.

Sleep Inn Hotel ★★★★, located on 7-Mile Beach, is popular with divers. It's the same chain as the Comfort Suites, but a less expensive version. There are 115 rooms, all with air-conditioning. Facilities include a swimming pool and Jacuzzi, bar and restaurant. The dive shop used is Treasure Island Divers, on the property. Room rates for a double range from about $126 to $140. Call (345) 949-9111; fax (345) 949-6699; e-mail: sleep inn@candw.ky; website: comfortinn.com.

Sunset House ★★★★★ is a dedicated PADI Gold Palm Resort that's really tops. It has just about everything—nice stretch of beach, boat dock, attractive beach-bar hangout, restaurant, spacious rooms, and Cathy Church's Underwater Photo Centre. The resort is located south of George Town in the more serene and scenic section of the West Side. Snorkeling and diving are excellent right from the beach. Choose from courtyard rooms, ocean-view rooms, suites, and apartment-style rooms. Phone (888) 281-3826; fax (345) 949-7101; e-mail: rsd@sunsethouse.com; website: www.sunsethouse.com.

Treasure Island Resort ★★★★, a PADI Resort, is in the heart of activity on 7-Mile Beach, which might be too much activity for some. The real bonus here is the excellent dive shop on premises—Bob Soto's—and the in-house photo shop. For diving Stingray City and the North Wall, you'll be picked up by bus and taken to the marina on the north side, to speed things along. The 278 rooms, all with air-conditioning, ceiling fans, balconies, and refrigerators, are spacious and comfortable. Facilities include a nice pool, restaurant, and bar. Room rates range from about $155 to $275, single or double occupancy. Call (800) 203-0775 or (345) 949-7777; fax (345) 949-8489; website: www.treasureislandresort.net.

Enriched Air Nitrox: Caymans' Designer Air

Dive professionals on-island, along with savvy visiting divers, are avid consumers of Enriched Air Nitrox, and almost every dive boat has at least a couple of bottles with the prominent green and yellow bands. Nitrox is readily available on all three islands for divers who are certified to use it. In classrooms throughout the islands, students are learning about partial pressures and atmospheres absolute. The most common certifying agencies are IANTD, TDI, and PADI.

Operators charge divers extra for the gas, but proponents claim it's worth it to reduce the effects of diver fatigue and nitrogen buildup. Although Nitrox can greatly increase bottom times, most divers seem to be using it to feel better, and therefore simply dive on regular air tables or use standard computers that calculate nitrogen buildup for normal air.

The mixture used here is almost exclusively EAN 32–32 percent oxygen (normal breathing air is 21 percent). Richer mixtures are possible, but as the oxygen percentages increase, the diving depths must decrease in order to avoid oxygen toxicity (which is extremely dangerous).

For years, the Cayman Islands Watersports Operators Association (CIWOA) frowned upon Nitrox use. With so many dive sites that plummet hundreds, if not thousands, of feet into the beyond, it's really not surprising that dive operators were at first hesitant to embrace an air mixture designed for shallow-to-medium depths. However, experience has shown that because Nitrox diving is a form of advanced diving, people who use it are generally well trained.

So sign up for that extra safety edge, not to mention the extra measure of comfort as you buckle up for the flight home.

Live-Aboard

If you want to live, sleep, and eat diving, the *Cayman Aggressor IV* is the place to throw your dive bag. This sleek, 110-foot live-aboard cruises Grand Cayman sites and, weather permitting, Little Cayman and Cayman Brac. It features nine staterooms with private head and shower, onboard photo lab, hot tub, Nitrox, and e-mail. These seven-day charters are all-inclusive—meals, tanks, weights, airport transfers. And you get unlimited diving. Call (800) 348-2628; fax (504) 384-0817; e-mail: info@aggressor.com; website: www.aggressor.com.

ISLAND LIFE ON GRAND CAYMAN

On Grand Cayman you'll drive along 7-Mile Beach, home to luxury resorts, condos, shopping centers, and even traffic jams. Getting into George Town, the capital and center of commerce, cruise ships loom in the harbor and multinational banks intermingle with duty-free shops. Still, this is hardly a metropolis, and within minutes you can be on an ironshore beach watching spewing blowholes. Enjoy a relaxing lunch at any number of attractive restaurants facing out to sea, and in the evening, catch a performance by Barefoot Man or simply watch for the sunset from a quiet beach.

For things to see, definitely try to rent a car and drive around (remembering to stay on the left). Visit **Bodden Town,** the old capital, and **Pedro's Castle,** the West Indian Great House. This eight-acre estate is located in the little settlement of Savannah, and in addition to the building re-creations, there are beautiful gardens with fruit trees, tropical plants, vegetables, and medicinal plants representative of a small West Indian plantation.

For more beautiful gardens, turn off to **Queen Elizabeth II Botanic Park,** where you could easily spend an entire pleasant afternoon strolling around. In the early evening, drive to **Rum Point,** order a refreshing Mudslide, and watch the sun drop below the horizon.

In George Town, visit the harbor and the **Cayman Islands National Museum,** an attractive restored nineteenth-century building. Divers will enjoy the natural history exhibit's three-dimensional map showing the dramatic panorama of undersea mountains and canyons that surround the islands. A gift shop sells handcrafted items.

Another terrific little shop for arts and crafts is **Pure Art Gallery and Gifts,** on South Church Street in George Town. If you're still in the shopping mood, or just exploring, stop in to see molten glass being shaped at the **Glassblowing Studio** just north of the Ferry Terminal.

Dining and Entertainment

Figure on spending about $30 per couple for a modest meal. For finer dining and nicer ambiance and service, expect to pay at least $50 per couple. Wine or cocktails will add quite a bit more. Restaurants frequently add gratuities to the bill, so be sure to check. Also, don't be alarmed to see turtle selections on the menus here. This is all farm-raised turtle and perfectly legal.

For a nice, romantic meal, dining at the **Almond Tree** on North Church Street in George Town is highly recommended. It has a pleasant courtyard with soft twinkling lights and excellent cuisine. **Bed Restaurant and Lounge** in the Islander Complex on West Bay Road gets high marks, as does **Edoardo's,** for Italian food, at Coconut Place on West Bay Road.

For family-type dining, with high decibel levels, try **Eat's Crocodile Rock Café** across from the Westin Casuarina Resort in the Cayman Falls

Centre on West Bay Road. The fare includes burgers, steaks, seafood, pizza, ribs, fajitas, and salads. On the same road, the **Lone Star Bar and Grille,** is a fun hangout with atmosphere. **PD's** pub, in Jalleria Plaza on West Bay Road, serves selections like buffalo wings (island famous, they claim), burgers, and quesadillas.

On a quieter note, for local Caymanian fare that's easy on the pocketbook, **Champion House I** and **Champion House II,** on Eastern Avenue in George Town, are good choices. On the menu you'll see curry goat, turtle stew, jerk chicken, etc. An interesting drink here is called Irish Moss and consists of seaweed, rum, cinnamon, and milk. Yum! Champion House I has no air-conditioning, no view, no liquor, and little in the way of decor, but it is less expensive than II.

Watch for occasional free Friday night buffets at the various hangouts—Lone Star, Hogsty, Big Daddies, and Deckers. You're liable to see your divemasters at any of these!

When you're touring, check out the **Crow's Nest** on the beach in South Sound. Anything conch is a good bet: conch chowder, conch fritters, conch salad, or conch stew. Also on the menu are turtle steak, coconut shrimp, red snapper, and lobster. Their Caesar salad is excellent.

Medical Facilities

George Town Hospital is a modern facility with an emergency room and 24-hour ambulance paramedic service. The hospital operates a two-person double-lock recompression chamber, which is staffed around the clock and supervised by a physician experienced in hyperbaric medicine. The hospital phone number is (345) 949-8600. In case of a diving emergency call DAN (Divers Alert Network) at (919) 684-4DAN (4326) or (919) 684-8111.

Cayman Brac

THE UNDERWATER SCENE

The Brac's dive sites (about 45 with moorings), although not as well known as those on Grand and Little Cayman, are pristine, beautiful, and exciting. There's little development on the island that might muck up the water, and cruise ships keep their distance. In fact, it's strange that the Brac has not received the same attention from divers and tourists that Grand Cayman and Little Cayman have experienced. But perhaps that's a good thing.

You'll find high underwater visibility and light ocean current at these sites. Fringing reef surrounds most of the island. Beyond the fringing reef are shallow sites that are perfect for snorkeling and diving, and they are as healthy and spectacular as those along the wall. Coral heads frequently reach to just 10 to 20 feet below the surface. Characteristic of most of these sites is gorgeous overlapping plate coral and lettuce coral—much more than you'll find on the other islands. Pillar coral and mountainous star coral are also abundant.

Off the north shore, a mini-wall starts at about 20 to 30 feet and drops to a ledge at 50 feet. Beyond this ledge begins the sloping main wall, which crests at about 60 feet and descends to an awesome 4,000 feet! The wall encircles the island.

Most of the dive shops are located on the south shore of the West End, which is somewhat protected from winds. Most of the 45 moored sites are also located on the West End, which means that you'll barely have time to don your wet suit before arriving at the dive site. East End sites take a bit longer to reach, but they are well worth the extra time.

For a while the *Tibbetts* wreck was the hot topic of conversation among divers on the Brac, but no longer, not since Spot arrived. Spot is a male bottlenose dolphin that once resided on Grand Cayman with his mate. After the female died, Spot moved off to make his home in the waters around Cayman Brac. Although he is a wild dolphin, evidently Spot is extremely approachable and playful, and even loves to be touched. Usually, such close dolphin experiences are with snorkelers rather than divers. Some marine animals, including dolphins and sea lions, exhale bubbles underwater as a sign of aggression. It is assumed, therefore, that a scuba diver's bubbles frighten away a lot of marine creatures. Spot, it seems, is undeterred; perhaps he recognizes these bubbles as nonthreatening. Hopefully, he'll still be around when you visit.

Recommended Level of Experience

The Brac's dive sites are appropriate for divers of all skill levels. If you're a new diver or thinking of getting some advanced training, this place is excellent. It's also ideal for group travel, simply because the sites are so perfect for every level of diver.

Great Dive Sites

Much of the diving is right around the West End of the Brac, just a short boat ride from the airport-area resorts, and within sight of nearby Little Cayman. In fact, *Airport Reef* and *Airport Wall* are so close that you can hear the tires screech as Cayman Air's direct-from-Miami flights touch down here. Airport Reef is particularly nice at night, where you're sure to see at least one octopus.

You'll love falling over the steep drop-offs at *Cemetery Wall, Airport Reef,* and *Rock Monster Chimney,* and following the rivers of sand down the mountainsides at *The Chutes.* Overlapping plate corals are particularly beautiful here and at *Garden Eel Wall* and *Rock Monster Chimney.* Garden Eel Wall displays stunning sea fans, tube and barrel sponges, sea whips, and gorgonians, as well as soaring shallow-water coral pinnacles and—of course—reclusive little garden eels.

East Chute and the wreck of the *Cayman Mariner* are other North Side sites that offer a choice of depths and photo lens opportunities. Don't be surprised to find at least one green moray in the wreck's engine compartment.

In the South Side shallows at *Sergeant Major Reef,* beautiful golden-brown elkhorn coral (some of it storm-damaged) attracts schooling fish, and the more solitary tropicals—puffers, triggerfish, butterfly fish, blue tang, and grouper—seem especially abundant. On a dive here, while I was trying to get as close as possible to snap off a picture of a slumbering stingray, a tiny yellow-headed jawfish popped straight up from its sandy burrow only inches away, to stare at me with big, ET-like eyes. The little stinker must have known I was using a wide-angle lens!

The newest wreck site in the Caymans is a Russian frigate now called the *Capt. Keith Tibbetts,* and for that you'll definitely want a wide-angle lens. Brought over from Cuba and sunk in 1996, the 330-foot-long vessel features dramatic turret guns both fore and aft. Snorkelers can look down and see the entire ship only 40 feet below. When I dived this in 1999, the ship was intact, but I've heard that it is now broken up. Since it's a new wreck, don't expect much marine growth.

The Brac's Shore Diving Sites

Many of the Brac's sites are excellent for snorkeling since coral heads are only 10 to 20 feet below the surface. Also, many, such as *Cemetery Wall, Radar Reef,* and *Bert Brothers Boulders* are easy to reach from shore. For Cemetery Wall, turn off onto Cemetery Road from the north shore road (just east of the airport and Tibbetts Square), and follow it to the end. Enter the water from either side of the jetty. Kick out to the mooring directly in front of the jetty, then drop down and follow the coral patches (about 50 to 65 feet) out to the main wall drop-off.

Radar Reef is also accessed from the north shore road in Stake Bay. Turn onto Kirkconnell Road, just east of the Cayman Brac Museum, and follow it to the end. Steps lead into the water from a jetty. Kick out to the end of the jetty, then drop down and turn east. Look for an underwater cable and follow it to the reef. The depth here is about 60 feet. And for Bert Brothers Boulders, look for a crafts store called NIM Things in Spot Bay. Follow the road directly opposite it and park in front of the boat ramp. Walk down the ramp and head out to the mooring ball. You'll be able to find the spur-and-groove system and have a great time looking under ledges and over-hangs for eels and lobster.

Brac dive operators make frequent runs over to Little Cayman, only five miles west, to dive the Bloody Bay Marine Park. Those are full-day outings.

DIVE SERVICES & PACKAGES ON CAYMAN BRAC

Brac Aquatics Dive & Photo Centre, housed at the Brac Caribbean Beach Village, is a real gem. The shop runs two comfortable boats, a 48-foot Reef Runner and a 55-foot Out Runner. It has a full line of rental equipment, including cameras and video. Nitrox is available. The Village Scuba School is located here, where you can get instruction through dive-master level with BSAC, NAUI, PADI, and SSI. Photo courses and other specialty courses are also available. For shore diving, just jump right off the dock. Trips are scheduled three days a week to Little Cayman. Call (345) 948-1429; fax (345) 948-1527; e-mail: info@brac-caribbean.com; website: www.brac-caribbean.com.

Retail Sales: *Adequate*	**Dive Boat Comfort:** *Excellent*
Rentals: *Extensive*	**On-Board Facilities**
Scuba Training: *Extensive*	**for Photographers:** *Superior*
Photo Services: *Extensive*	

Divi Tiara operates out of the Divi Tiara Beach Resort (a PADI Resort). Rental gear is available, as well as camera and video rentals. The shop has four 40-foot dive boats and one 38-footer, and they make runs to Little Cayman three times a week. Enriched Air Nitrox is pumped on the site. Classes are through divemaster level with NASDS, NAUI, and PADI. The Nitrox class is through TDI. This well-equipped shop has an excellent photo center with E-6 processing. Call (345) 948-1563; fax (345) 948-1316; e-mail: divitiara@candw.ky; website: www.diviresorts.com.

Retail Sales: *Extensive*	**Dive Boat Comfort:** *Excellent*
Rentals: *Extensive*	**On-Board Facilities**
Scuba Training: *Extensive*	**for Photographers:** *Superior*
Photo Services: *Extensive*	

Reef Divers is another excellent shop, operating at the Brac Reef Beach Resort (a PADI Resort). It's dive boats consist of two Newton 42s, a Newton 46, and a Pro 43—all beautiful vessels. Nitrox is available, as well as a full line of rental gear and camera and video rentals. There is a photo and video center, and courses are given through divemaster level with BSAC, NAUI, PADI, and SSI. Call (345) 948-1323; fax (345) 948-1207; e-mail: bestdiving@aol.com; website: www.braclittle.com.

Retail Sales: *Adequate*	**Dive Boat Comfort:** *Excellent*
Rentals: *Extensive*	**On-Board Facilities**
Scuba Training: *Extensive*	**for Photographers:** *Superior*
Photo Services: *Extensive*	

WHERE TO STAY ON CAYMAN BRAC

Brac Reef Beach Resort ★★★★★, a PADI Resort with 40 rooms, is a popular spot for dive groups. All rooms have air-conditioning, as well as ceiling fans and balconies. Features include an attractive swimming pool, Jacuzzi, restaurant, and bar. Besides diving and snorkeling, the resort offers fishing, biking, basketball, and tennis. Per person rates (based on double occupancy) for three nights, three dives per day, breakfast, dinner, tax, and service charge, range from $518 to $549. You can also get a package that includes lunch. Judging from all the exuberant driftwood signs made by guests, this place is well liked! Phone (800) 327-3835; fax (813) 323-8827; e-mail: bestdiving@reefseas.com; website: www.bracreef.com.

Brac Caribbean Beach Village ★★★★★ is an extremely comfortable and quiet place, on a gorgeous stretch of beach. It's particularly suitable for families and groups, since the accommodations are all extremely spacious condos with full kitchens, private balconies, air-conditioning, and ceiling fans. Facilities include a nice restaurant, bar, laundry, and swimming pool. The daily room rate for two adults is $185, but condos accommodate up to four adults ($245). Children up to 11 years old are free, and teens ages 12 to 17 are only $35 extra per night. Phone (345) 948-2265; fax (345) 948-1111; e-mail: info@brac-caribbean.com; website: www.brac-caribbean.com.

The **Divi Tiara** ★★★★★, a PADI Resort with 24 standard and 21 deluxe and luxury rooms, is one of the largest resorts on the Brac. Last time I was here, the place was looking a bit tired, but since then it has refurbished all rooms, plus the pool and deck. Plans were continuing to also fix up the restaurant and outside bar. The resort is located on the beach and uses the Peter Hughes dive operation, on the premises. This is an all-inclusive resort, with packages starting at $607 per person, double occupancy, for three nights. Phone (800) 661-3483 or (345) 948-1563; fax (345) 948-1316; e-mail: divitiara@candw.ky; website: www.diviresorts.com.

ISLAND LIFE ON CAYMAN BRAC

From Grand Cayman, "the Brac," as it's called locally, is 90 miles north-east. The island is tiny—only 12 miles by one and a half miles. You'll pass streets with names like Bluff Boulevard and Mango Tree Road. The pace is slower, and of the three islands, tourism is least evident here—no traffic, no cruise ships, no duty-free shops. Islanders, numbering about 1,500, will stop to chat. Much of the Brac is bird sanctuary, including a preserve for the personable little endemic Brac parrot.

Many of the residents will still head to caves in the island's bluff at the first signs of an approaching hurricane. Few homes here date from before 1932—the year of the last Big One. Look for signs along the road point-ing out caves that are appropriate for visitors to explore. **Rebecca's Cave** is one of the easiest to get to, being just off the road. It's on the south shore near the West End and was named after a young girl who died there. Also along the south shore road is **Bat Cave,** which is accessed by a ladder. **Peter's Cave** is high up on the bluff. Reach it from either Spot Bay or from a side road off the road that leads to the lighthouse. Steps and handrails go up to the entrance, but you'll have to duck down and almost crawl before you can get inside the large chamber.

Renting a car and driving around for a few hours is a lot of fun. Better yet, get in touch with Wallace Platts to give you a personalized tour. Wallace is active with the National Trust on the Brac and has contributed much to the island's preservation and conservation. But first, buy some of the delicious sugarcane in one of the grocery stores; you can munch and spit all along the way!

In Stake Bay go "Brac" in time to learn what island life was like in the old days at the **Cayman Brac Museum.** It highlights the shipbuilding era of the early twentieth century when the Brac was still fairly isolated from the out-side world. Also in Stake Bay visit Eddie Scott, who uses a dentist drill to craft jewelry from local **Caymanite.** Just look for several windmills in his front yard. Caymanite is a beautiful semiprecious stone found in the island's limestone bluff. Caymanite is also available at NIM (Native Island Made) Things on the East End. Hiking the nature trails on the East End bluff will introduce you to century plants, bright yellow shamrock, and glorious views.

Dining and Entertainment

One of my favorites here is **La Esperanza,** for their spicy jerk chicken bar-becued outdoors and served on paper plates. Eat it here or take it back to the room. Indoors can be fun unless you're not into high decibel levels. This is also where you can join the locals in a raucous game of dominoes. **Aunt Sha's** is another good spot for local food, especially fish, lobster, and conch, and is much more sedate. If you order any dish fixed Cayman-style, it will be cooked with bell pepper and onions.

When you're in the mood for fine dining (with a real tablecloth) go to **Captain's Table** at the Brac Caribbean Beach Village, where selections include rack of lamb, ribs, fish, lobster, crab cakes, bean soup, and the like. It's a nice, quiet place in a pleasant atmosphere. Unfortunately, none of the restaurants described here are on the waterfront.

Medical Facilities

Faith Hospital is located at Stake Bay. Phone (345) 948-2242. There is no recompression chamber on the island. In case of a diving emergency call DAN (Divers Alert Network) at (919) 684-4DAN (4326) or (919) 684-8111.

Little Cayman

THE UNDERWATER SCENE

If it's wall diving you want, this is where you'll get it. Bloody Bay Marine Park is the legendary home to these natural wonders. Surprisingly, the walls start very shallow, but their extreme vertical plunge makes you feel like backing away from the edge—just like looking down from a tall building. Generally, the underwater structure of all the Cayman Islands is similar, but here at the marine park it is unique. That's because the typical two-tiered shelf configuration is absent. Instead, the shelves merge into a single vertical wall—a spectacular geologic development. Also, some of the areas along the wall are undercut, due to the large amount of growth at the lip—truly an adrenaline rush!

Unfortunately, the marine park (North Side) is frequently undiveable, particularly in winter, because of winds and rough seas. When this happens you'll be taken to the South Side, where a 60-foot descent is often necessary simply to touch the reef. On two separate dive trips in December, we managed to dive the North Wall only a couple of times before bad weather set in.

To avoid stressing the popular Bloody Bay dive sites, diving in the marine park is limited to two 20-diver boats per day. The result is a very healthy reef. Even the shallow portions of the walls are in surprisingly good shape, considering their exposure to storms.

Just in case you don't have an opportunity to dive Bloody Bay Wall, you can always log on to www.bloodybaywall.com to see an enormous mural of the wall. The site consists of life-size photos of a portion of the wall 20 feet high and 60 feet wide. You can zoom out and see the grand scale, or zoom in and see the minute details. Underwater photographer Jim Hellemn is the creator.

Recommended Level of Experience

While Grand Cayman and the Brac cater to divers of all skill levels, Little Cayman is more popular with advanced divers who are willing to make the extra effort to get here. A typical diver on Little Cayman has 100 or more dives under his or her weight belt. One reason is depth. Although northern dive sites on Bloody Bay Wall and Jackson Bay have areas in which the wall begins at only 20 feet or so, their plunge is dauntingly vertical. Excellent buoyancy is necessary.

The larger problem, though, is that when winds and seas make the North Side undiveable, which is common through the winter season, diving must be done on the South Side, where the reef crest is very deep. If you're diving all three islands, try to save this one for last, when your diving skills will be better honed.

Great Dive Sites

I'd have to say that *Mixing Bowl,* at the westernmost end of Jackson Bay and the beginning of Bloody Bay, is my favorite dive in the marine park simply because of the incredible array of color. Fortunately, the wall is so shallow that this is a good second dive and a nice snorkel site, as well. But for the first dive, it's awesome! Descending a winding, sandy corridor on the Bloody Bay section (about a 45° angle), you'll follow it to 100 feet where an incredible array of color spreads out before you. Friendly grouper tag along while you weave through cuts and canyon passageways, and schools of jacks, chromis, schoolmaster, grunts, and snapper arch and flow all around. A stunning stand of pillar coral will greet you back up on top.

On my first dive here we managed to spot a well-camouflaged frogfish on this section of wall, and, incredibly, a tiny orange sea horse only a few feet away. With so much to take in at these prolific sites, it's easy to overlook some of these wonderful little critters.

Marilyn's Cut also has stunning displays of sponge life, especially yellow tube and trumpet sponges and bright red rope and cup sponges. The grouper here adore attention from divers, and visit with every one, practically begging to be stroked.

Be careful not to swallow your mouthpiece diving *Great Wall East* and *West.* The wall drops at a heart-stopping 90° angle below. At some locations it's actually undercut, due to the protruding growth near the top. Another humbling site on Bloody Bay Wall is *Randy's Gazebo.* First, you'll soar over an awesome vertical face, looking down on massive barrel sponges. At 40 feet you angle through a chimney that spits you out on the wall at 75 feet. Where the wall makes a wide inward curve, you fin through current (sometimes strong) and blue water to reach the other side. A little farther along, you'll locate the beautiful archway formed in a coral outcropping—the perfect photo, if you're not too narked to shoot it!

There's really only one good shore dive on Little Cayman—*Cumber's Caves*—and it's a blast. You'll feel like kids in a playground, weaving in and out of the narrow winding passageways through the reef and down the sponge and coral-encrusted wall. If you're shore diving, you can walk halfway to the buoy, then kick out the rest of the way. Drop down at the buoy, head for the reef, and look for a cut in the wall that actually has an anchor wedged in the sand. Fall right down through the cut—a 45° angle, and it'll spit you out at 85 feet onto the wall! The structure itself is wonderful, but you'll also see plenty of sea fans, rope sponges, and basket sponges. New divers can have just as much fun and plenty to see around the sand and reef area. The playmates there are rays, garden eels, conch, anemones, and even fish!

Boats run divers over to the Brac several times a week to dive the *Capt. Keith Tibbetts.*

DIVE SERVICES & PACKAGES ON LITTLE CAYMAN

Paradise Divers is the only shop on Little Cayman I have not dived with, but the reports are good. Guests staying at Paradise Villas are taken out via two pontoon boats—a 28-footer and a 43-footer—which are also used for Owen Island trips and sunset cruises. Paradise Villas is the only resort on the island which does not offer meals. There are 12 kitchen-equipped units. Nitrox air fills and a full gear-rental line are available. Instruction, with NAUI and PADI, is through divemaster level. Phone (345) 948-0001; fax (345) 948-0002; e-mail: iggy@candw.ky; website: www.scubatimes.com.

Retail Sales: *Adequate*
Rentals: *Extensive*
Scuba Training: *Extensive*
Photo Services: *Limited*

Dive Boat Comfort: *Good*
On-Board Facilities
for Photographers: *Good*

Pirate's Point Divers runs two-tank dives from a beautiful 42-foot Newton, the *Yellow Rose,* which is also used for trips over to the Brac to dive the *Tibbetts.* Gay and Ed are excellent underwater guides and will take care of all your needs. Gay is just about the best underwater communicator I've ever come across. Nitrox fills are available, as are gear rentals. Certification courses from NAUI, PADI, and SSI are given through the advanced level, and some specialties, including Nitrox, are offered. An underwater video of your diving experience can be ordered. Phone (345) 948-1010; fax (345) 948-1011.

Retail Sales: *None*
Rentals: *Adequate*
Scuba Training: *Moderate*
Photo Services: *Limited*

Dive Boat Comfort: *Excellent*
**On-Board Facilities
for Photographers:** *Good*

Reef Divers, at the Little Cayman Beach Resort (a PADI Gold Palm Resort), is the largest and most complete dive operation on the island. It features a full rental line, a photo and video center, and Nitrox air fills. Certification courses are through divemaster level, and Nitrox and photo classes are offered. Certifying agencies are IANTD, PADI, and TDI. Their boats are three 42-foot Newtons, definitely comfortable for trips to the Brac for diving the *Tibbetts*. Call (345) 948-1033; fax (345) 948-1040; e-mail: reefdive@candw.ky; website: www.braclittle.com.

Retail Sales: *Adequate*
Rentals: *Extensive*
Scuba Training: *Extensive*
Photo Services: *Extensive*

Dive Boat Comfort: *Excellent*
**On-Board Facilities
for Photographers:** *Superior*

Sam McCoy's Diving and Fishing Lodge runs two custom-built boats— a 28-footer and a 30-footer. Gear rentals and Nitrox air fills are available. For ease in getting to Bloody Bay Wall, this establishment is the place to be, with its north shore location. Phone (800) 626-0496 or (345) 948-0026; fax (345) 948-0057; e-mail: mccoy@candw.ky; website: www.mccoyslodge.com.ky.

Retail Sales: *None*
Rentals: *Adequate*
Scuba Training: *Limited*
Photo Services: *None*

Dive Boat Comfort: *Good*
**On-Board Facilities
for Photographers:** *Good*

Southern Cross Club (a PADI Resort) uses a 34-foot Crusader and a 36-foot Sea Hawk for diving. Terry Thompson is the affable guide, and will make sure you have a good time. Rental gear is limited; Nitrox fills are available. Trips go over to the Brac for diving the *Tibbetts*. Certification courses are through advanced, with PADI. The Nitrox IANTD course is also offered. Call (800) 899-2582 or (345) 948-1099; fax (345) 948-1098; e-mail: scc@candw.ky; website: www.southerncrossclub.com.

Retail Sales: *None*
Rentals: *Adequate*
Scuba Training: *Moderate*
Photo Services: *Limited*

Dive Boat Comfort: *Good*
**On-Board Facilities
for Photographers:** *Good*

WHERE TO STAY ON LITTLE CAYMAN

Little Cayman Beach Resort ★★★★★, a PADI Gold Palm Resort sister to Brac Reef Beach Resort, is one of the largest resorts on the island, with a whopping 40 rooms (gasp). Twenty-eight of the rooms have pool views with balconies, air-conditioning, and ceiling fans. Twelve are luxury oceanfront rooms with kitchenettes and balconies. Facilities include bar and restaurant, retail shop, game room, fitness center, tennis courts, Jacuzzi, and a health and beauty center. Guests can use bicycles for touring or take a guided tour. Per person rates for the pool-view rooms, based on double occupancy, range from $561 to $622 (depending upon season) for three nights and include breakfast and dinner and three dives per day. Meal plans with lunch included are also available. Call (800) 327-3835; fax (813) 323-8827; e-mail: bestdiving@reefseas.com; website: www.littlecayman.com.

Pirate's Point Resort ★★★★ (a PADI Resort) is a super-accommodating, friendly, laid-back place with attractive, spacious rooms and excellent cuisine. In fact, some of its clientele are nondivers who come for the dining alone. Owner Gladys Howard has studied with the best—Julia Child and James Beard. If you enjoy small resorts with lots of personal attention, you'll love this one. The ten rooms are in duplex cottages, and the little resort has its own swimming pool right on the beach. The lively dining room gets even livelier after dinner, with games and jokes—everyone joins in. Rates are all-inclusive: two boat dives and three meals per day, all alcoholic beverages, transfers, bikes, etc. Daily per person rates range from $210 to $230, depending on the season. Phone (345) 948-1010; fax (345) 948-1011.

Sam McCoy's Diving and Fishing Lodge ★★★, on the North Side (beachfront) close to Bloody Bay Wall, is a friendly, no-frills family-owned facility with only eight rooms. If you're not too fussy and are looking for very personalized service, this is the place to be. Chris McCoy will definitely show you a good time underwater, and he and his mom and dad are welcoming hosts. Have Chris take you out conching and try the univalve right out of the shell—it tastes like coconut and can't get any fresher than that! Gather around with them at the bar in the evening, and you'll hear some colorful island stories. Dinners are served family style at a single long table, which is a lot of fun. Before your stay has ended, you'll have several new friends. Even if you're not staying here, you might want to check out their Saturday evening barbecue and dine al fresco under the stars. The facilities include bikes, hammocks, and a swimming pool. The summer rate for divers is $160 per person, per day, double occupancy. The winter rate is $180. That includes room, three meals per day, a two-tank morning dive, unlimited afternoon shore diving, and optional night diving. Phone

(800) 626-0496 or (345)948-0026; fax (345) 948-0057; e-mail: mccoy@
candw.ky; website: www.mccoyslodge.com.ky.

Southern Cross Club ★★★★ is a super-attractive little PADI Resort, set
on a gorgeous stretch of beach, with 11 spacious and brightly decorated
air-conditioned beach cottages. Each is painted a different color (convenient for those of us who get lost easily) and spread out for maximum
privacy. The staff is friendly and accommodating, and the cuisine here is
outstanding. The resort also features bonefishing and has a guide on staff.
If you feel like getting some terrestrial exercise, you can grab a bike—any
bike—any time of day. Per person rates, double occupancy, range from
$2,254 to $1,445 (depending upon season) for five nights with two dives
and three meals per day. Packages are also available with three dives per
day. Call (800) 899-2582 or (345) 948-1099; fax (345) 948-1098; e-mail:
scc@candw.ky; website: www.southerncrossclub.com.

ISLAND LIFE ON LITTLE CAYMAN

From the Brac, Little Cayman is just five miles due west. To explore the
island, it's best to opt for a bicycle, or just ask someone to drive you
around. You'll travel unpaved, rutted roads and pass by signs warning you
to brake for iguanas. Just a few small dive and fishing resorts dot the island,
and except for the employees who work them, there are few islanders. In
your spare time you can visit the largest breeding colony of red-footed boobies in the Western Hemisphere, buy a handmade basket from Mrs. Reilly
(near the airport), or make a driftwood sign to leave for posterity. Then
again, an empty hammock might be impossible to resist.

Dining and Entertainment

Since there is only one restaurant (the **Hungry Iguana**) on the island,
meals are included in the resort's package price (with the exception of one
resort that is adjacent to the restaurant). In the evening, guests at all these
resorts have plenty to talk about while enjoying superb cuisine. In fact,
since word has spread, many nondivers come over primarily for the food
and relaxation. After dinner, they might watch diving videos, play dominoes, or simply read a good book. If you want more entertainment than
that, best stay on Grand Cayman.

Medical Facilities

A clinic is located near the airport, staffed by a nurse. Phone 948-1051. In
case of a diving emergency call DAN (Divers Alert Network) at (919) 684-
4DAN (4326) or (919) 684-8111.

Mexico's Cozumel

Physical Characteristics of the Dive Area

WATER & WEATHER CONDITIONS

Visibility	*Excellent*
Current and Surge	*Moderate*
Temperature	*Comfortable*
Storms	*Occasionally Stormy*

SITE CONDITIONS

Mooring Buoys	*N/A*
Fishing, Collecting, and Hunting Restrictions	*Widespread Restrictions*
Ease of Access	*Convenient*
Boat Traffic/Diver Congestion	*Light*

MARINE LIFE

Abundance of Invertebrates	*Prolific*
Abundance of Vertebrates	*Abundant*
Abundance of Pelagic Life	*Abundant*
Health of Reef/Marine Life/ Marine Structure	*Healthy*

Best Drift Diving South of the Border

Tell your friends you're going to Cozumel, and you'll receive green-as-guacamole scowls of envy. For years this little island off the coast of Mexico's Yucatán Peninsula has been North America's favorite international warm-water dive destination. That's because Cozumel has all the ingredients for a grand gringo holiday for both divers and nondivers: good food, lively nightspots, warm exceptionally clear waters, and sweeping white-sand beaches. Add to that mix ease of access–the island is less than two hours flight time from Miami and Houston–and an array of dive packages to fit any budget, and the result is a winning formula that keeps divers coming back year after year.

After a hiatus of 11 years, I recently returned to Cozumel and enjoyed it as much, if not more, than my first visit. Cozumel is more appealing than ever, with a vibrant *zocalo* (town center), an attractive harbor area, and long, pristine stretches of sandy coastline. For visitors who can't afford the time to hop over to the mainland to tour Tulum or Chichén Itzá, the little island even provides its very own Mayan ruins. And while tourists spend fortunes only 30 miles away in pricey Cancún, more discerning travelers to Cozumel can soak up Mexican culture along with warm rays of sunshine without depleting their savings accounts.

For comfortable diving and underwater beauty and excitement, this is about as close to perfection as it gets. While diving here in September, my computer registered a bathwater-warm temperature of 85°. None of the dive sites were crowded, and the marine life was abundant, healthy, and huge, from the French angelfish, queen triggerfish, and grouper to the lobster, anemones, and elephant ear sponges.

Most of the hotels lie along the island's western coast where the sea is calm, and this, as well as the southern tip, is where all the action is. Action, certainly, is the operative word. Divers don't fin much in Cozumel waters—they are propelled. Current simply sweeps you away. Want to get a workout? Forget it. This diving is effortless–that is, unless you have to swim up-current!

Even new divers might recognize names like *Palancar, Punta Sur,* and *Santa Rosa.* They all signify outstanding drift diving, where divers pass effortlessly by enormous coral pinnacles and soar through labyrinths of tunnels and passageways. Palancar's massive coral columns, Santa Rosa's enormous vertical wall, and Punta Sur's interconnecting tunnel system offer truly memorable diving experiences. Amazingly, after hosting several generations of divers and enduring the intrusions of weekly cruise ships, these reefs are still in excellent condition.

All of these sites and more are just a portion of the world's second largest barrier reef, which extends all the way down past Belize and off the coast of Honduras in Central America. From inshore coral gardens to enormous coral pinnacles and vertical walls, the sites offer a tremendous variety of marine life and exceptional underwater topography.

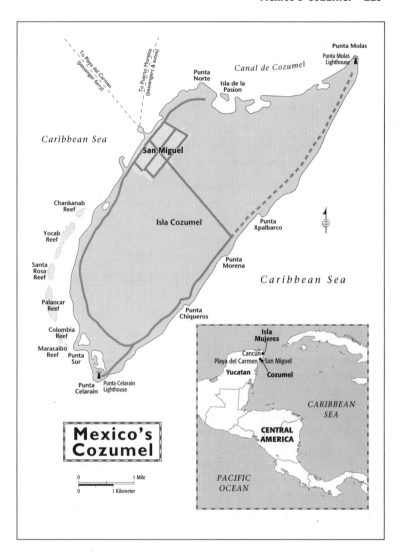

Mexico's Cozumel

Quick Stats

Pronounced   koh-zah-MEL

Size   10 miles wide and 30 miles long

Population   70,000

Location   12 miles off the northeast corner of Mexico's Yucatán Peninsula, which divides the Gulf of Mexico from the Caribbean Sea; in the state of Quintana Roo.

Time   Central Time Zone; Daylight Savings Time is not observed.

Language   Spanish, and a little Mayan, but most people understand English.

Electrical Current   U.S. standard, 110 volts AC, 60 cycles; not all hotels have three-pronged plugs, so bring an adapter.

Air Temperature   Normally mid-70s to low 90s; from December through February, the temperature can drop to the low 70s.

Rainy Season   June through October

Water Temperature   77° to 85°

Underwater Visibility   Averages 100 feet and often reaches 200.

Best Diving Months   Any time

PLANNING THE TRIP

Phoning Cozumel   From North America, dial the international number first, then the country code, the city code, and the local number. So it's 011-52-987+ the 5-digit number. From other destinations dial 001 first.

Getting to Cozumel and Getting Around   Many international flights are routed through Cancún, where passengers transfer to a flight to Cozumel. Flying is definitely the easiest way to get to Cozumel from mainland Mexico, since the ferry terminal is a costly taxi ride away. Both airports have excellent service and easy-to-read directions. All signs are in Spanish and English. The Cancún airport is gorgeous, with marble floors and air-conditioning. There are shops, restaurants, and car-rental agencies.

If you can't handle all your luggage yourself, carts are available for getting it through customs, but they cannot be taken out to connecting flights. You'll need to grab a porter to take them for you. It's handy to have plenty of $1 bills.

Cozumel International Airport is just a few minutes' drive from San Miguel. The major carriers flying into Cozumel are Mexicana, American, Continental, and Aeromexico. Contact Mexicana at (800) 531-7921 in the United States, (800) 531-7923 in Canada; www.mexicana.com.

A departure tax of $12 is collected on all international flights.

Ferries leave from the mainland's Playa del Carmen (about 40 miles from the Cancún airport) and deposit passengers at Cozumel's attractive downtown pier (not the cruise ship pier). Buy tickets at the little kiosks before queuing up. Tickets are around $7 per person, and ferry service is on the hour. The ferries themselves are well equipped with life rafts, large cushioned chairs, and even TV. If you're doing some cenote (sacred pool) diving around Tulum, the ferry is a pleasant and inexpensive way to get over to the mainland.

For the best car-rental rates, make a reservation before departing. Car-rental companies are located at the airport and at large hotels. Taxis are numerous and inexpensive. Red-colored cabs are reserved for locals, so don't bother trying to wave them down.

Entry Documents　A valid passport is required, or a certified original birth certificate (with a raised seal) along with a photo ID, such as a driver's license. Visitors are issued a tourist card free on arrival, which must be kept and returned to immigration officials before leaving the country. When going through customs (*Aduana*), you'll be shown a pole with a large button which you're instructed to push. If the green light comes on, you can move along, but if the red one lights up, be prepared to open your bags for inspection.

Currency　The Mexican peso is written as $, so don't confuse this with the American dollar. The exchange rate varies, but usually hovers around nine pesos to the dollar. U.S. dollars, credit cards, and travelers checks are widely accepted. ATMs dispense pesos.

Business Hours　Banking hours are 9 a.m. to 1:30 p.m., Mondays through Fridays, but currency exchange houses (*casas de cambio)* stay open later and some are open on weekends. Most shops close for siesta from 2 to 4 p.m.

Cozumel Tourist Office　When on island, pick up the free *Blue Guide to Cozumel.* From the United States, call the Mexican Ministry of Tourism at (800) 44-MEXICO.

THE UNDERWATER SCENE

To divers, the word Cozumel is practically synonymous with drift diving. Current is usually present, sometimes just giving a gentle boost, frequently a nudge, and occasionally a violent push. It can be so relaxing you'll feel like taking a siesta, or it can be adrenaline-rush ripping.

From the Mexican mainland, on the eastern Yucatán coast, the current runs from south to north and intensifies as it nears Cozumel. The flow definitely increases as it is funneled through the passage between the island and the coast. At the southern end of the island, the current is at its weakest. Toward the northern end, the channel narrows, so the flow is greatly intensified, approaching speeds up to ten knots.

The current does much more than provide us with a free ride, however. It is largely responsible for keeping the water clear and the food chain ever-nourished. Also contributing to the astounding water clarity is the absence of rivers, either from the island or the peninsula, flowing into the sea, which could deliver damaging sediments.

Rough windward seas generally pound the island's straight eastern shoreline; nevertheless, some areas on this side are dived occasionally. The western, leeward side is scalloped with sandy coves and surrounded with healthy reef structure, perfect for a number of diving environments.

Essentially, there are three types of underwater habitats off the western shore. Closest to shore are shallow coral gardens consisting primarily of patch reef on a sandy and rocky rubble bottom. Farther out are the coral pinnacles and deeper canyon-type coral buttresses surrounded by gorgeous fields of white sand and pocked with exciting tunnels, chimneys, caves, and caverns. Just beyond these (and frequently on the ocean side of them) are vertical walls that plummet far beyond safe diving depths.

The reef sites extend over large areas, and since there are no mooring buoys to use as starting points, the particular features of the sites are diverse and vary considerably from dive to dive. Essentially, each falls within one of the three types of environments described. Also, each site will have varying degrees of current. As a rule, the deeper sites will have the most interesting topography, frequently with tunnels, chutes, and all sorts of intricate passageways that make for thrilling experiences—sometimes challenging, always memorable.

The Cozumel reefs are known for their fabulous sponge formations, especially the venerable barrel sponges and the beautiful orange elephant ear sponges, both of which grow to enormous proportions. Spurs and patches of coral are habitats for lobster and crab, triggerfish and parrotfish, solitary grouper and schooling jacks. Huge coral pinnacles in all sorts of convoluted shapes soar above plains of brilliant white cascading sands. Decorating these massive coral structures are beautiful deepwater gorgonian corals that stretch out in fan-shape formation to catch nutrients and rays of light.

Because the reefs are protected by law from hunting and gathering, the marine life is free to grow. And grow they do, to enormous sizes. Particularly impressive are the massive lobster, eels, and grouper, the species that fall prey to humans so quickly in unprotected sites.

It is said that as many as 250 species of fish inhabit these reefs. One of them is the curious little splendid toadfish, which is endemic to the island.

Several different types of toadfish inhabit the Caribbean, but the splendid toadfish has been found only off Cozumel. It stays hidden under coral crevices, but you can hear little clicking noises when you're in the water, so you know it's around. Usually, with patience you can spot one, with its little bearded chin and flattened, zebra-striped head barely exposed in its hiding place. It would be unusual to see one out in the open, but it happens occasionally. Supposedly the unassuming little creature can devour an entire fish in six milliseconds.

Night diving off Cozumel is a definite *must*. During my last visit, a night dive at *Paradise* was one of the highlights of the trip. Under the illumination of dive lights and camera strobes, the reef's colors—particularly the elephant ear sponges—were brilliant. Little yellow stingrays scuttled along the sand, batwing coral crabs hugged the coral mounds, and hermit crabs hunkered inside abandoned shells. Whenever divers spotted anything interesting, they would clang on their tanks to signal to the other divers that they had found something. Because of the wonderful assortment of fascinating things to see, the banging was almost constant (and constantly annoying!).

Health Score Card

It's pretty amazing that the reefs here are in such good shape. After an absence of about 12 years, I noticed that some of the huge coral pinnacles that I had remembered were not as numerous. But the vertebrate life seemed more prolific than before. The sponges, certainly, were some of the healthiest I've seen anywhere in the Caribbean.

For years, cruise ship anchoring caused widespread damage in the Paradise region. The huge chains would sway back and forth, kicking up huge clouds of sand, smothering the corals and sponges. A second pier was constructed, which eliminated this practice. But in order to construct the pier, some reef area had to be sacrificed.

Storm damage is always evident in some shallow areas, an inevitable problem in hurricane country. Diver-damage usually occurs in the overhead environments—the tunnels, caverns and swim-throughs where it's so easy to kick up sand and knock into the structure itself. That's why good buoyancy skills are so important.

Diving Conditions

Cozumel's dive sites extend along the leeward western coast, which is protected from prevailing tradewinds. Drift dives predominate, and these can be extremely enjoyable or very frustrating, depending on your point of view. If you want to simply float along (and occasionally fly along) looking at the scenery, you'll love it. But if your goal is to observe or photograph a specific area, be prepared for disappointment. In many locations remaining stationary is difficult at best, and frequently impossible. Sometimes you can duck behind a coral head to get out of the flow—just watch that you don't knock into anything.

The currents vary from one knot to gusts of eight knots. Normally they run a comfortable two or three knots. All the boats here run "live;" that is, they do not anchor, but follow the divers' bubbles and pluck them out of the water when they surface. This type of diving can be tricky for any boat operator, but Cozumel's have really perfected the technique and for the most part do an excellent job.

Normally groups get off the boat and into the water quickly, and they stay together while a divemaster leads. Some operators are more flexible, especially with experienced divers, and will allow independent exploring. In such cases, you have to be willing to bob around in the water for a while as the boat travels from group to group picking up divers.

With this type of diving, carrying a safety sausage or some sort of visual marker is a good idea. Heads can be difficult to spot in the water, especially if conditions get rough, so popping up a colorful plastic tube will greatly increase your visibility to the boat captain. During my last trip to Cozumel I inflated my safety sausage twice. I'm sure I would have been spotted anyway, but the marker made it that much easier for the dive crew. If you find you're a long way from the boat without a safety sausage and become concerned, you can always hold up a fin, in a pinch.

Recommended Level of Experience

Cozumel is generally considered a good spot for any type of diver. However, there are many sites that should not be attempted by new or "rusty" divers. Several have extensive overhead environments that can make many divers uneasy, if not downright scared. Also, if divers don't have good buoyancy techniques they can do a lot of damage to the marine life. Don't forget: corals and sponges are living organisms and grow at extremely slow rates. Several of the dive sites are also very deep, and the deco stops are in mid-water, with no anchor line. Excellent buoyancy control is extremely important.

Always make your first few dives in shallow areas that have only modest current. Practice your buoyancy and get comfortable with the environment and your equipment, then move on to more challenging dives. It's best to let the dive shop know if you're an inexperienced diver.

I once saw a very experienced diver panic at Punta Sur, which is widely regarded as an advanced site. There are several other challenging sites, so make sure you find out what kind of diving is being planned before committing to a dive outing.

Dive Sites for the Adventurous

For divers who are comfortable in deep water and inside enclosed environments, the aforementioned Punta Sur is a blast. This beautiful and exciting dive features orange and purple rope sponges and branching gorgonians decorating the coral overhangs, and a maze of complex interconnecting tunnels and caves. Expect to reach depths of 115 feet or more.

On my last dive here, we all followed the divemaster down very quickly to a depth of about 80 feet. We entered a gradually sloping cave (technically a cavern), about six feet wide, that was heavily decorated with sponges and corals and absolutely beautiful. Several small openings above allowed narrow beams of light to shoot through. From the dark cave, it was a gorgeous sight to look up and see the brilliant blue above us. Snaking through the cave, we exited about 90 feet, then swam across a field of bright white sand topped with coral pinnacles and buttresses, and all decorated with a profusion of sea fans.

After finning over the sand for a few minutes, we made another downward dive through the coral and into a narrower sloping tunnel. This one, part of the *Devil's Throat* complex, was straight at first, then winding. A few openings from very high above allowed in some narrow shafts of light, illuminating sections of the wall. After winding around a bit, we reached an area where a wide chimney opened up into the coral structure above, with divers' bubbles moving up through it, creating a gorgeous smoke effect. At that point, straight in front of me, was a white sponge formation on the coral wall, in the perfect shape of a cross. I thought: OK, must be narked! Later the divemaster assured me that the cross did exist, and after developing my film, I knew for certain. After reaching another ethereal shaft of light, we exited the tunnel. While passing massive, soaring coral buttresses, we finned away from the wall over huge expanses of sandy plain. Far below I spotted a stingray and in the water column watched silvery jacks schooling. We all hung mid-water for several minutes before re-boarding.

Punta Sur (meaning South Point) is at the southern tip of Cozumel, where another wild dive site is located—*Maricaibo*. All of these deep dives require mid-water decompression safety stops. Maricaibo is considered even more advanced than Punta Sur, so divemasters generally avoid it. It is known for very strong and unpredictable currents and abrupt, very deep, drop-offs.

Columbia Reef and adjacent *Palancar Reef* both feature some skyscraper-proportioned coral pinnacles and flowing fields of white sand. Currents can be strong. They are both canyonlike in structure, with Columbia featuring successive terraces along the seaward-facing wall. The face of Palancar's wall is etched with winding canyons, deep ravines, and narrow crevices. It is a labyrinth of passageways, tunnels, and caves. Both sites have gigantic plate corals and huge sponges. Due to their complexity and size, it would require many dives to see all that these fantastic sites have to offer.

Santa Rosa has what is considered to be Cozumel's steepest wall, but I was as enchanted with the gorgeous white sandy plains, with their swirling patterns, as I was with the vertical wall and its cuts and swim-throughs. Because of the potential depths and strong currents, this is considered a dive for intermediate-level abilities. Starting at about 50 feet, coral heads jut out from the wall and all appears in enormous proportions. Orange elephant ear sponges, sinewy rope sponges, cascading plate coral, and queen angelfish are huge. Divers see fields of finger coral and bulbous translucent and yellow-tipped anemones. Windows through the coral outcroppings open to visions of brilliant white sand flowing down the wall. Swim-throughs all along beckon in vain as divers fly by, pulled by the strong currents. Atlantic spadefish and snapper school in profusion on top of the reef, among solitary or coupled triggerfish and French angelfish.

Ordinary Great Sites

Inshore, where maximum depths are closer to 70 feet, the dive sites are just as beautiful as those already mentioned, but the drop-offs are shallower and more gradual and the currents usually less fierce. Of these, *Maracaibo Shallows, Palancar Gardens, Yocab Reef* and *Tormentos Reef* are some of my favorites. *Paradise Reef South* is an excellent second dive and night dive. It's as though there's always a party going on here, with crowds of fish life all in motion.

At *Maracaibo Shallows,* jawfish and goatfish inhabit the sandy rubble between patch reefs. The lobster and French angelfish are especially numerous here, as are schools of grunts and snapper. In fact, there are so many species competing for space, it's a fascinating place to watch fish behavior. On a single dive here, I spotted those already mentioned, as well as a splendid toadfish, spotted drum, arrow crabs, and an enormous barracuda getting cleaned.

Palancar Gardens (15 to 70 feet) features wonderful pinnacles with winding, sinewy cuts. In swim-throughs and under ledges something is always hiding. The area is a kaleidoscope of brilliant azure vase sponges, multicolored rope sponges, and bright orange elephant ear sponges.

Yocab Reef (50 to 70 feet), which is fairly close to shore, has little current and is loaded with great numbers of lobster, queen angelfish, and other tropicals. Colonies of jawfish pop up from their burrows in the rocky rubble of the shallows. The marine life is exceptional here, and the reef is in very good shape. For close-up and macro photography, this is a perfect location.

A little farther out and a bit deeper is *Tormentos Reef* (50 to 80 feet), where coral heads dot the sandy bottom. Cut-out "windows" in the coral heads reveal the brilliant white sands beyond. Overlapping coral ledges are covered with bright green algae dripping from their undersides. Sponges of all varieties, but particularly rope sponges, extend in all sorts of convoluted formations, mixing with the gorgonian corals. Very large French and queen angels dart about, and a profusion of anemones sway in the ever-present currents.

Shallow Diving and Snorkeling

Chances are excellent that there is very good snorkeling at your resort. All that's needed on this side of the island is easy access, and the marine creatures are sure to be present. Walking out on a sandy bottom is fine, but as soon as it becomes rocky, snorkelers and shore divers should lie prone on the water, so as not to damage living coral. Some of the best snorkel spots on Cozumel have been destroyed because of ignorance.

Don't forget about the current, though, and make sure you plan your dive or snorkel carefully. If you drift along with the current, you'll need to exit at a convenient location. Also, make sure you have on booties, so you can walk safely on rocky terrain. You'll need fins without foot pockets, which are the most versatile for such situations.

Also, don't think you have to get to coral heads to find anything interesting. Sandy areas can be fascinating and attract entirely different creatures. You'll find crab, conch, flounder, tube worms, stingrays, and more. Once I marveled at something that looked like a leaf on its side, then realized by its behavior it was not vegetative matter. Sure enough, it was a leaf fish!

Chancanaab Park is a popular shore dive and snorkel spot, but if you're an experienced snorkeler, avoid it and the mobs that it attracts. Novice snorkelers and divers, however, will appreciate the calm water conditions and all the services, including gear rental, air fills, picnic facilities, and snack shops.

I have heard that *Playa Corona Beach Club* and *La Ceiba Reef* are excellent for shore diving, although I have not checked them out. The latter is the site of an airplane wreck that gets a lot of attention. The entire area encompassing *Paradise Reef* is also good for snorkeling, shallow diving, and night dives. Wherever you dive or snorkel, watch out for boat traffic. It's really best to not venture too far from shore for this reason. The Paradise area, in particular, has heavy boat traffic.

Marine Park

In 1996 the Mexican government designated as a National Marine Park Cozumel's 25-mile stretch of reef from the southern section of Paradise Reef (just beyond the newest cruise ship pier), all the way around the island to Punta Chiquero, on the east side. SEMARNAP—the environmental, natural resource, and fishing secretariat—administers the park. Financing is through several sources, including ANOAAT, the Cozumel association of dive operators. The association developed diving guidelines that outlaw spearfishing and limit the number of boats and dive operators permitted on the reefs. It emphasizes buoyancy control and respect for the reef and all sea life.

Boat divers and snorkelers pay $2 per day, which helps support the regulations. Since the boats run "live," there is no need to install mooring buoys.

DIVE SERVICES & PACKAGES

Years ago, after a long string of diving accidents, the federal government issued rules for increasing diving safety. The rules require that all divemasters be certified, that a divemaster is provided for every eight divers, that boat captains are licensed, and that all boats have marine radios. Most boats now also carry oxygen. When in doubt, don't hesitate to inquire about the safety features of dive boats. Also, check out rental equipment thoroughly before you get into the water.

Certified Nitrox divers will not have a problem finding mixed gas, since most operators now at least offer it, even if they do not pump it on site.

When dialing the on-island 987 numbers, remember to first dial 011-52-987, then the local five-digit number.

Aldora Divers is a PADI 5-Star IDC offering every level of certification, as well as many specialty courses, including Nitrox and DAN Oxygen Provider. With a fleet of five 27-foot boats, it runs morning, afternoon, and night dives around Cozumel. Nitrox fills are available. This is a charter operation with no retail shop. The Aldora is affiliated primarily with Fiesta Inn and El Presidente. Phone 987-2339; e-mail: dave@aldora.com; website: www.aldora.com.

Retail Sales: *None*	**Dive Boat Comfort:** *Good*
Rentals: *Adequate*	**On-Board Facilities**
Scuba Training: *Extensive*	**for Photographers:** *Good*
Photo Services: *None*	

Aqua Safari is a venerable PADI 5-Star IDC (operating since 1966). The business has two locations, one on the waterfront downtown (between 5th and 7th Streets South), and another on the premises of the Plaza Las Glorias resort. Boats of varying sizes, from 25 to 38 feet, run morning, afternoon, and night dives. Instruction is extensive, with certs from intro to scuba through advanced. Also, this is an instructor development center, so if you're thinking of going pro, this might be a shop to consider. Aqua Safari rents and sells gear and offers Nitrox fills. Above the shop is the Safari Inn, a modest 12-room hotel; all rooms at the Safari have air-conditioning and private bath. Nightly rates range from $35 to $50. Phone and fax 011-52-987-20101, 30101; fax 011-52-987-20661; e-mail: dive@aquasafari.com; website: www.aquasafari.com.

Retail Sales: *Extensive*	**Dive Boat Comfort:** *Good*
Rentals: *Extensive*	**On-Board Facilities**
Scuba Training: *Extensive*	**for Photographers:** *Good*
Photo Services: *Moderate*	

Dive House also has two locations, one at the Fiesta Americana and another at the Main Plaza downtown. The Fiesta Americana location is on the beach, and has its own boat dock. It operates a fleet of boats of varying sizes, from 28 to 46 feet, for morning, afternoon, and night dives. Nitrox and rental equipment are available. Certifying agencies are NAUI, PADI, SSI, and TDI. Call 987-21953; fax 987-23068; e-mail: dive@dive house.com; website: www.divehouse.com.

Retail Sales: *Extensive*	**Dive Boat Comfort:** *Good*
Rentals: *Extensive*	**On-Board Facilities**
Scuba Training: *Moderate*	**for Photographers:** *Good*
Photo Services: *Moderate*	

Scuba Du, on the property of the El Presidente Inter-Continental (a PADI Resort), has a very good reputation for service. The dive center runs two 28-foot, one 31-foot, and two 36-foot boats for morning, afternoon, and night dives. All boats have DAN oxygen units and VHF radios. Their certifying agencies are NAUI and PADI. Instruction is through the advanced level, and a number of specialties are offered. Nitrox fills are available. Phone 987-20322, ext. 6845; fax 987-24130; e-mail: scubadu@cozumel.czm.com.mx; website: www.lacozumel.net/diving/scubadu.

Retail Sales: *Extensive*	**Dive Boat Comfort:** *Good*
Rentals: *Extensive*	**On-Board Facilities**
Scuba Training: *Moderate*	**for Photographers:** *Good*
Photo Services: *Moderate*	

TTC Club Divers, affiliated with the all-inclusive Club Cozumel Caribe, has a very good reputation for both service and safety. Although the resort is located farthest from the primary dive sites, the boats are fast, roomy, and comfortable, ranging from 46 to 58 feet. They run morning, afternoon, and night dives, and offer Nitrox. Certifying agencies are PADI and ACUC. Call 987-24476; fax 987-25722; e-mail: ttc@cozumel.com.mx; website: www.clubdivers.com.

Retail Sales: *Adequate*

Rentals: *Extensive*

Scuba Training: *Moderate*

Photo Services: *Limited*

Dive Boat Comfort: *Good*

On-Board Facilities

for Photographers: *Good*

WHERE TO STAY

When dialing the on-island 987 numbers, first dial 011-52-987, then the local five-digit number.

Allegro Resort Cozumel ★★★★ (formerly Diamond Resort) has an excellent location on the southwest part of the island (km 16.5) right on San Francisco Beach. For divers, this means that some of the prime dive sites are just minutes away. The resort's 300 rooms are dispersed among thatch-roofed villas, with eight rooms per villa. All have air-conditioning and ceiling fans, balconies, satellite TV, phones, and safety deposit boxes. The resort also has two restaurants and several bars, a gift shop, car and motorscooter rental, tour desk, and more. There are four lighted tennis courts, equipment for non-motorized watersports, two swimming pools, and a Jacuzzi. The dive center is Dive Palancar, a PADI/SSI facility. Boats leave from the resort's own dock. All-inclusive packages cover room, meals, beverages, taxes, and gratuities. Rates are $127 to $154 per person based on double occupancy. Diving is extra. Call (800) 858-2258 or 987-23443; fax 987-21571; e-mail: internet@drcozumel.allegroresorts.com; website: www.allegroresorts.com.

Club Cozumel Caribe ★★★★, on San Juan Beach, is an attractive all-inclusive resort in the Spanish-colonial design. It is located north of town, which means that it's farther from the dive sites than many of the other resorts. I did not find this to be a problem, however. The dive operation is TTC Divers, a PADI facility, which has excellent boats. The time spent en route was always a pleasure and never seemed tedious. The resort has two swimming pools, a private pier, an open-air restaurant, two bars, a tour desk, a gift shop, and car rental. Rooms are spacious, and they have air-conditioning and large balconies. For an ocean-view junior suite, including diving, meals, drinks, etc., the nightly per person rate for a double is from $119 to $149. Phone 987-20100; website: www.clubcozumelcaribe.com.

The 172 air-conditioned rooms and 56 tropical casitas at **Fiesta Americana** ★★★★ (km 7.5) are across the street from the beach, where the dock and dive operation are located. Facilities at this PADI Gold Palm Resort include a swimming pool and tennis courts. Many types of watersport activities are offered. Room rates begin at $104 per night. The casita suites begin at $125 per night and include continental breakfast. Dive packages are available. Call 987-22622 and (800) 346-6116 from North America; fax 987-22680; e-mail: dive@fiestaamericana.com.mx; website: www.fiestaamericana.com.

Fiesta Inn Cozumel (km 1.7) is within easy walking distance of downtown. All of its 180 rooms have cable TV. Facilities include a huge swimming pool, three restaurants, and two bars. Dive shops are nearby, but none are actually on the property. Contact the resort for latest rates. Call 987-22900 and (800) 343-7821 from North America; fax 987-22154; website: www.fiestamexico.com.

El Presidente Inter-Continental Hotel Cozumel ★★★★ (km 6.5) always gets high marks from visitors. This PADI Resort is on the south end of the beach, and the dive operation is Scuba Du, which has a solid reputation. Each of the 253 air-conditioned rooms has a private terrace overlooking the Caribbean. Facilities include lighted tennis courts, a private beach and pool, and three restaurants and bars. Snorkeling and diving are right off the beach. Rates start at $220 per night. Dive packages are available. Phone 987-20322, ext. 6845 or (800) 327-0200 from North America; fax 987-21360; e-mail: cozumel@intercontl.com.

The all-inclusive **Reef Club** ★★★ is on the ocean, at the southern end of the island, near all the dive sites. Its 350 rooms are in two-story thatch-roofed bungalows. All have air-conditioning and ceiling fans, telephones, minibars, safety deposit boxes, satellite TV, and balconies or terraces. Loads of activities are offered, including some dive lessons in the pool. Otherwise, diving is extra. The resort has two large pools, four lighted tennis courts, several restaurants and bars, a disco, and activities for children. Per person per night rates for a double are from $125 to $152. The PADI dive center is on the property, and dive packages are available. Phone (800) 221-5533 or 987-43624; fax 987-60733; e-mail: iberostar@worldnet.att.net.

Scuba Club Cozumel ★★★★ (km 1.5) is a dedicated dive resort that's been around since 1976. Once called the Galapago Inn, its 55 rooms are all air conditioned. It has a Spanish-colonial design with a lovely courtyard and swimming pool. Its restaurant is perched right over the water, for terrific views. The dive shop, Scuba Cozumel, and boat dock are on the property. The per person rate for three nights, which includes two days of two-tank diving, all meals, and 24-hour shore diving, is $375 in summer, with double occupancy. Call 987-21133 or (800) 847-5708 from North America. Its website is www.scubaclubcozumel.com

ISLAND LIFE

Cozumel's early history is as romantic as its stunning natural environs. Once part of the advanced Mayan culture, it is said that Cozumel was the home of Ixchel, Mayan goddess of love and fertility. As such, Mayan women from the Yucatán mainland were obliged to make a pilgrimage to her shrine. The Mayas, assumed to have numbered 25 million in Mexico and Central America, were, for their time, surprisingly advanced in mathematics, astronomy, and writing. The civilization existed in several forms for an astounding 4,000 years, dating from about 2000 BC. In the Classic Period, from about AD 250 to 900, they built temples and massive stone structures nearly as grand as those in Egypt.

The Mayan culture began to decline in the tenth century. With the Spaniards' arrival in the sixteenth century, and particularly after Cortes' invasion in 1519, the island population was decimated by smallpox and other diseases carried by the Europeans. In the eighteenth and nineteenth centuries, Cozumel served mostly as a convenient hideout for pirates. Gradually the island was resettled, and its economy was given a boost with the exportation of chicle, the primary component of chewing gum. After Jacques Cousteau introduced Palancar Reef to American TV viewers in 1961, Cozumel's destiny was sealed. Today the island has around 60 dive operators.

More than 30 hotels are strung along the western coastline, but the hub of the island is the vibrant, attractive town of San Miguel, once a sleepy fishing village. The town's main plaza extends from the downtown pier, where ferries leave for the mainland. The streets (called *calles*) are odd-numbered extending south of the plaza, and even-numbered going north. Traffic going north/south has the right-of-way, so remember that when either walking or driving.

Life goes on all around the island—human life, that is. But the interior is the domain of the rest of the animal kingdom, hidden away in scrub jungle and swamp. A very small percentage of it is developed. There are no hills to speak of. A coastal road is the primary thoroughfare, providing wonderful seaward vistas. Much of the coastline on the eastern shore consists of hard ironshore, but on the west are spread incredibly beautiful and pristine white sandy beaches.

Topside Attractions

Definitely leave some time in your schedule to drive around and see the island, especially the wind-swept, pristine southern point and east side. Most of this coastline is under national park jurisdiction, so the beaches seem almost untouched. Anywhere along the way, you can park your car and take a refreshing swim.

Along the beach, you'll see attractive open-air *palapas* (structures with thatch roofs) that serve food and beverages. **Playa Bonito** restaurant has a particularly stunning location, on a long stretch of gorgeous beach. At **Punta Sur,** you can visit the lighthouse, but the area is now a private park, requiring an entrance fee.

Driving around to the east side, you'll find a lovely restaurant/bar called **Coconuts.** It's high up, so has a grand view of the ocean, and there's seating outdoors as well as under the *palapa.* Restrooms are very clean. Next door is the turtle farm, where eggs are incubated and the little tikes released a few weeks after hatching.

Farther along is **Mezcalito's Bar & Grill** at the intersection of the coastal road and the cross-island road that leads to the San Gervasio Mayan ruins. At this point, the paved coastal road becomes dirt, requiring four-wheel drive. Car-rental companies state that their insurance does not cover travel on this section. Shoppers might like to browse around here in the family-owned shops. There are lots of tourist-type items for sale, such as blankets, T-shirts, jewelry, and stone figures. Tours from the cruise ships are brought here, so on certain days it could be mobbed—although it was empty when I visited. Also, prices have been elevated exorbitantly. Definitely bargain. Most items are priced more than double their value.

Generally, the better shops in town have fixed prices, so bartering isn't practiced. You'll find duty-free shops selling perfume, jewelry, and the like. But regional products are the most fun—leather goods, hammocks, handcrafted clay products, blankets, and Mayan *huipiles* (wee-peels), or tunics.

Continuing on the tour, as you head back to town, you'll see signs for **San Gervasio,** where there are some of the island's Mayan ruins. They are modest compared to places like Chichén Itzá and Tulum on the mainland. If you are really into these, definitely book a tour; both are wonderful, but Chichén Itzá is by far the most impressive. San Gervasio charges a modest fee to enter, and you can hire a guide or just walk around on your own and

Sacred Places

To the ancient Mayas, the inland freshwater pools called *cenotes* (say-no-tays) were holy places, portals to a spiritual world below the earth. Well, they were absolutely correct. Although the cenotes can be explained in precise scientific terms, what they yield to those who explore them is nothing short of spiritual.

After experiencing a couple of cenotes recently with some very good friends, I thanked the gods, Mother Nature, and my original dive instructor for the opportunity to view such incredible beauty. The vast system of caverns that lie just below and beyond these somewhat innocuous circular pools of water almost defy description. But I'll do my best.

First, you should know that the majority of the cenotes that are dived are located in the Yucatán, not far from the ferry dock at Playa del Carmen. So an excursion is easy to arrange from Cozumel. Several dive operations, most of which have done extensive penetration through unexplored caves, specialize in taking divers through the caverns and in certifying them in cave diving.

Expert divemasters and instructors will give you extensive pre-dive instructions, then lead you through a magical, other-worldly vision that you're not likely to ever forget. After dropping down, frequently only 20 to 40 feet, you immediately enter limestone cathedrals adorned with brilliant white stalactites and stalagmites in all sorts of fantastic shapes. Long limestone columns drip from the ceiling to meet spires extending from the bottom. You'll float past these delicate behemoths, millions of years in the making, in water so clear that you'll swear your dive buddies are suspended in air. At each one, you'll want to linger, and you'll look longingly at the smaller chambers that lead off into the darkness and wonder about the treasures that they hold.

Don't expect these to be like caves in Florida. There is little similarity. Cenotes are far more diverse, and more beautiful, as well. They are also more exotic, surrounded by dense jungle and usually buzzing with mosquitoes (except in winter). In late summer months, several feet of algae bloom frequently lies on the surface of the pools, completely obscuring visibility. But, strangely, after getting below the haze, the water is surprisingly bright and clear.

Although the tours are cavern dives—always within daylight zone—you will go beyond sight of the cave openings. Maximum

Sacred Places (continued)

linear penetration is never more than 200 feet, which includes your depth. There are no small, restrictive environments; in fact, most of the caverns are big, spacious chambers, and the visibility is typically an incredible 350 feet!

Our excursion was with the well-run **Aquatech/Villas DeRosa** Technical Diving Facility, in Akumal. It is owned by Tony and Nancy De Rosa, who migrated to the area in 1984 from Salt Lake City. Tony and Nancy have explored and laid many thousands of feet of lines in two of the area's cave systems. Instructor Chris le Maillot, originally from the Dordogne region of France, known for its dry caves, picked us up at the ferry and took excellent care of our "large" group of five. Usually their groups are smaller.

Christophe explained that from a geological view, the cave structures are millions of years in the making. They start similar to a coral reef, consisting of limestone and dolomite, both porous, soft rock. Then they became dry caves, and all during the last Ice Age, drop by drop, evaporating water left minute deposits of calcium carbonate that accumulated over thousands of years to form the wonderful columns and spires. As the ice melted and the ocean levels rose, the dry caves slowly flooded again. That's the "nutshell" explanation, of course. The cenote itself is simply a sinkhole where the ground above a cavern has collapsed. The swampy look on the surface is due to tannins that are sucked from the organic material that falls into it—the leaves, trees, mangroves, water lilies, and such.

At the cenote called *Car Wash* (where taxis used to be washed), Chris gave us a thorough pre-dive briefing, going over hand signals, light signals, kicking techniques, and buoyancy control. Then we made sure we were properly weighted in the fresh water, and organized our camera equipment.

Descending briefly with no point of reference through the tea-like tannins, we dropped to the bottom. Our maximum depth for the dive was just over 50 feet. Chris gave us plenty of time to get oriented on the bottom, then started laying a line (there are no permanent guidelines) while slowly finning into the cavern. We followed him single-file, with dive lights turned on. In typical cave-diving fashion, we adhered to the rule of thirds for air management; that is, using one-third to go in and two-thirds to exit. Needless to say, we were very

(continued)

Sacred Places (continued)

careful not to touch any of the awesome spires that we passed—they deserved our utmost respect. We had 45 glorious minutes of bottom time and popped to the surface absolutely jubilant.

Thinking that nothing could possibly surpass that experience, we went on to dive *Grand Cenote,* and found it even more fabulous. We went farther into the cave and saw an even greater variety of architecture. Even the entrance was spectacular, with mangroves and vines and a faint light cascading into the shadowy water. The water level here is much deeper than at Car Wash, so to get down, we climbed a wooden ladder and geared up on a platform that sits on the surface. Fortunately, we did not have to carry gear and tanks down ourselves. An assistant took care of that.

You can experience the cenotes in a single day, like we did, or stay several days. Aquatech/Villas de Rosa facilities include 15 beautiful beachfront condos with kitchens and balconies, some beach villas, some hotel rooms, a large swimming pool, and a very pleasant rooftop bar and restaurant. Lodging prices start at a reasonable $65 per night. They offer full packages including lodging, maid service, meals, diving, guide service, and transportation. You can even arrange for explorer and photographer Steve Gerrard to accompany you on the dives and preserve the experience on film.

If you have any interest in getting cave-certified, this would certainly be the place to do it. Fax and phone 52-987-59020; e-mail: dive@cenotes.com. Check out the website at www.cenotes.com.

read the interpretive signs. One warning: bring bug spray and water. The heat and mosquitoes can be vicious.

About six miles south of town is **Chankanaab National Park,** which has a natural lagoon attracting both birds and marine life. The park also features a dive-with-the-dolphins experience.

For touring, you can either rent a car or hire a taxi. Taxi fares are government controlled and fairly reasonable. The *Blue Guide* lists sample fares you can expect to pay for a variety of destinations. For a tour around the island, they quote $30 pesos, and recommend that you tip the driver. They also advise to avoid paying in big bills and to agree on the fare before you get in. Meters are not used.

Locals warn against renting motorscooters, or even convertible Jeeps, because there are so many accidents. It's really best to rent a good car that can be locked. Local laws state that if you are driving east or west, you must stop at every corner. If you are moving parallel to the water (north/south), you have, theoretically, the right of way. However, be very cautious.

Should you break down, pray for a Green Angel. The Angels are a fleet of government-sponsored trucks bearing mechanics, gas, oil, and parts. They patrol Mexico's main roads, specifically to aid tourists. It's a free service, but tips are expected.

Just about every Mexican town has a town square, or *zocalo,* which is a focal point for socializing. All weekend, the *zocalo* is a hive of activity, but Sunday evenings are traditionally the most popular. Families stroll around the square and chat with friends, kids play, and teenagers flirt. Usually, a bandstand is in the center, where local musicians play and drinks and snacks are sold from vendors.

Cozumel's *zocalo* is a lot of fun, in addition to being very attractive, so definitely try to arrange an evening there. Free open-air concerts are held every Sunday evening from 7 to 10 p.m. The surrounding shops are open late, and there are several around the square and on the side roads that sell top-quality merchandise. Don't bother to come before 5 p.m., however, since many shops are closed for siesta from 1 to 5 p.m.

Finally, if at all possible, try to arrange an excursion to the beautiful Mayan ruins of Tulum on the coast, or better yet to Chichén Itzá, deep in the interior. The best way to arrange the latter is to book with a professional tour operator. Most of the resorts have at least one on the premises, and they will arrange transportation as well as guide services. Getting to Tulum is much simpler. Just take the ferry to Playa del Carmen, then hail a taxi for the short ride to the site.

Dining and Entertainment

You can eat well in Cozumel without emptying your wallet. If you're staying at a resort, definitely try to get downtown at least a couple of nights to sample some of the local restaurants. Most are wonderful places to just kick back and relax. Usually they are constructed to let in the natural breezes and also have ceiling fans whirring overhead.

La Choza, at 10th Avenue and Adolfo Rosado Salas, is excellent for traditional Mayan dishes and seafood. Just a couple blocks away is **Sonora Grill,** on 15th Avenue between Juarez and Calle 2 Norte. It's known for great fajitas, steaks, and seafood. **Las Tortugas,** at 82 10th Avenue Norte, is an attractive spot that's particularly good for red snapper dishes and chicken cooked in the Yucatán style. But there are many, many more to choose from, so ask around.

For nightlife, also, downtown is where the action is. Heard of **Carlos and Charlie's?** Who hasn't? You'll find it downtown, on the waterfront. Usually, all you need to do is walk around, and you'll find someplace fun to party down. For disco, **Neptuno's** is reputed to be the happenin' place, and there's even an Irish pub (called **Irish Pub**) on Adolfo Rosado Salas street between 10th and 15th Aves.

Medical Facilities

In addition to the main hospital (872-01-40), there are private clinics located around the island. For an ambulance call 872-06-39. Pharmacies dispense all sorts of over-the-counter drugs (e.g., antibiotics), which normally require prescriptions elsewhere. This can come in handy if you can't get to a doctor quickly.

The Cozumel Recompression Center is staffed by hyperbaric certified physicians 24 hours a day. The center is supported by donations from visiting divers, who pay $1 per day of diving with affiliated dive operators. In effect, this is dive insurance, since there is no charge for the hyperbaric services themselves. The center is located at Calle 5 Sur, #21-B. In case of a diving emergency call DAN (Divers Alert Network) at (919) 684-4DAN (4326) or (919) 684-8111

Curaçao

Physical Characteristics of the Dive Area	
WATER & WEATHER CONDITIONS	
Visibility	*Excellent*
Current and Surge	*Minimal*
Temperature	*Comfortable*
Storms	*Calm*
SITE CONDITIONS	
Mooring Buoys	*Extensive*
Fishing, Collecting, and Hunting Restrictions	*Widespread Restrictions*
Ease of Access	*Very Easy*
Boat Traffic/Diver Congestion	*Light*
MARINE LIFE	
Abundance of Invertebrates	*Prolific*
Abundance of Vertebrates	*Abundant*
Abundance of Pelagic Life	*Common*
Health of Reef/Marine Life/ Marine Structure	*Pristine*

Where Holland Meets the Caribbean

Imagine Arizona with an ocean view, lush coral reefs, and Dutch-inspired architecture. That's Curaçao in a nutshell. Although most people have heard of the sweet liqueur distilled here, few can find Curaçao on a map. It's located in the southern Caribbean, just off the northern tip of South America. For years, sister-island Bonaire attracted all the attention, and divers scarcely gave Curaçao a glance as they flew by, bound for Bonaire's world-class shore-diving sites.

Until recently, tourism has not played much of a role in Curaçao's destiny. As the capital of the Netherlands Antilles, and just a few miles from Venezuela's shores, Curaçao historically has been a pivotal center of commerce between North and South America. Container shipping, offshore corporations, and an oil refinery are part of the island's lifeblood. Amstel even brews beer—from desalinated seawater—in a large brewery on the island.

While the sight of all this industry may surprise some vacationers, it's also a blessing in disguise. Since tourism isn't the only game in town, locals aren't as apt to view travelers as prey. This means that visiting divers enjoy the benefits of low prices, unpressured dive sites, and almost no crowds, year-round. The island resorts still get many of their bookings from the Netherlands and Germany, and campaigns to capture the American dive-travel market are relatively new. Nevertheless, after you hear *bon bini* (good morning) from a friendly islander, you'll certainly be captivated by its charms.

Gradually, news is spreading to Americans of Curaçao's vast underwater treasures of the natural sort, as well as its magnificent shipwrecks. Packagers are stepping up their offerings to Curaçao and they also are arranging combo-trips with Bonaire. Consequently, dive resorts are getting to be almost as numerous as business hotels. Finally, Curaçao is getting the recognition it deserves, both as a vibrant, attractive destination topside, and an astoundingly beautiful landscape underwater. And unlike Bonaire, Curaçao offers much, much more than great diving and snorkeling.

A couple of years ago, I decided to make my third trip to Curaçao and take along some friends. A total of 16 people joined on, and everyone had an exceptional time. And why? It's because Curaçao has just about everything anyone could possibly want for a dive vacation, thus satisfying every type of diver and every type of traveler. I say "almost," because it does not have the tropical scenery that some might expect on a Caribbean island. What it does have are extremely healthy reefs with shallow walls just a few kicks from shore, warm waters, generally light currents, great visibility, terrific dive resorts with excellent boats and lots to see and do when you're not diving, including shopping and nightlife. And the pièce de résistance is its location—out of the hurricane belt. So it can be dived literally any time of year. That's a significant bonus.

Curaçao is the largest and most populated of the ABC islands (Aruba/Bonaire/Curaçao), which were all dominated at one time or another by the various nations of Europe. It is said that more than 40 nationalities now live on the island—truly a cultural stew.

Until 1986, when Aruba declared its independence, all three islands were members of the Netherlands Antilles. Although the official language is Dutch, and most islanders speak English and Spanish fluently, the native

language is a distinctive local blend called *Papiamentu,* which means "talking." Visitors are usually delighted when they first hear this musical patois, which combines elements from at least six European and African languages! The language originated on the west coast of Africa and was used by European merchants involved in the Caribbean salt and slave trade. It was adopted in Curaçao in the early eighteenth century by Portuguese Jews who wanted to communicate with their servants. In 1976, the Dutch government declared it to be the "Creole tongue of the people."

This rich European history seems strange for an island less than 50 miles from the coastline of Venezuela. Moreover, Curaçao does have a distinctly Southwestern look. Only occasionally, the arid landscape of scrub, cactus, and bonsai-like divi divi trees is interrupted by imposing plantation houses, called *landhuisen*, with their wide, welcoming staircases and gabled windows.

Of all the great cities in the Caribbean, Curaçao's Willemstad is my favorite. At its harbor, rows of Dutch-inspired pastel-colored houses edge the waterways and stone-walled eighteenth-century forts guard the entrance to the bay. An enormous floating bridge that spans the wide harbor entrance swings open like a giant garden gate, admitting cruise ships and small schooners laden with tropical fruit, fish, spices, and oils for the town's quayside floating market. Because of its trade status, shopping is excellent for crafts and fine art, electronics, jewelry, and clothing. At night, the Waterfort Arches provide the perfect venue for a romantic stroll. Twinkling lights, warm, soft trade winds, and lilting sounds of Papiamentu will chase away all your cares.

QUICK STATS

Pronounced cure-a-SOW

Size 182 square miles

Population About 150,000

Location Just 35 nautical miles north of Venezuela's coastline

Time Atlantic Standard, one hour later than U.S. Eastern Standard Time and the same as Eastern Daylight Savings Time

Government Curaçao is one of five islands that comprise the Netherlands Antilles, an autonomous part of the Kingdom of the Netherlands. The five islands are Bonaire, Curaçao, St. Maarten, St. Eustatius, and Saba. Locals are Dutch nationals and carry European Union passports.

Language Ninety percent of the local population speaks Papiamentu, a Creole language. Most official government documents and many signs are in Dutch, but most of the islanders speak English and Spanish as well.

Electrical Current 110–130 volts AC, 50 cycles. The majority of U.S. appliances will work, but some might overheat if used too long. Divers are advised to check with their hotel before charging sensitive equipment.

Air Temperature The average temperature is in the mid-80s. The island is in the tropics, just 12° north of the equator. It's warm and sunny year-round and outside the hurricane belt. Cooling trade winds blow constantly from the west, picking up in the spring months.

Rainfall   Total annual rainfall averages only 22 inches. The rainy season, October through February, is usually marked by short, occasional showers, mostly at night, followed by sunny days.

Water Temperature   Usually around 80°

Underwater Visibility   From 60 to 150 feet

Best Diving Months   Any time

PLANNING THE TRIP

Phoning Curaçao   The international code is 599-9. From the United States or Canada dial 011-599-9 and the local number.

Getting to Curaçao   Curaçao has daily nonstop flights on American Airlines and Air ALM from Miami, with connections available from all major U.S. gateways. American Eagle offers nonstop daily service from San Juan, Puerto Rico to Curaçao. There is also regular service from Atlanta on Air ALM. Flying time is about two and a half hours from Miami. Visitors pay a $20 departure tax for international flights, payable at the airport before check-in. Hato International Airport is located on the north coast, a 15-minute drive from the city center.

Getting Around   Car-rental agencies are available in Willemstad and at many of the resorts; driving is on the right-hand side of the road. Road maps are available at hotels, service stations, and bookstores throughout the island. Identify taxis by their sign and the TX on the license plate. Taxi stands are located at the airport, in Willemstad, and outside major hotels. They don't have meters, but taxis are government regulated and fares are standard. Be sure to confirm the fare before setting out. A 10 percent tip is customary.

Entry Documents   U.S. and Canadian citizens are required to have a return or continuing ticket and proof of citizenship, such as a birth certificate or valid passport, along with photo identification.

Currency   The Netherlands Antilles guilder (NAFL), also known as the florin, is roughly 1.78 to the U. S. dollar. U.S. dollars are accepted, as are travelers checks and major credit cards.

Curaçao Tourism Development Bureau   The address is Pietermaai 19, PO Box 3266, Curaçao, Netherlands Antilles. Call direct at (599-9) 461-6000; fax (599-9) 461-2305; e-mail, ctdbcur@ctdb.com. The website is www.curacao-tourism.com.

The on-island offices are located at Waterfort Arches in Willemstad, at the airport, and the cruise ship terminal. Tourist board offices are located in New York—(800) 3-CURAÇAO for brochures, and (800)270-3350 for information; e-mail, ctdbny@ctdb.com—and Miami (305) 374-5811; e-mail: ctdbmiami@ctdb.com).

THE UNDERWATER SCENE

There is a lot of activity in Curaçao's waters, and fortunately almost all of it is of the marine-animal variety. You'll find little traffic from dive boats and lightly visited sites. Local biologists claim that every hard coral in the Caribbean—55 species in all—is represented here, along with some 30 different soft corals.

Curaçao and its neighboring islands are all washed by the North Equatorial Current, which brings a constant source of warm, clear water and fish-sustaining nutrients to their shores. The underwater topography is more varied that on Bonaire and Aruba. It includes shallow reefs, gently sloping terraces, steep slopes, and walls that plunge to thousands of feet. Access to the reefs couldn't be easier. From many of the shore-diving sites the reef (and even the wall itself) is only a few easy fin kicks away. Curaçao's best shore dives are found on the serene southwest side of the island, in protected bays where there is exceptionally calm water and hardly any current. These conditions are also perfect for snorkelers, who will have a terrific time off of Curaçao's shores. Boat rides, also, are exceptionally short. All of the dive sites—and there are more than 65 to choose from—fall on the sheltered southern side of the island, sculpted along its length with small, sandy coves.

All along the southern shore is a gorgeous wall that is covered with enormous growths of mushroom-shaped star coral and prolific stair-stepping plate corals. The greatest profusion of these hard corals is usually found in water no deeper than 60 feet. Don't count on getting much exercise on these dives. There's little current to speak of, and with so much activity, you'll want to simply hang out at the edge of the wall and gaze in amazement at the multitude of schools swirling above and about the coral heads.

Going a little deeper, you can visit gigantic sponges and black coral before ascending to the more ample bottom times available in the shallows—where you'll still find enough brain coral, staghorn, elkhorn, meadow, and stone coral to keep your camera very happy. With an incredible assortment of tropicals, the scene resembles an urban landscape of skyscrapers and commuter traffic.

Photographers will find many wide-angle opportunities, but macro life is equally plentiful. Both close-up and macro photography are especially suited to night dives here. Shallow reefs and calm, clear waters make for pristine night diving. And at night the red cuplike tubastria coral opens up and provides a brilliant show, particularly on the shipwrecks.

Health Score Card

The corals and sponges here are some of the healthiest you'll see in the Caribbean. That's probably due in part to the infrequency of hurricanes, as well as protective measures coupled with light boat and diver traffic. During three dive trips here, I saw little coral bleaching and just isolated places where there was storm damage. Moreover, the marine life is prolific. In addition to fields and mountains of hard corals, divers will find healthy elephant ear and tube sponges. Prolific schools of tropicals flow over and around the invertebrate structures. Eels and pufferfish are plentiful, as are flowing anemones. The long cornetfish, usually seen in pairs, grow to huge proportions.

The more elusive frogfish and sea horses are fairly easy to spot here. In fact, during one visit, our group saw three sea horses in plain view right off the dock at Habitat Curaçao. Also, we were told precisely how to find the frogfish named Samsung, and sure enough, there he was, flexing his muscles as we approached! And this area is not even within the marine park!

Diving Conditions

The best diving conditions are at the "top" of the island, referred to as the Southwest. This is also where the best shore diving happens to be. There's no current to speak of, and little surge or wave action. The wind blows constantly, though, and as you progress down-island, conditions get rougher. At an area called *Seldom,* about mid-island, we experienced heavy swells on a boat dive. It was difficult, though not dangerous, to get up the ladder after the dive, and certainly well worth the effort, since the spot was covered with intricate coral formations and swarms of schooling fish. Ironically, where the underwater park stretches is usually the roughest section of the island.

Visibility is excellent, usually hovering around 100 feet, although the shallow sandy areas are generally more stirred up and visibility isn't as good. The water temperature typically hovers around 80°—perfect.

Recommended Level of Experience

Since the reefs are shallow here and there's no need to dive deep, Curaçao's sites are ideal for all levels of divers. The single exception is the *Superior Producer* wreck, which sits in deep water and frequently has a strong current running. It's not for new divers at all, and even experienced divers should make a few dives on the reef to get re-acclimated before diving here. Also, some of the dive sites within the underwater park are considered for intermediate or advanced levels, as the surface conditions are generally pretty rough and the current can be strong.

Curaçao is an excellent place to get certified and to acquire advanced certifications. Most of the dive shops are run in a professional manner, and you can be reasonably assured that their equipment is safe and well maintained.

Boat Dives

The *Mushroom Forest* could be considered Curaçao's signature dive spot, and one not to be missed, due to the prolific amount of mountainous star coral. The site is located toward the "top" of the island, where conditions are usually calm. All levels of divers will enjoy it. The mountainous star coral is found in many regions of the Caribbean, but what makes the Mushroom Forest unique is that the coral has assumed fantastic fairyland shapes. Vast expanses of it grow vertically on a sandy plateau. Sometimes it looks like great pyramidal pine cones, at other times like giant toadstools or (you guessed it) mushrooms. The unique shapes are said to be due to bio-erosion at the base of the coral heads. Essentially, boring clams and sponges have eroded the bases into narrow columns. You'll have plenty of time to appreciate and wonder at it all. Since it's possible to have a delightful dive here without exceeding 60 feet, bottom time is plentiful.

Frequently, dive boats will couple this dive with *The Cave*, which is just a short boat ride away. If you have at least 1,200 psi left after diving Mushroom Forest, that'll be *beaucoup* air for The Cave, which is technically a cavern (since you're always in range of natural light). You can surface in the air bell, emerging under a vaulted ceiling bathed in ethereal, sea-filtered sunlight. The lapping of the waves is amplified enormously by the curving petrified-coral walls.

Hell's Corner, so named because of the violent wave action on the rocky shore, looks more like heaven underwater. This is another beautiful wall dive, featuring large elephant ear sponges, brain coral, and tube sponges, with scads of schooling fish. Unfortunately, because of rough surface conditions, it is usually reserved for advanced divers.

Seldom Reef (which is seldom dived), is truly a spectacular wall dive about mid-island, but because the water is usually rough, it is recommended for experienced divers, or those (such as California divers) who are accustomed to a lot of surface wave action. Getting back on the boat can be a challenge, and knowledge of wave behavior is useful. At the top of Seldom's wall is a ledge that drops, seemingly, to infinity. The wall itself is covered with intricate hard-coral formations, but the top of the wall is the real highlight. Vast fields of hard corals spread out as far as you can see, with no break in sight.

Director's Bay, on the East End, is another thrilling wall dive, with a dark abyss that drops, as local divemasters are fond of saying, "to China." The drop-offs are steep dead vertical at times—and the wall twists and turns, so underwater photographers can easily silhouette a wall-side diver against the sun, regardless of the time of day. Morays and plate coral abound in this area of the underwater park, as do black coral and sponges. Turn away from the wall, and you're gazing down into the mesmerizing depths of the Big Blue. Surface conditions on this part of the island are generally wilder and less protected than the calm western sites, but that assures lush coral and sponge coverage on the walls. The currents coming in from the open seas bring a constant supply of fresh nutrients.

Not far from Director's Bay is *Beacon Point,* another advanced dive with strong current and rough waves. It is also called Kabes di Baranka (head of the rock) and lies within the underwater park. This is another steep wall, with a terrace at 20 feet, dropping down to a ledge at 110 feet. The wall is covered with lush growth, but the real highlight here is the incredible stand of pillar coral that can be found in shallow water near the buoy. If snorkelers are along on this dive, they'll really enjoy the sight. This vast city of coral skyscrapers is the largest I've ever seen. Nurse sharks are frequently found sleeping here.

For even more variety, day excursions can be booked to *Klein Curaçao,* a tiny island several miles to the southeast. You'll be rewarded for the effort with pristine walls, large fish, nurse sharks, and possibly even mantas and pods of dolphins.

Wreck Dives

On the East End, within the underwater park, is what must be the most-dived spot in all of Curaçao—*The Tugboat.* This cute little 25-foot tug rests level on a sandy floor in only 17 feet of water, so it is popular with divers and snorkelers alike. The site is particularly exceptional at night when the beautiful orange tubastria coral open up and "bloom." The tug glows like an enormous foil-wrapped Christmas package. In daytime, the tug is usually saved for the end of a deep wall dive, which can also be a drift dive depending on the conditions. Rather than anchoring, your dive boat will follow your bubbles and pick you up near the tug.

The deeper section is just a little southeast of The Tugboat and features an extremely vertical wall with no end in sight. Looking down over it, you'll see only the dark, dark blue beyond. You'll drift past a couple of huge rock slides that have carved channels through the wall. The tug sits on on top of the wall. Unfortunately, since this is such a popular spot, you can encounter other divers here, who have a tendency to kick up sand, spoiling the visibility. If you're lucky, and that's not the case, you should be able to capture it nicely on film.

Another wreck which shouldn't be missed is the *Superior Producer,* a 200-foot freighter sitting just off the entrance to Willemstad harbor. It's deep, though, and can have strong currents running, so don't attempt it if you're a new diver. All divers should get a few other dives under their belt before visiting the *Superior Producer,* just to check buoyancy and regain some confidence. You'll undoubtedly experience some narcosis on this one. I've dived the *Superior Producer* three times now, and each time I've been completely in awe at the sight of it. Certainly, this ranks among my top ten favorite wreck dives. Although the wreck rests 110 feet down, a diver floating on the surface can frequently see the entire wreck and the sea floor around it—testament to the clarity of Curaçao's waters.

In 1977 this former Dutch ship left the harbor, bound for Margarita island. Unfortunately, it was hopelessly overloaded with linens, alcoholic drinks, T-shirts, jeans, and tennis shoes. With a fierce wind blowing and the seas tossing, the ship's cargo hold flooded, and it sank (upright, fortunately for divers!) just west of the harbor entrance. The clothing was put to good use by the locals—who were not shy about pulling it out of the water—and divers have been just as grateful. The event is recorded in Papiamentu slang, which refers to everyday clothing as *panju salu,* or "salty clothes."

You'll see a lot of growth on the ship, especially tubastria coral. Divemasters say that because of the prolific amount of tubastria, this is a spectacular night dive. Fish school around the ship, and families of smooth trunkfish flutter about. The hull (about 100 feet deep) is easy and safe to penetrate, as is the wheelhouse (about 80 feet deep), which also makes a good photo op, with a diver peering out of the porthole.

Extra safety precautions are taken on this dive. Down lines are laid for reference and for deco stops, and tanks are staged at various depths. The divemasters do a thorough predive briefing and supervise the dive during the approximately 20 minutes that divers have to explore.

Great Shore Dives and Snorkel Sites

Shore dives are a real joy on Curaçao, because access is simple and safe, and the reefs are so incredibly beautiful! If you're comfortable arranging a dive yourself, definitely take advantage of the opportunity. After all, Curaçao (along with sister-island Bonaire) is one of the top shore-diving destinations in the world.

First, buy the island map, which spots and numbers all the dive sites, and the island dive guide called *Take the Plunge.* Both are produced by the Dive Improvement Program (DIP) of the Curaçao Tourism Development Bureau. As you drive around the island you'll notice the numbered DIP rocks, which correspond to the numbered dive sites on the map and in the book. When you see the one you want, simply pull in, park the car, and start gearing up!

Use *Take the Plunge* to do some advance planning. Locate the dive sites that are best for your group's abilities and that have facilities you might need. Some have restaurants, restrooms, showers, and rinse tanks. Others have no facilities at all.

Don't forget to bring towels for drying off and a tarp for keeping sand and dirt off your equipment while you're gearing up. Do not leave valuables in the car, and lock extra equipment, clothing, etc., in the trunk. Finally, wear hard-sole booties for walking out onto the sandy rubble. Our group did our own dive site cleanup and came back with some broken glass—so be careful while walking out to deeper water. Finally, don't forget to bring tanks—yes, we got halfway to a dive site once before we remembered them!

One of our favorite shore dives is *Port Marie,* located about one third of the way down the island. It is also called *The Valley,* due to a sandy valley that has formed between two parallel reefs. You can drive down to the beach area to unload your stuff, then put the car in the parking area higher up, behind the beach. The best way to dive this is to kick out to the mooring buoy (look for sea horses), then drop down and follow the sand patch to the large coral heads. The topography slopes gently from about 30 feet to 50 feet, and conditions are usually very calm. You'll see lots of schooling fish, puffers, and cornetfish as you progress over the first reef, past the valley and on to the next reef. You might even see grouper and eels hunting together. Look in crevices and under ledges for the black-and-white high hats and the smaller spotted drum. After the dive, relax at the little open-air beachside bar/café. They make a killer satay—chicken skewers with crunchy peanut sauce.

Toward the tip of the island is a cluster of excellent sites. Heading west (I always think of it as "up"), look for *Playa Lagun.* Marine life is particularly abundant at this site, and the mountainous star coral formations in some areas are built high atop one another, creating some underwater skyscraper-like architecture. Try hovering over one spot to watch the enormous variety of activity. You'll be amazed. On one dive here, Kris and I hovered over a range of coral heads for about 20 minutes, gazing at the multitude of schools swirling above and about the mushroom-capped structure. While transfixed, a manta ray sailed casually by. Kris hurriedly wrote something on his diving slate, then turned it around for me to see. I read: "Curaçao, WOW!" My sentiments exactly.

Again, gear up in the parking area, then walk down to the water. Enter at the left side of the cove. Kick out a short distance, then drop down fairly quickly, because there are some interesting things to see while finning over the pebbly bottom dotted with small coral heads. During the short

Shore Diving Tips

Because shore diving here is some of the best in the world—that is, both easy and scenic—you really should take advantage of it. It does require more planning, though, than boat diving, so here are a few tips to help ensure that your experience is safe and that you get the maximum enjoyment from it.

Car Rental   Before renting that cute little open jeep, remember that it will not be secure if you want to leave things in it while you're in the water. The tourism department doesn't like to advertise this on the island, but there is a problem with theft, and the shore-diving locations are prime spots for break-ins. While you're having a great time in the water, your vehicle is a sitting duck. So if you want to bring things along, it's best to rent a car with a trunk that can be locked. Definitely put all your personal belongings (especially valuables) in the trunk.

Valuables   Even if you do have a secure vehicle, take only what you'll really need and leave valuables behind. That means passports, airline tickets, identification, cash, cameras, and other expensive equipment.

What to Take   Be sure to take drinking water, sunscreen, a save-a-dive kit, and scuba tools Oh, yeah—the tanks! Sunglasses and a hat are also a good idea. If you're using an underwater camera, take along some fresh water for rinsing. Also take a tarp to put on the ground to keep your gear clean, and some towels. Finally, take an island map that shows all the dive spots.

Booties   It's usually a good idea to wear booties—preferably the hard-sole type—when you are shore diving. Sometimes you'll enter the water from a rocky or ironshore coastline rather than from a sandy beach.

Evaluate the Water Conditions   Most of the dive sites are on the lee of the island where the water is usually calm. You won't find strong currents or rough surf. Nevertheless, on some sections, and at certain times, you might find both—the current and surf can get pretty rough. So check it out carefully before getting in.

The Heat   Remember that this island is hot, hot, hot and very dry. Besides having plenty of drinking water, don't get overheated before you even begin the dive.

Shore Diving Tips (continued)

Plan Your Dive   Agree with your buddy how you intend to plan the dive. Usually you'll want to kick out to the buoy on the surface, then drop down. As you follow the slope down, check the direction of the current, then head into it. Usually it's best to turn around when you get to about 1,500 psi. Then, start to ascend gradually as you return. Since there's plenty to see in the shallows, you can play around and gas off at the same time.

Navigate   Remember, you have to get back to your point of departure on shore, so navigation is important. Take a compass heading and note natural landmarks before heading into the current. Also note the position of the sun.

---

kick out to the reef we saw a five-foot trumpetfish with a smaller mate, puffers, an eel, goatfish, and yellowtails! Out on the reef, which is about 40 to 50 feet in depth, we noticed a surprising number of French angelfish and very large anemones. There are restrooms, showers, a snack bar, and large shelter for shade.

Moving along up the coast are more good shore-diving sites, and finally you'll reach *Playa Kalki* (also called Alice In Wonderland), way up at the tip. The site is adjacent to the Kadushi Cliffs Resort (soon to be renamed Kurá Hulanda Lodge), but there are few facilities on the beach itself. Gear up in the small parking area near the road (not in Kadushi's parking lot), then walk down a few steps to the snack bar and sandy beach. Kick out, and in just a few minutes you'll be at the edge of the drop-off, where the corals grow in greatest profusion. You'll be in about 40 to 50 feet of water, where you're bound to encounter eels (frequently the small, speckled ones), puffers, trunkfish, and schools of juveniles. Along the edge of the wall are the familiar mushroom-shaped coral heads, and deeper down the wall stair-step are the flat sheet corals. If you're doing underwater photography, bring water for rinsing the camera.

Finally, don't overlook the shore diving from resorts. One of the best is off *Habitat Curaçao,* where a very long, thick rope hangs down the face of the wall to almost 200 feet. This makes navigation ridiculously simple. Just head either to the right or the left, explore the wall, then come back to the rope and follow it up the wall—brilliant! As you're heading out, you're likely to find sea horses at the buoys that lead out from the dock. Follow the ridges of coral across the sandy bottom to about 30 to 40 feet, where the wall starts to gradually descend. At the drop-off are yellow-tipped anemones, barracuda, pufferfish, mountainous star coral, and tube sponges in a variety of colors that provide perches for well-camouflaged frogfish. Tiny blennies hide among the valleys of mounds of brain coral. You could also encounter moray eels, lobster and stingrays, and schools of blue chromis.

Offshore from the Princess Beach Resort is an unusual collection of vintage cars—all underwater. A large barge and the entire pile of cars is called, appropriately, *Car Pile*. Divers (this one is not for snorkelers) kick out from the dock and go through the breakwater opening. It's a good idea at this point to take a compass heading for easier return. You'll want to veer to the right and follow the gradual slope of the wall down. First you'll come to the barge, then at about 90 feet begin to see the pile of cars. Coral and large tube and elephant ear sponges grow on the metal itself in this surreal scene. This is a deep dive, so don't admire the cars too long. Leave plenty of air for navigating your way back.

Marine Park

The Netherlands Antilles National Parks Foundation is referred to around the Netherlands Antilles by its Dutch acronym STINAPA. Founded in 1963, STINAPA cooperates closely with the Caribbean Marine Biology Institute (CARMABI), and operates several Antillean facilities, including Christoffel Park.

In 1983, STINAPA established the Curaçao Underwater Park, which protects coral reefs on the island's southeast coast from the high-water mark to the 60-meter (197-foot) depth contour beneath the reef. The park stretches from the Princess Beach Resort and Casino to the easternmost point of the island (12.5 miles), and includes under its protection more than 2,500 acres of reef and bay waters. The goal is to have the park encompass the entire coastline.

Within the park, nothing can be removed, and spearfishing is illegal. Fishing by hook and line, however, is allowed. Laws also prohibit killing sea turtles or taking their eggs. Conservation activities include turtle monitoring to gather data on their nesting habits. In fact, Shete Boka Park was developed as a result of the discovery of turtle nesting sites.

Every year just after the full moon in September and October, divers can observe corals and sponges spawning in the late afternoon and evening. As clouds of sperm are released into the water, the sponges and corals appear to be smoking. Volunteer divers participate in researching the phenomenon for an organization called Reef Care. It was formed to improve public awareness and carry out research projects and reef protection activities. Reef Care started the Kids for Coral project as well as Beach Clean-Up campaigns and the Reef Alarm Help Line. Any violations against the reef can be reported to them at 321-6666.

Recently, the Curaçao Dive Operators Association began implementing a new voluntary marine park fee. Divers willing to donate US$10 are given an anodized aluminum tag shaped like a scuba diver. The tag itself is an attractive souvenir—and it's also functional, since it works as a bottle opener. Proceeds generated by the fee will be used to help maintain and install moorings, fund CARMABI, support ongoing biological projects, and educate schoolchildren aboout marine ecology.

DIVE SERVICES & PACKAGES

Peter Hughes Ocean Encounters (formerly Underwater Curaçao) serves the Lion's Dive Hotel & Marina—a PADI Gold Palm IDC Resort with multi-lingual instructors. It has recently expanded its training to include professional-level courses. It operates two 40-foot dive boats, and sells and rents gear. Excursions are primarily within the underwater park. Call 599-9-461-8100; fax 599-9-465-7826; e-mail: lionsdive@ibm.net; website: www.divecuracao.com.

Retail Sales: *Adequate*   **Dive Boat Comfort:** *Good*
Rentals: *Extensive*   **On-Board Facilities**
Scuba Training: *Extensive*   **for Photographers:** *Good*
Photo Services: *Moderate*

Peter Hughes Ocean Encounters (formerly Princess Divers), at the Princess Beach Resort & Casino, operates two custom-built 41-foot dive boats with large dive platforms, for a maximum of 18 divers. The boats are equipped with oxygen, first aid, and radios for shore communication. Excursions are within the underwater park, on which the resort fronts, as well as to sites in the western area, farther up-island, and to Klein Curaçao. The shop sells, rents, and repairs gear. Its photo shop offers camera and video rental, E-6 processing, video editing, and instruction. PADI dive instruction is through the advanced level. Nitrox fills—both 32 and 36 percent—are available. Call them at (800) 992-2015 or (599) 736-7888; fax (599) 9-461-2432; e-mail: lionsdive@ibm.net; website: www.divecuracao.com.

Retail Sales: *Adequate*   **Dive Boat Comfort:** *Good*
Rentals: *Extensive*   **On-Board Facilities**
Scuba Training: *Moderate*   **for Photographers:** *Superior*
Photo Services: *Extensive*

Caribbean Sea Sports, on the beach at the Marriott (a PADI Gold Palm Resort), has a beautiful custom-designed Pro 42 dive boat with jet drive engines that can accommodate up to 20 people. The boat has a freshwater shower, camera tables, even towels! The shop also offers guided shore dives. It has dive gear sales and rentals, PADI instruction through advanced open water, and rentals of other watersports equipment. The Marriott is located at the eastern end of the island, adjacent to where the underwater park begins. Call 599-9-736-8800 or fax 599-9-462-6933; e-mail: css@cura.net; website: www.caribseasports.com.

Retail Sales: *Adequate* **Dive Boat Comfort:** *Excellent*
Rentals: *Extensive* **On-Board Facilities**
Scuba Training: *Moderate* **for Photographers:** *Superior*
Photo Services: *Moderate*

Habitat Curaçao, the 5-Star PADI IDC at the PADI Resort with the same name, is another one that is beautifully set up for diving freedom. There is even curbside tank availability, so you don't have to haul tanks up from the dive shop when you take off for shore diving. The dive boat is a Pro 42 with emergency equipment and is set up nicely for photographers. But if shore diving is more to your liking, it's just a matter of giant-striding off the dock, kicking out a short distance, then dropping down over the wall. They have wisely laid a long rope over the wall, down to about 200 feet (don't try to verify this), to make navigation easy. There's a complete line of diving equipment and camera rentals. Also offered are several photo and video courses as well as a Nitrox certification. Nitrox is pumped on the premises. Call (800) 327-6709 from North America, or call direct 599-9-864-8800; fax 599-9-864-8464; e-mail: curacao@habitatdiveresorts.com; website: www.habitatdiveresorts.com.

Retail Sales: *Adequate* **Dive Boat Comfort:** *Excellent*
Rentals: *Extensive* **On-Board Facilities**
Scuba Training: *Extensive* **for Photographers:** *Superior*
Photo Services: *Extensive*

Easy Divers Curaçao, (formerly Coral Cliff Diving) at the Sunset Waters Beach Resort Curaçao (formerly Coral Cliff Resort & Casino), operates a 38-foot custom dive boat. Diving is personalized and flexible. They offer PADI courses through assistant instructor level in both English and Dutch. Phone (800) 223-9815; phone or fax direct 599-9-864-2822; e-mail: info@easydiverscuracao.com; website: www.easydiverscuracao.com.

Retail Sales: *Adequate*
Rentals: *Extensive*
Scuba Training: *Extensive*
Photo Services: *Moderate*

Dive Boat Comfort: *Good*
On-Board Facilities
  for Photographers: *Good*

WHERE TO STAY

The following hotels are listed by their location from east, the lower end of the island, to the west. All offer diving packages. A 7 percent government tax is added to hotel bills, and a 12 percent charge is applied to all food and beverages.

Lion's Dive Hotel & Marina ★★★★ for years has been the dive resort of choice, particularly for visiting Europeans. It is conveniently located near the Marina, the Seaquarium, and the dive shop, Underwater Curaçao. Its 72 air-conditioned rooms overlook the ocean and sandy beach. Facilities include a swimming pool, a restaurant and lively bar, a dive retail shop, fitness center, windsurfing school, and a full range of water toys. A free shuttle bus runs into town. Room rates for a double range from $140 to $180. Call (800) 223-9815 or direct dial 599-9-461-8100; fax 599-9-461-8200; e-mail: info @lionsdive.com; website: www.lionsdive.com.

Princess Beach Resort & Casino ★★★★★, a PADI Gold Palm Resort adjacent to the Lion's Dive Hotel & Marina, overlooks the underwater park and is set on a long sweeping beach. It has several restaurants and bars, swimming pools, tennis courts, and a fitness center. All 341 rooms have air-conditioning and balconies. Ocean Encounters is located on the property and has its own boat dock. Room rates for a double for three nights range from $294 in summer to $382 in winter. Dive packages and honeymoon packages are available. From North America call (800) 992-2015; fax (305) 670-4948; e-mail, pbrbonet@cura.net. The direct number is 599-9-736-7888; fax 599-9-461-4131; e-mail: pbrbonet@cura.net; website: www. princessbeach.com.

Marriott Beach Resort & Emerald Casino ★★★★, a PADI Gold Palm Resort (formerly the Sonesta Beach Resort) on a stunning stretch of beach, is one of the most beautiful places to stay on the island and would be ideal for a honeymoon or special occasion. The buildings and grounds conform in an attractive way to the island's architecture and landscape. Fortunately, there are also two dive operations on the premises (Caribbean Sea Sport and Atlantis Divers), and you won't be competing for their services with hordes

Curaçao Seaquarium

This attraction, next door to the Lion's Dive Hotel and Marina, will please divers and nondivers alike. There are more than 3,000 examples of local marine fauna, including fascinating new species discovered in nearby waters. This is an excellent way to learn more about what you've been seeing underwater.

The Seaquarium's popular "Animal Encounters" consists of several large, open-water enclosures that bring visitors face-to-face with marine life. In one pool, snorkelers and divers swim, and feed, stingrays, angelfish, tarpon, grouper, etc. A word of caution here: if you get at all claustrophobic, don't try this. Swimming with these animals is one thing, but here they are fed, and they will mob you. Stingrays can grab hold of fleshy skin and rip—in fact, I still have a scar between my thumb and forefinger, caused by an agressive mature ray. The yellowtails can nip too, and they frequently draw blood.

In the other enclosure, you can feed nurse, lemon, and reef sharks by hand, behind thick mesh fencing that separates diver and shark. In one section of the enclosure, the fence has been replaced with three-quarter-inch clear Plexiglass, so participants feel they are swimming unprotected with the sharks. Feeding the nurse sharks is a blast; you will not believe the suction these guys have.

of other divers. Besides extensive recreational offerings, including tennis, health club and watersports, the resort has superb gourmet restaurants—something that is lacking at most of the other resorts. The 248 guestrooms and 34 suites have air-conditioning and balconies. The resort also has a swimming pool, kiddie pool, and whirlpools, a children's program, beauty salon, laundry, gift shop, and car rental. Call (800) 223-5388 or 599-9-736-8800; fax 599-9-762-7502; e-mail: mar-res@curacao.net; website: www.marriotthotels.com/curmc or www.offshoreresorts.com.

Habitat Curaçao ★★★★★ is a dedicated PADI Resort located about mid-island, which is perfect for accessing both underwater park sites, as well as sites at the calmer western end, and the excellent shore diving areas. This is one of the newer resorts, and I highly recommend it for die-hard divers. It is isolated, though, and those who don't dive or snorkel might go a little stir-crazy. The resort has car and jeep rentals, however, and offers regular, and free, shuttle service into Willemstad (about 30 minutes away). Set on a rocky bluff overlooking Rif St. Marie, its architecture and grounds are more southwestern than Dutch in style. Rooms, all with spacious balconies, are delightful, with tile floors and colorful fabrics. All rooms are suites, with either garden or ocean views, and have air-conditioning and fully stocked kitchenettes. There are also several two-bedroom cottages behind the resort and at a higher elevation (lots of steps). The resort has a large swimming pool, which seems to merge with the ocean, a restaurant, bar, and excellent dive shop with dock. Shore diving from the resort itself is superb, and 24-hour diving freedom is their motto. The per person rate for one night with two boat dives ranges from about $119 to 144, with two people sharing a room. Rooms accommodate up to four people, and the per person price decreases with added occupancy. Call (800) 327-6709 or 599-9-864-8800; fax (305) 864-8464; e-mail: habitat@cura.net; website: www.habitatdiveresorts.com.

Sunset Waters Beach Resort ★★★★ (formerly Coral Cliff Hotel & Casino) is another attractive dedicated-to-diving, cliff-backed beachside lodging, which over the years has obtained a following among Europeans. It has 100 rooms, which are all air-conditioned and have balconies. The all-inclusive resort has its own dive shop and boat dock, as well as tennis courts, miniature golf, beach volleyball, and a children's playground. The diving is excellent right off the beach. I remember a fantastic night dive here, where I saw a brilliant blue eel making its way over the white sandy bottom. Fantastic! The place is very laid back and casual—the open-air restaurant and bar overlook the sea, as does a new casino. There is complimentary airport transportation as well as a minibus shuttle to the downtown area. The resort also has laundry facilities and baby-sitting. Call (800) 223-9815 or 599-9-864-1233; fax 599-9-864-1237.

ISLAND LIFE

The Tourism Development Bureau suggests that Curaçao might have gotten its name from scurvy-stricken Spanish sailors. They were left to die on the island, but recovered when they ate the indigenous citrus fruit. Because of the miraculous healing, the Spanish named the island *Corazon,* meaning "heart," which later became Curaçao.

Be that as it may, Curaçao remained Spanish until the Dutch conquest of 1634. Then, from the end of the seventeenth century to the beginning of the nineteenth century, it changed hands several times between the Dutch and the British, with an attempt by the French thrown into the melee. The Dutch prevailed from 1815 until 1954, when Curaçao and the other Antillean islands became self-governing within the Kingdom of the Netherlands. Curaçao was a sanctuary for Jews during the Spanish Inquisition and later for runaway slaves; therefore, it has had a reputation for racial and religious tolerance.

All this prelude means that between dives, you can do much more than tan on the top-optional beaches. Some of you guys, however, might rank that particular activity high on your list of priorities.

Driving around Curaçao is the best way to get the flavor of this interesting cultural stew. North American visitors will find it easy, since driving is on the right-hand side. There is little traffic and the signage is excellent. Along the road, look for the mustard-colored VIP (Visitor Information Program) pillars, which identify various attractions and points of interest. All the pillars are numbered, and you will find the corresponding numbers on the excellent island map, produced by the Tourism Development Bureau. The map also provides color-coded driving routes and walking tours.

The western end of the island (I think of it as the top) is known to locals as Band'abou, which means downwind. This is the best area for exploring, where you'll find restored plantation houses, protected nature parks, and intimate beach coves. Driving through the island's semidesert countryside you'll see goats grazing among towering pillar cacti and scrubby divi-divi trees, bent over by the prevailing trade winds. Much of the eastern end of the island (Band'ariba or "upwind") is either developed or privately owned.

The long coastlines are distinctly opposite in character, as they are on most islands with elongated shapes. The southern coastline is dotted with dozens of sheltered inlets, where the calm turquoise waters are perfect for swimming, diving, and other watersports. In contrast, along the wild north coast, the pounding surf has carved out spectacular caverns in the jagged limestone terraces.

Sports on the island, other than diving and snorkeling, include fishing, sailing, and some of the best windsurfing on the planet. In fact, the world championships are held here each November. Horseback riding and tennis are also available, as is golf. The single golf course on this arid island is 18 holes with "greens" made of tightly packed and oiled sand.

Topside Attractions

Your first priority should be—well, diving, of course. But after that, plan to do a tour of **Willemstad.** You haven't really seen Curaçao until you've been to this capital city of the Antilles, for centuries a major international trade center and now a UNESCO World Heritage Site. Willemstad is split into two main sections by St. Anna Bay, a narrow waterway that leads to the bustling Schottegat harbor. The two sides—Punda and Otrabanda (the latter means "the other side")—are linked by the nineteenth century **Queen Emma pontoon bridge.** It's a lot of fun to just sit and watch as the bells ring and people scamper to the other side. The long arm of the bridge swings around to let in boats and ships, some dwarfing the tallest office buildings. If the bridge is open, and you're in a hurry to get across, a ferry runs back and forth on a regular basis.

From the Otrabanda side, you can click off some pictures of the **Handelskade** (Commerce Street), those colorful buildings along the waterfront with the curlicued gables and arched galleries.

If shopping interests you, then head for **Punda,** Willemstad's prime shopping district and the most scenic section of the city. You'll find jewelers, boutiques, and gift shops galore, with no duty or tax on any imported items. Also visit the **Floating Market,** opposite the Sha Caprileskade in Punda, where Venezuelan farmers and fishermen tie up brightly decorated boats to sell their produce. On Saturdays, visit the **New Market,** near the Post Office, where you'll find local products for sale.

Definitely take some time to stroll around the **Waterfort Arches,** the quarter-mile-long, barrel-vaulted seventeenth-century stone entryways set against the sea. Built originally as a series of storage chambers, these thick-walled bunkers once held slaves, but they now house boutiques and snack shops. At night the illuminated arches are a romantic place for dining and strolling.

Also downtown is the **Mikve Israel Emmanuel Synagogue,** said to be the oldest continually operating synagogue in the Western Hemisphere. Adjacent to it is the Jewish Cultural Historical Museum, which houses an impressive collection of artifacts reflecting the long history of the local Jewish community.

Watch potters go about their craft at **Arawak Pottery,** located on the way to the cruise ship terminal in Otrabanda. This is the perfect spot to find little gifts to bring home to friends and family, including ceramic candleholders, models of actual buildings around the island, refrigerator magnets, Christmas tree decorations, and a whole lot more. Also in Otrabanda is the new **Kura Hulanda Museum,** located in a former slave-trading yard. It displays African art and artifacts and is a sober reminder of Curaçao's active part in the slave trade.

To sample the local Curaçao liqueurs in the factory at **Landhuis Chobolobo,** just hop in a cab. This is the original distillery where the liqueur was first made, and you can watch the production process and get some free samples.

As you're driving around the island, you'll notice attractive **plantation houses** that dot the rolling countryside. Many of these can be toured. You'll see them marked on the island map. Visit the **Hato Caves,** with still-active stalactites and stalagmites and an underground lake with flowing waterfall.

I never miss the opportunity to head up to the "top" of the island on the rough northern shore to explore the coastal caves at **Boca Tabla.** Climb down the huge rocks to the wave-carved cave where roiling surf thunders in. It's awesome!

On the opposite end of the island is **Den Paradera,** a working herb garden with fascinating exhibits illustrating the traditional medicinal uses of local vegetation.

Dining and Entertainment

Dining and dancing in restored plantation houses is a unique experience here. **Landhuis Daniel,** which serves French-Caribbean cuisine on a garden terrace, has a band that plays on weekends. The beautiful **Landhaus Brievengat,** noted for the towers that flank the front entrance, has been restored and is used for private parties. At one time it was part of a vast plantation of 1,275 acres. It is also open for public view.

Willemstad is loaded with excellent restaurants, and the **Waterfort Arches** area is especially romantic, with its outdoor dining overlooking soft waves and shimmering waters. For some of the local specialties, such as goat stew, try the **Golden Star Bar and Restaurant** on Socratesstraat. Also, for local fare, along with lively activity in an open-air structure, don't miss the **Old Market** (Plasa Biew). Friendly cooks stir their huge kettles of steaming stews over open fires. You're likely to find goat, cucumber, and conch stews; fried fish, okra soup, fried plaintain, and funchi (corn meal). Yum—with a cold Amstel, you'll feel like a native. It's quite a fun show, and the price is right.

Another romantic setting with a spectacular view is **Fort Nassau Restaurant,** not far from Willemstad. For a special occasion, try the excellent **Portofino** at the Marriott Resort. This is definitely fine Northern Italian cuisine.

Up at the West End, on a cliff overlooking the ocean, is **Playa Forti,** for outdoor dining with an expansive view. Don't be surprised to see kids jumping off this high cliff into the ocean. The restaurant specializes in local dishes and seafood.

Medical Facilities

St. Elizabeth Hospital is staffed by European and U.S.-trained doctors and is located in the center of Otrobanda, across the street from the Colon Shopping Center. St. Elizabeth's is the site of the island's recompression chamber. Local emergency numbers: ambulance, 112; police, 114; tourism security assistance, 617991. In case of a diving emergency call DAN (Divers Alert Network) at (919) 684-4DAN (4326) or (919) 684-8111.

Fiji

Physical Characteristics of the Dive Area

WATER & WEATHER CONDITIONS

Visibility	*Excellent*
Current and Surge	*Moderate to Strong*
Temperature	*Comfortable*
Storms	*Occasionally Stormy*

SITE CONDITIONS

Mooring Buoys	*N/A*
Fishing, Collecting, and Hunting Restrictions	*Some*
Ease of Access	*Convenient*
Boat Traffic/Diver Congestion	*None*

MARINE LIFE

Abundance of Invertebrates	*Prolific*
Abundance of Vertebrates	*Prolific*
Abundance of Pelagic Life	*Prolific*
Health of Reef/Marine Life/ Marine Structure	*Pristine*

Soft Coral Fantasy

It is not easy for most first-time visitors to get a fix on the vast number of islands that make up what we collectively refer to as Fiji. When we say "I'm planning a dive trip to Fiji," it sounds as if we're heading out to a single exotic island somewhere in the Pacific.

Fact is, there are more than 300 islands that make up this archipelago. Together they trace a loose circular shape that sprawls over some 80,000 square miles of ocean, about 1,750 miles northeast of Australia. That's a whole lot of Fiji.

Seen on a map, Fiji is made up of two large islands: Viti Levu and Vanua Levu, with the other smaller archipelagos and island groups clustered around them like chicks around their mama hens. Only about 100 of all these islands are inhabited, which means that two-thirds of all Fiji is untouched by civilization and—most significantly—it's a fairly safe bet that much of the underwater wonders have probably never even been seen by another human diver or snorkeler.

Local scuba veterans, folks who have been diving these waters for 40 years or more, estimate that even with all the dives they've made on a daily basis all these years, they've seen probably only about one thousandth of one percent of what these waters contain.

Fiji's islands are the stuff of our tropical dreams: they're lush and green, some with lofty peaks etched by dramatic cascading waterfalls, some with shorelines scalloped by golden-sand beaches that curve to cup tranquil harbors. Groves of palm trees provide shade on almost every beach, shiny green breadfruit and banana trees grow larger than life, and every yard is decorated with at least one frangipani tree, its branches laden with those seductively perfumed star-shaped blossoms that Fijian women and men tuck behind their ears.

In this, the "Soft Coral Capital of the World," the underwater scenes are equally exotic, with fringing reefs, atolls, and lagoons lavished with everything from tunnels, grottos, and 100-foot-tall bommies to sheer drop-off walls. At shallow depths you'll find many seagrass beds and mangrove areas, both of which nurture and protect juvenile fish and corals. The classic atolls are famous for the breaks in their barrier reefs—the passes, through which the tidal surges sweep in and out of the lagoon. These passes make for some of the islands' most exciting dives, as the Pacific races through like a freight train, carrying along huge pelagic species and all sizes of their prey, while you hang on for dear life and ogle the passing parade.

Guidebooks to most destinations around the world all seem to fall back on the cliché about the "friendly locals" inhabiting these foreign lands. When we get there, however, it's a different story. All too often they turn out to be cranky folks who've just about had it with the tourist hordes cluttering up their countryside.

This, however, is not the case in Fiji. For whatever reason, the Fijians steadfastly remain among the friendliest and most hospitable people in the world. They're unfailingly delighted to see you each and every time you meet. Even if your paths crossed just minutes before, you'll still get a huge smile and a warm *Bula!* They're happy to share a bit of a chat or a bowl of

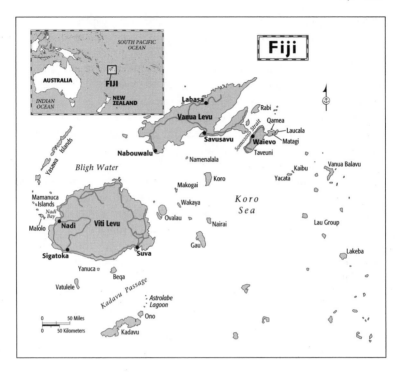

kava with you (more on this a bit later), and are so gracious and polite you'll thank your mom for drilling "please" and "thank you" into you when you were a child.

Fiji is considered an English-speaking country, but English isn't the mother tongue of most locals. The majority of Fijians speak Fijian at home, but, being infinitely gracious, they can also speak enough English to make their guests feel comfortable. Try returning the favor, even if only in a small way. The two words that will get you through most day-to-day situations are *Bula,* which is one of those catch-all greetings that means just about everything from "Hello, how are you?" to "Have a great day", and *Vinaka,* which means "Thank you."

International air passengers arrive at Nadi (nahn-dee), on the west coast of the main island of Viti Levu. Many tourists arrive here and never leave this island to explore other parts of Fiji. Viti Levu is large enough to have two "cities," Suva (on the southeast coast) and Nadi, both of which are bustling with commerce and choked with traffic. This main island also has its share of beaches, most of which have already been claimed by the large resort complexes. Scattered around the island's coastlines are dozens of hotels and resorts that range in price from super-luxury expensive to youth hostel affordable. The island also has plenty of natural sites to see, as well as those created specifically to appeal to tourists; and there are even a variety of shops and ethnic restaurants. In short, Vitu Levu makes an ideal tropical destination for the not-very-adventurous traveler.

Most romantics and most divers, however, can't wait to get out of town and over to one of the out-of-the-way islands, where there's probably nothing topside but a single resort, and where the underwater world teems with an endless variety of sites and sights.

There really is no "best Fiji diving," because the entire chain of islands yields a vast candy store of spectacular sites, blanketed in jellybean-colored soft-coral colonies, crinoids, gorgonians, and anemones that are visited by endless varieties of sea critters. Most dives are in currents, but the majority of these are well within the capabilities of any certified diver.

Given the vastness of the islands' sprawl and the almost limitless underwater opportunities, the idea of planning a dive vacation might seem, at first glance, a daunting project.

Happily, this is not an insurmountable problem. Fiji's best-known and best-loved sites tend to be grouped together within various regions. This is because they share in common specific underwater plateaus or atoll formations. Many of these sites are easily accessible from shore-based dive shops and resorts. To simplify planning for your dive vacation, we've broken down these shore-based diving options into four geographical groups.

But there's also a fifth group of dive sites—the remote and far-flung sites that can be accessed only by live-aboard boats that offer dive passengers not only speedy mobility but also the ability to avoid bad weather and other negative conditions by simply moving on to another location.

QUICK STATS

Size   Fiji's 300-plus islands are scattered across 80,000 square miles of the Pacific Ocean. The total landmass, however, adds up to only about 7,000 square miles; roughly the size of Massachusetts.

Population   Roughly 800,000 inhabitants. Of these, about 352,000 are pure Fijian and 337,500 are of East Indian origin. The rest are European, Chinese, etc.

Location   Seventeen degrees south of the Equator; about 1,750 miles northeast of Sydney, Australia

Time Zone   The same as New Zealand, 12 hours ahead of Greenwich Mean Time. Fiji is 20 hours ahead of Pacific Standard Time and 17 hours ahead of Eastern Standard Time. (Where Daylight Savings Time is observed, add one hour.) Travelers coming from North America will cross the International Date Line.

Government A republic, governed by a prime minister, and divided into 16 regional ministries. In May 2000, Fiji was rocked when the prime minister and several cabinet ministers, all of Indian descent, were taken hostage in a coup led by a native Fijian, George Speight. In July, Speight was arrested and the hostages were freed.

Language English is the official language, although Fijians speak Fijian, and Fijian Indians (who comprise about half of the native population) speak Hindi.

Electrical Current The current is 240 volts, with three-pronged Australian-type outlets. Some live-aboards and resorts supply 110 voltage or converters.

Climate In winter (June–October) the air temps range from 73° to 68°. In the rainy summer months (November–May) air temps are from 86° to 73°. Sudden afternoon showers are common, but these are usually followed by bright sunshine shortly thereafter.

Water Temperature Temperatures vary from around 80° in summer (October–April) to about 78° in winter (May–September).

Tides Tides play a huge role in Fiji diving, especially in the passes and cuts. In general, if the tide is rising, certain dive sites will be at their best; others are better on the reverse. The tides change every six hours.

Underwater Visibility Although vis varies greatly from site to site, in Fiji it is generally excellent (between 50 and 150 feet), especially in winter. Soft corals require plankton for feeding, so there will always be plankton where the corals are the most lush. Visibility is superb on the outer reefs.

Best Diving Months Winter

PLANNING THE TRIP

Phoning Fiji From North America, dial 011 + International Country Code (679) + local number. There are no area codes.

Getting There Most flights leave from Los Angeles and land at Nadi International Airport. Carriers include Air Pacific (Fiji's national carrier), Air New Zealand, and Qantas Airways. Flights take about 11 hours, depending on layovers. From North America, you'll cross the International

Date Line, so you'll arrive two days later. Most of the flights are set up to arrive in Fiji in the early morning hours. After arriving in Nadi and clearing customs, you can proceed to the domestic terminal to catch an interisland flight to your final destination. Sunflower Air and Air Fiji, Turtle Airways, and Vanua Air all offer convenient daily flights. Each has a baggage weight limit of 44 pounds per person. Remember to save $20 for your departure tax (children under age 12 are exempt).

Getting Around   In Fiji, buses run virtually everywhere. The open-windowed buses are great for taking in the sights and sounds of the islands. Taxis are inexpensive and metered. For instance, $2 will take you just about anywhere in the average town or city. Rental cars are available from Avis, Hertz, and other major local firms at the international airports and at most towns and resorts. Driving is on the left side of the road.

Ferries, launches, aircraft, helicopters, and seaplanes service an extensive network of docks and airfields throughout the islands and resorts. To islands off Nadi, the catamaran *Island Express* provides a twice daily service to resorts in the Mamanuca Group. A high-speed hydrofoil service, Drodrolagi, operates between Viti Levu and Vanua Levu with round-trip connections and transfers daily except Sundays.

Entry Documents   You'll need a passport that is valid for more than three months from date of entry. Also, you must be able to show a continuing or return air ticket.

Currency   The Fijian dollar is used throughout the islands. At press time US$1 equals about F$2. Credit cards are accepted at most resorts.

Fiji Visitors Bureau   In the United States, the Fiji Visitors Bureau is headquartered in Los Angeles. The address is 5777 West Century Boulevard, Suite 220, Los Angeles, CA 90045. Toll-free phone: (800) YEA-FIJI; website: www.bulafiji-americas.com.

THE UNDERWATER SCENE

North: Vanua Levu and Taveuni Islands

The swift and challenging waters of the Somosomo Strait, the narrow channel between Vanua Levu and Taveuni, make this area something of a Mecca for serious divers. The Rainbow Reef system, which stretches across the Somosomo Strait, is swept by strong tides bearing the rich nutrients that act like Neptune's own Miracle-Grow on the soft corals.

Savusavu, on a protected shore of Vanua Levu, is the unofficial headquarters for the Cousteau Society's Ocean Search Project, which gives a major clue as to the quality of the diving in these waters. The outer wall of Savusavu Bay is part of the barrier reef that runs up to the Somosomo Strait, so you can expect dramatic spreads of corals as well as just about everything that swims in the fish food chain.

Health Score Card As with most of Fiji's remote sites, damage from human divers has been minimal. Most dives in the straits are turbo-charged drift dives.

Diving Conditions Classic current/drift diving. Visibility is about 90 feet.

Recommended Level of Experience These high-speed drift dives are for experienced divers or intermediates who are willing to follow instructions. Pay serious attention to all instructions, re-boarding information, and site briefings. Bring along a current hook, and carry a surface signaling device and a safety sausage just in case you resurface out of range.

Dive Sites Taveuni's legendary *Great White Wall* is a vertical sweep of snowy white corals that really are, on close inspection, an exotic pale lavender. Time your dive so that the sun is in position to illuminate this spectacular blanket of coral. Your first view, appearing as if by magic at the end of a tunnel down about 120 feet, is a guaranteed dazzler.

Also off Taveuni, the Rainbow Reef, cut with endless nooks and crannies, has more than 30 extraordinary sites, including the *Yellow Grotto, Annie's Bommie,* and enough coral gardens to fill an entire vacation's worth of diving. Typical of this reef's bounty are sites like *Barracuda Point* and *The Zoo,* which teem with jacks, barracuda, turtles, eagle rays, and sharks; and *Blue Ribbon Eel* reef, where, of course, you just might spot the rare and elusive blue ribbon eel.

West: Mamanuca and Yasawa Islands

Off Viti Levu's southwestern Coral Coast, in the Mamanuca Island group, the diving is remarkably pristine, although the soft corals, for which Fiji is famous, are surprisingly few. The Mamanuca Islands form a miniature archipelago that arcs to meet the Yasawa chain. The Yasawa is yet another archipelago of 21 volcanic islands stretching northwest of Viti Levu and separated from it by a passage known as the Bligh Waters. This is where the Brooke Shields movie *Blue Lagoon* was filmed.

These islands are in the protected lee of a reef, so they harbor a virtual underwater paradise of coral gardens, caves, swim-through arches, and walls. Masses of marine life, including reef tropicals, turtles, dolphins, and lots of sharks love this area as well.

Health Score Card   Excellent. The waters surrounding some of these small islands have never been dived.

Diving Conditions   Visibility frequently exceeds 100 feet.

Recommended Level of Experience   There's something rewarding for all levels.

Great Dive Sites   *The Supermarket* is filled with lots of big, sharp-toothed "shoppers"—white-tip reef sharks and bronze whaler sharks by the dozens—as well as schools of barracuda. Many Fijians still believe the ancient myths that promise that their ancestors return to this world as sharks. One local character and diver, Api Bati, is a believer, and he loves to hug the sharks—certainly a uniquely Fijian sight to watch. This shallow (20-foot to 60-foot) dive is ideal for all levels of divers.

In the context of these waters, *The W* is not a trendy hotel; it's a diver's playground filled with ledges and overhangs carpeted in soft corals. Mantas and dolphins frequent the deeper edges (90 to 100 feet), as does the occasional whale shark.

The South: Vatulele, Kadavu, Beqa, and Yanuca Islands

The 50-mile barrier reef that surrounds Beqa (beng-gah) and Yanuca Islands forms the vast Beqa Lagoon, just south of Viti Levu. Divers find this lagoon riddled with cuts, passages, and overhangs. Yet it is the magnificent coral pinnacles that rise from a submerged plateau between the two islands that are legendary. These pinnacles, which have been dubbed such nicknames as *E.T.* and *Caesar's,* rise from a depth of about 90 feet and come to within 10 feet of the surface, making them almost as accessible and exciting for snorkelers as for divers.

Sheer-drop walls delight divers and are equally popular with vast numbers of sharks. It's all part of the deep Tonga trench, a geologically active area where volcanoes erupt frequently, releasing tons of nutrients into the currents.

Farther south, Kadavu stars on every diver's Top Ten list for its awesome Great Astrolabe Reef, a playground swarming with Tiera batfish, Maori wrasse, yellowfin tuna, and wahoo. Venture a bit deeper and you just might encounter the big guys—humpback whales, mantas, hammerheads, and white marlin.

Kadavu also has a legend that might (or might not) fascinate divers: in ancient times it was believed that Dakuwaqa, the Shark God, fiercely guarded the reef entrances to all the islands of Fiji. Once, a giant octopus tried to enter Kadavu and, despite his brute strength, Dakuwaqa proved no match for the eight strong tentacles of the octopus. So, sensing his own death, he begged for mercy, promising in return that he would never harm the people of Kadavu, no matter where they might travel in Fijian waters. Released unharmed, Dakuwaqa has kept his promise. So even today the people of Kadavu have no fear of sharks. Local fishermen, however, still respectfully pour a bowl of kava into the sea as a gift to their shark god.

Health Score Card   Excellent

Diving Conditions   Off the beaten tourist-track, so most are pristine.

Recommended Level of Experience   There's something rewarding for every level.

Great Dive Sites   In Beqa Lagoon, *Side Streets* is a wall that drops off into an abyss. Divers love it for its coral caverns, rainbows of sea fans, and such showy critters as lionfish, blue ribbon eels, and regal angelfish. *Tasu No. 2* is a submerged 200-ton Taiwanese fishing trawler. The swift currents at *Frigate Passage* pose some serious challenges to dive skills, but pay off in huge populations of sharks and schooling pelagics

Farther south, the Great Astrolabe Reef complex has some major brag dives. One such biggie is the Naingoro Pass, up in the northeast corner of Kadavu, where big-fish sightings—open-ocean hunters such as tiger sharks, hammerheads, tuna and billfish—are almost a sure thing.. *Aquarium No. 1* and *Aquarium No. 2* are small and challenging blue holes that plunge about 130 feet into the barrier reef. These are safe to explore only at high tides.

East: Lomaiviti Islands (Ovalau, Wakaya, and Gau)

This area takes in the group of islands east of Viti Levu in the Koro Sea, among them the islands of Ovalau, Gau, and tiny Wakaya. The Wakaya Pass sweeps through there, as does the Nagali Pass, which is regarded by many divers as primo dive site in all Fiji. Because these sites are so far-flung, this is ideal live-aboard territory.

Great Dive Sites   Nigali Pass, off the island of Gau, provides the ultimate drift dive. You should figure on nothing less than a three-to-four-knot ride. The minute you enter the water you'll immediately be swept along with vast schools of barracuda and jack, as well as mantas and hammerheads. The goal here is to reach *The Bleachers,* an area where the channel narrows to about 100 feet in width. Then settle yourself into a comfortable viewing position and become a spectator watching the passing parade of giant grouper (between 100 and 200 pounds each), sea snakes, and platoons of sharks patrolling the pass.

Wakaya Passage, in the Bligh Straits, is one huge photo op, with blue fusiliers and purple anthias against a rainbow background of corals. There are typically schools of jack, barracuda, coronet fish, and the occasional scalloped hammerhead.

WHERE TO STAY AND DIVE

Throughout Fiji are accommodations suited to every budget and every kind of traveler, from backpacker to sybarite. If you're looking for some outrageous pampering, this would be the ideal opportunity to check out one of those private island resorts for which Fiji is famous.

Remember, there are more than 300 islands here, and more than a few of those are privately owned. So, although there are plenty of "regular" hotels and resorts on the two main islands, you've traveled all this distance; why not experience what's really special about Fijian hospitality. Some of these resorts, such as the well-known celebrity haunts like Wakaya and Vatulele, are top-of-the-line expensive; others, like Toberua, are more moderately priced. But what they all share is the uniquely private setting that lets you indulge in the special fantasies that come with living on a remote island, cut off from mainland hustle and bustle.

Another wonderfully unusual feature of Fiji private-isle resorting is that you'll likely stay in a *bure* (boo-ray). Far from some gimmick dreamed up to pander to tourists, the bure is a traditional feature of Fijian life. It is a thatched-roof cottage, usually round in shape. Size varies: the more elaborate ones have several rooms; more traditional bures consist of only a single room. But all have a high-peak roof and a breezy, open-air design. Bures may be strictly traditional, but I've always found them so exotic that they're an integral part of my Fijian Robinson Crusoe fantasy.

Resorts in the South

Centra Resort Pacific Harbour ★ ★ ★ ★ is an excellent value for those not fixated on diving and for their nondiving companions. Part of a group of affordable vacation hotels that includes Parkroyal and Travelodge, the Pacific Harbour is a beachfront family resort on the south coast of Viti Levu.

There's plenty of diving off this coast, and the hotel offers a range of dive choices. One exciting option is to join the on-property Aqua-Trek Beqa aboard one of the high-speed boats to Beqa lagoon or to closer dive sites. Aqua-Trek is a PADI facility that offers courses through divemaster level. Other recreational pursuits include taking adventure excursions in a motor boat up the Navua River, or to white water raft and kayak this same river. Another tropical day trip is to picnic on Yanuca Island, sailing there aboard the resort's catamaran, *Longships*. In addition, there's an 18-hole championship golf course nearby, and a large swimming pool and tennis courts on the property.

Many of the 83 rooms face the resort's three-mile stretch of golden-sand beach; others are tucked into the tropical gardens. All have a private patio or balcony, and all have air-conditioning, phones, color TV, VCRs, coffeemakers, hair dryers, and irons and ironing boards. There is a restaurant, and a breakfast/dinner meal plan is $25 per day.

Rates run as reasonable as $84 in high season. Dive packages available. Resort phone (679) 450-022; fax (679) 450-262; e-mail: centrapacharb@ is.com.fj; website: www.sphc.com.au/hotels or www.aquatrek.com.

Retail Sales: *Adequate*

Rentals: *Adequate*

Scuba Training: *Extensive*

Photo Services: *Limited*

Dive Boat Comfort: *Good*

**On-Board Facilities
  for Photographers:** *Good*

Toberua Island Resort ★★★★ is a private island retreat just offshore from Viti Levu, the big island. It's a five-minute boat ride from a private dock at Nakelo, which is near the town of Suva (on the east side of the island). This resort is definitely more relaxed and casual than the typically plush private havens that characterize the Fijian islands. It's a lot more zany, too.

Guests at Toberua (tom-boo-roo-a) tend to socialize with one another almost immediately, joining up to dine together, chat over cocktails—and even play golf together. Turns out this tiny little four-acre island is internationally famous for its "reef golf." Regulars return, year after year, to challenge one another and to pit their skills against fellow guest arch rivals in the sport. All this because, every day when the mighty Pacific tides recede, Toberua Island's dry land suddenly expands to 20 acres of newly exposed surrounding reefs. And this new acreage immediately becomes the golf course. Happily, and somewhat surprisingly, this activity seems not to have had a disastrous effect on the reef.

The resort's 14 bures are set in the sand just inches beyond the high-tide mark. They are smaller versions of the traditional "chiefly" style bures, adapted to include such modern conveniences as a fridge and coffeemaker, and a well-stocked bar. Each comes with an outdoor open-air shower (discreetly hidden behind a bamboo privacy fence) and an indoor bathroom.

The public areas include a pool, an outdoor bar, and laundry facilities. The resort has only one restaurant and, even though this is a private island and there's no place else to go, meals are not included in the rates. However, you can sign on for a meal plan that includes three meals daily ($47 per person, per day) or another option that includes any two meals daily and costs $38 per person, per day. There are meal plans available for kids, too.

The best diving from the island is close by in the Toberua Passage, a nutrient-rich area that boasts everything from 60-foot walls to rainbow corals, and wide-ranging species of fish. Toberua has a resident PADI instructor, and offers resort courses through divemaster qualification. Dive plans are available (single dive costs $F60; ten dives cost $F500), with dive gear, boat, and guide included in cost. Phone (800) 441-6880 or (831) 335-5238. The Fiji phone is (679) 479-177; fax, (679) 302-215; e-mail: toberua@is.com.fj or toberuafj@aol.com; website: www.toberua.com.

Retail Sales: *Adequate*	**Dive Boat Comfort:** *Good*
Rentals: *Adequate*	**On-Board Facilities**
Scuba Training: *Extensive*	**for Photographers:** *Good*
Photo Services: *Limited*	

Wakaya Club ★★★★ is on the private island of Wakaya, east of Viti Levu in the Koro Sea. It is one of the first of Fiji's private-island resorts, and still one of the best. This is not only my opinion, but also the opinion of such publications as the *Hideaway Report* and *Conde Nast Traveler,* which consistently place it high on their Top Ten lists. Wakaya is also one of Fiji's more expensive and pampering havens. Be sure to save some time to check out the guest book, which reads like a Who's Who of Hollywood and Big Business. It's filled with handwritten rave reviews from people whose names usually appear in bold type in international columns.

On the island's 2,200 acres there is but one resort, with only nine bures strung out along its swimming beach of almost blindingly white sand. Do the math: nine bures, with only two guests per bure. That's right—18 is the maximum number of guests that can stay at this resort at any one time. No kids under the age of 16 are allowed.

Rates (brace yourself) range from $1,292 to $1,622, but this covers nearly every imaginable perk, including free-flowing French champagne, five-star meals, and outrageously luxurious and romantic accommodations. Diving, however, is extra. For jet-setter athletes there's a manicured croquet lawn, night-lighted tennis courts, and the three-hole Cheryl Ladd golf course set among the coconut trees. (Crave 18 holes? Play six rounds!)

There's also a "chiefly" bure whose roof soars to a 60-foot peak, believed to be the tallest in all the islands. Here is where guests gather for evening cocktails and for the nightly gourmet extravaganza that regularly runs to five courses.

The diving here is as unspoiled and pristine as it gets, and it is available whenever you want it to be. Dive equipment and instruction are available. Pana, the divemaster, usually wanders by as you're having breakfast in one of the oceanfront gazebos. "Bula," he greets you. "When would you like to dive today?"

Wakaya's surrounding waters abound with such treats as rare blue ribbon eels that live on a shelf at 85 feet and a purple leaf scorpionfish who seems to prefer a backdrop of yellow coral. The *Lion's Den* is named for the lionfish that hang out there. Divers also find blotched fairy basslet, long-nosed hawkfish, and unicorn surgeonfish. There are also visits from the big guys—the mantas, schooling barracuda, and schooling scalloped hammerheads, some of which measure 13 feet long.

After one especially spectacular dive I asked Pana what the site was called. "It has no name," he replied, adding with a smile, "until now. From now on, its name is *Brenda's Reef.*"

Call (800) 828-3454 or (213) 468-9100; fax (213) 468-9109; e-mail: reservations@tourismfiji.com; website: www.wakayaclub.com.

Retail Sales: *Adequate*	**Dive Boat Comfort:** *Adequate*
Rentals: *Adequate*	**On-Board Facilities**
Scuba Training: *Moderate*	**for Photographers:** *Good*
Photo Services: *Moderate*	

Resorts in the North

Jean Michel Cousteau Fiji Island Resort ★★★★ is tucked into a remote corner on the south side of the island of Vanua Levu, in the north. The Cousteau complex projects a cosseted ambiance similar to that of private island resorts. But in fact this resort shares this second-largest island with several other high-end resorts as well as lots of other commercial sites, including the dusty little town of Savusavu itself.

This PADI Resort follows the design of a traditional Fijian village, with 25 thatched-roof private guest bures scattered among the palm groves on the 17-acre property. Most of these front directly onto the resort's beach, and each features a split-level design that breaks the single room into a suite, with sumptuous furnishings and such amenities as a fully stocked bar and mini-fridge. Some are called garden-view bures, set one row behind the oceanfront bures. Seven of the oceanfront bures are family units. Rates range from $405 a night for garden-view bure ($310 for a single) to $625 for one of the oceanfront bures ($530 for a single). All rates include three meals daily as well as transfers to and from Savusavu airport.

All the resort services and public areas—reception, small gift shop, bar, and open-air dining room—are housed within the central high-peak-roofed bure. Everything here overlooks the pool and ocean. Because the restaurant is open to the public, it occasionally becomes crowded and hectic when large parties arrive. This tends to slow down the meal service, which can be a problem if you're trying to grab a bite before the dive boat departs.

Resort activities include intriguing rain-forest hikes with the resident naturalist/marine biologist, visits to a native Fijian village, educational trips to the mangrove lagoon, and tours of a copra (coconut processing) mill. The resort also offers kayaks, Hobie Cats and a glass-bottom boat. For kids, there's a complimentary Bula camp, with activities like coral reef exploration, fish printing, coconut-leaf weaving, village visits, swimming, snorkeling, beach combing, picnics, and various evening programs.

Diving is extra—$65 for a one-tank dive, $110 for two-tank dive. Equipment rental is available, for an extra charge. Dive packages are available. Instruction is from resort course through divemaster, and includes snorkeling. Specialty certifications are also available, including underwater photography and technical certifications such as Nitrox, advanced Nitrox, and staged decompression. Camera rentals include various lens rentals, and E-6 processing is available. The dive boat, *L'Aventure,* is a sleek, custom job.

Obviously, the Cousteau name is synonymous with ecologically sensitive diving, and you'll certainly see such politically correct elements as moored sites and supposedly well-trained crews. However (and I realize this is going to sound almost subversive, given the Cousteau mystique), during my visit things weren't always eco-correct. (The Man himself was off-island, so perhaps in his absence the standards lapsed a bit.)

My first disappointment involved a coral spawn, a not-to-be-missed phenomenon that my new dive buddies and I learned was taking place that very night. But the resort's dive staff was not impressed, virtually refusing to take us on the night dive to witness this event, claiming they'd never heard of a coral spawn and, besides, they were too tired to do a night dive. My second letdown was of a more general nature; it involved the dive personnel's ongoing disregard for their underwater environment. I witnessed any number of offenses—fins carelessly crashing into delicate corals, the dive crew standing on or otherwise manhandling the corals. Maybe that's no biggie out in the "Soft Coral Capital of the World," but it's a definite no-no where I come from.

Call (800) 246-3454 or (415) 788-5794; fax (415) 788-0150; e-mail: info@fijiresort.com; website: www.fijiresort.com.

Retail Sales: *Adequate*	**Dive Boat Comfort:** *Good*
Rentals: *Adequate*	**On-Board Facilities**
Scuba Training: *Extensive*	**for Photographers:** *Good*
Photo Services: *Extensive*	

Namale Island Resort ★★★★ is another of Fiji's super-luxurious getaways. In keeping with the concept of exclusivity and low-profile vacationing, there are only ten bures hidden away in the lush tropical garden setting that sprawls over the resort's 200 private acres. The terrain is very volcanic here in this part of the Savusavu peninsula of Vauna Levu, with lots of rocks, lava pinnacles, and rugged scenery—but not much in the way of sandy beach.

Each bure has a separate sitting area that connects with the bedroom and bath. Bathrooms are tropical and include one particularly romantic feature: a sliding glass door in the shower that opens directly onto a private deck or two-person hot tub. Also, each has a stocked refrigerator and coffee/tea-making provisions.

Namale is an all-inclusive resort that covers your every vacation essential except diving, which is an extra charge. Your rate makes sure you get three gourmet meals daily and all you can drink, round-trip airport transfers, as well as every activity from horseback riding to water skiing, from waterfall hikes to workout studio. The PADI Gold Palm Resort dive shop is at the edge of the marina. All gear is included in the rate.

The resort is located about a ten-minute ride from Savusavu Airport (a one-hour air hop from Nadi International.) A Tropical Bure runs $675 per night (double) or $575 (single) and can be made up with king or twin beds. No children under age 12 allowed; children over age 12 must stay in their own bure.

Call (800) 727-FIJI or (619) 535-6380; fax (619) 535-6385; e-mail: namalefiji@aol.com; website: www.namalefiji.com.

Retail Sales: *Adequate*

Rentals: *Adequate*

Scuba Training: *Moderate*

Photo Services: *Limited*

Dive Boat Comfort: *Good*

On-Board Facilities for Photographers: *Good*

Garden Island Resort ★★★★ On the island of Taveuni, this casual resort sprawls along the western coast facing the Somosomo Strait and the island of Vanua Levu, its back to a tropical rain forest. Accommodations in the 30-room resort are comfortable and predictable rather than posh. In an earlier incarnation the property was a Travelodge, so there's a kind of retro 1970s feel to the place (though rooms were refurbished in 1999). There's a freshwater swimming pool for those who find the currents in the strait too challenging for a casual swim.

All rooms open onto balconies, and most come equipped with air-conditioning and phones. The poolside restaurant overlooks the sea and serves a menu of Fijian and international favorites. There are the usual island-type activities to fill your surface hours—snorkeling, horseback riding, tennis, trips to the local village. But the one trip not to miss is the hike up to the waterfall. And, if you're feeling especially brave, join the local kids in the big plunge off the rocks into the waterfall's natural pool.

In 1999, Garden Island Resort won the *Rodale's Scuba Diving* Readers' Choice Award, ranked in the first 15 of the world's best dive resorts. It was the only resort in Fiji to be awarded this level. In the same poll, Fiji was ranked in the top five Indo-Pacific "Best Advanced Diving" destinations, and the top "Best Destination Value" for this region. More than 6,000 Rodale's readers participated in the poll.

Aqua-Trek, operating exclusively in the Fiji Islands since 1985, is the on-property dive operation. PADI courses are offered through the dive-master level, including enriched air specialty courses. Nitrox and Nitrox computer rental are available, and there is a full-service photo center with E-6 processing, camera rental, and film sales.

Room rates are based on occupancy: single is $73 and double is $92. There are also two dormitory-style accommodations, each with four beds, and this spartan bargain set-up goes for $15 per person, per night. In North America, phone (800) 541-4334 or (415) 398-8990; fax (415) 398-0479. The Fiji number is (679) 880-286; fax (679) 880-288; e-mail: info@aquatrek.com or garden@is.com.fj; website: www.aquatrek.com.

Retail Sales: *Adequate*	**Dive Boat Comfort:** *Good*
Rentals: *Extensive*	**On-Board Facilities**
Scuba Training: *Extensive*	**for Photographers:** *Superior*
Photo Services: *Extensive*	

Moodys Namena Island Resort ★★★★ lies about 15 miles off the southeastern coast of Vanua Levu, almost hidden away on a 110-acre private island. The 100 acres that are not occupied by the resort are a virtual nature preserve of ancient forests filled with myriad tropical creatures and palm-shaded beaches.

The resort consists of only six bures, five of which are perched atop dramatic cliffs that afford panoramic ocean views. The sixth bure is on the beach. Each hexagonal-shaped wood and bamboo bure is open to the sea breezes. Lighting inside is provided by gaslight or solar-powered brass cabin lights, like those aboard sailing vessels. The stunning centerpiece of each bure is a king-size four-poster bed carved and decorated by Fijian craftsmen. Each bure has a gas-powered coffee/tea maker and a tropical ceiling fan that runs on solar power. Best of all, perhaps, are the hammocks swaying on the private decks of each bure.

Although there are fabulous dive sites nearby, and plenty of opportunities to get out to them, the resort does not have any instructors on staff. So certified divers are the only ones who can take the plunge here. (Be sure to pack your C-card.) Also, the resort does not sell or rent dive gear or photo equipment. They can arrange with Aqua-Trek in Nadi or Eco Divers in Savu-Savu for rentals. Moodys uses a 33-foot cabin cruiser with a covered deck for diving, and they use a 20-foot Bertram for quick trips and small groups.

The Namea Barrier Reef that surrounds the island is an unspoiled underwater playground that offers everything from steep drop-off walls to gigantic coral-encrusted bommies. Every site is within a 15-minute boat ride. Their names tell their stories: *Grand Canyon, Fish Patch, Chimneys, Magic Mountain, Tetons, The Chunnel.*

On days when water conditions are calm, snorkelers join the dive boat at no extra charge. Other on-the-surface water sports offered by the resort include ocean kayaks, paddle canoes, paddleboards, and several different kinds of fishing.

The island's natural state is both breeding ground and habitat for almost limitless numbers of birds, making Namea also a birdwatcher's paradise. You'll likely see boobies, long-tailed tropic birds, lesser frigates, reef herons, barn owls, Fiji shrikebills, orange-breasted honeyeaters, and many more.

Each year between December and February, green and hawksbill turtles return to Namea's beaches to lay their eggs (there are a record number of between 40 to 50 nests each year). And just off the jetty is a clam farm, home to monster-size clams, some of which are 40 years old and weigh more than 50 pounds. Their mantles shimmer in dazzling shades of royal blue, violet, green, and amber. To accommodate those guests who are feeling too lazy to get into the water to see this exotic site, the resort has thoughtfully moved some into shallow water so you can just sit on the dock and do some"armchair snorkeling."

The rates here are $172 per person (double), an all-inclusive price that also covers all meals, snacks, and wine with dinner. There's a five-night minimum reservation requirement. Diving runs extra, about $41 per tank, and includes tank, weights, boat and crew, and dive guide. The resort closes during March and April every year. Phone: (800) 940-1712 or the Fiji number, (679) 813-764; fax (679) 812-366; e-mail: moodysnamena@is.com.fj; website: www.bulafiji.com/web/moodys.

Retail Sales: *None*	**Dive Boat Comfort:** *Good*
Rentals: *None*	**On-Board Facilities**
Scuba Training: *None*	**for Photographers:** *Good*
Photo Services: *None*	

Matangi Island Resort ★★★★★ Another private-island resort, this one covers 240 acres in northern Fiji, near Taveuni. Matangi is a horseshoe-shaped island that curls around an aquamarine lagoon and edges everything with a white-sand beach that stretches the length of the resort. Matangi is the only resort on the island, and it consists of only 14 bures.

Seven are deluxe, four are standard, and three are exotic little tree houses. All have great beach views and come with such amenities as coffee/tea-making, minibars, and daily cleaning service. A boutique is stocked with necessary short-term items, including toiletries and coffee.

Matangi Resort offers dive instruction ranging from an innovative "See The Sea" resort course to advanced courses, in both PADI and SSI. Rental gear is available, including underwater cameras and computers. E-6 film processing is available. The resort operates two dive boats (32 and 42 feet), each accommodating only ten divers. There are dozens of regular wonderful dive sites close by, but most of the truly awesome sites are within 40 minutes of the island by high-speed boat. Of these, a popular favorite is *The Edge,* a nearby atoll with a vertical drop of 30 to 1,000-plus feet, which boasts a generous array of just about everything: hard and soft corals, tropical reef fish, and pelagics. And then there's the *Great Yellow Wall,* another atoll garnished with sea fans, whips, and anemones, and populated with sharks, barracuda, tavelly, tuna, puffers, and fusiliers.

There are topside activities, too, ranging from guided bush treks, picnics with that special person or with new-found friends on your own deserted beach, and sunset cruises around Matangi and its island neighbors. For romantics, one surefire favorite is the short hike over the island's central hill to the totally deserted beach on the other side. There are village cultural tours to neighboring islands, bushwalks, waterskiing, snorkeling, sailing, windsurfing, and kayaking. Shore diving and snorkeling are right off the resort's beach.

Per person daily rates range from $166 to $218; for a double they are from $139 to $244. Rates include all meals, snacks, laundry, resort excursions, most activities, child care, and taxes. There are also special daily family rates. Dive packages range from five nights/eight tanks to seven nights/twelve tanks. Call (888) 628-2644; fax (303) 417-0557. The Fiji phone number is (679) 880-260; fax (679) 880-274; e-mail: info@matangi island.com; website: www.matangiisland.com

Retail Sales: *Adequate*   **Dive Boat Comfort:** *Good*

Rentals: *Adequate*   **On-Board Facilities**

Scuba Training: *Moderate*   **for Photographers:** *Good*

Photo Services: *Extensive*

Live-Aboards

Some dive purists will swear that live-aboards are the only way to fully appreciate the bounty that lies below Fiji's waters. There's no question that today's high-tech and high-speed dive yachts can zip divers out to unexplored and totally pristine reefs. Their mobility is a huge plus, and most are sufficiently luxurious to appeal to even the most finicky divers.

Nai'a is a live-aboard sailboat with dive itineraries that begin and end in Lautoka, a port city to the north of Nadi on the island of Viti Levu. The dive sites of the Bligh Waters lie on a straight course ahead. Islands typically visited during the *Nai'a's* trips include Namena, Wakaya, and Gau (in the Koro Sea), but itineraries include just about anywhere in Fiji.

The crew, the itineraries, and the spacious cabins (with their en suite bathrooms) of this 120-foot luxury get high marks from passengers. A few, however, expressed dismay over the onboard food saying that, with as many as 18 to feed, those passengers near the end of the line run the risk of coming away hungry. And I've heard complaints that some of the "non-drift" dives profiled by the crew were actually in such strong currents that divers were having to grab onto the coral so they wouldn't get swept away.

With such a large group (18 max), one nice feature is the twin chase boats—two 21-foot skiffs that speed small groups to different locations on the same dive, thus limiting the numbers and the impact on any one site. Dives are unlimited and promise such underwater features as walls, strong current drift dives, drop-offs, coral gardens, sharks (in both feeding and wild situations), and other pelagics. Among the rare species that have been spotted are the leaf scorpionfish and hell's fire anemone.

Among the most dramatic of the far-flung sites the *Nai'a* visits (and those not readily accessible from shore resorts) are *Save-A-Tack Passage,* off Namena Island, where schools of barracuda number 500 or more; Gau Island's fabled *Nigali Pass,* where divers wait in "the bleachers" as the pelagics stream by on the currents; and *E-6,* a stunning photo op of a site, aptly named by Captain Rob Barrel. At this last site, vast amounts of film are shot on masses of coral, schools of anthias and jacks, a swim-through grotto, nudibranchs, whip coral, giant clams, and vast anemone gardens.

Gau Island is also the site of one of the *Nai'a's* favorite topside activities—visiting Sawaieke, one of Fiji's remote and truly "unspoiled" villages. It is a special honor be invited by the village chief and elders to enter and visit Sawaieke.

Call (800) 903-0272; e-mail: naia@is.com.fj; website: www.naia.com.fj.

Sere Ni Wai, which is Fijian for "Song of the Sea," is one of the Mollie Dean Cruises vessels. This 101-foot custom-built yacht cruises the Bligh Waters, revealing this legendary passage's ultimate sites to its diver passengers.

Have you ever daydreamed about creating a perfectly user-friendly dive boat? An ideal design that would minimize the hassles involved with getting in and out of the water? One that would eliminate, or at least minimize, much of the awkwardness and heavy lifting? The design of the *Sere Ni Wai* comes close to that utopia. For one thing, you no longer have to waddle from bow to stern, bending over under the weight of your tank. *Sere Ni Wai* has equipped its almost-water-level stern dive platform with a waist-high tank rack. So all you have to do is descend one of the twin staircases to the platform, where your already-checked-and-assembled BCD and tank stand are waiting and ready to go. You then just back up to the rack, slide into your BCD, take one giant stride forward, and you're in the water—presto!

The *Sere ni Wai* has five twin cabins, each with its own private bathroom. That's a maximum of ten passengers. There's a crew of four. Also on board are facilities for E-6 processing, and video and still camera rentals.

Now want to design the perfect trip? This vessel is available for whole-boat charters, if you and your nine best dive buddies want to call the shots and orchestrate your own dream dive trip. "Owning" the ship in this way, means that for one week, you can dictate the course, pick the sites, and generally live your every dive fantasy. You can shoot out to some of the more distant island groups with their even more pristine and undiscovered sites. You might, for example, want to set up a "base" on *Sere Ni Wai*—owner Greg Lawlor's private 1,000-acre coconut plantation on the island of Vanubalavu, in the Northern Lau Group. Greg is a fourth-generation Fijian and one of the live-aboard pioneers. Or you might choose to steer a westward course and cruise around the Yasawa Group, stopping off to explore moviedom's famous Blue Lagoon.

Not interested in taking over the whole ship? Individual divers can choose from a set schedule of departure dates. The standard trips run seven nights. A sample itinerary for one of these standard cruises would include Gau and the Niglai Pass, Wakaya, E-6, and Namena. Extended trips are sometimes scheduled. And these would, subject to weather, venture farther into the northern waters, to Taveuni and the Northern Lau Group of islands.

Local phone: (679) 361-171; fax (679) 361-137; email: sere@is.com.fj; website: www.sere.com.fj.

Fiji Aggressor is a 105-foot high-powered catamaran that seeks out the exotic and remote dive sites of the northern islands of Wakaya, Korao, and Namenalala. A total of eight staterooms (all on the main level) on this PADI Resort assure a maximum of only 16 divers aboard.

The fleet's motto is "Eat, Sleep, and Dive!" And out in the Pacific, the benefit of the mobility of a live-aboard is never more evident than during turbulent tropical weather. As Wayne Hasson, owner of the Aggressor Fleet explains, "when weather is adverse we can move around to the lee side of the islands, while land-based operations are stuck with diving close by their resorts." He adds with classic diver understatement, "Lousy weather can really hamper a trip."

Each diver has his own dive station on the *Fiji Aggressor* as well as on the 30-foot skiff (which is raised and lowered by hydraulic lift). The dive deck also includes two freshwater showers, camera table with low-pressure air hoses, and E-6 photo lab.

Inside, there's a complete entertainment center with TV, VCR, CD player, and a library. On deck, the open-air hot tub is adjacent to the full-service indoor/outdoor bar, which is open around the clock. Underwater cinematographer Stan Waterman describes this luxury set-up as "Fat City Afloat."

The *Fiji Aggressor* is also totally handicapped-accessible, complete with HAS certified instructors and dive buddies, hydraulic wheelchair elevator, and other barrier-free modifications to ensure pleasurable diving.

The Saturday-to-Saturday seven-day trip includes a shore visit to a local Fijian village for a *meke* and a *kava* ceremony. Phone (800) 348-2628 or (504) 385-2628; fax (504) 384-0817, e-mail: aggressorfiji@is.com.fj; website: www.aggressor.com.

MV Solomon Sea was formerly an oceangoing fishing vessel. Now this 80-foot vessel is refitted with six air-conditioned cabins, each with an en suite bath. Four of these cabins have a queen-size bed (with twin upper bunk). Owners are Frederick Douglas, a Fijian who operated one of the first live-aboards in Fiji, and his wife, Corina, who is from the Solomon Islands.

A typical seven-day itinerary includes two days in Vatu-I-Ra Channel, a fairly new dive area that lies between Vauna Levu and Viti Levu in the Bligh Waters. There are lots of currents here, which means an overload of soft corals. The *Solomon Sea* has a "secret" site where schooling hammerheads hang out.

Another couple of days are spent diving *High Eight* and *E-6* sites, two huge pinnacles whose lush coverings of corals attract all sorts of tropicals and pelagics. One day is spent at the walls near Wakaya, and another at the Namena Barrier Reefs north of Wakaya. The final day of diving is at Charybolis Reef, off the west coast of Viti Levu, where the steep and deep drop-offs attract pelagics.

The *Solomon Sea* has E-6 processing facilities aboard, as well as gear and computer rentals. E-mail: info@solomonsea.com; website: www.solomon sea.com.

Dive Operators

The majority of recreational divers who visit Fiji are super-serious divers who have invested a lot of time and money to travel a long way to get to these

---

Happy Hour, Fiji-Style

The convivial custom of drinking Kava (yaqona) is a national passion, practiced by just about everybody in the islands on a regular basis. Part social gathering, part ritualistic ceremony, the custom is unique and something you definitely should not avoid if you're invited to participate. The drink is made by mixing the finely ground roots of the pepper shrub with water, and then straining the liquid through a filter of hibiscus bark. The resulting brew tastes something like clove-flavored dishwater, but produces a mellow buzz that somehow turns out to be remarkably pleasurable.

Everyone sits cross-legged in a circle and takes a turn participating in the ceremony. The kava is poured into a coconut shell bowl, which is then presented to each person in turn. Even the act of drinking is dictated by ancient ritual; the etiquette is exacting and must be strictly observed: Clap once, drain the bowl without pausing, clap three times, and then return the bowl.

---

islands. These divers invariably stay at either a resort that has its own superior dive operation, or they'll have booked space on a live-aboard dive vessel.

There are, of course, quite a few independent dive operators throughout Fiji whose main clientele are the "day-trip" divers, those vacationers who are interested in making only a couple of casual forays underwater during their stay in the islands.

Below is a representative sampling of those operators, along with their U.S.-based contact numbers and E-mail addresses.

Aqua-Trek Beqa, a PADI 5-Star IDC, has one boat that takes a maximum of 16 divers. It hits all the high spots of Beqa Lagoon. This company also has operations in Taveuni (2 boats carrying 27 divers, covering Rainbow Reef and Somosomo Straits), and in Mamanuca (3 boats carrying 36 divers,

---

Local Taboos

It is considered extremely bad manners to touch a Fijian on the head.

Fijians are quite modest and are offended by scanty clothing worn anywhere but in a beach setting.

All in Harmony

Seemingly born with perfect pitch, all Fijians sing—almost all the time. They sing in church, on the way to work, while they go about their work, whenever. And if you're truly lucky, they'll sing for you. Group singing is always a cappella and in breathtakingly sweet harmony.

The hauntingly beautiful "Isa Lei" was something that caught me completely by surprise. At the end of our first visit to Fiji, as we were leaving the resort to catch the flight back to Nadi, we noticed that the entire staff—gardeners, waitstaff, reception clerks—had all gathered next to the van. Suddenly they began to sing "Isa Lei," the traditional Fijian farewell song, in such glorious harmony we found ourselves weeping and sobbing. We didn't even understand the words; but there was no need to. Their open, sincere faces and their ethereal music spoke a universal language.

covering the Mananuca Islands). Call (800) 541-4334; e-mail: aquatrek@is.com.fj; website: www.aquatrek.com.

Crystal Divers has three boats and serves a maximum of 24 divers. It covers the Bligh Waters. Phone: (679) 694-747; e-mail: crystaldivers@is.com.fj.

Dive Sonaisali (a PADI Resort) has three boats with a maximum of 15 divers. It covers sites in the Mamanucas. Phone: (604) 261-4883; e-mail: aaron@sonaisali.com.fj.

Scuba Bula (a PADI Gold Palm Resort) has two boats and 20 divers, max. It covers sites in the Navula Passage and the Barrier Reef. Phone: (679) 706-100; e-mail: seashell@is.com.fj.

Eco Divers has four boats and can accommodate 30 divers. It covers sites around Savusavu. Phone: (679) 850-122; e-mail: ecodivers@is.com.fj.

ISLAND LIFE

What sets Fiji apart from other exotic south sea island destinations is its complete lack of artifice. Basically, what you see is the way things really are. For example, Fijians are naturally friendly. So the warm greetings you'll receive aren't some sort of tourist promotion. Fijians just can't help being welcoming, hospitable, and cheerful.

However, it would be naïve to suggest that Fiji has remained completely untouched or "unspoiled" by tourism. Obviously, foreign dollars have wrought significant changes on this ancient culture. And equally obvious, the Fijians have made concessions to ensure that this sort of tourist support will keep on coming in.

But regardless of all that, the Fijian way of life continues to flow placidly along the time-honored paths, despite the continual (and perhaps often intrusive) presence of visitors across the islands. For example, you might find it amusing, or even somewhat bizarre, that traffic cops in Nadi and Suva wear skirts. But this isn't some hokey costume they wear to wow the tourists; these skirts are the traditional *sulus* that are worn by all Fijian men, because loose breezy skirts make cool sense in this hot and humid climate.

Similarly, the exotic gear and rituals surrounding traditional ceremonies, such as the *meke* and *yakona* (kava) events, are the real thing. They have absolutely nothing to do with tourism, and everything to do with ancient traditions.

Even if you're the naturally shy type back home, don't be shy in Fiji; feel free to join in just about anywhere in Fiji, because you'll be most welcome.

One more tip: tipping is not encouraged in Fiji; it's really up to you. However, in lieu of daily tipping, some resorts operate a staff Christmas fund where "tips" are shared among everyone in the staff's village.

Topside Attractions

Please do not be put off by the idea of visiting something billed as a Cultural Centre, no matter how touristy you may think it sounds. This one happens to be a winner!

The **Orchid Island Fijian Cultural Centre** gives first-timers a one-stop, quickie overview of Fijian life—like Fiji in a nutshell. It's an outdoor experience in which you, the visitor, ride in a dugout canoe that makes stops at various illustrative sites which create a microcosm of Fijian history and life: a small and typical Fijian village, a craftsman making bark cloth, basket weaving, a chief's bure, and other traditions. One of my favorites is the witty, almost tongue-in-cheek demonstration of "100 Things We Do With Coconuts." Also on the site is Bure Kalou, a 50-foot native temple. Throughout the grounds' tropical gardens you'll encounter tame local animals. Also throughout the grounds are traditional dances and other shows, crafts shops, and places to picnic. The Cultural Centre is located in Veisari, on the Queens Highway, outside Suva. Admission is about $5 per person. Hours are Monday to Saturday, 8 a.m. to 4:30 p.m. The local phone is (679) 361-227.

A nice counterpart to this sort of hands-on lifestyle overview is to visit the **Fiji Museum,** which houses a collection that is fascinating and extremely eclectic. Along with such artifacts as the rudder of the *HMS Bounty* are impressive *drua* (double-hulled canoes), various weapons, and ceremonial kava bowls. There is even an old boot, which is all is that remains of the Reverend Baker, the Wesleyan missionary who evidently went into the cookpot fully clothed and shod. (That was back in the days when Fijians weren't quite so welcoming to strangers from foreign lands.) The museum exhibits include results of ongoing archaeological digs (some of the sites date back 3,500 years), oral histories, and other cultural elements of Fiji. It is located in the beautiful **Thurston Botanical Gardens,** in Suva. Hours are Monday through Friday, 9:30 a.m. to 4 p.m.; Saturday and Sunday, 1 to 4 p.m. Admission is about $1.50 per person. There's also a museum store and a café. The local phone is (679) 315 944

More than half of the Fijian population is made up of Fijian-Indians, so it makes perfect sense that the largest **Hindu temple** in the Southern Hemisphere, Shri Shiva-Subramaniya, is located in Nadi. It is dedicated to Lord Maruman, the deity of nature and guardian of seasonal rains. This three-part shrine is dazzling, covered with ornate paintings and sculptures of lotus blossoms, leaves, and deities. As a visitor you are welcome, but are requested to dress appropriately (modestly) and to show respect.

In addition to the more prosaic topside activities—tennis, golf, horseback riding—Fiji also offers activities that are a bit more exotic. There's trekking and bushwhacking into the highlands, where rushing rivers and streams plunge into deep lush valleys. There is also a local sport known as river jetting, the high-speed thrills of the famous Shooter Jet Fiji. Or you might want to experience the ultimate togetherness thrill of tandem skydiving. At the other end of the thrill spectrum, you could dress in white linen and join the locals in a bit of veddy proper Lawn Bowling.

You surely don't want to return home empty-handed from your trip to Fiji. Especially not when nifty gifts are so easy to find, and so affordable. You'll want several kava bowls—for yourself as well as for friends. And then there are the carved wooden war clubs, replicas of old "cannibal forks," and Fijian combs. Local handicrafts are always a good buy because they're, well, local and handcrafted. In Fiji, these made-by-hand goodies include woven baskets and mats, *mass* (tap/bark cloth), woodcarvings, and pottery. And, of course, the all-purpose gift for every single person on your list is the Fijian *sulu.* This one-size-fits-all wrap is appropriate for either sex, available in almost limitless varieties of colors and patterns, and packs flat to take up almost no room at all in your suitcase. Classical Indian gifts are plentiful, too, such as gold and other jewelry, spices, cottons, and silk sarongs.

In some locations (probably not in the boutique at your hotel, for example) bargaining is not only accepted, it's also part of the fun of the shopping experience. A great place to hone your skills would be in the shops and boutiques along Cummings Street in Suva.

Entertainment

Although most of Fiji's resident population is clustered on the two main islands of Viti Levu and Vanua Levu, some of its more exotic and more colorful traditions are tied to and centered on the smaller outlying islands. The famous fire walkers, for instance, all come from Beqa where, according to local legend, their ancestors were granted this ability to walk barefoot on white-hot rocks by a grateful spirit who was released from bondage by a Beqa villager many centuries ago. However, *Vilavilairevo,* which literally means "jumping into the oven," can be seen throughout the islands, because Beqa's modern-day fire walkers travel throughout Fiji to demonstrate their unique gift.

Happily, there are other traditions better suited to general participation, which visitors can readily enjoy and share with their hosts. Three traditions that you should try to take part in at least once during your visit to Fiji are the *meke,* a dance performance that illustrates traditional stories and legends; the *lovo,* a traditional feast where foods are wrapped in *bababa* leaves, buried in the earth and slow-cooked; and *yakona,* the kava ceremony.

Medical Facilities

Hospitals are located in major cities, and there are government Health Centres serving rural areas. Many hotels and resorts have a qualified nurse on the premises and a doctor on call.

The Fiji Dive Operators Association has a recompression chamber in the hospital in Suva. This facility coordinates the Fiji-wide Medevac system that transports dive accident victims by sea, road, or air to the recompression chamber for treatments. Treatment charges at present vary due to the type of transportation and the number of treatments required. The safest policy is to obtain adequate insurance to cover all eventualities before leaving home. In the future the facility hopes to provide free treatments.

In case of a diving emergency call DAN (Divers Alert Network) at (919) 684-4DAN (4326) or (919) 684-8111.

Florida: The Keys

Physical Characteristics of the Dive Area

WATER & WEATHER CONDITIONS

Visibility	*Adequate*
Current and Surge	*Minimal*
Temperature	*Comfortable to Chilly*
Storms	*Occasionally Stormy*

SITE CONDITIONS

Mooring Buoys	*Some*
Fishing, Collecting, and Hunting Restrictions	*Widespread Restrictions*
Ease of Access	*Very Easy*
Boat Traffic/Diver Congestion	*Heavy*

MARINE LIFE

Abundance of Invertebrates	*Abundant*
Abundance of Vertebrates	*Abundant*
Abundance of Pelagic Life	*Abundant*
Health of Reef/Marine Life/ Marine Structure	*Healthy*

America's Caribbean

The Florida Keys are truly America's Caribbean. Exotic flowers and fruits, sultry days, warm clear waters with gorgeous tropical marine life—it's all here, tucked away in this long necklace-string of coral and limestone islands. And, yes, they really are as wonderful as they sound. The Keys contain some of the best elements of the Caribbean—its beauty, its laid-back, relaxing atmosphere, its friendly disposition—with the advantages of the good old U.S.A.—an efficient touring infrastructure and affordable prices. That's a combination tough to beat, and you won't need a passport!

For divers, these are all great enticements, but the additional benefit is a welcoming underwater environment that's perfect for dive training and for casual, no-stress diving enjoyment. This is the ideal location for beginning divers. "I used to bring my students here to the Florida Keys when I taught diving in Fort Lauderdale," says Spencer Slate. "I came here for the clear, warm water, beautiful coral reefs, and the tremendous variety of fish." Slate, who has owned Atlantis Dive Center in Key Largo for donkey's years, estimates that half of his patrons are new to the sport. Atlantis likes to take its first-time divers to Pennekamp Reef State Park (the nation's first underwater state park) and Key Largo National Marine Sanctuary.

From Key Largo to Key West, this is the land of purple bougainvillea and pink hibiscus, juicy mangos and key lime pie, parrot-heads and wild sunsets. This is also the great vast land of dive shops, particularly in Key Largo, the area's premier diving site. Need dive gear? Definitely buy your supplies here; with so many dive shops, the prices are intensely competitive.

You'll also find a wide selection of lodgings, from the basic motel style to attractive resorts with dive shops on premises. But if you're traveling on a shoestring, don't worry about staying in a place that doesn't have a dive shop—just hook up with one nearby. You'll find that places to stay are a lot cheaper in Key Largo than in the rest of the Keys. Key West lodgings are the most expensive.

Word of Warning: When driving through the Keys, you'll be going over water as much as you will land. Roads and bridges get down to one lane each way for much of the long stretch, and traffic can be a challenge at times, particularly on weekends. US 1, called the Overseas Highway, is the only road that goes into and out of the Keys.

Get used to the mile marker system. Addresses and directions throughout the Keys are usually given in mile markers. Each mile along Route 1 is marked on a small green sign with white numbers. They begin with MM 126, just south of Florida City and end with MM 0 in Key West.

As you drive along, you'll notice that each section of the Keys has a distinctive personality. Key Largo is the biggest and the busiest, and therefore the least interesting. But sometimes strip malls can really come in handy, as do dive shops. And this is a diving Mecca, land of the big red flag with diagonal white stripe. As you continue to knock off mile markers, the landscape becomes more inviting and the concrete less dominant. Mangroves line the banks, but don't expect wide expanses of beach. There are several nice beach parks, however, such as the Long Key State Recreation Area and Sombrero Beach Park, in Marathon.

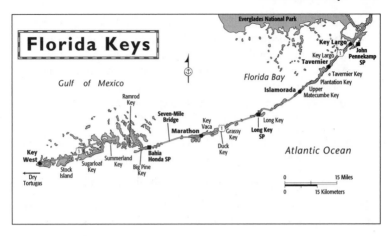

QUICK STATS

Weather   The average annual temperature is a low of 69° and a high of 83°. Average annual rainfall is 56 inches. In January the low is about 59°, the high about 75. In August, the low is around 77°, the high 89°. June gets the most rainfall—about nine inches—and December gets the least (less than two inches). Summer definitely is the rainiest time of year. The sun can be intense, so make sure you come prepared with sunglasses, sunscreen, and hat.

Water Temperature   Water temperature in summer can be as high as 85°. In winter, water temps are generally around 75°.

Underwater Visibility   Outside reefs have the best visibility—usually around 80 feet. Generally, the visibility ranges from about 30 feet when its stormy to 100 at its best.

Best Diving Months   The diving is year-round, but the best time is in summer and into September. Winter storms can often really muck up the visibility.

PLANNING THE TRIP

Getting to the Keys   American Eagle, US Air, and Continental Xpress all fly to Key West International Airport. American Eagle connects in Miami, Orlando, and Tampa/Naples. US Air connects in Miami and Tampa/Naples, and Continental Xpress connects only in Miami. Greyhound Lines runs between Miami and Key West, with stops in Homestead, Marathon, Ramrod Key, and Key West.

Getting Around   If you're only going to stay in the Key West area and need wheels, consider renting a Key West Cruiser. These are two- and four-seater electric cars with distinctive egg-like shapes and bright colors. You will be noticed. Don't try to pass anyone, though; the cruisers travel only up to 25 mph. On the bright side, you'll never get a speeding ticket! They are allowed on all Key West roadways except North Roosevelt Boulevard. Rent them at 1111A Eaton Street. Call (888) 800-8802.

Weather Service Reports   For the latest conditions, check the National Weather Service buoy reports at www.nws.fsu.edu/buoy/fl.html.

Diving Information   www.florida-keys.fl.us/diving.htm

Florida Tourism   For more information on diving in the Keys, call (800) FLA-KEYS or check out the Florida Keys website: www.fla-keys.com.

THE UNDERWATER SCENE

This is Ground Zero for divers searching for coral reef in North America. This is it, folks—the only one off the continental United States. Fortunately, there's a lot of it. The Key Largo area alone has about 150 moored dive sites, so getting bored is not an option.

About five miles offshore from Key Largo are several fertile reef systems that have been popular sites for years. Molasses, French, and Elbow Reefs are on the edge of a bank, where the Gulf Stream skirts by, constantly washing them with new water. They are fairly shallow reefs, ranging from 15 to 90 feet, but these are excellent areas for spotting pelagic life. Hawksbill turtles and spotted eagle rays are frequent visitors. Another bank of reefs is closer to shore and comes right up to the surface—perfect for snorkelers, as well as divers.

Divers will find a wonderful assortment of solitary tropicals such as French, gray and queen angelfish, rock beauties, wide-eyed pufferfish, beautiful parrotfish, triggerfish, and trumpetfish. The schooling fish also are prolific, especially since the advent of the Sanctuary Preservation Areas (SPAs). You'll find an array of grunts and snappers in hues of blue, yellow, and gray. Silvery tarpon, barracuda, Bermuda chub, and Atlantic spadefish often hang out at the dive sites. Also, the little guys school all about, and typically are found among the artificial reefs and around overhead environments. You'll see glassy sweeper, tomtates, and all types of little baitfish.

This would be the perfect area to get certified or to brush up on your diving skills. The water is toasty warm (except in winter) and usually calm; the visibility is very good; and most of the reefs are in shallow water. And this is also the perfect area to use Nitrox or to get Nitrox-certified. Courses are offered throughout the Keys, and the breathing air is widely available. Most classes now take only half a day.

Be aware that in June you might see jellyfish, and April is the typical season for the Portuguese man-of-war, a cousin to the jellyfish. The man-of-war stings are really painful, so be alert. A man-of-war looks like a blue bubble floating in the ocean and has very long tentacles with layers of stinger cells. Its larvae, known as sea lice, cling to swim suits and itch like crazy. Make sure you don't rub your eyes after taking off your wet suit. If you get a jellyfish sting, either vinegar, meat tenderizer, or ammonia can ease the pain. For the sea lice, just wash the area with soap and water, and try not to scratch!

Flags on the beach will tell you if there's a problem in the water. Red means no swimming, yellow means caution, green means get in and have a great time. One other important point: the water temperature in winter can be a very nippy 67°. That's cold. Definitely wear a nice warm wet suit.

Health Score Card

The area has experienced some coral bleaching, which is to be expected, since this is a natural phenomenon occurring virtually worldwide. Actually, in this area the corals appear to be bouncing back. Due to the Sanctuary Preservation Areas, the fish swarm around the Keys' shallow sun-kissed reef systems. It's a happy time for them—they couldn't be healthier.

Diving Conditions

Most of the reef systems here feature shallow spur-and-groove topography with little current. Patch reef formations are also common. The water is warm and most dives are leisurely with plenty of bottom time to really observe the marine life and take pictures. Visibility varies from around 40 to 50 feet in the near-shore areas to 60 to 80 feet at the outer reefs.

Although the water is clearer in the outlying areas, the dives there are typically more challenging because of the depths and strong currents. Divers will experience depths of around 100 feet, particularly at several of the wrecks. Also, the deeper dives can be cold, especially in winter, and a 3-mm wet suit is a good idea. Although these are deeper dives, they are still well within sport-diving limits, and they are within Nitrox limits, also. So to extend your bottom time at these sites, and have more time to really explore, definitely think about using Nitrox if you have the certification.

The diving in the Keys is all boat diving. I don't know of any good shore dives here.

Recommended Level of Experience

Every level of diver will enjoy the Keys. This is a wonderful destination to get certified and to hone your skills. More advanced divers will enjoy the deeper, more challenging, wrecks and drop-offs.

The currents of the Gulf Stream wash the deeper wrecks, and conditions at these sites can make the diving far more difficult. Only confident divers should attempt them. If your skills are rusty, make a few shallow dives to perfect your buoyancy and develop confidence, then attempt the more challenging dives. When you're diving in current, be sure to pull yourself down the descent line, rather than trying to swim through it. You'll save energy and air and have more bottom time.

Great Dive Sites

Key Largo Area   One of the most popular and best known areas in the Keys for training is *John Pennekamp Coral Reef State Park* off Key Largo at MM 102.5. Adjacent to it is the Florida Keys National Marine Sanctuary. These are perfect for new divers and ideal for practicing buoyancy skills while enjoying colorful marine life.

Several miles offshore is *Elbow Reef,* which generally has excellent visibility and a variety of sites with depths ranging from 20 to 65 feet. The Elbow is so called because of the angle of the reef that pokes out into the Gulf Stream. Spur-and-groove formations stretch out to deep ocean. The *City of Washington* wreck is here, as well as some Civil War wrecks. The *City of Washington* was a 320-foot-long steamship built in 1877 that ran aground in 1917.

North North Dry Rocks is a particularly fertile area with coral ridges and sandy channels. Fish are abundant. If you want to get some photos of angelfish, this is a good spot to find them. By the way, the extra "north" in the name is not a typo; the spot is located north of the site called *North Dry Rocks.*

Between *Elbow Reef* and *French Reef* is the wreck *Benwood*. This freighter, built in England in 1910, was 360 feet long but has been partially destroyed. Still, much of the ship is intact, such as the bow and part of the hull, so it remains an interesting wreck. Also, the site attracts large numbers of tropicals, including schooling fish. Depths here are nice and shallow—around 40 feet—so you have plenty of bottom time. It all makes for a particularly pretty night dive.

French Reef, with depths ranging from 10 to 90 feet, features coral spurs and sandy grooves but also has some intriguing arches, swim-throughs, caves, and caverns; so there's a lot of variety. Most of these features are in shallow water, and they're not intimidating or challenging. Typically, you'll find glimmering glassy sweepers schooling in the overhead environments.

Molasses Reef sites, such as *Winch Hole, Spanish Anchor,* and *Eagle Ray Alley,* offer opportunities for pelagic sightings, since these are in deeper water off the outer bank. That's one of the reasons that Molasses Reef is probably the most popular in the Keys. Spotted eagle rays, turtles, and sharks are frequent visitors. Schooling fish are also particularly abundant here. You're bound to find schools of grunts and Bermuda chub, blue tang, Creole wrasse, and horse-eye jacks. Pufferfish, cowfish, and barracuda are also common. The topography is typically spur-and-groove reef formation. Depths are mostly shallow—in the 30- to 40-foot range. Some areas are as shallow as 10 feet. This is a terrific area, but it can get crowded as a result.

An excellent wreck site for advanced divers is the *Duane,* a 327-foot U.S. Coast Guard Cutter sunk in 1987. Its depth, at 120 feet, as well as the typical strong currents here, makes it a fairly challenging dive. It sits upright in the sand, and due to its age exhibits a pretty carpet of corals. Schools of tropicals are ever-present. I spotted a nice fat scorpionfish here, waiting motionless for a meal. About a half-mile from the *Duane* is its sister ship the *Bibb,* an even deeper dive. Divers will find the wreck lying on its starboard side at 130 feet, and it, too, is prone to strong currents. Some well-fed jewfish live aboard. Only the upper cabins of both wrecks are open to divers.

Conch Reef has probably the best wall site in the Keys, and it's also an easy dive. You'll start out on sandy bottom and grass flats, which is where you should look for the conch tracks. Swim out toward the wall, and at about 60 feet it drops down to 90 feet. At the edge of the wall are healthy barrel sponges and sea fans. You'll probably see some stately pillar coral here, as well.

Islamorada Area Another wreck, the *Eagle,* was sunk in 1985 and now lies at 110 feet. The *Eagle* was 287 feet long and constructed in Holland in the early 1960s. Divers (this is an advanced dive) will find half of the wreck lying on its starboard side and covered with corals and schooling fish. There are areas where the ship can be penetrated, but that, of course, can be dangerous given the depth here. Only wreck-certified divers should attempt it. If you're lucky, you might be able to see some huge jewfish that make the *Eagle* their home.

Marathon Area Two sites—*Thunderbolt* and *Coffins Patch*—are often dived together. *Thunderbolt* was a 188-foot cable-layer and research vessel that now sits upright in about 110 feet of water. It's very open and easy to penetrate. You can safely enter the wheelhouse and the engine rooms. Remember, though, that this is a deep wreck, so only experienced divers should attempt it. *Coffins Patch,* on the other hand, is very shallow and offers a convenient contrast to the wreck. Coral patch reefs are scattered about, surrounded by a sandy bottom. You'll also find pretty pillar coral here. This is one of the few types of coral that has its polyps exposed during the daytime. Wave your hand by the coral, without touching it, and you can see the movement of the fuzzy polyps. You'll also find a lot of brain coral here. The angelfish seem to love the place; you'll see every species right here.

Sombrero Reef is popular with local dive shops because it accommodates both divers and snorkelers. With depths ranging from 20 to 25 feet, it is shallow enough to keep the surface conveniently at hand, but deep enough to hold the full range of tropical corals and marine life. Among the tongue-and-groove topography (which extends perpendicular to the shoreline) you'll see lobster, pufferfish grunts, tangs, and perhaps nurse sharks. In the shallow depths are beautiful stands of elkhorn and staghorn coral.

Big Pine Key Area   *Looe Key* is a large reef system with about 50 moored sites. This is where the Looe Key National Marine Sanctuary is located, consisting of about five square miles of reef. Much of the reef is classic spur-and-groove coral formation, with long fingers (spurs) alternating with channels of sand, extending out to sea. Depths range from the shallow (practically at the surface) to about 80 feet, which gives divers plenty of bottom time. And there is plenty to see, from nice big brain and star corals to sea fans and barrel sponges.

A 210-foot island freighter named *Adolphus Busch, Sr.*, is the newest piece of tonnage in the Keys. This is another advanced dive, since the ship lies at 100 feet about six miles southwest of Big Pine Key. Fortunately, the currents here are not as strong as at the northern wreck sites.

Key West Area   *Western Dry Docks* is a shallow area featuring coral mounds and spur-and-groove configurations. Both kinds of topography attract large fish populations. This site is a good area for snorkeling, as is *Eastern Dry Docks,* which has shallow ridges of coral. Nearby *Sand Key* features an actual lighthouse underwater.

A wreck dive to practice on before tackling the *Duane, Thunderbolt,* and other advanced wrecks, is *Joe's Tug.* It's a popular dive, and many of the dive shops put it on their itinerary. The depths are in the 50-foot range, but the area can experience strong currents. The harbor tug is 75 feet long and sits upright at 65 feet. It attracts clusters of grunts and jacks, as well as barracuda and angelfish.

Snorkeling Sites

Snorkeling is terrific all around, since the inshore shelf is so shallow, and most sites are in the 25-foot range. Most of the dive shops offer special snorkeling trips, and snorkelers are welcome on most of the dive trips. Just make sure they're not scheduled to do any of the deeper dives, such as on the *Duane* or the *Bibb* shipwrecks.

Snorkelers should watch out for stinging fire coral. It is a golden-brown color and grows in vertical columns, in folds. Also, since sun-loving staghorn coral frequently comes right up to the surface, be very careful you don't bump into any and damage the branches.

Carysfort Reef, off Key Largo, is a pleasant snorkeling area, with beautiful elkhorn coral. *Dry Rocks* is where you'll find the Christ of the Abyss statue, certainly a fascinating underwater spectacle.

A new twist on the snorkeling excursion is being offered by Dolphin Cove, located at MM 102 bayside in Key Largo. They can arrange eco-snorkeling tours through the Florida Bay backcountry, where you'll learn all about the marine life and their habitats. A pontoon boat is used that holds 25 people. Excursions are twice daily at 11 a.m. and 1:30 p.m. Dolphin swims may also be included. Call (877) 365-2683 or (305) 451-4060; website: www.dolphinscove.com.

Marine Park

Both federal and state legislation safeguard the coral reef ecosystem in much of the Florida Keys area. Adjacent to Everglades and Biscayne National Parks is the Florida Keys National Marine Sanctuary. This encompasses the John Pennekamp Coral Reef State Park, which is run by the state. Pennekamp is particularly noteworthy for being America's first undersea park.

John D. Pennekamp was a Miami newspaper editor instrumental in establishing the Everglades National Park and the Pennekamp Coral Reef State Park. Together, the National Marine Sanctuary and the Pennekamp park protect and preserve a portion of the only living coral reef in the continental United States. The protected areas extend three miles in length and cover approximately 178 nautical square miles of coral reefs, seagrass beds, and mangrove swamps.

Also, 18 Sanctuary Protection Areas (SPAs) surround the major reefs. Looe Key, which was designated a National Marine Sanctuary in 1981, is among the SPAs. In these regions hook and line fishing has been prohibited since 1997, allowing a resurgence of fish. These are also no-touch, no-take, and no-anchoring zones. Most of the dive sites described in this chapter are located in these SPAs.

The Dry Tortugas are also among the Florida Keys National Marine Sanctuary and the Dry Tortugas National Park. Conservationists hope that an additional 185 square nautical miles of the region will also soon be converted into an ecological reserve. Researchers have found that snapper, grouper, and shrimp are being overfished in the area, which is a rich breeding ground for the species.

DIVE SERVICES & PACKAGES

The following dive shops are listed starting from the north and progressing south down to Key West.

Atlantis Dive Center (MM 106.5), a PADI Dive Center in Key Largo, is owned by Spencer Slate, the guy who likes to pose for unique photo opps. Spencer will actually feed a barracuda (or at least he used to) who takes mackerel from his mouth! Needless to say, Slate is quite a character. His dive center is located in the center of Pennekamp Coral Reef State Park and the Key Largo Marine Sanctuary. Atlantis uses three 42-foot custom built dive/snorkel/glassbottom boats with broad beams (ideal for people who are prone to seasickness). Want to get married? Atlantis will do the honors, in an underwater ceremony with family and friends watching through the windows of the glass-bottom boat! Special snorkel trips go out three times daily for only $26.50, which includes the gear. Instruction is with all the major agencies, and you can even go pro here, since this is a YMCA Instructor Training Career Institute. You'll find everything you need at Atlantis, including Enriched Air Nitrox mixes. Atlantis is partnered with the nearby Howard Johnson Resort, where divers will get a reduced room rate. These partners are even travel agents, and can make your airline reservations and book your car rental. Phone (800) 331-3483 or (305) 451-3020; e-mail: captslate@reef net.com; website: www.pennekamp.com/atlantis.

Retail Sales: *Extensive*	**Dive Boat Comfort:** *Good*
Rentals: *Extensive*	**On-Board Facilities**
Scuba Training: *Extensive*	**for Photographers:** *Good*
Photo Services: *Moderate*	

Coral Reef Park Company (MM 102.5) operates all the concession services within John Pennekamp Coral Reef State Park, including the diving and snorkeling activities. The training facility at this PADI Gold Palm IDC Resort is located directly across the channel from the Main Concession, from where the glass-bottom boats and snorkel tours leave. Instruction is through the advanced level. Scuba tours are a reasonable $37 per person; scuba and snorkeling rentals, also, are reasonable. Besides dive tours, there are special sailing and snorkeling tours from a 38-foot catamaran, glass-bottom boat tours, and boat rentals—19-footers to 28-footers. Call (305) 451-6322; website: www.pennekamppark.com.

Retail Sales: *Adequate*

Rentals: *Extensive*

Scuba Training: *Moderate*

Photo Services: *Limited*

Dive Boat Comfort: *Good*

On-Board Facilities
for Photographers: *Good*

Ocean Divers is located next to the Marina Del Mar Resort & Marina at 522 Caribbean Drive in Key Largo. The owners also have **American Diving Headquarters** at MM 105.8, which has some excellent dive packages with dorms and apartments. The PADI Career Development Center offers courses from Discover Scuba to instructor. It runs 50-foot custom dive boats with camera benches and freshwater showers and a 47-foot Newton with all the frills, including fresh fruit for the aprés-dive. Enriched Air Nitrox is available. The shop offers rentals and repairs, as well as gear for sale. Also, there's a locked storage area for gear—a nice feature. Call (800) 451-1113; fax (305) 451-5765; e-mail: info@oceandivers.com; website: www.oceandivers.com. For American Diving Headquarters, call (877) 451-0037.

Retail Sales: *Extensive*

Rentals: *Extensive*

Scuba Training: *Extensive*

Photo Services: *Moderate*

Dive Boat Comfort: *Excellent*

On-Board Facilities
for Photographers: *Superior*

H₂0 Adventures, at MM 94.5 oceanside in Key Largo, runs a shop at Snappers Waterfront Restaurant. Here, all sorts of watersports equipment can be rented (Hobie Cats, Waverunners, kayaks, etc.) as well as power boats. You can rent one of these boats to do your own diving or go out with their crew. The Global Positioning System self-guided tours supply you with coordinates for diving, snorkeling, and eco-tours. H₂O Adventures will also deliver boats to area hotels and rent out snorkel and fishing equipment. NAUI and PADI instruction is through the divemaster level. Call (305) 853-0600; website: www.h20.adventures.com.

Retail Sales: *None*

Rentals: *Adequate*

Scuba Training: *Extensive*

Photo Services: *Limited*

Dive Boat Comfort: *Good*

On-Board Facilities
for Photographers: *Good*

Tilden's Scuba Center is on the property of, and offers packages with, Hawk's Cay Resort & Marina at MM 61 oceanside on Duck Key. PADI instruction is from the intro course through divemaster level. The shop sells gear, does repairs, and provides equipment rentals. Tilden's runs a comfortable 40-foot dive boat with hot-water shower, and a marine head. The boat holds 40 passengers, but no more than 20 are taken out at a time. Special snorkel trips are scheduled, as well as scuba trips. Call (877) FUN-DIVE or (305) 289-4931; e-mail: diving@hawkscay.com; website: www. divingathawkscay.com.

Retail Sales: *Extensive*	**Dive Boat Comfort:** *Excellent*
Rentals: *Extensive*	**On-Board Facilities**
Scuba Training: *Extensive*	**for Photographers:** *Good*
Photo Services: *Limited*	

Abyss Pro Dive Center, a PADI Dive Center in Marathon (MM 54), carries no more than six divers on its boat, the *Vitamin Sea*. The shop offers dive-vacation packages with a number of lodging options, including most of the motels in the area, as well as the gulf-front Sheraton Key Largo Resort. Rentals are available, including underwater cameras, and there is a repair service. Instruction is offered to the divemaster level. Phone (800) 457-0134 or (305) 743-5929; fax (305) 743-7081; e-mail: info@abyss dive.com; website: www.abyssdive.com.

Retail Sales: *Extensive*	**Dive Boat Comfort:** *Good*
Rentals: *Extensive*	**On-Board Facilities**
Scuba Training: *Extensive*	**for Photographers:** *Good*
Photo Services: *Limited*	

Hall's Diving Center and Career Institute, in Marathon, is located on the property of Ferro Blanco Marine Resort at MM 48. Guests literally have the dive service at their doorstep (or their dock, as many of Ferro Blanco's "rooms" are spacious houseboats). Trips are on Hall's 40-foot custom dive boat. The shop provides rentals and repairs, and sells gear. Instruction ranges from learn-to-snorkel trips to advanced diving certifications. Phone (800) 331-HALL or (305) 743-5929; fax (305) 743-8168; e-mail: hallsdive@aol. com; website: hallsdiving.com.

Retail Sales: *Extensive*	**Dive Boat Comfort:** *Good*
Rentals: *Extensive*	**On-Board Facilities**
Scuba Training: *Moderate*	**for Photographers:** *Good*
Photo Services: *Limited*	

Down at Ramrod Key (MM 27.5), halfway between Key West and Marathon, is **Looe Key Reef Resort and Dive Center.** It is a PADI Gold

Palm Resort and 5-Star Dive Center, and a BSAC facility. Rental gear is available, and instruction is extensive—virtually anything you would want. Snorkeling instruction is free. The location is convenient to the Looe Key National Marine Sanctuary, consisting of approximately five square miles of spur-and-groove reef. Looe Key is also the site of one of the most unusual diving events ever: the Lower Keys Underwater Music Festival, a zany annual event that takes place in July. The center uses a 45-foot catamaran equipped with soft drinks and shower. It leaves for dive trips directly behind the resort's guest rooms. Dive/lodging packages are available. Call (800) 942-5397 or (305) 872-2215; fax (305) 872-3786; e-mail: looekey dive@aol.com; website: www.diveflakeys.com

Retail Sales: *Extensive*

Rentals: *Extensive*

Scuba Training: *Extensive*

Photo Services: *Limited*

Dive Boat Comfort: *Good*

On-Board Facilities
for Photographers: *Good*

WHERE TO STAY

Reservations services might be helpful if you're having problems getting a booking: AA Accommodations Center (phone (800) 732-2006) provides free information on hotels, condos, and guest houses; Mile Marker Zero Accommodations Center (phone (877) 800-3200) provides information on lodgings as well as watersports activities. The following lodgings are listed starting from the north and progressing south down to Key West.

Amoray Dive ★★★★, in Ley Largo (MM 104.2), is a small plantation-style dedicated dive resort overlooking the bay. Accommodations range from rooms with refrigerators to efficiency suites with full kitchens. The dive shop is right here, just steps from the rooms. Facilities include a swimming pool and spa, small beach, dock, boat basin, sun deck, and barbecues. Special wedding plans are offered. A locked dive equipment storage and rinse area is close to boat docks. The dive shop uses a 45-foot catamaran. Both PADI and NAUI instruction is through the divemaster level, and various specialties are taught. There is also a BSAC (British Sub Aqua Club) school. Room rates range from $65 to $200 per night and include continental breakfast. Call (800) 4-A-MORAY or (305) 451-3595; fax (305) 453-9516; e-mail: amoray@pennekamp.com; website: www.amoray.com

Howard Johnson Resort ★★★, in Key Largo (MM 102), is right on the bay, and diving is through the nearby Atlantis Dive Center. The 100-room resort features a white sandy beach, swimming pool, restaurant, lounge, and water activities that include kayaking, parasailing, and sunset cruises. Rooms have refrigerators and coffeemakers, and the poolside rooms have microwaves. Divers have a special room rate that ranges from $59 to $165 (single or double) depending on the season. Those are great rates, and to get them you must stay for a minimum of two nights and sign up for two half-day charters—pretty reasonable. Call (800) 947-7320 or (305) 451-1400; fax (305) 451-3953; e-mail: hjkeylargo@aol.com; website: www. islandfun.com/hojokeylargo.

Marina Del Mar Resort & Marina ★★★★ is located on the waterfront in Key Largo (527 Caribbean Drive). All rooms and suites (one- , two- ,and three-bedroom) have balconies, air-conditioning, and refrigerators. Facilities include a full-service marina, dive shop, gift shop, waterfront restaurant and cocktail lounge, swimming pool with whirlpool, lighted tennis courts, fitness center, and outdoor entertainment facilities. A variety of water sports and diving packages are available. The adjacent dive shop is Ocean Divers. Call (800) 451-3483 or (305) 451-4107; fax (305) 451-1891; e-mail: marina-del-mar@msn.com; website: www.marinadelmar.com.

On Plantation Key at MM 90.5 is the **Tropic Vista Motel ★★★**, not far from Pennekamp Coral Reef State Park. It has both large and small efficiencies, a heated pool, sun deck, Jacuzzi, and restaurant. The desk people are not the greatest, but for divers, the place is convenient and affordable. The Upper Keys Dive & Sports Center is also located in the motel and offers dive packages. The shop runs a 38-foot dive boat and offers PADI open water and advanced certifications, as well as Nitrox and other specialty courses. The shop also has rental equipment and arranges sailing charters. Standard rooms run about $68 a night. Waterfront efficiencies range from $73 to $85 per night. Call (800) 537-3253 or (305) 852-8799; fax (305) 852-4605; e-mail: tropickey@aol.com; website: www.florida/keys.fl.us/tropicvista.

Cheeca Lodge ★★★★, in Islamorada, is an upscale Rockresort, so a budget property this is not. But if you're looking for something special, this should work perfectly. The on-site dive operator is Caribbean Watersports, which can get you certified or give you a resort course. The shop uses a 49-foot catamaran, which visits such sites as Cheeca Rocks, about a mile offshore; Alligator Reef, known for morays and barracuda; and the sunken *Eagle,* a 287-foot freighter lying 110 feet down. A package called "Dive or Snorkel the Purple Isle" includes nightly accommodation, a one- or two-tank dive or snorkel trip daily, 50 percent off Camp Cheeca (an environmentally oriented day camp for children ages 6 to 12), and a few other tidbits to sweeten the pot for $310 per room for a double. Call (800) 327-2888 or (305) 664-4651.

On the more affordable side in Islamorada is **Lookout Lodge,** a place designed especially for scuba divers. It sits on Florida Bay at 87770 Overseas Highway in Islamorada Village of Islands. The lodge has studios (accommodating up to four people) and one- and two-bedroom suites (up to six people), some with sunset views. Each is air-conditioned and has a refrigerator, microwave, coffee percolator, toaster, and utensils. The suites also have electric ranges. Outdoor gas and charcoal grills are located near the waterfront. There is no pool, but the resort has a private swimming and sunbathing area, with chickee huts and lounges, beside the lagoon. A dive shop, Lookout Lodge Dive Resort, is on the property and the *Sea Raven* dive boat sits at the dock, just steps from the rooms. The shop offers scuba instruction and guided dives. Snorkelers are welcomed, too. There are gear rinse barrels and a secure overnight storage area. A restaurant just next door (MM 88) is open for dinner. Most of the year, there is a two-night minimum for divers. Nightly room rates range from $65 to $149 (depending on the season) for studios; they can range from $110 to $169 for the suites. Room tax is 11.5 percent. Dive packages are available. Call (800) 870-1772 or (305) 852-9915; fax (305) 852-3035; e-mail: mail@lookoutlodge.com; website: www.lookoutlodge.com.

Hawk's Cay Resort ★★★★ is an extensive place at MM 61 oceanside on Duck Key. There are 135 two-bedroom villas, 160 guest rooms and 16 suites. On the premises are a marina, four restaurants, a swimming lagoon, two swimming pools, a watersports concession, glass-bottom boat, children's program, fishing charters, tennis courts, bicycle rentals, an interactive dolphin program, and finally—a dive shop! It's Tilden's Scuba Center, which offers dive packages. The resort also features a fly-fishing academy (call (888) 809-7305, ext. 3570) with weekend courses designed for beginning and experienced anglers ages 16 and older. You'll learn how to cast and tie flies as well as casting techniques. Call for latest prices. Phone (800) 432-2242 or (305) 743-7000; website: www.hawkscay.com.

Ferro Blanco Marine Resort ★★★★, in Marathon, is a sprawling place with the Atlantic on one side and gulf waters on the other. Hall's Diving Center is right on the property. You can stay ashore or tie up your own vessel at the marina. The lodgings include cottages, houseboats, and condominiums. You can even stay in a lighthouse apartment. Several excellent restaurants here have been favorites with the divers for years. Angler's Bar has nightly entertainment and gets a lot of activity. Also on the property: laundry facility, playground and picnic area, dive gear storage lockers, swimming pool, boat rentals, and boat basin. The best dive package rate is

$67 per person, double occupancy. Phone (800) 759-3276 or (305) 743-9018; fax (305) 743-2918.

A new 79-unit **Hampton Inn & Suites** is located at MM 48 oceanside in Marathon. Every room has a private balcony and ocean view. There are 55 guest rooms and 24 suites, either one- or two-bedroom, with fully equipped kitchens. On the site are a restaurant and bar, swimming pool and whirlpool, fitness center, dock, boat ramp, and dive shop. In addition to diving and snorkeling, fishing charters and eco-tours are scheduled. Boats and waverunners can be rented. Nightly rates start at $109 for a garden-view room, $119 for a marina-view room, $129 for a gulf-view room, $149 for a garden-view suite and $180 for a gulf-view suite. Call (800) HAMPTON or (305) 743-9009; fax (305) 743-383; e-mail: hamptoninns @aol.com; website: www.thefloridakeys.com/hamptonsuites.

Looe Key Reef Resort & Dive Center ★★★★ (MM 27.5), a PADI Gold Palm Resort at Ramrod Key, is halfway between Marathon and Key West. This is truly a dedicated dive resort, on the canal, with dive shop, boat ramp, and dockage, and the dive boat just in back of the guest rooms. There's a swimming pool, restaurant, and open-air Tiki Bar that features live entertainment. Packages are available. The nightly room rate (with two double beds) ranges from $70 to $150. Call (800) 942-5397 or (305) 872-2215; fax (305) 872-3786; e-mail: looekeydive@aol.com; website: www.diveflakeys.com.

Campgrounds

John Pennekamp Coral Reef State Park (MM 102.5) has 47 full-facility camping sites for both tent and RV campers. Reservations are recommended and may be made by phone or in person only. They are not accepted more than 11 months in advance of the check-in date. Phone (305) 451-1202.

On the beach (one of the few) at Bahia Honda Key is an excellent place to pitch a tent or bring an RV. The 524-acre **Bahia** (folks here pronounce this bay-ya) **Honda State Park** (MM 36 and 37) has camping sites and rental cabins, and a 19-slip marina on the bayside. This is a terrific area for snorkeling, with a wonderful, extensive sandy beach. There's no diving here, but you can take off in any direction and hook up with a nearby dive shop. The facilities are clean and attractive, and the park even has a nature trail for a self-guided tour of the natural dunes. Call (305) 872-2353.

Topside Attractions

Before starting off to explore, there are a couple of essential bits of information to get you started. First, the Overseas Highway (US 1) is the only main road connecting the Keys. Most of US 1 is a narrow, two-lane high-way, with some wider passing zones. As you drive along, remember that the mile marker number identifies most places of business here. The markers start with MM 127 just north of Key Largo and end with MM 0 in Key West. The town of Marathon is at MM 50, about halfway. To drive the length of the Keys will take about three and a half hours.

Secondly, do not pronounce the "s" in Islamorada; it is silent. Now practice—EYE-luh-moh-RAW-duh. Great, now just get rid of the sun-burn, and no one will recognize you as a tourist!

The **Florida Keys Wild Bird Center,** at MM 93.6 bayside in Tavernier, is quite an active place, with birds, of course, claiming it as their own. The center treats and rehabilitates sick and injured wild birds and has a board-walk that winds past caged birds. Another one winds through a native hammock featuring a variety of plants and trees, such as poisonwood, cac-tus, and air plants. There's also a red mangrove solution hole. Hours are 8 a.m. to 6 p.m. daily, and admission is free.

Now that you know how to pronounce Islamorada, you can go there to the **Somewhere in Time Treasure Museum,** located oceanside (MM 82.4). It features an extensive exhibit of Spanish weaponry, a display on slavery, paintings of famous pirates who inhabited the Keys, ship models, and arti-facts. Hundreds of Spanish coins are on display, and others are for sale. While in Islamorada, stop by the **Theatre of the Sea** (MM 84.5), one of the oldest marine parks in the world and still giving entertaining dolphin shows.

Moving on down the Keys, the **Dolphin Research Center,** at MM 59 bayside on Grassy Key, has an interactive program known as Dolphin Splash. As participants stand about waist-deep in the water on a submerged platform, dolphins swim up to greet them, and the staff is there to tell you all about the dolphins. You have only ten minutes in the water, but that's plenty of time to interact with them. The entire program is a half-hour ($60) and also includes an educational walking tour of the center. Call (305) 289-1121 or (305) 289-0002. Website: www.dolphins.org.

Key West has a lot to keep you occupied, and one of the best activities is simply walking around. The architecture in the Old Town has come to be known as "conch style" and echoes Bahamian architecture. The Chamber of Commerce on Wall Street has walking guides of town.

Some folks (namely Parrot-heads) might enjoy a guided walking tour called **Trails of Margaritaville.** You'll visit all the sites made famous by musician Jimmy Buffett, and in the process learn a lot about Key West. The tour starts at **Captain Tony's Saloon** (428 Greene Street) at 11 a.m. and 4 p.m. The cost is $18. Call (305) 292-2040.

Key West's historic **Custom House** contains the **Key West Museum of Art and History.** The building dates from 1891 and is an interesting piece of architecture itself. Definitely stop by to see it at 281 Front Street near Mallory Square. And be sure to visit the **Ernest Hemingway Home and Museum** at 907 Whitehead Street, where the author wrote many of his best works. Yes, the cats still have six toes (on each foot). Key West has an aquarium, of course, and no doubt you've heard of **Mel Fisher's Maritime Heritage Society Museum** (200 Greene Street). Watch out—it'll make you downright depressed, with all the gleaming coins and sparkling gold- and jewel-studded artifacts. Really amazing!

Last but not least, don't forget to catch the sunset at **Mallory Square**— and the quirky ambience that comes with it.

Dining and Entertainment

Key limes have almost disappeared from southern Florida. But if you can manage to find some key lime pie in the area, you're in luck. The key lime is a small yellow lime with a distinctive tart flavor. Try it also in sorbets and ice cream, as well as flan, souffles, and cheesecake. Delicious!

An excellent family style restaurant just outside the Everglades and on your way to the Keys is **Angie's Café,** in Florida City (404 SE First Avenue). At the end of the Florida Turnpike, drive a quarter-mile south on US 1. My personal favorite is the Crabby Crabber sandwich. Take-outs are available.

For a nice dinner in Key Largo, go to **Sundowner's** (MM 103.9). The glass-walled dining room faces the bay for scenic views, providing your evening entertainment. For chili, pita concoctions, steaks, and down-home food try the popular **Mrs. Mac's Kitchen** at MM 99.4.

For a special occasion, dine at **Pierre's Restaurant** in Islamorada, or have a cocktail in the **Green Flash Lounge,** which is located at MM 81.6 on the bay. In the Marathon area, Ferro Blanco Resort, at MM 48, has diver's hang-outs both at the **Angler's Bar** and **Kelsey's,** overlooking the marina. The bar, with windows all around, has terrific harbor and bay views.

Down south at MM 25 is **Monte's Restaurant and Fish Market,** with good old-fashioned seafood platters—baskets with fries, cole slaw, etc.— you get the picture. You can sit outside on the porch while munching on conch fritters, beer-battered shrimp, stone crab, and such. A little farther, at MM 20, is **Mangrove Mama's,** which is surrounded by banana trees. The decor leaves a lot to be desired, but the menu is inventive.

Down in Key West, **Kelly's** (owned by actress Kelly McGillis) has very good food and a spacious, attractive courtyard for enjoying it. The **Rusty Anchor,** across from the dog track on Stock Island, is another popular and moderately priced spot. If you have a hankering for something that hasn't lived in the sea all its life, try their finger-lickin' baby-back ribs. Finally, after the sun goes down in Key West, both **Captain Tony's,** at 428 Greene Street, and **Sloppy Joe's,** at 201 Duval Street, are a lot of fun and reminiscent of the days of old when Hemingway called this home. The latter also has live music most of the time.

DETOUR TO THE EVERGLADES

Everglades National Park is the largest remaining subtropical wilderness in the continental United States, and, happily, it's less than an hour's drive from Miami. If you love great escapes underwater, then you'll probably also fall in love with this vast wilderness escape (one and a half million acres) and the awesome beauty that exists here. From silent, sunning alligators and rare American crocs to leggy great blue heron and flamingoes, the wildlife dominates this beautiful world.

If you only have a few hours to spend in the area, don't worry. There's a wonderful visitors center where you can see the wildlife in its natural environment quickly and easily. However, if you have an extra day or two, try to get a reservation at **Flamingo Lodge,** about 38 miles inside the park. This will give you an opportunity to absorb so much more. What you should *not* do is simply drive through the park; you'll see only miles of rather uninspiring prairie grassland. In this type of environment, you really need to get out and walk, kayak, or canoe in order to see the highlights.

Naturally, most visitors who come to the Everglades are anxious to see the alligators, and they won't be disappointed. The gators certainly are in no danger of becoming extinct any longer. And there are fair number of crocodiles, too. But after you see your fill of these, you'll start to look around and notice the birds, which thrive here in profusion. That took me a bit by surprise.

The other surprise was the absenc of airboats in the park. For years, my vision of the Everglades was that of strange vessels skimming over the surface, with Spanish moss dripping from the trees, and alligators scurrying up mud banks. In fact, motorized vessels are not allowed in the park at all. If you want to ride one, you can visit the alligator farm outside the park, which gives rides that are a lot of fun, but they're along well-worn "paths." The wildlife is constantly being fed, to keep them ever-present and make the route seem more exotic. Frankly, although the farm is interesting, that is hardly the way to experience the Everglades.

Although the park can be enjoyed year-round, remember that this is mosquito heaven, so guess what happens during the rainy season? There are

43 species of mosquitoes here—and no bats! Definitely bring some repellent. May is a good month to visit, since it is the breeding season for crocs and gators. You'll see large concentrations of them at that time; later in the summer, during the rainy season, they tend to be more spread out.

If you're coming from Miami, take the Florida Turnpike south to the last exit, then follow the signs to Everglades National Park. The entrance fee is $10. You'll first see the Ernest Coe Visitor Center, where you can get information, but I highly recommend continuing four miles farther to the **Royal Palm Visitor Center,** open 8 a.m. to 4:15 p.m. An elevated boardwalk here (Anhinga Trail) winds over swampland and through tall saw grass and sedge for half a mile. It's a terrific way to view the wildlife up close and get some great pictures. You'll see everything from grasshoppers to long-necked anhingas, from air bromeliads to water lilies. The great blue heron, with its long legs sticking high up out of the water, will stare down intently, waiting to snatch a fish; an anhinga will toss a stick into the air and catch it over and over, practicing its technique. And it all happens right in front of you.

If you want to continue through the park and head down to Flamingo Lodge, there are several scenic stopovers along the way. At **Paurotis Pond** I spotted white wood storks high in the trees, and a huge croc on the shore, its mouth wide open. It was so still it hardly looked real. Herons were perched in the trees, including a species that fishes by throwing bits of bread into the water, as bait. Driving down to **Nine Mile Pond,** a soft-shell Florida turtle sat beside the road. This species has a long snout that sticks up out of the water, to breathe.

Snake Bight Trail, just over a mile and a half in length, is very popular, and a good location for spoonbills. A little farther along is **Mrazak Pond,** an excellent spot to see more birds. There are white pelicans, heron, spoonbills, and more. And it's all set in a still, peaceful world that seems almost magical. Come to think of it—it's a lot like diving!

Flamingo Lodge the park lodging concession, is managed very well and has a beautiful location on Florida Bay. There are 103 motel rooms, 24 cabins with kitchens, a restaurant, cafe, and marina. The meals in the Buttonwood Café and Restaurant are excellent. You can rent kayaks and canoes here and take a back-to-nature ride for three miles down Buttonwood Canal. Red and white mangroves line the banks, and cool trees bend low over the water. On my trip down the canal we saw owls, herons, turkey vultures, turtles, snakes, and gators, and heard only the soft sounds of nature. Houseboats and bicycles are also for rent.

For reservations, call (305) 253-2241. National Park information is (305) 242-7700; website: www.nps.gov/ever.

Detour to the Tortugas

Seventy miles from Key West in the Gulf of Mexico is another island that looks more like an artificial movie set. This somewhat surreal vision is a combination island/military fort. The fort is the island, and the island is the fort. Fort Jefferson was a nineteenth-century, Civil War—era prison, and its harbor was a supply site for U.S. Navy battleships. Now it is the **Dry Tortugas National Park,** and the waters surrounding it are part of the Florida Keys National Marine Sanctuary.

The site is fascinating, and snorkelers will have a terrific time playing in the surrounding waters. There are reputed to be at least 200 shipwrecks in the area. This is where I saw my first flying gurnard, its multicolored "wings" outstretched, skimming over the fringing reef. I felt that the gurnard alone was worth the time and expense to come over. Divers have reported that the biodiversity here is impressive. With Gulf Stream waters bringing in nutrients from the deep, the marine life remains healthy and prolific. Many species of corals exist here that can no longer be seen elsewhere in the Keys. Unfortunately, fishing is still allowed, but there is a strong movement to establish an ecological reserve to protect certain sections. Let's hope the effort is successful. The fishing "lobby" in the Keys is at least as strong as the diving promoters.

One way to get to the Tortugas is by seaplane, but another (which is better for nitrogen-loaded divers) is on *Yankee Freedom II,* an all-aluminum ocean catamaran ferry. The boat travels at an average speed of 30 m.p.h., so trips run about two hours. It carries 250 passengers and features an air-conditioned main cabin, sun and observation decks, a fully equipped galley, and two bars. Daily trips leave at 8 a.m. from Lands End Marina and return by 5:30 p.m. That will leave you about four and a half hours to explore the island. The adult fare is $95. Call (877) 327-8228 or (305)294-7009. The website is www.yankeefleet.com.

The best way to dive the area is to book onto a live-aboard. The *RV Tiburon* (Taylor Made Excursions) is a 63-foot vessel with eight cabins and carries a maximum of 14 passengers. It features Nitrox fills and E-6 film processing. Its port is Key West. Call (800) 211-9598 or (305) 293-9183. E-mail: taylormade@scubaworld.com; website: www.scubaworld.com/taylormade. Also, Sea-Clusive Charters runs a 60-foot motor yacht with four staterooms, carrying a maxium of 11 passengers. Call (305) 872-3940; fax (305) 872-0111; e-mail: seaclusive@compuserve.com; website: www.seaclusive.com.

Medical Facilities

The most central hospital to all of the Keys is Mariner's Hospital in Marathon (call (305) 852-4418), which has a recompression chamber. There's also Mercy Hospital in Miami (call (305) 854-4400), which has a recompression chamber (call (305) 854-0300). In case of a diving emergency call DAN (Divers Alert Network) at (919) 684-4DAN (4326) or (919) 684-8111.

Florida: Miami Beach

Physical Characteristics of the Dive Area

WATER & WEATHER CONDITIONS

Visibility	*Good*
Current and Surge	*Minimal*
Temperature	*Chilly*
Storms	*Occasionally Stormy*

SITE CONDITIONS

Mooring Buoys	*Some*
Fishing, Collecting, and Hunting Restrictions	*Widespread Restrictions*
Ease of Access	*Convenient*
Boat Traffic/Diver Congestion	*Light*

MARINE LIFE

Abundance of Invertebrates	*Common*
Abundance of Vertebrates	*Common*
Abundance of Pelagic Life	*Common*
Health of Reef/Marine Life/ Marine Structure	*Mixed*

Artificial Playgrounds

Miami is a big, busy place. Both greater Miami and Miami Beach are spread out over 2,000 square miles at the southeastern tip of the Florida peninsula. But that's about all the two have in common. Essentially, Miami is big city and big business; Miami Beach is laid-back, hip, and playful.

To the traveler, Miami Beach appears to be one long, narrow peninsula paralleling the mainland. In fact it is a series of islands, all connected by highway and bridges. One bridge extends for seven miles. The Intracoastal Waterway completely separates Miami Beach from the Miami mainland; consequently the two could not be more disparate—high-rise office buildings on the mainland, beach playground across the waterway. And which side would *you* rather be on?

The waterway provides a nice sheltered area for harboring boats, which can zip through a couple of different passages to get over to the Atlantic side. It's on the Atlantic side, of course, where all the diving takes place, as well as jet-skiing, parasailing, windsurfing, and now the exciting new sport of kite surfing. Beyond the swarms of people on the sandy beaches, the waters are extremely shallow for a long way out, and a typically gentle surf rolls up to the beach. So this is a terrific place to bring the kids. You won't have to worry about them getting pounded by rough waves.

Diving off Miami Beach is just about as zany as the area is topside. Besides a wealth of shipwrecks, there are all sorts of objects that have been placed in the water, creating terrific habitat for marine life and providing us divers with opportunity to have a lot of fun. You can see radio antennas, an oil rig, Army tanks, and even a tequila bar! The clear, warm water, shallow wrecks, and excellent dive shops are wonderful for novice divers. This would be an excellent place to get certified. Yet out in deeper waters are wrecks that would be sufficiently challenging to technical divers.

Located just a few degrees above the tropic of Cancer, this is truly America's Caribbean, with exotic fruits and flowers, a tropical climate and mixed culture. Beyond that sort-of-cliché image, Miami Beach is something of an enigma. I have to admit to being annoyed when I got a recording in Spanish as I tried to check my messages at the hotel one night. Nearly half the population here speaks Spanish as their native language.

Without a doubt, Miami Beach is a watersports playground; beyond that, it gets a bit confusing. The art deco district at the southern tip of Miami Beach is getting all the attention these days. This is a popular area (especially for young singles) to see and be seen. Restored pastel-colored boutique hotels from the 1930s and 1940s, cafés, and palm trees line one side of the street; on the other is the long stretch of gorgeous white beach. While walking along the beach boardwalk one morning I passed a guy with a python wrapped around his shoulders, as well as numerous glistening, beautiful bodies either rollerblading or jogging. Even the waiters are gorgeous. Every night there was a fellow dancing by himself on the beachside, gyrating around to the music emanating from the hotel.

The sidewalk cafés are perfect for people-watching. In fact this place really can't be beat for ogling the passing parade. At night, though, it's very crowded and noisy, so be forewarned.

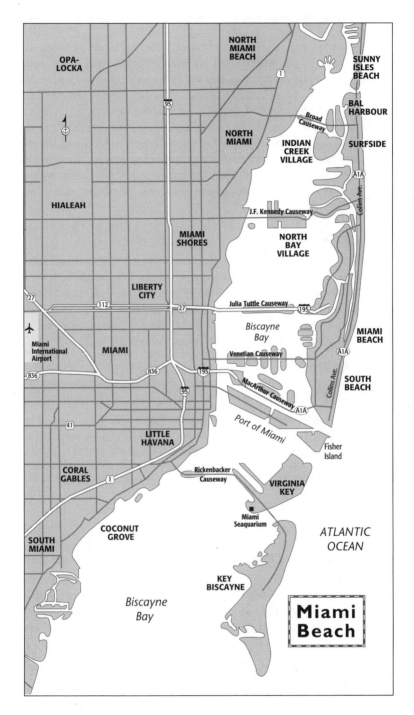

If you want a quieter, calmer area along with your beach activities, stay farther north in the Surfside, Bal Harbour, or Sunny Isles Beach areas. These are more family-oriented, and you could always pop down to the art deco district for a few hours to check it out. Also, these more northern spots are better locations for accessing the offshore wrecks.

If there's time to spare in your vacation, definitely try to get down to the Everglades and Biscayne National Park—you won't be sorry. Along the way are some wonderful stopovers that are a nice counterpoint to the trendy artificiality of Miami Beach. There's more about Biscayne in the Marine Park section of this chapter. To learn about the Everglades, refer to the Florida Keys chapter.

QUICK STATS

Weather   The average annual temperature is about 76°. The average annual rainfall is 56 inches. In January the low is about 59°, and the high about 75°. In August, the low is around 77°, the high 89°. June gets the most rainfall—about nine inches—and December gets the least—less than two inches. Summer definitely is the rainiest time of year. The sun can be intense, so make sure you come prepared with sunglasses, sunscreen, and hat.

Water Temperature   In summer the water temperature can be as high as 85°, but in the Miami area it can drop dramatically in winter, all the way down to a chilly 67°—heavy wet suit temps.

Underwater Visibility   Generally the visibility is very good between 50 and 80 feet. Because there is so much sand, however, it can get mucked up easily, especially when the weather is stormy.

Best Diving Months   From June through September is hurricane season in this part of the world, so during the shoulder season—spring or fall—would be the best. The chances for storms are reduced, and the water is still calm and warm.

PLANNING THE TRIP

Calling Miami Beach   There are two area codes used in Miami and the Beaches area: 305 and 786. The latter is the newest one, so most numbers will have the 305 prefix. You always have to dial the area code no matter where you're calling from. So even if you're in the 305 area, you still need to dial the area code.

Getting to Miami   Just about every carrier imaginable flies into Miami Beach. This is the easiest part!

Transportation   From the airport to Miami Beach is about 14 miles and takes around half an hour to 45 minutes, depending on traffic. All the major car-rental agencies have desks at the airport, but you'll have to take a shuttle out of the airport to pick up your car.

A taxi will cost about $41 to get to the Sunny Isles Beach area, about $24 to get to the art deco district in South Beach. These are flat-rate fares from the airport and are based on a rate of about $1.75 per mile. You can also take the *Supershuttle,* which has door-to-door transportation from the airport. Per-person rates are around $10. Advance reservations are not necessary. For information call (305) 871-2000; website: www.supershuttle.com.

Getting Around the Art Deco District   Definitely get out and walk here, but for long distances, consider taking the *Electrowave,* an all-electric transit system. Shuttles run 32 designated stops approximately every 10 to 15 minutes along Washington Avenue between 17th Street and 5th Avenue. The fare is 25 cents each way.

Tourist Office   Greater Miami Convention & Visitors Bureau, (800) 283-2707 or (305) 539-3063; fax (305) 539-3113; website: www.tropi coolmiami.com

THE UNDERWATER SCENE

You should be aware, that the reefs in the Miami Beach area are mostly artificial. Also, some of the wrecks are legitimate, but many were deliberately placed in the water, and they are all within three miles of the shoreline. Before you go *awwww* and start to skip this section, know that 1) they are wonderful dive sites in their own right and fascinating to explore, and that 2) they attract a surprising amount of growth in a short period of time. You'll see the full range of tropical fish here, including barracudas, eels and rays, and even nurse sharks. Believe me, you won't be disappointed. The artificial reef program began officially in 1981, so there has been ample time for marine life colonies to grow.

The dive businesses also go out to areas of natural reef, most of which are in the 30-foot to 45-foot range. Some patch reef is in the 70-foot to 90-foot range, and all of these run north/south, which is also the way the currents run. The area has experienced some coral bleaching, an expected natural phenomenon. Actually, in this area the corals appear to be bouncing back.

Be aware that in June you might see jellyfish, and April is the typical season for the Portuguese man-of-war, a cousin to the jellyfish. The man-of-war stings are really painful, so be alert. A man-of-war looks like a blue bubble floating in the ocean and has long tentacles with layers of stinger cells. Its larvae, known as sea lice, cling to swim suits and will cause extreme itching.

Make sure you don't rub your eyes after taking off your wetsuit. If you're stung by jellyfish, either vinegar, meat tenderizer, or ammonia can ease the pain. For the sea lice, just wash the area with soap and water.

Diving Conditions

The water is toasty warm and usually calm, the visibility is very good, and most of the reefs are in shallow water. Miami Beach is a dive destination unto itself, but if you're on your way to the Caribbean and find yourself with a long layover, you might think about staying an extra day or two having fun underwater rather than being miserable at the airport. If you stay shallow and use Enriched Air Nitrox (that is, if you're certified), all the better.

Flags on the beach will tell you if there's a problem in the water. Red means no swimming; yellow means caution; green means get in and have a great time. One more important point: the water temperature in winter can be a nippy 67°. That's cold. Definitely wear a nice warm wet suit.

Recommended Level of Experience

This would be the perfect area to get scuba certified or to brush up on your diving skills. Technical divers also will find plenty to keep them busy. Some interesting wrecks in this area are around the 200-foot range. For this, the northern part of Miami Beach, around the Sunny Isles area, would be the best base of operations. Adventure Scuba Diving is one shop that runs special technical diving trips. Some of these deep sites are mentioned in the next section.

This is also a good area to learn to spearfish. None of the Miami Beach shoreline is protected, so underwater hunting is popular. Most of the dive shops teach this as a specialty course and will rent spearguns. The lobster (a.k.a. bugs) season runs from August through March. To hunt, you'll have to get a Florida saltwater fishing license and learn about the rules for size, bag limits, etc.

Because there isn't much natural reef in this area, it is not a particularly good environment for snorkeling. Snorkelers would probably be happier going down to the Florida Keys.

Great Dive Sites

At the northern end of Miami Beach, dive boats moored in the Intracoastal Waterway use the passage called Haulover Cut to get through to the Atlantic side. The name Haulover comes from the early pre-bridge days when mules were used to haul boats over land. In either direction from the cut, there are about 30 wrecks less than two miles offshore, taking only a few minutes to reach.

Most of the wrecks dived here are in the 55-foot to-135-foot range, but many are in the 200-foot range and require technical diving certification.

Tenneco Reef   An advanced dive and a truly exciting one, *Tenneco Towers* is an old oil rig consisting of five huge towers and a platform. It is located north of Haulover Cut, near the Dade County/Broward County line. Two of the towers are side by side at 105 feet. Another tower is about 150 feet away at the 115-foot depth. Hurricane Andrew pushed it over to a 45° angle, which actually makes it a more interesting attraction. Divers can get on top of the platform at 60 feet to adjust equipment prior to descending to the towers. Two towers are way beyond sport-diving depths; one is at 185 feet and the other at 205 feet. In these clear waters, the structures are magnificent—truly an awesome sight—but the bonus here is the tremendous amount of growth on them.

The towers were put down in 1985, so they've had plenty of time over the years to attract huge spiny oysters, sponges, and soft corals. Barracuda reign supreme among the struts of the tower, as though they're taunting, "This used to be yours—mine now." The structure also attracts large tarpon and angelfish. Schooling fish are all about—around the towers, in the open ocean, and under the platform. This is also home to a few bull sharks.

Nearby is the *Cruz del Sur,* a deep dive for technical divers only. This is a 287-foot steel ship sunk in 1986. It rests at 240 feet, and the working deck is way beyond sport-diving limits.

Haulover Reef   Directly east of Haulover Inlet, less than two miles offshore, are two steel freighters, the *Narwal* (137 feet long) and the *Andro* (165 feet long), both sunk in the mid-1980s. The *Narwal* rests at 115 feet in a collapsed state, and the *Andro* is at 103 feet. The *Andro's* stern section was torn off and collapsed during Hurricane Andrew. Both wrecks are decorated with corals and sponges, and have attracted a prolific gathering of fish. Another site that is frequently used for training dives is called the *Rock Pile,* an excellent place to see nurse sharks.

Sunny Isles Reef   This reef is in close proximity to Haulover Reef. At least two wrecks are found here, both sunk in the early 1990s, and other smaller vessels are scattered all about. The *Concepcion,* a 150-foot Haitian freighter, was sunk in 1991 on an underwater plateau officially designated as the Sunny Isles reef site. Also at this location is a 120-foot steel-hulled tug called the *C-One,* sunk in 1990. Both sit in about 70 feet of water. The *C-One* is intact, and divers can penetrate the engine area. Be careful not to kick up any silt, though. Very big tarpon gather at these sites, as well as stupendous morays. Tropicals such as angelfish, triggerfish, and butterflyfish are typically milling about. Swirling balls of baitfish are also common.

Pflueger Reef   On this reef are two big freighters, the *Tortuga* (180 feet long) and the *Deep Freeze* (210 feet long). Now lying in 110 feet of water, the *Tortuga* was blown up in 1994 as part of the closing sequence of the movie *Fair Game,* with Cindy Crawford and Billy Baldwin. It stretches about 40 feet from the sandy bottom to the top of the wheelhouse, which can be penetrated easily. You'll see barracuda and tarpon here, as well as a lot of little critters, such as tiny trunkfish. It has not been down long enough to attract a great deal of growth. *Deep Freeze,* however, was sunk in 1976, and so displays quite a bit more growth.

Anchorage Area   Farther south is a popular area that is perfect for novice divers. Called the *Wreck Trek,* it consists of seven different sites, all in about 55 feet of water and within easy finning distance of one another. They are linked by a marking system that allows a diver to find the sites during a single dive. Some of the attractions include radio antennas, an old Haitian shrimp boat, a 110-foot steel barge, and a couple of tugs—the *Miss Patricia* (65 feet long and intact) and the *Miss Karline* (85 feet long but broken up).

I made this dive with a group of divers at night, which is not such a terrific idea. Everyone got lost, including several divemaster-guides! Navigation to the various features is by vertical stakes on which divers visually line up. They are placed too far apart, however, to be able to see at night, so navigation is impossible by this means. Despite that little problem, it was a great dive. I enjoyed seeing a huge hermit crab carrying its home along the sand, and an enormous scorpionfish. The radio antenna, soaring skyward, was particularly eerie at night. It and other structures were covered in bright red cup corals, which would not have been visible in the daytime.

Nearby is *the ultimate two-tank dive.* Sitting upright on the sandy bottom in 48 feet of water are two Vietnam-era M60 Army tanks only 50 feet apart. You won't believe your eyes! This is quite an unusual dive and, of course, a great photo op. All instruments were removed from the tanks, and they were completely scrubbed clean before being sunk in 1994. It's easy to stir up the sand, here, so watch your fins. Although the tanks are too "young" to have collected much growth, you might spot crabs taking up residence in the gun barrels, and you're bound to see tarpon and barracuda.

Exciting night dives take place at a site called *The Trench.* This is an east/west cut, about 25 feet wide, which starts at a depth of 45 feet and descends to 60 feet. As divers make their way along the trench, the shadows of dive lights play on the walls rising high above them. Dramatic! To add to the excitement are morays—lots of them—some six and seven feet in length.

The newest addition to the zany underwater spectacle is the *Jose Cuervo Margarita Bar,* sunk with great fanfare on "Sinko de Mayo" 2000 during the Watersports Festival. It lies just offshore from the art deco district in only 20 feet of water. Where else would you be able to sidle up to a bar, sit down on a bar stool, and wave to snorkelers above you? The 16-ton concrete and steel structure is about eight feet high, with a base of 10 feet by 12 feet. You can't miss it—just look for a yellow and red (Jose Cuervo colors, of course) structure with a red top and diagonal white stripe (remind you of anything?). To be politically correct, there are admonitions posted at the bar to refrain from drinking and diving!

Around the bar are a bunch of tetrahedrons made of recycled materials. These are the latest methods used to help to prevent beach erosion, as well as to attract marine life.

Artificial Reefs

Don't think of these artificial reefs as just junk in the water, because there are some very good reasons for them beyond the fun diving aspect. They can help restore natural habitat systems that have been damaged by storms, by ship anchors, or by dredging projects. The objects can be steel ships, concrete pipes, or other demolished concrete structures, vehicles, towers, and so on.

When the materials are put at depths that permit sufficient sunlight, they are colonized and covered by a variety of organisms, such as algae, soft and hard corals, sponges, sea anemones, and marine worms. These organisms, in turn, provide an abundant food supply (and shelter) for such marine critters as crabs, lobsters, shrimp, brittle stars, and all types of juvenile and smaller fish. They also filter water and improve water quality.

In time, this diverse ecosystem becomes almost identical to those that exist on natural coral reefs. Like the coral reefs, they will attract and provide a stable food supply for all types of adult reef fish, such as grouper and snapper, as well as pelagic species, like mackerel, dolphin, and bluefish. In a short period of time, the reef material transforms a previously somewhat barren ocean bottom into a thriving marine community.

Marine Park

Biscayne National Park, just south of the Miami Beach area, is a 180,000-acre sanctuary for birds and marine life. Ninety-five percent of it is underwater, and the remaining 5 percent includes 44 keys that form a north-south chain 18 nautical miles long. The mangrove shorelines, coral reefs, shallow bays, and undeveloped islands are all protected, but, strangely, fishing (including spearfishing) is allowed in the park, as well as the use of motorboats. Canoes and kayaks can be rented.

A park concessionaire provides snorkeling and scuba excursions in a glass-bottom boat. You can also buy and rent dive and snorkel gear. The dive operation is located within the Convoy Point Visitor Center, which is open from 8:30 a.m. to 5 p.m. daily. Call (305) 230-1100. One of the favorite destinations is about seven miles offshore, at Elliott Caye (nine miles long and two miles wide). Around the seagrass beds, you can generally spot stingrays, yellow rays, and eagle rays, and the area is a virtual nursery for barracudas. The little guys will actually school right along with the swirling masses of baitfish.

Within the park is a wall dive called, appropriately, *The Wall.* The top of the wall is at a depth of about 60 feet, and it drops vertically to a little more than 100 feet. Large barrel sponges are definite highlights. Another site called *Virginia Reef* is shallower, with branching hard corals near the surface. Slightly deeper are boulder corals and gorgonians.

Camping facilities (albeit primitive) are located at **Elliott Key** and at **Boca Chita Key.** Campsites are $10 per night. Call (305) 230-1100. The park also maintains a 66-slip harbor at Elliott Key, where boaters may spend the day or night. Docking is on a first-come, first-served basis, and there is a $15-per-night fee.

Biscayne National Park is open daily from 8 a.m. to 5:30 p.m. There is no entrance fee. The Convoy Point Visitor Center is located seven miles east of Florida Turnpike exit 6 (Speedway Boulevard) or nine miles east of US 1 on SW 328th Street (North Canal Dr.). Phone (305) 230-PARK; website: www.nps.gov/bisc.

DIVE SERVICES & PACKAGES

Dive centers are listed from north to south. Unless they are on resort property, none have lodging/dive packages. Most, however, work with nearby hotels to serve the guests.

Adventure Scuba Diving, run by Ted Gawronski, is located in the Newport Beachside Hotel and Resort in the Sunny Isles Beach area. Dive/lodging packages are offered. It also runs the watersports activities at the resort, including rentals of waverunners, kayaks (and dive kayaks), rafts, boogie-boards, snorkel sets, and sea-scooters. Banana boat rides, jet boat rides, snorkel trips, "snuba" diving, and scuba resort courses are offered. All scuba rentals, sales, and air (including Nitrox) are available at the resort. The shop uses a 15-foot Nautica (hard-bottom inflatable) that carries up to six passengers; a 25-foot Privateer, which is Coast Guard certified; and a 50-foot catamaran. Divers are driven over to the dock, about one and a quarter miles off the property, in the protected Intracoastal Waterway. They don't do a huge dive business, however, which can be a good thing for visitors. The instruction offerings, including technical courses, are extensive. All levels of NAUI certifications are offered, as well as numerous NAUI, PADI, and TDI specialties, including Nitrox. Technical diving courses include advanced Nitrox, mixed gas, extended range diving, and wreck diving. Phone (305) 949-1194; fax (305) 949-0722; e-mail: ted@adventure scubadiving; website: www.adventurescubadiving.com.

Retail Sales: *Extensive*

Rentals: *Extensive*

Scuba Training: *Extensive*

Photo Services: *Limited*

Dive Boat Comfort: *Good*

On-Board Facilities for Photographers: *None*

Mermaids, a PADI 5-Star Dive Center at 16604 NE Second Avenue in North Miami, uses a variety of boats, depending on the need at the time. Excursions extend all the way north to Ft. Lauderdale and south to the Keys. The shop is both a retail and rental facility; Nitrox is available. Its rental line includes spearfishing equipment and Sea Scooters. PADI instruction is through the divemaster level, and a training pool is on the premises. Phone (305) 940-0927; fax (305) 944-1506; e-mail: nmarti@bellsouth.net; website: www.mermaidsdive.com.

Retail Sales: *Extensive*

Rentals: *Extensive*

Scuba Training: *Extensive*

Photo Services: *Limited*

Dive Boat Comfort: *Good*

On-Board Facilities for Photographers: *Good*

H₂O Scuba is a PADI 5-Star Dive Center in the community of Sunny Isles Beach (160 Sunny Isles Boulevard) near the Miami-Dade County line. The oceanfront shop provides daily dive trips aboard a sleek 30-foot Island Hopper (with a flybridge) kept docked behind the shop. Excursions are made to the North Canyon, which features 12-foot high parallel walls, as well as the popular nearby wrecks. It provides instruction up to assistant instructor level and equipment sales, rentals, and service. Divers can use Nitrox, and even Trimix, with the proper certifications. Phone (888) 389-DIVE or (305) 956-3483; fax (305) 956-9405; e-mail: divemaster@h2o scuba.com; website: h2oscuba.com.

Retail Sales: *Extensive*

Rentals: *Extensive*

Scuba Training: *Extensive*

Photo Services: *Limited*

Dive Boat Comfort: *Good*

On-Board Facilities for Photographers: *Good*

South Beach Divers is located in the heart of South Beach, at 850 Washington Avenue. This is a PADI 5-Star Dive Center that provides lessons for guests at nearby hotels, and features three-day certification classes starting every Friday. The shop also conducts beach dives and takes excursions to the Keys. Dive gear is available for both sale and rental. Equipment repair is available, but there is no dive vessel. Phone (305) 532-1445; e-mail: info@southbeachdivers.com; website: www.southbeachdivers.com.

Retail Sales: *Extensive*
Rentals: *Extensive*
Scuba Training: *Moderate*
Photo Services: *Limited*

Dive Boat Comfort: *N/A*
On-Board Facilities for Photographers: *N/A*

Tarpoon Lagoon is located in the Miami Beach Marina (850 Washington Avenue), down in South Beach. It's one of Miami's oldest full-service dive centers, providing sales, service, and rentals. This is a PADI Dive Center facility. PADI and NAUI specialty courses are also offered, including the Nitrox course. A heated pool is on the premises. The shop uses a 42-foot Delta for its half-day and full-day trips. Phone (888) 331-DIVE or (305) 532-1445; fax (305) 532-8928; website: www.tar poondivecenter.com.

Retail Sales: *Extensive*
Rentals: *Extensive*
Scuba Training: *Extensive*
Photo Services: *Moderate*

Dive Boat Comfort: *Excellent*
On-Board Facilities for Photographers: *Good*

Bubbles Dive Center (2671 SW 27th Avenue), a PADI 5-Star Dive Center, offers courses with pool work at the Venetian Pool in Coral Gables. Classes are given through the assistant instructor level and in Nitrox and technical diving. Instruction is available in both English and Spanish. The shop rents, repairs, and sells gear. Dive trips on the 50-foot dive boat are scheduled to the reef on Saturdays, to the wrecks on Sundays, and there are night dives on Wednesdays. Phone (305) 856-0565; e-mail: bubbles1@ gate.net; website: www.bubblesdive.com.

Retail Sales: *Extensive*
Rentals: *Extensive*
Scuba Training: *Extensive*
Photo Services: *Moderate*

Dive Boat Comfort: *Good*
On-Board Facilities for Photographers: *Good*

WHERE TO STAY

Hotels are arranged from north to south. Unfortunately, unless dive shops are on the premises, there are no dive packages with the hotels.

Newport Beachside Hotel and Resort ★★★, in the Sunny Isles Beach area in northern Miami Beach, has a welcoming, open lobby with chattering exotic caged birds and the beach beckoning just outside. All 350 rooms are mini-suites with refrigerator, microwave, safe, and private balconies. Facilities include a spa and salon, game rooms, fitness center, large swimming pool, and watersports center. The scenic Newport Fishing Pier is also part of the property. For activities, there are kayaking, snorkeling, and a beautiful wide beach with waving palm trees. Two outdoor thatched-roof snack bars are convenient to the pool and beach. There are two restaurants, a coffee bar, and a lounge with evening entertainment. The on-property dive shop is Adventure Water Sports, with a lobby retail shop and a full dive center on the lower level.

This is an attractive resort, perfect for either families or couples, but during my visit it was experiencing personnel shortages and management problems. Hopefully those have been straightened out. When I asked for a rate sheet, I was told that the room rates change on a daily basis, so there was none. Room rates, however, seem to range from about $125 to $150 per day. Diving packages are available, which bring the room rates down considerably. The address is 16701 Collins Avenue. Phone (305) 949-1300; fax (305) 956-2733; e-mail: newportbeachsideresort@msn.com; website: www.newportbeachsideresort.com.

In Surfside, **Beach House Bal Harbour** is directly on the ocean and around the corner from Bal Harbour Shops. The resort has 170 rooms and suites, and features a swimming pool, spa, gym, oceanfront restaurant, and bar that actually has hundreds of live sea horses (let's hope they breed in captivity). Room rates range from $175 to about $250 per day. The location is 9449 Collins Avenue. Phone (305) 535-8600; fax (305) 535-8601; e-mail: reservations@rubellhotels.com; website: www.rubellhotels.com.

The Avalon/Majestic Hotel, at 700 Ocean Drive in the art deco district, has 108 rooms with a lively art deco decor. All are air-conditioned and have refrigerators and safes. This is a casual beachfront property with a restaurant, A Fish Called Avalon, and a lobby bar. Room rates range from $65 to $175 per day, which include a complimentary continental breakfast. Phone (800) 933-3306 or (305) 538-0133; fax (305) 534-0258.

Southern Extremities—Horticultural Heaven

If you're heading down to the Florida Keys or out to the Everglades, you'll be driving through an extremely fertile area called **Redland.** The towns of Homestead and Florida City are in this region (driving time from Miami Beach is about half an hour). The look and the feeling here are completely different from the Miami area; you could compare it to the difference between California's Malibu and Napa Valley. The folks are friendly and welcoming, the attention is on the earth and all that is produces. And this is where the growing season is nonstop. From exotic orchids to fields of strawberries, tomatoes, and corn, this is a horticultural paradise like few other destinations in the world.

The best way to learn about this area, and about any tropical plant you might be interested in, is to stop off at the **Redland Fruit and Spice Park** in Homestead. The park is 35 acres of herbs, vegetables, and exotic fruit. Guided tours are given daily at 11 a.m., 1 p.m., and 2:30 p.m. The park is located at 24801 SW 187th Avenue. Phone (305) 247-5727; e-mail: fsp@co.miami-dade.fl.us; website: www.co.miami-dade.fl.us\parks\fruitandspice.htm.

Another local treat in Homestead is the ever-ebullient Robert, owner of **Robert is Here Fruit Stand.** When Robert was a young lad of seven, his farmer-father gave him his first job selling produce by the roadside. The only problem was, no one stopped—Robert was simply too small to be noticed. So Robert's ingenious father placed signs on either side of his son that read "Robert is here." Robert was finally noticed, the cars stopped, and Robert has been selling like crazy ever since. Besides a wonderful fruit selection (try lychee, mamey, carambola, and mangos), he now features an enormous assortment of honey and delicious fresh fruit milkshakes. His wife's parrot has his own perch and loves to show off for anyone interested. Out back are tortoises and iguanas. The stand is open from 8 a.m. to 7 p.m. and is located at 19200 SW 344th Street. The website is: www.robertishere.com.

For a formal tour of the area (not in summer, though), contact **Tropical Tours** at (305) 248-4181. And if you'd like to stay here, there's no better spot than the **Grove Inn Country Guesthouse,** with 14 homey, air-conditioned units. Every room is different, but all are efficiencies to some extent, with refrigerators, microwaves, and coffeemakers. The courtyard, beautifully landscaped with exotic plants, has a hot tub and lounge furniture. Delicious country breakfasts are included in the rate, and while you feast, Paul Mulhern (an owner) will entertain you on keyboard and vocals. This talented guy once toured as a musician with Tina Turner and entourage. Believe me, his music will send chills up your spine—it's quite a bonus for staying here! In the evening you can hear him again during Friday Happy Hour. Paul also enjoys showing off the area and takes it upon himself to be an unofficial tour guide. From the lodging it's just a few minutes to the Everglades. The nightly room rate is $65—a bargain. The address is 22540 Southwest Krome Ave., Redlands. Phone (305) 247-6572.

Hotel Edison South Beach is located in the heart of popular art deco mecca, at 960 Ocean Drive. Across the street is the beach, and all up and down the sidewalk, on either side of the hotel, are excellent restaurants and nightspots. Rooms are rather spartan, which seems to be typical of the small renovated circa-1930 lodgings. Also, with all the activity on the street, noise is a definite problem (especially on weekends). There are 60 rooms with refrigerators and air-conditioning. The swimming pool has bar service, and dining is indoor and out at the Official All Star Café sports bar. Rates start at $125 from mid-April to mid-December, and the rest of the year they start at $145. Phone (305) 531-2744; fax (305) 672-4153; e-mail: info@edison-hotel.com; website: www.edison-hotel.com.

Topside Attractions

Ocean Drive is getting a lot of attention these days. Cruising Ocean Drive, walking Ocean Drive, café-ing on Ocean Drive—actually, just being on Ocean Drive seems to be the idea. If you don't like crowds, how-ever, *not* being on Ocean Drive is also a good idea. It is busy, trendy, and high-energy. That is, except in the early morning hours. This is a late-night venue, so you won't find too much activity before noon. So what's the attraction? Beyond the pastel-colored art-deco hotels and cafés, the main attractions are the people who come here (those beautiful bods), that aqua ocean, swaying palm trees, and the gorgeous stretch of sandy beach.

The beach area here is officially **Lummus Park,** which extends from 6th to 14th Streets, but most people just refer to it as South Beach. In addition to lots of palm trees, there are little "chickees" for shade and a snack bar. North of South Beach is North Shore (76th to 87th Streets along Collins Avenue), featuring a fitness course, wooden boardwalks, and barbecue facilities. Farther north is Haulover Beach, with picnic facilities and lifeguards. The northern one-third mile of beach is designated a clothing-optional section in the signed area only. No gawkers, now!

Besides the beach, there's a lot to keep you occupied within a half-hour's drive south—the **Miami Seaquarium, Parrot Jungle and Gardens,** and **Monkey Jungle,** for example. The latter is particularly interesting, because throughout most of the area visitors are caged while the monkeys run freely! You move through the habitats via screened walkways, and you never really know what could pop up (or down)! This is also a serious research facility and breeding sanctuary for South American primates. Some of the wonderful species include crab-eating macaques, cute little squirrel monkeys, beautiful swinging gibbons, and rare tamarins and lemurs. Monkey Jungle, at 14805 Southwest 216th Street, is open daily 9:30 a.m. to 5 p.m. Phone (305) 235-1611.

Dining and Entertainment

Being in a cosmopolitan area, you'll find that many restaurants here add the gratuity to the final bill, so be sure to look it over first before paying.

Cuisine in this part of Florida is a real delight, due to the extremely fertile growing area in the south and the multicultural diversity, which blends European, Caribbean, and Latin influences. Fresh seafood is particularly abundant. And you'll find a lot more than Florida orange juice here. Exotic fruit are wonderful and a delight to sample. Ever heard of mamey (mahmay)? It's sweet and delicious! You'll find big and juicy mangos, papayas, sapodillos, avocados, guavas, etc. The selection seems endless.

In the Sunny Isles Beach area, a terrific spot for good cuisine, **Christine Lee's,** is about three blocks from Newport Beachside Hotel, tucked back in a shopping area. It specializes in steaks and Asian food, and has an attractive decor and pleasant evening entertainment. Definitely try the huge stone crab claws if they are in season (October to May). The fresh fish specialties cooked Asian-style are very good, and the service is excellent.

For dining, there's no dearth of possibilities here. Just look around—the choices are overwhelming! Down in South Beach, the **Official All Star Café** in the Edison Hotel has a nice outdoor dining area, perfect for people-watching, and inside has all the accouterments of a good sports bar. It serves up some delicious peel-and-eat shrimp, salads, sandwiches, pasta, burgers, ribs, and fish specials. Good fries, too.

Some other favorites are **Penrod's Seafood Grill,** well known for its seafood, oceanfront view, and scenic location, at One Ocean Drive; **Joe's Stone Crab Restaurant,** a landmark at 11 Washington Avenue that has been serving since 1913; **Hard Rock Café Miami,** at Bayside Marketplace, which you can reach by water taxi.

In the Lincoln Road area of shops and galleries is the **Van Dyke Café** (846 Lincoln Road), which has entertainment in the evenings. Lincoln Road is South Beach's artsy area, with the South Florida Arts Center, Miami City Ballet, recording studios, and much more.

Medical Facilities

Call 911 in an emergency. The Coast Guard-Marine Emergencies number is (305) 535-4368.

Mercy Hospital (call (305) 854-4400) at 3663 S. Miami Avenue has a recompression chamber. The South Florida Hyperbaric Medical Center phone is (305) 854-0300.

In case of a diving emergency call DAN (Divers Alert Network) at (919) 684-4DAN (4326) or (919) 684-8111.

Hawaiian Islands

Physical Characteristics of the Dive Area

WATER & WEATHER CONDITIONS

Visibility	*Good to Excellent*
Current and Surge	*Minimal*
Temperature	*Chilly to Comfortable*
Storms	*Occasionally Stormy*

SITE CONDITIONS

Mooring Buoys	*Some*
Fishing, Collecting, and Hunting Restrictions	*Widespread Restrictions*
Ease of Access	*Convenient*
Boat Traffic/Diver Congestion	*Light to Heavy*

MARINE LIFE

Abundance of Invertebrates	*Abundant*
Abundance of Vertebrates	*Abundant*
Abundance of Pelagic Life	*Abundant*
Health of Reef/Marine Life/ Marine Structure	*Healthy*

Beautiful Isolation

The Hawaiian Islands are just far enough from the U.S. mainland for visitors to feel as though they are making a significant excursion; indeed, escaping from the ho-hums of everyday life. Adding to the effect are the islands' exotic physical features, so wonderfully unique and enchanting. The visitor is totally taken in by the full effect—outrigger canoes riding the waves, waterfalls cascading down deep ravines, red *iiwi* birds calling to one another, the almost indescribable scent of a lei. It's no wonder people hunger to visit the islands, to marry, to explore, to learn, relax, and play.

But the Hawaiian Islands offer more to us than simply a handy destination for a quick escape. They're endowed with a wonderful culture that we can experience, and certainly from which we can learn. For about a thousand years, the islands had a relatively isolated native population that developed a unique culture in harmony with the land and the sea. Fortunately, many of the old Hawaiian ways have been embraced by modern-day islanders and seem to be held more dear as the islands are developed and ever more visitors come over. We can learn the stories that the hula dancers tell without speaking. We can learn about fishponds, the ancient method of aquaculture. We can also learn to relax and to slow down a bit.

Despite the rampant development around Honolulu, the sprawling high-rise resorts and strip malls, there are still plenty of stunning isolated beaches, plenty of rain forest with wild orchids growing all about, volcanic craters spewing lava into the ocean, and quaint villages where someone might be crafting a ukulele or building an outrigger canoe. There still is much for us to discover, and for Americans this exotic land is ours very easily. We don't need to renew our passport, change money, learn a new language, or drive on the "wrong" side of the road.

The islands are, of course, volcanic. Millions of years ago lava began spewing into the sea, forming a series of seamounts. It continues even now, and visitors can see its dramatic force on the Big Island of Hawaii. The first island that was formed is the northernmost island in the archipelago—Kauai. Its volcanoes, now extinct, are the oldest. And the youngest of them all, the southernmost island, is Hawaii.

This interesting evolution, coupled with the fact that the Hawaiian Islands are the most isolated islands in the world, presents a truly unique environment on land and underwater. Rather than vast fields of coral, divers will find a fascinating convoluted topography, all created from molten lava. You've probably heard of *lava tubes*. These are underwater tunnels in an infinite variety of shapes and sizes. Most are not solid; they'll have numerous holes, or skylights, where light can shine through. They make wonderful habitats for eels and crabs. Other lava formations are ledges and archways, pinnacles and caverns. And these provide resting spots for white-tip sharks and turtles. Most of the lava structures are coral-encrusted, some carpeted, others lightly dusted. It all depends on their age and the amount of nutrients and sunlight they get. Soft corals are not prevalent in the islands.

Although the lava tubes provide quite a sight, the Hawaiian fish are the star attractions. Their extreme isolation has allowed them to evolve in unique ways, and today about 30 percent of the species are endemic to the

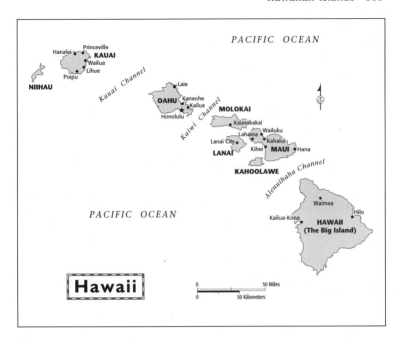

Hawaiian Islands; that is, *they are found nowhere else on the planet.*
Snorkelers and divers will have a wonderful time discovering these colorful, fascinating species. Besides the fish, which are immediately obvious,
you'll have to hunt a bit to find colorful nudibranchs, Hawaiian lobster,
Spanish dancers, sea stars, urchins, octopus, and eels. Turtles make an
appearance on most dives here, and it's always thrilling to see these grace-
ful, curious creatures.

The islands themselves are quite different, so don't think that because
you've seen one you've seen them all. Between the Big Island, with its vast
ranch land, rolling green hills, and black volcanic plains, and Kauai's verdant valleys and rain forests, there are dramatic differences. Try to visit
more than one, if possible. The islands appeal to all ages and, although
prices are higher than on the mainland, it's still possible to find reasonably
priced accommodations.

QUICK STATS

Size   Hawaii, the Big Island, at 4,038 square miles, is almost twice the
size of all the other Hawaiian Islands combined. Maui is 728.8 square

miles; Oahu 597 square miles; Kauai 552.3 square miles; Molokai 260 square miles; Lanai 141 square miles.

Population   Oahu 836,231; Hawaii 143,135; Maui 103,000; Kauai 56,603; Molokai 6,745; Lanai 2,800

Location   The islands are about 2,000 miles from California.

Time   Hawaiian Standard Time never changes. There's no daylight savings time, so it's two hours behind California and five hours behind New York during standard time. During daylight savings time, it would be an additional hour behind.

Air Temperatures   In winter and spring highs are usually in the 80s and lows in the 70s. In summer and fall, temperatures are around the mid-80s.

Water Temperature   Hawaii water temps are not toasty warm, so be prepared to wear some protection. At least a 3-mm neoprene suit is wise, and in winter a 6-mm suit is a good idea. Summer water temps are around 77°; in winter they're in the low 70s.

Underwater Visibility   Visibility usually is best in summer and fall, reaching well past 100 feet; in winter and spring it drops below 100, but rarely below 80 feet.

Elevations   The islands are all volcanic and all have summits that reach thousands of feet above sea level. Divers need to decompress at sea level prior to ascending mountainous areas. With altitudes of 8,000 feet or more, the general rules of flying apply. For most divers, that means waiting at sea level for at least 12 hours.

Best Diving Months   Diving is year-round, but storms are more common in winter.

PLANNING THE TRIP

Getting to the Hawaiian Islands   All the major airlines fly regular schedules to Honolulu, Oahu. Flying time from Los Angeles or San Francisco is five and a half to six hours. Hawaiian and United Airlines have direct flights from Los Angeles to Kona (Big Island). American and Delta fly direct from Los Angeles to Kahului, Maui. Otherwise, for getting around the islands, either Hawaiian Air or Aloha Airlines run regular schedules out of Honolulu.

Getting Around   Definitely rent a car in all of the islands and drive around. On Oahu, The Bus has excellent service all over the island.

Phoning the Islands   The area code island-wide is 808.

Tourist Offices

Big Island Visitors Bureau   Call (808)886-1655; fax (808) 961-2126; website: www.bigisland.org

Maui Visitors Bureau   (808) 244-3530; fax (808) 244-1337; website: www.visitmaui.com

Destination Lanai   (800) 947-4774 or (808) 565-7600; fax (808) 565-9316

Oahu Visitors Bureau   (808) 524-0722; fax (808) 538-0314; website: www.visit-oahu.com

Kauai Visitors Bureau   (808) 245-3971; fax (808) 246-9235; website: www.kauaivisitorsbureau.org

To contact the island-wide Hawaii Visitors and Convention Bureau, call (800) GOHAWAII or (808) 923-1811; fax (808) 922-8911; and the helpline: (800) 353-5846.

HAWAII'S MARINE PARKS

The underwater parks in the Hawaiian Islands are called Marine Life Conservation Districts, established to protect and preserve the unique ocean resources found there. Each area is set aside for the enjoyment of swimmers, snorkelers, and scuba divers. Generally, fishing is restricted, and in some cases taking anything at all is prohibited. More details about these districts are included in each island section that follows.

A huge conservation milestone occurred in December 2000, when President Bill Clinton issued an executive order creating an enormous nature reserve in the waters along the northwestern stretch of the Hawaiian Islands. The expanse of 84 million underwater acres is now the nation's largest official nature reservation. It's estimated to include about 70 percent of the nation's coral reefs, as well as pristine remote islands, atolls, and submerged lagoons. Named the Northwestern Hawaiian Islands Coral Reef Ecosystem Reserve, it's larger than the states of Florida and Georgia combined. Clinton's order bans the removal of coral from the region and caps both commercial and recreational fishing at existing (already limited) levels.

The reserve also includes two existing National Wildlife Refuges—Midway Atoll and the northwest Hawaiian Islands—and designates 15 reserve preservation areas (totaling about 4 million acres) where all fishing, anchoring, and touching of coral are prohibited. Also banned are oil and gas drilling and production.

Hawaii (The Big Island)

THE UNDERWATER SCENE

On the Big Island, the Kona Coast should be your diving destination. This is on the west side, which is the lee of the island, so the water is usually flat and calm. On the other side, huge volcanic peaks rise thousands of feet and lava is still flowing down to the shore, creating ever more landmass.

Boat and shore diving and snorkeling are superb here, and there are plenty of good dive shops for renting tanks and gear and getting repairs. Healthy accumulations of hard corals are in many areas close to shore in shallow waters.

Sea turtles are especially prolific. They can migrate hundreds of miles from their feeding areas to nesting beaches in the Northwestern Hawaiian Islands. It is feared, however, that the green sea turtle is nearing extinction. Whereas once there were tens of millions, now it is estimated that only 350 females nest each year. All sea turtles in Hawaii are protected under state law and under the federal Endangered Species Act. These regulations prohibit harassing, harming, killing, or keeping sea turtles in captivity.

The other pelagic species that you'll want to see here are the elegant manta rays, and one of the best ways to observe them is at night. Of course, always keep an eye out for Hawaii's wonderful endemic species, and keep that camera loaded with film.

Health Score Card

Fortunately, development has not run amok on the Kona Coast, so the shoreline is pristine. Kona is on the leeward side of the island, so it doesn't receive the brunt of storms that can damage shallow corals. Still, plenty of ocean currents wash by, dumping a good supply of nutrients on a regular basis. The hard corals seem to be in no danger of being smothered by sand and remain in excellent condition.

Diving Conditions

This is pleasant and easy diving. Under normal conditions, you won't encounter strong currents or heavy surf. In fact, much of the time the water is glassy. Most of the dive spots are fairly shallow, but an offshore shelf can send you plummeting more than 100 feet, so there's deep diving here, as well. The visibility is usually excellent, and the water temperatures vary from warm to chilly. A 3mm wetsuit is recommended.

Shore divers beware, however. This is the great land of volcanic rock, and it can be exceptionally sharp. Do not even attempt to shore dive here unless you're wearing hard-soled booties. Be careful when you enter the water. The lava rock is not only sharp, but uneven, and you can easily slip and get some nasty cuts. Never wear your fins into the water. Carry them in; then when you get to water about waist deep, put them on.

Also, having a tarp to put on the ground is a good idea. This will help keep everything clean while you're gearing-up. Most shore diving areas do not have facilities, so bring fresh water with you to drink and to rinse camera gear.

Recommended Level of Experience

Divers of all levels will enjoy the diving here. This would also be an excellent place to get an open-water certification or go a little further and take an advanced course.

Elevations on the island soar to more than 13,000 feet. After diving, do not ascend these slopes on the same day. If you intend to ascend to an altitude of 8,000 feet or more after diving, the general rules of flying apply. For most divers, that means waiting at sea level for at least 12 hours.

Great Dive Sites

One of my favorites on the Kona Coast is called *Place of Refuge,* a wonderful shore dive, as well as a snorkel site. The coral here is especially abundant and close to shore—you won't have to wear yourself out to get to it. To find the shore-diving location, you'll head to Place of Refuge National Historical Park, about 20 miles south of Kailua. From Highway 11, take Middle Keei Road. Turn left on Painted Church Road. At the dead end, turn right. Turn left into the entrance to the heritage site, but don't enter it. Make the first right and follow the road down to the boat dock.

Be careful getting into the water; it is exceptionally rocky and slippery. When I was here, someone had arranged cinder blocks on the sand to form the word "aloha." After entering the water, veer to the left to find a huge stretch of gorgeous plate coral and other hard branching corals. Spotted eagle rays and turtles are common, as well as Hawaii's colorful assortment of tropicals.

Another excellent place, called *Amphitheater,* is near Keei Point, and is best accessed from a boat with a guide. You'll see soft coral here, which is somewhat unusual in the islands. I found a gorgeous reticulated butterfly fish here, with a multicolored tail, yellow spots all over the body, and a black vertical band over the eyes. Spectacular! From the water, head toward the cliff on shore, finning over large boulders and into shallow water. The surge gets stronger as you approach shore. Then enter the amphitheater. Go up to the surface and take a look around. You'll find that it is a very large lava tube with a beautifully chiseled ceiling. Descend again and follow the contour of the cliff and watch underwater as the surf pounds the rock—the effect is explosive. Finally, enter the swim-through, which narrows a lot as you go along. It has a pretty "skylight" up above, nicely illuminating the tunnel. The passage then dips down a bit before presenting you with a superb scenic exit—photographers take note. Watch for well-camouflaged frogfish and turtles.

Another spot, which can be either a boat or a shore dive, is at *Keei Point,* just south of Honaunau. Large pinnacles and rock masses predominate in the shallow sections. A rocky wall starts at about 60 feet, and the depth to the sandy bottom is about 135 feet. There's little coral here, but plenty of tropicals, mostly solitary or in couples. You'll see many crown-of-thorns all about, which look like leafy green starfish. Unfortunately, this sea star is a voracious eater of algae and other invertebrates, and it's therefore destructive to coral reefs.

A popular area with dive shops is called *Red Hill,* where there are several sites. Red Hill is south of Keauhou Bay and just north of Kealakekua Bay. It features an interesting topography of ridges, lava tubes, achways, and caves. Also, the marine life varies from the tiniest critters like ghost shrimp and Spanish dancers to turtles and manta rays.

South of Red Hill is beautiful *Kealakekua Bay.* Captain Cook didn't enjoy it much, though, at least not on the day he was whacked to bits here in 1779. This is a great spot for coral. Also, it's protected and perfect for snorkeling as well as deep diving. A variety of butterfly fish, angelfish, spotted pufferfish, and turtles hang out here. This is a Marine Life Conservation District, so everything here is protected.

Up north off the *Kohala Coast* are some excellent turtle-spotting areas and healthy pinnacles. Although this area doesn't receive as much attention from divers, it nevertheless offers superb diving. This section of the leeward coastline is relatively barren, with only a handful of resorts. Some, however, have dive shops on-property, which is the best way to dive the area. From the Mauna Lani hotel, I dived both *Finger Reef* and *Turtle Reef,* both of which were superb dives. Finger Reef (at Makaiwa Bay) features wonderful lava formations and abundant coral. Morays, turtles, and tropicals are plentiful. Turtle Reef was fun for its caverns and lava tubes of interesting formations. It featured abundant coral, also, including tube coral. Shy, but large, pufferfish were very evident and usually alone.

Without question, though, the most awesome dive on the island is the *Manta Ray Night Dive.* But it's also a snorkeling experience, so everyone can join in. Take a look at the sidebar called "Night Flight" for more details on this wonderful experience.

Shallow Diving and Snorkeling

All three of the conservation districts (next section) are excellent places for shore diving and snorkeling. Waialea Beach is especially popular with the locals. It can get pretty churned up in winter, though, and the beach will

Night Flight

As each day draws to a close along the tropical Kona Coast, Lee and Dinah Rodgers (from Manta Ray Divers) start loading up *Rainbow Diver II*. It's a pre-dive ritual, getting tanks and gear ready and launching her for a dive site that will take them all of about five minutes to reach. Though just a few yards from the Kona Surf Resort's craggy volcanic cliffs, this singular site is the Big Island's most popular dive. Other dive operators will do the same, because as sure as night falls, there will be divers and snorkelers wanting to see the gentle giants.

As the sky darkens, both divers and snorkelers make their way to an amphitheater-like area. Divers find their places, kneeling among large rocks that provide some stability against the strong surge, and snorkelers look down from above. Their dive lights, all shining upward and toward the group's center, illuminate the blackness below. It's a surreal, but beautiful, scene in itself—like some mystical ritual to attract the water gods.

Hands clutch the rocks, bodies bend in the surge, and anticipation grows as the dive lights reveal masses of tiny plankton. Yes—dinnertime!

From out of the blackness an enormous white creature swoops in, wings gracefully curved, establishing its rightful place at the table. Huge mouth agape, it climbs, then banks, and performs a series of loops, around and around, in mesmerizing rhythmic circles. Other mantas appear in the lights, flying through the water column just over the heads of the crouching divers and beneath the snorkelers also watching the show.

The mantas take their turns in the spotlight, swirling about over and over, swooping up masses of tiny plankton. If a tune were to accompany the performance, it would surely be Beethoven's "Ode to Joy." These great white bodies appear to be having a grand time.

Meanwhile, their audience watches in awe, without touching the mantas or swimming up through the water column, all of which can drive them away. In fact, on this dive, you can break all the rules. Divers don't wear snorkels (which might hurt the mantas), they do wear extra lead to help stay on the bottom, and they not only touch, but grab onto, anything they can! Lee and Dinah actually provide kneepads to protect wet suits.

Except for the dive lights, which encourage the congregation of plankton, this is a pure marine encounter. The manta's staple diet

(continued)

Night Flight (continued)

consists of this microscopic brine shrimp (a type of plankton), and because divers aren't feeding the mantas directly, their behavior is natural. Mantas use their winglike fins to funnel water into their cavernous mouths, which then filter out the organisms. The swirling motion of their somersaults causes the plankton to accumulate into a mass, which they can then swoop up as they come back around.

Although the Pacific manta ray can grow to more than 14 feet, it is perfectly harmless (no teeth or stingers) and even has a shy disposition. The greatest danger for divers here is getting seasick in the surge. For the mantas, though, the possibility of getting harmed by divers is a definite concern.

Most dive operators schedule one or two night dives per week, but for Lee and Dinah, every night is a night dive. If you're prone to seasickness, definitely take some medication several hours before going out. Also, if possible, try to leave time to dive here more than once. This isn't an amusement park, where everything is perfectly calculated. Occasionally the mantas simply don't appear. If that happens, you'll want to go out and try again.

You can contact Manta Ray Divers at (800) 982-6747 or (808) 334-11154; their website is at www.rainbowdiver.com.

actually disappear then. Nevertheless, it's an excellent spot for viewing the visiting humpback whales that make their annual journey here to mate and calve.

Marine Park

On the Big Island, there are three Marine Life Conservation Districts: Kealakekua Bay, consisting of 315 acres south of Kailua-Kona; Lapakahi, 45 miles north of the Kona airport; and Waialea Beach, frequently called Beach 69, because the turnoff to it is by a telephone pole marked with the number 69 (or so they say).

Kealakekua Bay is known not only for its underwater life but also as the place where Captain James Cook, the British navigator, was killed in 1779. A 27-foot white obelisk stands as a memorial. The bay is located south of Kailua-Kona and features dramatic cliffs rising above the water. Honeycombed in the cliffs are ancient Hawaiian burial caves. The bay's protection began in 1969, and it now teems with fish. The only access by car is to Napo'opo'o Beach. From Kailua-Kona drive south to the Napo'opo'o turnoff, then drive four miles to the bay.

Lapakahi, which extends from the ocean four miles to the 1,900-foot elevation, is a 262-acre historical complex. Hawaiians first came to Lapakahi during the 1300s. The land park has trails, self-guided tours, and the remains of ancient Hawaiian settlements. In 1979, the state declared the waters offshore of the park a protected area. Huge boulders and caves are the subterranean features. From Kailua-Kona take Highway 19 north to Kawaihae and follow Highway 270 to the park.

Off the beaten path, Waialea Beach is popular with local residents for snorkeling, diving, and whale-watching. From Kailua-Kona take Highway 19 north and turn on Puako Beach Drive. Then take the first right to Old Puako Road and watch the numbers on the telephone poles. Turn left between poles 69 and 70 onto the rough road.

DIVE SERVICES & PACKAGES ON HAWAII

Manta Ray Divers runs nightly manta dives (see the sidebar "Night Flight") in Keauhou Bay from the 28-foot glass-bottom *Rainbow Diver II.* The ride is only a few minutes. The shop can provide snorkeling equipment and rent dive gear. It also leads groups to sites during the day, including snorkel tours. Groups are limited to 10 divers, and they are Coast Guard certified for 14. Groups of six to eight are most common. PADI instruction is through the advanced level. Call (800) 982-6747 or (808) 334-1154; fax (808) 334-1158; e-mail: rainbow@rainbowdiver.com; website: www.rainbowdiver.com.

Retail Sales: *None*	**Dive Boat Comfort:** *Good*
Rentals: *Extensive*	**On-Board Facilities**
Scuba Training: *Moderate*	**for Photographers:** *None*
Photo Services: *None*	

Kona Coast Divers has been in business since 1967, and now is a PADI 5-Star IDC facility. This would be a superb place to go pro. The shop operates two custom-built boats: a 42-footer (for 18 divers) and a 32-footer (for 10 divers). Both have shade, freshwater showers, and camera buckets. Kona Coast provides transportation to and from the boats and pickups from the Kailua-Kona area. You'll recognize the shop by the distinctive lighthouse (it is located at 74-5614 Palani Road in Kailua-Kona). There's a retail area, an excellent repair facility, rental center, classroom, and pool. The shop pumps its own Nitrox. Every certification level is taught (NAUI, PADI, and SSI), plus specialty courses. Call (800) KOA-DIVE or (808) 329-8802; e-mail: divekona@ilhawaii.net; website: www.konacoastdivers.com.

Retail Sales: *Extensive*   **Dive Boat Comfort:** *Excellent*
Rentals: *Extensive*   **On-Board Facilities**
Scuba Training: *Extensive*   **for Photographers:** *Good*
Photo Services: *Moderate*

Red Sail Sports, on the property of the Hilton Waikoloa (a PADI Resort), has a complete dive and watersports program. A 38-foot dive boat has a regular schedule, including night dives. A complete scuba equipment rental package is $20. The NAUI and PADI scuba school offers just a basic certification and some specialty courses. The company also uses a 50-foot sailing catamaran for snorkel sails, whale-watch cruises, and sunset sails. Call (800) 255-6425 or (808) 886-2876; fax (808) 886-4169; e-mail: info@redsail.com; website: www.redsail.com.

Retail Sales: *Adequate*   **Dive Boat Comfort:** *Good*
Rentals: *Extensive*   **On-Board Facilities**
Scuba Training: *Limited*   **for Photographers:** *Good*
Photo Services: *Limited*

WHERE TO STAY ON HAWAII

An excellent place in the budget category is **Kona Magic Sands,** on Aliii Drive next to the Magic Sands Beach Park. There are 37 condo units right on the beach. The studio units are not large, nor are they luxurious, but each has a kitchen, lanai, and a dynamite view. There are laundry facilities and a restaurant on-site. Rates are from $75 to $95 for a double in high season, from $65 to $75 in low season. No diving packages are available. Call (800) 622-5348 or (808) 329-3333; fax (808) 326-4137; website: www.konahawaii.com.

Another great budget spot is the **Kona Tiki Hotel,** also on Aliii Drive about a mile from downtown Kailua-Kona. This one, also, is located on the beach. It has only 15 rooms, but each has ceiling fans, mini fridges, and private lanais overlooking the ocean. They do not have TVs or phones. Really great deals are the doubles with kitchenettes. Rates are $56 for a double and $62 for double with kitchenette. No diving packages are available. Note that there is a three-night minimum. Call (808) 329-1425; fax (808) 327-9402.

Up north on the Kohala Coast are some of the islands' finest resorts. Of course, the prices are vastly different from those already mentioned, and diving is far from being their top concern. Nevertheless, I would recommend a couple, because they do have dive shops and the properties are incredible.

The 3,200-acre **Mauna Lani Bay Hotel and Bungalows ★** (350 units) is not only the perfect place for pampering, it is also the site of some very interesting historic remains. Trails lead to ancient fishponds and petroglyphs, and have signage explaining their significance. You can keep very busy here golfing, playing tennis, boating, or just vegging out on the beach. Of course, you can also dive and snorkel! Although diving is not given much emphasis here, the hotel will arrange it for you. Rates, of course, are steep—anywhere from $325 to $575 a night for a double room. If you'd like to pay more, you can get a villa or a bungalow. Phone (800) 367-2323 or (808) 885-6622; fax (808) 885-4556; website: www.maunalani.com.

The **Hilton Waikoloa ★★★** is another big PADI Resort (1,240 units) with lots of activities, including an active dive program. Red Sail Sports has a full dive and watersports facility on the property. Guests get around the resort on trams and boats. Its 62 acres feature tropical gardens, waterfalls, wildlife, and a one-acre pool with hidden grottos and man-made lagoons, including a dolphin lagoon. There is a swim-with-the-dolphins program. Rates are from $250 to $520 for a double. No diving pagkages are available. Call (800) HILTONS or (808) 886-1234; fax (808) 886-2900; website: www.hilton.com/hawaii/waikoloa.

LIVE-ABOARD

The **Aggressor Fleet** operates a 120-foot live-aboard along the Kona Coast. Carrying a maximum of 18 passengers, it features nine staterooms, each with private head and shower. The vessel features an onboard hot tub, photo lab, and e-mail access. The charters are all-inclusive—meals, tanks, weights, airport transfers—and you get unlimited diving. Nitrox is available. Call (800) 348-2628; fax (504) 384-081; e-mail: info@aggressor.com; website: www.aggressor.com.

ISLAND LIFE ON HAWAII

Hawaii was first discovered by voyaging Polynesians nearly 2,000 years ago and is considered the cradle of Hawaiian civilization. Fortunately, many wonderful cultural and historic sites have been preserved, and it is those, along with ancient legends, that will fascinate visitors.

The Kona Coast is pleasantly laid-back; the locals are friendly and the touring easy. You won't encounter much traffic; also, prices are reasonable.

Definitely visit **Pu'uhonua O Honaunau (Place of Refuge) National Historical Park,** which is also where one of the top dive spots is located. This site was a sixteenth-century sanctuary for defeated warriors. You can see reconstructed thatch huts, canoes, and other fascinating elements of the old civilization.

When in Kona, don't miss the opportunity to try real Kona coffee. On your way to or from Place of Refuge, stop by **Bay View Farms and Mill,** which gives informative tours and has a particularly attractive gift center. These are very friendly folks, and you'll learn a lot of interesting tidbits about coffee production. It's a pleasant stopover for an hour or so.

Pele, the fire goddess, made her home in Hawaii's mighty volcanoes—Kilauea, Mauna Kea, and Mauna Loa. To see some of her violent legacy, go to **Hawaii Volcanoes National Park.** It takes a long time, since it is 95 miles from Kona, and the place is huge. Several days would be needed to see it all. The summit is 4,000 feet above sea level, so be sure to take a windbreaker or rain jacket. After reaching the Kilauea Visitor Center (admission is $10 per vehicle), take the Crater Rim Drive for the full effect. Along the drive are the sulphur banks, steam vents, Halemaumau Crater's edge, the Thurston Lava Tube, and a lot more. If you follow Chain of Craters Road down to the end, you might get lucky and see the lava flowing. Kilauea has been erupting almost continuously since 1983, covering thousands of acres of lowland and rain forest, and obliterating entire towns and historic structures. On the upside, the volcano has added hundreds of acres of new land to the island. Also in the park are several hiking trails. Pick up a park map at the visitor's center to get the details.

Up north on the **Kohala Coast,** drive into some of the small towns, get out, and just browse. Places like Hawi and Kapaau have some top-quality art galleries and craft shops. In Hawi, visit the Kohala Koa Gallery inside the Bamboo Restaurant. It features gorgeous furniture, fabrics, prints, and fine art. The restaurant is also highly recommended. In Kapaau, visit **St. Augustine's Church,** also known as the "Little Church on the Hill." It is particularly striking—you can't miss it. The church was founded in 1884 by English families that emigrated to the island to manage the sugar plantations. Also in Kapaau is the statue of Hawaii's great King Kamehameha I, who lived and ruled here from the late eighteenth to the early nineteenth century.

In the town of Kamuela in up-country **Waimea,** Parker Square has several shops. One that particularly impressed me was Silk Road Gallery, which sells fine antiques, textiles, baskets, and such. Equestrians will enjoy taking a trail ride from the **Parker Ranch.** Don't expect to see the entire ranch, though; it covers 225,000 acres!

Hawaii was where our knowledge of **surfing** originated; indeed, it was the sport of royalty. Today the boards are much shorter and lighter, but the theory is still the same. When "surf's up," the rules change and serious surfers will drop everything, grab a board, and get to the beach. On the Big Island, the Hilo area generally gets the best surf.

These are just a few of the highlights. Definitely pick up more literature to learn about all the other possibilities on the Big Island. For those interested in horticulture, for instance, there are some wonderful botanical gardens and nature trails.

Dining

Cuisine in Hawaii is better than ever. With so many influences from the Asian nations and the availability of fresh produce and seafood, the combinations are nothing short of exciting. What is usually termed Pacific Rim Cuisine can either be very expensive or, fortunately, very inexpensive, as well. The noodle shops are great buys. They're not only easy on the pocketbook, but the food is tasty and nutritious. Healthy fast food!

Oodles of Noodles, in the Crossroads Shopping Center in Kailua, has delicious food and an eclectic menu in a pleasant atmosphere. You'll find Chinese, Japanese, Vietnamese, and Thai influences, all at reasonable prices. I can personally attest that the noodle bowls are superb. My favorite has slices of ahi on top—mouth-watering!

If you want your meal beachside, you'll enjoy **Beach Tree Bar and Grill** in the Four Seasons Resort at Hualalai, Queen Kaahumanu Highway, Kaupulehu-Kona. From the thatched bar on the sand you can watch the sun set while dining on coconut-marinated chile prawns or an albacore tuna sandwich. The atmosphere is fun and casual. Their Saturday evening barbecue (with entertainment) on the beach is a crowd-pleaser.

In South Kona check out the **Keei Café,** on Highway 11, and have the fresh catch for dinner (lunch is not served), or try the **Manago Hotel Restaurant,** also on Highway 11 in Captain Cook.

The resorts, particularly those along the Kohala Coast, all have superb restaurants. There's **Batik,** in the Mauna Kea Beach Hotel, **Brown's Beach House,** in The Orchid at Mauna Lani, the **CanoeHouse,** in the Mauna Lani Bay Hotel and Bungalows, and **Roy's Waikoloa Bar and Grill,** in the Waikoloa Beach Resort. This is just a small sampling, since each grand resort has several wonderful restaurants, and they're all vying for attention.

Medical Facilities

The phone number for Kona Community Hospital is (808) 322-9311. The closest recompression chamber is in Honolulu (808) 523-9155.

In case of a diving emergency call DAN (Divers Alert Network) at (919) 684-4DAN (4326) or (919) 684-8111.

Maui

THE UNDERWATER SCENE

Maui is one of those rare places that can seem bustling and overcrowded, yet has sufficiently serene corners that are quaint, quiet, and inviting. It also has a wild side to it underwater, with vast expanses for exciting exploration. You can be milling about T-shirt shops, being jostled by the tourist throngs along a seemingly endless shopping strip, yet within a few hours meet up with a family of gray sharks and a convention of barracuda so massive in proportion that they throw a 747-size shadow on the ocean floor.

Maui was once connected to the islands of Lanai, Molokai, and Kahoolawe (ka-ho-uh-lah-vay). Over time, the basin between the islands filled with water, so there are four islands where once there was only one. Four islands and much more underwater diversity—great news for divers.

Tourist accommodations are clustered on the leeward western and southern shores, where you'll find the majority of the dive operations and the dive sites, as well. Fortunately, in addition to some spectacular sites that need to be reached by boat, the shore diving here is also a lot of fun and easily accessible.

Diving Conditions

You would think that with all the development along the coast, the shore diving would be pretty sad, but that's not the case at all. The big problem is getting to the shore diving spots, due to the large resorts. *Black Rock,* an old shore-diving favorite, is accessible to guests staying at the Sheraton Hotel in Kaanapali, but difficult for others. Also, parking is expensive. Just down the coast off the Hyatt Regency is another good spot with numerous turtles. Again, it is difficult to access.

Divers won't find much coral in the near-shore areas, but there are plenty of turtles and indigenous tropicals. Caves and caverns dot the shoreline. Farther out to sea, around Molokini and Kaho'olawe, are great soaring walls, ledges, and mysterious cobalt depths.

Along the coast, conditions are generally calm, with little current. Summertime gets the best conditions, with warmer and less choppy water. If you go out beyond Molokini, though, the seas can get pretty choppy, so don't get in over your head, so to speak. Also, remember to take that seasick pill!

Recommended Level of Experience

All levels of divers will enjoy the sites here, although some are best reserved for very confident divers. Remember to decompress at sea level for several hours before going to high elevations. If you intend to ascend to an altitude of 8,000 feet or more after diving, the general rules of flying apply. For most divers, that means waiting at sea level for at least 12 hours.

Great Dive Sites

Molokini gets top billing here. This is the beautiful crescent-shaped island, which is actually a partially eroded crater, located three miles off Maui's southwest coast. Its height above water is 160 feet. Underwater it drops down 35 feet, then gradually slopes to 70 feet before plunging right off into the deep deep blue.

There are several dive areas here with distinct personalities. Shallow areas, perfect second dives, are inside the crater rim. The deeper dives are along the outer seaward wall. The current along the wall frequently makes good drift diving. So Molokini offers something for every level of diver.

Because this is a marine preserve, it attracts everything from schooling fish in miniature to majestic manta rays. In winter, from November to April, you'll hear some beautiful sounds underwater—the songs of the migrating humpback whales.

On the less-than-positive side, this popular spot can get crowded. You're likely to find several other boats anchored here along with yours.

My favorite spot is off the island of *Kaho'olawe*. Because of severe restrictions on diving, the underwater environment is wild and exciting. For years the Navy used this area for testing ammunition; consequently, dive boats are discouraged from making the area part of their regular itinerary. Nevertheless, while diving off Halona Point here, our group immediately spotted several white-tip sharks and gray reef sharks congregating near the bottom, which was well over 100 feet. As we descended they scooted off. Then an amazingly huge school of barracuda darkened the skies above us, like an enormous rain cloud looming overhead. On that single dive I spotted a tinker's butterfly fish, which is very rare, as well as a bandit angelfish, an endemic species. At 90 feet black coral trees billowed from the wall. In shallower waters were several varieties of nudibranchs. And as if to say aloha, an octopus pulsated through the water column at about eye level! Experienced divers who have an opportunity to come here will really enjoy it.

Most of the Maui dive shops will also make runs over to some of the diving highlights around the island of Lanai. Those sites are described in the Lanai section, which follows this one.

Shore Diving and Snorkeling

Makena Landing, is the perfect shore dive here. You'll even find showers and restrooms. This area is on the southern end of the leeward side. As you're driving south to Makena, take the Makena Road turnoff. Drive down to the parking area. Gear up in the parking lot, then walk the short distance to the rocky shoreline. Although there is a small beach here, the entry over lava rock is easy. Go either right or left; if you enter here, it's really too far to get to the caves.

Experienced divers might like to enter in front of the grave site area, a bit north and around the point. Known as *Five Caves,* this is where the best diving is, and you'll find the caves, coral heads, and large green sea turtles. By the way, I believe the original name for this area was *Five Graves,* because of that grave site. Also, I personally have not identified five caves. Don't forget—if you are not cave-certified do not enter the caves.

When I dived here at Makena Landing, we noticed a family camping along the shore. After we came out of the water and changed out of our wet gear, a gentleman came over to our car and handed us two heaping plates of food! We were definitely touched by his thoughtfulness (also, quite sure that would never occur in California). Robert, once again—*thank you!*

Anywhere around Makena Landing is good diving. I made a dive about two miles south of the landing, just before the huge lava fields. Called *La Perouse Bay,* it's a marine reserve. You'll enter the water just past the house that's on the beach. It's not difficult, and novice divers wouldn't have a problem here. We had fun dinking around the combination rocky/sandy bottom, since the visibility was not good at the time we were here. Nevertheless, we saw gorgeous blue trunkfish that looked like velvet. Also, many butterfly fish, surgeonfish, and sargeant majors. Kick out a bit from shore and you'll see some very pretty coral heads.

Just adjacent to this spot, on the other side (north) of the rocky point is *Ahihi Bay,* another marine reserve. Entry from the bay itself is easy, and you'll find lots of fish and coral—great for snorkelers.

Marine Parks

Maui has four underwater parks, or Marine Life Conservation Districts as they are called in the islands. Beginning on the northwest shore there is Honolua Bay and the adjoining Mokuleia Bay, which have been protected since 1978. You'll find Honolua Bay slightly more than half a mile past mile marker 32 on Route 30, north of Kapalua. A narrow dirt road leads down to it. The snorkeling and diving are good here when conditions are calm (usually in summer), but in winter the giant waves will be attractive only to surfers and onlookers.

The entire island of Molokini is an underwater park and can only be accessed by boat. This is Maui's most popular dive site.

Down on the southwest coast, past Makena Landing, are Ahihi Bay and La Perouse. Both are small, scenic bays that have very good snorkeling and diving, but receive few visitors (other than fish).

DIVE SERVICES & PACKAGES ON MAUI

Ed Robinson's Diving Adventures runs two dive boats, a 30-footer and a 32-footer. Each is certified for 16 people (but only carries 12), has a head, and freshwater rinse. The larger vessel is more camera-friendly, with a camera storage table and freshwater camera rinse tub. They like to have small groups of certified divers who have been in the water within the last two years. Divers receive a Biology 101 natural history and animal talk prior to and after each dive, and each dive is a guided nature tour. There is no retail business (since this is not a store location), but rental equipment is available for guests who dive with them. Also available is a reasonably priced cottage for rent with full kitchen and lots of amenities. Call (800) 635-1273 or (808) 879-3584; e-mail: robinson@maui.net; website: www.mauiscuba.com.

Retail Sales: *None*

Rentals: *Adequate*

Scuba Training: *Limited*

Photo Services: *Limited*

Dive Boat Comfort: *Good*

**On-Board Facilities
for Photographers:** *Good*

Maui Dive Shop is the big kahuna on the island, with six locations: two in South Maui and four in West Maui—you can't miss em! Each location has gear rentals, a retail center, and activity center. The shop has discounted prices with the Maui Coast Hotel in Kihei. For dive trips a Pro 48 is used, and there are special snorkel trips as well. PADI instruction is through all levels, and you can go pro with their PADI 5-Star IDC. In South Maui there are shops in the Kihei Outlet Center and Kamaole Shopping Center. In West Maui, the locations are Lahaina Cannery Mall, Kahana Gateway, Whalers Village in Kaanapali, and Honokowai Market Place. Phone (800) 542-3483 or (808) 879-3388; e-mail: mauidive@ maui.net; website: www.mauidiveshop.com.

Retail Sales: *Extensive*

Rentals: *Extensive*

Scuba Training: *Extensive*

Photo Services: *Extensive*

Dive Boat Comfort: *Excellent*

**On-Board Facilities
for Photographers:** *Superior*

Lahaina Divers, Inc., located at 143 Dickenson Street in Lahaina, is a PADI Gold Palm IDC Resort. They also teach SSI, NAUI, YMCA, and NASDS courses. So just about whatever you want, they got! You can also get your Nitrox cert here and even learn to use a rebreather. Definitely a fascinating specialty course (there are several) would be the Hawaiian Naturalist Specialty. The shop runs two custom dive boats: a 43-foot Reliant, certified for 22 passengers, and a 50-foot Endeavor, certified for 49 passengers but limited to 24. Each accommodates photographers and has freshwater rinse hoses and soaking barrels and a marine head. Nitrox is available. The shop offers interesting package tours, depending on your skill level. There's the Open Water Training package, the New Diver/Rusty Diver package, and the Experienced Diver package. The latter includes dive trips to Lanai or the Molokini wall. Call (800) 998-3483 or (808) 667-7496; e-mail: lahdiver@maui.net; website: www.lahainadivers.com.

Retail Sales: *Extensive* **Dive Boat Comfort:** *Excellent*
Rentals: *Extensive* **On-Board Facilities**
Scuba Training: *Extensive* **for Photographers:** *Superior*
Photo Services: *Extensive*

Mike Severns Diving runs small, personalized trips for divers who are comfortable in the water (translated: no newbies). Mike and Pauline Fiene are biologists and about the best guides you can get. Mike is also a professional underwater photographer. They do not sell gear or give instruction, but they can provide rental equipment. Phone (808) 879-6596; e-mail: severns@mauigateway.com.

Retail Sales: *None* **Dive Boat Comfort:** *Good*
Rentals: *Adequate* **On-Board Facilities**
Scuba Training: *None* **for Photographers:** *Good*
Photo Services: *None*

WHERE TO STAY ON MAUI

Maui has some incredible resorts, which are also incredibly expensive. Here are a few examples, as well as some options that are a little easier on the pocketbook. Few lodgings in Maui offer dive packages.

Starting up at the northwest is the moderately priced **Kahana Sunset** (4909 Lower Honoapiilani Highway), located at the northern end of Kahana, almost in Napili. The resort is nice and private, stair-stepping down the side of a hill to a white sandy beach. The 79 one- and two-bedroom units have kitchens with dishwashers, washer/dryers, sleeper sofas, and lanais with great views—perfect for families. There's also a small pool and spa. High-season rates (three-night minimum) are from $160 to $180 for a one-bedroom unit, from $165 to $265 for a two-bedroom unit. Each sleeps up to six people. Call (800) 669-1488 or (808) 669-8011; fax (808) 669-9170; e-mail: sun2set@maui.net.

A little farther south is **The Whaler on Kaanapali Beach** ★ (2481 Kaanapali Parkway), which will give you privacy, luxury, elegance, and incredible ocean and mountain views. There are 360 units, each with complete kitchen, washer/dryer, marble bath, ten-foot beamed ceilings, and a blue-tiled lanai. The resort has a pool and spa, exercise room, tennis courts, and watersports. Next door is Whalers Village, where both Maui Dive Shop and the Hula Grill and other restaurants are located. High-season rates for a studio are from $195 to $210. There are also one- and two-bedroom units with rates ranging from $235 to $500 (paradise doesn't come cheap!). Phone (800) 367-7052 or (808) 661-4861; fax (435) 655-4844; website: www.tenio.com/vri.

In Lahaina, on ten landscaped acres and three blocks from the beach, is the **Aston Maui Islander** ★ (660 Wainee Street), with 372 units. Units are spacious (another good one for families), and most have either full kitchens or kitchenettes. On the property are tennis courts, swimming pool, sundeck, and barbecue and picnic area. The resort doesn't offer dive packages but does have an association of sorts with Lahaina Divers. High-season rates: $99 double, from $125 to $135 for studio with kitchenette, $155 one-bedroom with kitchen (sleeps four). There are also two- and three-bedroom units with kitchens. Call (800) 92-ASTON, (800) 367-5226, or (808) 667-9722; fax (808) 661-3733; website: www.aston-hotels.com.

Maui Coast Hotel ★★ is another pleasant, moderately priced property (for Maui, at least), located in Kihei one block from Kamaole Beach Park. There are 265 one- and two-bedroom suites, swimming pool, spas, tennis courts, gift shop, restaurant, and sushi bar. Besides snorkeling and diving, you can arrange to kayak, sail, or windsurf. Guests who dive with Maui Dive Shop can get discounted prices. The hotel also features an extra-value package that includes a rental car. Single standard rates are from $145 to $165. Doubles are from $165 to $205. For a discount, be sure to mention Maui Dive Shop. The address is 2259 South Kihei Road. Call (800) 895-6284 or (808) 874-MAUI; e-mail: mch@maui.net. Log onto the Maui website for more info: www.visitmaui.com.

Punahoa Beach Apartments is only 12 units on a quiet street in Kihei with ocean frontage. All units have lanais with ocean views and fully equipped kitchens. The location is 2142 Iliili Road, off S. Kihei Road and 100 yards from Kamaole Beach 1. Rates for a double: studio from $66 to $93, one-bedroom from $85 to $127, and two-bedroom from $94 to $130. Call (800) 564-4380 or (808) 879-2720; fax (808) 875-3147; e-mail: pb6110@aol.com.

Hawaii's Special Species

One of the most exciting aspects of diving here is the opportunity to find new species. It is commonly stated that there are about 450 species of fish in the islands, which isn't a really a huge number. What is significant is that about one-third of these are endemic; that is, they can be found nowhere else on the globe.

New divers will have a more difficult time spotting these unique species, simply because everything looks new to them anyway. More experienced divers will notice a lot of them immediately. To help identify the endemic species, go to a bookstore and buy a fish ID guide to the islands. A good one is *Hawaiian Reef Fish, the Identification Book* by Casey Mahaney, published by Blue Kirio Publications (call (800) 863-2524) in Kailua-Kona.

Hawaii's famous fish-with-the-long-name—humuhumu-nukun-uku-a-pua'a—is known as the Picasso triggerfish, and is not one of the endemic species. Nevertheless, it's a beauty, and fun to encounter.

Some of the unique species you're sure to encounter are the various wrasse species: the blacktail, saddleback, belted, psychedelic, and shortnose wrasse. An easy wrasse to spot is the Hawaiian cleaner wrasse, with its bright-yellow front half and magenta back half. Naturally, you'll see it at cleaning stations, where you might spot other endemics getting groomed.

Hawaii's butterfly fish are as prolific as they are vibrant and colorful. The tinkers butterfly fish, generally found in deep water, was once thought to be endemic but has been seen in the Marshall Islands. This one is mostly white with a large black triangular stripe running down the back and a yellow stripe through the eyes. Some butterfly endemics include the bluestripe butterfly fish (yellow body with iridescent blue horizontal lines), the pebbled butterfly fish, and the lemon butterfly fish. The latter is often called a milletseed and has the unusual behavior of schooling and grazing in large numbers. Typically, such butterfly fish travel only in pairs or are solitary.

Several angelfish are endemic, such as the bandit, with the lateral black stripe that crosses the eyes like a bandit's mask; and the potter's, with grayish blue and orange hues. There are endemic damselfish, pufferfish, filefish, parrotfish, goatfish, and even scorpionfish. It's a whole new world for divers and snorkelers to discover.

Makena Landing is on the ocean, adjacent to a terrific dive spot—can't get much better than that. Too bad there's no dive shop nearby! But it's easy enough to pick up a few tanks, come back and do some great shore diving. This is actually a bed and breakfast that has been owned by the same family for seven generations. There are two units at opposite ends of a two-story cedar house. Each has a full kitchen, and outside is a barbecue area and a sundeck. Want to see whales, sunsets, and views of Molokini? This is the place. The nightly rate is $95 for a double, with a three-night minimum. Phone (808) 879-6286.

ISLAND LIFE ON MAUI

Beyond the tourist centers are absolutely gorgeous valleys, beaches, forested mountains, and grasslands. Then there's **Haleakala,** the world's largest dormant volcano. It's so big, it has its own ecosystem within the crater, which visitors can tour. If you're sated with sun and surf, drive up to the summit, which is nice and cool (in fact it can get downright cold). Several little towns on its slopes are interesting artists' communities—towns such as Makawao, Haiku, and Kula.

Note: Diving and driving up to Haleakala the same day would be very dangerous. The summit is 10,023 feet above sea level. Wait at least 12 hours after a dive (at sea level) before ascending.

Serious surfers should head for **Honolua Bay,** one of Maui's four marine preserves. This is also an excellent shore diving and snorkeling spot. The bay is toward the north end of the windy east side. Drive slightly more than half a mile past mile marker 32 on Route 30, north of Kapalua. Look for a narrow dirt road that leads to the bay, where there is an old boat ramp. Beginners can rent surfboards and take lessons at calmer **Kaanapali Beach** on the leeward side.

Whale-watching tours go out between December and April. Remember, under law the operators must keep a certain distance from the whales. Also, with nature as it is, it's always possible that you won't see anything. No, you don't get your money back. The warm shallow waters off west Maui must be heaven for the whales after their 5,000-mile journey from their Alaska feeding grounds. Mid-February is the height of whale season, when you can see them easily from shore.

The **Road to Hana** is always a great escape. If you haven't gotten queasy on the high seas yet, just wait till you've been around a few of the 617 hairpin curves! The drive is lush and wild, and at its terminus you can take a dip in the Seven Pools or rest your tummy on the red sand beach.

Maui has a terrific 2.5-million-liter walk-through aquarium—the **Maui Ocean Center.** This is perfect for divers and snorkelers to be able to ID all those species they're seeing. It's perfect, also, for those companions who would never dream of communing with these critters in their own environment. The aquarium is located in Maalaea Harbor Village at the triangle between Honoapiilani Highway and Maalaea Road, and is open every day from 9 a.m. to 5 p.m.

Contact **Trilogy Excursions** for snorkeling or kayaking trips. They do an excellent job, providing transportation, gear, and even arranging lunch. Call (888) MAUI-800 or (808) 661-4743; website: www.sailtrilogy.com.

Dining and Entertainment

The small waterfront town of Lahaina is a popular tourist draw during the day, with its art galleries, shops, and scenic harbor. It's also the perfect spot to head to in the evening, for a meal and entertainment. There are restaurants with varying price ranges, so just nose around until you find something that appealing. **Maui Brews** has live entertainment most nights, and the open-air cantina **Cheeseburger in Paradise** always gets a good crowd after dark. Lahaina is also the best place to find a wonderful, authentic luau. The **Old Lahaina Luau** takes place at a one-acre site just oceanside of the Lahaina Cannery. For reservations call (808) 667-1998.

In Kihei, **Carelli's on the Beach** attracts the cognoscenti for pasta, pizza, seafood, and sunset. **Hapa's Brew Haus** is the venue for good food and beer and great live entertainment, which is usually jazz or blues.

On the bay at Ma'alaea, a new place called **Bamboo Bistro** is getting a lot of attention. On the way to upcountry Maui, stop at **Haliimaile General Store** for lunch or dinner. The menu is interesting and eclectic. Like ribs? Try these.

Medical Facilities

Maui Memorial Hospital is located in Wailuku (221 Mahalani) in central Maui. Phone (808) 244-9056 or (808) 667-9721. The closest recompression chamber is in Honolulu; call (808) 523-9155.

In case of a diving emergency call DAN (Divers Alert Network) at (919) 684-4DAN (4326) or (919) 684-8111.

Lanai

THE UNDERWATER SCENE

Lanai has wonderful dive spots that do not see as many divers as those popular areas around Maui. This is simply because there are few resorts and dive operations on this island, which once was the pineapple-producing capital of the world. However, many of the Maui dive operators will schedule trips over here. The travel time is about 45 minutes from Lahaina.

On the south shore, the underwater cave formations and pinnacles are the highlights of Lanai dive sites. These have been formed by the molten lava solidifying in a latticework pattern. This allows light to shine through, casting beautiful designs on the rocky ocean floor. Much of the area around Lanai has not been thoroughly explored, so in all likelihood there are many wonderful spots that simply are not identified.

Due to a combination of modest development on the island and few divers visiting underwater sites, Lanai's marine life is in superb condition. You'll see turtles here and swarms of tropicals, as well as nudibranchs, lobsters, cowries, and moray eels.

Recommended Level of Experience

You do not need a vast amount of experience to dive here. Dive sites are fairly shallow and water conditions are generally calm.

All divers, however, need to be careful about heading straight up to Lanai City after diving. For diving purposes, it's considered to be at an altitude of 2,000 feet. Consequently, you should wait at sea level for at least four hours after a dive before going up the mountain. Also, avoid strenuous exercise for a while, and do not drink alcoholic beverages right away.

Great Dive Sites

Cathedrals I and II are beautiful dive spots located outside Manele Harbor and Hulopoe Beach. They get their names from the intricate structures that let splashes of light shine though in interesting patterns. Of course the complex structure also makes great habitat for all sorts of crustaceans and critters. Spend some time poking around, and take a dive light if you can. You'll also find that eels like the little crevices.

Cathedral II features a large pinnacle that rises from about 55 feet to within 15 feet of the surface. It, too, is interwoven with openings, tubes, and crevices. Orange cup coral covers the undersides, and schools of snapper throng all about.

Both of these sites make good night dives, also. The depth is about 60 feet. At night you'll see plenty of shrimp, and beautiful phosphorescence if you turn off your dive light.

Shallow Diving and Snorkeling

Both bays on the south end of Lanai (Hulopoe and Manele) are protected, and have easy entries and lots to see—perfect snorkeling conditions.

Marine Parks

Lanai's marine life conservation areas are at Hulopoe Bay, Pu'upehe Cove, and Manele Bay. Fearing that the anchors from visiting yachts and commercial passenger boats from Maui would damage the corals in these bays, Lanai's residents pressed for preservation and prevailed. Manele Bay, once the site of an ancient fishing village, is now a small boat harbor.

DIVE SERVICES & PACKAGES ON LANAI

Trilogy Excursions is a Maui-based ocean-sports operation, but it has a staff member who works permanently at the Manele Bay Hotel (a PADI Gold Palm Resort) and arranges all the trips. The company offers sailing, diving, and snorkeling trips, all on a large catamaran. It also provides snorkeling and diving equipment. Trilogy also organizes shore dives. Call (800) 874-2666 or (808) 565-9303; website: www.sailtrilogy.com.

Retail Sales: *None*

Rentals: *Adequate*

Scuba Training: *Limited*

Photo Services: *Limited*

Dive Boat Comfort: *Good*

On-Board Facilities for Photographers: *None*

Adventure Lanai Dive Center, located in Lanai City, organizes kayak-scuba (one-tank dives) and kayak-snorkel trips. In winter a whale-watch kayak adventure (northeast part of the island) goes out to the remains of a giant Liberty ship. And in summer there are trips to the western side of Lanai to see sea arches, secluded coves, and sea caves. The company will teach you how to kayak and supply dry bags, towels, water, and snacks. You can rent kayaks if you want to go out on your own. Call (808) 565-7737 or 565-7373; website: www.kayakhawaii.com.

Retail Sales: *Adequate*

Rentals: *Adequate*

Scuba Training: *None*

Photo Services: *None*

Dive Boat Comfort: *N/A*

On-Board Facilities for Photographers: *N/A*

WHERE TO STAY ON LANAI

For old salts, there really are just two options, but both are on the beach! **Hulopoe Beach Park** has six campsites run by the Lanai Company, each of which can accommodate up to six people. Facilities include restrooms, showers, barbecue areas, picnic tables, and fresh water. There's a registration fee of $5, and the nightly rate is $5 per person. Call (808) 565-3982. Website: www.lanai-resorts.com. To rent camping equipment, call Adventure Lanai Dive Center, (808) 565-7737 or 7373.

You can also stay in the lap of luxury at the **Manele Bay Hotel ★**, a beautiful PADI Gold Palm Resort situated on a hillside overlooking a gorgeous stretch of sandy beach, and a bay where dolphins come to nurse their young. While staying here I phoned home to inform my family that I could see dolphins playing in the bay that very moment! The resort has 250 units, all luxuriously appointed. There are various watersports, plus tennis, golf, jeep tours, snorkeling, and diving (with Trilogy Excursions; see above). The sister-hotel is the scrumptious Lodge at Koele, up in the mountains. Guests at either resort can enjoy the facilities of the other and get free transportation. Brace yourself: rates are from $295 to $575 for a double. Call (800) 321-4666 or (808) 565-7700; website: www.lanai-resorts.com.

There is another place to stay that get a lot of praise, but it's not on the beach. This is the **Hotel Lanai,** right in Lanai City. It has only 11 small units, but they are clean and pleasant. For years this was the only place for visitors to stay on the island. Divers staying here should keep in mind that the elevation requires several hours of decompression time after diving. Rates are from $95 to $105 for a double, $140 for a cottage double, and $200 for a nearby two-bedroom house that sleeps six. These rates include continental breakfast. Call (800) 795-7211 or (808) 565-7211; fax (808) 565-6450; website: www.onlanai.com.

ISLAND LIFE ON LANAI

For years Lanai consisted of one enormous pineapple field, a single village, and just a few miles of paved road. And all of it was owned by the Dole company. About ten years ago, that all changed. Dole moved out and the fields began converting to other crops. When the two luxury resorts were constructed (Manele Bay Hotel and Lodge at Koele), the island began to draw tourists (build it and they will come, right?). Nevertheless, just a small fraction of the island is developed. There still are only a few miles of paved road, there is no traffic light, and the resident population numbers only around 3,000. Lanai definitely attracts those looking for a place to get away from noise, glitz, traffic, and commotion.

Besides diving and snorkeling, visitors hike the trails that weave up and over the island, ride horseback, golf, fish, sail, and explore. Contact Lanai EcoAdventure Centre—(808) 565-7737—if you want to rent a mountain bike or a jeep. **Lanai City** is a fascinating little town, a throwback to old 1920s Hawaii. Banana palms and papaya trees stand before clapboard homes with tin roofs. Sounds of roosters and birds predominate. It is a place where you can easily stop and chat with residents. I found it enchanting.

Note: For divers, Lanai City is considered to have an elevation of 2,000 feet above sea level. After completing a dive, wait about four hours at sea level before returning to Lanai City. Also, it's wise to lounge around rather than do any strenuous activity. Avoid alcoholic beverages.

If you can spare the time, try to check out the **Luahiwa Petroglyphs,** which are considered to be among the best-preserved ancient rock carvings in all the islands. They're not easy to find, though, so your best bet is to arrange with the EcoAdventure Centre for an excursion. Another interesting detour, which would need to be by jeep, is to **Kaunolu Village,** once the summer retreat of Kamehameha the Great and now a national historic landmark. It's full of archaeological treasures and the ruins of more than 80 houses—a veritable ghost town. You'd need to get precise directions, or else go with a tour.

Dining and Entertainment

Sumptuous resorts usually propagate equally scrumptious restaurants, and Lanai is no exception. There is truly wonderful dining at both **Manele Bay Hotel** and **Lodge at Koele.** Of course, most of the restaurants are very expensive. Manele Bay has Hulopoe Court and the Ihilani for fine dining. But you can also have a very good meal for a lot less at the Pool Grill. This is the most casual of the hotel's restaurants, located poolside. The salads, especially, are excellent, and you can get grilled ahi, tuna, and other fish specialties. Both resorts have a regular program of live entertainment.

Lanai City has a few less expensive restaurants. There's **Henry Clay's Rotisserie** in the Hotel Lanai and **Blue Ginger Café** on 7th Street.

Medical Facilities

The phone number for Lanai Community Hospital is (808) 565-6411. The closest recompression chamber is in Honolulu; phone (808) 523-9155.

In case of a diving emergency call DAN (Divers Alert Network) at (919) 684-4DAN (4326) or (919) 684-8111.

Oahu

THE UNDERWATER SCENE

Don't overlook Oahu (uh-wah-hoo) for diving in the islands. I've had wonderful experiences here. The water can be surprisingly clear and the conditions excellent. Sure, it's the most populous of the islands (about 836,000 people) and a major center of commerce, but there still are plenty of out-of-the-way gems and even some terrific dives in areas that are really congested.

You'll find everything here that you can see on the other islands—turtles, eels, tropicals, lava tubes, and coral. But here you'll also find some interesting shipwrecks, a facet the other islands do not offer.

As on the other islands, most of the diving takes place on the lee of the island—the west and southwest. Conditions are far more favorable here year-round. The north shore has some great diving, with wonderful caverns, enormous lava formations, and tunnels, but it can be very dangerous. There are no protected bays, and the surf can be ferocious.

Snorkeling on Oahu is superb. Beautiful beach parks ring the island, and most have restrooms and other facilities. Entry is usually from a sandy beach, and the depth is fairly shallow for a long way. Just watch the surf carefully for a while before getting in, to see how the waves are behaving. Carry your fins into waist-deep water before putting them on.

Recommended Level of Experience

Most dive sites off Oahu are perfect for novice divers. They're in sheltered areas with clear, calm water. Just remember that the farther you are from shore the chancier water conditions become, even on the leeward side. Only experienced divers should dive the north shore most of the year. And during much of the winter, the north shore is off-limits to everyone. That's when you hang up your regulator and become a topside spectator.

Oahu would be a wonderful place to become certified. In fact, many of the dive shops on the island specialize in certifying new divers, and especially those who have completed their classroom work elsewhere and have a referral from their instructor to do the ocean dives in Hawaii.

Remember to decompress at sea level for several hours before going to high elevations. If you intend to ascend to an altitude of 8,000 feet or more after diving, the general rules of flying apply. For most divers, that means waiting at sea level for at least 12 hours.

Great Dive Sites

Jackie James of Aloha Dive Shop once told me that "Hanauma Bay is one of the most misunderstood parks in Hawaii." This First Lady of Diving in the Hawaiian Islands explained that most divers will pooh-pooh Hanauma as a snorkeling spot that has deteriorated from too many bodies and too much suntan lotion. She explained that you simply have to know where to go. And if you find it, divers will have a terrific time. Yep, she was right!

In fact, *Hanauma Bay* today is probably a better diving spot than snorkeling spot, even though it is generally regarded to be Oahu's primo snorkeling park. So à la Jackie James, here's what you do: locate the lifeguard stand on the right side of the beach and enter the water directly in front of it. You can either save your air by snorkeling out or drop down, since it is shallow for a long way. Look for the underwater cable that extends from the beach straight out to sea. Simply follow the cable over the sandy bottom through the channel and fairly quickly you'll start to see staghorn and elkhorn coral, as well as a gorgeous assortment of tropicals.

On my first dive here on Christmas day the bay was completely flat. We followed the cable on snorkels until we started to see coral. At that point I noticed a small turtle watching us from the surface. Amazingly, it came right over to us! When we deflated our BCDs, it dropped right down with us. And throughout that dive, the turtle was our constant companion. Of course, it had to surface occasionally for air, but would always find us again. That was when I learned to "talk" to turtles. I made sounds (through my regulator of course) and the little guy came up and put its head so close to mine that we were almost touching. When I talked, its head cocked to one side and he watched me intently—definitely listening! So that's a hot tip that you can try; Jean's "talking to turtles" trick.

I've experienced several wonderful days of diving in the bay and found white-mouthed morays, big-eye squirrelfish, goatfish, bird wrasse and saddle wrasse, triggerfish, scorpionfish, octopus, pufferfish, and trumpetfish. The butterfly fish were magnificent, especially the endemic species. We found milletseed, threadfin, raccoon, and bluestripe varieties. Photographers, grab your cameras and come to Hanauma Bay! The area around *Witches Brew,* which is part of the outer reef, has a prolific amount of hard corals. You just need to venture out a bit farther toward the point to reach it.

On one dive, however, we decided to drop down before getting to the reef, and to explore the rocky rubble and turtle grass area on the way out. Even that was terrific. We spotted a bluespine unicornfish, a convict tang, and an Achilles tang. I noticed a small leaf waving about in the water column and watched it for a while, because its movement seemed unleaf-like. Sure enough, I was told later on by a naturalist that it was a leaffish! So experiences like these make Hanauma Bay loads of fun.

The park is about nine miles east of Waikiki. Take Highway 72 to Koko Head and watch for the Hanauma Bay sign. There's a large parking area, but get there early because it does fill up. You'll have to pay an entrance fee to use the park. There is no dive shop here, so rent tanks and bring them down with the rest of your gear. Fortunately, a tram at the top of the hill makes the trek a lot easier, since it's quite a steep walk.

Before heading off to the park, you can get everything you need in the Koko Marina Shopping Center, just west of the Hanauma turnoff. Rent tanks and scuba and snorkeling equipment from Aloha Dive Shop. Grab some sushi at Kozo Sushi, a terrific little take-out place, and buy a Hawaiian Reef Fish ID book at the bookstore. Then you're all set!

In the vicinity of Hanauma Bay are two dive sites where the shops like to take students and "rusty" divers. These are *Coco Craters* and *Turtle Canyon*. On both of these shallow dives, the odds of seeing turtles are very good.

If you like seeing metal underwater, hook up with a dive shop to go out to three great wrecks not far from Waikiki Beach. There's also a good chance of seeing pelagic species around them, such as eagle rays, mantas, and sharks. All of the following dives are for divers with deep-diving experience, and certainly not for novice or "rusty" divers.

The *YO-257* is a 175-foot U.S. Navy ship that sits at 100 feet. Atlantis Submarines sank the vessel in 1989 as part of the artificial reef program. It has been submerged long enough to display an impressive amount of coral growth. Before its sinking, large openings were cut in the hull, so exploring the interior is safe. Look for marine life that has taken up residence, especially morays. Swarms of schooling fish typically put on a beautiful show here. Trips to this wreck leave from the Kewalo Basin boat harbor. Recently, Atlantis sank another ship called *Sea Tiger*. So ask about that one, as well.

Following the coastline going west, you'll find two more artificial reef wreck sites—the *M/V Mahi* and *The Plane*. The *Mahi* was a 185-foot minesweeper sunk in 1982. It, too, has several large openings that were cut into it, so you can penetrate the wreck easily. You can go into the wheelhouse and the cargo area, venture up the stairways, see the masts and the big cable-layer. Remember to keep one eye searching the blue for pelagic species on all these wrecks. This one also sits at a depth of 100 feet.

The Plane is not far from the *Mahi* and sits at 75 feet. Divers can actually go right into the cockpit and play "pilot." Trips to the *Mahi* and The Plane leave from the Waianae Boat Harbor.

Shallow Diving and Snorkeling

Hanauma Bay and Pupukea Beach Park are excellent spots for shallow diving and snorkeling. Refer to the next section for directions to the parks.

In the Pupukea Beach Park, *Sharks Cove* and *Three Tables* (named for the flat sections of reef that are exposed at low tide) have interesting lava formations and plentiful marine life. Divers should kick out well beyond the flat tables, to get into deeper water. Snorkelers should stay just beyond the tables. Since this park is on the north shore, visit only in summer when conditions are calm. Also, stay out of the caves unless you're cave-certified and there's no dangerous surge.

Other beaches and beach parks with good snorkeling are Diamond Head Beach Park (see next section) and nearby Halona Cove Beach, (near Halona Point). Up north on the windward coast is a tropical paradise that also happens to be a state recreation area—Malaekahana. Just offshore is idyllic Goat Island (no goats), a bird refuge. You can camp at either place. And the snorkeling is very good.

Marine Parks

Hanauma is one of Hawaii's most beautiful bays, once a fishing site for Hawaiian royalty. The name means "curved bay," and the bay consists of a pair of volcanic craters, outside of which is a shallow fringing reef. This creates a sheltered environment, perfect for fishing. The surf can be raging outside the bay when inside it is nice and calm. When the underwater park status was given to Hanauma in 1967, there were hardly any fish—the spot was just too tempting to anglers. Now it teems with fish. Unfortunately, the snorkelers have loved it a little too much and there's very little living coral along the shoreline. Farther out, however, is another story altogether. Refer to "Best Dive Sites" above for a description of the diving here. The city bus can take you to Hanauma or you can drive and park in the large lot. Take Kalaniana'ole Highway to Hanauma Bay Road. You'll have to pay before going down to the bay. There's even a tram to take you down the hill, if you are so inclined. Lifeguards are on duty, and facilities include restrooms and showers.

Up on the north shore is Pupukea Beach Park, which includes two of the best swimming and snorkeling beaches on the island: Shark's Cove and Three Tables. Don't worry about sharks—there are few anywhere around Oahu. Read the description about these beaches in the previous section. The city bus can take you to the park, or you can take Kamehameha Highway from Haleiwa to Waimea. It's just north of Waimea Bay and adjacent to Sunset Beach Fire Station.

A 75-acre section of Waikiki Beach is protected. It lies at the Diamond Head end of the beach in front of the Waikiki Aquarium and the War Memorial Natatorium. This is a flat, shallow reef area that harbors an abundance of fish. A little farther out, it drops off into deeper water, where the structure gets more interesting. There are lifeguards, restrooms, and showers.

DIVE SERVICES & PACKAGES ON OAHU

Aaron's Dive Shop is one of the oldest shops on the island. The retail location is in Kailua, at 602 Kailua Road. Several different boats are used from around the island, and sites visited are virtually everywhere—leeward, south shore, windward, and north shore—including the *Mahi,* The Plane, and *YO-257* wrecks. The shop also organizes shore dives. As a PADI 5-Star IDC, all levels of courses are offered. Many specialty courses are taught, including Medic First Aid and Enriched Air (Nitrox) Diver.

Associated with the shop is a studio apartment for rent for $65 a night. It has a microwave, refrigerator, cable TV, and VCR and is a short distance from Kailua Beach. For the studio, call (888) 847-2822 or (808) 261-6037;

fax (808) 262-4158. For the dive shop, call (888) 84-SCUBA or (808) 262-2333; e-mail: aarons@aloha.com; website: www.hawaii-scuba.com.

Retail Sales: *Extensive*	**Dive Boat Comfort:** *Good*
Rentals: *Extensive*	**On-Board Facilities**
Scuba Training: *Extensive*	**for Photographers:** *Good*
Photo Services: *Moderate*	

Aloha Dive Shop, a PADI 5-Star Dive Center established since 1970, has certified thousands of divers through NAUI, PADI, and SSI. It specializes in bringing new people into the sport and helping reintroduce skills to those called "rusty" divers. Instruction is through rescue-diver level. Aloha is a full-service retail, rental, and repair facility. The 32-foot dive boat leaves from right behind the shop and takes divers to shallow locations just offshore. All equipment is included. Aloha offers free pick-up from all Waikiki hotels and can arrange to have your dive videotaped. They're located at Koko Marina in Hawaii-Kai Shoping Center. Phone (808) 395-5922; fax (808) 395-8882; website: www.alohadiveshop.com.

Retail Sales: *Extensive*	**Dive Boat Comfort:** *Good*
Rentals: *Extensive*	**On-Board Facilities**
Scuba Training: *Moderate*	**for Photographers:** *Good*
Photo Services: *Moderate*	

Ocean Concepts has five locations around the island and is a PADI Career Development Center, Dive Center, and 5-Star IDC. So you can learn just about anything you'd like here. They also have retail sales, rentals, and repairs. Transportation is provided from all Waikiki hotels. Charter trips go to the *Mahi* wreck and other west coast sites, as well as to south shore, windward, and north shore sites. There is a veritable fleet of dive boats, including a 40-foot custom boat for 32 divers, a 38-foot custom boat for 28 divers, an 85-foot glass-bottom snorkel and dive boat, and another 85-foot snorkel boat. There's also a 40-foot Portafino Executive for private charters that sleeps four and a 28-foot Hawk for private charters or for tech dives that accommodates up to six. A special gear-rental price is $16. Enriched Air Nitrox is pumped with 32 percent and 36 percent oxygen mixes. Special snorkel trips include instruction. There are also guided beach dives, with all gear included. Night dives are scheduled throughout the week. An extensive repair facility is staffed by IAST technicians. Call (800) 808-dive or (808) 677-7975 or (808) 682-2511; fax (808) 682-1031; e-mail: info@ocean concepts.com; website: www.oceanconcepts.com.

Retail Sales: *Extensive*

Rentals: *Extensive*

Scuba Training: *Extensive*

Photo Services: *Moderate*

Dive Boat Comfort: *Excellent*

**On-Board Facilities
for Photographers:** *Good*

South Seas Aquatics is another PADI 5-Star Dive Center, so you can get almost any instruction and specialties you want here. It's a full-retail sales, rental, and repair shop. Tours range from beginner introductory dives and snorkeling to advanced dives at the wreck sites. The 38-foot custom dive boat has freshwater showers, rinse tanks, a marine head, and a nice wide swimming platform. The shop offers free round-trip hotel pickup and return and reasonable rental rates. There are two locations: in Waikiki at Kalakaua Center and in Kapahulu. Call (800) 252-6244, (808) 922-0852, or (808) 735-0437.

Retail Sales: *Extensive*

Rentals: *Extensive*

Scuba Training: *Extensive*

Photo Services: *Moderate*

Dive Boat Comfort: *Excellent*

**On-Board Facilities
for Photographers:** *Good*

WHERE TO STAY ON OAHU

Very few hotels and resorts on Oahu (or the other islands) have diving packages. You need to pick your lodging-of-choice, then contact one of the dive shops. Several will provide free transportation. There are many luxury beach-side resorts on Oahu, which you can book easily through a travel agent. The following, however, are some suggestions for good quality places that are more affordable. Remember that an 11.42 percent tax will be added to your bill.

If you're just on Oahu for a short time and do not care whether you're on the beach or not, check out the **Best Western Plaza Hotel,** near the airport (3253 N. Nimitz Highway). It's an attractive, comfortable place and reasonably priced. There are 274 air-conditioned rooms surrounding a courtyard, a 12-story tower, pretty swimming pool in a tropical setting, a sundry/souvenir shop, sports-theme lounge with satellite-live sporting events and live entertainment, and an attractive restaurant. You can request a room with microwave and refrigerator. And you won't be nickel-and-dimed to death (if you know what I mean). There is free 24-hour airport shuttle service as well as free parking. You'll be about 25 minutes from Waikiki, but only 8 minutes from Pearl Harbor and 12 minutes from the Arizona Memorial and Iolani Palace. Room rates for a double are generally from $110 to $132, but occasionally they are reduced. Call (800) 528-1234 or (800) 800-4683. From neighbor islands call (800) 327-4570 or call the hotel directly at (808) 836-3636; fax (808) 834-7406.

The **Outrigger Hotels and Resorts** chain has 20 properties in the Waikiki area, ranging from deluxe to economy. Many have kitchenettes. Naturally, those on the beach are the most expensive, but don't forget that the beaches are all public, so by taking a short walk to sink your toes in the sand, you could save a bundle. The **Outrigger Waikiki Surf** (302 rooms) and **Outrigger Coral Seas** (109 rooms) are both economy properties with kitchenettes and not far from Waikiki Beach. Room rates are under $100. There are many in the standard category, as well, which is just a bit pricier, and many of these have kitchenettes also. Call (800) OUTRIGGER or (303) 369-7777. The website is www.outrigger.com.

Condos are another good bet on Oahu, especially when traveling with kids. Call Condo Rentals of Waikiki for some recommendations; (800) 927-0555 or (808) 923-0555. One of these that gets rave reviews is **Patrick Winston's Waikiki Condos** (417 Nohonani Street, Suite 409), a five-story condominium hotel between Kuhio Avenue and Ala Wai Boulevard. There are 14 one-bedroom apartments with extra sofa beds and full kitchens. Most have a washer and dryer. On the site are a cocktail lounge and tropical courtyard with pool. Waikiki Beach is two blocks away. Be sure to ask for Patrick Winston's units (as opposed to Hawaiian King Hotel). Rate range for a double is from $85 to $119 in high season, from $65 to $99 in low season. Call (800) 545-1948 or (808) 924-3332; fax (808) 924-3332; website: winstonswaikikicondos.com.

On the north shore, **Ke Ike Hale** has 19 one- and two-bedroom duplex cottages on one and a half acres with 200 feet of beach. This stretch of beach just happens to be smack between Waimea Bay and Banzai Pipeline, and the Shark's Cove snorkeling and diving area is very close. In winter, the breakers here can get enormous, and you would not want to be in the water. In summer it's a different story. The units are modest but comfortable, with kitchens, barbecues, and hammocks (sans TV and phones). There are laundry facilities. A double unit is $85. Call (800) 377-4030 or phone and fax (808) 638-8229.

For campers who want to get away, look up at the stars, and view paradise, get a reservation at **Malaekahana Beach Park** and **Goat Island,** way up on the northeast side. Tent camping is allowed at these sites, with a state permit. Malaekahana also has some rustic beachfront cabins. You'll need all your own bedding and cooking gear, but you'll be right on the edge of a tropical dream, and the only other items you'll need are mask, snorkel, and fins! The park is in Laie, about 23 miles north of Kaneohe on the Kamehameha Highway.

ISLAND LIFE ON OAHU

Considering that it's less than 600 square miles, there's a lot packed into this gathering place (which is what Oahu means). Before we get started, here's a hot tip: if you want to save a bundle of money here, don't rent a car. **The Bus** will take you anywhere; in fact, you can circle the island (#52 or #55) for a buck! It's an efficient, reliable system. Call (808) 848-5555 for recorded information or check out the website at www.thebus.org.

When it's time to explore Oahu, it seems that there's a magnetic force always pulling me to the north shore, and there's no better way to get there than taking an island circle tour, heading counterclockwise from Honolulu. You'll drive along some gorgeous white-sand beaches on the windward coast. But first check out some important sights in the Honolulu area.

Visit **Iolani Palace** in downtown Honolulu. This Renaissance-style mansion was the royal residence until Queen Liliuokalani was overthrown in 1893. Across the street is the **Kamahameha Statue,** honoring Hawaii's first king, who united the island in 1795. Also visit **Pearl Harbor** and view the sunken *U.S.S. Arizona,* just below the water's surface. The museum is directly above the ship, right in the middle of the harbor. National Park Service Rangers provide historical insights.

Now put pedal to the metal and get thee to the hills! Head over to **Diamond Head** and hike up it. You'll get great coastal views and see some of the hillside bunkers. After driving past Hawaii Kai and Hanauma Bay, you'll actually be able to see Molokai and Lanai on the horizon. You'll see an overlook at **Halona Blowhole,** and between December and April this is a good whale-watching spot. Watch the surfers at popular **Sandy Beach,** then make your next destination **Makapuu Point,** the beginning of green-velvet mountain ridges falling upon miles of windswept beaches. Watch the windsurfers at Lanikai Point, then follow the Kahekili Highway to **Haiku Gardens** and the **"Valley of the Temples"**—memorials to the Japanese. Kaneohe Bay is known for its offshore barrier reef as well as its near-shore ancient fish ponds. These ingenious rock-bound enclosures were constructed by the early Polynesians for raising fish—really fascinating.

If the tummy starts rumbling, stop at the **Paniolo Café** in Punaluu for good fresh seafood and ribs. Now head on around the point toward the north shore surfing spots. If you've ever watched any of the old surfing movies like *Endless Summer,* undoubtedly you've heard of **Sunset Beach** and **Waimea Bay.** They are legendary, but whatever you do, don't even think about tackling the big guys on the North Shore when the surf is really rolling, which is in winter. Just come on up to watch. It's truly breathtaking to see the experts play on these unbelievable walls of water. Once those waves break, a surfer can be submerged under a mountain of foam for too many lung-aching seconds, or even minutes. Instead, try Makapuu or Sandy Beach.

There are two good vantage points for watching the surfers: **Ehukai Beach Park,** just off Kamehameha Highway, and **Puu O Mahuka Heiau,** an ancient Hawaiian temple above Sunset Beach on Pupukea Road. Waimea Bay can get absolutely monster waves, but when I saw it, it was glassy calm. So it can also be a great place for swimming and picnicking. In **Haleiwa,** grab a bite to eat at Café Haleiwa, a local favorite. On a hot day Haleiwa's famous shaved ice concoctions in tropical-fruit flavors are heavenly.

For some great hiking, go to Manoa Valley and take the **Manoa Falls Trail.** The valley is only 15 minutes north of Waikiki. In this rain-forest experience you'll see a lush, cooling retreat, complete with a waterfall and assorted bird life.

Dining and Entertainment

You'll find on Oahu that restaurant meals are expensive. But guess what, any food here is expensive; just go to one of the markets and check out the prices. It's really surprising. One way to economize on meals here is to have a kitchen wherever you're staying and fix some of your own meals. But, let's face it, you're on vacation, so who wants to do that all the time? Another alternative—a delicious one—is to feast on *saimin,* the Hawaiian noodle soup. There are many varieties, so try several. Best of all, they're nutritious, inexpensive, and kids love em. They're also plentiful, so just ask around to find a place near your hotel.

It's always fun to see some entertainment, especially Hawaiian-style. Rainbow Lanai of Waikiki's **Hilton Hawaiian Village** puts on a good show on Fridays that is free, and should you decide to also have dinner, it'll be less than $20. Many of the Outrigger hotels have good beach-type entertainment. For a great view of Diamond Head with fresh seafood and Hawaiian music, go to Duke's Canoe Club in the **Outrigger Waikiki Hotel,** which is very reasonably priced. Also check the *Honolulu Weekly* to see what's going on around town.

Medical Facilities

There are several medical centers on Oahu, and a recompression chamber in Honolulu. For the chamber, call (808) 523-9155.

In case of a diving emergency call DAN (Divers Alert Network) at (919) 684-4DAN (4326) or (919) 684-8111.

Kauai

THE UNDERWATER SCENE

Kauai is the oldest and northernmost island in the Hawaiian chain. There are areas with good diving, but my advice is not to come here solely to dive. Your primary motivation for visiting Kauai should be to experience and luxuriate in this lush, tropical Garden of Eden. But while you're here, why not dive!

The reason for this caveat is that diving conditions can be rough. The island frequently gets high winds with corresponding heavy ocean swells. That tends to play havoc with visibility, and access to the dive areas is made difficult. However, the south shore, in the Poipu Beach area, generally has stable conditions and is a favorite for dive operations. In the summer, when conditions usually are best, other areas are also fair game.

Recommended Level of Experience

In most circumstances, novice divers won't have a problem—snorkelers either, for that matter. It's only when conditions get rough that only more experienced divers should be in the water. Usually, though, the dive operations simply won't go out in those circumstances.

Divers should not combine diving and hiking to high elevations on the same day. If you intend to ascend to an altitude of 8,000 feet or more after diving, the general rules of flying apply. For most divers, that means waiting at sea level for at least 12 hours.

Great Dive Sites

Sheraton Caves, near Poipu on the south shore, is the spot dived most often. It is fairly shallow (20 to 60 feet) and perfect for novice and intermediate divers. The site consists of interconnecting lava tubes. My dive bud and I had a great time swimming in and out of tunnels and through arches—an underwater playground! There were plenty of fish hanging out, as well as a friendly spotted moray and some brilliantly colored Hawaiian lobsters hunkered down in holes.

A site nearby called *General Store* doesn't have such an impressive structure, but it features lots of fish. You'll see plenty of butterflyfish, including the interesting long nose variety. This is a good spot for underwater photographers.

If conditions are optimal, dive operators might take you directly opposite, to the north shore. This will really be a treat, since this is Kauai's lush, amazingly beautiful rain forest. I kayak-surfed here in Hanalei Bay, with the craggy green-embossed cliffs rising dramatically from the shoreline.

Spectacular! To the east, around Kilauea Point National Wildlife Refuge, is another reputedly good dive spot with a huge arch and several caves. Such pelagic species as sharks, turtles, and dolphins frequently visit.

Shallow Diving and Snorkeling

Besides the *Sheraton Caves* area, several other very good dive sites are scattered along the south shore. They just don't get as much attention. *Koloa Landing,* also near the Poipu resort area, is one of these. To get down to the landing you'll drive toward the Spouting Horn, then turn onto Ho'onani Road. Take the rough little road down to the landing. This protected inlet is also a good spot for snorkeling. The shallow sandy area features a horseshoe-shaped reef that is covered with coral and a terrific assortment of Hawaii's finest tropicals. *Tortugas,* directly in front of Poipu Beach Park, is the place to spot green sea turtles, all protected by state law. Remember to never grab hold of one; they need to come up for air too!

Up on the north side, shore diving and snorkeling from *Tunnels Beach* is very good in summer. The correct name for the place is Makua Beach, but the surfers who come here like to call it Tunnels. It's very accessible, being just off of Highway 560 and west of Hanalei Bay. The site consists of some interesting structure—lava tubes, crevices, and ledges—at depths ranging from 15 feet to about 65 feet. Look for Hawaii's endemic cleaner wrasse at any of the numerous cleaning stations you'll find here. Remember that this side of the island attracts the pelagic species, so keep an eye out for reef sharks, turtles, and dolphins.

DIVE SERVICES & PACKAGES ON KAUAI

Bubbles Below Scuba Charters works out of Port Allen (there is no physical storefront) and offers personalized outings with small groups (six to eight). Divers interested in learning about marine biology (or at least finding out what's going on down there) will enjoy their trips. Bubbles uses a 35-foot custom dive boat equipped with a hot (say *hot*) shower, a freshwater camera rinse bin and a marine head. The shop caters to divers but will accept snorkelers if space permits. A special all-day trip in summer takes experienced divers to the "forbidden" island of Niihau, 25 miles west of Kauai. This is a three-tank dive, and ascent and descent is in open ocean without an anchor line. The 90-minute ride is usually choppy (consider taking seasick meds) and the current can be strong, but the rewards are great—a dramatic vertical drop-off, huge caverns, and resident sharks. Bubbles has a complete line of rental equipment. Call (808) 332-REEF (7333); e-mail: kaimanu@aloha.net; website: www.aloha.net/~kaimanu.

Retail Sales: *None*

Rentals: *Adequate*

Scuba Training: *None*

Photo Services: *None*

Dive Boat Comfort: *Excellent*

**On-Board Facilities
for Photographers:** *Good*

On the south side is **Fathom Five Adventures,** (3450 Poipu Road) in Koloa, with 15 years on the island. It's about five minutes from Poipu Beach and Kukuiula Harbor. Dive sites are only 10 to 15 minutes from the harbor. More than 20 sites are dived ranging from 30 to 90 feet. This is a PADI 5-Star IDC facility, specializing in scuba training for newbies to instructor wannabes. NAUI and SSI open-water certs are also possible. A couple of custom-built Radons take a maximum of six divers each, which allows them to divide the groups into experience levels. The shop also organizes night dives, shore dives, refresher two-tank dives, refresher one-tank shore dives, and even noncertified two-tank boat dives and one-tank shore dives. Rental equipment is available. Call (800) 972-3078 or (808) 742-6991; e-mail: fathom5@fathom-five.com; website: www.fathomfive.com.

Retail Sales: *Extensive*

Rentals: *Extensive*

Scuba Training: *Extensive*

Photo Services: *Moderate*

Dive Boat Comfort: *Good*

**On-Board Facilities
for Photographers:** *Good*

WHERE TO STAY ON KAUAI

Although expensive, the **Hyatt Regency Kauai Resort & Spa** (1571 Poipu Road), in Koloa, really delivers in terms of service, facilities, and activities. It evokes a plantation-era ambiance, on 50 acres overlooking Shipwreck Beach. The four-story, 602-unit resort is built into the oceanside bluffs and manages to carry out a casual, comfortable atmosphere despite its luxurious appointments. Rooms are large and most have private lanais overlooking the ocean. The swimming possibilities, alone, are impressive. These include an elaborate freshwater fantasy pool complex, and two additional pools, plus five acres of saltwater swimming lagoons with island and a manufactured beach. Other facilities include a lavish spa and tennis courts. An excellent guest-activity program will get you out kayaking, horseback riding, and dune-walking. There are several restaurants, bars, and entertainment. No dive packages are available, and there is no dive shop on the property. Rates are from $310 to $520 for a double. Call (800) 55-HYATT or (808) 742-1234; fax (808) 742-1557; website: www.hyatt.com.

Another high-end luxury resort, although much more intimate, is **Whalers Cove** (2640 Puuholo Road), in Poipu. There are only 38 suites on a beautiful secluded cove. The suites are either one-bedroom or two-bedroom and feature washers and dryers, Jacuzzi tubs, and walk-in closets. Each living room opens to a private lanai, which overlooks the ocean and Turtle Cove, once the docking site for whaling ships. Turtles, monk seals, and whales are frequently spotted offshore. Each suite also has a fully equipped kitchen. Facilities include an oceanfront swimming pool, spa, and barbecue area. Golf, tennis, and horseback riding are available close by. Restaurants are a mile away. No dive packages are available, and there is no dive shop on the property. The nightly rate for a one-bedroom ocean-view suite for two is $310; the two-bedroom ocean-view suite that accommodates up to six people is $380. Phone (800) 225-2683 or (808) 742-7571; fax (808) 742-1185; e-mail: whalers@hawaiian.net; website: www.premier-resorts.com.

Now for a dose of reality, still in the Poipu area. The **Poipu Kapili Resort** (2221 Kapili Road), in Koloa, is an oceanfront cluster of 62 condos with ocean views. The nearest sandy beach, however, is a block away. The units are large and have fully equipped kitchens. Facilities include swimming pool, tennis courts, barbecues, and an herb garden. No dive packages are available, and there is no dive shop on the property. The one-bedroom apartment, which sleeps four, is from $170 to $200. There are also two-bedroom apartments. The minimum stay is three nights, and special package rates are available. Call (800) 443-7714 or (808) 742-6449; fax (808) 742-9162; website: www.poipukapili.com.

Classic Vacation Cottages (2687 Onu Place), in Kalaheo, is about a seven-minute drive to Poipu beaches, but the five units are beautifully decorated. Also, each has a fully equipped kitchen and a private lanai. Classic Vacation even supplies snorkeling equipment, boogie boards, and beach towels. It's in a pleasant, peaceful location in the hills, complete with hiking trails. The room rate for a double is $70. Call (808) 742-7522 or (808) 332-9201; fax (808) 332-7645; e-mail: clascot@hawaiian.net.

If you're looking for an inexpensive condo, definitely call **Grantham Resorts,** which handles condos and vacation homes. The condos all have a three-day minimum stay. Call (800) 325-5701 or (808) 742-2000; fax (808) 742-9093; website: www.grantham-resorts.com.

ISLAND LIFE ON KAUAI

It's no wonder that Hollywood loves Kauai. Watch *Jurassic Park, Raiders of the Lost Ark, King Kong,* and *Lord of the Flies,* for starters, and you'll see Kauai. It can only be described as fantastic—a lush, natural magical fantasy. My first view of Kauai was just a couple of months after Hurricane Iniki virtually wiped out the island, and it was still beautiful. That was in 1992, and of course now it is fully recovered. Nature recovered very quickly; the man-made structures took a bit longer.

This Garden Isle is 70 miles northwest of Oahu across a channel that can get violent. Most of the island is forest preserve and little of it is crossed by roads. In the island's center is the wettest spot on earth. Mount Waialeale is an extinct volcano and the source of Kauai's five rivers.

Definitely strike out and explore. You'll find fields of taro, sugarcane, guava, papayas, bananas, coffee, and macadamia nuts. There are vintage villages like Hanapepe, in the Waimea area, and Hanalei, up north. And there are botanical gardens, beach parks, and wildlife refuges.

I love to kayak here, and admire the craggy mountain cliffs and the way they fall in downy green folds to the coastline. Hikers, especially, like Kauai, and most of the trails are around the Na Pali Coast and Waimea Canyon-Kokee regions. The 11-mile trail to Kalalau, along the rugged Na Pali Coast, is a favorite of Kauai aficionados. Call the State Department of Land and Natural Resources for more information about hiking trails: (808) 241-3444.

Note: Elevations here soar above 5,000 feet. Divers should not dive and hike these high elevations on the same day. Wait at least eight hours before heading up to the mountains.

Dining and Entertainment

The grand resorts have fabulous restaurants with the very best Pacific Rim cuisine. But for casual dining, it's fun to just get out, explore, and sample what the locals like to eat.

Even right after Iniki devastated the island, **Hamura's Saimin Stand** still stood and still served, while most establishments around it shut down. This is a well-regarded, although humble, place with excellent steaming bowls of noodles, vegetables, and an almost infinite variety of condiments. There are just a few U-shaped counters. Hamura's is at 2956 Kress Street in Lihue.

For more dishes-on-the-run, try the "plate lunch" counters that serve two scoops of your choice: rice, potato, or macaroni. With it comes a meat or fish entree, and most of the time that's fried. Don't forget shave-ice for a refreshing treat.

Island music is mostly concentrated in the resorts, unless it's coming from feathered vocalists high up in the trees. One spot in Hanalei, however, has an entire variety of musical choices: reggae, jazz, blues, and rock. It's **Sushi & Blues** in the Ching Young Village. Oh, yes, contemporary Hawaiian music is featured during Sunday afternoon Happy Hour.

Medical Facilities

Wilcox Memorial Hospital, at 3420 Kuhio Highway, is in Lihue. Call (808) 245-1100. The closest recompression chamber is in Honolulu. Call (808) 523-9155.

In case of a diving emergency call DAN (Divers Alert Network) at (919) 684-4DAN (4326) or (919) 684-8111.

Honduras:
The Bay Islands

Physical Characteristics of the Dive Area	
WATER & WEATHER CONDITIONS	
Visibility	*Excellent*
Current and Surge	*Minimal*
Temperature	*Comfortable*
Storms	*Occasionally Stormy*
SITE CONDITIONS	
Mooring Buoys	*Extensive*
Fishing, Collecting, and Hunting Restrictions	*Widespread Restrictions*
Ease of Access	*Very Easy*
Boat Traffic/Diver Congestion	*Light*
MARINE LIFE	
Abundance of Invertebrates	*Prolific*
Abundance of Vertebrates	*Abundant*
Abundance of Pelagic Life	*Prolific*
Health of Reef/Marine Life/ Marine Structure	*Pristine*

Tropical Corner of the Caribbean

Just a geographical stone's throw from Belize, the Bay Islands of Honduras (Isla de Bahia) rise out of the ocean on the edge of visual range from the Honduran mainland. Lush mountain ranges and tropical jungles that seem to spill into the sea distinguish this Central American beauty and its Caribbean Bay Islands. In 1998 Hurricane Mitch came tearing through Honduras wreaking terrible havoc, from which the mainland is still suffering. But for the most part, the Bay Islands have recovered nicely and many of the old tired structures have been rebuilt and now look better than ever. Step into Roatan's modern air-conditioned airport, and you *know* that something's going on here that's not happening in the rest of Honduras. The answer, of course, is tourism, and that means dollars.

Despite the Central American location, the cultural nature of these islands—four major ones and a plethora of smaller islands and cayes (pronounced keys)—is decidedly Caribbean. Roatan, the largest island, is about 40 miles long with a central ridge running along its length. It is covered in lush vegetation and has plenty of freshwater runoff from the hills. Roatan is completely encircled by the enormous barrier reef that is also shared by Cozumel and Belize. Dynamic diving lies just body lengths from shore. Plummeting walls decorated with an abundance of coral varieties, sponges, and other invertebrates characterize Honduras diving generally. In addition, Roatan offers several good wreck dives as well as an opportunity to snorkel with dolphins.

The "lesser" islands of Utila, Guanaja, and Barbareta all have dive resorts and epitomize the Bay Islands' tucked-away type of experience. In fact, neither Guanaja nor Barbareta have roads.

Utila and the island grouping called Cayos Cochinos are the most remote and undeveloped of the Bay Islands and therefore have the most pristine underwater conditions. They both feature vertical walls and a greater abundance of fish than the more developed islands, as well as healthy giant sponges and monumental formations of elkhorn coral. Is a whale shark still on your wish list? dolphins, perhaps? Utila just might work for you. Shipwrecks and labyrinths of lava rock characterize Guanaja diving. Only three-by-seven miles in size, this island offers more than 50 moored dive sites, including a 6,000-foot wall.

Although Spain historically dominated Honduras, the Bay Islands were influenced primarily by England; therefore, English is the primary language. For decades British pirates plundered Spanish ships, colonies on the islands, and countries neighboring Honduras. The famous, or infamous, Sir Henry Morgan was among them. Pirating was a lucrative enterprise throughout the 1600s, until the raiding was curtailed by the British military. Many of the pirates settled on Roatan and turned to farming. In the 1800s there was an influx of settlers from Grand Cayman, of Scottish and English descent.

On the Honduran mainland, San Pedro Sula is the capital and center of activity. From this city, as well as from La Ceiba, excursions can be made

to the ancient Mayan temples of Copan, to banana plantations, waterfalls, and rainforests. Whitewater rafting in Honduras is among the most exciting in the world.

If you're looking for a place to get away from it all and enjoy a touch of rusticity, this is it—the perfect diver's hideaway. You won't find shopping malls or nightclubs. Après-dive activity in the Bay Islands consists of doing time in a hammock, enjoying the warm tradewinds blowing through the fronds of palm trees, and sipping on a tropical drink.

Warning: The Bay Islands are in the tropics, which means two things: wonderful wildlife and bothersome bugs. Sand fleas and mosquitoes are as evident as gorgeous butterflies and hummingbirds. Be sure to bring insect repellent and lightweight clothing to keep covered up in the evening. Malaria is a possibility in the islands, especially during the rainy season.

QUICK STATS

Size   The Bay Islands consists of 3 large islands and about 65 smaller islands. Roatan, 40 miles long, spans almost 50 square miles; Guanaja, 11 miles long, measures 29 square miles; and little Utila measures only 7 miles by 3 miles.

Population   Around 50,000

Location   The Bay Islands are from 10 to 35 miles from mainland Honduras in Central America. Roatan, the largest and most populated island, lies between the neighboring islands of Guanaja (Isla de Guanaja), to the east, and Utila, to the west.

Time Zone   Central Time Zone

Government   Great Britain restored the Bay Islands to the Honduran government in 1861. Honduras has a democratic form of government.

Language   English and Spanish

Electrical Current   110 volts AC, 60 cycles—same as in the United States.

Weather   It is generally sunny, with the air temperature usually in the 80s and the humidity near 80 percent. Cooling trade winds blow most of the year. October through January is the rainy season, when there can be churned-up seas, poor underwater visibility, and swarms of mosquitoes. Hurricanes are a possibility any time from June through September.

Water Temperature   78° to 80°

Underwater Visibility   Ranges from 75 to 150 feet.

Best Diving Months   Try to avoid the rainy season, from October through January, when mosquitoes are most likely to appear and underwater visibility can be reduced.

PLANNING THE TRIP

Phoning the Bay Islands   From North America, first dial the international access code (011), then the country code (504), then the local phone number.

Getting to the Bay Islands   TACA Airlines (800-4-ROATAN) has direct flights to Roatan from Houston, New Orleans, and Miami. TACA also has one-stop flights to San Pedro Sula or Belize City, with connections to Guanaja, Roatan, or Utila on local carriers (Rollins, SOSA, and Islena). Flying time from Miami to Roatan is only two hours. The airport on Roatan is excellent—modern and air-conditioned. There is a $2 fee collected upon entry and a $20 departure tax.

Getting Around   On Roatan, taxis, rental cars, and public transportation are all available. The larger resorts offer airport shuttle service.

Entry Documents   A valid passport and return airline ticket are required. U.S. and Canadian citizens do not need a visa.

Health Warning   Although not a huge problem, cases of malaria do occur here, especially during the rainy season, from October through January. Typhoid and hepatitis A should also be considered. Contact the Center for Disease Control (www.cdc.gov/travel) for updated warnings. Bring a good insect repellent and clothing to cover arms and legs.

Currency   The Lempira is used throughout Honduras; conversion is around 14L to US$1, but it fluctuates.

Tourist Office   Honduras Institute of Tourism, P.O. Box 140458, Coral Gables, FL 33114-0458. Call (800) 410-9608. You can get more information from the website: www.roatan.com. Another good site is by the *Coconut Telegraph:* www.bayislands.com.

THE UNDERWATER SCENE

Geologically, the Bay Islands belong to the volcanic and coral mountain range that skirts the coastline. Called the Bonacca Ridge, it consists of a core of volcanic rock surrounded by an ancient limestone shelf. The underwater topography consists of fissures, cracks, tunnels, and other features that are unique to such volcanic geology. This interesting terrain provides a healthy habitat for marine life, with all sorts of areas for invertebrates to thrive and for fish, eels, and other marine life to find shelter.

Along the northern side of the primary island chain, a large lagoon spreads out between the islands and the reef. Beyond the lagoon lies an almost solid wall, with just a few narrow channels running through it. On the south side, which has no lagoon, the reef begins right at the shoreline and both patch reef and spur and groove configurations slope gradually down to a steep precipice. Several sea mounts lie within a few miles of Utila's coast. Most reach up to within 30 to 45 feet of the surface and slope down to as deep as 200 feet. These are loaded with soft corals, and pelagics definitely cruise by. Utila is also known for the awesome whale sharks that feed in the area year-round.

The Cayos Cochinos are the only islands that are not part of the primary chain. This group, also known as the Hog Islands, is located between the mainland and Roatan. The entire Cochinos archipelago is a protected biological reserve. Refer to the sidebar in this chapter for more information about this incredible group of islands.

The Bay Islands claim more than 800 species of fish and 60 species of corals—elkhorn, star, brain, lettuce, and pillar, as well as bushes of black coral. Guanaja, especially, is known for its gorgeous stands of pillar corals that rise up from the reef ridges. Although it's a hard coral, pillar corals expose their polyps in the daytime, so you'll see the tentacles waving in the current, catching any plankton that might be drifting by.

Bluebell tunicates in the Bay Islands are absolutely stunning, and in my opinion are one of the great rewards of diving here. You'll find them in clusters and usually in shallow areas. Photographers take note—they stand still! You'll be able to get some really great shots. Try to capture some billowy black coral (which is white) in the composition, as well. The tunicates are not as plentiful around Roatan, but you'll see them in the Cochinos area and in Utila and Guanaja.

Roatan's north and south coastlines each offer 30 miles of excellent diving possibilities. Dive sites are all around the perimeter of the island. Guanaja has around 50 dive sites and has put in about 30 mooring buoys. Utila features around 100 dive sites, 40 with mooring buoys, and has gained a reputation for its exciting pelagic sightings, especially the whale sharks. Banks rise up from the ocean floor and surround the island, offering divers adrenaline-producing drop-offs into the abyss. The deep-water seamounts provide even more variety and excitement. About 80 percent of Utila is mangrove swamp, the perfect environment for marine nurseries.

Health Score Card

For the most part, the area is extremely healthy. The more pristine areas are generally the most remote. For example, the waters around Utila and the Cayos Cochinos are some of the most biologically diverse marine ecosystems in the Caribbean.

On the south side of Roatan, the area around French Harbor should be avoided. This is a center for commercial fishing; also, squatters living along the water's edge dump raw sewage into the water. Storms, particularly Hurricane Mitch from 1998, have caused some damage to corals and sponges, but evidence of this is primarily in the shallow areas.

Diving Conditions

Diving conditions here are excellent, for the most part. The dive sites that are farther out in open ocean are subject to stronger currents and rougher seas. Generally, however, currents are mild and the visibility is exceptional.

Due to the rough ironshore along the beach, most dives are from boats. If you do dive from shore, be sure to wear hard-soled booties.

Recommended Level of Experience

Any level of diver would have a superb time in the Bay Islands.

Great Dive Sites

There are many dive sites in these waters, and most of them are exceptional. The following selection is intended solely to offer an idea of the types of terrain you might encounter. Dive resorts usually visit the sites that are close by, thereby avoiding long boat rides, so where you dive largely will depend on the resort you choose. That's especially true on Roatan, where diving is all around the island.

Roatan Sites   Along Roatan's north shore on the west end are numerous sites that receive the benefits of protection by the marine park. West End Wall, beginning at about 60 feet, features a colorful, healthy concentration of corals and huge overhanging barrel sponges. The following sites start from the south side and progress around the west end to the north shore, then go east.

Mary's Place, on Roatan's south side, is an unusual dive that's best for intermediate-level divers, due to the overhead environments. The top of the reef starts in only 20 feet, along a wall. Divers will find a protrusion from the wall that can be entered through a volcanic fissure. Enter the fissure and follow it (to about 70 feet) to another one that meets it at a right angle. Swim through this one, which is shallower, back out to the wall. It's a sort of circuitous route, which your divemaster will undoubtedly lead. Inside the fissures at shallow depths, copper sweepers and grouper hang out among bushes of black coral. The wall here is beautiful but tends to be overshadowed by this intriguing structure.

Also on the south side is CoCo View Wall, which has a number of excellent sites and some sunken wrecks.

Hole in the Wall is a really fun but deep wall dive on the north shore that is best for advanced divers. You'll start off by following a sandy slope to 60 feet, where there is a large crack in the wall. After entering this fissure, you'll make a steep descent to another sandy area that is also sloping. It's important to level off at this point, which is at about 120 feet. If you were to continue down the slope, your computer might "wig out" and the divemaster probably would not be happy. Although this is called "*hole* in the wall," actually there are several holes. One is at about 180 feet, and when you ascend the wall you'll be alongside another one. Wonderful, dramatic coral ledges project way over the wall. At shallower depths you'll enter more tunnels and swim-throughs. Look for lobster, juvenile blennies, and angelfish. While making your safety stop, look around in the water column. I noticed buttercup jellyfish here, about the size of large thimbles, and fascinating pelagic tunicates with shimmering lines running down the length of their translucent bodies.

Bear's Den is a cave dive and among my favorite sites on Roatan. However, because of the overhead environments it can be intimidating, and novice divers should avoid it. The dive begins by entering a nice tunnel through the coral, beginning on a gravel bottom. Weaving around, you'll then ascend through the tunnel and out onto the wall. Brilliant blue chromis school along and on top of the wall. Ascending to a depth of only 25 feet, you'll enter the cave. It snakes in, narrowing at first, then opening a little with a shaft of light shining through. You'll veer off to the left, losing sight of the entrance, and enter a short tunnel, which then opens into a wide chamber. Shafts of brilliant light enter through openings in the top, illuminating the walls and the white sandy bottom. It's an ethereal effect that will have you wishing you could stay longer.

Barry's Reef and *Four Sponges,* both on the north shore, are like the Grand Canyon gone aquatic. An enormous plateau of coral—a flat, table-like formation—features fantastic cuts and tunnels. Shelves of hard corals stairstep down to a sandy bottom at about 175 feet. Pillar coral and large sponges decorate *Lighthouse Reef,* also on the north shore.

Wrasse Hole is a wall with a series of shelves down to the sandy bottom at about 150 feet. It's shot through with cuts and swim-throughs and is loaded with healthy corals and reef fish. Down at about 104 feet I spotted some eagle rays here. Nurse sharks are also common. Big, friendly grouper hang out here and at *Peter's Place.* They'll follow divers along the wall and into crevices and canyons watched over by moray eels. At *Deep Eel Garden,* both garden eels and chimneys through the coral structure are the highlights of this wall dive.

Guanaja Sites   January and February when the moon is full, *Devil's Cauldron* is the venue du jour, when many species of grouper migrate here to spawn. Divers comfortable diving deep and in heavy current will enjoy being voyeurs at this wild orgy. The top of the reef, however, is about 100 feet, descending to ravine depths of 140 feet. There is a mooring buoy, which helps.

For a more benign (but still deep) dive, the 240-foot *Jado Trader* rests at 100 feet on the south side, and the wall continues to plummet into the great beyond. Large grouper, jewfish, and morays call the *Jado* home.

Black Rocks is a series of caverns and tunnels weaving through the volcanic wall for more than a mile. If you like overhead environments, as I do, you'll love this. Otherwise, forget it. You'll see lots of ins and outs—tunnels, swim-throughs, caverns, and caves—inhabited by all the creatures that love these environments, namely lobster, glassy sweepers, and squirrelfish. But don't expect to see a lot of coral growth or an abundance of fish and other marine life.

Utila Sites   On the north side of the island, on the edge of the continental shelf is where whale sharks frequently are spotted, and occasionally pods of pilot whales. *Willy's Hole* is on this side in the Turtle Harbor Marine Reserve, and divers can often see these gentle giants on the way out. Willy's starts in only 15 feet of water, then suddenly plummets—all the way down, way farther than you should think about going. There are fun swim-throughs and a cavern at about 70 feet, so you don't really need to dive deep.

Black Hill on the southeast side is another site that holds promise for spotting pelagic life. You could find whale sharks or hammerheads anywhere around this ocean seamount. Typical of many other dive sites in this area, you'll drop down the side of the pinnacle (about 80 feet), then work your way up to the top at around 40 feet.

Cayos Cochinos Sites The *Pelican Wall,* just off Pelican Point on Grande Cochinos, has some magnificent vistas and a wonderful array of marine life. The shallow wall, which drops to about 110 feet, is festooned with black coral bushes and covered with a prolific amount of hard corals. On top of the wall are several types of brain coral. Look for the little critters, such as banded coral shrimp, flamingo tongue, plume worms, and feather duster worms. But watch out, there's a lot of fire coral on top of the wall, as well. Blue chromis swarm all about. A bit deeper are yellow tube sponges, yellow tunicates, clumps of bluebell tunicates, and azure vase sponges. At one of the sites along this wall I was amused, watching French angelfish biting at the air bubbles emitted by my dive buddy. Farther down the wall are huge mounds of plate coral, an assortment of tube sponges of all colors, and giant yellow anemones. Encrusting sponges look like patchwork quilts in colors of peach, orange, and blue. Terrific crevices and chimneys slice through the wall, illuminated by shafts of light entering the openings.

Pelican III is a particularly beautiful site for wide-angle photography, with lots of photo ops from "inside" the wall—in the cuts and swim-throughs—looking out into open water. The top of the wall here has some stunning mounds of hard corals and also branching elkhorn coral where schools of blue tang dance over the golden antlers. Groups of copper sweepers hang out in the crevices and tunnels.

Flamingo I, off of Grande Cochinos, is another huge and impressive wall site. Incredible mounds of plate coral build on top of one another in skyscraper structures. Green leafy algae glistens in the sunlight. Lettuce and sheet corals grow in healthy and huge proportions, along with mountainous star coral.

Shallower sites (about 56 feet), such as *Bunker Cove* and *Lion's Head,* about 75 yards off of Grande Cochinos, will give you plenty of time to check out the unique species in this area. At *Lion's Head* I noticed under a rocky ledge a glass-eye snapper that actually turned a brighter red as the divemaster approached it. Amazingly, he was actually able to touch the fish. He then coaxed a reclusive sailfin blenny from its rocky habitat. The blenny popped out, dramatically flaring its colorful dorsal fin. While my dive buddy was following the trail of a conch on the sandy bottom, I happened to notice a cute little whiskered burrfish with wide green eyes. As I approached it, in a slow, nonthreatening manner, the little guy just hovered over the sand watching me. A member of the puffer family, it looked like a put-together, eight-inch-long jigsaw puzzle that might break apart into a hundred pieces if it ever actually moved. Puffers are normally very shy. But that's the beauty of diving in pristine, protected waters. Fish have no reason to fear humans, so mask-to-eyeball encounters like this are possible, as long as your movements remain careful and nonthreatening. This site also had some large coral heads, surrounded by white sand, bluebell tunicates, yellow tunicates, flowing white feather dusters, and garden eels. Look out for large torpedo-shaped cobia with remora tagging along underneath.

The surface intervals alone in this area are worth the effort to get out here. This part of Grande Cochinos is gorgeous, with white sandy beach, palm trees, and rocky cliffs.

Charlotte's Choice off one of the small cays in the Cochinos is absolutely loaded with layer upon layer of hard corals. The spot is incredibly healthy. It was here that I spotted a cryptic teardrop crab, a round and reddish little thing that had a living sponge on its carapace! At *Sand Cay* we barely spotted a golden-brown large eye toadfish. It was well camouflaged, but its barbells hanging out from its rocky home gave it away.

Shallow Diving and Snorkeling

Off of Roatan, all of the following sites are along the north shore, which is the calm, leeward side.

Over Heath Reef in daylight is a paradise for photographers. On top of the reef are schools of blue chromis and numerous angelfish, pufferfish, and trunkfish. The depth of 54 feet makes this an excellent night dive, as well.

Green Outhouse Wall is a wonderful shallow dive on the north shore of Roatan with enormous grouper. Watch them lying on the sand getting their daily cleaning by purple-banded shrimp. Schools of chub soar up, over and around spectacular stands of pillar coral. There's one grouping of pillar coral here that reminded me of a medieval castle in a storybook enchanted kingdom. On a night dive I was able to hold a little trunkfish gently in the palm of my hand. The octopus were numerous, including one enormous one that moved along the side of the wall, extending its long arms way out over the edge. Dive lights reveal eels and lobster and the glimmering eyes of fast-moving shrimp.

White Hole, also on the north side of Roatan, has long deep ravines of brilliant white sand cutting through meadows of coral. As you fin across the sand, the coral walls rise up on either side of you as much as 20 feet. The shallow depths and white background make this an excellent spot for photographing your dive buddy. The pillar coral is beautiful here, also.

Snorkeling around the Bay Islands Beach Resort is excellent. There are several areas, including Spooky Channel and a buoyed snorkel trail, which will take you through a number of different marine habitats, to see the full range of marine species.

From the other islands, snorkeling is excellent around all of the resorts, most of which are on the leeward (calm) side. Snorkelers will have an opportunity to see plenty of sea fans and other soft corals, as well as elkhorn and staghorn coral. You'll see schools of grunts, snappers, blue tang, and a plethora of the more solitary tropicals. Look for moray eels and octopus. And don't forget to search the shallow sea grass beds for seahorses, crabs, and spiny lobster.

Marine Park

Residents remember a time when the area now encompassing Roatan's Sandy Bay-West End Marine Reserve had deteriorated to an alarming extent. "Several years ago, this area had been seriously depleted of fish, lobster and conch. The coral reef was also deteriorating from anchor and boat damage and over-exploitation," according to the Bay Islands Conservation Association, which now supervises the reserve, established in 1989.

Today, the coral reefs within the Marine Conservation Sanctuary are teeming with life, and offer researchers and snorkel and scuba diving enthusiasts an opportunity to experience an exciting, colorful, and highly biologically productive and diverse coral reef ecosystem.

Persons anchoring on the reef, collecting live shells, spearing, dumping trash, or engaging in other reef-threatening activities are liable for fines and up to 90 days in jail. Mooring buoys are common on Roatan sites, and are becoming even more so thanks to efforts by the Bay Islands Conservation Association, Reef Relief, and the U.S. Peace Corps. To discourage touching or grabbing corals, divers and snorkelers may not wear gloves.

In 1996 the Guanaja Marine Reserve was established and encompasses the waters surrounding the island. It is said that more than 95 percent of the coral varieties in the Caribbean are found in the fringing reef system. Thirty reef mooring buoys have been installed to prevent anchor damage.

Recently, the Honduran government decreed the whale shark a protected species in its territorial waters, with severe penalties for violators. Passage of the new law makes Honduras the first nation in the Caribbean to protect whale sharks.

DIVE SERVICES & PACKAGES

Roatan

Anthony's Key Resort has a fleet of six 42-foot boats, each with a capacity of 18 divers. A 35-foot boat is used for dolphin dives, and a 48-foot custom dive boat takes divers on remote offshore trips. A 51-foot flattop dive cruiser is dedicated to snorkel tours. Certifying agencies are PADI and PDIC. Anthony's is a PADI Gold Palm IDC Resort, so all levels of instruction are offered, from open water to instructor. For youngsters, the SASY program is offered for children from five years old; the Bubble Makers program for children ages eight to ten; and the Junior Open Water certification for children over ten years old. The shop has a complete photo facility (Photo Roatan) with camera, lenses and strobe rentals, custom shoots, photo instruction, and print and E-6 film processing. Enriched Air Nitrox is available, with several levels of certification, along with 11 other specialty courses. Rental equipment is extensive and includes dive computers and lights. Shore diving or night channel diving can be done every day, but are limited to the dive shop's hours of operation. Shore diving is done in the lagoon in front of the dive shop, where there is a reef that bottoms out at about 35 feet, and an airplane wreck. Snorkeling packages include two daily boat trips with guide, reef ecology lecture, fish ID slide show, dolphin encounter/swim, and fish and coral underwater ID cards. Phone (800) 227-3483 or (954) 929-0090; fax (954)922-7478; e-mail: akr@gate.net; website: www.anthonyskey.com.

Prior to the first dive, Anthony's gives a complete dive operation orientation, and divers are required to perform a short orientation dive to ensure that they are comfortable with their equipment and buoyancy before going out to the open reef. A divemaster goes into the water with them and runs through some of the basic skills. This is a done quickly, and I didn't feel at all inconvenienced by it. In fact, I think more dive shops should follow suit.

Retail Sales: *Adequate*   **Dive Boat Comfort:** *Good*

Rentals: *Extensive*   **On-Board Facilities**

Scuba Training: *Extensive*   **for Photographers:** *Good*

Photo Services: *Extensive*

Bay Islands Beach Resort (a PADI Resort) offers diving and snorkeling with two 33-foot dive boats to sites within the marine reserve and all along the north shore. All boats carry emergency oxygen and two-way radios. A 22-foot Boston Whaler is also available for diving and fishing. There is unlimited shore diving from the resort property in the marine reserve and the Spooky Channel. Snorkelers can join the dive boats or explore the Natural Aquarium Buoyed Snorkel Trail, which takes you through a number of marine habitats. Certifying agencies are NASE, NAUI, PADI, PDIC, and SSI. Dive classes through the advanced level are offered, as well as several specialties, including Enriched Air Nitrox. This is a NAUI Technical Training Center with many technical courses offered, including technical Nitrox, Trimix, decompression techniques, extended range diving, and technical wreck penetration. Guided technical diving can be arranged. The shop has E-6 film processing and rents still cameras and lenses. There is a repair section and a rental facility with dive lights and the new SASYs for kids. Enriched Air Nitrox is available, and a special Nitrox package can be purchased. Facilities include guest bathrooms, showers, rinse tanks, and gear storage. Phone (800) 476-2826 or (561) 624-5774; fax (561) 624-7751; e-mail: bibrusa@aol.com; website: www.bibr.com.

Retail Sales: *Adequate*   **Dive Boat Comfort:** *Good*

Rentals: *Extensive*   **On-Board Facilities**

Scuba Training: *Extensive*   **for Photographers:** *Good*

Photo Services: *Extensive*

CocoView Resort/Dockside Dive Center (a PADI 5-Star Dive Center) is on the south shore on a private peninsula, with several dive sites just minutes away. PADI dive instruction is through the divemaster level, and specialty courses are offered, including Enriched Air Nitrox and DAN

Oxygen Provider. CoCo View Wall is a beach dive just 100 yards off the resort. Four dive boats include two heavy-duty 50-foot vessels once used by the U.S. Navy. The shop has a 150-bottle tank rack for air 24 hours a day. Tanks, backpacks, and weights are provided with every dive package. Gear rental (including computers and dive lights) and repair services are available. An extensive photo service has E-6 slide processing, still and video camera rentals, strobe and lens rentals, and several photo courses. Custom underwater videos can be arranged. Enriched Air Nitrox is also available. Phone (800) 282-8932 or (352) 588-4131; fax (352) 588-4158; e-mail: ccv@roatan.com; website: www.roatan.com/cocoview.htm.

Retail Sales: *Adequate*   **Dive Boat Comfort:** *Excellent*
Rentals: *Extensive*   **On-Board Facilities**
Scuba Training: *Extensive*   **for Photographers:** *Superior*
Photo Services: *Extensive*

Fantasy Island Beach Resort, Dive and Marina has a fleet of six custom 42-foot boats adjacent to the guest gear storage area, underwater photo center, compressors, and equipment rental facility. All the sites along the south shore are visited, and a private dock along the north shore allows easy access to those sites as well. Shore diving day or night is facilitated by a unique "dive gazebo" with a shipwreck, sunken airplane shallow reef, and wall, all close to shore. A full line of rental gear includes dive lights and computers. The use of gear bags is complimentary. Certifying agencies are PADI and SSI, and courses are offered through the advanced level. The shop offers E-6 film processing and Enriched Air Nitrox. Phone (800) 676-2826 or 011-504-455-5191; fax (813) 353-0154; e-mail: sarai@fantasyislandresort.com; website: www.fantasyislandresort.com.

Retail Sales: *Adequate*   **Dive Boat Comfort:** *Excellent*
Rentals: *Extensive*   **On-Board Facilities**
Scuba Training: *Moderate*   **for Photographers:** *Superior*
Photo Services: *Extensive*

Utila

Laguna Beach Resort (a PADI Resort) on Utila runs two custom 34-foot Newton dive boats for visiting a multitude of sites around the island, including the deep-water seamounts. The vessels are equipped with freshwater tanks for cameras. From the resort, there is unlimited shore diving. PADI open water and intro courses are offered. The dive shop provides a full line of gear rentals, as well as camera rentals. Nitrox is not pumped on-site, but the shop can get it. A hanging gear storage area is just steps away from the boat dock. Phone (800) 668-8452 or (337) 893-0013; fax (337) 893-5024; e-mail: awhite@utila.com; website: www.utila.com.

Retail Sales: *None*	**Dive Boat Comfort:** *Good*
Rentals: *Adequate*	**On-Board Facilities**
Scuba Training: *Moderate*	**for Photographers:** *Good*
Photo Services: *Moderate*	

Utila Lodge (a PADI Gold Palm IDC Resort) runs a 41-foot Morgan, with fly bridge (great for spotting whale sharks), as its primary dive boat. PADI instruction is offered through the divemaster level and includes numerous specialty courses. The full line of rental equipment includes dive lights. Enriched Air Nitrox is available, and the Nitrox specialty course is offered. Phone (800) 282-8932 or 011-504-425-3143; fax (352) 588-4158; e-mail: utl@roatan.com; website: www.roatan.com/utilalodge.

Retail Sales: *None*	**Dive Boat Comfort:** *Good*
Rentals: *Extensive*	**On-Board Facilities**
Scuba Training: *Extensive*	**for Photographers:** *Good*
Photo Services: *Limited*	

Guanaja

Bayman Bay Club on Guanaja takes divers out to around 30 different dive sites, all just a few minutes from the resort and within the marine reserve. It uses two custom dive boats, a 37-footer and a 40-footer. Equipment rentals are available, as is diving instruction. Phone (800) 524-1823 or (954) 572-1902; fax (954) 572-1907; e-mail: info@baymanbay club.com; website: www.baymanbayclub.com.

Retail Sales: *None*	**Dive Boat Comfort:** *Good*
Rentals: *Adequate*	**On-Board Facilities**
Scuba Training: *Limited*	**for Photographers:** *Good*
Photo Services: *Limited ve*	

Posada del Sol operates three comfortable 42-foot dive boats with waterline dive platforms and walk-through transoms and large freshwater dip tanks for photo gear. Fifty different dive sites are visited, and the resort has unlimited shore diving. The PADI and PDIC shop offers instruction through the advanced level. A photo lab has E-6 processing and rentals of video and still cameras. Phone (800) 642-3483 or (352) 588-4132; e-mail: pds@roatan.com; website: www.posadadelsol.com.

Retail Sales: *None*
Rentals: *Extensive*
Scuba Training: *Moderate*
Photo Services: *Extensive*

Dive Boat Comfort: *Good*
On-Board Facilities
for Photographers: *Good*

Cayos Cochinos

Plantation Beach Resort on Grande Cochino, in the Cayos Cochinos, is a small operation that serves the limited number of guests staying at Plantation Beach. Dive service is exceptional, in an equally exceptional marine reserve. A couple of boats are used, including a very nice Pro-42 that is perfect for transporting divers from the mainland. PADI instructors teach through the advanced level and also a number of specialties. Equipment rentals include dive computers. Phone (800) 628-3723 or (504) 442-097; e-mail: pbr@hondurashn.com; website: www.plantationbeachresort.com.

Retail Sales: *None*
Rentals: *Adequate*
Scuba Training: *Moderate*
Photo Services: *Limited*

Dive Boat Comfort: *Good*
On-Board Facilities
for Photographers: *Good*

WHERE TO STAY

Hotel tax is from 12 to 16 percent. Most of the resorts in the Bay Islands are dedicated dive resorts.

Roatan

Anthony's Key Resort ★★★★★, a PADI Gold Palm IDC Resort on the northwest coast of Roatan, is a little slice of jungle paradise, melding beautifully with its lush surroundings. Years ago, I remember looking longingly at the ads for it in dive magazines and thinking, "Some day…." Well, I did go, and really loved it. Planning a honeymoon? Special occasion? This would be perfect for both. There are 56 wooden bungalows (with and without air-conditioning), most located on a small cay facing a calm lagoon. All were refurbished and upgraded after Hurricane Mitch roared through. Directly across are the resort's public facilties. A little skiff awaits to take you and your dive gear the short distance to the resort's center. There is a lovely tropical open-air restaurant and bar with parrots, macaws, toucans, and other exotic birds (watch those bare toes!). Scheduled activities, including a dolphin camp, keep kids busy, and there are baby-sitting services. The dive center, docks, and boats are all on the premises, as well as the Institute for Marine Sciences, which offers extensive snorkeling and diving with dolphins programs. The dives are done in the open ocean off Bailey's Key, which also has a nature trail. Other activities include horseback riding, windsurfing, kayaking, canoeing, birdwatching, deep sea fishing, beach picnics, and hiking. The resort even has its own hyperbaric chamber and Photo Roatan, a complete photo shop right next to the dive shop. This is truly a dedicated dive resort. The nightly room rate (double occupancy) is $190. Extensive diving and snorkeling packages are available. Phone (800) 227-3483 or (954) 929-0090; fax (954) 922-747; e-mail: akr@gate.net; website: www.anthonyskey.com.

Bay Islands Beach Resort ★★★★, a PADI Resort on Roatan's north shore, is a 45-acre property that stretches from its 600-foot sandy beach into the hillside. On six beautifully landscaped acres are an estate house, villas, a beachhouse, and lodge. There are 18 air-conditioned rooms, a restaurant, and beach bar. Activities include horseback riding, parasailing, hiking, rafting, and sightseeing. The resort also offers a number of festive events, such as the lobster buffet, a free tour of the Wild Cane Historic Village (which is on the property), and a party in the village with island food and dancing. For kids ages 6 to 14, there is a daily camp program, where they learn about the reef, and fish, kayak, swim, and explore the island. Besides diving, the resort offers an extensive snorkeling program, with instruction and guides. The Natural Aquarium and Buoyed Snorkel Discovery Trail lead snorkelers from spot to spot to see the highlights of the reef. There's an inner trail and an outer trail, where different marine habitats can be observed. Their packages include air-conditioned accommodations, airport transfers, use of kayaks, three boat dives daily, one boat night dive, unlimited shore diving, and three meals daily. The nightly room rate (double occupancy) is $60. A seven-night package for divers and snorkelers is $775 per person, double occupancy. Rates do not include taxes. Phone (800) 476-2826 or (561) 624-5774; fax (561) 624-7751; e-mail: bibrusa@aol.com; website: www.bibr.com.

CocoView Resort ★★★★, on Roatan's south shore, features 25 air-conditioned oceanfront rooms, ranging from over-the-water bungalows to beach rooms. All have porches or balconies. There's excellent diving right off the front porch—shallow reefs, ship and plane wrecks, and two walls. A restaurant is on the premises, with meals served buffet-style, and an over-the-water bar. Besides its human guests, the resort caters to sea turtles with its unique Turtle Raise and Release Program. Hawksbill Cay (formerly Picnic Island) is now dedicated to the protection and preservation of sea turtles—both hawksbill and green. A number of island excursions are offered, such as a rainforest/waterfall hike, horseback rides on the beach, eco-tours, flats fishing, and deep-sea fishing. The seven-night package rate of $800 to $825 per person, double occupancy, includes all meals, ten boat dives, ten drop-off boat dives, unlimited beach diving, use of kayaks, etc. Taxes are not included in these rates. CoCo View also offers dive packages with Utila Lodge. Phone (800) 282-8932 or (352) 588-4131; fax (352) 588-4158; e-mail: ccv@roatan.com; website: www.roatan.com/cocoview.htm.

Fantasy Island Beach Resort, Dive and Marina ★★★★ is on a private island on the south shore of Roatan. The 84 air-conditioned rooms have modern communications amenities, refrigerators, and cable TV. A restaurant and indoor/outdoor lounge overlook the sea. A small swimming pool is on the premises, but who needs it with a private-island beach. Excellent snorkeling is right off the beach and shore diving just 40 yards out. The resort also has Roatan's only lighted tennis courts. An extensive Watersports Center has boats for rent, including speedboats, wave runners, Boston Whalers, fishing boats, sailboats (including catamarans), and sea cycles. Canoes and kayaks are complimentary. Activities include island tours, moonlight cruises, beach dancing buffets, and barbecues. The daily diver's rate (double occupancy), which includes meals and three boat dives, is $150. A seven-night diver's package (double occupancy) is $770 to $840, depending on the season. This includes airport transfers, all meals, three boat dives daily and a night dive, unlimited snorkeling, and use of kayaks. These rates do not include 16 percent tax. Phone (800) 676-2826 or 011-504-455-5191; fax (813) 353-0154; e-mail: sarai@fantasyisland resort.com; website: www.fantasyislandresort.com.

Utila

Laguna Beach Resort ★★★★ (a PADI Resort) on Utila is on a gorgeous sandy peninsula with the Caribbean on one side and a calm mangrove lagoon on the other. There are 12 air-conditioned rooms in 5 duplex and 2 individual natural wood bungalows. Each waterfront room has a private deck. The natural wood lodge with restaurant and bar has a soaring open-beam ceiling with sweeping views. Boats and the dock are right out back. Access to the resort is by boat only. That's isolation! A dive complex includes gear storage and rinsing facilities. The diver rate of $795 per person (double occupancy) for seven nights includes round-trip airport transportation, all meals, three boat dives daily, two night boat dives per week, unlimited shore dives, and unlimited use of kayaks, canoes, and windsurfers. The daily per person rate for divers is $125, with double occupancy. These rates do not include taxes. Phone (800) 668-8452 or (337) 893-0013; fax (337) 893-5024; e-mail: awhite@utila.com; website: www.utila.com.

Utila Lodge ★★★★, a PADI Gold Palm IDC Resort, is a seaside diver's retreat at the western end of little East Harbour Town on little Utila. The

Caribbean-style oceanfront lodge has a restaurant, bar, and gift shop. The screened porch overlooks the harbor and boat slips, and another porch upstairs has a sun deck. Behind the main house is a rinse and gear storage area. A two-story wing has only eight air-conditioned rooms—that's it! Facilities include a bar and the on-premises dive operation. Other activities include off-shore and flats fishing, kayaking, spelunking, lagoon excursions, whale shark expeditions, picnicking, and sightseeing. Laundry facilities are available. A seven-night package for $750 (per person, double occupancy) includes three meals and three boat dives daily, two night boat dives, unlimited shore diving, use of kayaks and canoes, airport transfers, etc. It does not include 12 percent tax. Utila Lodge also offers fishing/diving packages and duo packages with CoCo View on Roatan. Phone (800) 282-8932 or 011-504-425-3143; fax (352) 588-4158; e-mail: utl@roatan.com; website: www.roatan.com/utilalodge.

Guanaja

Bayman Bay Club ★★★★ on Guanaja has a funky island style with wooden fan- and breeze-cooled cabanas spread across a tropical hillside overlooking the water. On the edge of a sandy beach and bordering a national forest, it is nestled on 100 acres of private property. Each cabana has a private veranda with a view of the Caribbean and is shaded by tropical trees. Facilities include a three-story central lodge (clubhouse) with bar and dining area, pool tables, library, gameroom, and observation deck. Other facilities include a gift shop, laundry, and water taxi. There's excellent snorkeling right from the 650-foot-long beach. One- and two-person kayaks can be used for excursions to such sites as the rainforest area of the Soldado River, near the beach where Columbus landed in 1504. Hiking jungle trails and tours to the mainland are other possibilities. A seven-night diving package is $699 per person. Included in the rate are airport transfers, all meals, two boat dive trips daily (three tanks), unlimited shore diving, use of kayaks, etc. Taxes are not included. Phone (800) 524-1823 or (954) 572-1902; fax (954) 572-1907; e-mail: info@baymanbayclub.com; website: www.baymanbayclub.com.

Posada del Sol ★★★★ on Guanaja features a distinctive Mediterranean villa design among 70 acres of gorgeous landscaping. From the airstrip, it can only be reached by water. Facilities include 23 guest rooms, either poolside, oceanfront or hillside. Each guest room has tile floors, marble baths, and native woods. Amenities include a swimming pool, marina, dive shop, gym, massage area, and tennis court. Saltwater flats lie directly offshore—perfect for bonefishing. Fishing guides are available, and the resort has a well-stocked pro shop. Other activities include kayaking and windsurfing. There's also excellent hiking—to high mountain waterfalls or to an archaeological dig. Couples can be dropped off on a secluded uninhabited island with a champagne lunch and hammocks. A tour company can arrange mainland trips. The daily diver's rate for double occupancy is $170, which includes three meals, airport transfers, three dives, unlimited shore diving, and use of kayaks. Seven-night packages are available for $900 per person. Room tax is not included. Phone (800) 642-3483 or (352) 588-4132; e-mail: pds@roatan.com; website: www.posadadelsol.com.

Cayos Cochinos

For serious divers, **Plantation Beach Resort** ★★★★ on Grande Cochino in the Cayos Cochinos islands is an absolute gem. It's a very small and very special place, smack dab in the middle of a biological reserve. This is the only lodging and the only dive shop allowed in the Cochinos Cayes. Check out the accompanying sidebar for more information about this group of islands. Accommodations are simple but comfortable, and the small staff couldn't be more helpful. Since these islands are much closer to the mainland than all the others, you'll probably be brought over by boat, but there is a small landing strip, so air travel is also possible. Two primary structures face the sea and the boat dock and are surrounded by lush vegetation. One is the single-story main lodge with dining and lounge area, and the other is an attractive two-level stone and mahogany building with four guest rooms. Some smaller buildings up the hill provide six additional rooms. The seven-night diver's package is $895, which includes all meals, three boat dives daily, unlimited shore diving, a night boat dive, etc. It does not include taxes or transfers. Boat transfers (Wednesdays and Saturdays) are $80 per person, round-trip. Phone (800) 628-3723 or (504) 442-0974; e-mail: pbr@hondurashn.com; website: www.plantationbeachresort.com.

Live-Aboard

The **Aggressor Fleet** operates the *Bay Islands Aggressor IV* (a PADI Resort) and visits sites throughout the Bay Islands, including Cayos Cochinos. The 120-foot live-aboard carries a maximum of 20 passengers. It features eight "Queen" staterooms with queen-sized berths, private head and shower, TV/VCR, hair dryer, and large window. There are two larger "King" staterooms. All are air-conditioned. On board are photo lab, hot tub, Nitrox, and e-mail. The charters are all-inclusive—meals, tanks, weights, airport transfers—and you get unlimited diving. Call (800) 348-2628; fax (504) 384-0817; e-mail: info@aggressor.com; website: www.aggressor.com.

ISLAND LIFE

You'll find stunning white sandy beaches on all the islands, as well as vast areas of swampy mangroves. Vegetation is green and lush. Gumbo limbo trees, coconut palms, Caribbean pines, and sea grape trees are just a sampling of what you'll find here. Settlements are small and most of the businesses very modest.

Here's a little slice of island life: during one of my visits to Roatan, I was driving back to my little resort in the Sandy Bay area after a day of island exploring. Motoring slowly along the dirt road, I noticed a group of islanders watching a softball game. As I drove along, I spotted a flat object placed in the middle of the road, and it wasn't until after I had passed it that it suddenly dawned on me that I had driven right over Third Base!

On Roatan, you'll find most development around this Sandy Bay area, which is on the northwest side. Several resorts are located here, including Anthony's Key and Bay Islands Beach Resort. The island's beautiful air-conditioned airport is located on the southwest side, and a few resorts are spread out along the south side, including CoCo View and Fantasy Island.

A good paved road runs most of the length of Roatan, and visitors can tour from west to east to gape at the view or stop at some tucked-away gem for food and drink. Unfortunately, there are also some pockets of extreme poverty. Most of these are located around the harbour areas, where some actual slums exist. The little villages, although very modest, are clean, and the residents have a pretty decent standard of living.

Guanaja, to the east of Roatan, is just nine miles long and the second largest of the Bay Islands. It's the hilliest, with some steep mountain elevations, waterfalls, and Caribbean pine trees. What it does not have is roads. Several cays encircle Guanaja, and on two of these is the main settlement called Bonacca. It's a crazy maze of streets and alleyways where all the building are on stilts over the water.

The main island itself has few settlements. A man-made canal cuts through the island and serves as the main road. All transportation is either by boat or walking. Although Hurricane Mitch really tore through Guanaja, destroying everything in its path, the island has regrouped and recovered nicely. Swimming and snorkeling from white sandy beaches, sport fishing, kayaking, and hiking are popular activities when you're not diving. Hiking trails wind amid mango, pine, and breadfruit trees and from sandy beaches into verdant jungles. For fabulous views, climb to the highest point in the Bay Islands—1,400 feet (not right after a dive, though!).

To the southwest of Roatan is Utila, equally lush in vegetation and perfect for hiking and bird watching. It's more flat than the other islands, and much of it consists of huge areas of swamp and mangroves. The island is neat and tidy, with brightly-painted houses, most with gingerbread trim, wide porches, and a colorful assortment of plants and flowers. Although Utila is one of the smallest islands, you'll find plenty of restaurants, cafes,

The Bay Islands' Best-Kept Secret

If you were to devise a scenario for the perfect dive spot, I bet it would go something like this: take an isolated island that has no development, no agriculture, and no roads. There would be a single place to stay with an excellent dive operation. Around the island, fishing, spearing, and collecting would be prohibited (except for local subsistence), and the diversity of marine life would be unparalled in the Caribbean.

Welcome to Cayos Cochinos. Located about nine miles north of mainland Honduras, the Cochinos are a tropical mini-archipelago of two hilly islands, Cochinos Grande and Cochinos Pequeño, and several completely flat, palm-tree-studded sandy cayes. Except for a handful of tiny fishing villages, some island-residents who obviously enjoy solitude, and one dedicated dive resort with a few attractive mahogany-and-stone cottages, you won't find any development whatsoever.

This area is so pristine that in 1993 the entire archipelago was declared a protected biological reserve, financed by the Honduran Coral Reef Fund and operated by the Smithsonian Institution. After careful inspection of Cayos Cochinos and surrounding waters, the Smithsonian determined that the territory was in a sufficiently primitive state to be operated as an outpost of the Smithsonian Tropical Research Institute.

Under the reserve protection, no new construction is allowed, and most nonendemic species of flora and fauna will be removed. Enforcement is provided by special squads from the Honduran Navy, trained as park rangers.

The reserve's director, Hector Guzman, is a marine biologist and active diver who sees scuba diving, along with hiking and birding, as one of the few activities compatible with the reserve's protected status. Under a grandfather clause, Plantation Beach Resort is the only resort permitted to exist within the reserve.

Once in the water, divers immediately see why this place is so unique. Bushes of black coral billow in only 40 feet of water, and brilliant clusters of bluebell tunicates decorate fringing reefs that have layer upon layer of life. Mounds of boulder star coral and ledges of plate coral, lettuce, and sheet coral cover the reef tops. Critters like large-eye toadfish, web burrfish, cryptic teardrop crab, and sailfin

---

The Bay Islands' Best-Kept Secret (continued)

blennies are all here, along with flying gurnards, sea horses, frogfish, and batfish.

Time out for island exploration means hiking across the island to visit the lighthouse and Garifuna fishing villages. Dugout canoes, heaps of coconut husks, and thatched-roof wooden huts all characterize the simple lifestyle of these people of African heritage. The path can be a bit obscure at times, but if you take Nike along (the resident golden retriever) it'll be *no problemo.*

---

markets, hotels, and shops in East Harbour, the primary settlement. Indeed, it's quite cosmopolitan—there's even a movie theater!

Topside Attractions

On Roatan, rent a car in Sandy Bay, then head inland to higher ground for some fabulous ocean vistas. The farther east you drive, the more remote the landscape becomes. Or cruise the islands and coral reefs with **Far Tortuga Charters.** Full and half-day cruises are given on the trimaran *Genesis.*

On the West End, you can swim or dive with dolphins at **Anthony's Key.** Find the Institute for Marine Sciences and sign up for one of their Discover the Dolphins programs. Also at Anthony's is a beautiful nature trail on Bailey's Key.

Near Sandy Bay is another area that will attract naturalists: the **Carambola Botanical Gardens,** which showcases a wide variety of exotic plants. Along the banks of Mahogany Creek, bridges connect walkways that lead through areas of flowering plants, ferns, spices, fruit trees (such as cashew and carambola), hardwoods (including the Honduran mahogany), and an extensive orchid collection. From the garden a path leads to the summit of Carambola Mountain, a 20-minute hike. Along the way is a natural iguana and parrot breeding ground and ancient Indian archeological sites that date back to the Mayan civilization. At the top, you can visually absorb all the colors of the reef and see Utila, 25 miles west.

The most spectacular land tour in the Bay Islands is Guanaja's natural waterfall, the only constant flow of water on any of the islands. There are no formal tours, but visitors to Guanaja can follow the somewhat grueling (and sometimes sloppy) trail into the higher elevations to this picturesque waterfall and pool.

On Utila, hiking and biking are popular to sites such as the cave on Brandon Hill and the summit of Pumpkin Hill. The views are worth the effort.

While in the Bay Islands, try to find a copy of the excellent *Coconut Telegraph* for more information about what's going on and what the future brings for this dynamic area.

Dining and Entertainment

There's an eclectic mix of cuisines here, none of which is exactly "haute." Most local restaurants serve the traditional Caribbean and Creole dishes. Definitely try some of the local specialties. One of these is called baleadas, which are homemade tortillas filled with refried beans, cream, cheese, and onions. Honduran coffee is excellent, and makes a nice gift to take to the folks back home.

For an island excursion combined with lunch, head for **Paya Bay Resort** high on a cliff on the northeast corner of Roatan. Better ask for directions before starting off. You can dine al fresco, overlooking a gorgeous stretch of pristine coastline with verdant hills beyond, stretching for miles. When I visited a few years ago, there were only four rooms, each with a private balcony overlooking the sea. If you really want to get away from everything for a few days, call (504) 924-2220 to make reservations.

Medical Facilities

A 24-hour hyperbaric chamber and medical center are located at Cornerstone Mission on Roatan, funded by a $2 per dive day donation requested of every diver using a Bay Islands charter. In case of a diving emergency call DAN (Divers Alert Network) at (919) 684-4DAN (4326) or (919) 684-8111.

North Carolina:
The Outer Banks

Physical Characteristics of the Dive Area

WATER & WEATHER CONDITIONS

Visibility	*Adequate*
Current and Surge	*Strong*
Temperature	*Chilly*
Storms	*Occasionally Stormy*

SITE CONDITIONS

Mooring Buoys	*Some*
Fishing, Collecting, and Hunting Restrictions	*Some*
Ease of Access	*Moderate*
Boat Traffic/Diver Congestion	*None*

MARINE LIFE

Abundance of Invertebrates	*Common*
Abundance of Vertebrates	*Abundant*
Abundance of Pelagic Life	*Abundant*
Health of Reef/Marine Life/ Marine Structure	*Healthy*

Graveyard of the Atlantic

Miles offshore from windswept sand dunes and beneath a hundred feet of
seawater lies a mariner's nightmare and a diver's dream. Where North

Carolina protrudes from the eastern coastline, scores of vessels, from the Civil War era to the modern day, perished on shallow shoals, in foul weather, or during wartime attacks. Referred to dramatically, but aptly, as the Graveyard of the Atlantic, this area is undoubtedly one of the best-kept secrets in the United States—and the mounds of metal are only half the attraction.

As a West Coast gal, I never thought much about the possibility of moving east; that is, until I visited Carteret County and an area called the Crystal Coast. This is where I fell in love with Beaufort and Morehead City, Cape Lookout National Seashore, and the southern Outer Banks.

Visitors will find here the perfect mixture of serene escapes and vacation-oriented entertainment. Sand dunes with sea oats waving in the breeze line more than 65 miles of beaches. Offshore this is a watersports playground for such activities as windsurfing and bodyboarding. The calm waters of Bogue Sound are perfect for kayaking and casual boating. The pace is gentle and relaxing, and the atmosphere is casual. And fortunately there's still a plentiful supply of Southern hospitality.

In addition to attracting divers, the area would certainly appeal to families, history buffs, and anyone who appreciates pure natural beauty. Whether you're walking the shoreline searching for seashells or exploring Beaufort's restored historic homes, you'll find that the pleasures of the Crystal Coast come with a modest price tag. The value-per-dollar ratio here is excellent. Accommodations and restaurants are affordable, making a diving vacation here within easy reach.

When dive boats enter the glassy waters of Bogue Sound early in the morning, they leave behind stately homes on the banks of Beaufort and pass fishing boats returning from their long journey at sea. In summer, the air at 7 a.m. is already very warm and the humidity high. Water droplets fall from the underside of the bimini, and it's impossible to keep anything dry. But it doesn't really matter, since soon enough you'll be wet anyway, and getting chilled isn't a problem.

The dive boat's wake trails past Carrot Island and Shackleford Banks, where wild horses still roam—the descendants of Spanish mustangs that belonged to seventeenth-century explorers. These are the very waters that Edward Teach (Blackbeard the Pirate) prowled, and it is believed that the wooden remains of his ship were discovered near the Beaufort Inlet in 1996.

I heard a diver here say that "unless I see metal, it seems like I'm not really diving." And that's the attitude of a lot of divers who come to the graveyard to dive its watery wrecks. Nevertheless, there's a lot more than metal to hold your interest underwater. The Gulf Stream sweeps by bring-

ing warm waters and tropical fish. Huge schools of baitfish swirl about wrecks that also attract sand tiger sharks, barracuda, grouper, bonito, Atlantic spadefish, jacks, turtles, and eels, just for starters.

QUICK STATS

Location   The Crystal Coast is in the southern Outer Banks of North Carolina.

Time   Eastern Standard

Air Temperature   April to October are the warmest months in North Carolina, with temperatures from the mid-70s to the high 80s.

Water Temperature   As low as 50° in the winter, rising to the low 80s in summer. During most of the diving season, a 2- or 3-mm wet suit should be sufficient.

Underwater Visibility   Can exceed 100 feet, but in stormy conditions (mostly in winter) can also drop precipitously to less than 20 feet. Typical visibility on the outer wrecks is 60 feet.

Best Diving Months   The prime diving season runs from May through early October; after that, winter storms rough up the seas and reduce visibility.

PLANNING THE TRIP

Getting to the Crystal Coast Major carriers fly into Raleigh-Durham International Airport, which is about three hours away by car. There are also small airports in Jacksonville and New Bern, North Carolina, which are closer. Private aircraft can fly right into the Beaufort-Morehead City Airport, located on the Beaufort side of the channel.

Getting Around A rental car would be your best bet. Access to Cape Lookout National Seashore is either by private boat or by ferry. There are no roads or bridges to the islands.

Tourist Offices Carteret County Tourism Development Bureau, phone (800) SUNNY-NC; website: www.sunnync.com.

THE UNDERWATER SCENE

If you were to look at a chart of North Carolina that labeled all the shipwrecks lying offshore, there would be a thick string of marks paralleling the length of the coastline. In fact, a map that was published by National Geographic ("Ghost Fleet of the Atlantic") in 1970 plotted more than 500 wrecks. The earliest dated from 1585; the most recent was 1969.

Since that time many more shipwrecks have been located, including Blackbeard's ship, near the Beaufort Inlet, and the Civil War–era *Monitor.* The *Monitor,* one of the world's first ironclad vessels, sank off Cape Hatteras during a storm in 1862 while it was being towed to Beaufort. Now it is a National Marine Sanctuary, but at 240 feet, well beyond sport-diving limits.

The experts say there are as many as 5,000 documented wrecks in North Carolina coastal waters. Several modern ships have been scuttled for artificial-reef building.

The best way to understand why there are so many wrecks is to peruse a good map of the area. You'll see an elbow of land that juts way out into the Atlantic. Around this area for about 11 miles in length and two miles in width are shallow shoals just a few feet deep—dangerous conditions for shipping. This, coupled with heavy maritime traffic and collisions, storms, and limited visibility, have taken a heavy toll.

One of the most fascinating stories, however, is that of submarine warfare in the early years of World War II. During the war and for years afterward, Americans knew little of what was going on along our own eastern coastline. In 1942, when U.S. merchant ships hauled cargo for transatlantic convoys, they had to travel around the dangerous shoals. Well aware of this, German submarines lay in wait in deeper waters to the east and to the south. For a while, they had a field day picking off the U.S. ships one by one. Eventually, our navy stepped up its defense and deep-sixed many of the U-boats. Two very interesting wrecks of this era—the *Papoose* and the *U-352*—are described a little farther on.

On a brighter note, the jutting landmass south of Cape Hatteras extends directly into the flow of warm Gulf Stream waters, bringing warm-water species this far north. So, although coral reefs do not develop, many of the same tropical species found in Florida and the Caribbean are here as well.

Of course, pelagic species appear also, including turtles, amberjack, Atlantic spadefish, barracuda, and sharks. The sharks seen on the wrecks are usually sand tigers, but the occasional bull shark appears. So don't think you have to travel to the Bahamas and participate in a shark dive to see them. The abundance of food here makes chum unnecessary for shark viewing. When I dived the Outer Banks, I saw sharks in their natural environment—not as part of a contrived program—on nearly every dive I made. Some wrecks seem to attract them more than others. At one time, they congregated on the *U.S.S. Tarpon,* but now the *Papoose* seems to be their ship of choice.

If you would like more information about the shipwrecks, there are several good books from authors Rob Farb and Gary Gentile.

Health Score Card

There is no coral reef here, but beautiful invertebrates cover many of the wrecks as well as the rocky pinnacles. These, in turn, attract reeflike species, which then bring in the pelagic species. The area teems with marine life, including huge schooling masses that at times completely blot out the wrecks from view.

Diving Conditions

The warm Gulf Stream waters nearly create Caribbean-like diving here— that is, warm water, great visibility, and lots of colorful marine life. However, most of the exciting dives off Cape Lookout are miles from shore in open ocean; this is not reef diving. Many are more than 100 feet deep, but the visibility is usually around 60 or 70 feet. Although deep, the wrecks are still shallow enough for using Nitrox mixes. In fact, Nitrox is popular here. It's especially nice for the "feel good" benefit when the waters are choppy and you might be feeling a bit queasy anyway.

The depths of these wrecks, combined with the very conditions that sent some of them to their graves—storms, rough seas, and strong currents—can be serious factors for divers here. So taking a few extra precautions with equipment is a good idea. Extra pre-dive time should be spent checking air mixtures, dive light batteries, getting extra tanks for hanging overboard (including pure oxygen), clipping on line reels, etc. Although the warm waters are teeming with tropicals, this is not your typical roll-off-the-boat type of diving.

Also, those who are prone to turning green on pitching boats should take a wise precaution before going out: seasick medication. Debbie Boyce, owner of Discovery Diving in Beaufort, suggests that divers begin taking pills the day *before* they're going out, as an extra safeguard.

Ocean currents at many of the sites can be strong. Remember to use the anchor line to get down and to come up, in order to expend less energy and save precious compressed air. Also, if you find that the current is really strong below, it will help to hug the bottom, to get as close to the wreck or the sand as possible, and to pull yourself along while kicking.

Be sure to dive with some surface signaling equipment. A whistle, safety sausage and light, or light/strobe combo, would be excellent. If a diver were to get swept away, it would be difficult to see his or her small form from a boat that's being pitched around by ocean swells. Almost all the boats used for diving here have flybridges, which do make it easier for captains to spot divers.

Also, be aware that there are many sharks in these waters, and it would be very surprising if you didn't spot at least a couple. So if that idea bothers you, this might not be your kind of dive destination.

Recommended Level of Experience

This is an area for advanced divers and for technical divers. Though not always present, all of the elements that can make diving difficult are generally here: deep water, currents, chop, and churned-up visibility. Normally, however, the visibility is very good, ranging from 50 to 100 feet. Also, although surface conditions can be rough, once you descend it's not usually a problem. Currents can range from slight to strong, so it's important to assess your own ability under these conditions.

The descriptions of the following wrecks include information about penetrating the interiors. Do not, however, penetrate them unless you are wreck-certified. Without the proper training, this can be very dangerous, especially at the extreme depths.

Great Wreck Sites

Papoose   About 30 miles from shore and 125 feet down lies the *Papoose*, a 412-foot tanker. It had carried fuel from Texas to the East Coast in the early years of World War II. Unfortunately, this was also the time (1941 and 1942) when German submarines (U-boats) patrolled these waters, sinking merchant ships with abandon. As the *Papoose* hugged the coastline down from New York, the *U-124* sent a torpedo first into its port side, then another into its starboard side, and the crew scrambled to abandon ship.

The wreck lies upside down at a depth of 130 feet. The keel, however, rises to within 85 feet of the surface. Generally the visibility here is excellent, but currents can sometimes be strong. The hull can be penetrated in a couple of places, but note that the ship is lying upside down.

Frankly, I think it's a lot more interesting, and certainly more exciting, to survey the exterior of the ship. And the reason? Sand tiger sharks! At least a couple can be found hanging out here at any time. On my last *Papoose* dive, eight sand tigers were counted. These are not pretty sharks. They have pointy snouts and ugly snaggle-toothed dentures, but they are not aggressive, which is comforting.

About midship, in a dramatic, cavernous opening where the hull is broken in two, you're likely to see huge grouper, silvery jacks, and barracuda. As I was exploring this area, a lone sand tiger shark lay on the sandy bottom, back under the tilted railing. As my dive buddy swam in to take some close-up shots, the sand tiger decided to make a quick exit into open ocean—straight at me. I watched it come within just a few feet, at eye level, before it swerved off in another direction. Whew!

Later when we were back on board, Robbie Purifoy from Olympus Dive Center laughingly told us that while we had intently kept watch over our single sand tiger, another one had casually passed about five feet behind me. Robbie also informed us that sand tigers are active at night, and during the daytime tend to have placid demeanors. The one we disturbed was probably annoyed we interrupted his nap.

While making a slow ascent to the surface, we passed through a dense swirling show of schooling baitfish. And as we hung onto the deco line, they kept us entertained. While flowing in one direction, in an instant they would flash their silvery bodies, turning to swirl about in the opposite direction. The synchronized dance was beautifully hypnotic—better than any laser show.

U-352   This German submarine and another one, the *U-85* north of Cape Hatteras, are perhaps the graveyard's most popular wrecks. During World War II, German subs terrorized the East Coast, sinking dozens of ships operated by the U.S. Merchant Marine. Several German U-boats were sunk, as well.

In 1942, while the *U-352* patrolled the North Carolina coast, it fired a torpedo at a small U.S. ship, the Coast Guard cutter *Icarus*. But the torpedo missed its mark, and the intended target, armed with depth charges,

Safety Guidelines for Diving in North Carolina

(Courtesy of Discovery Diving website: www.discoverydiving.com)
North Carolina wreck diving can be more strenuous than Florida
diving, due to potentially rough sea conditions and currents. Only
capable, experienced divers should dive the deeper, offshore wrecks.
The inshore wrecks, however, are suitable for most divers.

To promote diving safety, Discovery Diving posts the following
guidelines, which were originally issued by the now-defunct North
Carolina Dive Charter Association:

Requirements

No consumption of alcohol before dives.

No two-stage decompression dives.

Certification by a nationally recognized organization.

Recommendations

Do not make decompression dives.

For dives deeper than 80 feet, divers should have one logged ocean
boat dive within the last 12 months or 5 logged dives.

Do not exceed 130 feet.

Make a safety stop at 15 feet for at least 3 minutes on all dives.

---

quickly deduced the sub's location. Depth charges were released and con-
cussive explosions chased the sub to the surface, where it was met with a hail
of machine-gun fire. Most of the crew escaped through the hatches, but a
few went down with the sub, where they remain entombed today. The
Icarus picked up the surviving U-boat crew, and in 1992 George Purifoy
(who discovered the wreck of the *U-352*) hosted a reunion and memorial
service at the site for the German survivors and members of the *Icarus*.

Because of these historical circumstances and the fact that it is a war
grave, the *U-352* is an emotional wreck site, equal to those in Hawaii's
Pearl Harbor. While shining my dive light through the open hatch on my
first dive on the sub, I was surprised to see tropicals swimming through the
wreckage-strewn hull. And while straining to see farther inside, I literally
started to feel the ghosts within. The final agonies of the dead seemed to
be pouring from the sub. Instead of wonder and curiosity, suddenly I felt
their terror and anguish as the shells struck the hull and the dark sea rushed
in. Was it just narcosis? I wonder. . .

On this particular dive, in October, the visibility was only about 20 feet. On our descent, masses of tomtate baitfish were so thick that we hit the hull before we saw it. The current was strong, and we had to hug the structure and pull ourselves along the length of the hull. My second dive here was in August, and the conditions were far better—at least 80 feet of visibility and only a slight current.

The *U-352* is submerged in sand at about 115 feet, some 25 miles from the Beaufort Inlet and in the same vicinity as the *Papoose*. Although it is possible to penetrate the hull through the hatches, heavy silting zeroes-out the visibility, creating potentially dangerous conditions. But the sub's interesting exterior, coupled with colorful tropicals, provides more than enough to explore. The conning tower is a definite attraction, as are the open hatches and deck gun. Look inside the various orifices for morays that like to be tucked away. You'll probably see triggerfish, squirrelfish, and angelfish, as well.

USS Schurz   This is a World War I German cruiser now lying in the same body of water as the *U-352* and the *Papoose*. Originally named the *Geir*, it was confiscated by the Americans and recommissioned as a U.S. Navy ship. The cruiser patrolled the East Coast until 1918, when a tanker, the *S.S. Florida*, accidentally rammed it during heavy fog and it went down in about 110 feet of water. The ship is 295 feet long, and its location usually has very good visibility. Because of its age and because it gets fewer divers, there's far more growth here, and as a result, more marine life as well. You'll probably see angelfish, parrotfish, silver snapper, amberjacks, and flame scallops. The occasional turtle might cruise by, and sand tiger sharks, as well. Of course, moray eels love wrecks, and this one is no exception.

Aeolus   This was a modern-day cable layer scuttled intentionally in 1988 to provide structure for marine growth. Although without the historical drama that makes the other ships so intriguing, it is still an interesting ship to explore. It's in the same general vicinity as the previously described ships, but closer to shore. Once a little more than 400 feet long, the *Aeolus* is now broken into several sections as a result of storm action and lies at around 100 feet.

Indra   This is another artificial reef site located closer to shore and in shallow water. The area, which consists of a cluster of wrecks, is a nice alternative if conditions are too rough farther out. The *Indra*, 316 feet long, was formerly a U.S. Navy landing craft repair ship. It was scuttled in 1992 and lies intact at 70 feet, part of it within 35 feet of the surface. The primary attraction is the enormous congregation of marine life, from thick schools of baitfish to very large barracuda. Bluish-gray conger eels peek from the

Queen Anne's Revenge

During the Golden Age of Piracy (1689–1718), when North Carolina was still a colony, privateers and pirates wreaked havoc on the seas along the Atlantic coast. Among them was none other than everyone's favorite loathsome, fearsome pirate, that wascally Edward Teach, a.k.a. Blackbeard. With his tall, burly physique and bushy black beard, Eddie swashed and buckled and generally struck fear into the hearts of even his most unpleasant compatriots.

Because he was such a "good" pirate, he was awarded a grand prize—the *Concorde,* a French slave vessel. The *Concorde* was captured in 1717 while transporting 516 West Africans to Martinique. Obviously, such an aristocratic name would never do for a pillaging pirate, so he renamed the vessel the *Queen Anne's Revenge*—much better. And he increased the weaponry from 14 guns to 40.

With his ship, Blackbeard was in hog heaven. This was one of those (many) times when England and France were not getting along, and it was war—Queen Anne's War—that gave Blackbeard an opportunity to do what he did best: plunder. And this he did at will, all along the Atlantic coast. In the process, he amassed more ships and made more pirate friends. He attacked merchant ships and captured gold and other booty. With his flotilla of four ships and 400 pirates, he even blockaded Charleston, South Carolina, for a week in order to restock his medicine chest. Pirates, it seems, were not a healthy lot, being plagued with scurvy, syphilis, and dysentery, among other ailments. (No wonder they were so disagreeable!)

Finally, his luck ran out in June 1718. Beaufort Inlet's shallow shoals claimed another "turtle in the net." *Queen Anne's Revenge* ran aground, as did a smaller sloop, *Adventure,* that was trying to free her.

The year 1718 was not a good one for Blackbeard. In November he was "taken out" by the Royal Navy's Lt. Robert Maynard. Maynard had Blackbeard beheaded and hung his bushy black head from the bowsprit of the sloop as proof that he was indeed done-in.

Edward had been a pirate captain for only one year, but he made quite an impression in the pirate milieu. If there were a Pirate Hall of Fame, he certainly would have made the cut.

In 1996 a wreck was discovered in Beaufort Inlet that was believed to be the *Queen Anne's Revenge.* To date, marine archaeological research on the wreck site has produced such evidence as an appropriate number of cannon (21) and specialized ammunition,

Queen Anne's Revenge (continued)

eighteenth-century medical supplies (for syphilis), and stoneware pottery traceable to period artisans. Conservation of the artifacts is underway at the North Carolina Maritime Museum, in Beaufort, where preserved artifacts are on display.

Mike Daniel, director of operations for a Florida-based research company called Intersal, Inc., is credited with the ship's discovery. He is now president of Maritime Research Institute, a nonprofit corporation working in partnership with the State of North Carolina to excavate the site. The state will retain ownership of all artifacts. Diving at the wreck site is under the control of the Underwater Archaeology Unit (UAU) of the North Carolina Division of Archives and History.

hatches. In the sandy bottom area surrounding the ship lie huge sand dollars. When I dived this wreck, the visibility was only about 20 feet, so we attached a line to the wreck and reeled out to search for the sand dollars— easy navigation! Along the way we spotted some striking black-and-white high hats and bluish conger eels among the rocks.

W.E. Hutton   This was another victim of the German *U-124,* which sank the *Papoose.* The *Hutton* was torpedoed in 1942. Deemed a menace to navigation, it was subsequently depth-charged and wire-dragged by the Coast Guard, leaving a field of twisted metal. It lies in 72 feet of water, not far from the *Indra.* Broken wreckage covers a large area. Nearby are some rocky pinnacles that are covered with multicolored invertebrates and surrounded by soaring schools of baitfish, Atlantic spadefish, and amberjack. When I dived this wreck, my buddy and I were spearfishing, which attracted a bull shark. When another bull shark joined the party, we figured the fun was over and decided to get back to the boat. First, however, we had to sacrifice our entrée for the evening barbecue, since this duo was not about to let *its* dinner get away.

The **Caribsea** was another U.S. freighter torpedoed in 1942 by the German *U-158.* It lies around on the other side of the "elbow" and much closer to shore than many of the other war ships. It went down quickly with a heavy cargo of manganese ore and left only seven survivors. One who went down with the ship was engineer James B. Gaskill, of Ocracoke. As the story goes, his family first learned about the sinking when the

Caribsea's nameplate washed ashore on Ocracoke. The official announcement came weeks afterward. The bottom of the wreck is at about 90 feet and the bow rises to within 45 feet of the surface, so divers have plenty of time to explore. That's fortunate, because there is much to see, with the broken hull providing a perfect habitat for a variety of marine life. It's beautifully decorated with invertebrates and attracts masses of schooling fish. The loner-type tropicals meander all about, as well.

Shore Dives and Snorkeling

Although there are a few possibilities, in truth this is not the best area for shore diving and snorkeling. That's because there is no coral reef here. The main attractions, the shipwrecks, are in deep and frequently rough water. Snorkelers would not have much fun on most of the boat dives.

Radio Island, however, is an excellent spot for both shore diving and snorkeling. There is a bit of a hike, though, from the parking lot to the jetty. The island sits in the middle of the channel that separates Morehead City and Beaufort, and has a couple of marinas where you can get supplies and information. The sandy shoreline drops off to about 35 feet, where the tropicals are plentiful. Unfortunately, the visibility averages only around 15 feet.

The *Cape Lookout Jetty* is another good spot for snorkeling, with easy access from the beach. Tropical fish brought in from warm Gulf Stream waters are common here. The jetty is oceanside, and you can expect visibility to be about 20 feet. In July and August the water temperature stays a toasty 82°. All transportation to Cape Lookout is by boat, and most boat services for snorklers depart from Beaufort. The *Shackleford Jetty* is another spot that attracts shore divers and snorkelers.

Marine Protection

North Carolina prohibits the taking of artifacts within three miles of the shore. The loggerhead sea turtles, their nests in the sand dunes, hatchlings, and carcasses are protected under the Endangered Species Act. To learn more about them, visit the North Carolina Aquarium's exhibit in Pine Knoll Shores. Also protected here are the sea oats. This large grain-headed grass helps anchor the sand dunes; therefore it's illegal to pick either the live or dead stalks.

Dive Services & Packages

Both of the following dive shops have excellent websites, with a wealth of information about the diving here as well as the local area. You'll have access to maps, driving directions, weather information, and much more.

Olympus Dive Center (a PADI Dive Center) is a spacious, well-organized shop on the waterfront (713 Shepard Street) in Morehead City, with a special area for displaying artifacts brought up from years of dives on these wrecks. Owner George Purifoy discovered several of the wrecks himself, including the awesome *U-352*. The shop has a large retail area as well as equipment rentals and service. Among the rental selections are spearfishing gear and underwater cameras. Nitrox is mixed on the premises and custom breathing blends can be ordered. All dive boats carry emergency equipment. Olympus has both NAUI and PADI courses, as well as some specialty courses, including underwater hunter, photographer, medic first aid, DAN oxygen provider, and wreck diving. Professional-level NAUI courses are offered, as well as NAUI and IANTD technical diving courses. Basic Nitrox is another specialty. The shop also has a diver's lodge two blocks away. There are 32 bunks in five separate rooms, a large lounge area, microwave and refrigerator, and separate male/female restrooms with showers and toilets. Phone (800) 992-1258 or (252) 726-9432; fax (252) 726-0883; e-mail: olympus@olympusdiving.com; website: www.olympusdiving.com.

Retail Sales: *Extensive*	**Dive Boat Comfort:** *Excellent*
Rentals: *Extensive*	**On-Board Facilities**
Scuba Training: *Extensive*	**for Photographers:** *Good*
Photo Services: *Moderate*	

Discovery Diving in Beaufort (414 Orange Street) is run by the indefatigable Debbie Boyce. Debbie is part diveshop owner, part tour guide. She wants to make sure that everyone enjoys the area. Debbie came here from out of state to do some diving in her college years and liked it so much she decided to stay. Eventually she bought the dive shop. Discover Diving offers equipment service and repairs, and has an extensive retail selection. Rentals also are substantial, including scooters, buddy phones, and underwater cameras. A Nitrox system has just been installed. For training, just about every PADI certification is possible, including the professional levels, since this is a PADI 5-Star IDC. Some of the specialty courses include medic first aid, deep diving, underwater hunter, DAN O_2, Nitrox, photography, and, of course, wreck diving. The shop uses several dive boats ranging from 6- to 16-passenger capacity, and all are equipped with emergency equipment. In addition to dive trips, special snorkel excursions are made to Cape Lookout, one of the barrier islands. Discovery Diving has two diver's lodges available for groups, with a very reasonable $11 per-person nightly rate (min. group rate $77 per night). Phone (252) 728-2265; fax (252) 728-2581; e-mail: dive@discoverydiving.com; website: www.dis coverydiving.com.

Retail Sales: *Extensive*
Rentals: *Extensive*
Scuba Training: *Extensive*
Photo Services: *Moderate*

Dive Boat Comfort: *Excellent*
On-Board Facilities
 for Photographers: *Good*

WHERE TO STAY

The following hotels and motels offer special diver's rates, but none has a dive shop on the premises. Rates listed here are the approximate nightly rates for rooms and might change depending on the time of year.

Best Western Buccaneer ★, in Morehead City: 91 rooms; restaurant, outdoor pool, full breakfast; $64. Phone (800) 682-4982 or (252) 726-3115.

Best Western Crystal Coast Resort ★, in Atlantic Beach: $117. Phone (800) 733-7888 or (252) 726-2544.

Comfort Inn ★, in Morehead City: 100 rooms; outdoor pool; $88. Phone (800) 422-5404 or (252) 247-3434.

Econo Lodge ★, in Morehead City: 56 rooms; outdoor pool; $60. Phone (800) 533-7556 or (252) 247-2940.

Days Inn ★, in Atlantic Beach: 90 rooms; refrigerators, balconies, outdoor pool, boat ramp, slips; $80. Phone (800) 972-3297 or (252) 247-6400.

The **Hampton Inn Hotel** ★★ on Bogue Sound in Morehead City (4035 Arendell Street), has very good dive packages with both Olympus and Discovery Diving. It has a swimming pool, exercise room, and features free continental breakfast. Many of the rooms have views of the sound. The two-room suite has a separate living area, microwave, wet bar, and refrigerator—nice for a small group or for families. Standard room rates are from $74 to $82 per night. Call (800) HAMPTON or (252) 240-2300; fax (252) 240-2311; website: www.hamptoninns.com.

Campground

Whispering Pines is a well-tended, peaceful place in Newport, about eight miles west of Morehead City, on Highway 24. Divers get a 10 percent discount. Call (252) 726-4902.

Live-Aboard

Olympus Dive Center runs a 65-foot custom dive boat that holds 12 passengers. Sleeping is in bunks in the main salon. Phone (800) 992-1258 or (252) 726-9432; fax (252) 726-0883; e-mail: olympus@olympusdiving.com; website: www.olympusdiving.com.

LIFE IN THE OUTER BANKS

With the multitude of choices for what to see and do in the area, my numero uno would be to take a boat ride through **Bogue Sound** in the late afternoon. Perhaps it seems strange, after diving all day and spending hours on a boat getting to and from dive sites, that another boat ride would hold any appeal. But it really does provide a wonderful change of pace.

On these glassy-calm waters, you'll motor past serene estuaries with colonies of shorebirds and islands completely devoid of development other than interpretive trails. The setting sun illuminates miles of pristine beaches along its path.

Another way to enjoy these islands is to hop a ferry over to **Shackleford Banks** and **Cape Lookout National Seashore** for hiking and swimming. You won't find any concessions or services on the islands, so bring along picnicking supplies. Fifty-five miles long, the national seashore consists of wide, barren beaches with low dunes, flat grasslands bordered by dense vegetation, and large expanses of salt marsh alongside the sound. It extends from Ocracoke Inlet down to Beaufort Inlet. There is a ferry service from Front Street in Beaufort and a ferry landing at the picturesque Cape Lookout Lighthouse. For more information about the park, you can drive to the visitor's center and park headquarters on Harkers Island. The island is 17 miles east of Beaufort, and is reached by taking Highway 70 to the Harkers Island turnoff and following the signs to Cape Lookout National Seashore.

While on Harkers Island, stop by the **Core Sound Waterfowl Museum,** which is keeping alive the generations-old art of waterfowl decoy making. It features decoy exhibits and carving demonstrations, and has a gift shop and gallery.

Another pristine area is the **Rachel Carson Reserve** at Tidal Bird Shoals and Carrot Island, practically within stone-skipping distance of Beaufort. Shelling and hiking are the attractions, including a half-mile interpretive loop trail. The trail is marked with numbered posts keyed to a descriptive brochure and introduces some of the plants and animals that live in the area. Following the trail at low tide is advised. Probably the best way to get here is to rent a kayak from one of two businesses located on Front Street in Beaufort, directly across from the Rachel Carson Reserve.

For island exploration on **horseback,** contact Outer Banks Riding Stables, which organizes a variety of rides and trips on the beach at Cedar Island. Call (252) 225-1185.

Definitely spend some time walking around **Beaufort,** a seaport town founded in 1709. Its 21-block historic district shows off nearly 100 restored homes. Another option is to take the English-style double-decker bus on a one-hour narrated tour. Catch it at the Beaufort Historic Site at

138 Turner Street. In the evening, enjoy a long, tall cold one at an open-air bar on the docks.

You'll certainly want to spend some browsing time in the wonderful **North Carolina Maritime Museum.** It features fascinating displays of historical life-saving equipment, wooden boat building, and collections brought up from shipwrecks, including what is assumed to be Blackbeard's ship, the *Queen Anne's Revenge.* The museum is at 315 Front Street, just off the Intracoastal Waterway on the Beaufort waterfront.

Bogue Banks, where **Atlantic Beach** is located, is the focus for tourist-type activities. From Morehead City you take Highrise Bridge, which deposits you on the eastern end, in Atlantic Beach. This is where the kid-type amusements are found, like miniature golf, bumper cars, and a ferris wheel. At the eastern tip you'll come to **Fort Macon State Park,** a Civil War fort surrounded on three sides by water. You can explore the fort and the surrounding salt marshes and estuaries. Driving west there are motels and restaurants interspersed with fishing piers and miles and miles of beaches.

Another must-see is the **North Carolina Aquarium** at Pine Knoll Shores, five miles west of Atlantic Beach in the Theodore Roosevelt Natural Area. Some of the interesting features are the Living Shipwreck display, a live alligator exhibit, and a touch tank.

About 45 minutes outside this area is **New Bern,** founded in 1710. Named after its mother city, Bern, Switzerland, it also has a terrific historic district.

Dining and Entertainment

Fresh seafood here is wonderful. One of my favorite combinations, which I've never seen anywhere else, is shrimp and grits. Another local specialty, which makes my mouth water to write about it, is the lowland barbecue, otherwise known as a pig pickin'—definitely not for vegetarians. An entire pig is slowly cooked over wood chips while basted frequently with a vinegar-based sauce. This type of barbecue is usually done for large groups. To get individual plates, head for **Roland's** in Beaufort, and in Morehead City try **McCall's** or **Smithfield Barbecue.**

For excellent seafood, go to Clawson's in Beaufort and the Sanitary Fish Market in Morehead City. **Clawson's 1905 Restaurant,** at 425 Front Street (on the waterfront), is popular with divers and features fresh local seafood, ribs, and pasta. It also has the best beer selection on this part of the coast. The original dining room was once Mr. Clawson's 1905 grocery store. Check out the memorabilia. Next door to Clawson's is **Fishtowne Java and Ice Cream,** serving gourmet coffees, baked goods, and desserts.

The **Sanitary Fish Market and Restaurant** is an institution here (more than 60 years) on the waterfront at 501 Evans Street. Enjoy fresh seafood, chicken and steaks, homemade chowders, soups, and desserts along with great views of Bogue Sound. Come on down to this area during the North Carolina Seafood Festival (the first weekend in October each year) and you can even participate in a crab race.

A lively divers' hangout downtown in Morehead City is **Raps Grill and Bar.** It's a great place for trading dive stories, ordering pitchers of beer, and getting down to some serious eating—ribs, steamed crabs, pasta, sandwiches, seafood, and steaks.

Medical Facilities

Carteret General Hospital, at 3500 Arendell Street in Morehead City, is the area's closest facility; phone (252) 247-1439 or for emergencies (252) 247-1543. The nearest recompression chamber is the FG Hall laboratory at Duke Medical Center, which is also the home of DAN (Divers Alert Network). Phone (919) 684-8111 for emergencies. For general diving questions call (919) 684-2948.

To reach the local Coast Guard Station at Fort Macon, call (252) 247-4598. For on-the-water emergencies, standard procedure is to call on Channel 16 (marine radio) to reach the Coast Guard.

Palau

Physical Characteristics of the Dive Area	
WATER & WEATHER CONDITIONS	
Visibility	*Adequate to Excellent*
Current and Surge	*Minimal to Ripping*
Temperature	*Comfortable*
Storms	*Occasionally Stormy*
SITE CONDITIONS	
Mooring Buoys	*Average*
Fishing, Collecting, and Hunting Restrictions	*Some Restrictions*
Ease of Access	*Moderate*
Boat Traffic/Diver Congestion	*Light*
MARINE LIFE	
Abundance of Invertebrates	*Prolific*
Abundance of Vertebrates	*Prolific*
Abundance of Pelagic Life	*Prolific*
Health of Reef/Marine Life/ Marine Structure	*Healthy*

Underwater Wonder of the World

After diving Palau, whatever is highest on your list of top-ranked dive sites will be knocked right off its pedestal, guaranteed. This truly is a diving mecca—the ultimate, numero uno, top dog. In fact, in 1989, CEDAM International (an organization dedicated to conservation, education, diving, archeology, and museums) selected Palau as the best of the seven diving wonders of the world. Jacques Cousteau once named Palau's Ngemelis Wall as the world's best wall dive. Not too shabby.

Palau's amazing cluster of islands and barrier reef offer diving experiences in all possible facets—interesting, beautiful, exciting, and thrilling. You can explore wreck sites and caves, fall off vertical walls, and soar through swift currents. You can also see species of marine life found nowhere else on the planet. It is said that Palau's waters hold 1,500 species of fish and 700 varieties of coral.

On the surface, Palau is as exciting and beautiful as it is underwater— truly a tropical paradise. Most of this island-nation is in its natural state, with dense tropical forest, mangroves, rivers, waterfalls, and vast stretches of brilliantly white sandy beaches. But there is also just the right amount of development to satisfy tourists, as well as a traditional culture that remains an integral element of Palauan life.

Most of the 300-odd islands that comprise the Republic of Palau lie around and inside an enormous lagoon, its waters ranging from ethereal blue-green to shades of blue you never knew existed. Want to plan a wedding? celebrate an anniversary? give someone a memorable birthday gift? This would be the place for that special occasion. Stay at a nice (perhaps elegant?) resort on the beach. Hike through forests of ironwood, banyan, coconut, pandanus, and broadleaf hardwood trees to reach waterfalls; kayak the mangrove forests to see crocodiles lounging in the shallows, and visit ancient ruins and local villages. In the evening, lie in a swaying hammock and search for the Southern Cross. What could possibly be more romantic?

Now that you're hooked, you probably want to know where Palau is located. That's not easy to answer, because this 400-mile-long archipelago really isn't *near* anything. To start, it is in the westernmost part of Micronesia. On your globe it'll be a tiny speck surrounded by a whole lot of water. But the easiest way to locate Palau is to find the Philippines, then look to the right of Mindanao. Palau is about 600 miles east.

When you land at the airport, you'll be in the state of Airai, which is the southern-most section of the island called Babeldaob. Although Babeldaob is the largest island, the three-and-a-half-square-mile Koror is Palau's capital and center of commerce. This is also where most of the dive centers and resorts are located. A paved road extends from the airport to Koror, and causeways connect Koror to its neighboring islands, Arakabesang and Malakal. Some of the small islands much farther south, such as Carp, Angaur, and Peleliu have small dive resorts and modest guest houses.

To visit the other states (16 altogether) you'd need a four-wheel-drive pickup and a guide. The far-flung islands both north and south of Koror and Babeldaob are accessible by boat. One of these, Peleliu, does have a paved runway and regular air service with Paradise Air. The southernmost states are some 250 miles southwest of Koror.

Palau

Philippine Sea

Ngarchelong

Ngaraard

Ngardmau

Ngeremlengui

Ngiwal

Melekeok

Ngatpang

Ngchesar

Aimeliik

Airai

Ngerekebesang

Koror

Ulong

The
Rock
Islands

Chankanab
Reef

Ngerukewid
(Seventy Islands)

Ngermeaus

Mecherchar

PACIFIC
OCEAN

Ngemelis

Omekang
Island

Ngercheu
(Carp Island)

Peleliu

PALAU

SOUTH PACIFIC
OCEAN

PAPUA
NEW GUINEA

AUSTRALIA

INDIAN
OCEAN

NEW
ZEALAND

Angaur

421

Quick Stats

Pronounced   puh-LAOW

Size   Palau is an archipelago of 343 islands spread over hundreds of miles (anywhere from 325 to 500 miles, depending upon the information source); the land area is 196 square miles.

Population   19,000

Location   7° 30' north latitude, 133° east longitude; between Guam, the Philippines, and Papua New Guinea. It is 800 miles southwest of Guam and 600 miles east of the Philippines.

Time   In the same time zone as Tokyo, which is 14 hours ahead of New York and 17 hours ahead of Los Angeles. When traveling west, you'll cross the International Date Line, so you lose a day going and gain it coming back.

Government   The Republic of Palau (it's called *Belau* by its inhabitants) became self-ruling in 1994. It had been a postwar U.S.-administered Trust Territory of the Pacific Islands for 47 years; now it has a Compact of Free Association with the United States.

Language   The official languages are Palauan and English, but Japanese is also spoken widely.

Electrical Current   Single phase, 60 cycles, 115/230 Volts AC, same as in the United States.

Climate   Essentially warm and humid, with virtually no seasons. Average air temperature is 82°, and the humidity stays at 82 percent. Annual average rainfall is 150 inches, and rain is frequent throughout the year. The driest time is February to May. Palau is considered to be outside the typhoon zone.

Water Temperature   Averages 83° near the surface.

Currents   Expected at most dive sites, and can be very strong both at depth and at the surface. Most dives are drift dives.

Underwater Visibility   50 to 200 feet

Best Diving Months   December through March, but any time is fine.

Planning the Trip

Phoning Palau   The country code is 680. From the United States, dial the international access number (011) + country code (680) + the local number.

Getting to Palau   Continental Micronesia, a subsidiary of Continental Airlines, flies to Palau from Guam, the international air service hub for the Micronesia region. Continental Airlines flies to Guam from Honolulu, Los Angeles, and San Francisco. Maximum luggage allowance is two bags, 70 pounds each, and one carry-on up to 11 pounds. Departure tax is $20. You'll have to go through customs and immigration.

Airport Transportation   Arrange to have your hotel pick you up at the airport. If this doesn't work out, you can always get a taxi. Most of the accommodations are in or near Koror, which is only a 30-minute drive from the airport.

Getting Around   There are taxis, car rentals, bicycle rentals, and boat and plane charters. Driving is on the right; some roads are not paved.

Entry Documents   Proof of citizenship (passport or birth certificate) and an onward or return airline ticket are required of U.S. citizens. Visas are not required unless the stay is longer than 30 days. Non-U.S. citizens must have a valid passport.

Immunizations   None are required; however cholera and yellow fever immunizations are required for those arriving from infected areas.

Currency   U.S. dollar

Tourist Offices   Palau Visitors Authority, PO Box 256, Koror, Palau 96940. Phone (680) 488-2793/1930; fax (680) 488-1453/1725; e-mail: pva@palaunet.com; website: www.visit-palau.com.

THE UNDERWATER SCENE

These islands, which are mostly volcanic in origin, lie atop a huge subterranean mountain ridge. A few are very shallow coral atolls, lying inside an enormous and stunningly beautiful lagoon. The lagoon and most of the islands are completely surrounded by barrier reef. For divers, this interesting diverse topography means infinite diving experiences, as well.

The exciting wall dives begin with a boat ride from Koror (typically) through the shallow lagoon and its breathtaking Rock Islands, to reach sites along the western edge of the barrier reef and islands toward the south. It usually takes anywhere from 45 minutes to one and a half hours to get to the sites, but no one complains. On the other hand, most of the wreck sites and the Chandelier Cave site are within the lagoon, among the Rock Islands, and conveniently close to Koror.

The individual Rock Islands appear to be clusters of small mushroom-shaped masses of lush green growth floating upon the water's surface. They reminded me of bunches of broccoli popping up all around, but surrounded by water colors that seemed too beautiful to be real. The chiseled, undercut shape of these shallow islands is said to be caused by a combination of acidic water (seeping through the vegetation) and marine organisms, all eating away at the limestone base. These Rock Islands, alone, would be sufficient reason to come to Palau. And that's only the prelude to your dives!

Most dive centers are located in Koror. Many of the operators cater to the Japanese diving market. Make sure you choose one that caters to Westerners or at least provides bilingual divemasters. All those listed in this chapter have English-speaking divemasters.

Dive boats usually combine the surface interval with lunch on the beach at one of the uninhabited Rock Islands. After lunch you're usually free to snorkel around or explore the island at your leisure. Frequently there is little shade, so a hat, cover-up, and sunscreen are a good idea.

For marine life, you'll have an opportunity to see it all: hundreds of species of tropicals and corals, sponges and pelagics. At the drop-offs and along the walls are snappers, blue fusiliers, pyramid butterfly fish, triggerfish, surgeonfish, and unicornfish—and several species of each, just for starters. You'll also see marine life in enormous proportions—huge spreading sea fans, monster anemones, manta rays with eight-foot wingspans, and fat, five-foot-long Napoleon wrasse. And there are sharks, lots and lots of reef sharks. Both silver-tips and white-tips patrol off the walls. Of course, there are plenty of little creatures too, such as the nudibranchs, in an array of exotic colors.

Health Score Card

When I dived this area in 1994, it was absolutely pristine. The lush coral growth was an underwater fantasy, and the vast numbers of fish and other reef and pelagic marine life were absolutely overwhelming. The only area that appeared to be a bit worse for wear was the shelf on the Blue Corner dive, which is where divers cling to watch the blue water parade. My guess is it probably looks a lot shabbier now. The hooks, however, should be more environmentally friendly than the method of old, which was to simply grab onto a piece of dead (hopefully) coral. I have heard that coral bleaching has hit even Palau, but that the areas have already recovered. Unfortunately, bleaching is a worldwide phenomenon, due to exceptionally warm water temperatures. As soon as the temperatures get back to normal, the reefs recover quickly.

Diving Conditions

The conditions vary from benign shallow lagoon waters to raging currents with intimidating ocean swells, and from 300-foot visibility to only 40 feet of vis. This huge range of conditions is due to the tremendous diversity of diving environments here.

Most of the sites that divers come all this way to see are those that can have pretty dicey conditions at times. The wall sites have at least a mild current running and occasionally it will go full speed and sprint. Generally, there's a direct correlation between wind and ocean swells: the stronger the wind, the heavier the swells will be. That can make for rough boat rides and difficulty getting back on board after dives.

On the other hand, the water temperature is bathwater warm and the visibility is frequently well over 100 feet. In fact, it can be over 200 feet. But then, where there's a sandy bottom, such as in channels and harbors, visibility can really get mucked up, to the extent that it's reduced to about 40 feet.

Recommended Level of Experience

Divers need to be confident and experienced. Most of the best dives here are challenging drift dives and deep dives. It's necessary to have very good buoyancy control and the experience and presence of mind to remain calm if you suddenly make a rapid ascent or descent due to the currents.

Since most dives along the walls are drift dives, the boats do not anchor but simply follow the divers' bubbles. With this type of diving, you have to do your safety stops in open water without a handy anchor or decompression line to hold on to. So it's important to be able to do that without any particular difficulty, since safety stops, and occasionally decompression stops, are absolutely necessary on these deep dives. So, again, good buoyancy control is a prerequisite to diving in these waters.

Everyone should dive with a few pieces of emergency equipment: a whistle, an inflatable safety sausage, and a small light or combination light and strobe that can be slipped into a BCD pocket. Actually, it's always good to dive with these, but they're particularly useful for drift diving, especially in an area where you could drift off to the Philippines.

The waters of Palau are perfect for advanced divers, and surprisingly, for snorkelers, also. Because the water is so clear, even some of the wall sites would be interesting for snorkelers. Jellyfish Lake is one area where you must snorkel—diving is not allowed. Snorkelers can also see the giant clams at various sites. Some of the wreck sites, too, are fairly shallow.

Great Dive Sites

Blue Corner is undoubtedly the most exhilarating, yet at the same time the most frustrating, dive site I have ever experienced. Frustrating because there is so much activity that it is impossible to grasp it all, savor it, then try to remember it for the logbook. I dived Blue Corner three times, and each time I told myself, "OK, this time I'm really going to get it, to take it all in and keep it locked in a corner of my brain." Wrong.

The problem is, during this swift drift dive you'll have a fraction of a second to admire anything. Just as soon as you take a look at it, it's gone, replaced by something else. You want to say, "Now, wait a minute!" Don't plan to take any pictures as you're being propelled along the wall, and definitely tether your camera to your BCD. Later in the dive, you'll have an opportunity to find some terrific subjects in less frenzied conditions.

Actually, Blue Corner starts off pretty much like any other wall dive here. You'll follow the steep wall down to about 114 feet, admiring the astounding variety of hard and soft corals and giant sponges. You'll see clownfish darting in and out of their anemone-protectors. As the dive progresses you'll start to ascend, little by little, perhaps thinking to yourself: *OK, what's the big deal? This is great, but where's the pizzazz?*

That's about when you'll literally start to turn the corner along this underwater peninsula, and then an incredible thing happens. Serenity turns into a madcap, tumultuous scene of motion. You're swept into and among huge schools of jacks, snappers, butterflies, Pacific silversides, and more tropicals you can ever expect to remember, many intermingling with one another. You don't drift, you soar along that face. As you rush into the schools, about all you can ID is . . . big fish . . . little fish . . . more little fish . . .

With visibility around 150 feet, you can survey the blue water, and what you see accelerates your breathing rate. Sharks, sleek and regal, cruise along, with their pilotfish in hot pursuit. You have only seconds to admire them before they're behind you. You turn to look behind you, and as soon as you turn back around you see more up ahead, as well as yellow fin tuna, manta rays, and the occasional sea turtle. You desperately want to put the scene into slow motion, to savor the brilliant colors and enjoy the swirl of movement—to check out those sharks!

At times you might encounter sudden downdrafts, where currents will sweep you up then throw you right back down again. I've never experienced it, but I'm sure it could be intimidating. Just be forewarned and remember to breathe!

At a ledge along the wall, divers are holding onto rocks and dead coral, their bodies flowing like diver-down flags, in order to watch the colorful feeding-chain parade of tropicals and pelagics. Many of the divemasters here provide special hooks to divers that they can cram into a dead area. You'll feel like an underwater windsock, with the still-strong current sweeping past you.

But it's time to ascend toward the top of the reef, where the show continues. Enormous schools of shimmering barracuda hover like overhead cloud cover. The schools of tropicals are fewer now, but more reef sharks patrol the sandy flats. On my first dive here, I spotted one that appeared to be napping. I moved up on it, snapping off pictures until I was close enough to touch it. Sensing my presence, the shark popped up, gave a little shiverlike shake, and darted off with incredible speed.

If Bonaparte, the enormous narcissistic Napoleon wrasse, is still in residence at Blue Corner, you can't possibly miss him. In fact, if you're taking pictures, he'll probably cruise in front of your lens, coming between you and whatever you're trying to photograph. But then, he's a terrific subject, himself. You'd swear he's thinking something like: *Admire me, I'm big and beautiful.*

Divemasters frequently precede Blue Corner with the adjacent *Blue Holes* site. Along the vertical wall in shallow water, four very large holes on the top of the reef lead to four separate vertical chimneys that plummet more than 80 feet and spit you out along the wall at a depth of 135 feet. What a way to start a dive!

Blue Corner is located along the *Ngemelis Wall,* where several other terrific dive sites, such as *New Drop-off,* are located. A popular surface-interval retreat is on the beach at Ulong Island. Boats anchor in the bay's shallow aquamarine waters. Everyone leaps off the boat and wades to the beach, which with brilliant white sand and a palm tree backdrop seems just too good to be true. Be sure to wear your booties or tennis shoes before jumping into the water anywhere around here. That sharp coral can really do a job on bare feet. It's likely you'll have this entire spot to yourself, to lounge and to explore. It's fun to walk out onto an enormous sand spit that runs far out into the bay.

New Drop-off, at the southern end of Ngemelis Island, is another deep wall dive. This is a nice site to follow Blue Corner, because it's more relaxing and you'll have time to appreciate some of the wonderful species found in this part of the world. A gentle current provides effortless drift, propelling you along at about the 100-foot depth. Giant gorgonian fans and vase sponges protrude into the blue. Soft corals come in varied shades of pink, purple, and orange. Brilliant orange-and-purple anemones harbor little orange-and-black clownfish among their tentacles. Out in the misty blue water, gray reef sharks cruise along at about 150 feet. You'll have plenty of bottom time for exploring the mysteries within the walls' cuts and crevices.

Also off Ngemelis Island is *Big Drop-off,* another deep wall dive (dropping to nearly 1,000 feet) with gentle currents. It's another knock-your-booties-off gorgeous site with a wonderful variety of fish and coral species. The shallow section here is most impressive, with spectacular colors of hard corals, sea fans, and coral whips of all colors. Definitely bring the underwater camera on this dive.

Just a few minutes from Big Drop-off is *German Channel,* the place to spot manta rays. They like to come in and hover over the rock outcroppings to get their daily grooming by tiny cleaner wrasse. On my dive here, our depth was about 90 feet, but the visibility was poor—only around 40 feet. Nevertheless, we spotted an enormous manta. A member of our party approached it, and so scared it off, and unfortunately we never saw another one. If you wait for them to approach you, you'll have greater success and probably see several mantas. If you're lucky, you might also spot a shark-cleaning station.

The island of *Peleliu,* located at the southern end of Palau's lagoon, features several adrenaline-producing sites. Be forewarned: the currents can really scoot, and if the seas get churned up, bag the dive. You could literally float to the Philippines if the dive boat doesn't locate you. Definitely clip a safety sausage to your BCD.

The currents at the southern tip of Peleliu, which is wild, open ocean, bring in a constant supply of nutrients that form the base of the food chain. That's what attracts the swarming schools of tropicals and their pelagic predators. Sharks keep well nourished here. Sea fans, crinoids, corals, and sponges all reach out from the plunging walls to snatch their share of nutrients.

This sheer wall at the southern tip, which is frequently called *Peleliu Corner,* plummets hundreds of feet, so don't drop that camera! The individual sites include *Peleliu Cut, Peleliu Express, West Wall, Orange Beach,* and *Yellow Beach.* The top of the wall at these sites is shallow, ranging from about 35 to 60 feet, so you do not need to dive deep. Peleliu Cut is located closest to the corner and therefore receives the strongest currents. Orange Beach combines diverse reef life with leftover relics from World War II, now merged with the reef structure. Please, do not think about pocketing anything.

Huge gorgonian soft corals in all sorts of colors cover the length of the wall, joined occasionally by stony cup corals and brown barrel sponges. Schools of snapper, sennet, sea bream, barracuda, and Moorish idols fill the water column. Large triggerfish, lionfish, crocodile fish, and hawkfish are a few of the residents that work the reef. Purple carpet anemones billow from their anchors and small orange-and-yellow clownfish dart in and out among the anemones' waving tentacles. Resting in the alcoves and caverns are turtles, nurse sharks, and tiger sharks.

This is biodiversity at its finest. Certainly, making the trek to Peleliu is well worth the effort.

Wreck Dives

In the lagoons around the Rock Islands, warship and plane wrecks have been submerged for so long they've developed their own ecosystems. The wrecks themselves are interesting from a historical perspective, and the artificial reef structure with its marine-life inhabitants provides the finishing touches. These wrecks are now havens for yellowtails, batfish, and lionfish, among others.

Several wreck sites are right in Malakal Harbor, near the commercial port. One of these is the *Helmet Wreck,* a.k.a. Depth Charge Wreck. The ship is an unidentified Japanese World War II freighter and lies at about 90 feet. Visibility here can be poor, so bring a dive light, because there's lots to see. You'll find stacks of helmets, bits of bottles and crockery, a machine gun, urinal, etc.

The *Iro Maru* was a Japanese fleet supply vessel sunk in 1944. You can see a large hole in the bow where the ship was torpedoed. This is another deep one, with the rudder and propeller beyond 100 feet, but most of the area you'll be exploring will be shallower than 90 feet. You can see the large bow gun, and at the stern is another gun. It's possible to explore the cabins and the holds. Water conditions here are generally very good, with little current.

The *Upside-Down Zero* is a Japanese airplane sitting at about 63 feet. You can see the prop and various parts of the plane. Visibility can be poor here, so bring a dive light for this one, too. Although the plane is interesting, I was more entranced with the lovely fields of stony corals nearby. Beautiful tabletops and ledges of lacy white stony corals were obviously thriving in the shallow waters.

Overhead Environments

These islands are a combination of volcanic material and porous limestone, and consequently riddled with caves and caverns. Two wonderful sites that are commonly dived are shallow and safe enough for divers with no cave-diving experience (as long as a guide accompanies you). Be sure to take a dive light.

Siaes Tunnel is along another plunging wall on the outside of the barrier reef, this one dripping with soft corals. A point along the wall juts out into the Philippine Sea (another right-angle turn like at Blue Corner), which is where this horizontal tunnel passes, at about 90 feet. It's huge, estimated to be about 30 feet in diameter, 50 feet high, and 100 feet in length. On the way it will take you to a beautiful cavern bathed in an ethereal blue light and adorned with sea fans and bushes of black coral. On the white sandy bottom, watch for white-tip reef sharks taking a snooze, and up on the ceiling look for inverted lionfish.

Shallow *Chandelier Cave* features a series of underwater chambers, some filled with ancient stalactites and flowstones. Bring your dive light along and peer at these huge formations, thousands of years in the making. The cave is located on the uninhabited island of Ngarol inside the lagoon and very close to Koror. If you get squeamish thinking about overhead environments, or are at all claustrophobic, better skip this one. The dive begins with a swim through a ten-foot diameter tunnel that leads from the lagoon into the bowels of the island. A twisting horizontal passage, about 400 feet in length, connects five large chambers, none deeper than 60 feet. It is possible to come up to the surface and breathe fresh air in most of these chambers.

Great Snorkeling Sites

There's no place quite like *Jellyfish Lake* anywhere in the world. Imagine bobbing around inside a lava lamp and you'll come close to understanding this unique experience. Jellyfish Lake is a brackish inland body of water about the size of a football field located on Eil Malk Island, just a 30-minute boat ride out of Koror. Surrounded on all sides by the limestone of the island, by thick mangroves, hanging vines, and dense tropical forest, the lake is a predator-free environment for the hundreds of thousands of jellyfish that inhabit it.

Before going *yuuck, jellyfish,* listen to this: after untold eons in this benign environment, the cauliflowerlike jellies (species *mastigias*) have shed their defensive mechanisms—that is, they don't sting. As a result, these normally fearsome creatures take on a rather beautiful aura in Jellyfish Lake. Their slow, steady pulsating and golden hues produce a peaceful hypnotic effect, especially when they are all around, coming at you from every direction. They're really soft and friendly, and if they weren't water creatures, might be considered cuddly.

Evidently, when the Rock Islands rose, waters became landlocked, thereby forming several lakes. The resident jellyfish, and a few other species that inhabit the lake, evolved over centuries and lost their need for stinging tentacles. Rather than stinging and feeding upon stunned marine life, they grow their own food through photosynthesis.

After the boats drop you off, you'll take a 15-minute hike to the lake, with some hindrances along the way, so don't take much with you. Do take a towel. Photographers, on sunny days you'll get your best shots in these naturally turbid waters sans strobe, so do yourself a favor and leave it behind. You'll enter the water in a murky freshwater creek, then progress to the main body of the lake, which is extremely salty. This is where the jellies congregate. If at first you don't find them, just follow the rays of the sun, which is what the jellies are after.

Although this is widely heralded as the sole locale for these interesting creatures, divemasters confessed that there are at least two other lakes in the republic that hold this variety of jellyfish. But local operators have agreed to restrict diving pressure to boat-ride-convenient Jellyfish Lake, thereby according the other lakes an unofficial nature-preserve status.

Scuba equipment is discouraged here. You can't go deeper than about 50 feet anyway, due to the toxic concentrations of hydrogen sulfide beyond that depth. Actually, scuba isn't necessary. On sunny days, the lake's inhabitants come right up to the surface. They are fragile, so as you swim through them, be careful not to hurt them with fins, snorkel, and camera gear. The best technique is to simply float motionless on the surface and let the clouds of sunlight-hungry invertebrates join you.

Marine Life Protection

It is illegal to purchase, import, or export any listed threatened or endangered species, such as sea turtles, dugong (a type of manatee), saltwater crocodiles, and some corals. Palau's water falls under the restrictions of the Endangered Species Act, the Lacey Act and the Convention on International Trade in Endangered Species (CITES), and the Marine Mammal Protection Act. To avoid anchor damage to the reefs, a mooring system has been in place since 1992, developed by the National Marine Sanctuary Program, and now implemented by Palauans.

Among the dive permits required is the $15 permit for all visitors to the Rock Islands, which assists with the mooring system, beach and island cleaning, and protecting the dive sites from illegal fishing. Angaur requires a dive permit of $75 per person. And a new $15 permit is now required by the State of Peleliu. Permits are valid for seven days. Check with the Palau Visitors Authority for details: phone (680) 488-2793; website: www.visit-palau.com.

DIVE SERVICES & PACKAGES

Fish 'n Fins, adjacent to the Marina Hotel (a PADI Resort), at M-Dock in Koror, is one of the oldest dive centers in Palau, having been established in 1972. The shop offers airport transfers, and provides diving and snorkeling tours and outrigger canoe rides. Rinse tanks and secure gear storage are provided. They even offer e-mail service and Internet access a the dive shop. On dive boats, divers are placed in groups of six to eight, based on experience. Boats have cabins with toilets and showers. All have marine radios, oxygen, and shelter from the sun. All employees have PADI divemaster certification, and instruction is with IANTD, PADI, and TDI. Nitrox is available. Technical diving courses include Advanced Nitrox and a Deep Air course. Photo services include video and still camera rentals (Nikonos and Sea 'n Sea), a wide selection of lenses, and E-6 processing. A complete photo shop is in the planning stages. A repair technician is on staff. Finally, also associated with the shop is the six-passenger live-aboard *Ocean Hunter Palau*. Phone (680) 488-2637; fax (680) 488-5417; e-mail: fishnfin@palaunet.com; website: www.fishnfins.com.

Retail Sales: *Extensive*	**Dive Boat Comfort:** *Good*
Rentals: *Extensive*	**On-Board Facilities**
Scuba Training: *Extensive*	**for Photographers:** *Good*
Photo Services: *Extensive*	

Neco Marine, based in Koror, runs a couple of custom dive boats with shallow drafts for getting into those hard-to-reach areas. The boats have camera tables, freshwater rinse, and wet/dry storage. Each boat carries an oxygen kit, long-distance marine radio and first-aid kit. Rental gear is available. This is a PADI 5-Star Dive Center. It's also an IANTD facility, so technical courses are given as well. Nitrox is pumped on the premises. The photo shop has E-6 processing, camera and video rentals, including a variety of lenses, and housing rentals, repairs, and photo instruction. Two-tank dives also include a "freebie" afternoon dive or snorkel at places like Chandelier Cave, Jellyfish Lake, or Soft Coral Arch. There's a dedicated photo boat for serious underwater photographers, allowing the freedom and type of diving needed to get good underwater pics.

Neco Marine also offers Big Island Adventure tours to Babeldoab to see native villages, waterfalls, and the traditional bai meeting house, with opportunities for shopping. A picnic lunch features authentic Palauan food. Phone (680) 488-1755 or 2009; fax (680) 488-3014 or 5245; e-mail: neco marine@palaunet.com; website: www.seapalau.com. Check out their website for terrific weather information.

Retail Sales: *Adequate*	**Dive Boat Comfort:** *Good*
Rentals: *Adequate*	**On-Board Facilities**
Scuba Training: *Extensive*	**for Photographers:** *Superior*
Photo Services: *Extensive*	

Palau Diving Center is Koror-based and caters to visitors staying in various Koror hotels, as well as those at the Carp Island Resort, near Peleliu. The shop offers equipment rentals, scuba instruction with NAUI and PADI, and a variety of land tours as well as fishing and kayaking. The primary boat used is a 29-footer. Dive/lodging discounts are with Carp Island Resort. It also provides airport transfers. Phone 488-2978; fax 488-3155; e-mail: carpcorp@palaunet.com.

Retail Sales: *Adequate*	**Dive Boat Comfort:** *Good*
Rentals: *Adequate*	**On-Board Facilities**
Scuba Training: *Moderate*	**for Photographers:** *Good*
Photo Services: *Limited*	

Sam's Dive Tours is a PADI 5-Star IDC, which means you can get just about any training you want here, including an instructor rating. They even offer a specialty course that they created called Blue Corner Specialty Diver. Other specialty classes include Enriched Air Nitrox and DPV (Diver Propulsion Vehicle). The shop has extensive rental and retail lines (including fish ID books) and offers Nitrox fills (32 percent and up). Dive boats usually are limited to eight divers and are equipped with VHF radios and oxygen kits, and have sun canopies. Snorkelers are welcomed and accommodated. Sam's tours cover most of Palau's dive sites, including Peleliu. KD Photo Shop at Sam's Tours has E-6 processing, camera and video rentals, repairs, and photo instruction. A certified (IAST) repair technician is on staff. Equipment storage is available at the shop.

In addition to diving tours, Sam's has kayak tours (with **Planet Blue**), fishing tours (with **International Anglers Palau**), and Rock Island and land tours. Camping gear can be rented and tickets purchased on Belau Air (and boat charter) to Peleliu and Anguar. Associated with Sam's is **Palau Sea Ventures,** which runs the charter sailing yacht *Eclipse*. This is a 48-foot sloop that carries a compressor and tanks for divers, sea kayaks, and fishing gear. Guests pitch in, becoming part of the crew and doing various tasks.

Sam's offers dive/lodging packages with Carolines Resort, Sunrise Villa, West Plaza Hotel, and Palasia Hotel, and can arrange reservations. Phone (680) 488-1062; fax (680) 488-5003; e-mail: samstour@palaunet.com; website: www.samstours.com.

Retail Sales: *Extensive*	**Dive Boat Comfort:** *Good*
Rentals: *Extensive*	**On-Board Facilities**
Scuba Training: *Extensive*	**for Photographers:** *Good*
Photo Services: *Extensive*	

Splash Diving Center is on the property of the Palau Pacific Resort, which is on Arakabesan Island, across the causeway from Koror. Splash is a PADI 5-Star IDC with a boat dock, classrooms, and pro-shop. If you're staying at the Palau Pacific, just walk out of your room, down to the beach, and the boat's waiting for you—nice! The main dive boat is a twin-diesel custom craft, and another smaller, but faster, boat has twin outboards. Boats carry oxygen and first-aid kits. Splash is another Instructor Development Center, so you can take courses from Discover Scuba all the way to instructor. The shop also offers a number of specialty courses, including Enriched Air Nitrox, Medic First-Aid and the DAN Oxygen course. The Pro Shop has gear for sale, including safety sausages and reef hooks. There is also an equipment repair service. Photo Palau is the in-house underwater digital video and photo center. They offer E-6 and print processing, photo instruction, custom underwater videos, equipment sales, and still and video camera rentals and repairs. Phone 488-2600; fax 488-1741; e-mail: splash@palaunet.com; website: www.divepalau.com. The website has superb information about the island and dive sites, including some useful maps.

Retail Sales: *Extensive*	**Dive Boat Comfort:** *Good*
Rentals: *Extensive*	**On-Board Facilities**
Scuba Training: *Extensive*	**for Photographers:** *Good*
Photo Services: *Extensive*	

WHERE TO STAY

Palau has a variety of accommodations, including luxury resorts, hotels, motels, and guest houses. The following are particularly suited to divers. To research the smaller properties, log on to www.visit-palau.com.

Carolines Resort ★★ has seven island-style hillside bungalows, surrounded by tropical landscaping. Each has a verandah and expansive views. On the property is Pacific Treasures, a nice little shop for picking up gifts. There is beach access, a pool, restaurant, and bar. Dive packages are available with Sam's Tours. Caroline's is located on the island of Arakabesan (near the Palau Pacific Resort), just over the causeway from Koror. The nightly room rate of $150 includes airport transfers. Phone (680) 488-3754/3755; fax (680) 488-3756; e-mail: carolines@palaunet.com.

If you're looking for isolation but want to be in good proximity to the exciting wall sites, **Carp Island Resort ★★★★★** could be the perfect spot. Its physical location is spectacular; to get to the beach, just step out of your room. The three-acre Carp Island is a part of Peleliu State, and only a 15-minute boat ride from Peleliu Island. It's about 45 minutes to Koror by speedboat. The resort is particularly popular with Japanese divers, but the staff is bilingual.

When I first saw the resort, it looked like an upscale camping site. Now it has a number of different room options, including seaside cottages (duplexes), new cottages (independent), a deluxe single bungalow (ideal for honeymooners), and suite rooms. All have showers and toilets. A dive house with seven rooms has showers and toilets at an adjacent building. A separate restaurant facility serves all meals, with menus to suit both Eastern and Western tastes. Boat charters and land tours can be arranged; kayaks can be rented, with or without a guide. Diving is with the Palau Diving Center, associated with NAUI, JP, and PADI. The shop offers daily two-tank dives and can provide all equipment. There are dive package discounts on room accommodation and two-tank dives. Room rates: $85 for the seaside and new cottages, $95 for the deluxe bungalow, $140 for the suite, and $65 for the dive house. Camping rates are $15 per night for up to 5 nights and longer. Tents are not provided. Call (680) 488-2978 or 6337or 5177; fax (680) 488-3155; e-mail: carpcorp@palaunet.com.

D.W. Motel ★ is one of several economy lodgings located in Koror. This one, which is popular with divers, has 17 rooms. Rates range from $35 to $55 per night. Phone (680) 488-2641; fax (680) 488-1725.

Palasia Hotel ★★ is located in Koror near government offices and the central business district. There are 165 rooms, shops, restaurants, a swimming pool, and fitness center. The nightly room rate starts at $182. Airport transfers are $20 per person. Dive packages are available with Sam's Tours. Call (680) 488-8888; fax (680) 488-8800; e-mail: reservations.palsia@ palaunet.com.

Palau Pacific Resort ★★★★ is the most upscale of all the lodgings in the islands. It is expensive, but you do get a lot for your money. It would be perfect for a honeymoon or observing a special occasion. The resort covers 65 acres of tropical gardens on Arakabesang Island, just across a causeway from Koror (a ten-minute drive). Located on a long beach of glistening white sand, it has a fabulous view. Catch sweeping rainbows over the water just after a rainfall and in the evening watch the sun dip below the horizon. There are 160 rooms, either oceanfront or garden view, with air-conditioning and ceiling fans, patios, and balconies. Facilities include two restaurants, swimming pool and poolside bar, Jacuzzi, fitness center, floodlit tennis courts, hiking trail, shops, and beauty salon. Splash is the on-property dive center, and their boats depart from the resort's dock. Nightly room rates range from $215 to $255. Airport transfers are $20 per person. Call (680) 488-2600; fax (680) 488-1606 or 1601; e-mail: ppr@palaunet.com; website: www.panpac.com.

Storyboard Beach Resort ★ has a terrific location on Peleliu Island— terrific because it's so close to the top dive sites. Not terrific if you want access to shops, restaurants, etc. Six thatch-roofed beachfront cottages, set among coconut trees and tropical plants and flowers, line a white sandy beach. Each unit has a private lanai overlooking the ocean, complete bathroom facilities, and electricity during the evening. The resort has an open-air restaurant serving Palauan, American, and Japanese cuisine and a tree bar, perfect for trading dive tales while watching the sunset. Land tours of Peleliu's World War II battle sites are offered, as well as to remote beaches and snorkeling areas. The nightly rate is $85. Phone (680) 345-1019; fax (680) 345-1058 or 488-1725.

Sunrise Villa ★★, on a hillside overlooking the water, features spacious rooms with views. The Villa has a pool, Jacuzzi, poolside bar, indoor bar, and restaurant. Diving packages are available with Sam's Tours. Room rates range from $130 to $160 per night and include airport transfers. Phone (680) 488-4590/4591/4592; fax (680) 488-4593; e-mail: sunrise@palaunet.com.

West Plaza Hotels ★★ has four locations: Desekel (15 rooms), located in downtown Koror; Malakal (22 rooms), near Sam's Tours; Coral Reef (11 rooms) and By the Sea (34 rooms), both located two miles from town center and on the water (no beach). All rooms are air-conditioned; some have kitchenettes. Nightly room rates range from $70 to $100 and include airport transfers. Diving packages are available with Sam's Tours. Phone (680) 488-5355; fax (680) 488-1783/2136; e-mail: west.plaza@palaunet.com.

Live-Aboards

The **Aggressor Fleet** operates the 120-foot live-aboard *Palau Aggressor II,* which carries a maximum of 18 passengers and features nine staterooms with private head and shower, onboard photo lab, hot tub, Nitrox, and e-mail. The charters are all-inclusive—meals, tanks, weights, airport transfers—and you have unlimited diving. Call (800) 348-2628; fax (504) 384-0817; e-mail: paggressor@palaunet.com; website: www.aggressor.com.

Big Blue Explorer is the new kid on the block. This is another upscale liner, 167 feet long with nine cabins accommodating up to 18 divers. Four 24-foot skiffs take divers to the sites; as many as five (or more) dives a day are possible. Nitrox is available. The ship has a dedicated camera room, and E-6 processing is done on board. Dive gear, accessories, and photo equipment are all available to rent, and instructors can get you certified in advanced and specialty courses. Each cabin has its own head and hot-water shower. Also onboard are sea kayaks, and additional activities include island excursions and beach barbecues. Day trips are also possible for divers staying in resorts; transportation to the ship is provided. Contact Ultimate Dive Travel toll-free at (877) 348-3475 or (562) 865-7198; fax (562) 865-7198; e-mail: explorer@palauscuba.com; website: www.palauscuba.com.

Ocean Hunter Palau is a sleek, six-diver live-aboard that has been a family-run operation (with the same crew) for four years. Packages are for seven full days of diving, with 95 percent of diving done from the main boat. The 60-foot-long vessel has three separately air-conditioned cabins. Cabin 1 has two single extra-wide beds and a semi-private bathroom and shower. Cabin 2 has a king-size bed, a single bed on top (for a couple or two singles), and a semi-private bathroom and shower. Cabin 3 has a master stateroom, king-size bed, a single bed, and a private bathroom and shower. There's a salon and dining room, bar, marine library, CD player, TV, and VCR. Three Nitrox mixes are blended on board, and divers can even earn their Nitrox certification. Phone (680) 488-2637; fax (680) 488-5418; e-mail: ocean.hunter@palaunet.com; website: www.oceanhunter.com.

Peter Hughes Diving, Inc. operates *Sun Dancer II,* a PADI Gold Palm Resort which puts you in the lap of luxury with morning coffee in your cabin, plush terry bathrobes, and evening turndown service. Staterooms all have bathrooms and are air-conditioned. Among the services offered are daily E-6 processing, Nitrox fills, and 24-hour day crew service. Among the facilities: audio/video entertainment center, photo and video labs with light and worktables, and open-air sundecks with covered areas. The package includes airport transfers, all meals and snacks, all beverages (alcoholic ones, too), up to four or five dives daily. Call (800) 9-DANCER; (305) 669-9392; e-mail: dancer@palaunet.com; website: www.peterhughes.com.

ISLAND LIFE

The underwater excitement of Palau has a tendency to overshadow everything else. It's inevitable, since you've traveled a long way and the primary purpose is to dive. Nevertheless, this is a fascinating country to explore topside whenever you need a surface interval, or perhaps for a few hours after your diving day is finished. Also, nondiving companions will have plenty to keep them occupied while you're submerged and should have a wonderful time exploring (and probably won't miss you a bit).

Topside Attractions

Tour operators are ready to take visitors to several of the Palauan islands to offer a glimpse of the old culture which to some extent is still practiced. Also, active treks can be made into the jungle to view some stunning natural scenery.

The tours will take you to ancient *bai,* the men's meetinghouses. These served as places of training and learning, and were important elements in this culture that experienced constant intervillage warfare. History was carved into the beams and gables of the bai, and this was the origin of the storyboard woodcarvings. You can also see an ancient amphitheater where warriors competed and where there are some mysterious ancient stone monoliths.

Palau is where people from the neighboring islands of Yap once mined quartz for their money. Incredibly, they traveled some 400 miles of open ocean in outrigger canoes to obtain this "currency," which, by the way, was enormous—sometimes more than a meter in diameter! So this was a major effort. They cut the huge chunks of stone from the rock, then carved them into wheel-like shapes before they were taken off the island. Today you can visit the quarry and see some of the disks that broke and were left behind. You'll be impressed.

Kayak treks are wonderful for seeing Palau's flora and fauna. You can kayak the Ngermeskang River, starting with its mangrove forest and progressing to dense jungle. See crocs lounging in the mangroves and exotic birds in the overhanging branches. Speaking of exotic, you'll see plenty of it in the tropical trees and ferns, and the wild orchids, which flourish here.

You won't need a guide to visit the Ngatpang Waterfall, a popular day-hike outside of Koror. Just pack a lunch and hike down a forested river valley to the base of the waterfall. Have lunch, then swim in the Tabecheding River. Other more strenuous hikes will take you to higher waterfalls and through more difficult terrain, but a guide would be necessary.

Definitely put shopping on your agenda before heading for home. The **Belau National Museum** in Koror has a gift shop and bookstore, in addition to having fine exhibits of anthropology, art, history, and natural history. You can get the carved storyboards here, as well as jewelry, handicrafts, posters, T-shirts, and books about Palau and Micronesia. Another excellent spot for shopping is the **Ormuul Gift Shop,** also in Koror, on main street in the Senior Citizens Center. This is a super place to bring the kids and your camera. Crafts are made here, and you can watch exhibits of basket weaving, canoe carving, dancing, and other skills. On sale are baskets, storyboards, and jewelry, and proceeds go directly to fund the senior citizens' programs.

A new place to shop and to learn about traditional Palauan culture is the elegant **Etpison Museum** in Koror. While there, have lunch or dinner at **Kramer's Café** on the third floor. In the museum are displays of prehistoric pottery and tools, heirloom items donated by Palauan families, rare seashells, original Palauan money beads, antique maps, and paintings. There are also two full-size canoes and a miniature bai, all built in the traditional manner. The gift shop/art gallery, on the third floor, carries souvenirs, art prints, original paintings, handicrafts, and books. The museum is open 9 a.m. to 9 p.m., and admission is $5.

Trips to some of the **remote islands** can be arranged through tour operators. Some islands, such as Peleliu (see sidebar) and Angaur are fairly close and easy to reach. The northern-most island, Kayangel, is about two hours away from Koror by boat. It is a low-lying atoll, criss-crossed by sandy

Storyboards

A storyboard is a carved wooden plank depicting some event, and it is one item you'll want to take home with you. The stories usually depict scenes of native life. The boards themselves come in all shapes and sizes—mine is shaped like a fish. Most boards depict stories about the sea, which is not surprising in this culture where the sea has been the source of livelihood for centuries.

You can find storyboards at the gift shops and museums, and you can also purchase them at the jail (yep, the jail), where inmates make most of the carvings sold in Palau. The jail is open several hours a day for visitors.

Since these are such an integral part of Palauan culture, I'll tell you a story called "Ngemlis—The Discovery of the Egg-Laying Cycle of the Turtle":

Though the shell of the turtle is prized in the islands of Palau as material from which is made money used by women folk, the people did not know how to catch turtles in ancient times.

There once lived a young man of Peleliu and a maiden from Ngerkebsang who fell in love. As the distance between the two islands is great (via canoe), the couple decided to meet on Ngemlis island, which lies somewhere between the two. As they had promised, they met on Ngemlis on the night of the new moon. They talked far into the night of their plans for their future.

When the girl awoke the next morning, she found that her back skirt had disappeared. They searched the whole island but could find no trace of the skirt. Beside the spot where she had been sleeping, however, they could see the prints made by a turtle during the night. Finally, the girl had to gather leaves from coconut palms for another skirt. She said goodbye to her lover and both promised to meet again on the island at the full moon.

The youth was waiting on the appointed evening when the girl arrived and ran to embrace him. They were sitting on the beach talking when they saw a turtle crawling toward them. They could see that something was entangled in its flipper. They looked more closely and discovered that is was the missing skirt which the girl had lost on the night of the previous new moon.

They learned by this that turtles in Palau space their egg laying about 15 days apart.

pathways and shaded by coconut palms. Fishing is the primary activity here, and it is also where the pandanus weaving is done. The Southwest Islands are a collection of atolls about 200 miles southwest of Koror. They're sparsely populated, and islanders live in homes made of woven palm fronds and still build canoes. Fishing and diving are reputed to be superb in these islands. It's a natural sanctuary for sea birds, green and hawksbill turtles, and marine life.

Dining and Entertainment

Due to its heavy Western and Asian influences historically, Palau cuisine is varied, with menus including everything from ramen to hamburgers. Fresh fish á la Pacific Rim (Asian style) can't be beat. Try the local micro-brewed beer called Red Rooster. Koror is where most of the restaurants are located, including a number of Japanese restaurants and sushi bars.

For divers, a fun spot to grab a bite and exchange dive tales is the **Bottom Time Bar and Grill,** located dockside at Sam's Tours in Koror. The fare ranges from burgers and sandwiches to sashimi. Also, near Fish 'n Fins is the new **Bar-ra-cu-da Bar and Mediterranean Restaurant,** facing the Rock Islands. The **Rock Island Café** is another good spot to hang out. It's an American-style diner featuring pizzas.

For romantic dining any time of day, the **Coconut Terrace Restaurant** at the Palau Pacific is wonderful. Enjoy the soft sounds of surf and refreshing breezes while dining alfresco. Buffet breakfast, lunch, and dinner are served daily. Every night is a special theme dinner with live entertainment. For especially fine dining, the **Meduu Ribtal Restaurant,** also at the Palau Pacific, features Pacific Rim cuisine and nightly live entertainment. Every Saturday and Sunday at PPR is a barbecue (burgers and dogs) at the **Mesekiu Waterhole.** An ice-cream cart gets a lot of attention.

For bars and nightlife, visit the hotels in Koror. In the neighboring island of Arakabesang, there are **Images** and **Larry's Bar,** as well as the poolside bar at the **Palau Pacific Resort.** On nearby Malakal (all of these islands are connected by causeways and just a few minutes from one another), **Storyboard** and **Hightide** are both popular.

Medical Facilities

Palau has two private medical clinics and a public hospital. The phone for Palau National Hospital in Arakabesan (very close to Koror) is (680) 488-5550; the hospital emergency number is 488-2558; and the ambulance number is 488-1411. The police emergency number is 911. There is a one-person hyperbaric chamber located at the public hospital.

In case of a diving emergency call DAN (Divers Alert Network) at (919) 684-4DAN (4326) or (919) 684-8111.

Visit to Peleliu Island

During World War II, Japanese and American forces fought one of the bloodiest battles of the Pacific here on this four-and-a-half-mile-long stretch of land that forms the southern boundary of Palau's enormous lagoon. It would have been impossible for them to imagine that one day Japanese and American divers would explore these islands together and share the wonders of the waters around them, bonding in that special way that naturally happens with divers.

In 1944 the island was literally on fire. The U.S. forces had launched an amphibious assault, expecting to rout the Japanese within a few days, take control of the airstrip, and complete the job with few casualties. But the Japanese had been firmly entrenched here for years; indeed, it was a center for their defense forces. Enormous limestone caves provided them with excellent cover and protection for equipment and armaments. Entire centers of communications, hospitals, and command posts were housed within these caves.

The **Battle of Peleliu** lasted more than two hellish months, and at least 15,000 soldiers died. Napalm destroyed all vegetation; flamethrowers and shelling completed the job. When it was over, it looked as though a nuclear bomb had hit it. Fortunately, islanders had all been evacuated prior to the fighting, but their homeland was a site of complete devastation.

Today, you can charter a boat or fly into Peleliu, landing on the very airstrip that each army wanted desperately to control back in 1944. From the air it looks like a razor has shaved a long thin section out of the jungle. Every now and then while driving around, you'll see a rusting jeep, a tank, or an anti-aircraft gun barely visible in the thick brush.

Local guide and historian Tangie Hesus can show you the sights and put you up in his guest house. Hop into his flatbed and you'll see monuments to the Americans and shrines to the Japanese. You'll climb hills now thick with vegetation and explore the caves used by the Japanese, caves that once had electricity and ventilation. You'll survey the crescent-shaped beaches where the American forces landed. He can even show you photographs of the island taken immediately following the battle.

Fortunately, the currents of time heal all wounds. At Orange Beach where U.S. landing craft came ashore, divers find relics of that time, now coral-encrusted and barely discernible among the new and beautiful life forms.

Saba

Magnificent Deepwater Monoliths

Tiny Saba rises from Eastern Caribbean waters like a brilliant cone-shaped emerald. Most travelers to this part of the world are sublimely unaware of the five-square-mile gem, as they skirt right by heading toward its far more popular neighboring islands: St. Maarten, St. Barts, Statia, and Anguilla. And that's just fine for those fortunate divers who have discovered this rare outpost of the Dutch Antilles and are quite happy to have it all to themselves.

The Saba Tourist Office estimates that the island sees fewer than 25,000 visitors per year. That's partly because the first and only airport here opened in 1963, and it wasn't until 1972 that the pier was constructed.

Visitors don't come to Saba to lounge on its beaches—not because there's so much to do, which there is, but simply because there are no beaches. Saba is composed almost entirely of a 2,900-foot volcanic peak—Mount Scenery. Its base is washed by waves and its top almost always capped by clouds.

Underwater, divers find mirror images of this soaring verticality. Like Saba itself, a dormant volcano rising from the seabed, submerged pinnacles rise hundreds of feet from the depths and soar to within 80 feet of the surface. Almost mirage-like in misted blue water, these sentinels are piled high with layer upon layer of plate-like corals and gaping barrel sponges. Swarming around them is a prolific amount of marine life, fed by relentless ocean currents and protected by Saba's no-spearing regulation.

Any adventurous hiker can reach Mount Scenery's peak, but only scuba divers can experience her magnificent deep seamounts—truly an experience of a lifetime. Saba is definitely on my Top Ten list for dive destinations. In fact, it's one of those special places I'm hesitant to revisit, for fear that any of the magic will be dispelled.

Why? This place is truly unique. Where else would you find a single road called The Road? a single peak called Mount Scenery? and a capital city called The Bottom? Even its runway is named Flat Point.

The aforementioned road is noteworthy. Once referred to as "the road that couldn't be built," it consists of nine miles of switchbacks, plunges, and hairpin curves. After its designer completed a correspondence course in engineering, local Sabans toiled 20 years to complete it. But before you get The Road initiation, you have to tackle yet another white-knuckle experience—the landing.

Here you'll have the pleasure of landing on one of the world's shortest runways (1,312 feet), flanked by facing cliffs and terminated by the deep blue beyond. When you leave the island, the special DeHavilland STOL (Short Take Off and Landing) will rumble and shake as the pilot gives it full throttle while holding the brakes. Suddenly, brakes are released and, thankfully, the plane bolts down the runway and soars over its watery edge.

When you arrive on the island, you'll be greeted by fragrant trade winds and genuinely friendly locals. With bags loaded into a comfortable taxi van, you'll be whisked along The Road and experience a half-hour roller-coaster ride across the island, where almost too-perfect gingerbread houses dot verdant green hillsides. Every last structure is painted white and has

green shutters and a red tile roof. Saba is among five islands that comprise the Netherlands Antilles, hence this Dutch-inspired architecture.

Traversing the island might be difficult, but getting a great view isn't. Lodgings, all relatively small and of course built on hillsides, have terrific views—views of yellow birds flying along the tops of poinciana trees that bloom bright red. And views of huge elephant ear palms that bend over and roar when the winds blow. And, of course, there's the cobalt-colored sea wherever the eye wanders.

The island's natural beauty inspires visitors to lace up their hiking boots and strike out on foot. Indeed, for nondivers, hiking along established trails and strolling about the villages are definitely recommended, preferably with camera in hand. Saba is short on glamour but high on natural endowments.

Lodgings and restaurants mirror Saba itself. They are generally small, attractive, and clean, with comfort and service given high priority. They are not inexpensive, however, and travelers looking for a budget vacation should search elsewhere. Children and nondiving companions, also, might not find the activities here that they would enjoy in more populated destinations. Beaches and beach activities are all nonexistent; shopping and nightlife are minimal. If you're the type that enjoys natural beauty, peace, and quiet pleasures, however, you'll find them here, both high and low.

QUICK STATS

Pronounced SAY-bah

Size 5.1 square miles (13 sq. km)

Population 1,200

Location Northeastern Caribbean; east of Puerto Rico and the U.S. Virgin Islands, and 28 miles south of St. Maarten

Time Atlantic Standard

Government Part of the Netherlands Antilles

Language Officially Dutch, but everyone speaks English

Electrical Current 110 volts, U.S. standard

Air Temperature Low 70s to high 80s

Water Temperature 76° to 82°

Underwater Visibility 100 to 120 feet

Best Diving Months May to October

PLANNING THE TRIP

Phoning Saba From the Unites States and Canada: dial 011-599-4 + the local number. From other destinations, dial 001 rather than 011.

Getting to Saba and Getting Around Major carriers such as American, Continental, US Airways, Air France, AOM, ALM, and Liat provide regular daily service to St. Maarten (airport code SXM). Connections to Saba (SAB) are via Windward Island Airways, called Winair (phone (800) 634-4907). Five flights service Saba on a daily basis. Flying time is only 12 minutes; moreover, the flights are conveniently nonpressurized and flown at around 1,500 feet for the safety of divers.

There is regular ferry service between St. Maarten and Saba aboard the *Edge* (599-5-42640) and the high-speed *Voyager I* (599-5-24096). The round-trip fee is $60 for both.

Although rental cars are available, I don't advise driving around, unless you really love hairpin curves. Far easier (and healthier) is walking within the villages and taking a taxi between villages. The taxi drivers have comfortable, modern vans and are usually more than happy to provide island tours.

Entry Documents A valid passport or original birth certificate (with a raised seal) is needed, as well as a return or ongoing ticket.

Currency The official currency is the guilder, written as NAfl. The exchange rate is about NAfl1.80 to US$1. Traveler's checks, U.S. dollars, and major credit cards are widely accepted.

Saba Tourist Office For information, check out their website or contact the on-island tourist office by phone or fax. After you arrive, stop by the office in Windwardside for the latest island news. It's located at Lambee's Place. To contact them phone 599-4-62231/62232; fax 599-4-62350; e-mail: iluvsaba@unspoiledqueen.com; website: www.turq.com/saba.

THE UNDERWATER SCENE

Saba is a dormant volcano, and its surrounding structure underwater is similarly the result of volcanic action. This is evident when you look at the sand—not the characteristic Caribbean pure white but sort of a blackish gray.

Whereas Saba's steep-sided mountain might also suggest plummeting walls below the surface, in fact, a narrow shelf rings most of the island, so there are plenty of excellent shallow dive and snorkel spots. On the north and northwest coast the shelf extends outward for more than a nautical mile before depths plummet to 1,000 feet and more. These same depths are reached within only a half-mile from shore off the East Coast and northwest part of the island.

This means that divers should not expect the precipitous walls of the Cayman Islands and the Bahamas. Nor should they expect typical reef structure; that is, a reef composed entirely of living corals. Don't worry, there *are* corals in profusion—both soft and hard—but these are typically found encrusting volcanic rocks and boulders. The coral growth is so prolific, in fact, that it has fused the boulders at several locations, forming a wonderful labyrinth of tunnels and galleries.

Gorgonians, those soft corals that include the beautiful sea fan, are prolific. Even huge colonies of elkhorn coral encrust these volcanic rocks, lying in very shallow water. Also abundant here are sponges, such as the encrusting brown volcano sponge, barrel sponge, and tube sponge.

Beyond this encircling shelf lies the enormous pinnacles that are the raison d'être for most divers venturing to Saba. To see these in their entirety is truly a thrilling experience, but remember, they are deep. They begin on a seabed hundreds of feet down and top out at about 90 feet at the *shallowest.*

Life on these pinnacles is very different from the shallow near-shore sites that get plenty of light and wave action. The deep pinnacles not only receive less sunlight, but they are far enough down in the water column to be beneath most wave action. They are, however, subject to strong ocean currents. The result is lots of black coral and deepwater gorgonians—two types of coral that thrive in nutrient-rich ocean currents.

Also, because deepwater corals need more area to collect the sun, the plate-type corals tend to predominate and are massive on the plateaus of the dive sites *Third Encounter, Twilight Zone,* and *Outer Limits.* If you were to drop down off the plateaus and dive along the sides of the pinnacles, your divemaster might frown, but you would find these plate corals shelving out horizontally in an effort to collect more sunlight.

Lettuce corals, also, are larger on the pinnacles than they are inshore, with less sediment to inhibit growth. Barrel sponges grow large, particularly on *Eye of the Needle,* in part because there is no wave action to rock a massive sponge off its holdfast, and in part because sponges grow larger when there is little sediment to clog their filter-feeding systems.

As for animal life, look into the nooks and crannies of the pinnacles to see a variety of eels, including green morays. Wonderful encounters with hawksbill turtles are common. Sponges are their main food source, so the high density of sponges here provides good feeding grounds.

Nurse sharks lurk beneath boulders, and Nassau grouper patrol the fringes of the plateaus. And they are all huge, fed by the constant ocean currents. Especially on the up-current areas southwest of the pinnacles, fish congregate in large numbers, often attracting barracuda and black-tip sharks. Even on the up-line, divers making their safety stops are apt to be passed by wahoo, jacks, tuna, and other bluewater fish. The occasional bottlenose dolphin sometimes shows up, probably just to check out these strange-looking bubble blowers.

Health Score Card

The marine species found in Saba's waters are healthy, big, and abundant. A major reason for this is the lack of significant development along its shoreline. Consequently, there is little runoff to murk up the waters and impede the growth of corals and sponges. But considerable credit must go to the early establishment of the Saba Marine Park, which completely encircles the island. Protection began in the late 1980s, restricting fishing, anchoring, and collecting, and permanent mooring buoys help prevent anchor damage.

Unfortunately, mother nature occasionally makes a harsh statement, with tropical storms, hurricanes, and violent groundswells. All of these have an impact on reef development. White-band disease and coral bleaching, too, have made their presence known here, as they have throughout the Caribbean. Fortunately, these are signs of stress, and recovery usually follows.

Diving Conditions

Most dive sites are situated on the West Side, in the lee of the island, and close to shore. Boat rides are rarely longer than about 20 minutes. Prevailing trade winds coming from the east frequently cause the north, east, and south sides to be too rough for comfortable diving. In winter months, however, groundswells can greatly reduce the visibility at West Side sites, so dive operators will use the South Coast.

The current normally runs from east to west and is not strong. Occasionally, though, currents will pick up at certain sites, including the pinnacles.

Depth is the most important consideration here. The pinnacle dives are all very deep, usually about 110 feet. Moreover, the entire dive is spent at the maximum depth, unlike most dives, which have both deep and shallow features. Furthermore, some of the pinnacles are reached by taking a compass heading and swimming into blue water without any point of reference.

Having said that, however, keep in mind an important point: of the approximately 28 permanently moored sites within the marine park, only a handful are really considered to be advanced deep dives. Most of the dive sites consist of gentle slopes. A favorite spot of both novice and experienced divers, *Torrens Point*, is only 40 feet at its deepest section.

Recommended Level of Experience

Saba offers something for everyone—new divers, snorkelers, the "rusty" diver, and the seasoned diver. Anyone could dive here at the shallow sites and be deliriously happy for the entire trip. Nevertheless, it would be a shame to come all this way and not experience the deepwater pinnacles, which are the primary attractions.

That's why I would recommend Saba for advanced divers. Make sure you have enough dives under your weight belt to feel really comfortable in the water. You should be able to remain relaxed and control your buoyancy perfectly while finning in blue water, exploring the pinnacles, or admiring a black-tip off in the distance.

If possible, bring your own dive gear (making sure that it's serviced before you leave), and be familiar with it. A dive computer is highly recommended.

Dive Sites for the Adventurous

We'll start with my favorites—the deepwater pinnacles. Three of these—*Third Encounter, Twilight Zone,* and *Outer Limits*—are promontories on a subsea mesa about a mile west of Ladder Bay. The shallowest of these tops out at 90 feet, and waters more than 1,000 feet deep surround them all. So these are very deep dives, and only experienced divers should attempt them. Typically, divemasters will test for current before the dive begins, and lower a hang-bar and extra tanks for mandatory decompression stops.

The magnificent site called *Third Encounter,* just a short boat ride away, starts at 100 feet and drops off dramatically. Along its slopes are several spectacular pinnacles. Follow your divemaster out into blue water and swim on a compass heading for a couple of minutes to reach the highlight of the dive, *Eye of the Needle.* This slender pillar appears, mirage-like, as you approach, and rises majestically up from the depths to within 90 feet of the surface. It is akin to watching the Sears Tower suddenly forming before your eyes; the sight is astounding. Barracuda and huge grouper patrol sentrylike all around, and schooling fish swarm up and over the peak. To actually see the "eye" of this structure, you'll have to dive way deeper than your divemaster would approve, but even without that detail, this singular site is worth the price of your airfare.

Flattened forms of mountainous star coral, leaf and sheet coral, and giant brain coral cascade down the walls of all these underwater skyscrapers. Lacy sea fans and sponges of all types are prolific. Enormous grouper, yellowtail snappers, triggerfish (including the beautiful queen triggerfish), schoolmasters, jacks, chromis, and Creole wrasse are all likely visitors. Turtles, too, are not uncommon.

On one of these dives I saw a black-tip shark cruising along, then watched in astonishment as it suddenly arched its back and bolted like a missile to the surface—150 feet above. In the clarity I could easily see the entire scenario, as well as the dark object on the surface that was its intended target. The shark's sheer force and speed definitely sent the adrenaline flowing! As it turned out, there was no attack, and I never discovered what the dark object was—apparently, it wasn't on the lunch menu after all. It is said that white-tips, reef sharks, and bull sharks also cruise the area, along with whale sharks, humpback whales, manta rays, and hammerheads.

On the same seamount is *Twilight Zone,* a series of rocky outcrops that run east-west along parallel lines. The most shallow of these is at 80 feet, and the mooring line is attached at 100 feet. The peak drops straight down from about 100 feet to la la land. Pinnacles are covered with deepwater gorgonians, elephant ear sponges, and black coral. Black-tip sharks frequently encircle the pinnacles and grouper seem to be everywhere. The third site here is *Outer Limits,* which features several extremely vertical promontories.

North of these sites is another pinnacle, *Shark Shoal,* that lies about half a mile west of Well's Bay. It rises from the seabed at 300 feet and comes to within 90 feet of the surface. And, yes, you could very well see sharks here, as on most of Saba's mounts, as well as a spectacular amount of fish—jacks, snappers, and silvery pelagics that venture in from the deep ocean. Dripping from its vertical sides are giant tube sponges, deepwater gorgonians, and black coral varieties.

A new pinnacle site called *Monte Michel* lies a little farther to the west. It, too, begins at a depth of 90 feet, and word has it that sharks and turtles are common. Should be fun!

When diving these pinnacles, it is easy to go too deep, so maintain neutral buoyancy and check your depth gauge frequently. Of course, your ears usually let you know when you're descending, also. Leave plenty of air for a slow ascent and a four-minute safety stop at 15 feet (assuming you haven't exceeded the no-deco limits).

Ordinary Great Sites

Diamond Rock and *Man-of-War Shoals* are spectacular shallower pinnacles north of the deeper ones. If you need to hone your diving skills before tackling the big boys, these are good spots to start.

Diamond Rock sits on a sandy bottom between 70 and 80 feet and juts right up out of the water. Covering its steep walls at the shallower depths are encrusting sponges and corals. Farther down are deepwater gorgonians and barrel sponges. You'll also notice many anemones with pink-tipped tentacles. On the sandy bottom look for southern stingrays that are usually rooting around for crunchy crustaceans. Sergeant majors are abundant. Look for their round patches of purple eggs that frequently become feasts for blue tangs and rock beauties. You'll also encounter all these species at *Man-of-War Shoals,* which is similar, except that this pinnacle is totally submerged.

Moving southward along the West Coast, several of the following dive sites have hot vents through the sea floor. Even in these tropical waters, the warm sand can feel wonderful at the end of a dive. One of these sites is *Ladder Labyrinth* (50 feet). Look for bare flats amidst the coral and sulfur-stained volcanic sand. Stick your fingers into the sand and you'll immediately feel the heat. Volcanic lava flow here created a natural labyrinth of spur and groove formations. Nearby, *Babylon* (47 feet) also has this warm volcanic sand, as well as a preponderance of mountainous star coral, tall pillar coral, and staghorn coral.

Custom's House Reef (65 feet) is a deep patch reef that you can circumnavigate. It's inhabited by dozens of barracuda, which are fairly small and won't bother you. Although the top of the reef is at 65 feet, it drops down abruptly to 90 feet.

Of the approximately 28 buoyed sites commonly dived around Saba, only *Giles Quarter* (85 feet) and *Greer Gut* (60 feet), on the south side of the island, are parts of the only true coral reef complex. Toward the southeast is *Hole in the Corner* (50 feet), which features a beautiful shallow-water elkhorn forest.

Shallow Diving and Snorkeling

Saba is not just a destination for "deep freaks." There are excellent opportunities for snorkeling and for shallow diving with long bottom times— perfect conditions for photographers. Unfortunately, access from shore is difficult, but boat operators run special trips just for snorkelers, and your lodging can help you make arrangements.

Two of the favorite snorkeling sites on the leeward side are *Wells Bay* and *Torrens Point*, which are usually well protected. Torrens Point also features a snorkel trail. Patch reefs with a variety of swim-throughs extend from the shoreline and harbor an assortment of eels and juvenile tropicals. At *Tent Reef*, located just outside the harbor, garden eels cover the sandy bottom, swaying in the surge, and southern stingrays cruise around looking for a meal.

Hole in the Corner, on the windwardside, is also excellent. The sandy bottom is white, compared to the volcanic gray on the opposite side. Also, if weather conditions are good, the visibility is usually better here. This is one of the best sites to see beautiful stands of elkhorn coral. Due to the shallow depths, these corals fall victim to storm damage easily, but fortunately they are among the fastest growing coral species and can quickly recover.

Marine Park

Saba's Marine Park can serve as a model for islands around the world. Planned by dive-park pioneer Tom Van'T Hof, and established in 1987, it is the world's first underwater park to become self-supporting through charitable contributions, souvenir sales, and hidden-tax use fees (which are a part of every dive-charter fee paid in Saba). To help keep the park healthy and solvent, many divers elect to contribute one day of their dive vacation to the park, volunteering to help in any way needed.

When I talked to Tom a few years ago, he noted that diver-damage on Saba was insignificant. "The kind of people coming to Saba are looking for a different experience," he said. "They are much more environmentally conscious and careful." If *you* feel like volunteering some time during your trip, just call the park at 63295. It could be a rewarding and memorable time spent.

The marine park encircles the island, protecting all waters and seabed to a depth of 200 feet. Fishing and anchoring are prohibited throughout the five recreational diving zones. The park maintains a system of permanent mooring buoys, and it administers the Saba Marine Park Hyperbaric Facility, a four-person recompression chamber. It also maintains a small information office at Fort Bay and gives slide presentations free of charge to all dive groups visiting the island.

A total of 41 permanent buoys bob in waters around the island. White buoys (24) are for small dive boats up to 50 feet long, orange buoys (12) are reserved for large dive boats up to 110 feet long, and the yellow buoys (5) are for visitor yacht moorings.

DIVE SERVICES & PACKAGES

Because of the structure of the island, all diving on Saba is done from boats that depart from the harbor in Fort Bay. Only two dive shops service the entire island, and both are located at the harbor, where there is a restaurant (the In Two Deep) but no lodgings. Unfortunately, this means that you have to find transportation from wherever you're staying to get to the dive shops. If you book a dive package, your transportation to the harbor might be included—be sure to check. Otherwise, taxi service is fairly reliable, but just to be safe, make sure you tell them when the dive boat is leaving, so they know the timing is critical. I had a taxi arrive a half-hour late, and there were a lot of disgruntled passengers on board, anxious to get going.

Sea Saba, the granddaddy of the two dive centers, has been in operation since 1985, and demonstrates professional, reliable service. There is a second store at Lambee's Place in Windwardside, where you can stop in to purchase gear. Rentals are at the Fort Bay location. The scuba training ranges from resort course through divemaster, as well as specialty courses, including Nitrox certification. If you're Nitrox-certified, you'll be able to place your order with them. Sea Saba is a universal referral center for NASDS, NAUI, PADI, SSI, YMCA, etc.

The dive center operates two 38-foot boats that are U.S. Coast Guard certified, and so are well equipped with safety features—VHF radios, a land-based radio system, oxygen, first aid, flare systems, etc. Moreover, Sea Saba specializes in taking out small groups (about ten) accompanied by two instructors, one of whom is available for in-water guided tours. Dive boats leave the harbor at 9:30 a.m., and between-dive surface intervals take place on the boat in a sheltered area.

Having the two smaller boats allows the flexibility to accommodate divers of differing skill levels. One boat can take out an experienced group, which won't be hindered by the short bottom times of the newer or less-experienced divers. Also, Sea Saba offers divers the freedom to dive on their own and to establish their own dive plans. That's an attribute that's getting more and more difficult to find, and one that more veteran divers, and dive photographers, will enjoy. Similarly, novice divers can feel more comfortable, having greater supervision from attentive instructors.

Both boats have a platform and ladder, freshwater rinse bins, cameras-only rinse bins, hanging facilities, and dry space for photographers. Drinking water and lemonade are provided, as well as cold storage for box lunches. An upstairs flybridge has more seating, for both sun and shade.

The group is particularly sensitive to the needs of dive photographers, to the extent that they have a special charging facility available at the dock—for 110 volts or 220 volts. Very nice!

All divers are provided with safety sausages, which is an excellent service. Should you surface and find yourself far from the dive boat, you simply inflate the tube and partially submerge the base in the water, so that it pops straight up. That way the dive crew will be able to spot you easily. This is especially helpful when the seas are rough, and swells can easily obscure divers. Sea Saba takes divers to both the leeward side and the less-dived windward side of the island.

Sea Saba arranges transportation for divers who have dive packages with selected lodgings. Package plans are available with the Cottage Club, El Momo Cottages, the Gate House, Juliana's, Queen's Gardens Resort, Scout's Place, and Willard's of Saba. To contact them, phone 599-4-62246; fax 599-4-62362; e-mail: divemaster@seasaba.com; website: www.seasaba.com.

Retail Sales: *Extensive*	**Dive Boat Comfort:** *Excellent*
Rentals: *Extensive*	**On-Board Facilities**
Scuba Training: *Extensive*	**for Photographers:** *Superior*
Photo Services: *Moderate*	

Saba Deep runs three dive boats that specialize in accommodating small groups of divers, or divers with specialized needs or requests. All of the boats are equipped with VHF, first-aid kits, and oxygen kits. Dives are regularly scheduled at 9 a.m., 11 a.m., and 1 p.m.; night dives are by request. The boats are designed for speed, and they return to the dock between dives.

The Fort Bay harbor location provides freshwater rinses, drying, and overnight storage facilities. BCDs, regulators, masks, and fins are available for all dives at no extra charge. Also at harborside is the shop's restaurant, In Two Deep, and a small boutique.

At the shop in Windwardside, you can get scuba instruction, have film developed (E-6 processing), and purchase dive gear, clothing, and literature.

The dive training is extensive, with courses ranging from Discover Scuba through instructor training and certification. The technical certifications available include Nitrox training and Drager rebreather courses. The certifying agencies represented are IANTD, NASDS, NAUI, PADI, SSI, and TDI.

Saba Deep's dive/lodging package plans are with Juliana's, the Gate House, the Cottage Club, El Momo Cottages, Queen's Gardens, and Willard's. Package prices include airport and dock transportation, marine park fees, and taxes.

From North America call toll-free at (888) 348-3722. The local phone number is 599-4-63347; fax is 599-4-63397; e-mail: diving@sabadeep.com or sabadeep@unspoiledqueencom; website: www.sabadeep.com.

Retail Sales: *Extensive*   **Dive Boat Comfort:** *Good*
Rentals: *Extensive*   **On-Board Facilities**
Scuba Training: *Extensive*   **for Photographers:** *Good*
Photo Services: *Moderate*

WHERE TO STAY

Unfortunately for divers, there are no lodgings at Fort Bay, near the dive operations, so it's necessary to hop in a cab or van to get down to the dive shops. Keep in mind that the farther your lodging is located up the hillside, the longer your ride will be in the morning. Most of the hotels, guest houses, and cottages are located in Windwardside, definitely the most scenic community. The Bottom, however, is the most convenient town for divers, and also has several nice places to stay. Wherever you stay, you'll be hit with a five percent government room tax that is automatically added to the bill.

Most of Saba's lodgings have dive packages with the two dive operators. Usually airport pickup and Marine Park fees are included in the package price.

Starting at **The Bottom** (literally) and working up, the following are some accommodations that are particularly well suited for divers. **Cranston Antique Inn ★** in The Bottom has six rooms furnished with four-poster beds and antiques, a restaurant, bar, and large swimming pool. Rates are $99 in summer, $125 in winter. Phone 63203.

On **Troy Hill,** overlooking The Bottom, is **Queen's Gardens Resort ★★**, with restaurant, outdoor bar, large pool, fitness center, and conference room. The 12 luxury units, set among lush gardens, have fully equipped kitchens, cable TV, and telephone. Rates are $200 for the one-bedroom units and $300 for the two-bedroom units. Weekly rates are offered. Phone 63494 or 63496; fax 63495; e-mail: info@queenssaba.com.

Windwardside is a lovely community of lodgings, shops, and restaurants, about three miles from Fort Bay Harbor (a 10- to 15-minute taxi ride). Here you'll find some charming places to stay. If you're interested in renting an apartment or cottage, contact the Saba Office of Tourism for a list of possibilities.

The **Cottage Club** ★★ consists of ten gingerbread-type cottages nestled among tropical landscaping with kitchens, private balconies, and great views. The cottages are spacious (ideal for large dive bags) and are equipped with cable TV and phone. There's a natural stone swimming pool but no restaurant or bar. Rates are $95 in summer, $145 in winter. Phone 62486 or 62386; fax 62476; e-mail: cottageclub@unspoiledqueen.com.

Juliana's ★★ is an attractive gingerbread-and-garden complex of nine guest rooms (with outside access), a two-and-a-half-room apartment, and two two-bedroom cottages, all with traditional Caribbean decor. Built in 1986, the complex was renovated in 1999. Each room has a balcony and a small refrigerator, and the apartment and cottages are each equipped with a full kitchen and patio. There's also a swimming pool and Tropics Café, overlooking the pool, with a spectacular vista of the mountainside terrain and blue ocean beyond. The café serves breakfast, lunch, and dinner daily, except Monday, when they are closed for dinner. The rooms are $90 and up in summer, $115 and up in winter. The apartment and cottages are $115 in summer, $135 in winter. Phone 62269; fax 62389; e-mail: julianas @unspoiledqueen.com.

Scout's Place ★★ is a hillside inn with 15 units, each with bath, balcony, and fantastic views. There's also a pool, bar, and restaurant with balcony. Rates (which include breakfast) are $79 and up in summer, $85 and up in winter. Phone 62205; fax 62388.

El Momo Cottages ★★, located on Booby Hill, just outside of Windwardside (a ten-minute walk), are great for the budget-minded. They are six gingerbread-style private cottages surrounded by tropical plants, with balconies overlooking the hills and the sea. One important point: a single bath facility serves all the cottages. There is also a pool and barbecue area, and there is daily maid service. Cottages are $40. Phone or fax 62265; e-mail: elmomo@unspoiledqueen.com.

Willard's ★★, also on Booby Hill, is decidedly more luxurious than El Momo, with a corresponding price increase. The resort has a spectacular setting, perched on a cliff 2,000 feet up, with a 270-degree panoramic view. This is an intimate resort, with only seven rooms. There's also a large pool, hot tub, restaurant and bar, lounge with TV, and tennis court. The restaurant is excellent but could set you back a week's salary. Rooms range from $250 to $500 in summer, and $300 to 700 in winter. Phone 62498; fax 62482; e-mail: willard@sintmaarten.net.

Up and over the hills is the secluded village of **Hell's Gate,** where the **Gate House** ★★ is located. This is an attractive two-story gingerbread-style guest house with six rooms (with balconies), a swimming pool, and dramatic views of neighboring islands. Two rooms have kitchenettes. A café, serving breakfast and dinner, features authentic Saban Creole dishes. Rates are $85 in summer and $110 in winter. Phone 62416; fax 62550; e-mail: sabagate@aol.com.

Live-Aboard

The 16-passenger *Caribbean Explorer* provides weekly access to the Saba Marine Park. Based in Philipsburg, St. Maarten, the vessel departs on Saturdays for week-long excursions around St. Kitts, Saba, and occasionally Statia. It is owned and operated by Explorer Ventures Ltd., and was established in 1987. For information and reservations call (800) 322-3577 from the United States and Canada. Elsewhere, call +1-903-887-8521 or fax +1-903-887-8526. Their website is www.caribexplorer.com.

ISLAND LIFE

Saba has little crime or poverty and no pollution or political unrest. Apart from the occasional boisterous groups of inebriated individuals, especially on weekends, it's a peaceful place. Also, the island is safe to explore on foot, and islanders are for the most part exceptionally gracious people.

Like so many Caribbean islands, Saba was ruled by several foreign cultures—English, French, Spanish and Dutch—until it came under the dominion of the Dutch Crown in 1816. It's now one of five islands that comprise the Netherlands Antilles. Saba, St. Maarten, and Statia (St. Eustatius), known as the Windward Islands, are clustered in the mid-Caribbean. The others, Bonaire and Curaçao (both of which also have excellent diving), are located close to South America, not far from Venezuela. Saba's Dutch influence is particularly evident in its architecture. English is spoken everywhere, but Dutch is the official language. The capital of the Antilles is Willemstadt, a picturesque and cosmopolitan city in Curaçao.

Temperatures are typically mild, averaging about 80°, and the island is continuously swept by easterly trade winds that keep Saba from becoming oppressively hot. Mosquitoes can be a problem at times, but the winds help keep them from becoming a constant nuisance. An active cloud movement also means occasional showers, so it's a good idea to keep a lightweight jacket with hood handy, especially when climbing Mount Scenery.

Climbing Mount Scenery

Sooner or later Mount Scenery will lure you to its cloud-capped peak. Don't worry, it's not that difficult—only 1,064 hand-carved steps to climb. You'll get some great exercise and a sweeping view (when the clouds part) of the red-roofed Saban villages of Hell's Gate, Windwardside, St. John's, and The Bottom—definitely worth a few aching muscles. Allow about three hours to make the round-trip pilgrimage, and don't be surprised to see your divemasters *running* up; that's how they keep in shape.

Even if you arrive to find the summit socked in, the journey is extraordinary, taking hikers through a number of climates and environments during the ascent. At the mountain's foot, near the villages, steep grass pastures are swept by the steady onslaught of trade winds. Higher up, tree cover begins, and tiny *anolis sabis* lizards, endemic to the island, scamper across the stone paths.

The foliage is unbelievably dense and lush. I was only a couple of feet from a donkey that was standing just off the trail, but I never noticed it until my eyes focused on a strikingly beautiful butterfly that had alighted nearby. Only then did I see the donkey's wide eyes, staring straight at me through the dark, thick canopy of palms.

When the winds pick up, enormous elephant ear palms in swaying motion let out long, deep roars that echo along the mountainside. In upper regions, washed by precipitation from the cloud cap, a canopied rain forest holds tree frogs, ankle-deep humus, and enormous ferns. And finally, at the top, where sunlight is at a premium because of the perennial cloud cover, the mists part to reveal an elfin forest—the rain forest in miniature.

Note for Divers

The peak of Mount Scenery is approximately 2,885 feet above sea level, and it does require strenuous activity to get there. Both of these factors contribute to decompression sickness. To be safe, follow the recommended rules for flying after diving: at least 12 hours of surface interval for less than two hours total accumulated dive time in the previous 48 hours, or 24 hours of surface interval for multiday unlimited diving.

Topside Attractions

Strolling around the villages here should be high priority. They're clean, crime-free, and super-scenic. **The Bottom** is Saba's capital city and the business center of the island. It is also assumed to be the volcano's crater. Stop by to see the governor's house and visit **Heleen's Art Gallery.** Her watercolors of life underwater and in the rain-forest are impressive. There's also the Saba Artisans Foundation, where you can shop for silk-screened fabrics and watch Saba lace being made. You'll probably find places that sell Saba Spice, a sweet rum-based liquor that's bottled on the island and is also homemade in many Saba kitchens.

Windwardside is a charming little town of cute (and very expensive) old gingerbread cottages with gabled roofs and immaculate gardens. It even has a little shopping center—**Lambee's Place**—with boutique-type shops and galleries. You'll find the Breadfruit Gallery, which represents all local artists, as well as El Momo Folk Art and the Carmel, which offer unique gift items. Jobean Designs has beautiful glass objects, including glass jewelry. There's a nice little restaurant with rooftop seating called YIIK. And this is also where you'll find the tourist office. Be sure to stop in for maps of the island and more information.

For outdoor adventurers, hiking rivals diving on Saba. From rain forest to elfin forest, the island's magnificent vegetation zones offer unparalleled beauty and diverse species of reptiles and birds. You'll see racer snakes, (which are harmless) as well as the resident anole lizards scuttling about everywhere. Flying high among the trees are banana quits, pearly thrasher, tremblers, and the Antillean crested hummingbirds. You'll walk among breadfruit and banana trees, fig trees and elephant ear palms, begonias, hibiscus, and cilantro—nothing short of paradise.

When you stop by the tourist office in Windwardside, pick up a *Saba Nature Trails* brochure. You'll find directions to excellent hiking trails, including the one up Mount Scenery. Most are fairly strenuous. Directional signs and interpretive placards have been placed along many of the trails. For a historical perspective, the Ladder trail will show you how people used to travel before The Road was constructed. The 800-step stairwell was the only route from the dock at Ladder Bay into town. After climbing this, you'll understand why the locals love The Road.

Dining and Entertainment

Excellent restaurants are located in all the villages, and you'll find a wide variety of choices. Also, there are plenty of relatively inexpensive ones. You don't have to worry about spending a fortune on meals. Before leaving a tip, remember that a service charge of 10 or 15 percent will be automatically added to restaurant bills.

If you want to really economize on dining, choose one of the lodgings that has cooking facilities. You can fill the fridge from the **Big Rock Market** located in the heart of Windwardside.

Dining out is an excellent way to learn more about the culture, so don't be afraid to try some of the native dishes, including the delicious native blend of Indonesian and West Indian Creole. Most restaurants have outdoor patios, where you can enjoy the grand vistas, and a friendly bar-cum-local-gathering-spot. What to wear? Tasteful, casual sportswear is fine, but definitely cover up swimsuits in restaurants and in the villages.

In Windwardside, at Lambee's Place, the **YIIK Grill and Bakery** is a good place to stop in prior to your hike up Mount Scenery. Here you can order croissants and turnovers for breakfast, and sandwiches and pizza for lunch, as well as gourmet coffees. The establishment is a pleasant place for outdoor dining, too, with a shaded gazebo and rooftop umbrella tables. You'll probably smell the wonderful aromas well before you see the place. Another good casual choice is **Guido's Pizzeria,** also in Windwardside. The pizza dough is made fresh daily. It's open weekdays only, beginning at 6 p.m.

For dinner in Windwardside try the **Brigadoon,** located in an 1800s Saban home. It serves Caribbean/American cuisine, as well as Greek and Lebanese specialties. Up the hill is a really good Chinese restaurant called **Saba Chinese Restaurant** (what else?).

In St. John's, closer to The Bottom, is **Lollipops,** known for local specialties. I particularly enjoyed the outdoor dining, soft breezes, and unobstructed views of the ocean and surrounding hills. Give Lollipop a call, and she might be able to pick you up.

Overlooking the harbor in Fort Bay is the **In Two Deep,** a welcoming spot for divers. From breakfast to dinner, this is the place to fill the tummy, trade tales, and meet friendly folks.

On weekends and during Carnival in late July and early December, steel bands frequently entertain outdoors. The soft sounds of steel drums echo over the hillsides. But if your taste is more for disco, that's available too, at Guido's and Lollipops.

Medical Facilities

The A.M. Edwards Medical Center is located in The Bottom. The local phone number is 63239 or 63288 or 63289.

The Saba Marine Park Hyperbaric Facility, located at Fort Bay, serves the entire Eastern Caribbean region. This four-person recompression chamber is administered by the Saba Marine Park (63295) and is operated by a staff of specially trained volunteers.

In case of a diving emergency call DAN (Divers Alert Network) at (919) 684-4DAN (4326) or (919) 684-8111.

Turks and Caicos

Physical Characteristics of the Dive Area

WATER & WEATHER CONDITIONS

Visibility	*Excellent*
Current and Surge	*Minimal*
Temperature	*Comfortable*
Storms	*Occasionally Stormy*

SITE CONDITIONS

Mooring Buoys	*Some*
Fishing, Collecting, and Hunting Restrictions	*Widespread Restrictions*
Ease of Access	*Convenient to Moderate*
Boat Traffic/Diver Congestion	*Light*

MARINE LIFE

Abundance of Invertebrates	*Abundant*
Abundance of Vertebrates	*Abundant*
Abundance of Pelagic Life	*Common*
Health of Reef/Marine Life/ Marine Structure	*Mixed*

Passages through the British West Indies

"Turks and What?" is the typical response from nondiver friends when I tell them about this unique cluster of islands. Although still obscure to most of the world, the Turks and Caicos Islands (call them TCI) are actually not far from the mainland United States—just an hour and 15 minutes by air from Miami, and only 30 miles southeast of the Bahamas. In fact, the nine primary islands and umpteen cays that comprise TCI are an extension of the Bahamian archipelago, but separated by the 4,000-foot-deep Caicos Passage.

Two groups that have certainly discovered the Turks and Caicos are 1) savvy divers-in-the-know, and 2) investment bankers; the former searching for marine treasures, the latter hoping for riches from offshore finance.

The islands are flat and somewhat lacking in physical beauty, but they more than make up for this deficit with stunning beaches, warm turquoise-hued waters, glorious wall diving, and plentiful options for nondivers. So many unique islands present myriad opportunities for diversions, making everyone happy—even those who wouldn't dream of getting wet after taking their morning shower.

It's important, straight away, to understand how these islands are grouped. When I visited the excellent little museum on Grand Turk, I was told that visitors can rarely point out the island's location on the big wall map at the entrance. That isn't surprising, given the confusing scatter.

Essentially, you need to understand that the separation between the Turks islands and the Caicos islands is caused by an extremely deep (more than a mile) 22-mile-wide trench called the Columbus Passage (formerly Turks Island Passage). The Caicos grouping is far more numerous and diverse. Among its many islands are Provo (Providenciales), essentially the Miami Beach of TCI, along with North, Middle, and South Caicos, which have few inhabitants (the human variety, anyway). In the little Turks grouping, the primary focus is Grand Turk, where TCI's capital city, Cockburn Town, is located. Assuming that Provo is TCI's equivalent to Miami Beach, you could think of Grand Turk as Key West. Tiny Salt Cay, not far from Grand Turk, should also be mentioned, since it draws divers to its single resort and dive operation.

Essentially, that translates into a lot of folks in the tourism and banking industries flying into Provo on large jets, with a few hard-core divers and government types zipping over to Grand Turk on six-seater props. Forget boat travel on a regular basis between the two island groups—the distance of 75 miles is just too far.

The first half-hour on these two distinct islands tells everything: after touching down on Provo, I entered a modern, efficiently run terminal and was whisked off to my resort in an air-conditioned taxi-van, its cell phone ringing incessantly while passing sprawling all-inclusive resorts and elegant condominiums. In contrast, Grand Turk's rather dilapidated-looking terminal seemed to be in complete confusion (in a charming kind of way), with locals hanging out and chatting at the bar, and luggage and cargo items strewn about. While my taxi driver described in detail the previous

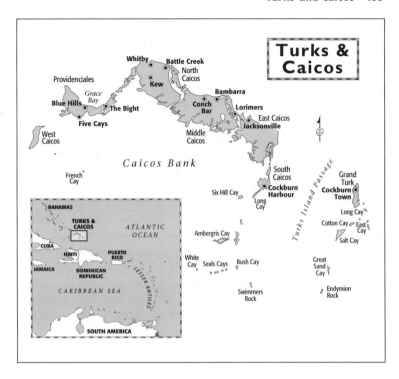

night's dart tournament, she waved and honked her horn at friends, while passing a gridwork of salinas, now filled with water, and donkeys and horses wandering around freely in the streets.

The majority of islanders are descendants of Africans that were brought to the Caribbean to work the plantations and salt flats. Now there is a growing number of expats, both European and North American. The native Arawak Indian population was enslaved to work in salt production and was quickly all but eradicated.

This is a sunny, arid climate, with little rainfall, so you'll find more cactus than palms and tropical plants. In fact, the word Turks stems from the barrel-shaped Turks Head cactus, which looks like a Turkish fez. Caicos is derived from the Spanish word *cayos,* meaning small island. This type of climate promotes fewer problems with pesky mosquitoes and no-see-ums.

As TCI is a British Crown Colony, driving is on the left and English is the primary language. Similar to the Bahamas and the Cayman Islands, TCI reaps the benefits of a stable government and a tax-free investment environment. Oddly, the local currency is the U.S. dollar.

Exciting, beautiful wall diving is what attracts most divers, and whether you stay on Provo or on Grand Turk, it makes little difference—you'll have access to excellent wall sites at either location. However, if you're a novice diver or traveling with nondiving companions, especially kids, Provo, with its calm bay, condos and all-inclusive-resorts, would be your best option.

Dive aficionados tout Grand Turk for its ease of access to walls, since most dive sites are just minutes from shore. It's true that the excellent wall sites require more travel time from Provo, especially those sites on West Caicos, but most Provo operators have large, comfortable boats that can really scoot. Also, I've never considered it much of a hardship spending a surface interval on a beautiful boat in gorgeous Caribbean waters, where you're likely to see anything from dolphins to flamingoes!

Most of the dive areas throughout TCI are under national park protection. You'll see mooring buoys at almost all the sites, to eliminate the possibility of anchors damaging the reef. As in other areas of the Caribbean, storm damage and coral bleaching are evident, especially in some of the shallow areas. Generally, dive operations are safe, professional, and conservation-minded.

Because the islands are so different, try to sample both Provo and Grand Turk if you can spare the time. A third option is the little island of Salt Cay, just south of Grand Turk and accessible by boat or by air. It's far less developed than Grand Turk, with only one small dive shop and lodging. You'd feel like a pioneer!

QUICK STATS

Pronounced   turks and KAY-kohs

Size   193 square miles total; Grand Turk, 10.5 sq. mi.; Salt Cay, 2.5 sq. mi.; Providenciales, 37.5 sq. mi.; North Caicos, 41 sq. mi.; Middle Caicos, 48 sq. mi.; South Caicos, 8.5 sq. mi.

Population   25,000, about half on Providenciales

Location   575 miles southeast of Miami, 90 miles north of Haiti and the Dominican Republic

Time   Eastern Standard Time

Government   British Crown Colony

Language   English

Electrical Current   115 volts, 60 cycles; 3-prong plugs

Air Temperature   75° to 95°

Water Temperature   75° to 82°

Underwater Visibility   80 to 150 feet

Best Diving Months   Winter

PLANNING THE TRIP

Phoning TCI   From the United States and Canada, dial 011 + 649 + the local number. From other destinations, dial 001 rather than 011.

Getting to TCI and Getting Around   American Airlines flies twice daily between Provo and Miami. The flight from Miami is one hour and 15 minutes. Travel to the islands is also possible by way of Jamaica, New York, Nassau, Cuba, Haiti, and the Dominican Republic. There are four international airports in TCI. Departure tax is $15.

Interisland connections are provided by Turks and Caicos Airways (TCA-946-4255), SkyKing (941-5170/ 5464), and InterIsland Airways (946-4999). A round-trip flight between Provo and Grand Turk is about $120. Provo's airport is air-conditioned and has a nice restaurant, clean bathrooms, and a couple of shops. It is also a good place to find books about the island's marine life and history. I found service at the Sky King desk to be excellent, and the employees exceptionally accommodating.

Taxis are available at most of the airports. As an example, the fare from Provo airport to Ocean Club for up to three people is $18. Additional passengers are $8 each. Call Tina's Taxi and Tour for touring around Provo (941-0200). On Grand Turk, ask for Delphine to take you around the island; everyone knows her.

There are car rental agencies on both Provo and Grand Turk. In addition to mandatory insurance, which costs about $14, you'll have to pay a government tax of $10. Remember that driving is on the left.

Entry Documents   A passport and a valid return ticket are normally required for entry, but visitors from North American may enter with an original birth certificate (with a raised seal) and one piece of ID bearing a photograph.

Currency   U.S. dollar

Turks & Caicos Islands Tourist Board   You can contact them directly on Grand Turk by phone (649) 946-2321; fax (649) 946-2733; e-mail: tci.tourism@tciway.tc. They also have a small office on Provo at Turtle Cove Landing: phone (649) 946-4970; fax (649) 941-5494; website: www.turks andcaicostourism.com.

The U.S. office is in Florida: phone (305) 891-4117; fax (305) 891-7096; e-mail: tcitrsm@bellsouth.net. The European office is located in Middlesex, England: phone 0181-350-1000; fax 0181-350-1011; e-mail: mki@ttg.co.uk; website: www.ttg.co.uk/t&c.

Providenciales (Provo)

THE UNDERWATER SCENE

These limestone islands are actually portions of sprawling banks that cover an area about ten times the size of the total land area. Consequently, most of the shoreline is composed of rough ironshore that's been weathered by wind and rain. These shallow waters of the limestone and coral banks provide important habitat for marine life.

Diving from Provo, however, typically takes place in three locations where the shoreline drops fairly abruptly. All are under national park protection. These are Grace Bay, Northwest Point, and West Caicos. A few operators will also encompass distant French Cay, a national sanctuary. Grace Bay and Northwest Point are the closest and also have the most promising water and weather conditions.

For snorkelers, beginning divers, and "rusty" divers, Grace Bay is the perfect playground. This sweeping crescent-shaped stretch of powder-soft sand is on the calm north side of the island, where most of the resorts are located. While staying at Ocean Club, I watched a small class of students practicing their skills in an attractive swimming pool and garden setting. When they were ready for their ocean dives, the sandy beach and super-clear waters were just a few yards away, and showers, bathrooms, and an outdoor restaurant near at hand. It certainly seemed preferable to a cold, murky quarry in Wisconsin!

Underwater, Grace Bay features shallow spur-and-groove coral formations; that is, long fingers of coral that stretch perpendicular to shore, separated by sandy channels. The coral heads reach to within 25 feet of the surface, getting a bit deeper and more compact as they extend out to sea. At about 40 feet they meet a mini-wall that descends to a sandy plateau at about 100 feet.

Because of the enormous stretch of sand here, the visibility in the bay can be seriously diminished during stormy conditions, or with a strong outgoing tide. Usually, it's excellent, though, and the marine life is plentiful, due in great measure to the establishment of the Princess Alexandra Land and Sea National Park in 1989.

At Northwest Point and the west side of West Caicos, it's all wall diving, in many respects similar to the Cayman Islands and Cozumel (without the current). Boat rides to Northwest Point take about 45 minutes from the dock at Turtle Cove, which is about mid-island. Trips to West Caicos, an uninhabited island ten miles southwest of Provo, are at least twice that, but well worth it.

The typical structure at Northwest Point consists of a patch reef that slopes to the edge of the wall at 40 to 50 feet, followed by either a sloping or sheer wall that drops to a ledge at 130 to 150 feet. Each site has unique features in terms of cuts and swim-throughs, arches and chutes, as well as the variety and abundance of marine life present.

The walls start a bit deeper at West Caicos—50 to 70 feet—and feature dramatic vertical drops, sometimes from undercut ledges, into the Caicos Passage. The structure is also more convoluted and canyonlike. Along the edges of these walls you might see turtles, mantas, hammerheads, and reef sharks. You'll definitely see more schools of fish here, particularly chromis and horse-eye jacks.

Inshore from the walls at both locations are sand flats with isolated coral heads—patch reef structure, rather than the spur-and-groove of Grace Bay. On these sandy plains you'll find exciting discoveries such as southern stingrays, colonies of garden eels, and beautiful stands of pillar coral, with their hairlike polyps flowing in the surge.

Health Score Card

The walls and deeper sites of these areas are in excellent condition. Some of the shallow areas show some coral bleaching or sand damage, or possibly a combination of the two. With marine park protection, there are restrictions against anchoring; nevertheless, there is still a problem with boaters who are not aware of the laws and throw their anchors over the side.

Diving Conditions

So little rain falls in these islands that there are no rivers or streams to cloud up the inshore waters with sediments. When it isn't stormy, visibility is excellent in winter, and this is when you might encounter the humpback whale migrations. Storms and strong outgoing tides can kick up sand, especially on Grace Bay. In spring, plankton blooms can impair visibility, but these little critters also attract hungry mantas. Summertime has calmer seas and warmer waters, but, of course, you always take your chances during hurricane season. Strong currents are not an issue here at all.

Recommended Level of Experience

The shallow walls are perfect for every level of diver. Novice divers can explore the inshore sandy areas, the drop-offs, and shallow sections of the walls. Experienced divers will enjoy it all, including the exciting deeper parts of the walls with their intriguing cuts, chutes, tunnels, and ledges. Grace Bay is perfect for snorkelers, new divers, and those who need to hone their skills a bit before tackling the walls.

Great Dive Sites

Just about any site off the west side of **West Caicos** is an adventure, and the boat ride out can be as well. You frequently see nurse sharks in the fringing reef and turtles in the deeper ocean.

At *Driveway,* noteworthy for its huge number of barrel sponges, I hung out with a turtle on top of the reef, then after descending to only 60 feet spotted a black-tip shark. A large barracuda sentry positioned itself directly under the boat, eyeing divers on their safety stop.

The site called *Gully* features a sandy chute-like tunnel that winds down from the top of the reef to about 90 feet, right on the wall. With various breaks in the surface, this is not a solid overhead environment, so it gets plenty of light and is a lot of fun to ride down. On the wall itself, the sponge life reigns supreme, with enormous barrel sponges, encrusting volcano sponges, and magnificent bright-orange elephant ear sponges. The latter is what really distinguishes these wall dives from others in the Caribbean, although the elephant ear are also fairly abundant in the Cayman Islands. Large lobster strut about in broad daylight and gorgeous multicolored queen triggerfish go their solitary, regal way. Large schools of tropicals flow up and over the lip of the wall.

Off Provo's **Northwest Point** are several excellent sites, both underwater and topside for the surface intervals. At *Eagles Nest,* a sandy channel leads to the wall, which starts at about 45 feet. Several cuts in the wall are bordered with layer upon layer of swirling plate coral, draped with red-and-orange rope sponges. On top of the wall are lobster, queen triggerfish, and large pufferfish. During my surface interval here, I was watching the shoreline and spotted a pink cloudlike mass moving over the point. It turned out to be a huge flock of flamingoes—flying! And on the ride back to Provo, bottlenose dolphins joined us to play in our wake and ride the bow. Quite a morning.

At *Amphitheater* another sandy channel drops right over the wall. Farther down is a spectacular ledge, where the wall is severely undercut, with a multicolored mosaic of corals and sponges. Marine life ranges from enormous grouper to tiny flamingo tongue clinging to the sea-fan gorgonians. Tube sponges, basket sponges, and layered sheet coral blanket the face of the wall.

At *Pine Cay* you're likely to see eagle rays flying over sandy channels and swarms of baitfish around the wall. Near the lip of the drop-off are schools of Bermuda chub and families of silvery Atlantic spadefish.

Shore-side during the surface interval, dive boats usually head to a stretch of beach called *Malcolm Roads Beach,* where exotic-looking but dilapidated Tiki huts are the sole remains of a silly, and dangerous, French TV game show.

Shallow Diving and Snorkeling

In an area called The Bight, which was one of the first developments on the island, is a popular snorkel site called *White House/Coral Gardens.* To access it, drive to The Bight, just a short distance east of Turtle Cove. Go to the end of Stubbs Road and park—you'll see the Coral Gardens condos. Then follow the dirt road to the beach. The area is loaded with marine life, from moray eels to eagle rays and turtles. You might spot them all. In the Turtle Cove area is another good snorkeling spot called *Smith's Reef.*

For shallow diving, *Grace Bay* is a perfect spot to play around the patch reefs. You're likely to see schools of blue chromis, plenty of yellowtail snappers, white-spotted triggerfish, and families of Atlantic spadefish. Cute little turtles frequently come along to check you out. Try "talking" to them through your regulator; you might be surprised at the response!

Marine Park

In 1988 the National Parks Ordinance was passed in TCI, which led to the development of 11 national parks, 11 nature reserves, 4 sanctuaries, and 7 areas of historical interest, covering some 270 square miles. On Provo alone there are eight protected areas covering approximately 30 square miles of land and sea.

Chief Parks Warden Ezekiel Hall admits that enforcement of the laws has been a continuing problem and that the department has had to rely on fisheries and the marine police to keep watch. This problem was addressed in 1998, with the establishment of the Coastal Resources Management Project, funded by a grant from the British government (Department for International Development) and from accommodations tax monies. The department will soon have its own patrol boats and surveillance should be far more aggressive. Fines will be imposed on transgressors, including divers and operators, which could range from $50 to $10,000. The island also requires better sewage control, both from the island and from boats in the marina. Hall is a hydrogeologist with specialized training in environmental impact assessments. To contact the office, phone (649) 941-5122; fax (649) 946-4793; e-mail crmpgarland@tciway.tc.

DIVE SERVICES & PACKAGES ON PROVIDENCIALES

Provo has seven dive operations, with most located along the north shore. They will pick you up and take you to their boats, docked at Turtle Cove, Sapodilla Bay, or Five Cays. A few operators keep boats at the docks of the resorts.

Caicos Adventures is based at the Turtle Cove Marina and Caicos Café Plaza, a PADI Resort. The shop uses a 36-foot dive boat, equipped with a camera rinse bucket and dry storage, for daily trips to West Caicos and, as weather permits, to French Cay. This operation is known for its small groups and is very service-oriented, providing water and other beverages, along with lunch, in the surface interval. It is also less expensive than some other shops that do not provide the extra service. PADI dive instruction is through the divemaster level. Packages are available with the following resorts: Caribbean Paradise Inn, Comfort Suites, Erebus Inn, Ocean Club, Sands Resort, and selected island villas. Call (800) 513-5822; fax and phone (649) 941-3346; e-mail: divucrzy@tciway.tc; website: ww.caicosadventures.tc.

Retail Sales: *Adequate*	**Dive Boat Comfort:** *Good*
Rentals: *Adequate*	**On-Board Facilities**
Scuba Training: *Extensive*	**for Photographers:** *Good*
Photo Services: *Limited*	

Dive Provo, another popular shop, maintains three offices: in the Ports of Call shopping center, at the Leeward Marina, and in the Allegro Resort (a PADI Gold Palm Resort). Rentals include cameras and video. Trips go out to West Caicos, Northwest Point, Grace Bay, and Pine Cay. The shop also provides scuba safaris, with three tanks, and specialty dives. Boats have a camera rinse bucket, and drinking water is provided. Longer trips include lunch. PADI instruction is given, and rentals are available. Dive packages are available with the Allegro Resort, Comfort Suites, Le Deck resort, the Ocean Club, and Club Med. Call (800) 234-7768, or (954) 351-9771, or (649) 946-5040; fax (954) 351-9740; e-mail: diveprovo@gate.net; website: www.diveprovo.com.

Retail Sales: *Adequate*	**Dive Boat Comfort:** *Good*
Rentals: *Extensive*	**On-Board Facilities**
Scuba Training: *Extensive*	**for Photographers:** *Good*
Photo Services: *Limited*	

Flamingo Divers is located on the ground floor of the Erebus Fitness Centre building and provides packages with the Erebus Inn (a PADI Resort). It features a maximum of eight to ten divers per boat, with two divemasters aboard each boat. Trips go out to French Cay, West Caicos, Northwest Point, and Grace Bay. Soft drinks, snacks, water, tea, coffee, and muffins are served on Mondays (at least, that's what I've heard). The shop offers a full rental line and PADI dive instruction. Phone and fax (649) 946-4193; e-mail: flamingo @provo.net; website: www.provo.net/flamingo.

Retail Sales: *Adequate*

Rentals: *Adequate*

Scuba Training: *Moderate*

Photo Services: *Limited*

Dive Boat Comfort: *Good*

On-Board Facilities for Photographers: *Good*

Provo Turtle Divers is a full-service PADI facility that has been operating since 1970. Turtle Divers' main shop is at the Turtle Cove Marina. A smaller one is on the property of Ocean Club, near the East End. They run three boats, including a beautiful 42-foot Newton that carries up to 20 divers. A nice table and shelf area for cameras is out of spray range, and they provide a freshwater tank for soaking. The bridge topside has extra seating, with comfortable cushions. The other two boats are 30-foot Island Hoppers. All have oxygen and first-aid equipment. Turtle Divers rents and sells equipment and cameras. It offers a full range of PADI certification courses, including a free Discover Scuba class. Dive packages are with Comfort Suites, Erebus Inn, Grace Bay Club, Ocean Club, Turquoise Reef Resort and Casino, and Turtle Cove Inn. Call (800) 833-1341 or (809) 946-4232; fax (809) 941-5296; e-mail: provoturtledivers@provo.net; website: www. provoturtledives.com.

Retail Sales: *Extensive*

Rentals: *Extensive*

Scuba Training: *Extensive*

Photo Services: *Moderate*

Dive Boat Comfort: *Excellent*

On-Board Facilities for Photographers: *Superior*

For camera rentals, E-6 processing, and photo courses, contact **Fish Frames** at 946-5841; e-mail fishframes@tciway.tc; website: www.fishframes.com.

WHERE TO STAY ON PROVIDENCIALES

Variety is what you'll find here, from budget to elegant, but the balance definitely tips toward all-inclusive resorts. I call these the ABC resorts— Allegro, Beaches, and Club Med.

If lots of activity is what you seek, then **Allegro Resort & Casino** ★★★★ should be just right. Located on Grace Bay, this PADI Gold Palm Resort provides watersports activities (kayaking, sailing, windsurfing), three lighted tennis courts, a Kid's Club, a casino, and nightly entertainment. Dive Provo provides training, rents gear, and runs trips. Covered under the all-inclusive rate are all nonmotorized watersports and Discover Scuba classes. There are 36 deluxe oceanfront rooms and 150 superior rooms. They all have air-conditioning, phone, cable TV, and either balcony or terrace. Facilities also include two restaurants, two bars, and swimming pool. Their per-person adult rates, for a two-night stay, range from $490 to $580. To contact them, phone (800) 858-2258 or (649) 946-5555; fax (649) 946-5522; website: www.allegroresorts.com.

Beaches Turks & Caicos Resort & Spa ★★★★ also sits right on popular Grace Bay and is liked by couples as well as families. This all-inclusive place has 177 large, air-conditioned ocean-view rooms, each with TV and phone. There are several bars and lounges (with entertainment) and five restaurants. A complete range of watersports and recreational options includes two lighted tennis courts, a fitness center, and European spa. The Beaches on-property dive center provides all gear needed, rents cameras, and gives instruction. Dive boats depart from the resort's dock. Just for kids is Pirate's Island, a huge wood beam ship surrounded by a swimming pool with water slides and —get this—a kiddie swim-up bar. There's even a restaurant just for kids. For two nights, adult per-person rates from January through April range from $780 to $935, and from May through December, $755 to $910. Phone (888) BEACHES or (649) 946-8000; fax (649) 946-8001; website: www.beaches.com.

Comfort Suites ★★★ is a popular spot with divers, although it is not on the beach. Provo Turtle Divers, in its swing around the resorts to pick up divers in its large bus, stops by Comfort Suites and always picks up several divers. The resort is across the street from Grace Bay Beach, at the Ports of Call. There are 98 air-conditioned junior suites with refrigerators, coffeemakers, and in-room safes. Phones have data ports and fax capability. Facilities include a swimming pool with Tiki bar and the Provo Turtle Divers on-site tour and watersports desk. The Ports of Call shopping complex has four restaurants and bars, a fitness center, beauty salon, gift shops, liquor and convenience store, boutiques and car, scooter and bike rental agency. Room rates range from $140 to $190, depending on the season, so if you're splitting the cost with a dive buddy, this is a good deal. Continental breakfast is included. Call toll-free (888) 678-DIVE or (649) 946-8888; fax (649) 946-5444; e-mail: comfort@provo.net; website: www.provo.net/comfort.

Erebus Inn ★★★★★, a PADI Resort, has a perfect setup for divers; it is located on a hill overlooking Turtle Cove, just steps from the marina. There are 21 air-conditioned rooms, four cottages, and a two-bedroom villa. The spacious rooms have ceiling fans, cable TV, phones, patios, and superb views. Also on the property are restaurant and pub, swimming pool and sun deck, and two clay tennis courts. The dive shop, Flamingo Divers, is just below, where guests can store their gear. Per-room nightly rates are from $140 to $190 January through April. The rates do not include government tax (nine percent) or service charge (ten percent). Dive packages are with Flamingo as well as Provo Turtle Divers. Phone (800) 323-5655, (800) 742-4276, or (649) 946-4240; fax (649) 946-4704; e-mail: erebus@tciway.tc; website: www.erebus.tc.

Ocean Club ★★★★ is by far one of the nicest, most comfortable places to stay on the island. Comfortable, because this condominium/resort features spacious individually decorated suites with fully equipped kitchens, large screened balconies, cable TV, phones, and air-conditioning. For groups and families it's a great way to go. You have the convenience of multiple bedrooms (up to three), while saving money by cooking some of your own meals. Located on Grace Bay, the beach is only steps away, as is a lovely meandering swimming pool set among flowers and tropical plants. You also have the option of eating at the casual outdoor Cabana Bar and Grill and an excellent restaurant, the Gecko Grill. Provo Turtle Divers has a small shop near the pool where you can rent and purchase gear, book trips, and arrange for classes. They collect divers from Ocean Club and several other lodgings in large buses and transport them to Turtle Cove Marina, where the boats are docked. Also on the property are lighted tennis courts, fitness center with massage therapist, boutique, convenience and gift store, duty-free shop, and auto, scooter, and bicycle rentals. The island's golf course is adjacent to Ocean Club. A new section, Ocean Club West, is just a mile away and features more ocean-view suites. Summer rates range from $165 for a studio suite for two to $550 for a 3-bedroom suite for six people. In winter they range from $215 to $865. These rates include government tax and surcharge. Dive packages are available with Provo Turtle Divers. Call (800) 457-8787 or (649) 946-5880; fax (649) 946-5845; e-mail: oceanclb@tciway.tc; website: www.ocean-club.com.

Turtle Cove Inn ★★★★, a PADI Resort near the marina, is a perfect location for divers. Thirty air-conditioned rooms, each with patio, cable TV, phone, and ceiling fan, have either poolside, marina, or ocean views. The pool and sundeck, surrounded by gardens, are the centers of attention, as is the dock and tennis courts. Two restaurants are popular with locals as well as guests. Per-room rates in summer range from $85 to $125, and from $95 to $150. Dive packages are available with the on-property Turtle Inn Divers. To contact them, phone (649) 946-4203 or (800) 887-0477 from the United States and Canada; fax (649) 946-4141; e-mail: turtle coveinn@provo.net; website: www.provo.net/turtlecoveinn.

A great little get-away on North Caicos is **Pelican Beach Hotel,** an excellent rustic family-oriented place. This is where Ocean Club's GM says he loves to go with his family to escape and relax. It is rustic, very friendly, and quietly tucked away on a gorgeous stretch of beach. Rates, which include breakfast and dinner, are $160 in summer, $225 in winter. Phone (649) 946-7112; fax (649) 946-7139; e-mail: reservations@tciway.tc; website: www.pelicanbeach.tc.

Live-Aboards

The *Turks & Caicos Aggressor* leaves from Provo for weeklong trips all around the island, including South Caicos, French Cay, and West Caicos. The 120-foot live-aboard carries a maximum of 18 passengers. It features nine staterooms with private head and shower, onboard photo lab, hot tub, Nitrox, and e-mail. The charters are all-inclusive—meals, tanks, weights, airport transfers—and you get unlimited diving. Call (800) 348-2628, or fax (504) 384-0817; e-mail: info@aggressor.com; website: www.provo.net/ aggressor or www.aggressor.com.

Peter Hughes' *Sea Dancer,* a PADI Gold Palm Resort based out of Provo, was completely refurbish-ed in 1999 with deck expansions, stateroom reconfigurations, and an updating of amenities. Call (800) 932-6237; website: www.peterhughes.com.

ISLAND LIFE ON PROVIDENCIALES

On my flight from Miami into Provo, I struck up a conversation with a lovely young Jamaican woman working at the Beaches resort. About Provo, she said: "It's growing fast; every time I wake up, there's something new going up."

"Like Grand Cayman?" I asked.

"Worse," she said. "It's not bad now, but it will be, because of the easy access. It's so close to the States."

If the locals, the "Belongers," as they're called, are somewhat dismayed about all this development, tourists and those working in the tourism industry are loving it. Most of the activity is centered around the crescent-shaped, 14-mile stretch of beach on the north shore called **Grace Bay.** This is home to Ocean Club, Grace Bay Club, Beaches, Allegro Resort, and

JoJo, the island's friendliest dolphin.

Grace Bay's pristine waters are typically dotted with any number of kayakers, sailors, and windsurfers. Resorts are nicely spaced out along the bay, so there are long stretches of empty beach—you can walk along it for many peaceful miles, in glorious serenity. JoJo, the wild Atlantic bottlenose dolphin who enjoys the company of humans more than his own species, frequently makes an appearance when you're on or in the water, and seeing this dolphin can be a thrilling experience.

For touring, the choices are few, but it's fun just to drive around for half a day. Have a guide take you to **Sapodilla Hill** to see the rock carvings made by marooned sailors watching for ships passing by. They date from the 1760s and consist of both drawings and written inscriptions. It's a pleasant little walk up a dirt path, and at the top you'll be treated to some panoramic views of the harbor and small inlets.

The **Caicos Conch Farm,** on the way to Leeward Development at the East End, is quite a production, with huge lagoons filled with the mollusk in various stages of growth. Unless you're really interested in the process, there's little to see—after all, conchs are not the most exciting creatures to watch. These are raised for consumption and shipped off.

Leeward has some attractive homes and a marina. This is where you catch Allen Ray's **Sand Dollar Cruisin'** tours and fishing trips (946-5238), which I strongly recommend. For some boutique-type shopping, head over to **Ports of Call** near the Comfort Suites Hotel. You can grab a quick lunch there, also.

The Leeward Highway takes you to just about any point on the island. If you continue around to the south, you'll reach what I think is the prettiest part of Provo—**Chalk Sound National Park.** This is an inland saltwater lake that's dotted with hundreds of tiny cays. The striking azure water makes the site spectacular. This southern shoreline of Provo features numerous winding inlets and channels, with shallow lagoons, so different from the long sweep of beaches along the north shore.

Believe it or not, there's an 18-hole golf course on the island. The **Provo Golf Club** has a 6,560-yard, par 72 championship course on the east end, not far from Grace Bay.

Dining and Entertainment

So many resorts are all-inclusive on the island, but if you're on your own dining-wise, definitely check out some of the places the locals like. Island food features almost limitless ways of cooking conch—conch fritters, conch salad, conch chowder, steamed conch, cracked conch. The locals love it, and if you do too you'll be in conch heaven. Barbecue ribs are also popular, as well as snapper and chicken. These are typically served with fried plaintain,

Sand Dollar Cruisin' with Allen Ray

Cruisin' with Allen Ray is not just fun—it's an experience. A native of these waters, Allen Ray teaches about island life through personal stories, and his humor is priceless. If there's time in your itinerary, I highly recommend his tour to **North Caicos,** the garden spot and bread basket of TCI. The tour is also leisurely and flexible. Allen Ray is an amiable guy, and he's also a sharp boat captain.

Shoving off from the dock at the Leeward Marina, or the beach at your resort, don't be surprised to see **JoJo.** Allen Ray claims that JoJo knows his boat. Sure enough, on my outing with him and just two other guests, this dolphin-without-a-pod came straight to the boat, and after Allen Ray killed the motor, JoJo hugged the side of the boat and looked up inquisitively, as if beckoning us to come on in and play. "But only pregnant women can touch JoJo," claimed Allen Ray.

It was a spectacular setting, in clear pale-blue-to-turquoise waters with the white sands of curving Grace Bay as a backdrop. When we started up the motor, JoJo followed for a bit, then leaped out of the water and leaped again—a proper dolphin farewell.

Motoring near the coastline, we quickly came to **Little Water Cay,** a sanctuary for Turks and Caicos rock iguanas. Allen Ray made a beach landing and, wondering if we would actually see any iguanas, we climbed up to the wooden walkway that two-footed visitors must use, since this island is not inhabited by humans. A single iguana was sunning itself right underneath the signpost for the sanctuary, as though waiting to greet us. This trip was getting too amazing.

Back in the boat, Allen Ray pointed out **Big Water Cay** and the half-moon-shaped beach that's unofficially designated for nudists. Next is **Pine Cay,** which connects to Big Water Cay. As we slowly followed the shoreline, Allen Ray explained that technically the islands are not in the Caribbean. "On the right side is the Caribbean, and on the left is the Atlantic," he said.

Pine Cay is a private island and favorite playground of movie stars and others seeking privacy and exclusivity. Its Meridian Club is both unpretentious and super expensive, a back-to-nature sort of place with no phones or TVs- where you can truly disappear. But, then, that's possible at just about any of these islands, and for a fraction of the cost!

Approaching **Sand Dollar Point** and **Fort George Cay,** Allen Ray asks if we would like to snorkel in the shallow bay. In this pristine spot, the only sights are sun, sand, and water, as well as some good-size sand dollars and five old cannons, coral-encrusted and lying on the sandy bottom. They date from 1700, and were origi-

Sand Dollar Cruisin' with Allen Ray (continued)

nally on the coast, as part of Fort George, which belonged to the British. The fort's few remains are protected by the Fort George Land and Sea Park.

In just a few minutes, we arrive on North Caicos and hop in Allen Ray's car parked at the dock. The island is lush with vegetation, and you immediately notice the difference between this place and the more arid Provo. While coating ourselves with insect repellant, we walk down a mosquito-infested pathway through heavy vegetation to explore the crumbling remains of **Wade's Green Plantation.**

After the American Revolution, loyalists to the British Crown, who lost land in the Americas—primarily Georgia, the Carolinas and Florida—were granted large amounts of land in the Caicos Islands. Wade Stubbs, originally from Cheshire, England, was among them. He lost close to 1,500 acres of land in Florida. In 1789 he was granted 860 acres on North Caicos, where he grew cotton and sisal for export to England and America. All this is explained on some rough signboards at the entrance to the plantation. Stubbs was an industrious guy, because when he died he owned 2,040 acres of land and 384 slaves.

Next stop is **Flamingo Pond,** where it's best to have some good binoculars. Three little huts are there for viewing the lake far in the distance.

Farms on North Caicos produce bananas, sugarcane, mangoes, and avocados, among many others. While walking along, Allen Ray points out the sapadillo fruit (similar to a kiwi) and sugar apples. He'll show you the Turks Head cactus and describe numerous ways of cooking conch ("TI-man's Viagra," he laughs). This is Allen Ray's element. He grew up here on North Caicos, and he particularly likes to talk about his mother.

"I listen to my mom, and I remember everything," he says, almost reverently. His mom, for instance, taught him to keep a "Little Bitters Bottle" on hand for extra energy. "It's for those times when you're too tired (like when you've been out fishing) to do the mommy/daddy type of thing." He explains that it's a mixture of extracts from seven different bushes. He'll also tell you what to use for headaches, toothaches, burns, and cramping.

He obviously loves North Caicos and with this priceless quote provides the essence of the island: "You can leave anything you want here, it's safe—anything but your wife or your girlfriend."

To contact him, and experience some of these gems for yourself, phone or fax (649) 946-5238.

potato salad, cole slaw, or peas and rice. **Caribbean Kitchen** is a good spot for trying the local temptations.

Popular eateries around the Turtle Cove area are **Tiki Hut** (chicken or rib special every Wednesday) and the **Terrace Restaurant,** both at Turtle Cove Inn. Also try the Caribbean grill at **Banana Boat Bar and Grill** near the marina.

For truly innovative dishes in a warm and friendly atmosphere, go to Ocean Club's **Gecko Grill.** It has a popular bar with evening entertainment. Also at Ocean Club is the **Cabana Bar and Grille,** a casual spot for a light meal that will please the senses, with sea breezes at your back and sounds of soft island music and surf rolling up on the beach. As it grows dark, a kerosene lantern will be brought to the table. Watch out—the flickering light just might lull you to sleep.

Medical Facilities

The island-wide emergency number is 911. On Provo, the Menzies Medical Practice & Interisland Medical Services is in the John Delisser Building on the Leeward Highway (946-4242). This is also where the recompression chamber is located. There's also the government-run Myrtle Rigby Health Clinic on the Leeward Highway (941-3000).

In case of a diving emergency call DAN (Divers Alert Network) at (919) 684-4DAN (4326) or (919) 684-8111.

Grand Turk

THE UNDERWATER SCENE

Grand Turk's submarine wall stretches the length of the island's west shore, from about 400 yards out and starting in only 40 feet of water. It drops quickly to about 130 feet, and from there it's a free fall all the way down the Turks Island Passage—7,000 feet. Mooring buoys all bob in full view of Duke Street and its narrow strip of sandy beach, where most of the hotels are located. The entire west coast of Grand Turk was protected by marine park status in 1991, prohibiting fishing, collecting, and anchoring.

Dive operations on Grand Turk favor little 24-foot Carolina Skiffs, which can be maneuvered easily and brought right up onto the beach. Divers wade out into the water and hand up their gear, but usually it's already on the boat. Service is excellent. At the dive site, back-rolls are the entry of choice, and the typical dive profile is about 80 feet for the first dive, followed by 50 feet for the second. You can have as much or as little underwater guidance as you like. There's a strong emphasis on diving freedom, and divers here tend to be more experienced and self-reliant than those diving Provo. About one-quarter to one-third of the divers use Enriched Air Nitrox, which is a good indication of the general skill level.

Underwater bottom compositions vary between hard coral bottom and sandy bottom, averaging a depth of about 35 feet out to the wall before dropping off. Huge healthy coral heads usually cap the top of the wall, which is a magnet for all sorts of marine life. The walls themselves are similar to those off of West Caicos but are more sheer and vertical. Some are concave, and can be quite a thrill, giving you the feeling of falling off a cliff, into the dark blue void below.

Reef topography frequently features tunnels, caves, chimneys, or archways through these large coral heads, leading right out to the face of the wall, sometimes as deep as 85 feet. There's always the possibility of encountering large pelagics cruising the Grand Turk Wall; in summer when the visibility can reach 150 feet, you might encounter the awesome manta ray, and in winter glimpse migrating humpback whales heading out to the Mouchois Silver Banks. Imagine seeing them in the water—an experience of a lifetime!

According to Cecil Ingham, who is with Sea Eye Diving, deciding the best time to dive really depends on what you want to see. "Although winter is the season for migrating humpbacks," said Cecil, "it's also when cold fronts come through, creating wave action and reducing visibility. The vis could be 50 feet or less. When it's not stormy, the vis can be excellent, but it can also change suddenly, even while you're diving. Typically, the rough side of Grand Turk is the East Side, but in winter, it switches. The weather comes from the northwest, and the East Side is calm then."

Dropping off the wall, then looking back toward the top, you might see waves of flowing, billowy gorgonians stretching out into the water column and glowing in the sunlight. Schools of Atlantic spadefish like the drop-offs. Butterfly fish and angelfish weave in and out among the hard coral ledges and around the barrel sponges. In shallower areas are families of cute little trunkfish, and occasionally you'll see the well-camouflaged scorpionfish patiently waiting for a meal.

In coral recesses you can usually find the juveniles. It was on a Grand Turk dive that I spotted just about the tiniest fish I'd ever encountered—a tiny trunkfish that looked more like a rolling little Pac-Man, almost microscopic in size. It's as exciting to see these little critters as it is to come upon the big guys.

Elkhorn and staghorn coral grow in the abundant sunlight of shallow areas, but can be easily damaged by storms. At several sites, the shallow areas have taken a beating from storms and coral bleaching. A few looked like a vast white wasteland. Fortunately, the walls are healthy. There are no currents to speak of any time of year, and the water is a very warm 80° plus.

Recommended Level of Experience

Everyone from novice to advanced will enjoy the area. But new divers, or those who haven't yet perfected their buoyancy, should avoid the narrow swim-throughs, where tube sponges and plate corals can easily be kicked and damaged. Also, some of the walls have steep drop-offs, and it's easy to sink down below the recommended depth. So watch your gauges carefully and try to avoid sawtooth profiles—repeated up-and-down patterns.

Great Dive Sites

Tunnels is an exciting and also particularly beautiful wall dive, toward the south end of the island. A sandy bottom at about 30 feet slopes down to some large coral heads. At about 55 feet, a tunnel cuts through the coral face, gradually sloping down to 75 feet. Following it takes you right out over the wall, which then drops off precipitously to a ledge at about 170 feet. Exciting! Be sure to turn around toward the wall and look up to the light. You'll see gorgonians literally dripping over the sides and delicate-looking sea fans stretching out to catch the rays of light—an underwater cathedral. At the end of the dive, notice the beautiful stand of pillar coral, with its tiny polyps waving in the surge, and the garden eel, popping up out of the sand. This is a particularly healthy area, loaded with invertebrates, and schools of tropicals, as well. You're just as likely, though, to spot a solitary scorpionfish, motionless and waiting for a passing morsel.

The *Annex,* also appropriately called *Alpine Meadows,* is typical of another particularly beautiful feature at these Grand Turk sites. Huge meadows of glistening white sand cascade out to sea, then spill through coral passages, sloping down to the wall. Overlapping the sandy passages are swirling plates of hard corals and gorgeous bright-orange elephant ear sponges, which provide convenient shelter for shy marine life. Large angelfish dart in and out the coral outcroppings over the wall, and turtles often stop by. A barracuda or two would not be unusual, and it's surprising how closely you can approach them.

Good-size, friendly grouper are the attractions at *Coral Gardens.* If you stroke their sides and scratch under their chins you'll halfway expect them to start purring. Odds are, you'll cringe next time you see them on a restaurant menu. They seem to have their territories, and they will follow you up to a certain point (as you travel along the wall), then stop short and watch while you swim on. Now that you're in new territory, a different grouper might sidle up for some attention.

Excursion to Gibbs Cay

Don't miss a half-day excursion to *Gibbs Cay*, and be sure to take the kids and anybody else in your group, particularly if they're snorkelers. Like Grand Cayman's Stingray City, this is your opportunity to get in the water and actually play with the rays. Don't worry, they won't hurt you. Their barbed tails are purely for defense, and since they know they're going to be fed, they certainly have no intention of biting the hands that feed them, so to speak.

Hold bits of conch or fish by making a fist, and the rays will come right up to you and attempt to literally suck it up, which they can do with vacuum-cleaner efficiency. You don't really need to have any food, though. They'll be swarming all around anyway, just in anticipation of food. Your boat operator might attach a container of chum to the boat's anchor line.

Feel the rays' soft, silky bellies and rub them between their eyes. You'll be their best friend. Food, of course, also draws other marine life, so don't be surprised to see fish stop by for a snack. During my visit a little lemon shark tried to nose its way in for lunch, but the rays did a good job of protecting their turf.

Nearby, some small coral heads look more like marine condos, with eel, grouper, and triggerfish residents piled high. On one little coral head I counted eight eels! The fish are usually opportunists and hang out to catch remnants of whatever the eels might scarf up food-wise.

Your boat operator probably will pull the boat right up on the beach and set anchors in the water and in the sand. So where you'll hang out is in shallow water just offshore—only knee- to waist-deep. All you'll need is a mask and snorkel—you won't even need fins. Usually the trip is combined with a picnic lunch on the sandy beach and time to stretch out in the sun and relax. This is a pleasant family-oriented activity and the perfect way to off-gas before your trip home.

The trip out to the little island takes about half an hour, and since it's over open ocean, it can get bumpy, wet, and windy. Be sure to take something to sit on for cushioning, as well as a windbreaker or even a sweatshirt to keep you warm for the ride back to Grand Turk.

For snorkeling, a site near St. Mary's church off Front Street is recommended, as well as the popular uninhabited island Gibbs Cay.

Salt Cay Sites

This little two-and-a-half-square-mile island lies south of Grand Turk, and for adventurous divers is a great getaway. For hundreds of years its raison d'etre was to produce salt; now it's to thrill divers. Most elect to fly over, but you can also be transportd by boat. The wall diving is similar to Grand Turk, with lush, healthy hard and soft corals. One of the most exciting sites here is actually an hour away, across open water, so it frequently gets blown out. It's the 1790 *Endymion,* a 40-gun British warship, sitting in about 40 feet of water, so snorkelers can enjoy it also. You can still see the cannons, the anchor, and other relics, which are all under government protection.

DIVE SERVICES & PACKAGES ON GRAND TURK

The following dive centers, located on Duke Street, have all been operating on Grand Turk for many years. They can combine packages with almost any of the island's lodgings. Boats are small, so even groups of eight can seem like a crowd. Since dive sites are only a few minutes from shore, there isn't the need for extensive emergency equipment or special amenities.

Blue Water Divers runs two 24-foot Carolina Skiffs and a V-hull cabin cruiser. It rents dive gear and cameras, both still and video. PADI classes range from Discover Scuba to divemaster. Blue Water also puts together what it calls eco-tour adventure packages to South Caicos (62 miles away) and the wreck of the *Endymion* (27 miles away). And they organize special snorkel trips. Blue Water partners with the Salt Raker Inn (a PADI Resort) to provide dive packages. The local number is (649) 946-1226; e-mail: mrolling@tciway.tc; website: www.microplan.com/bluerake.htm.

Retail Sales: *Adequate*	**Dive Boat Comfort:** *Adequate*
Rentals: *Adequate*	**On-Board Facilities**
Scuba Training: *Extensive*	**for Photographers:** *Good*
Photo Services: *Limited*	

Oasis Diving has four 28-foot dive boats, with shaded areas. On board are freshwater, drinks, and towels. Snacks are served between dives. Nitrox mixes of 32 percent and 36 percent are available. The shop rents equipment and has camera and video rentals. PADI instruction is through the advanced level, and a number of specialty courses are offered (including

Enriched Air Nitrox). Oasis also provides film processing and runs a small boutique. Packages are available with Island House, Osprey Beach Hotel, Turks Head Inn, Salt Raker Inn, The Arches Condominiums, and Arawak Inn. Phone (800) 892-3995 or (649) 946-1128; e-mail: oasisdiv@tci way.tc; website: www.oasisdivers.com.

Retail Sales: *Adequate*	**Dive Boat Comfort:** *Adequate*
Rentals: *Adequate*	**On-Board Facilities**
Scuba Training: *Moderate*	**for Photographers:** *Good*
Photo Services: *Moderate*	

Sea Eye Diving runs several 24-foot Carolina Skiffs with Bimini tops for shade. There is some dry storage, and a tub for cameras is filled with saltwater to keep the cameras wet. Boats go back to shore for the surface interval, and divers can relax on the beach, grab a bite to eat, and reload cameras. Sea Eye also has a new 42-foot boat that it plans to equip with a compressor to enable further exploration out on the northeast reef. Sea Eye pumps its own Nitrox, both 32 percent and 36 percent, as well as custom mixes for extended ranges.

Cecil Ingham is a NAUI course director and PADI master instructor, so this is a great place for training, including Nitrox certs. The two shops are practically side by side. One is for gear rental, storage and repair; the other houses the retail shop, reservation center, and classroom. Packages can be arranged with any lodging on the island. To phone or fax call (649) 946-1407; from the United States and Canada call (800) 810-3483; e-mail: ci@caribsurf.com; website: www.reefnet.on.ca/grandturk.

Retail Sales: *Adequate*	**Dive Boat Comfort:** *Adequate*
Rentals: *Adequate*	**On-Board Facilities**
Scuba Training: *Extensive*	**for Photographers:** *Good*
Photo Services: *Moderate*	

WHERE TO STAY ON GRAND TURK

Most of the hotels are on or across Duke Street from the beach. So divers need only roll out of bed, walk across the street, and wait on the beach until boats are loaded. Though the island is sparsely vegetated, the hotels are in a lovely area, with colorful hibiscus, bougainvillea, sea grape, etc.

Island House ★★★, the newest lodging on Grand Turk, is a special treat, due to the beautiful accommodations and gracious owners. Decorated

Mediterranean-style, all rooms are suites equipped with cooking facilities, cable TV, air-conditioning, and direct-dial phones. Most have spectacular views because the house is located on a rise. Although Island House is off to itself, away from the dive shops, it's a blast to throw your dive gear into one of its golf carts and scoot down the hill, passing wandering horses and waving to friendly locals. After you get settled in, Colin gives you a personal island tour, pointing out restaurants and grocery stores, since Island House itself has no food service. Guests have access to a gorgeous courtyard, barbecue area, and swimming pool, as well as laundry facilities. Your only obligation is to make sure to lock the front gate when you come in, to keep out errant horses and donkeys and thereby spare the stunning gardens. Rates per person, based on double occupancy, range from $130.80 to $152.60 in winter and $109 to $130.80 in summer. They're a bit higher during Christmas and New Year's. Rates include government tax but no service charge. Phone (649) 946-1519/1388; fax (649) 946-2646/1388; e-mail: ishouse@tciway.tc; website: www.islandhouse-tci.com.

The **Salt Raker Inn** ★★★★★ (a PADI Resort) is a quaint 12-room oceanfront gem that's popular with divers. It was built more than 150 years ago as the private home for a Bermudian shipwright. Rooms are categorized as economy, superior, and suites. Some face seaward, others are garden-oriented; some have balconies, others patios. Upstairs rooms have ocean-view balconies with hammocks. Also available are rooms with air-conditioning, refrigerators, TVs, and phones. Dive packages are with the dive shop Blue Water Divers, which also includes unlimited shore diving. Meal plans can be arranged. The courtyard harbors the Secret Garden Restaurant, bar, and barbecue area. Live musical entertainment is on Wednesdays and Sundays. There are bicycles for rent. Nightly rates for a double are from $90 to $155 plus 18 percent taxes and service. Single rates are less. Phone (809) 946-2260; fax (809) 946-2432; e-mail: mrolling@tciway.tc; website: www.microplan.com/bluerake.htm.

Turks Head Hotel ★★★★, dating from the 1840s, at one time did duty both as the governor's guest house and the American consulate. Six large restored suites are decorated with antiques; they all have been equipped with air-conditioning, cable TV, and minibar. There's also a bar and restaurant on the premises. Located on Front Street, the Turks Head is barely 50 feet to the beach and within easy walking distance of dive shops. Rates are per person, based on double occupancy. They range from $55 to $82 in summer, and from $64 to $96 in winter, including tax and continental breakfast. There is no service charge. Call (649) 946-2466; fax (649)946-1716; e-mail: tophotel@grand-turk.com; website: www.grand-turk.com.

ISLAND LIFE ON GRAND TURK

Generally flat and treeless, the six-and-a-half-mile by one-and-a-half-mile Grand Turk is scored by numerous salinas—the salt flats that kept the economy humming for several centuries. It was primarily Bermudians who settled in the islands, cleared the land, and created the large salinas. In fact, TCI was better known on an international basis back in the late 1800s because of its salt works.

Divers will be well acquainted with **Duke Street,** flanked on both sides by stone walls, and more than 500 years old. And for most, this narrow street bordering the ocean will be all you'll really need, since this is where all the dive operations and most of the lodgings are located. But definitely walk around and do some exploring on this most unusual island. Nondivers, however, might exhaust the available activities and attractions quickly, so unless they're content with a good book and some of the simple pleasures of island life, they might yearn for the activity of Provo.

Exploring the island, you'll see the **Archbishop Cathedral,** which serves both TCI and the Bahamas, and **St. Thomas Anglican Church,** dating from 1823. The stately house behind the wrought iron gates is the governor's residence, named **Waterloo,** and dates from 1815. Surprisingly, on the grounds is a nine-hole *public* golf course. You'll undoubtedly come across the lighthouse (not operational), built in England and shipped in sections in 1852. Exploring some of the old structures near the lighthouse might spark images of sailors and pirates, slaves and landed gentry, salt and cotton—many stories to tell.

While exploring, you'll see cedar trees and a lot of cactus, as well as sugar apples and sea grapes growing all about. When sea grapes are ripe, they turn purple—try some! Watch where you step, because horses and mules wander about at will. You'll undoubtedly pass people who will take the time to greet you pleasantly. And what you'll probably find, as you explore, is that this rather run-down scrubby-looking island grows on you.

Don't miss the excellent **Turks and Caicos National Museum** in Cockburn Town, the capital of Turks and Caicos. It will give you a good sense of what these islands are all about—the salt industry, the slavery, the maritime history. The building itself is an interesting relic. It's more than 150 years old, constructed by Bermudians from the lumber of wooden ships. Bermudian "wrackers," as they were called, would intentionally lure ships by signaling them from shore, thereby causing them to run aground. Displays about the **Molasses Reef wreck** are some of the most interesting in the museum. The Spanish caravelle dates from before 1515, making it the earliest European shipwreck discovered so far. The site was excavated in the 1970s by the Institute of Nautical Archaeology at Texas A&M University.

The island's beaches are fairly narrow, and even more so at high tide, but the sand is soft and inviting, especially for anyone wanting simple relaxation—sans personal watercraft and parasailing. If there's any "racket," it's probably being made by shore birds.

Dining and Entertainment

This place is super casual. There's absolutely no need to dress up. In fact, you might look a bit strange if you do! Night life consists of getting together with friends in open-air restaurants, discussing the wonders of the day's diving, and comparing it to exotic locales around the world.

Most of the hotels have their own restaurants. Among the independent establishments, there's **Waters Edge** Restaurant on Duke Street, across the street from Oasis Divers, where you can sit outside on the wooden deck and dream of being back in the water. The **Regal Beagle,** on Hospital Road, offers fish, conch, hamburgers, and chicken, served with rice or french fries, and it is usually about half the price of the establishments on "the strip." There is also the **Diplomat,** on the town end of Airport Road, and the **Poop Deck,** near the museum, which is good for lunch.

Medical Facilities

The Grand Turk Hospital (946-2040/2110) is on the north side of the island, and a government-operated clinic is downtown (946-2328).

In case of a diving emergency call DAN (Divers Alert Network) at (919) 684-4DAN (4326) or (919) 684-8111.

Index

Unofficial Guide
to the World's Best Diving Vacations
Reader Survey

If you would like to express an opinion about your diving vacation
or this guidebook, complete the following survey and return to:

Unofficial Guide Reader Survey
P.O. Box 43673
Birmingham, AL 35243

Date/duration of trip: Today's date:

Diving destination(s) visited:

Please circle one of the following:

—*Was this your*   1st   2nd   3rd   4th   5th   6th or
more dive trip?

—*Would you dive again at this destination?*   Yes   No

—*Recommend it to a friend?*   Yes   No

—*Do you plan to dive*   within 6 months   within 1 year   longer?

—*Your age:*   teens   20s   30s   40s   50s   60s   70s or over

—*You are:*   employed   self-employed   retired

—*Line of work:*

Please score items below from 1 to 10 with 10 being the highest or best.
Feel free to add your comments.

Value for money:

Total diving experience:

Your overall impression of the dive destination *(beauty, accessibility, weather,
convenience, friendliness and helpfulness of locals, variety and skill level of dive sites,
diver congestion, number of dive shops and other resources):*

Your overall impression of the dive resort or other accommodations *(appearance,
appeal, furnishings and decor, cleanliness, comfort, diver-friendliness, diving facilities
and resources, dive packages):*

Your overall impression of the dive shops and dive operations *(knowledgeability
and expertise of staff, level of service, quality of equipment and dive boats, retail and
rental stock):*

Quality of diving instruction:

Confidence level in expertise of diving instructors:

Ratio of dive instructors to dive students:

Friendliness & accessibility of local diving community:

Local attention to environmental concerns:

Local attention to diving concerns:

General friendliness to foreign tourists:

Ease of processing through customs:

Non-diving touring options:

Dining & restaurants:

Entertainment:

Any other comments:

Your hometown:

How did you learn about your dive destination?

How did you learn about this book?

Where did you buy your dive package or trip?

When and where did you buy this book?

(Optional) If you are available for a telephone interview, please give us your name, address, telephone number, and a convenient time to call.

THANK YOU!

For all your dive travel needs.

**Visit your PADI Dive Center or Resort
or contact PADI Travel Network to
arrange your dive vacation today.**

PADI
padi.com
email: ptn1@padi.com